The Life Insurance Sales Management Handbook

The Life Insurance Sales Management Handbook

Planned and Edited by

JACK C. KEIR, Ph.D., C.L.U.

Professor of Insurance

School of Business Administration,
Temple University

*With the co-operation of seventy-five
outstanding American Life Insurance
and Sales Management Authorities*

PRENTICE-HALL, INC.   ENGLEWOOD CLIFFS, N. J.

PRENTICE-HALL INTERNATIONAL, INC., *London*
PRENTICE-HALL OF AUSTRALIA, PTY. LTD., *Sydney*
PRENTICE-HALL OF CANADA, LTD., *Toronto*
PRENTICE-HALL OF INDIA PRIVATE LTD., *New Delhi*
PRENTICE-HALL OF JAPAN, INC., *Tokyo*

LIBRARY OF CONGRESS
CATALOG CARD NUMBER: 71-134686

PRINTED IN THE UNITED STATES OF AMERICA
ISBN-O-13-536102-8
B & P

CONTRIBUTING AUTHORS AND CONSULTING EDITORS

Robert A. Adams, Director of Advertising and Sales Promotion, Provident Mutual Life Insurance Company of Philadelphia, Philadelphia, Pennsylvania

George F. Albright, C.L.U., Senior Vice President, The Life Insurance Company of Virginia, Richmond, Virginia

Kent L. Babcock, Jr., C.L.U., General Agent, Emeritus, Aetna Life & Casualty, Philadelphia, Pennsylvania

Bruce Bare, C.L.U., General Agent, New England Mutual Life Insurance Company, Los Angeles, California

Edward B. Bates, C.L.U., President, Connecticut Mutual Life Insurance Company, Hartford, Connecticut

Brent N. Baxter, Executive Vice President and Director of Research, American Institutes for Research, Pittsburgh, Pennsylvania

Dr. John S. Bickley, Professor of Insurance, University of Alabama, Alabama

James S. Bingay, Executive Vice President, The Mutual Life Insurance Company of New York, N. Y.

Dr. Kenneth Black, Jr., C.L.U., C.P.C.U., Dean, School of Business Administration, Georgia State University, Atlanta, Georgia

Dr. H. Randolph Bobbitt, Jr., C.L.U., Associate Professor of Management Sciences, The Ohio State University, Columbus, Ohio

Joseph E. Boettner, C.L.U., President, Philadelphia Life Insurance Company, Philadelphia, Pennsylvania

Wallis Boileau, Jr., Vice President (retired), The Penn Mutual Life Insurance Company, Hi Nella, New Jersey

Donald Bramley, C.L.U., Executive Vice President, Life Insurance Agency Management Association, Hartford, Connecticut

Dr. Richard H. Buskirk, Professor of Marketing, University of Colorado, Boulder, Colorado

Robert W. Carey, Second Vice President, Personal Health, John Hancock Mutual Life Insurance Company, Boston, Massachusetts

G. Frank Clement, C.L.U., President, Shenandoah Life Insurance Company, Roanoke, Virginia

E. C. Danford, C.L.U., Vice President, The Mutual Life Insurance Company of New York, New York, N. Y.

Dr. James H. Davis, Professor of Marketing, College of Administrative Science, The Ohio State University, Columbus, Ohio

B. W. Dornbirer, C.L.U., Vice President, Marketing Research, The Ohio National Life Insurance Company, Cincinnati, Ohio

Walter L. Downing, C.L.U., General Agent, New England Mutual Life Insurance Company, Boston, Massachusetts

Philip H. Dutter, Director, McKinsey & Company, Inc., New York, N. Y.

Robert E. Dye, C.L.U., President, National Insurance Marketing, Inc., Santa Monica, California

William T. Earls, C.L.U., General Agent, The Mutual Benefit Life Insurance Company, Cincinnati, Ohio

Darrell D. Eichhoff, C.L.U., Senior Vice President, Metropolitan Life Insurance Company, New York, N. Y.

Coy G. Eklund, C.L.U., Senior Agency Vice President, The Equitable Life Assurance Society of the United States, New York, N. Y.

Carl T. Furniss, C.L.U., Manager, Connecticut General Life Insurance Company, Bloomfield, Connecticut

Charles E. Gaines, C.L.U., Vice President—Marketing. Research and Review Service of America, Inc., Indianapolis, Indiana

Dr. James Gatza, Director of Management Education, The American Institute for Property and Liability Underwriters, Inc., Bryn Mawr, Pennsylvania

Herbert C. Graebner, C.L.U., President, Building Owners and Managers Institute, International, Bryn Mawr, Pennsylvania

Paul C. Green, C.L.U., Vice President National Sales Division, Continental Assurance Company, Chicago, Illinois

Dr. G. Victor Hallman, C.L.U., Director of Examinations, The American Institute for Property and Liability Underwriters, Inc., Bryn Mawr, Pennsylvania

Gordon K. Harper, C.L.U., Senior Vice President and Director of Sales, Phoenix Mutual Life Insurance Company, Hartford, Connecticut

Wm. Eugene Hays, C.L.U., General Agent (retired), New England Mutual Life Insurance Company, Boston, Massachusetts

John A. Hill, C.L.U., President (retired), Aetna Life & Casualty, Hartford, Connecticut

William B. Hoyer, C.L.U., General Agent, John Hancock Mutual Life Insurance Company, Columbus, Ohio

Solomon Huber, C.L.U., General Agent, The Mutual Benefit Life Insurance Company, New York, N. Y.

John M. Huebner, Senior Vice President, The Penn Mutual Life Insurance Company, Philadelphia, Pennsylvania

Roger Hull, C.L.U., Chairman, The Mutual Life Insurance Company of New York, New York, N. Y.

Dean W. Jeffers, Vice President, Nationwide Mutual Insurance Company, Hartford, Connecticut

William G. Kashnig, Research Manager, Aetna Life Insurance Company, Hartford, Connecticut

Dr. Jack C. Keir, C.L.U., Professor of Insurance, Temple University, Philadelphia, Pennsylvania

Harry Krueger, C.L.U., The Northwestern Mutual Life Insurance Company, Milwaukee, Wisconsin

Frank B. Maher, President, John Hancock Mutual Life Insurance Company, Boston, Massachusetts

James R. Martin, C.L.U., President, Massachusetts Mutual Life Insurance Company, Springfield, Massachusetts

E. J. Moorhead, F.S.A., Vice President, Integon Corporation, Winston-Salem, North Carolina

Alvin E. Mulanax, Professor of Marketing, Kansas State University, Manhattan, Kansas

Robert V. Nally, J.V., Director of Examinations, The American College of Life Underwriters, Bryn Mawr, Pennsylvania

Kenneth C. Nichols, Senior Vice President, The Prudential Insurance Company of America, Newark, New Jersey

Elmer L. Nicholson, President, The Fidelity Mutual Life Insurance Company, Philadelphia, Pennsylvania

Paul A. Norton, C.L.U., Senior Vice President, New York Life Insurance Company, New York, N. Y.

Dr. Jeremiah J. O'Connell, Assistant Director for Academic Affairs Centre d'Etudes Industrielles, Geneva, Switzerland

Gerald W. Page, C.L.U., General Agent, Provident Mutual Life Insurance Company, Los Angeles, California

Frederic M. Peirce, C.L.U. Chairman, General American Life Insurance Company, St. Louis, Missouri

Lyle B. Pelton, C.L.U., Management Consultant, A. V. Nelson Associates, Highland Park, Illinois

Henry W. Persons, Senior Vice President (retired), The Lincoln National Life Insurance Company, Fort Wayne, Indiana

Robert B. Pitcher, C.L.U., General Agent, John Hancock Mutual Life Insurance Company, Boston, Massachusetts

Carr R. Purser, Consultant, Brevard, North Carolina

Fredrick E. Rathgeber, Executive Vice President, The Prudential Insurance Company of America, Newark, New Jersey

Charles F. B. Richardson, F.S.A., Vice President, Bowles, Andrews, & Towne, Inc., Atlanta, Georgia

Bernard S. Rosen, C.L.U., General Agent, State Mutual Life Assurance Company of America, Denver, Colorado

Dr. Hugh G. Russell, Professor of Management, School of Business Administration, Georgia State University, Atlanta, Georgia

Howard Dana Shaw, President, Institute of Management Services, West Chester, Pennsylvania

Thomas C. Simons, C.L.U., Agency Vice President, Connecticut General Life Insurance Company, Hartford, Connecticut

TO

*The General Agents and
Managers throughout
America whose dedication
to excellence in sales management
has contributed so much
to the progressive achievements
of life insurance marketing.*

PREFACE

An outstanding achievement of the life insurance industry has been the successful marketing of its products. The continued expansion of sales is the great challenge of the future. Organizing, planning, activating and controlling the future sales effort in this selling business demand an increasing competence and excellence on the part of sales management.

The building of excellence and the strengthening of competence in life insurance sales management are the purposes of this volume. Thirty-six company executives, successful agency managers, educators, and institutional leaders have joined together to contribute toward this objective. The intent has been to integrate principles with practice in the presentation of each of the chapters. The guiding philosophy has been that principle without practice is barren theory and practice without principle habituates management to inefficiency. The emphasis on principle, however, has not been at the expense of practice. In the main, the authors are practitioners with many years of experience. The articulation of principles by these practitioners is eloquent testimony to the acceptance of scientific management in life insurance sales management today. This embracement of management principles by practitioners augurs well for the future of the life insurance business.

The thirty-six chapters are grouped logically into ten major sections. Section I describes the life insurance marketing environment of today and contrasts it with those earlier years when sales management principles were being developed. Section II discusses the important functions of sales management performed by the home office and indicates the interrelationships that must be effectively maintained between home office management and field management. Section III sets forth the important principles of management that must be followed by sales management at all levels. Section IV describes the principles and practices of organization as these principles are practiced both in the home office agency department and in the individual agency. Section V is concerned with market planning (including marketing research) for life and health insurance sales at both the home office and the individual agency. Section VI discusses the principles and practices of public relations and sales promotion. Section VII is devoted to the manifold problems of sales manpower development: recruiting, selection, education and training. Section

VIII describes the principles and practices of motivation, supervision, and retention of manpower. Section IX deals with the principles and practices of business conservation as an important responsibility of home office and agency sales management. Section X is concerned with financial management for the achievement of profitable sales operations.

When the idea of a handbook in life insurance sales management was first considered, the Consulting Editors recognized that differences in management philosophy among the members of such a large group of practitioners were inevitable and would be readily apparent to the reader. As the book evolved, the apprehensions of the editors were allayed as the similarities in the expressed philosophies became more pronounced than the differences. The minor differences are understandable and expected among practitioners.

An attempt has been made to obtain uniformity of terminology throughout the book. Some differences in terminology, however, must be accepted in the writings of such a large group of practitioners. Most of these differences are of no great significance. For example, it would seem to be of no great significance whether the man responsible for the management of an agency (general agency, branch office or some oblique combination of both) is called an "agency manager" or "agency head" or any other similarly respectable title.

The Contributing Authors and Consulting Editors comprise a prestigious group. Their achievements are abundantly documented in their companies' and agencies' successes. Their willingness to risk their national reputations by writing and editing these chapters for their industry associates attests to their exemplary and unselfish dedication to industry wide attainment of excellence. A profound and heartfelt appreciation goes out to these men for their authorship and editorship of this volume.

In addition to the Contributing Authors and Consulting Editors, many friends have been helpful in the structuring and editing of this volume. Dr. Davis W. Gregg, President of The American College of Life Underwriters, originally suggested the idea of a handbook to present the fundamental principles of life insurance sales management. His enthusiasm for the handbook approach provided the motivation for undertaking the project. Wm. Eugene Hays, former General Agent for New England Mutual Life Insurance Company in Boston, has been an invaluable counsellor, author and editor. Acknowledging his tremendous assistance in a Preface is an inadequate tribute to his enormous contribution to this volume. Dr. H. Randolph Bobbitt, Jr., Associate Professor of Management Sciences at The Ohio State University, has given generously of this talent as an editor, management scholar, and insurance teacher.

His contribution to the organization and editing of this volume is recognized with deep appreciation. William G. Wilson, former Agency Manager for New York Life Insurance Company in Philadelphia, has been a dedicated contributor, consultant, and editor during the many months of this volume's development. Dr. H. Wayne Snider, Consulting Editor for Prentice-Hall, Inc. and Chairman of the Department of Insurance and Risk, School of Business Administration, Temple University, has been of tremendous assistance in the final editing of this volume. A special thanks goes to Mrs. Grace Tappert of the Harry A. Cochrane Research Center, Temple University, whose cooperation was invaluable in the scheduling of typing and retyping of the many pages of manuscript that flowed through her office. Finally, it is a pleasure to acknowledge the excellent cooperation and competence of Prentice-Hall, Inc. in handling the many details associated with the publishing of this handbook.

CONTENTS

Nature, purpose, and tools of communication (68) Communications responsibilities of the home office (69) Coordinating communications channels (70) Centralizing responsibility (70) Person-to-person communication (71) Field visits (73) Letters (74) Opinion research and complaint analysis (75) Communications responsibilities of the regional sales officer (76) Communications responsibilities in departments outside the agency department (77) Attitudes necessary for effective communication at all levels of life insurance sales management (78) Benefits of effective communication (80)

Types of agents (81) Important characteristics of agents (82) Corporate planning (84) Relating the agent to corporate plans (87) Other corporate objectives involving the agent (90) Conclusion (94)

Interdependence of sales management objectives and other company goals (96) Interdependence of sales management and other company functions (98) Top management's responsibility for sales management (101) Sales responsibility of the agency department and the field (102) Effects of sales management on long-term company growth (110)

Section III
FUNDAMENTAL PRINCIPLES

Common denominators for success (113) The two fundamental and unique tasks of management (114) Establishing objectives (114) Achieving objectives (116) Variations in applying management principles (120) Role of company management (121)

Section VI
PUBLIC RELATIONS AND SALES PROMOTION

The nature of public relations (297) Does performance precede publicity? (301) Building the agency's own plan (302)

The dimensions of sales promotion (317) Company structuring (317) Objectives of a sales promotion department (318) Responsibility (318) Structure (319) Functions of sales promotion (319) Advertising (322) Keeping the agent informed (322) Using sales aids (324) Preparing the budget (324) Company communication (325) Summary (326)

Section VII
MANPOWER DEVELOPMENT

The need for manpower (327) Essentials for manpower development and growth (329) Manpower planning (333) The interaction of all forces in manpower development (338) Summary (341)

Importance of manpower (343) The planning function in the management of recruiting (346) Selling the opportunity (356) Organizing, implementing and controlling recruiting (359) Conclusions (360)

The selection process (362) The selection ratio (363) Selection devices (364) The application blank (364) Per-

Section VIII
MOTIVATION, SUPERVISION AND RETENTION OF MANPOWER

Section X
FINANCIAL MANAGEMENT

The Life Insurance Sales Management Handbook

Section I

THE LIFE INSURANCE MARKETING
ENVIRONMENT: PAST & PRESENT

The Life Insurance
Marketing Environment

Benjamin N. Woodson

The marketing environment in which life insurance sales management must operate is similar in many ways to that confronting the sales management of any industry. The life insurance marketing environment, however, does have several unique aspects which this chapter will describe.[1]

The sales volume for any product or service is a function of (1) the number of consuming units, (2) the attitudes of the consuming units toward the product or service and (3) the purchasing power possessed by the consuming units. These three factors are the essential features of any marketing environment. The following discussion will emphasize the unique significance of these factors to life insurance sales management.

THE NUMBER OF CONSUMING UNITS

Families and business units are the principal consuming units for life insurance. Until the development of group insurance and qualified pension plans, most life insurance was marketed on an individual contract basis insuring the life of the family head. The family is said to be the philosophical heart of life insurance, and in the final analysis the purchase of most

---

[1] The author gratefully acknowledges the substantial contribution in the preparation of this chapter of Dr. H. Randolph Bobbitt, Jr., Associate Professor of Management Sciences, The Ohio State University.

life insurance is for family needs. However, in recent years business units have purchased a considerable amount of life insurance, and the magnitude of the annual premiums that business units pay for life insurance will increase substantially in the future. The income tax rate structure and the deductibility of premiums for group insurance and qualified pension plans as a business expense provide great incentive for arranging, wherever possible, for the business unit to pay life insurance and annuity premiums instead of the individual employee.

The Continued Importance of the Family

The family has been described as man's most remarkable social institution.[2] It is remarkable not only because historically it has endured so long, but also because it continues to provide the most effective arrangement for achieving "certain societal imperatives." Every man, woman, and child needs a haven to which to return from life's embattlements for comfort, understanding, sympathy, counsel, judgment, and love. The close interrelationships that develop over the years of living together give the members of a family a feeling of security and confidence that is provided by no other institution.

To what address does the escaped prisoner usually return? To what group does the college freshman tell his troubles when he has been expelled from school? With whom do we all typically want to be when we have been elected to office, crowned king of the golf links, won a scholarship or failed a C.L.U. examination?

Through the medium of the family great educational and cultural achievements can be realized. The child may learn to distinguish right from wrong, to participate in social relationships, to respect the rights of others, and to develop basic attitudes toward life in general. The home is a combination school, church, hospital, restaurant, hotel, night club, laundry, dry cleaner and psychiatric clinic. In fact, the home will usually provide just about any service on some basis although perhaps in an unprofessional manner.

Some writers have expressed concern for what is described as "the decline in the cohesiveness of the family unit." They refer to the increase in the number of divorces, the apparent trend toward sexual promiscuousness outside of marriage, the increase in the percentage of married women in the labor force, the generation gap and the lack of respect on the part of children for family discipline. The conclusion of these pessimists is that

---

[2] Kephart, William M. *The Family, Society, and the Individual,* Houghton Mifflin Company, New York, 1966, p. 2.

the family is rapidly losing its importance and effectiveness as a social institution.

The pessimists may be right, but as of now there is not much statistical evidence to support their thesis. The number of divorces is increasing principally because of the increase in the number of family units. There has been only a small increase in divorces as a percentage of total married couples.[3] Sex outside of marriage is difficult to measure, but the divorce rate would suggest that either the increase is not being detected by the other spouse or if detected it is being compatibly tolerated!

It is true that there has been a substantial increase in the percentage of married women who are employed outside of the home, but this may be a factor that will contribute to strengthening the cohesiveness of the home. The increased income may remove an otherwise serious financial problem that could impair family harmony. The increased income permits the family to enjoy together the standard of living of the upper middle class, which might be impossible on the husband's income alone. Domestic help once or twice a week may remove most of the drudgery of housework for the wife. With labor saving appliances and part-time domestic help, the wife may actually work less than if she had no outside employment. This may permit her to have more time, energy and good spirit to devote to her children during their non-school hours which coincide with her off-work hours.

The implications of all this for life insurance sales should be obvious. The working mother has a more visible and tangible economic value to be insured than does the stay-at-home mother producing no clearly measurable dollar income. Furthermore, the working mother possesses the dollars with which to pay premiums. The fact that a wife is working does not reduce a husband's human life value, but it may increase the wife's. Generally, a wife's working income would not be adequate if anything happened to her husband.

Finally, the behavior patterns of the younger generation do not appear to pose a serious threat to the long-term functioning of the family. Any significant decline in the strength of the family organization appears to be confined in the main to the lower income families in the ghettos. The solution to this latter problem must lie in improving economic opportunities for these families. In fact, one of the strongest arguments for preserva-

---

[3] Wattenberg, B. J., *This U.S.A.*—An unexpected Family Portrait of 194,079,296 Americans drawn from the Census, Doubleday and Co. Inc., Garden City, N.Y. 1965, p. 36. More recent census data does show a greater increase in the divorce rate than earlier census data. This more recent data has persuaded one U.S. Census Bureau Official to comment: "What we are seeing now is a steady uptrend that appears bound to continue." *The Wall Street Journal* page 1, June 3, 1970.

tion of the family type society is the fact that a good family background appears to be largely self-perpetuating. The broken home appears to be a seed-bed for juvenile delinquency and discipline problems. Life insurance obviously can play an important part in preserving the family entity when disintegration may be threatened as a result of death of the breadwinner.

The Formation of New Family Units

The preceding paragraphs have emphasized the realistic expectation that the family will continue to be the accepted social institution for achieving important social imperatives. Therefore, since the family will represent the predominant consuming unit for economic security, any attempt to measure the future demand for economic security to be provided through the medium of life insurance, must begin with a determination of the expected growth in the formation of new family units.

The formation of new family units will be primarily a function of population growth and the prevailing marriage age. Each of these two factors is, of course, affected by a large number of social, economic, religious and political factors. Population growth depends on (1) utilization of birth control information and techniques, (2) society's attitude toward the number of children considered desirable, (3) the income level of the family unit, (4) religious attitudes toward family size and birth control and a whole host of national and international political factors, including wars, military service in peace time, government welfare benefits and even the nation's tax structure.

The interrelationship of all these factors is to a large extent conjectural. However, the United States population has been growing at a rapid rate and is expected to reach 230 million by 1980.[4] It is true that there has been some slowing down from the rapid growth that took place after World War II. However, this has been more in the nature of modifying the "explosion" to a mini boom rather than a significant reversal of a trend. The consensus among demographers and sociologists is that the formation of new family units will increase during the 1970's. This will be due primarily to the fact that the teen-agers and young adults—13 to 34—will become large groups.

---

[4] For data on the population of the United States as well as projections of the population of the United States, see tables #2 and #3 in the U.S. Bureau of the Census, *Statistical Abstract of the United States: 1965* (86th edition; Washington, D.C., 1965), pp. 5 and 6. See also *U.S. News and World Report,* Jan. 12, 1970, pp. 32 and 33: "Population now is growing at little more than 2 million a year, compared with 3 million in the early 1960s. But the pace will quicken again in the late '70s. Reason: A boom in weddings, now under way, promises an increase in the yearly baby crop soon."

This phenomenon is mainly attributable of course to the high birth rate since 1945. If the average marriage age remains the same, the increase in the number of teen-agers and young adults in our population means a substantial increase in family units during the 1970's.[5]

Regional Shifts in Population

One of the major characteristics of the American population is its high degree of mobility. Because of this, the increase in population since World War II has not been shared equally by all sections of the United States. There have been three aspects to the shift in population that has taken place since World War II: (1) a movement toward the southwestern and western states, (2) a movement away from the rural areas and (3) a movement from the center city to the suburbs of metropolitan areas.

As a result of these changes in population densities the home office marketing departments of life insurance companies have increased their efforts in the geographical areas experiencing population growth by making appropriate adjustments in the number and location of agencies as well as in the focus of their sales promotion activities. At the agency level, the agency manager has responded to these population changes by intensifying efforts in the suburban communities and in many cases opening separate offices in these areas.

Further changes in population densities will require careful review of the existing location and staffing of existing agencies. These population changes are likely to have considerable significance for the many aspects of life insurance sales management in the future, including recruiting, training and supervision.

THE CONSUMER

The most important element of the marketing environment is the consumer, whether it be an individual or a corporation. It is to captivate and persuade the consumer that products are designed and market planning initiated. To understand the marketing environment, marketing management must understand the consumer.

The considerable importance of the consumer is emphasized today by two concepts: (1) the marketing concept and (2) consumerism. The marketing concept embraces two fundamental ideas: first, the company should be customer oriented in all aspects of its management and operations; and, second, within this customer orientation management should strive for profitable sales volume.

---

[5] *Ibid.*, p. 33.

Consumerism, on the other hand, espouses the idea that management is not meeting the needs of the consumer but, instead, is using the latter's ignorance to exploit him. Peter Drucker says, "Consumerism is the failure of marketing." [6] The radicals increasingly noisy protestations under the banner of "consumerism" are an indication that marketing management must make whatever changes are necessary to assure the consumer that he can trust what he gets. The problem for the consumer is one of bafflement in selecting from among so many products and services, concerning many of which he has little knowledge and information for responsible and informed choice.

The problem for marketing management is to achieve profitable sales volume by supplying what the customer needs. "If one cannot make money, even though the demand is there, one is not supplying what the customer needs. And then one had better start thinking: 'What is it the customer really needs?' " [7]

Consumer Acceptance and Enthusiasm for Life Insurance

Life insurance has enjoyed a prestigious and venerable acceptance in the United States. More persons own life insurance than own their own home. More persons purchase a new life insurance policy every year than purchase a new automobile. Life insurance has grown in stature and in public favor through several periods of national and international trauma including two world wars, the economic debacle of the 1930's, congressional investigations, muckraking journalism, a quarter of a century of inflation and it will probably survive the campus revolts and the new morality. One cannot help wondering why a prestigious product, that has been honored and revered by the lower class, the middle class and the upper class family has always been purchased with such steadfast reluctance. The answer must be found in the same book that explains why we give so sparingly to religious, charitable, and educational institutions. A footnote in that book may startle the reader by raising the questions: "Why does a man bet more at the horse races than he sets aside for his daughter's education? Why does he spend more for cigarettes for a day or a week than for his wife's Christmas present?"

Consumers spend their money in response to other than noble motives. Nobility, respectability, and prestige are not enough to assure a product's marketability. Life insurance is the shining example of this axiom of consumer behavior. Prestige in the marketplace, however, is a valuable acces-

---

[6] Drucker, Peter F. "Insurance Opportunities in an Era of Change." *The Journal of Insurance Information,* July–August 1969, p. 3.

[7] *Ibid.,* p. 4.

sory that enhances a product's marketability. The Cadillac maintains an impressive sales volume year after year to a large extent because of the prestige of the product among automobile buyers. Despite its high prestige, however, the Cadillac is not purchased by every family that can afford one any more than life insurance is purchased in the quantities that middle income and higher income families can afford. Thus, something more is needed in addition to the high prestige of the product to assure a successful market for the product.

The high prestige enjoyed by life insurance in the years immediately following the Great Depression has diminished to some extent in more recent years because of the erosion of the purchasing power of the dollar. Life insurance provides its greatest benefits in an economic environment characterized by stable prices. It is to be expected that the public will not be greatly enamored by a contract that promises to provide a benefit which may prove to be of less and less value the longer the contract is in force. A life insurance renaissance can be achieved by either the life insurance industry modifying its product so that it more nearly reflects changes in economic values or by a government program to stabilize prices. As a matter of fact both of these approaches are currently (1970) being implemented. The life insurance industry is rapidly restructuring its product line to provide mutual funds, variable annuities and equity reserves. The federal government is striving to bring inflation under control through appropriate monetary and fiscal policies. Both of these efforts may result in an improved marketing environment for life insurance.

Reasons for Purchase Reluctance

There are three basic reasons why families have typically postponed the purchase of life insurance while at the same time allocating purchasing power to other products and services.

1 THE BENEFIT IS LONG DEFERRED

The purchase of life insurance requires an immediate sacrifice for the enjoyment of a retirement income thirty or forty years hence, or to provide one's family with a death claim check on an unpredictable date the insured believes will be in the distant future, and which he wants to be in the distant future.

2 THE EVENT INSURED AGAINST SEEMS REMOTE

The second reason for purchase reluctance is that the event against which life insurance insures seems remote. Life insurance assures the purchaser that he will not be penniless in his old age, and that his family will not be penniless in the event of the insured's premature death. But to the younger man, at least, old age is hidden in the mists of the future, ten generations away from him, and although his reasoning tells him that while he must do something about financial security for his later years, his feeling tells him that he has all the time in the world to do so.

A person quickly perceives that he must have fire insurance this hour, because his house can burn as readily as his neighbor's. He knows also that he must not put the key into his automobile ignition until he has bought liability insurance. Even though he is the most cautious driver in all America he could still strike down a youngster darting out between two cars parked at the curb. In contrast, he feels there is no hurry about purchasing life insurance because he is in excellent health and will surely die in bed in his nineties! Therefore, a man feels no sense of urgency in purchasing life insurance.

3 HUMAN INERTIA

The third reason why men do not readily buy life insurance, even though they need it and know they need it, can afford it, and intend to buy it, is plain old-fashioned, everyday human inertia. This, of course, is a problem encountered daily by every salesman of consumer goods and services of every sort. Yet most of the purveyors of other goods and services have something working for them that the life insurance agent does not have: pressure of natural human want, or the pressure of a desire so clearly seen, so readily recognized, so strongly held, that the inertia is overpowered.

The above three reasons explain the prevalent consumer attitude toward the purchase of life insurance even when the person needs it, knows that he needs it, intends to buy it and can afford it. These reasons emphasize that life insurance must be a selling business. Success or failure in the life insurance business depends almost entirely upon the intensity of the selling effort. Enormous amounts of attractively priced life insurance were dropped by servicemen at the end of each world war because the idea of maintaining those policies was not sold strongly enough.

The basic reasons why Canada and the United States outstrip the rest of the world in the distribution of life insurance is that in our countries we *sell* it, whereas in other countries it is *offered for sale*. The United States and Canada have approximately 7 per cent of the world's population and approximately 70 per cent of the world's life insurance in force. This is *not* because we have different, or better, forms of life insurance, or because our companies are fundamentally different or better managed, or because our people are more conservative or thrifty, or more ardent in their search for security. It is simply because we have developed good agency departments which have developed good marketing plans and sales forces, because those good sales forces have taken our product into the market and *sold* it *hard*.

The more than one trillion dollars of life insurance in force contributes immeasurably to the economic stability and financial security of American families today. Without the hard sell approach, most of the life insurance would not be in force. The record of life insurance sales in other countries should convince us that life insurance must be sold. The record of non-agency companies in America proves that life insurance will not be selected by customers at the supermarket. The nature of the human animal conclusively suggests that people in great numbers will not walk into a bank and open an annual premium account.

Development of Attitudes and Purchase Behavior

Psychologists emphasize that a person's attitudes are learned. Each of us has learned his attitude toward political parties, religion, racial structure, education, marriage, and life insurance. We learned these attitudes from our parents, our teachers, our friends and our business associates. We frequently attempt to emulate the attitudes of our friends or the attitudes of persons we respect and admire.

The story is told of three college freshmen from three widely separated geographical areas. All three joined the same fraternity and almost immediately in small but perceptible ways began to emulate the dress, speech, and social habits of the president of the fraternity. On their return to their respective homes at the end of the first semester their parents were amazed at the noticeable changes that had occurred. Upon graduation the three students accepted junior executive positions in three different corporate organizations. Within a few days after joining their respective organizations small but again perceptible changes began to take place in their dress, grooming, and social habits as a result of their attempt to emulate the "prestigious" vice president to whom each reported. Each of the young men would deny that he was an organization man. However, the desire to emulate a "prestigious" person is the obvious explanation as to why one of the young men grew sideburns and wore a sport coat and colored shirt to the office, while another in a different corporate organization daily wore a dark gray, three-piece suit with striped tie.

People learn their purchase behavior from group association. We all have a strong desire to become accepted and integral members of our social, religious and cultural group. We believe that we achieve such acceptance to a large extent by purchase behavior that the group approves or even applauds. The college freshman knows that he wins the approval of his peer group if he has a sports car on campus rather than a conservative sedan.

People pattern their consumer hehavior in accordance with their conception of the accepted purchase behavior. For example, we dress differently for a civic or community group meeting in the evening than for the day-time routine at the office. People frequently dress differently for a church group meeting than a business or social group meeting.

A product which can be readily made visible to other persons with whom we wish to associate, or identify, may be purchased with greater enthusiasm than a product which is less readily visible. If a $25,000 life insurance policy were as clearly visible to our neighbors and peer group as a new Cadillac convertible, the former would unquestionably be purchased with greater enthusiasm than it is today.

Family Attitudes

Since life insurance is a product which is designed to protect the family, the quantity of life insurance that will be purchased depends to a large extent on how keenly the premium payer desires to provide for the economic needs of his family. The extent of the insured's desire to protect his family is a function of (1) his love and affection for his family, (2) his sense of responsibility for his family's financial welfare, (3) his evaluation of the capacity of the members of the family to provide for themselves, (4) his evaluation of the extent to which other people or other institutions will provide for the members of the family, (5) his aspirations for the future education and development of his children and (6) the effective pressure that his wife can apply to him to organize the family's financial affairs. With respect to items (1), (2), and (5) most men would respond affectionately, responsibly and with profound aspirations for the future education and development of their children. With respect to item (3) most men would wish for their children to finish college before having to go to work. In case of their premature death, most men would wish for their wives to be able to remain at home until after the children are at least through elementary school.

With respect to item (4) men in the middle income brackets and above recognize that benefits provided by Social Security, group life insurance and other employee benefit programs are often inadequate, and they would like to supplement these programs by purchasing additional life insurance, if they could arrange for the premium dollars. It must be recognized, however, that this desire varies in intensity among men. Also, there is considerable variation in disposable income that is available for life insurance premium payments.

Most men recognize that we have outlived the era of the agrarian economy, when it was possible for the widow and her children to find economic support at the farm or homestead of relatives and friends. Finally, most men do not wish to leave their families dependent upon private charities or governmental welfare programs.

With respect to item (6) men today are more frequently including their wives as partners in the decision-making process of the family business. Wives also are more frequently demanding that they be included in the decision-making process. Some of this change is the result of the wife's providing part of the family's income and savings. But even among the stay-at-home wives there is a general increase in participative management. The wife is frequently as well educated as her husband and probably more keenly aware of the financial problems of home management. The wife today is frequently the custodian of the checkbook, the principal shopper, and the advance planner for social, recreational and educational activities. The wife is becoming more and more the key person in deciding on additional life insurance. Since she is a more active participant in family financial management, she is more likely than in the past to provide the necessary motivation and continuing pressure on the husband to arrange more adequate life insurance.

POLITICAL, SOCIAL AND LEGAL ENVIRONMENTAL FACTORS

The family's attitude toward the purchase of additional life insurance is influenced by a number of political, social and legal environmental factors. The government is becoming an increasingly important public supplier of goods and services. Probably no American industry has had its product supplied to the public by the government more extensively than the life and health insurance industry.

Veterans Insurance

During World War I and World War II the government provided servicemen with $10,000 of low-cost life insurance. The amount of government term life insurance owned by servicemen during World War I reached a maximum of $40 billion. Most of this coverage was not converted to permanent insurance despite the attractive conversion privilege available to servicemen. A similar experience occurred during World War II. Under the provisions of the National Service Life Insurance Act servicemen purchased a maximum of $125 billion of term life insurance. Most of this was also lapsed after World War II.

The government has continued to supply life insurance at a low cost or gratuitously to servicemen during the Korean War and Vietnam conflict. Servicemen are now covered under group life insurance provided by private United States companies under a master contract with the Veterans Administration. Servicemen may convert their term insurance to permanent with one of the approximately 600 companies participating in the group plan. It will be interesting to observe the conversion experience of this new type of group life insurance over a period of years as the servicemen are discharged from active duty.

Social Security

In 1935 Congress passed the Social Security Act, which inaugurated a broad program of social benefits. Congress has expanded the program from time to time with the result that the following coverages are available currently: (1) old-age and survivors insurance, (2) disability income insurance, (3) hospital insurance for the aged, (4) supplementary medical insurance for the aged.

It is a matter of conjecture as to the effect that Social Security legislation has had on the sale of life insurance. It has been argued that the providing of Social Security benefits called the attention of the American family to the need for additional survivorship and retirement benefits. Since Social Security benefits are not adequate for the needs of the vast majority of American families, additional purchases of life insurance are recommended. The existence of Social Security benefits has encouraged the use of the programming approach to selling life insurance, and this has pointed up the inadequacy of the program of most families. Many of those who are fearful that continued expansion of Social Security benefits will reduce the market for private insurance agree that Social Security has been, up to this time, an important factor in the growth of private life insurance. These persons argue, however, that, since Social Security taxes now represents 5.2 per cent of a wage earner's income below $7,800, there is available only a small number of additional wage dollars for the purchase of private life insurance.

The future for life insurance sales among families with incomes below $7,800 is reduced, when viewed in terms of the need to replace a respectable percentage of the family's net income after deduction of the wage earner's taxes and cost of self-maintenance. For example, 60 per cent of $8,000 annual wages would mean $4,800 of survivorship benefits for the family. A family composed of a wife and two children will be assured of more than this amount as soon as the wage earner has been in covered employment long enough to qualify for maximum Social Security benefits. However, $4,800 a year is below the poverty level of a family of four according to some estimates.

Group Insurance

The increasing amounts of group life insurance available to families in all income groups also tend to shrink the market for individual policies. Some control over future expansion of group life insurance exists as a result of the limitations imposed by law, federal or state. Several states limit the amount of group life insurance to 150 per cent of the employee's earnings when the life insurance coverage exceeds $20,000, and provide for a maximum of $40,000 of coverage. The IRS requires the employee to report as taxable income all premiums paid by an employer on annual renewable term group life insurance in excess of $50,000.

Despite these controls and limitations, however, increasing amounts of group life insurance are available to families through professional associations, credit bureaus, banks, mutual funds and insurance companies themselves. The availability of large amounts of group insurance may further restrict the market for future sales of ordinary life insurance.

Political pressure makes it almost inevitable that Social Security and welfare benefits will be increased. Likewise, group life insurance, pensions and other employee benefits will be increased as a result of pressure from unions and as a result of management's continued recognition of a social responsibility.

Legal Environment

A few brief comments should be made concerning the legal environment as it affects the marketing environment for life insurance. Both federal and state laws are generally favorable to life insurance. A well established code of case law assures the favorable interpretation of the life insurance contract for the insured and his family. Litigation is minimal and decisions have served to build the confidence of the public in the liberal attitude of the courts toward insureds and beneficiaries.

One specific area of the legal environment deserves special attention. This is the area of federal income, estate and gift taxes. Through its liberal tax treatment of family owned life insurance, Congress has apparently sought to encourage American families to provide for their own economic security. Life insurance proceeds paid by reason of death are generally free of federal income taxes. The annual investment income earned on the savings element of permanent life insurance is not currently taxable. When the death proceeds are paid to a widow under one of the installment settlement options, the first $1,000 of annual investment income on the proceeds is not taxable income. There are no special privileges accorded life insurance under the Federal estate and gift taxes. However, through the appropriate use of trusts it is possible to achieve considerable estate and gift tax advantages for the estate owner and his family. For example, through the establishment of a short term reversionary trust a father may pay the premiums with income tax free dollars for ten years on a substantial amount of life insurance on the life of the son.

Life insurance and annuities receive favorable tax treatment also when the business unit pays the premiums. As previously described, the business unit may deduct as a business expense group life insurance premiums. Such premiums are not taxable income for the employee when group term life insurance is purchased and the amount of the insurance does not exceed $50,000. Premiums paid to fund a qualified pension plan are deductible as a business expense by the corporation and are not taxed currently to the employee. Premiums paid to fund a non-qualified deferred compensation plan are not taxable income to the employee if the benefits are non-vested and forfeitable. The details of appropriate use of specific devices and techniques to minimize the tax bite is beyond the scope of this treatment of the life insurance marketing environment. However, it is obvious that the use of these tax saving arrangements is a favorable aspect of the life insurance marketing environment.

THE PURCHASING POWER POSSESSED BY CONSUMING UNITS

The amount of a family's purchasing power available for the purchase of life insurance is a function of net income after taxes and the expenditure pattern of the family with respect to all other available products and services.

There has been a spectacular increase in disposable personal income in the United States in recent years. Disposable personal income increased from 207.7 billions of dollars in 1950, to 340.9 billions in 1960, and to more than 631.6 billions in 1964.[8] Personal incomes were at the annual rate of 801 billions for the second quarter of 1970.[9]

The average income per family has also shown a rather spectacular increase in recent years. For example, average family personal income has increased from $4,969 in 1950 to $8,151 in 1962.[10] With the upward trend in disposable personal income and average income per family there has been a more equal distribution of income per family. This would sug-

---

[8] Bureau of Census, *op. cit.*, p. 325.
[9] Reported by Commerce Department, *Federal Reserve Bulletin,* September 1970.
[10] Bureau of Census, *op. cit.*, p. 340.

gest that there is a broadening of the market for life insurance as more and more families attain an annual income that provides an increasing amount of discretionary spending power.

A family's purchasing power available for the purchase of life insurance may be considerably diminished by the family's expenditures for automobiles, color television, travel, cocktail parties and other established ecstasies not easily eliminated. The life insurance industry must compete for the consumer's dollar with the products and services of a variety of industries. However, statistics indicate that life insurance in force varies directly with disposable personal income.[11] The high positive correlation that exists between life insurance per family and disposable personal income per family is not surprising. It is logical to expect that the families with higher incomes would be purchasing larger amounts of life insurance. Premium dollars for new life insurance are more readily available from the higher income and middle income family than from the lower income families. Sales management attempts to direct its activities increasingly to the segment of the market possessing the higher disposable income. It should not be overlooked, however, that the more equal distribution of income that we are achieving today is broadening the market for life insurance.

Economists and statisticians have observed for many years the American family's propensity to increase its consumption by less than its increase in disposable income. There is a remarkable stability in the percentage of disposable personal income that families direct to personal consumption expenditures. This means that if only the same percentage of disposable personal income goes into savings, the amount of savings dollars will increase absolutely. This is significant to life insurance marketing because family dollars directed into life insurance come from the excess of disposable personal income over non-discretionary personal consumption expenditures.

It has been indicated previously that life insurance marketing organizations are in competition for the consumer's income with the marketing organizations of every other industry. However, since statistical evidence indicates the considerable stability of consumption expenditures as a per cent of disposable income, the life insurance industry's competition apparently comes primarily from other savings and investment media. As a matter of fact, the life insurance industry cannot obtain much solace from the considerable continued expansion in funds being directed into savings and loan associations, mutual funds and new issues of common stock.

---

[11] Institute of Life Insurance, *Life Insurance Fact Book*, 1969.

In the nine year period from 1960 through 1968 the assets of mutual savings banks increased 77 per cent, mutual funds 210 per cent, savings and loan associations 115 per cent. In the same period life insurance companies increased their assets only 57 per cent. As a nation we have reduced the per cent of disposable income going into life insurance from 6.28 per cent in 1935 to 3.81 per cent in 1967. Also, life insurance's share of the nation's savings dollars has declined from 47 per cent in 1948 to 14 per cent in 1968.[12]

The success of other forms of savings and other institutions of thrift, equities in particular, no doubt accounts for the entry of many life insurance companies into the mutual fund field. According to the Investment Company Institute, life insurance companies in 1969 had 20,000 agents registered with the N.A.S.D. to sell mutual funds. The number is expected to approach 50,000 by the end of 1970.

The great challenge to life insurance marketing is the challenge of increasing the percentage of disposable personal income saved as well as increasing the life insurance industry's share of family savings.

Premium Paying Capacity of Business Units

Business units in the future probably will become even more extensive purchasers of life insurance, pensions and other employee benefits. This increase in the provision of employee benefits by business units will be attributable to several factors, including the continued pressure from organized labor, the increased sense of management responsibility for economic security for employees and their families, favorable tax treatment of business units and employees and the liberal social spirit of the times.

The extent that business units will be willing to contribute to employee benefit programs will depend on the level of income earned by business firms. An extremely important factor in the tremendous growth of premium volume paid by business units in recent years has been the high level of corporate earnings which business was willing to share with its employees. Most economists are optimistic concerning the future outlook for corporate earnings. Therefore, the future looks bright for a continued capacity of business units to pay premiums. There is always the possibility, however, that labor costs will become so high that the squeeze on profits will leave the business unit with such reduced earnings that it may have to reduce

---

[12] *Fortune* magazine, October, 1968. Cited by Dr. Harry J. Loman "Developing Trend in Environmental Security and their Impact on Insurance," *Proceedings Fifth Annual International Insurance Seminar on Insurance Company Management and Seminar Security,* 1969, p. 49.

its commitment of funds for fringe benefit programs.

Business units have recently become so fond of each other that conglomerate marriages are occurring with increasing frequency. The justice department and other governmental agencies have raised the cry of monopoly power and restraint of trade. The final decision on these two issues is best left to the legal mind. We will only note that larger business units, whether size is achieved by growth or merger, may have significance for life insurance sales. A favorable effect of the increased size of business organization is an increased tendency to provide economic security programs for employees. This may result from (1) an increased financial capacity to provide these benefits, (2) a self-conscious feeling that its size requires it to do more, (3) a more socially responsible management than is typically associated with small business and (4) unions being more aggressive in their demands on larger business units. Whatever the explanation, the growth of a business firm is likely to produce an increase in available premium dollars to fund employee benefits.

A possible negative effect of such growth is an increased disposition to self insure employee benefits rather than use the facilities of life insurance companies.

The increases in the size of the business organization may mean fewer individual business units. This may mean less of a market for key-man life insurance, less need for business continuation agreements funded by life insurance and fewer deferred compensation plans to hold key employees.

SUMMARY

The ability to adapt to a changing marketing environment is mandatory if the life insurance business is to continue its established growth pattern. Adaptation to changes in consumer attitudes and buying habits is already apparent in the increased marketing of variable annuities and mutual funds and in proposals for the marketing of variable life insurance. It is devoutly to be hoped, however, that responsiveness and consumerism and the marketing of "balanced investment programs" does not result in the abrogation of the life insurance business' important responsibility to its market, and that the business continues to emphasize that security is its most important product.

2

Historical Developments in Life Insurance Sales Management and Institutional Relations

Charles J. Zimmerman

Until about the time of World War I, life insurance selling and sales management methods were largely a matter of hunch and guesswork. If a company developed a better method of selling than its competitors, the secret was jealously guarded. There was little or no cooperation among companies in regard to mutual problems; little or no exchange of information.

No one in those days seriously tried to find out what kind of men made good life insurance salesmen. No one did much about training men to succeed. Management technique was to hire a large number of agents in the hope that enough would pull through to enable the company to build a sales force. Training of sales managers was unknown. Men were named managers usually because they were good salesmen.

These conditions hampered effective distribution of life insurance. Annual sales volumes were not high by today's standards and buyers of life insurance were likely to let their policies lapse.

To comprehend the distance the life insurance industry has come, it is useful to look all the way back to its founding days.

EARLY HISTORY

The Agent In Absentia

Life insurance marketing and marketing management in America have had their extremes ever since the industry was off to its real start in the 1840's. Before that time, life insurance had been marketed through the passive approach. At first there were no agents at all. No one was actually paid for bringing life risks to the companies. And even when the first agents were hired, they did not aggressively go out to seek business.

The earliest life companies were content to do without any life insurance marketing program. This abstaining from any selling effort obviated the need for salesmen and the need for any sales management. The companies secured the power to underwrite lives; but did nothing to attract business. However, in the late 1830's and early 1840's the companies recognized that making the product available to the public was not an adequate or appropriate method to merchandise an intangible product such as life insurance. Consequently, a few companies in the 1840's did embark upon rather mild and conservative efforts to promote life insurance sales. Life insurance marketing began with modest announcement advertising. All business was transacted by mail or in person at the head office of a company.

The start of the insurance agent in this country dates back to about 1807 when a committee was appointed to consider the matter of agents in the Insurance Company of North America, organized in Philadelphia in 1794. At that time the committee authorized the president of the company, "to appoint suitable and trusted persons at such places as he shall think it advisable to act as surveyors of the company."

The early agent announced his presence and his wares to the people of his community; then waited for customers to come. Agents were often prominent local citizens, doctors, merchants, politicians. They accepted an agent's assignment evidently with little, if any, intention of working at the job. They were merely available. The companies made no effort to educate, train or supervise these "prominent citizens" so that an effective sales effort could be achieved.

These "big names," as some called them, soon dropped out of the business, their places being gradually taken by men who needed the commissions received for selling life insurance policies. And some of the latter gradually gave up all or most of their other business activities. In some of the larger cities a company's agents would have sub-agents to work part-time.

This does not mean, however, that the company's agents became general agents in the modern sense, but they tended to approach that status as success changed their circumstances and responsibilities.[1] "In spite of the loose contractual arrangements, territorial assignments caused little friction; for travel was not easy, and agents tended to handle just the business of their immediate communities. There were a few traveling agents, but mostly their prominence came at a later period."[2]

Introduction of Person-to-Person Solicitation

The initiative and intensity of marketing activities were enormously stepped up with the introduction of person-to-person solicitation of risks by agents who called upon prospective buyers at their homes and offices. Soon thereafter a gradual rise in agency compensation attracted more and abler men, many of whom made life insurance marketing their main or only business interest.

The Arrival of the General Agent

As the sales forces grew in numbers the need for direction increased, and the general agency system became the most popular mode of fixing local sales management responsibility. That system lent itself readily to the development of national selling organizations, the home office management group concentrating on general agency appointments and the general agents concentrating within their respective territories on the appointment of soliciting agents.

The Influence of the Mutual Companies

The coming of the "mutual" principle to the life insurance industry was a revolutionary influence in many ways. The marketing programs of the life and trust companies, which predominated prior to the mutuals, were simple and nonaggressive. The volume of life sales was relatively unimportant to them. This was not true of the mutuals. Stock companies had capital to fall back on for early death claims and expenses. To defray such costs, the mutuals had to rely on premium income, and therefore needed a sustained volume of business immediately to provide an adequate cash flow. A flow of early premiums for the mutuals was the difference between success and failure.

With the advent of the mutuals, therefore, came an immediate expansion in the range of life insurance marketing activities, and an increase in the intensity with which sales efforts were executed.

---

[1] Stalson, J. Owen, "Marketing Life Insurance," Richard D. Irwin, Inc., Homewood, Illinois, 1969, p. 9.

[2] *Ibid.*, p. 160.

One of the great pioneers of life insurance in America was Morris Robinson, first president of the Mutual Life Insurance Company of New York, and actually founder of person-to-person selling. When Robinson called on his friends and acquaintances to persuade them to subscribe for policies in his newly incorporated Mutual Life, he inaugurated a new era in selling. Taking insurance to the market via personal solicitation of prospective buyers was virtually unknown in America then. For Robinson it was evidently a method inspired by necessity. Mere announcement of plans had won him scant support, even among his co-incorporators. After months of working alone, he came to realize that the task was so huge that he would have to get the help of many aggressive solicitors; not until they, too, had gone into action were applications secured and premiums paid for enough business to permit the company to begin operations in February, 1843.

By 1848 there were upwards of a dozen companies selling through agents: most of these companies were mutuals less than three years in business, there were a few English companies soliciting business in our eastern States, and the old life and trust companies remained upon the scene without becoming aggressive seekers after business or representation. Even these few first years, however, had taught management something about life insurance marketing and its accompanying sales management problems.

Early Education and Training

In these early years, the average agent of an insurance company received little help from the home office or from the general agent. The agent in those days was expected to educate himself.[3] "He learned by doing. His first need was thought to be knowledge of insurance principles; these were set down for him in the booklets which the company issued. Not all modern marketing men believe in giving agents training in principles before sending them into actual selling work. They teach sales talks first, principles later. This method has a degree of efficiency in it, for the situation which it is designed to serve is that of getting the impecunious new man quickly on an earning basis. In 1845, however, the idea of life insurance was not as well-known as it is today; it could not be taken for granted; people frequently challenged its logic."[4]

Educating the agent was a process which went hand in hand with the educating of the public. In early booklets actuarial discussions were brief and the more essential "selling-argument" sections were substantially

---
[3] *Ibid.,* p. 177.
[4] *Ibid.,* p. 177~178.

longer. The latter attempted to answer the doubtful or objecting applicant and supplied the agent with the answers to spoken objections. There were infrequent articles, tracts, and in the early 1850's, even books that gave practical advice to prospective or beginning agents as to how they could prepare themselves for work and how they should conduct their business. Actual formal training was, of course, unknown.

Quite early there developed both home office officials and general agents whose experience in the business qualified them to give sound and expert guidance to beginning and inexperienced agents. But such instruction in person-to-person exchanges was available to but a limited number of men; most agents lived and worked in small communities, and even "the traveling agents" could do no more than visit them at infrequent intervals. Moreover, the traveling agent was chiefly a recruiter of new agents and a salesman of his own account rather than a supervisor, stimulator, and educator of previously appointed agents.

Five per cent of the premium was the usual commission paid by the mutuals during their first years of business. "This rate, according to company literature and letters, was continued in use as the 'typical' rate for a number of years after 1842. But exceptions were not only frequent in number but important in character, since the extra benefits which *were granted* in 'special' cases tended to influence bargaining with the result that the special rates gradually became typical."[5]

The Influence of Henry B. Hyde

One of the most forceful personalities that helped build the early agency marketing system was Henry B. Hyde, founder of the Equitable Life Assurance Society. The dynamic Hyde, for many years, personally directed the hiring and sales efforts of his agents. He was a prolific letter writer. It was not uncommon for him to stay at his desk until late, writing long letters of direction to people in the field.

Hyde seemed to sense what the public wanted; he devised the means for informing them that he had what they wanted.[6] "His charm, his energy, his self-confidence, the persuasiveness of his logic and the obvious good sense of his merchandising plans, as well as the high commissions he paid, attracted the best agents in the field to the Equitable. But Hyde had staying qualities as well; he not only won men to the company, he inspired them to performance beyond their normal capacities. He could make men excited about life insurance selling. He is considered to be the inventor of the contest concept by virtue of the fact that he was the superb exploiter

---

[5] *Ibid.,* p. 254.
[6] *Ibid.,* p. 364.

of it. Where he led, competition had to follow. He became, therefore, both prophet and teacher-leader of the insurance marketing fraternity."[7]

MARKETING DEVELOPMENTS AFTER THE CIVIL WAR

Despite the fact that outstanding progress was made in the life insurance industry after the Civil War in the selection and education of agents, many companies fell by the wayside. Basically, the cause for these company failures was the inability to market their product. No effective marketing organization was established. The typical complaint of management was that the agents were not selling life insurance as they should. Apparently, it did not occur to management that organizing, planning, leading and controlling the sales process were important management responsibilities. In other words, marketing management in those early years paid little attention to management principles. Competition among those companies that survived encouraged the search for new and more effective means of increasing the sales of one company over another. The nation's population was booming. Each company wanted to boom with it. The tendency of all companies was to search for sales gimmicks. However, this was consistent with the management thinking of the period. The application of management principles and concepts and the development of sound marketing structure, embracing effective training and supervision procedures, did not emerge in this country until the twentieth century.

Increase in Competive Tempo

The marketing of the Tontine policy[8] soon after the Civil War was probably the most important life insurance development in a period in which new ideas were eagerly sought. The asset-swelling possibilities of the plan for the company induced its leading advocates to concentrate selling effort upon that policy—a concentration which became a powerful and disturbing marketing influence in this period.[9]

The coming of the Tontine life insurance system increased the competitive tempo in life insurance selling. Agents were hired promiscuously; high pressure methods often resulted; a buying public, eager for security

---

[7] *Ibid.*, p. 364.
[8] The Tontine policy provided for payment of deferred dividends to policyowners whose policies remained in force for minimum periods, such as ten, fifteen or twenty years. Policyowners received no dividend if they terminated their policies before the end of the designated minimum time period. The sale of Tontine policies was promoted by projecting tremendous dividends to be payable because of the poor persistency of most policyowners. In other words, the terminating policyowner forfeited his investment values to the policyowners who continued.
[9] Stalson, J. Owen, *op. cit.*, p. 487.

and willing to gamble for a fortune, bought Tontine policies even though many were unable to maintain them.

The agent became more aggressive; forceful; reckless. He combed the cities and towns of the nation, selling his product, often with an excess of zeal that characterized the age itself. The era of high pressure sales tactics was in full bloom. It was at this time that the agent stereotype developed. In those days, many office buildings posted notices barring, "Peddlers, solicitors, and insurance agents."

One writer reported to his readers the common concept of the mythical insurance agent:

> He was a mixture of the royal good fellow, the hypnotist, the slight of hand performer, the poet, and the genial pirate; whichever of these constituent parts would be most effective with a certain type of customer, that part instinctively assumed temporal command over him. He charmed you with his personality, until you couldn't say no . . . he boarded you unaware, batted you down with his booming statements, and leaving you dazed and helpless, carried off his loot in the shape of a signed application for a policy . . .[10]

"It appears that life insurance company officers of the 1850's and 1860's permitted themselves to be farther and farther removed from the problems of the agents,"[11] J. Owen Stalson writes:

> ". . . They interposed the authority, and of course, therefore, sometimes the venality, of the general agent between the soliciting agent and themselves. They washed their hands of the agent, so to speak. The long-range viewpoints which characterized the development of underwriting, actuarial, and investment policies under the guidance of the home office executive group were in consequence but little applied to the development of the sales management, especially the agent management, policies of the company. The company officers who did well by the work and the workers in underwriting, mathematics, and investment appear to have left the agent and his development to the tender mercies of the general agents, whose interests too often conflicted with those of the agent, the company, and the policyholder."[12]

Nobody had any idea how many agents were selling life insurance and little idea of how they were doing it. It was estimated by its President in 1884 that Connecticut Mutual had four or five hundred men in its field force. In 1905, New York Life had 10,000 agents. Home offices, regarding general agents as partners of the companies, had little desire to look

---

[10] Ascribed to "a popular writer in 1906." Quoted by Mildred F. Stone, *A Calling and Its College,* Richard D. Irwin, Inc., Homewood, Illinois, 1963, pp. 10—11.

[11] Stalson, J. Owen, *op. cit.,* p. 354.

[12] *Ibid.,* p. 354.

closely at their operations, as long as they responded to the constant prodding for more agents and more production. Too many field men were agents in name only. They submitted applications for their friends and relatives who wanted to buy a policy. They were not organized for any aggressive sales effort. Phoenix Mutual, for example, found that in 1913 eighty percent of the company's business was produced by fifteen per cent of its agents. Some 660 of the company's agents had been licensed, supplied with rate books and literature, but had not done one dollar's worth of business. Over sixty per cent of the company's field force were part-timers, and there was no standardized agent's contract.

Industrial Life Insurance

One of the early landmarks in life insurance marketing was the development of industrial life insurance. Industrial life insurance was essentially a marketing innovation. It was not a new system of life insurance. In fact, its special handling of the marketing function constitutes its only serious deviation from what had come before. The features which distinguish industrial from ordinary life insurance are associated in the main with its ready availability to most working men and women without a medical examination. Sold door-to-door and serviced in the same manner, industrial life insurance reached directly to the wage earner whose economic status and knowledge of life insurance were both limited. The industrial life insurance agent not only was able personally to sell the idea of life insurance; but also provided a personal service not usually available.

The important characteristics of industrial life insurance are (1) its availability in small units; (2) its availability to all members of the family from age one day to seventy years; (3) its sale through house-to-house and person-to-person soliciting effort by agents who also call in person each week or each month to collect premiums; (4) its issuance in most cases without medical examination. Each of these departures from ordinary life insurance practices was closely associated with and was significant to the marketing of industrial life insurance.

The start of industrial life insurance in the United States thus had its basis in the fact that it served a clientele which, prior to the 1870's, had not been reached by company marketing techniques.

The marketing structure that developed out of the sale and servicing of industrial life insurance became known as the "debit system." It originated in England in the mid 1850's and subsequently was adopted in the United States. The "debit system" has been used to some extent in the United States to market ordinary as well as industrial life insurance.

The debit system, and the marketing management organization inevitably associated with it, have had both favorable and unfavorable effects on the development of the present day life insurance marketing structure. The favorable effects include: (1) the strong home office direction given to the sales effort of the branch offices, (2) the emphasis on favorable client relations, (3) development of career agents, (4) a carefully structured sales management organization that demands effective leadership at all levels of the structure, (5) emphasis on sales and service to the families of America's most important population group—the families of industrial wage earners, and (6) emphasis on agent loyalty to the company and its products.

The unfavorable effects of the debit system include: (1) recruiting of agents to sell and service primarily the families of industrial wage earners whose limited incomes did not permit extensive purchases of life insurance, (2) education and training of agents were limited to what were considered necessary to sell and service the average family of industrial wage earners, (3) toleration of mediocrity in agent production results, (4) emphasis on collecting premiums and conserving existing business rather than imaginative and dynamic growth of new sales and (5) preservation and continuation of a sales organization that was appropriate for the "blue and grey-collar" market but inappropriate for the higher income market that developed after World War II. Happily an enlightened management in the combination companies has taken steps to correct the major inadequacies of the older marketing structure while preserving its important strengths.

A NEW ERA OF PROGRESS

Public Criticism, Investigation and Reform

The era of the Tontine inevitably had its end in a period of public criticism, investigation and reform. The Armstrong hearings and new state legislation that followed in 1905, actually stand between two eras in the evolution of American life insurance thought. For management and marketing alike it tolled the time of a grand conversion. Asserting their long unexercised authority, the people summoned a new order of management, under strengthened government regulation, and the course of developments changed. Tontine methods were outlawed.

Group Life Insurance

Group insurance was introduced around 1911. One of the first major cases was an insurance contract between the Montgomery Ward Company and the Equitable Life Assurance Society of the United States. Some 2,912 employees were thus covered for $5,946,564 of insurance.

The tremendous growth in group life insurance after World War II has had significant effects on the organizational structure of the home offices and the marketing operations of the agencies. Because of the technical and specialized nature of group insurance marketing, home office and field specialists must be available to assist brokers and agents in selling and servicing group insurance. The group insurance buyer is usually a well-informed and sophisticated buyer. A knowledgeable and sophisticated specialist is needed at each step in the sales process. The group market for the large employer group cases exists primarily in the large metropolitan areas. One reason for this is the vesting of authority to arrange the group coverage in the national offices of the large corporation. Therefore, the principal group writing companies have found it necessary to establish group offices in the major metropolitan areas. Each metropolitan area group office will have a manager reporting either directly to the company's home office or to a regional office. Although there is frequently little relationship between the local group office's operations and the company's individual sales, both offices can be helpful to the other in building prestige for the company and its products as well as in communicating sales opportunities. However, the relationship between the group office personnel and the individual agency personnel is sometimes strained. The "vertical" and "horizontal" extension of group sales is criticized by the individual agency as cutting into its market. The placing of a few group cases on a direct basis without agent commissions further irritates the individual agent.

With the coming of group insurance and the many legislative developments discussed below, it soon became apparent that to function as effective counselors to their clients, life agents needed far more than "just a rate book and a pat on the back" with which they had traditionally been sent "out into the field."

Progress in Education and Training

The scattered training schools that existed in company home offices around 1910 helped to underscore as well as serve the knowledge and skill requirements of the new marketing mode.

To make a beginning on the educational work that confronted them, the field forces of the industry, acting through their national association, commissioned Dr. S. S. Huebner to prepare a text on life insurance. It was published in 1915 and received much favorable comment.

According to Griffin Lovelace, a pioneer in life insurance marketing,

> It is hard to say which company was the first to start educational and training work for the agent. The Travelers was the first Connecticut company to have a formal department. The Equitable of New York was the first of the New York companies. The Connecticut Mutual was perhaps the first in my time to introduce some aspects of need selling and the psychology of selling. Vice President Winslow Russell of the Phoenix Mutual was the company leader in promoting educational facilities for agents that resulted in our schools at Carnegie Tech and New York University ... you can't be too definite about which was the first company to start educational work for the agents.

Looking back over this formative period, Vincent B. Coffin, one of the early students of the Carnegie Institute of Technology in Pittsburgh, stated:

> In the judgment of the writer, the one individual most responsible for the new ideas ... was Griffin M. Lovelace ... Mr. Lovelace introduced a new concept ... completely accepted today ... that life insurance ought to be sold on the basis of definite and specific needs. If it seems incredible to you that this truth was revolutionary, then you need to be reminded that up until about this time, companies had distributed their wares almost exclusively on the comparative merits of one policy contract over another. ...

Recognition of the Counseling Aspects of Marketing

With the passage of regulatory laws in the beginning of the 20th century, salesmen increasingly assumed the roles of counsellors as well as salesmen. The marketing of life insurance increasingly became more of a service than the merchandising of a product. The idea gained ground that marketing life insurance is a complicated service and science, requiring training, understanding and dedication. There was a sharp shift from over-powering opposition in a sales situation to studying the needs of clients. There is every indication that this will continue to be the sales approach of the future for those who are truly committed to a career of professional service in life insurance selling.

INSTITUTIONAL COOPERATION FOR IMPROVEMENT OF LIFE INSURANCE MARKETING

Competition Leads to Cooperation

The rapid growth of an industry inevitably means strong competition within the industry. Life insurance in force grew from $97,000,000 in 1850 to $204,000,000 by 1860; to $1,522,000,000 by 1880 and to $3,522,000,000 by 1890 and was over $7 billion by 1900. Parallel to this growth was an increasing competition within the life insurance industry. This competition appeared in the form of (1) establishment of new companies, (not always on a sound financial basis); (2) establishment of new general agencies; (3) recruiting of new agents; (4) payment of high commissions rates; (5) projection of high dividend rates by mutual companies; (6) contractual guarantees of high non-forfeiture values; and (7) a general vying among agents and agencies for increased sales volume. One author has described life insurance agency operation in the period following the Civil War as follows:

> The offices were run on a high-pressure system. Solicitors extolled the merits of their own and depreciated those of rival companies in almost every town and village in the country, aided by pamphlets, periodicals, and prospectuses, picturing in magnificent figures the attractive features of the new philanthropy. . . . Excessive outlays and defective management were alike concealed by the enormous volume of new business which every enterprising office was able to report at the end of successive years, and the suggestions of speculation, reaction, and a possible collapse were unheeded in the rich harvest that was being reaped. [13]

As early as 1858 thoughtful men in the industry recognized that there were mutual benefits to be gained from cooperatively working together instead of villifying each other in an intensely competitive marketing environment. The establishment of The Life Convention on a permanent basis in 1859 in one indication of the early attempts toward cooperation. Over the years great progress has been made so that today it can truly be said:

> Probably no business in the country is served, as is life insurance, by so many associations having members so well schooled in cooperative endeavor, or so willing to volunteer services in a community cause. [14]

This occupational attitude of cooperation, which flourishes today under the profound respect which most life insurance men have for their business, may be considered as part of the civic awareness of this century, yet it is still so unusual in other industries as to inspire comment from people outside the life insurance business. The institutional climate today is in direct contrast to conditions of 100 years ago when hatred and suspicion were not unusual between competing agents, when promises frequently exceeded the ability to perform, when "traveling agents" rode the strains with the hardware and soft goods drummers, and when slander was sometimes the language between companies.[15]

---

[13] Nichols, Walter, "Annals of American Insurance, 1771 to 1876," *The Insurance Blue Book for 1876~187* (New York, 1877). pp. 57~58.

[14] *Why an Institute?* by Board of Managers, Institute of Life Insurance, 1938.

[15] Stalson, J. Owen. *op. cit.,* p. 485.

The Organization of the National Association of Life Underwriters

Although a few tentative steps had been taken toward cooperation among companies, the first as early as 1859, none of these had as direct an influence on the marketing of life insurance as the yeasting at the point of sales, which led agents to realize they had interests as a group to try to better their condition and improve their stature before the public. Probably the earliest recorded reference to such group action by agents was that reported by the *Chronicle* (an insurance publication) in November, 1869, in describing the proceedings of a meeting of the Life Underwriters' Association of Chicago. From time to time through this period, the activities of other associations in Ohio, Maine, and the southern states were mentioned, but the most significant development was in Boston, where these local associations organized themselves in 1890 into the National Association of Life Underwriters. This action by agents had no measurable influence on the companies at first, but there can be little doubt that it furnished a pattern, a justification, and a motive force for the institutional cooperation which came into being after the Armstrong investigation in 1905, and for the desire to improve life insurance marketing, which crystalized in 1916.

Under the leadership of Winslow Russell of Phoenix Mutual and Edward A. Woods of the Equitable Society, the membership of NALU launched a campaign in 1912 to educate the public and interest colleges and civic groups in life insurance. Early work on the college campus was done by Dr. Solomon S. Huebner of the Wharton School of Finance at the University of Pennsylvania, who became the best known teacher of insurance in the country, and eventually head of the American College of Life Underwriters. Woods, one of the most famous of general agents, whose agency had $100 millions of insurance in force in 1910 and $250 millions in 1920, was an innovator in the search for new markets. For instance, in 1909, he pioneered the sale of life insurance for business partnerships and other business purposes. He was a widely quoted speaker, and a moving force in the NALU. In 1915, he became NALU president and chairman of a newly formed committee on scientific salesmanship. He is credited by authorities with having inspired the Equitable's home office schools, which began in 1902, and the company's early exploration of scientific salesmanship.

The Founding of the Association of Life Agency Officers

Woods and Russell had already been collaborating for some time when they shared the platform at the World Salesmanship Congress in Detroit in July, 1916. Woods, who headed the life insurance section, spoke on schools for salesmen, while Russell repined the wasteful methods in use in the hiring and firing of agents and called for rigid selection and careful training by expert teachers. He urged the home office agency department executives at the Congress to support the idea of organizing an association of their own. The idea was discussed at length at an informal luncheon meeting for the executives, sponsored by the Detroit Association of Life Underwriters. As a result of this session sufficient interest was generated, and an organizational meeting was held in Chicago on October 16, 1916. Here was born the Association of Life Agency Officers.

Up to this point, agency department men had had little opportunity to meet and discuss their common problems. It would be hard to estimate how much Russell's geniality was the instrument which broke down their mutual suspicion, but it was evident in the early meetings that the conferees accorded to him unquestioned leadership, which they were slow to grant anyone else. The discussions were wide-ranging in the first annual meeting, but there were also indications that, in regard to some information, the conferees remained relatively uncommunicative. Even so, these early meetings hammered out an effective platform for institutional cooperation in the management of life insurance sales.

From the beginning, Russell was imbued with the idea of research, based on an industry-wide sharing of marketing information. The ALAO, to him, was only a first step. The organization was a nominal one, with only a $10 dues structure, based on individual members rather than company memberships. Its annual meeting, and the distribution of a printed proceedings of that meeting, were its only activities, other than some committee work. Through one of these groups, the ALAO worked with the Federal government to set up insurance education programs in the armed forces in 1918. The effectiveness of the ALAO was largely in channeling the marketing leadership of the industry into some sort of cooperation where none existed previously. One indication of this was that 14 company presidents among the charter members were responsible for the operation of their companies' agency department functions. The 1919 annual meeting considered, among other things, the first proposal for a national cooperative advertising program. The greatest attention, however, was given to Russell's insistence on the need for a central research facility and the establishment of uniform standards in selection and training.

The Establishment of the Life Insurance Sales Research Bureau

At the 5th annual meeting of ALAO, in 1921, Russell's reiteration of his research theme paid off. "The problem of distribution," he told the conference, "is now before the American business house." Wood's work in Pittsburgh had paved the way for a life insurance research program being set up as part of the research facility at Carnegie Technological Institute. The ALAO voted to form the Bureau of Research, with 13 charter member companies pledging their support. John Marshall Holcombe, Jr., lawyer son of the president of Phoenix Mutual, who had started as a legal counsel for the company, but who had moved over to handling agency department problems under Russell's direction, was named the business manager of what soon came to be known as the Life Insurance Sales Research Bureau. By March, 1922, when the organizational meeting of LISRB was held in the building of Union Central Life in Cincinnati, Holcombe had signed up 22 member companies to support a $15,000 budget.[16]

Participation of Canadian Companies

It is interesting to note that one of the original 22 member companies of LISRB was a Canadian company. From the very beginning, both the LISRB and the ALAO were truly international organizations. Nine Canadian companies were members of ALAO at the time of its first annual meeting in 1917. Participation of the Canadian companies had an enormous influence on LISRB research. They formed a homogeneous group and, secondly, they were and continued to be greatly interested in research. Consequently, they were often used for pilot programs. For instance, when the Central Scoring Unit was first set up in Hartford, Canadian selection tests were scored for a full year before the service was extended to United States companies.

The LISRB and the ALAO Merge to Form LIAMA

The bureau, as the offspring of the ALAO, was under the latter's constant scrutiny. Holcombe, too, was vitally interested in keeping a close relationship to member companies because all of Russell's influence had been for the creation of a viable arm of the industry which would be useful in dealing with the real problems of the market place. The bureau started operations at Carnegie Tech, but Holcombe was somewhat restive in the academic atmosphere and there are some indications that he felt the specific problems of the life insurance business might be swallowed up in the broad gauge business research program in effect at Carnegie Tech. Within a year, he resolved to break the ties with the college and move the bureau to New

---

[16] John Marshall Holcombe, Jr., correspondence, Library of Life Insurance Agency Management Association.

York, to be nearer the center of the industry.[17] One year later, in 1924, the bureau made the move to Hartford.

LISRB was an operating organization with a professional staff, while ALAO continued as a discussion forum. The bureau, in this context, was the institutional center for research in life insurance marketing, while the ALAO served as a means for directing attention to the areas in which research was needed. It was natural, in the course of events, for both organizations to merge, in 1945, into the Life Insurance Agency Management Association. In another phenomenon of the times, some of the subjects that preoccupied the minds of agency officers at the early ALAO annual meetings led, eventually, to the formation of other special purpose insurance associations of companies—and also associations of individuals who would confer together on their particular specialized functions in home office operations. Examples of the latter are the Association of Life Insurance Counsel, the Association of Life Insurance Medical Directors, the Home Office Life Underwriters Association, the Society of Actuaries, and the Life Advertisers Association.

The Services of LIAMA

LIAMA, currently staffed by over 150 people, including approximately 50 professional researchers, psychologists, economists, statisticians and management consultants, produces a broad range of services for its member companies. The research department usually has underway more than fifty research projects involving markets, finances, and human resources.

In the *market* area the research division conducts surveys to learn about the consumer—the kind of person he is, his motivation for buying, his buying characteristics and his habits. The research division obtains economic market data to help planners of sales strategy, it keeps abreast of developments affecting business persistency and attempts to pinpoint important distribution trends.

Financial research is conducted on a continuing basis to establish facts and industry norms that will increase returns from company investments in sales development and public service and attempts to develop methods of functional cost analysis which will improve supervision of field operations. Other objectives of financial research are the development of methods of investing in new agents and methods of compensation for established agents that are effective and appropriate for the present economy.

The third area, *human resources* research covers selection, training, job attitudes, public opinion, leader behavior, company practices, products and

---

[17] Holcombe correspondence, LIAMA.

services, and manpower research. The *Aptitude Index* is the best known test to indicate if a man has an aptitude for selling ordinary life insurance. A continuous program of research—checking and revising—is maintained to take into account significant changes in economic and other factors.

LIAMA strives to keep its members aware of the findings and results of research and of its program through the Company Relations Division —publications and the annual visit to each company by a trained management consultant. The company consultant maintains close liaison with research activity and has direct contact with many member companies. A typical relationship involves an average of 32 contacts—personal visits, correspondence and telephone—a year. Consultants staff LIAMA's various schools and seminars for field management, agency development, and executive development. Consultants are also responsible for contributions to the Association's growing publications operation, which includes a monthly handbook, two quarterly magazines, four newsletters and over 140 agent and management texts.

IMPORTANT INSTITUTIONS DIRECTLY OR INDIRECTLY SERVING MARKETING MANAGEMENT

Many institutions have contributed to and continue to aid the multiple phases of life insurance sales management. The following paragraphs describe the services provided by those institutions that have been particularly significant in (1) finding solutions to common problems, (2) providing information and (3) inspiring management to strive for greater accomplishments in life and health insurance marketing.

Institute of Life Insurance

The Institute of Life Insurance, which serves as the public relations spokesman of the life insurance business, while not involved with the sale of life insurance, performs an invaluable service through its data collection and publications programs. The *Life Insurance Fact Book* is a case in point. Reporting annually on major industry trends, the *Fact Book* is a valuable adjunct to the total marketing information process.

Also of interest are the informational services of the Institute, which are designed to bring about a better understanding of the use of life insurance by the public. This is done by cooperating with newspapers and magazines, community organizations, and schools and educators.

Through programs of national advertising, the Institute speaks for the business as a whole in trying to inform and educate the public about how life insurance works, and about its unique advantages as a form of savings and protection. This and other educational efforts of the Institute are continuing public conditioners that support the efforts of agents of all life companies.

In its research function the Institute has published studies of consumer attitudes and characteristics that have been of background value to those concerned with distribution. The *Life Insurance Public,* published in 1955, provided information on the characteristics of the owners of life insurance; age, sex, income, occupation, educational status, family status, place of residence, attitudes toward ownership, and ownership related to other protection programs such as social security, pension plans, veterans' insurance, and group insurance. In 1961, the Institute surveyed male heads of households of two or more persons under age 55. This study covered many facets of personality, economic behavior, experience with and attitudes toward life insurance, all analyzed in terms of the differences between groups who varied in the amount of life insurance carried in relation to personal income. The Institute has also surveyed the ownership of life insurance and related characteristics in the older population and, for a number of years, published tabulations and analyses of life insurance ownership among American families.[18]

The American College of Life Underwriters

The American College of Life Underwriters was established to provide a system of professional education and certification for persons engaged in the process of insuring human life values. Founded in 1927, the American College is an independent, non-profit educational institution located in Bryn Mawr, Pennsylvania. The "Life Underwriters" portion of the College's name is interpreted to include all persons engaged in activities related to insuring human life values. Candidates in the educational programs of the College include practicing field underwriters, field management personnel, home office personnel holding management or technical positions, collegiate teachers of insurance, insurance regulatory personnel, corporate risk managers, and employees of life and health insurance institutional organizations.

The professional educational programs of the College are in three general areas. The Charter Life Underwriter Diploma Program, which is the major activity, is provided for individuals seeking professional knowledge related to the insuring of human life values and certification through attainment of the C.L.U. designation. The program is based on recognition of the neces-

---

[18] *Catalog of Research and Statistical Projects of Life Insurance Organizations, 1950~1965,* Institute of Life Insurance.

sity for a life underwriter to have a broad business education. This includes knowledge of economics; taxation; wills; trusts and estates, in addition to life and health insurance. The College provides Study Guides, Teacher's Manuals, and other study materials; administers examinations for each of the ten courses; and assists in establishing classes and study groups.

The other two general areas of education provided by the College are the Certificate Course Program and the Continuing Education Program. The Certificate Course Program is provided for persons interested in specialized areas of study. This program includes courses in Agency Management, Company Management, Estate Planning, Group Insurance, Health Insurance, Pension Planning, and Personal Investments.

The Continuing Education Program is jointly sponsored with the American Society of Chartered Life Underwriters and is designed to further the professional education of Chartered Life Underwriters. In addition, the College, in cooperation with the Society, establishes and endeavors to assure the maintenance of high standards of professional conduct.

The McCahan Foundation, established for research in security, risk, and insurance, also is part of the College structure. The College also conducts experimental classes, lectures, and seminars, and engages in research regarding the adult learning process.

American Life Convention

This organization of life insurance companies endeavors to advance the economic and social objectives of life insurance and gives continuing attention to the multiple management problems confronting the life insurance industry. The ALC has lent continuing support over the years to the initiation and passage of constructive state and federal legislation and the establishment of sound administrative measures.

Life Insurance Association of America

Another cooperative organization of life insurance companies, the LIAA, maintains a large staff of professional people whose continuing responsibility it is to advance the interests of life insurance policyholders and the life insurance industry. It works closely with the ALC in supporting state and federal legislation of interest to policyholders and the life insurance industry.

Life Office Management Association

This organization is devoted to the continuing improvement of life insurance management through a program of research and educational courses.

Member companies cooperate in sharing research results and management innovations. The Association conducts an educational program for office employees, completion of which is recognized with the professional designation FLMI (Fellow Life Management Institute).

Life Underwriter Training Council

This is a national organization that sponsors locally administered courses in sales techniques for agents marketing life and health insurance. Since its establishment in 1947, LUTC has trained more life insurance salesmen than all other institutions in life and health insurance. It emphasizes practical sales techniques in actual case situations.

Million Dollar Round Table

This is an international organization of top life insurance salesmen dedicated to the maintenance of high standards for marketing personnel in terms of sales volume and professional ethics. The MDRT annual meeting is an outstanding symposium presented by life insurance marketing specialists skilled in all sales aspects of the business. The resulting publication makes a noteworthy contribution to life insurance sales literature.

National Association of Life Underwriters

This is a national organization of life insurance salesmen devoted to the encouragement of the sound growth of life insurance sales through the sponsorship of local life underwriter associations whose monthly meetings strengthen the dedication of all life insurance sales personnel to the objectives and purposes of the National Association. Tremendous accomplishments have been achieved by the Association over the years to advance the life insurance agents' professional status through the quality of their service. The General Agents and Managers Conference of the National Association of Life Underwriters sponsors classes in agency management and each year conducts a national seminar and a national institute at which the nation's outstanding leaders in agency management articulate the most recent developments in management concepts and practice.

Association for Advanced Life Underwriting

With expansion of business life insurance and estate planning concepts, there was growing interest in an association devoted to the more sophisticated applications of life insurance. The AALU was formed in 1957 by a group of men who specialized in advanced underwriting. It operates as a conference of the NALU.

EXAMPLES OF INSTITUTIONAL COOPERATION

There are many examples in recent years of a viable spirit of cooperation among the various institutions contributing to the increased sophistication of life insurance marketing and sales management. The Institute of Life Insurance and LIAMA have cooperated in: (1) the 1946 study of employment trends in the industry; (2) the 1956 study of premium volume, ordinary life insurance in force, weekly premium sales, group sales and ordinary sales; (3) the 1960 report, *The Growth of Term Insurance in 1950's*; and (4) the 1966 study, *Life Insurance Attitudes* and *Expectations of American Youth.*

The Life Underwriter Training Council and the General Agents and Managers Conference of NALU have participated in joint projects with LIAMA, including: (1) the 1953 publication of *Managerial Practices* which summarizes the day-to-day operational practices of agency managers in the recruiting, selection and training of agents; (2) the 1952 study relating characteristics of agents attending LUTC classes to their sales methods, marketing patterns and performance; (3) the 1955 study of LUTC students successful and unsuccessful sales interviews; (4) the 1956 evaluation of *The LUTC Lesson-Plan Technique,* (5) the 1961 report, *Health and Life Sales Methods of Ordinary and Combination Agents;* (6) the 1960–64 five volume series, *Life Insurance in Focus;* (7) the 1966 publication of *The Family Financial Officer;* (8) the NALU-LIAMA biennial *Survey of Agency Opinion,* which provides a current source of information relative to (a) reaction of the field force to recent developments in the industry, (b) agency morale, and (c) job attitudes.

The establishment of the Research and the Inter-association Statistical Group is an outstanding example of institutional cooperation. The purpose of the organization is to coordinate the research activities of the associations represented in the Trade Executive Association and thereby prevent duplication of activity in data collection. The organizations which compose the group include NALU, LIAMA, LOMA, Institute of Life Insurance, Health Insurance Association of America, Life Insurance Association of America, American Life Convention, Canadian Life Insurance Association, and Life Insurers Conference.

Probably the most impressive aspect of institutional cooperation in life insurance marketing is the cooperation of companies in providing each other with a central well of information concerning marketing procedures and marketing results. For example, data from the companies furnish the raw material for the main thrust of LIAMA's research. The statistical surveys of LIAMA are based upon company supplied data. These statistical surveys have been keeping score for the industry since the early days of the LISRB. They provide a measure of the progress being made from year to year on a number of fronts including sales, in force, lapse and market characteristics. They are useful to companies as a standard against which to measure company performance. In a sense, they create a context in which to operate and a point of departure from which to plan.

Perhaps most of all, the statistical surveys are important in the recording of history. If history is instructive in helping the industry to assess better how it arrived where it is now, then the statistics of the past may point directions for the future. If the portents are not palatable, the industry at least has the chance to try to do something about them.

For over 200 years now, the agent has been the key to life insurance marketing. Experiments to sell through other means have largely failed.

So it is the agent—today better educated, more knowledgeable, better able to serve public needs than ever before—who is responsible for the fact that by the 1970's, American families were protected by more than one trillion dollars of life insurance guarantees. The bulk of this protection was individual policy ordinary, followed by fast growing ownership of group life. Industrial insurance was slowly phasing out.

At the same time, as inflation and high interest rates continued to plague the economy through the 1960's, and as competitive forms of savings and investment came to the fore, life insurance companies began to re-examine both their markets and their marketing traditions. Well before 1970, the move to diversification was on. Without de-emphasizing the importance of life insurance and its traditional guarantees in any way, companies were adding equity-type products such as mutual funds and variable annuities. In 1970, New York Life became the first major U.S. company to announce its intent to introduce a variable life insurance policy.

It looked as if product diversification was here to stay for most life companies, as it was for so many other businesses.

At the same time, there was no question about the continuing essentiality of life insurance and the fact that for most men it would continue to be the best means of guaranteeing financial security for themselves and their families. It was also clear that, even though group and other mass distribution methods were likely to have an increasing impact, the professional, well informed, career life underwriter would continue to be the key to life insurance marketing.

Section II

HOME OFFICE FUNCTIONS

3

Significance of the Home Office Functions to Life Insurance Marketing

Roger Hull

Although there is a lack of unanimity as to a definition of marketing, one view that may be taken is that marketing is a process wherein a company analyzes its internal strengths and brings them all to bear on the external forces in such a way that the company will achieve both its short-range and long-range objectives. In particular, marketing is the process by which the demand structure for insurance, or more broadly financial services, is anticipated or enlarged and satisfied through the conception, promotion, exchange and physical distribution of such services.[1] It is for this reason that marketing is frequently said to be the key to the successful operation of a life insurance company.

If the marketing process is to be successful, however, management must see that a proper relationship exists among all home office functions. Each home office executive who is responsible for a particular functional department must understand the role of his department in the marketing process and its contribution to the objectives of marketing as well as overall company goals. Therefore, if the home office departments of a life insurance

---

[1] This definition has been adapted from Theodore N. Beckman and William R. Davidson with the assistance of James F. Engel, *Marketing* (Eighth edition; New York: The Ronald Press Company 1967), p. 4.

company are to make a significant and continuing contribution to the marketing process, top management must establish a sound foundation for these departments. This foundation can be provided by well-defined objectives.

COMPANY-WIDE OBJECTIVES

The first step in providing this foundation is for top management to define the company-wide or overall objectives of the firm. This is necessary to provide a guide to departmental decision making and goal setting. For example, assume a company president calls in his vice president of underwriting and tells him that *the objective* of the company this year is to have the smallest number of losses in the company's history. He then calls in the agency vice president and tells him *the objective* is to have the greatest sales volume in the company's history. It is evident that the vice president of underwriting and the vice president of agencies will be in conflict. They have been placed in an over-defined situation. The only resolution to this conflict is for the president to determine what the primary objective of his company is. Given this primary objective, the vice presidents can then make their plans and can determine the contribution needed from them to accomplish this objective. In this way their efforts can be coordinated rather than placed in opposition to each other.

Objectives, of course, will differ among various companies, depending upon how management views the firm's respective strengths and weaknesses. The traditions and environment of the company, its geographical scope, the kind of people who make up the organization, and the philosophy of management also will affect the objectives. There are some general objectives, however, that should be germane to nearly all life insurance companies. These might include:

(1) *Growth.* To maintain the company's vitality as a growing enterprise and to be an ever-improving company in which to own insurance and to work.

(2) *Service.* To strive continuously to improve products and services in order to give the best possible coverage to the public at the lowest possible cost.

(3) *Market position.* To maintain and improve the company's competitive position among the companies with which it compares itself.

(4) *Financial strength.* To maintain adequate financial strength as measured by surplus, reserves, and stability of asset values.

(5) *Personnel.* To maintain its competitive position in matters of compensation of employees, field underwriters and in other areas of personnel policy and to encourage and to maintain the

development of adequate and competent manpower for future as well as present needs.

(6) *Social responsibility.* To see that all areas of the company's operations are conducted in accordance with public policy.

It should be recognized that the above objectives are neither mutually exclusive nor independent. Thus, management must not only define the objectives but in addition place a priority as to which objectives are the dominant ones.

Within the above framework of company-wide objectives, management must define its marketing objectives and the means for attaining them. It should be noted that many of the company objectives are marketing oriented, for example, growth, service and market position.

MARKETING OBJECTIVES

As was true with company-wide objectives, marketing objectives will vary among companies. A few examples that might be applicable to most companies are:

(1) *Volume of business.* To obtain new business and to maintain existing business on the books so that the company experiences a growing volume of premium income and life insurance in force.

(2) *Promotion.* To develop and to maintain effective recruiting, training and merchandising programs for use by the sales manager, and to develop and to maintain effective sales tools and promotion aids for use by field underwriters.

(3) *New products and marketing techniques.* To develop, in cooperation with other departments, new products and marketing techniques so that the company can better serve the insuring public and promote a continuing client-practitioner relationship between the field underwriter and the policyowner.

(4) *Manpower.* To create and to maintain field management and manpower development programs necessary to attain the marketing objectives and to compensate such personnel on an incentive basis for quality as well as quantity of business.

(5) *Product mix.* A company that sells ordinary and group insurance as well as health insurance will have to determine the mix it desires among these different types of insurance.

THE SIGNIFICANCE OF HOME OFFICE FUNCTIONS TO THE ACHIEVEMENT OF MARKETING OBJECTIVES

After management has established the company-wide objectives and defined the marketing objectives within this framework, policies and procedures must be defined for the attainment of these objectives. Procedures must be established for (1) the periodic review of objectives and policies, (2) the evaluation of actual results in light of the objectives and (3) the adjustment of activities as required in order to bring actions in line with objectives. This can only be accomplished if the objectives, policies, and procedures are communicated to the people responsible for attaining them. Thus, each department must be made aware of its role in the attainment of objectives.

These four elements: (1) overall company objectives, (2) marketing objectives, (3) communication of objectives, and (4) policies and procedures for review and evaluation, provide the basis of a management program. They provide a common foundation on which the management and personnel of all departments can bring to bear their specialized skills, as actuaries, underwriters, lawyers, and investment men, to make their company a better company for which to work and for which to sell. These elements provide internal direction to a company.

This chapter is not intended to be a catalogue of particulars precisely useful to all readers. In general, larger companies employ a large number of people who perform precisely defined specialties. Medium-size or smaller companies employ fewer people and each person frequently performs combined specialties and a broader range of individual activities. For example, in some companies market research and public relations might be functions of sales promotion and development. Underwriting and medical services might be combined with actuarial. Or, group and health insurance sales might be completely disassociated from the ordinary department. In other companies a different set of relationships might exist.

This chapter, therefore, will analyze the effects of the various home office functions on the achievement of marketing objectives regardless of the size of company or the location of the particular function on an organization chart. Attention will be focused on three methods of attaining marketing objectives:

    (1) Development of products that will attract buyers.
    (2) Distribution of the products in as effective and economical manner as possible.
    (3) Provision of services that will keep the buyer sold.

Development of Products

All product development must be guided initially by a life insurance company's pricing and dividend philosophy. This philosophy must come from the company's top management. For example, in a mutual life insurance company management must decide: Will the going-in price be high or low? Should the dividend scale be steep in order to bring increasing benefits to the continuing policyowners, or will early dividends be declared to benefit the newer policyowners? Is the dividend scale set this year something that management expects to maintain next year, or will the company be concerned about next year? Will management seek to keep surplus close to permissible limits, or will it allow the ratio to fluctuate widely from year to year?

Once top management makes the basic decisions relative to product development, those decisions provide the premises for derivative planning and, therefore, must be communicated to all departments that are concerned with product development.

In developing products that will be attractive to buyers, the marketing personnel will play key roles. They must attempt to anticipate future trends, analyze the marketing efforts of other financial institutions as well as life insurance competitors, test the new products before recommending their adoption or rejection and estimate the impact of new products or changes in price. They should be joined by the actuarial and underwriting personnel in analyzing the company's experience with its product portfolio and in comparing their experience with that of competing companies.

THE AGENCY DEPARTMENT

The agency department often will be the originator or innovator of marketing ideas. It feeds back to company management the views of field underwriters, policyowners, competitors and others. It thus acts as the direct liaison—in both directions—between the home office and the field force, thereby assisting in the determination of priorities of action.

THE ADMINISTRATION DEPARTMENT[2]

The administration department is involved in product development to assure that any new product has simplicity of concept and is amenable to simple administrative procedures. The administrator is not only interested in seeing that the policyowners are served quickly, satisfactorily and economically, but he is also concerned with efficient service to field underwriters. A life insurance company that is capable of giving prompt and accurate service to its field underwriting force will be placed in a strong competitive position.

THE ACTUARIAL DEPARTMENT

The actuary has the ultimate responsibility for the financial soundness of new products, new provisions and new pricing. He relies on the underwriting department for asssurance that a proposed product can be and

---

[2] This title will vary among companies and in some companies its functions may be scattered among different departments.

will be underwritten on a sound basis. In writing the language of new policies, the actuary and underwriter will work closely with the law, agency and public relations departments. In many cases these departments will form a policy writing committee.

THE CONTROLLER

In the development of new products, the aid of the controller will be enlisted in estimating and controlling the costs of experimentation, installation and operation of new programs as well as in the revision of any existing products.

THE INVESTMENT DEPARTMENT

Product development also is influenced by the financial strength of a company. Such strength comes about through the gains realized from the company's investments and the control of operating costs by all departments.

Adequate financial strength, particularly as shown by surplus and reserves, has permitted many companies to broaden their scope of operations by embracing the concept of a multi-functional financial institution. Dramatic evidence of this is the revitalization of the role of life insurance in the pension market, the increased marketing of variable annuities, mutual funds, and, in some cases, expansion into the property and liability insurance market. The achievement of high investment yields on portfolio assets is an important objective of the investment department, since this has a significant impact on the pricing of the company's products and therefore has a substantial effect on the company's competitive position.

SUMMARY

Product development[3] is essential to a life insurance company that desires continued growth and success. Although the marketing personnel will play key roles in the development of new products, all home office departments must contribute to and be coordinated with the work of the marketing department if the sale of new products is to function with economy and effectiveness.

Distribution of Products

As was pointed out above, the second step in attaining the marketing objectives is the effective and economic distribution of the company's products. Here again management must first make some basic decisions:

---

[3] See Chapter 12 for a discussion of product planning.

(1) Will the company distribute its products primarily through its own field force of full-time underwriters or will it encourage and accept business from other sources, including brokers?

(2) What types of products will be distributed? Will the company market health insurance as well as life insurance, substandard as well as standard life insurance, association group as well as regular group, segregated funded pension plans as well as conventional group annuities. The company must also decide its desired product mix. That is, which type of business will be the company's principal line and what percentage of each of the other types is desired?

(3) Will special markets be developed and cultivated? For example, will the company attempt to develop a market among (i) college students, (ii) professional men, (iii) business firms, (iv) blue collar employees on a payroll allotment plan?

(4) Will the company that is marketing medical expense insurance, disability income insurance, group insurance, and mutual funds develop each of its lines through specialists, or will the lines be handled in ways that will provide increased opportunities for the company's full-time field underwriters?

Once these questions have been answered then all departments in the company can devote their specific talents in assisting in the development of the manpower needed to distribute the company's products efficiently and economically.

MANPOWER DEVELOPMENT

The marketing department will be primarily responsible for determining the market areas and the sales potential of each area for the company's products. It should keep a close watch on what life insurance and non-life insurance competitors are doing. With the assistance of the controller and the actuary, the marketing department should estimate the manpower needed to carry out a given level of marketing activity. It should also be involved in studying and "casting out" the number, type and location of sales outlets. In addition, the department should analyze the size, quality, productivity and survival pattern of the current sales force. Finally, the marketing personnel should seek to determine the best sources of manpower and the most effective methods for the selection of manpower.[4]

The agency department should have the responsibility for developing the field management necessary to recruit, select, train, and supervise an ever-growing sales force. It should provide the tools and programs needed to fulfill these obligations as well. It also should be involved in the design of the merchandising programs and the selling tools to be used by the field underwriters.

[4] See Chapter 21, for a discussion of the problem of finding agency manpower and Chapter 22, for a discussion of selection of manpower.

One of the most important jobs of the agency department is the establishment of methods for supervising the operation of its program, i.e., control.

The actuary should provide answers to questions concerning initial costs, strain on the company's surplus, the effect of manpower development on asset growth and other such related problems. In addition, he should assist in projecting the company's future position with respect to assets, insurance in force, expenses, earnings and other matters. The actuary also acts as the engineer in constructing the compensation methods for field underwriters, managers, or general agents, as well as other members of the field force.

Another important contributor to the efficient and economical distribution of products is the home office underwriter. He plays an important role in seeing that the company's underwriting practices are understood by the field force. This is accomplished through field visits, participation in business and educational conferences, training programs, correspondence and other communications media.

The underwriter should review his department's practices continuously and be sure that the requirement rules are as liberal as possible while remaining consistent with the company's underwriting policy. A final task of the underwriter is the study of the problems of the field force, the underwriting differences among geographical areas and market segments and the practices of competitors.

MANAGEMENT DEVELOPMENT

Although the development of sales manpower in quality and quantity is an important aspect of product distribution, management development also is of primary importance. In fact, some would say that the key to effective sales manpower is effective management. This author firmly believes:

> Although machines and automation will help solve problems now and in the future, the greatest single hope is in the field of human relations—trying to find ways to motivate people, to set examples for them, to teach them and to learn from them, to train and to supervise them, to move them toward their intellectual and physical capacity, and to project them into responsibility as they earn it. For all the advances in automation, people still remain a corporation's greatest asset, and the yield from such assets will be in direct proportion to the way in which people use their most valuable tools—time and intelligence.

This objective can only be achieved with management manpower that is well-versed in the management of human resources. Success hinges on:

(1) A careful selection of candidates.
(2) The developing and conducting of training and educational programs that are practical, comprehensive and intellectually stimulating.
(3) Personnel policies that create an atmosphere for job satisfaction through adequate compensation, individual recognition and opportunities for advancement.
(4) Leadership that is knowledgeable, dynamic and exemplary.
(5) Disciplines that insist that a manager spend his time managing, i.e., getting work done through other people, rather than doing it himself.
(6) Financial support and incentives for continuing education and development.

Once all departments are manned by well-trained and educated management, the task of accomplishing the company's marketing as well as overall objectives will be well on its way to success.

MANPOWER SUPPORT

Now, let us assume that a company has created products, recruited adequate manpower, developed people to manage the manpower and trained all of them well. What additional is needed?

The need now is for instruments that will bring together a salesman and a prospect. These tools will be created by a variety of talents within the company—merchandising, sales promotion, advertising, market development and publicity. Close coordination among all such departments is needed to assure that all parts are in harmony for the sales message. Pretesting as well as follow-up evaluation should be employed to see that the sales instruments are effective.

Merchandising and sales promotion, however, involve more than advertising, direct mail and related devices. Other home office departments also make important contributions. For example, consider the influence of:

(1) The actuary when he designs, jointly with the legal department, the provisions and language of the company's policies and options; when he determines dividend allocations and interest assumptions year after year; and when he provides field underwriters with technical assistance, draws up illustrations and makes competitive comparisons.
(2) The underwriter when he supports the development of non-medical coverage, family policies, add-on riders, triple indemnity and automatic inclusion of waiver of premium and accidental death benefit provisions.
(3) The controller, or treasurer, when he induces banks to permit policyowners to pay premiums through pre-authorized check withdrawals.

These are but a few examples of the role of home office departments. Merchandising strength is indeed developed from many sources. Nearly every home office department can make and should make a contribution.

SUMMARY

The distributive process, step number two in the attainment of objectives, thus consists of manpower development, management development and manpower support through merchandising. The catalyst in this process is the agency department. Its officers must provide motivation and leadership to make the programs *live*.

Results are frequently influenced more by the "climate" of an organization than by the nature of its tools. A group of average people with poor procedures but superior leadership can usually produce more than superior people with the best procedures but poor leadership.

A sense of excitement, a sense of commitment and an atmosphere of approval are vital to the achievement of marketing objectives, and this dynamic spirit should emanate from the agency department.

Provision of Services

The third step in achieving the marketing objective is providing services that will keep the buyer sold. Here again management must first make some basic decisions. It must establish a proper balance between service and cost. It must give priorities to those things it judges are the most important to the greatest number of people it serves. It must review its operations continuously and decide which services are necessary and which are not. It must decide which services can be routinely mechanized and which must remain personal in nature. Finally, management must determine which services require immediate and speedy action and which do not.

Management must recognize, of course, that in the final analysis high persistency is achieved when policyowners are given the greatest possible number of reasons to stay with the company. Nearly every home office department has opportunities to provide such reasons.

A good impression at the time of the sale reflects the agency department's careful selection and sound training of the field underwriter. In advance of this, a prospect is likely to have been influenced by such factors as:

    (1) an advertisement (public relations),
    (2) a piece of direct mail (sales promotion),
    (3) a telephone call (sales training),
    (4) a favorable remark by a friend (referred lead technique), or
    (5) a story in the local newspaper (public relations).

At the time of the delivery of the contract, a policyowner is exposed to other conditions that assist him in developing his impressions of the company:

(1) speedy issue of the policy (underwriting),
(2) an explanation of the policy provisions by the agent (field underwriter training),
(3) an accompanying booklet that explains how his insurance works (public relations and sales promotion),
(4) an attractive format and clear language of the policy (actuarial, public relations and law),
(5) an accompanying review of his security program (field underwriter training),
(6) a welcome letter from the company's president (public relations),
(7) a convenient way to pay premiums automatically each month (office operations), or
(8) options to add to his basic coverage (actuarial, underwriting, law, and merchandising).

As time passes the policyowner experiences more reasons why he should stay with the company:

(1) Premium notices. They arrive on time (office operations). They are friendly and clear (public relations). They give him additional important information, including the amount of the dividend and the increase in the cash value of his policy (office operations and electronics).
(2) Reminder calls from his field underwriter (training and electronics). Such calls should be made on the following occasions: an option date; age change; rating removal; addition to family; new job; new home; expansion of business; other reasons to review his program.
(3) Efficient servicing of his policy (office operations and electronics). Such servicing is appropriate whenever there is a change in: beneficiary; address; method of premium payment; options for settlement; or policy loan. Follow-up questionnaires (public relations) should be used to find out whether he was satisfied with the service.
(4) Other communications with or about the company and the field underwriter. Such communications would include: birthday and holiday greetings; friendly and clear letters; magazines; annual reports; advertising materials; and publicity releases.

The policyowner who is satisfied with his program can have a pervasive influence. His satisfaction may induce friends to come with the company, and influence his family to stay with the company after his own insurance has served its purpose. The satisfied life insurance policyowner is likely to buy health insurance from the same company. The satisfied group certificate holder is likely to buy individual coverage—and so will his co-workers. The satisfied employer is likely to buy personal protection.

Persistency, therefore, is an important part of the total marketing concept and the attempt to achieve it should enlist the talents of the major departments of the company.

Role of Law Department

Although this chapter has touched on the role of the law department, some additional observations are appropriate because of the special challenges and responsibilities that confront this department in helping a company accomplish its objectives.

The insurance industry is infused with the public interest; thus it is subject to detailed regulation by federal, state and local governments, and a morass of administrative, statutory and common law.

Furthermore, the business of insurance consists of the purchase of one type of legal document (investments), the sale of another type of legal document (policies), and the issuance and administration of a third type, contracts with field underwriters.

The law department's success in supporting marketing objectives relies on its ability to (1) exercise preventative law, and (2) apply constructive legal analysis.

PREVENTATIVE LAW

Corporate lawyers who devote their entire time and energy to the affairs of a single company are in a position to see the overall picture. They are consulted in advance of decisions and form part of the team in the decision-making process. Their function is to pilot the objectives through the legal shoals and to prevent violations and legal involvements during the journey.

LEGAL ANALYSIS

Legal analysis applies sound legal principles to construe the law as it is found. It searches for legally acceptable alternatives when a particular course of action is not permissible or involves a risk a company should not assume.

It also recognizes that the law is not static. Thus the law department might, in some cases, counsel against an action that may be legal at the moment, if the law appears to be developing to the point where the activity may soon be curtailed by the courts or the legislature. On the other hand, the law department may seek a change in the law or other legislative or regulatory relief, for the benefit of the company and the industry.

Effective understanding and support by the law department are vital to the success of life insurance marketing.

Summary and Conclusion

To obtain a perspective of the significance of home office functions to life insurance marketing, management must first set company-wide objectives and policies, and within this framework determine the company's marketing objectives and policies. We have described some of the factors that will be significant in the achievement of varying objectives among different companies.

Next, the company must decide on the methods it will use to achieve the defined objectives and then must see that these decisions are communicated to all of the people responsible for carrying them out. Finally, management must establish procedures for periodic review, evaluation and adjustment of objectives, policies and methods.

These principles really must become a management platform on which all departments can base their activities and bring to bear their respective talents toward the achievement of the objectives. They help familiarize key members of each department with overall company policies, so that they can relate their own activities more closely to central objectives. They also give each department a better understanding of the policies of all other departments, and therefore help to promote better coordination of inter-departmental activities. They also provide an orderly way for policies to be changed from time to time to meet changing conditions, needs and objectives.

In the last analysis, it is the successful application of these principles that will bring the company to the achievement of its planned objectives.

4

Coordinating Home Office Functions for Life Insurance Marketing

Frederic M. Peirce

THE NEED FOR COORDINATION

The distinctive characteristic of the marketing concept is the recognition that the activity that results in the ultimate purchase by a consumer begins, not with the selling effort, but at the earliest point of creation of the product or service that is to be sold. From this point forward, every step of business activity that is undertaken should be channeled and directed toward the ultimate goal—the purchase of the product or service by the customer. In essence, that is why it is essential to the growth and prosperity of any life insurance company that its management embrace the philosophy that marketing is everybody's business.

Coordination is the process through which individual actions are synchronized and the above philosophy is made effective. Coordination may be defined as *"the orderly arrangement of group effort to provide unity of action in the pursuit of a common purpose."*[1] Thus, a primary task of

---

[1] James D. Mooney, "The Coordinative Principle," *Management, A Book of Readings,* eds. Harold Koontz and Cyril O'Donnell (New York: McGraw-Hill Book Company, 1964), p. 5. Original appears in James D. Mooney, *The Principles of Organization* (New York: Harper & Row Publishers, Inc., 1947), pp. 5~13.

management is to reconcile the differences among home office functions in order to provide a unity of action toward marketing objectives.

As an organization becomes more complex, necessitating the fragmentation of functions, and the separation of personnel into distinct units each with its separate customs, outlooks and vocabularies, coordination becomes increasingly difficult to achieve, and correspondingly more important. For large companies of every kind, coordination is a major management problem.

It has been generally conceded among the students of management that the essence of coordination is the involvement in the decision-making process of all individuals who have major responsibility for the various functions that are directly affected by pertinent policies of the organization.[2] Although the techniques by which management may strive for such involvement are many and diverse, they may be grouped into major categories for analysis.

TECHNIQUES OF COORDINATION

Organization Structure

The size and objectives of a company should determine the kind of organization structure it will need. Since different life insurance companies vary in size and possess different objectives, their organization structures will vary. Yet, all effective structures should contain certain basic elements and should meet certain basic principles. They should reflect clear lines of authority from the top to the bottom; they should establish the responsibility and authority of each supervisor or manager; and they should provide for accountability to a single superior. The inclusion of each these elements in the organization structure recognizes the fact that each person works best with others when he knows (1) for what he is responsible, (2) to whom he is responsible, and (3) why it is important to practice cooperation and coordination in his relationships with others.

One basic test of the soundness of an organization chart or structure is the degree to which it facilitates effective, coordinated relationships. The organization structure can provide an environment that either facilities or hinders coordination.

In formalizing the structure of an organization, it is not merely enough to chart it. The structure must be brought to life, the skeleton must be augmented by tissue, muscle and tendon. These are most often reflected in a written "Manual of Duties and Responsibilities" that describes the func-

---

[2] Ordway Tead, *The Art of Administration* (New York: McGraw-Hill Book Company, Inc., 1951), p. 183.

tions of each organizational unit, the duties that its manager and each of his supervisors are charged with performing and the responsibilities for which they are accountable.

In stating the specific responsibilities with which each member of management is charged, the areas requiring coordination should be highlighted. The manuals of some companies even go so far as to define these areas of coordination and specify at whose initiative the coordination must take place, and with whom.

Life insurance companies are typically viewed as function type organizations, i.e., the work at the primary level of a life insurance company is usually divided into various functional groups, such as accountants, actuaries, investment specialists, lawyers, underwriters, and, of course, sales representatives. To achieve maximum effectiveness all of these specialists, grouped into departments, must work closely and be coordinated with all other departments.

In contrast, many large industrial organizations are organized along product or geographical lines at the primary level so that coordination, except for broad matters of policy, occurs principally, within the divisions. The functional type of structure creates special problems of coordination because it must take place along a wider front and normally at higher levels of management. The organization structure of a life insurance company, therefore, requires that a number of additional mechanisms of coordination be utilized. Many of these take the form of communications facilities.

Communications

Open and free communication not only stimulates action but in addition acts as a coordinating mechanism in linking the decision centers of the organization into a synchronized pattern.[3] The form of these communications may be either written or oral.

Typical examples of written communications are official memoranda circulated through the entire management staff by a department head charged with the origination of the action. These may be in the form of progress reports, or they may simply be management newsletters. In any form, however, they should be officially recognized as established channels of communication and methods of achieving coordination.

Verbal, or oral communications take place in meetings, conferences, or conventions that bring together experts whose specialties may be utilized

---

[3] William G. Scott, "Organization Theory: An Overview and an Appraisal," *Readings in Management,* eds. Max D. Richards and William A. Nielander (second edition; Cincinnati: South-Western Publishing Company, 1963), p. 656.

in finding the solutions to business problems. Such group meetings may be for the express purpose of achieving coordination or for another purpose, with coordination being a side benefit. Management must recognize when such meetings afford the opportunity for communicating the needs for coordination.

Committees

Standing committees and special ad hoc committees are devices commonly used by many managers in attempting to achieve the integration of viewpoints and the coordination of efforts. Despite the disparagements to which committees have been subjected in the literature, a committee remains, perhaps, the most effective method available for focusing the collective knowledge and judgment of qualified people on a single problem. It should be employed in instances when individuals occupying established positions cannot carry out one or more of their responsibilities without affecting the capability of others to discharge their responsibilities. Committees offer the additional impetus of group dynamics in the development of new policies and projects.

Behavioral scientists have found that the lack of participation in the planning stage is often the forerunner of resistance to change, and to the adoption of new policies. Participation via open discussion, suggestions, and criticism will often result in the development of cooperation instead of resistance. Such participation can be effectively implemented through the use of committees.

A special form of committee that has recently become prevalent is the so-called "task force." For example, a few years ago a "task force" representing the various home office departments of a life company evolved a program for marketing a lower premium policy for women. The program involved developing new electronic data processing procedures, new forms, new sales promotion material and a sales campaign, to be followed by meetings in the field and continued supervisory attention. It was a total merchandising effort involving representatives from the agency, actuarial, electronics planning, law and public relations divisions. The net result was that a markedly larger proportion of the company's agency organization became more active in the women's market.

Similarly, some years ago the fieldmen in the same company reported that there was a growing need for life insurance on the part of college students, many of whom were marrying while still in school. Months, and even years before these young men graduated, they had already assumed family responsibilities—without having earned incomes of any significant amount. This was, and is, particularly true of medical students and others pursuing professional or graduate education. The problem was that they had a high need for life insurance with the expectation of substantial earnings within a few years after graduation. They did not have, however, the present ability to pay premiums. The company's managers, actuaries and attorneys were organized as a committee and jointly studied the problem and came up not only with a method of financing the premiums for a few years, but with an entire marketing package that included special sales training for the company's sales representatives. This united approach achieved an increased share of the college market for the company and gave the young clients an opportunity to enjoy security and peace of mind at prices they could afford.

A special form of committee that promotes integrated effort is the Advisory Council. Typically, a field Advisory Council is composed of representatives of the selling organization, whose function it is to bring to management their experiences in selling and the reactions of their prospects, to interpret the emerging needs of their clients, to make recommendations as to product design and to react to contemplated programs and policies of the company.

Another type of special committee, found in many companies, is the Marketing Committee, composed of the heads of the appropriate operating divisions, including the sales division, who meet and pool their knowledge and experience. Out of their discussions can come a common understanding, resulting in a solid support of new products and marketing approaches. This committee utilizes sub-committees composed of men in the lower echelons of the various divisions, so that integration can take place vertically as well as horizontally. Each division of the company thus becomes directly involved in the marketing process.

Thus, committees can play an important role in achieving coordination by getting all individuals with responsibility involved in the decision-making process.

Informal Organizations

Entirely apart from the structure of the organization, as it is defined in manuals and by the organizational chart, there exists organizations within the organization, labeled by modern management as "informal organizations." These represent the social structures of groups. They evolve out of the social and personal interactions of the work force. Their existence is natural because man has a basic need for association and friendship. This is sometimes referred to as man's "gregarious instinct"; it represents his need for belonging. Within every corporation, the group as a social entity, provides a setting that encourages or discourages cooperation and as such can affect coordination.

Well aware of the motivating quality of group dynamics, social scientists have demonstrated that individual interests and desires, biases or prejudices may subordinate the goals of the firm to personal or group goals. This is especially true when behavior is influenced by the norms or pressures of the group. This may even take place at the highest level of corporate activity. When officers regard themselves as competitors, unexpected behavior may be evoked by rivalry. Their judgments may be narrowed and they may be unwittingly swayed toward a course from which they, rather than the organization, will be the principal beneficiaries. On the other hand, cooperation necessarily reflects itself in collaborative behavior, requiring the suppression of individual drives and goals to the attainment of the overall company objectives.

If proper coordination is to be achieved, management must see that there is a proper balance between the goals of individuals, groups and the total company goals. Thus, a primary task in coordination is the achievement of good congruence among the elements that make up the organization.

The Agency Officer

The agency officer, by his attitudes, generates a most potent force in the organization. If he wears the hat only of a sales officer, concerned solely with his responsibility for building a sales organization, which will produce the amount of business desired by the company, he inhibits the growth of a total group spirit. But if he wears a second, and equally important, hat as a general officer of the company, he encourages cooperation and facilitates coordination. As a general officer, he must involve himself in matters of general company concern. He must manifest a sincere interest in the investment philosophy of the company, the results of which affect the company's long range welfare as well as the competitiveness of its rates and policy values. As a general company officer, he must be concerned with the company's administrative effectiveness, not only from the standpoint of service to the field organization, but also because of its importance in controlling the operating costs of the entire company, which ultimately affect the competitiveness of the company's products. He must be concerned constantly about costs and about the profitability of his own operation. He should be thoroughly familiar with the financial facts of company life, and the impact that sales results have on the company's results. He must identify himself as a general officer whose overriding concern is the welfare of the company as a whole. Such an agency officer recognizes that a company is not truly agency-minded or marketing-minded if it overspends its energies and financial resources in agency activities and undernourishes others.

THE COORDINATING ROLE OF THE CHIEF EXECUTIVE

Over and above the techniques of coordination that may be employed by life insurance companies in their marketing efforts, there is a requirement that only the chief executive can fulfill. Not only must the form of coordination exist, but the spirit of cooperation as well. Such a spirit is an elusive quality that stems from many places, but primarily from the personality and leadership of the corporation, i.e., the chief executive. As one management expert states: "If management wants the results of coordination, it has also to want to give the lead as to ways and means."[4]

Top management generates this spirit when it listens to what is said, when it invites comment and suggestion, when it encourages collaboration, when it fosters established channels of communication, when it adopts goals for the organization to which worthy people can rally and when it shares those goals with other members of the management team.

The concept that marketing is everybody's job must begin with top company management and must then be accepted by every area of company operations. A company does not achieve the successful distribution of its products by inspiring only the valiant efforts of some of its able people. All personnel must understand that in performing their functions they have a basic obligation to bend their collective efforts toward the main objective, the successful pursuit of their most important partner—the public —the consumer—the user—to whose best interest their joint efforts must always be dedicated.

The chief executive helps to create this understanding and acceptance not only by his observations and pronouncements, but by the sense of balance he exhibits in dealing with questions of policy.

Most chief executives make it a practice to bring the principal officers of the company together at regular intervals to discuss and to reach a concensus on matters of company-wide significance. This is a coordinating mechanism of prime importance, for its influence penetrates the entire organization. From these meetings of the senior officers, each officer may go better equipped to communicate and to consult with the responsible management members of his own operation, and they in turn with theirs,

---

[4] Ordway Tead, *op. cit.*, pp. 192~193.

about the marketing affiairs of the company that have an impact on their functions. Through such means, each operation can also grow in its comprehension of the effects that it has on sales and their mutual inter-relationship.

To help his principal lieutenants understand each other better, develop respect for each other and share the common purpose, some chief executives have invited them to secluded two or three day "talkfests" at a lodge or quiet resort. Following a prepared agenda, long-range company policies, including the marketing philosophy, are illuminated by unstructured, informal and extensive discussion. Out of such exercises, collective dedication to the common purpose can readily emerge.

The chief executive may also bring the sales message personally to the entire management team by direct exposure to its members in meetings, or through written communications. Some even use a microphone connected to speakers located throughout the building for direct audio-communication to the full home office staff.

In these and other ways that challenge the ingenuity of the chief executive, he fosters and nurtures the spirit of company-wide cooperation that gives meaning and vitality to the home office staff's participation in marketing.

The ways in which this spirit of cooperation can be manifested in specific areas of coordination that have an important bearing on marketing effectiveness is treated below.

AREAS OF COORDINATION

Product Development

In most companies product development is a direct responsibility of the actuarial staff. Yet, it is important that this activity be adequately coordinated with the agency organization. Such coordination may be achieved through a standing Marketing Committee, or, as indicated earlier, by the appointment of special task forces.

Ideas generated in the field, either through Advisory Councils or by individual contact of agency supervisory personnel with field representatives, should be directed to the actuarial staff via established procedures within the home office agency organization. Some companies designate specific individuals within the home office agency staff as liaison with the actuarial staff. An active and functioning Marketing Committee, composed of representatives of various home office functions, in addition to actuarial and agency, provides a more highly developed and comprehensive form of coordination.

Underwriting

Another area of particular consequence to field organizations' attitudes and effectiveness is underwriting. The degree of understanding of the company's underwriting policies and procedures by the field force can be directly related to both the quality and quantity of business obtained. The agency organization's responsibility to train and to supervise the field force in field underwriting gains strength through a close inter-relationship in the home office between the agency and underwriting administrative staffs. Both the field force and the home office underwriting department gain from the attendance at, and participation in, agency conferences and meetings by home office underwriters.

Within the home office, such coordination is nurtured by membership of an agency department representative on the Selections Committee. This convenient and constant avenue of two-way communications adds both flexibility and dimension to the underwriting process.

Claims Administration

The methods by which claims are handled can directly affect the climate for sales. Claims must, of course, be settled in accordance with contract provisions, with due, but not undue attention to the marketing effects of claim decisions.

A clear understanding of the underlying claims philosophy of the company is an essential element of proper field indoctrination. Alertness on the part of claims personnel to the marketing implications of their decisions in individual cases should lead to consultation and communications with the agency supervisory staff. Here, too, it has been found helpful to provide for established liaison between the home office agency and claims operations.

Policyowners Service

Policyowners service that is prompt, considerate, and efficient has major sales implications. Although there are problems in balancing service and costs, much can be achieved by impressing upon members of the policyowners service operation the importance and significance of their roles in the marketing process. Frequent contact between representatives of both the agency and service operations at all echelons of management should be encouraged.

Many companies build sales campaigns around policyowner service efforts on the part of the field organization in order to encourage the greater cultivation of their policyowners as sources of new business. The planning and launching of such campaigns offer excellent opportunities to achieve a desirable level of cooperation. Policyowner service representatives can be helpful in identifying specific types of policyowners for cultivation during such a campaign. Electronic data processing can be used to provide the field with status print-outs relating to specific policyowners. Automated procedures for service to policyowners, with adequate communications to the field, represent a highly sophisticated form of coordination that electronic data processing has made possible.

Investment

The investment philosophy of a company has a direct impact upon the product competitiveness and sales results of the company. As one authority states:

> Experience has proved, however, that the investment and agency departments should work closely together . . . Agency people in the field are very much interested in investments which are being made in the various territories. They are concerned with which banks are used as depositories. If the company makes mortgage investments, local agencies should be in a position to cultivate them as sources for leads for mortgage protection insurance sales . . . The agency department has a vital stake, of course, in the level of investment yield because of the eventual effect upon basic premium rates and the dividends payable to policyholders.[5]

The chief agency officer and the chief investment officer should work together to develop a balancing of interest and coordination of viewpoints through frequent interaction on a face to face basis, with the chief executive lending an encouraging hand.

Multiple Line Areas

The coordination of individual insurance and group insurance activities presents particularly complex problems for multiple line companies. Specialized skills are, of course, required in each area, but united efforts are necessary for the maximum marketing impact.

In some companies, the marketing of all lines is under the direction of a single executive, and sales coordination is thus provided for along vertical lines. In most companies, the group sales organization and the individual sales organization are under the direction of different executives. In such

---

[5] Paul A. Norton, "The Role of the Agency Department," *Life Insurance Sales Management*, ed. Dan M. McGill (Homewood, Ill.: Richard D. Irwin, Inc., 1967), p. 28.

cases, the president himself, or a designate at the senior level, may well act as the coordinating personality, assisted by special committees representing all interested departments that he may appoint to consider the more involved and perplexing aspects of the conflicts that are inherent in the gray areas where individual and mass marketing concepts collide.

Public Relations

Public relations are both a cause and a result of marketing activity. The activities of the agency organization in contacting, selling and servicing the public represent one of the major forces that establish the public relations image of the company.

Conversely, other public relations activities have a direct bearing on the acceptance accorded to the field organization by the public. The mutuality of interests is apparent. Coordination is achieved by the frequent interchange of viewpoints and free consultation among representatives of the public relations and agency departments together with other interested departments.

Responsibility for initiating the necessary contacts should be clearly placed. One control mechanism lies in the requirement for approval of mass communications by interested operations in the company, including the agency department, prior to publication or issuance by the public relations department.

In this area, as in so many others, successful coordination can be attributed more to to cooperative attitudes than to coordinating mechanisms.

CONCLUSION

The mutuality of relationships between the agency department and the other departments in a life insurance company extends into many other areas of activity too numerous to delineate in a single chapter. This mutuality permeates the entire marketing process and involves a constant sharing of information, of conviction and of purpose. Its essence is found in the mental approach with which each member of the management team embraces his task. True coordination is a state of mind.

5

Effective Communications Between Home Office and Field Management

James S. Bingay

To communicate is "to impart, convey, make known." Perhaps the best dictionary definition is: "To be connected." That suggests, quite properly, a receiver and a sender . . . a taker and a giver.

Communication provides the only way in which it is possible to get work done through others . . . and this is the very essence of business management.

In order to examine systematically the important matter of deliberate, effective communication as it applies to the various elements of life insurance sales management, it is best to deal with the component considerations in the following order; (1) the nature, purpose, and tools of communication; (2) the communications responsibilities of the home office; (3) the communications responsibilities of the regional sales office; (4) the communications responsibilities in departments outside the agency department; (5) attitudes necessary for effective communication at all levels of life insurance sales management.

Nature, Purpose, and Tools of Communication

If clear communication between all members of a management force is one of the central requisites of effective, efficient business practice, nowhere is this more apparent than in the management sector of life insurance sales, where written and spoken communication—a world of words—lies at the very heart of the industry. The major communications objectives here are (1) to provide field-management with information from the home office that field representatives need to help the company achieve its objectives; (2) to obtain from field management information the company needs to help it reach sound decisions, determine objectives, establish policies; (3) to assure that field management is effectively relaying information to and from field force and field office staffs; (4) to evaluate and improve continually the effectiveness of communications media within the total organization, tying field management more closely to other members of the company in the home office and field offices.

Although there are many tools that men can employ to communicate with their fellow men, two essential means—and the ones most pertinent to a discussion of communications in life insurance sales management—are formal, public writing and person-to-person communications, be they written or spoken. The usual vehicles of formal written communications include company newspapers or magazines, directives, bulletins, and annual reports. Person-to-person methods include letters, advisory committees, business conferences, field visits, induction and indoctrination programs, and refresher training programs. Additional devices for expediting communications include opinion research and centralization of complaints for analysis. All such vehicles deserve the strictest attention of all members of the management team, the same sort of managerial attention now devoted to production and marketing: these vehicles should never be taken for granted. For while every intelligent businessman is aware that skillful listening, observing, note-taking, and composition are fundamental prerequisites of good communication, and while many are also aware that clarity, simplicity, and careful repetition make for the most effective writing and speaking, the greatest single problem in the area of business communication is the illusion that it has been achieved.

In considering how to use the various available vehicles most effectively in communicating with field management, a company will need to make at least two basic decisions: (1) Should responsibility for communications be centralized? (2) Are field management and the field staff receiving, through existing channels, information promptly, and is this information sufficiently unambiguous, accurate, and complete? Or should an accelerated and more comprehensive method be used?

Communications Responsibilities of the Home Office

Communication is a two-way street, but the home office bears the greater part of the responsibility for directing and maintaining the flow of traffic on that street. Without intelligent planning in the home office, communications failures are bound to result, and the larger the company, the greater the danger of such failures.

Many companies have discovered that as they grow and diversify, they inevitably lose some of the all-around personal contacts that are possible in small organizations. Such companies come to depend, for their efficiency and morale, on their methods of communication and their ability to relay information through successive layers of authority.

Perhaps the most obvious failure of communication is *under-communication*. Under-communication occurs when management and staff (1) are not getting sufficient information, (2) are not getting information quickly enough, or (3) are receiving distorted versions of information as it is transmitted from one layer of authority to another. These three forms of under-communication are not mutually exclusive, of course. In fact, (3) occurs most frequently in conjunction with—and as a result of—(1) or (2).

Although under-communication is the most obvious failure of communication—and the one of which management and staff are likely to be aware —the opposite problem, *over-communication,* is equally dangerous and less easily recognized by home office management. When over-communication occurs, key people are compelled to read information not once, but two, three or more times in a variety of publications, memoranda, circular letters, and other media. Over-communication is often the result of company expansion and diversification, for as companies grow, new areas of activity add new communications media to those already in existence. As a result, field management and field staffs are force-fed information and written materials they often do not need and cannot use.

Along with under-communication and over-communication, another communication failure which can be avoided by intelligent planning in the home office is *uncoordinated communication.* When a company issues a number of uncoordinated communications, the same information tends to be repeated a number of times, and it tends to be slanted differently for different audiences. As a result, people in diverse areas of the company will form disparate interpretations of one set of facts or one situation; and this disparity can easily lead to misunderstanding, confusion, mistrust, and serious loss of efficiency in the entire operation.

Closely related to uncoordinated communication is the problem of uncoordinated channels of communication. In the case of uncoordinated channels, the receiver becomes confused because he does not know where to look for information. Will it come to him in a magazine, a directive, a bulletin, a newspaper, a letter? Should he, if he is a field manager, relay it to his staff, or will this be done for him? To be effective, communications must be as familiar to a receiver as his daily newspaper. The reader of the *New York Times,* for example, knows each day almost precisely where he can find editorials, obituaries, financial news, classified ads and other departments. Similarly, field managers (and other personnel in the company) must know what types of information they will find in the various communications they receive and where in these communications each type will be found.

Coordinating Communications Channels

A truly effective internal communications system will coordinate the various channels it uses, assigning appropriate functions to each and preventing the waste and confusion of overlapping functions. Even the channels of external communication must be considered. Morale within an organization will deteriorate quickly if company people learn about a vital change or development from outside sources before it has been announced internally. Thus, in most cases central coordination of external and internal communications is necessary to assure the proper timing of announcements.

The first step in coordinating channels of communication is to evaluate existing channels to determine how well they fulfill their functions in the context of the particular organization in question. Different organizational structures and situations call for different communications media, and even a single organization, as its structure and situation evolve, will require changes in its communications procedures. Recently, for instance, a number of companies have discovered that they are no longer able to rely upon monthly publications to transmit pertinent information to field management. For their present needs, a monthly publication is not frequent enough to be timely, and it does not offer enough space to be comprehensive. As a result, these companies have all added weekly newspapers—some as replacements for their monthly publications, some as complements to them. In each case, the problem determines what solution is most appropriate.

Centralizing Responsibility

In most cases, we see that *centralization* is the key to well coordinated communication. One company has recently centralized all of its general information for all members of the company—field management, field force, and employees—into a single weekly newspaper. It has also centralized in the same department the responsibility for issuing external information, thus preventing conflicts in timing or substance between the two agencies.

Such centralization for communications naturally requires first the establishment of policies and procedures which will insure its success. A suggested guide has been developed which spells out clearly who makes announcements, how they are coordinated, who writes the material and obtains clearances, and who decides the medium for transmitting information. The guide also points out the deadlines for material and suggests how the copy should be prepared. Through such policies and procedures, this company has been able to coordinate its internal communications so that (1) the weekly newspaper transmits all information of general interest to all members of the company, and (2) bulletins, circular letters, and related media contain only directives, instructional and procedural detail, or material of interest to specialized groups of people (e.g., group field force, advanced underwriting specialists).

This centralized program has reduced by at least 75 percent the amount of information which field managers were formerly required to relay to their field staffs. It has also saved field managers, home office managers and supervisors a great deal of time formerly wasted reading duplicate material in several publications. Furthermore, such a company newspaper fosters a view of the company as a whole, rather than as a loose organization of fragmented parts seen from a departmental perspective. It relates the activities of various departments to each other and to the field staff. Home office and field people become identified with one another and better aware of the company as an integrated whole. Finally, a company newspaper has these additional advantages: (1) readability; (2) frequency of publication, which permits important matters to be repeated and emphasized whenever that is necessary or desirable.

Person-to-Person Communication

Written communications—particularly formal "mass media" such as newspapers, magazines, bulletins, directives and related vehicles—are important for transmitting information, but they are usually one-way devices. They typically transmit information from the home office *to* field management, but do not obtain information for the home office *from* field management. An excellent means of obtaining this information from field management is *person-to-person communication*. Such person-to-person communication is achieved through the following avenues:

1. Field Visits
2. Business Conferences
3. Advisory Committees
4. Induction and Indoctrination Programs
5. Refresher Training Programs
6. Letters
7. Complaint Analyses
8. Opinion Research

However, something more than mere awareness is required if such avenues are to be used to improve the effectiveness of two-way communications with field management. Here a pre-planned and organized program will accomplish the following objectives: (1) it will centralize and analyze all the information obtained through these avenues; (2) it will report back to field management that adjustments have been made or that experiments and studies are being conducted; or it will see to it that explanations of why changes are impossible are forwarded promptly to field management.

In addition, a program for studying on a continuing basis the information and views obtained from these person-to-person media will enable a company to discern patterns of criticism or complaint. If any such pattern is discovered early enough, the company can take steps to remedy the situation before it becomes a serious problem. Lacking such a program, on the other hand, a company can delude itself into believing that criticism is isolated or fragmented when, in fact, it may be widespread. A program of this kind has a number of advantages for all home office personnel who engage in person-to-person communication with field management: (1) it causes people to be profitably curious, to ask questions, to find out what field management likes and dislikes, and what their field staffs like or dislike; (2) it suggests a sense of urgency on the part of the listener so that he is paying active attention to what he hears and reads, that he is willing to initiate some action, including conferences with the appropriate departments to consider remedial measures; (3) it encourages a sense of obligation on the part of the listener or reader to report back to the field manager the results of his efforts.

To be fully effective, a program of communication with field management requires that field management and home office management work jointly and carefully in establishing agenda for all business and educational conferences, including advisory committee meetings. Although members of advisory committees should understand clearly that they do not represent field management as a whole, they should be asked to give their individual, personal views on all proposals on which their guidance is sought, whether such proposals originate with committee members or with home office management. Summary reports of such meetings should be made, approved by the committee, and transmitted to field management as a whole. If the company subsequently takes specific actions as an outgrowth of advisory sessions, announcement of these actions should include credit to the advisory groups concerned.

At a general business conference with field management, the company should provide for the following: (1) spontaneous questions from the floor about any and all aspects of the company's policies and operations; (2) attendance at the meetings by home office management representing a sufficient cross-section of operational areas to answer all such spontaneous questions. At these conferences, it is recommended that the listener make written notes about what he hears and that he report back to the questioner at the earliest possible opportunity. It is also helpful for a complete record of the questions and answers to be circulated among the respective home office departments. Above all, home office departments should understand clearly that their prime duty at such conferences is *to inform* and *to be informed*. This might mean early breakfast meetings, late evening conversations, chats during recesses, and patient listening during so-called "free" afternoons. This is all part of—and an important part of—the communicative process.

Field Visits

Two of the most effective methods of person-to-person communication are (1) visits to individual field offices and (2) meetings with small groups in various sections of the country. Such direct contacts provide a way to translate generalizations into particulars at the local level in the light of particular local problems or needs. They also are a way to view directly the operation and difficulties of Agency X and Field Underwriter Y, instead of seeing all such matters as part of the vague generic term "field management."

But field visits can also be a most damaging and demoralizing form of communication if they are not carefully prepared and coordinated. Such planning should provide for the following: (1) the agency department and regional sales officer, among other key personnel, should be informed well in advance of all proposed field office visits, regardless of what home office department is making such trips; (2) the visiting officer should send to all his peers in the home office an advance copy of his itinerary and should ask his associates two simple questions:

1. Are you experiencing any problems with the field offices at which I'll be calling?
2. Are you engaged in any experiments, special correspondence or conversations with these field offices, about which I should know?

Thoughtful advance preparation for field visits can have several beneficial effects: (1) it can help convince field management that the visiting officer is knowledgeable about and interested in areas of company operations outside his own; (2) it can impress field management with the coordinated efforts of the home office department; (3) it can put the visiting officer in a position to answer questions on the spot, thus obviating many of the shortcomings of much written communication outlined earlier in this chapter.

Few things are more discouraging to field management than an impression that Officer A knows little and cares less about what Officer B is doing in the field, particularly when A and B are both involved in situations affecting the field office being visited. But through carefully planned and organized field visits, such demoralizing situations can be eliminated almost entirely. For example, if an investment officer is visiting a field office, the company's agencies department could brief him in advance on the status of important insurance business from the agency or agencies he will be visiting. Conversely, if the visitor is from the agencies department, it would be helpful to him to learn from the investment department that a sizable loan is being developed or has been approved in the area he will be visiting. It is obvious, then, that such advanced visit planning contributes much to effective communication between home office and field offices.

The value of training programs—induction, indoctrination, refresher courses, and related activities—is self-evident. Most companies have excellent syllabuses and bring fine direction to such programs. An adequate follow-through procedure can add to the value of these communications media in the following ways: (1) the programs could be evaluated immediately after the completion of each session—by all participants; (2) the company's opinion research specialists could be most helpful in fashioning questions that will produce meaningful appraisals; (3) results of these evaluations should then be added to the ever-growing store of home office management knowledge about what field management and field underwriters think of company policies or procedures.

Letters

Except for face-to-face discussion, no form of communication is more personal than letters, and none requires a greater degree of individualization. Recognizing this fact, many insurance companies have developed excellent programs for improving correspondence with policyholders. The objectives of such programs are (1) to produce letters that are friendly, simple, and clear; (2) to produce letters creatively written to make a good impression upon readers; (3) to make letters so completely responsive to readers' questions that embarrassing (and expensive) follow-up explanations are unnecessary.

These same principles and the same methods that have resulted in better letters to policyholders are also applicable toward improving correspondence with field managers. However, although most companies today are aware of the importance of effective correspondence with policyholders, far fewer have taken sufficient pains to improve correspondence with field management. To be truly effective, a program of correspondence within the company should extend the principles of the company's policyholder correspondence program into two crucial areas of internal communication: (1) letters written *to* field management; (2) letters written *by* field management. As in the case of letters to policyholders, letters to field management can and should be personalized and humanized, even when they are mass-produced. In order to accomplish this, the writer must bear in mind the interests of the readers and the particular personality of the subject or subjects involved in the letter.

Opinion Research and Complaint Analysis

Letters are an indispensable component of a communications program, because they are the most personal form of written communication. However, letters alone are not sufficient to provide a thorough program of effective written communication. Two additional methods, which are vital supplements to any effective correspondence program are (1) opinion research and (2) complaint analysis. These methods, if employed in conjunction with a carefully directed program of correspondence, enable a company to keep its finger on the pulse of the field managers, field underwriters, home office and field office employees, policyholders, the general public, and even competitors.

The use of opinion research in the life insurance field was pioneered by Clifford B. Reeves, senior vice-president of Mutual of New York, with whom the author was privileged to be associated for twenty-two years until Mr. Reeves' retirement in January, 1967. On frequent occasions, Mr. Reeves remarked:

> Everyone agrees that every business should know what *people* are thinking. The only real question involved is how to find out. One way is to sit in your office, and try to guess changes in attitudes and preferences that may affect your business in this fast-changing world. The other way is to develop definite methods for measuring opinions accurately.

Complaint analysis is actually a form of opinion research, and like other forms of opinion research, it should (1) rest on a *broad base,* (2) be

conducted on a *regular basis,* and (3) be *centralized* under a single authority. In most companies, complaint analysis appears to be limited to the
study of letters addressed to the company's president, chairman, or chief
executive officer. Such complaints generally come from policyholders, and
the responsibility for answering them usually falls upon the department
of public relations. This type of procedure for dealing with complaints
is useful as far as it goes, but it is by no means fully adequate.

A broadly based program of complaint analysis should study and analyze
all complaints regardless of their sources, their destinations, or their form.
Possible sources of complaints are (1) policyholders, (2) field underwriters, (3) field managers, or (4) field employees. A broadly based
program will deal with complaints from all of these sources, and it will
deal with them regardless of who receives them or what department that
recipient represents. A broadly based program will also cover all of the
various forms of complaints—letters, telephone calls, individual or group
meetings, and casual conversations.

Once this broad base of complaint coverage is established, the other two
principles of effective complaint research—*regularity* and *centralization*—
must also be applied. In a broadly based program, unless there is regularity
and centralization of complaint analysis, individual complaints tend to
become isolated and minimized within individual departments. As a result,
a general pattern of discontent can remain undetected by central management until it has developed into a major problem.

The complaint analysis program, then, occupies a vital place in a company's communications system; for the more knowledge a company can
obtain about the problems that trouble people, the more effectively it can
communicate, and the more efficiently and profitably it can progress. Informed by a comprehensive program of complaint analysis, home office
management will communicate more effectively with field management and
with all other elements of the company. Field management, in turn, can do
a more effective job with field underwriters, policyholders, and employees.

Communications Responsibilities of the Regional Sales Officer

In a company which has a centralized program of direct communication
with field management and field underwriters, the regional sales officer is
relieved of some of the logistics duties otherwise associated with his job. He
is, at least, relieved of the task of relaying to the field force the bread-and-
butter information they need in their daily activities. And yet, in any life
insurance company organization, the regional sales officer has an unusually
difficult role—perhaps a unique role—in the communications process.

To be an effective communicator, the regional sales officer must simultaneously be field management and home office management. He must be as intimately familiar as top management with his company's long-range and short-range objectives, with the factors that have led the company to its decisions, and with the underlying philosophy which guides its operating policies. On the other hand, he must have as much knowledge and understanding of the objectives of each of the field offices under his supervision as does the manager of that office. He must know the weaknesses that inhibit one office from reaching its goals and the strengths that enable another to surpass them.

The regional sales officer has a twofold task in interpretation, requiring him to play two roles at once: (1) he must interpret the home office to field management, a task he can perform effectively only if he has a role on the home office management team, helping to construct the objectives he is expected to meet and contributing to the development of the tools he will need to meet these objectives; (2) he must interpret field management to the home office, a task he can perform effectively only if he has a role in the field office operation—only, that is, when field management invites his partnership and counseling in their problems and respects his special experience and know-how. In interpreting field management to the home office, the regional sales officer must see beyond the imagined problem and formulate an accurate, pragmatic description of the real problem —together with a proposed solution. In interpreting the home office to field management, he must be strengthened by the knowledge and conviction that the company's decisions, objectives, and policies are in the best interests of the company's policyholders.

The regional sales officer is like the baseball manager in the dug-out, the coxswain in the shell. He is the only officer who is able directly, on a daily basis, to convert company objectives, decisions, and policies to the inspiration, the example, and the supervision that develop manpower, produce sales, strengthen persistence, and encourage service. No conferences are more important in the communicative process than those that put the regional sales officer on the home office management team or those that put the regional sales officer on the field management team.

Communications Responsibilities in Departments Outside the Agency Department

Although the field manager is a member of the sales department staff, his responsibilities, problems, and concerns frequently cross departmental lines. The field manager is frequently involved in direct communication with non-sales departments about situations requiring his attention. Typical examples of such situations are (1) an underwriting problem, (2) a medical examination, (3) a situation involving an employee, (4) a question about the company's participation in a local charity drive, (5) a proposal for local newspaper and television advertising. In each of these cases, the field manager must communicate effectively with the appropriate non-sales department.

Policies and procedures governing a company's communications should require that the appropriate section of the sales department, including the regional sales officer, be notified about all .communications with non-sales departments. The simplest method is for the originating department to send the sales department copies of the communications. If the project involved will necessitate extensive correspondence over a long period, it might suffice for the originating department to provide the appropriate sales section with occasional status reports.

From the communications standpoint, the important thing to remember is that the sales department should have an interest in *every* relationship between a field manager and the home office. The field manager's representation of the company as an investor, employer, and corporate citizen also affects his representation of the company as an insurer. In many companies the field manager and the home office people have become so well known to one another over the years that rapport between them assumes a very personal air. They tend to lose sight of the fact that they are engaged in the communication process and that the sales department has a vital interest in knowing about the situation.

All these lines of necessary inter-departmental communication must be kept open and working: (1) the sales department must be notified about communications between the field manager and non-sales departments; (2) the sales department should have an interest in communications between a field manager and the home office; (3) the field manager should be posted on all correspondence between the home office and policyholders for whom his agency is responsible. If any of these avenues of communication is neglected, the entire operation is likely to suffer.

Attitudes Necessary for Effective Communication at All Levels of Life Insurance Sales Management

Communication is, in the last analysis, simply the way one human being relates to another. As a result, the effectiveness of the written or spoken word depends to a great extent on the attitudes the sender and receiver adopt in the communications process. The following suggestions have proved extremely useful and profitable in developing the attitudes necessary for effective communication at all levels of life insurance sales management:

1. *Be a good listener.* The prominent author and lecturer Mortimer Adler has stated: "If you asked me what is most important for successful communication, my answer is ... the ability to *listen well* to the other person's point of view, to hear what the other fellow says. This is much more difficult than any of us realizes."

2. *Be a good observer.* Meyer Berger, late star reporter for the *New York Times*, in commenting about the necessity for a writer to be a good observer, advised: "Watch the person you are writing about when he is in action. Watch for little gestures. Live the other person's life ... look and listen. Some stories you see, some you hear, some you feel, and some have all of these." Mr. Berger's advice is as sound for a good listener as it is for a good writer.

3. *Be courteous, pleasant, warm, thoughtful.* Warmth brings human personality and persuasiveness to communication. Thoughtfulness elicits interest in your reader or listener. Does a bright "hello" convey a message at the office in the morning? Does the lack of a greeting also carry a message? Does a prompt response to a telephone call or letter mean something? How about the tone of voice, or the tone of the letter (which so many otherwise good writers overlook)? Courtesy, warmth, and thoughtfulness all *communicate* a message to the reader or listener: they say, in the most believable terms, "I am sympathetic and interested." Conversely, their absence also conveys a message—a clearly undesirable one.

4. *Be knowledgeable; avoid guessing.* Obviously, it is desirable to be well informed on every matter that comes to your attention. But this ideal, like all others, is impossible to achieve in every instance; it is simply the standard toward which one must work. In those cases when a matter comes up about which you are not sufficiently well informed to speak authoritatively, an honest "I don't know, but I'll get the information," is far more effective than an obvious guess at an answer.

5. *Be prepared and organized.* From the simplest telephone call to the longest interview or the most detailed and complex letter, it is always helpful to outline in writing in advance the information you want to transmit or the information you want to obtain.

6. *Be accurate.* Few things are more discouraging to field managers —or to any correspondent for that matter—than to be misled by the wrong information or by insufficient information.

7. *Recognize differences among individuals and groups.* In his book *The New Society*, Peter Drucker makes this point:

> Each of the groups in industry sees the same thing—
> the enterprise—from a different viewpoint and within a
> different angle of vision. What one group sees as obvious
> and plain fact, the other cannot see at all. Each group,

though seeing only part of the picture, fancies that it sees the whole. And each group, convinced that it sees the whole, is convinced that its viewpoint is logical and fair.

Remember that it is extremely unlikely that the other groups and persons with whom you communicate will see things exactly as you do. Try to understand and appreciate their positions, even when they differ from your own or from the ones you have been accustomed to hearing.

Benefits of Effective Communication

None of these communications techniques—and no techniques of any kind—will lead to effective communication between home office and field management unless this prerequisite has been met: *the company must have something sound, good, and worthwhile in the shape of policies, beliefs, and principles of management to communicate.* In the words of retired steel executive Clarence Randall, "no marvel of science can change the fact that what a man says should be wise and true."

Assuming, however, that a company has met this prerequisite, effective communication will have far-reaching benefits. It will enable an insurance company to accomplish the key objectives outlined at the beginning of this chapter: (1) to provide field management with quick, accurate, and complete information from the home office, thus enabling the field representatives to do their part fully in helping the company achieve its objectives; (2) to obtain from field management the information necessary for the company to reach sound decisions and to determine and adjust company policies and objectives; (3) to expedite communication between field management and field office staffs; (4) to evaluate and improve the effectiveness of communications media within all sectors of the organization.

In the insurance industry, there is no substitute for the effective communications program. Such a program will produce more knowledgeable field managers. It will encourage loyalty and confidence; for everyone in a firm wants to feel he is part of what is going on—everyone wants to be "in the know"—and when communications channels are operating efficiently, everyone will know what is going on and will therefore feel more loyalty for and confidence in his company. Moreover, an effective communications program will improve coordination among departments in achieving company objectives. It will provide a continuous check on the effectiveness of company policies and objectives. It will doubtlessly lead to substantial savings in time and costs. It will, in the end, enhance tremendously the value and meaning of a life insurance company's most important operations.

6

Functions of Agents and Their Relationship to Total Corporate Goals

John A. Hill

The mainspring of the life insurance industry is the agent. When an agent sells a life insurance plan, the sale brings into action corporate personnel all the way from the clerk in the field office, through the underwriter in the home office, to the investment department and ultimately to the claims department. The agent and the sales which he makes, therefore, are the primary reasons for the existence of the agency and sales promotion departments, and for the agency manager or general agent, and his staff. The agent is the base upon which the achievement of corporate goals rests. For that reason it is important that the agent be understood. Who is this person we call an agent? What kind of person is he?

TYPES OF AGENTS

There are four principal types of agents. First, there is the full-time life agent who sells for one life insurance company. He is normally housed and serviced by the company and devotes virtually his full time to the sale of life insurance. If his company provides the coverages, he may also be involved in the sale of health insurance and group coverages. His sales major is the personal lines.

Another type of agent is the agent who sells all lines of insurance but primarily represents one life insurance company. He usually provides his own office and staffs it. He may represent several property insurance companies, but he gives one life insurance company first call on the life insurance business he sells. He generally produces a substantial amount of life insurance sales.

The broker represents a third type of agent with whom a life insurance company may do business. A broker generally sells all lines of insurance and maintains and staffs his own office. His sales major is the general lines of insurance. Life and health insurance and group coverages are usually a minor part of the broker's sales activity. A broker represents not one but several companies.

Another type of "broker" must also be considered. This is the full-time life agent who occasionally brokers a piece of business to another life insurance company. Generally, such business is surplus business, i.e., business that his own company cannot underwrite.

The final type of agent in our typology is the part-time agent. As the name implies, this agent sells life insurance on a part-time basis. The sale of insurance is normally not his primary business activity. Typically, he works out of his home and the volume of sales he generates is not high. It should be noted that not all companies nor field offices permit the employment of part-time agents.

The above four types of agents, together with the field management staff (in many companies), constitute a life insurance company's "sources of business." The success of any plans for insurance company growth depends on the number and the quality of these sources of business and their loyalty to the company. It is impossible to set realistic corporate goals unless they are based upon these agents. Because of this, it is important to understand the agent's interests and motivations.

IMPORTANT CHARACTERISTICS OF AGENTS

The typical life insurance agent is a proud, independent, ambitious, dedicated individual. His work is self-created. Business is not put before him; he must create it himself. He decides what markets he will develop and how he will develop them. Then, through his own initiative, the agent sets about the important business of making sales in the chosen market. It is basic that the agent regards his work as a means of a livelihood or a means of becoming an independent business man, but primarily he sees in what he is doing an opportunity to perform a worthwhile service for his clients.

Agent's Goals

An agent's ambitions and goals are varied. For most agents a primary goal is a higher standard of living or the satisfaction of building his own business. For others it may be qualification for a company or industry club or convention. Agents are motivated by these goals and by a desire for the prestige and ego-recognition that accompany them.

Skilled management can and does play an important role in igniting these ambitions and goals. A good general agent or manager invests a great deal of time in stimulating and motivating his agents and brokers to produce more business. He can do this in a variety of ways. He guides the agent as he makes his plans and sets his goals. He introduces him to new marketing areas, and then educates and trains him in marketing methods to reach and be effective in those areas. With some agents he assists them in raising their sights from one-half million dollars of production to a million dollars and to membership in the Million Dollar Round Table. With others he sets tangible goals, such as a new and more expensive car, a larger home in a better neighborhood, a long coveted trip or the liquidation of a personal debt. With still others he uses pride, pressure or protest to stir up and get them started to a higher level of production. In doing this he employs such means as personal conferences in the office, over the luncheon table or at home; sales contests; app-a-week and other prestige clubs or private offices for better producers. The techniques are many and varied, depending on the imagination of the general agent or manager and the personality and objectives of the agent.

Agent's Loyalties

It is important that a company's management understand the loyalties of these individual sources of business. The company's loyalty to an agent and the agent's loyalty to his company stem from self-interest. The degree to which each identifies with and accommodates to the other establishes the scope and depth of that loyalty in both directions. An attempt by either to make "loyalty street" one way destroys the very foundation on which this important quality is built and maintained. An inseparable mutuality must exist.

The first loyalty of agents generally is to their clients and to themselves. Competent agents feel a high degree of responsibility for their clients' best interests and in serving them they realize they are also serving their own interests. What is best for their clients is nearly always best for them and, incidentally, for their companies.

In addition to the above mentioned loyalties, there is usually a feeling of loyalty between these sources of business and the field office with which the agents do business. This is often a strong feeling, even though sometimes it is directed toward the general agent, manager or staff man who works closely with the agent or broker.

Finally, we should mention the agent's loyalty to his company. However, this loyalty may be a phantom virtue. As a matter of fact it is frequently difficult for the individual agents or broker to identify himself with corporate problems or goals. The gulf is often too great. If this is the case, real loyalty to the company may be minimal.

Companies, however, can and do frequently bridge this gulf. Structuring open lines of communication between field and home office by such means as company and regional meetings, home office and field schools, company field publications, field visits by home office staff, field advisory councils, agents and field staff recognition programs, broad policy portfolios, competitive rates and underwriting, fair and prompt claims payments may be helpful in achieving this desirable goal. The belief that the company *does* care and *is* sincerely interested in the individual agent can be built, and with it loyalty is earned. This climate can be created only by the efforts of the company through well-conceived programs and the active and imaginative support of its field management personnel.

On the other hand, if the gulf between the home office and the agent is not bridged, these all-important sources of business may well regard the company as a remote corporate entity, impersonal and cold, which is not really concerned with their well being, except as it affects their ability to produce business. Sometimes the agents question even this. They scrutinize corporate actions and statements with suspicion and cynicism. In this climate there is little room for the loyalty or *esprit de corps* that is so vital for company growth.

In corporate planning, these subjective elements, i.e., agent's goals and loyalties, should be evaluated as carefully as possible because the ultimate success of most planning may very well rest upon these elements.

CORPORATE PLANNING

Long-range corporate planning is relatively new. Formerly, if any planning was done, most businesses planned for only a year or two at a time. At best it was based on minimal research. Now many companies' long-range planning is based on extensive research and includes the process of setting objectives five, ten or more years into the future. The computer has made a great contribution to this advance in planning, and techniques of planning are constantly becoming more sophisticated.

The Need for Planning

In long-range planning it is important to point out that present actions on the part of life insurance companies have strong long-range effects. Whether such actions are concerned with underwriting risks, pricing policies, investing funds, controlling expense, making sales or building the force that makes them, they are molding the company's ability to meet long-range objectives and to make a profit. It should be noted that the profit, if any, generated by sales today will not be realized for many years in the future. Competition among companies tends to narrow profit margins and this, in turn, makes the need for long-range planning more apparent. This profit measure is equally pertinent in a mutual or a stock company.

Important, too, is the need for extensive research in product design, markets, buying patterns, selection of sales and management personnel, personnel performance, sales promotion, costs, compensation, public and in-company attitudes toward the company and its sales and public relations policies. Such knowledge of a company's operations is necessary if it is to maintain a strong competitive position and a satisfactory sales volume while making sure of its future strength. The problem each company is trying to solve through planning is how to achieve an optimum rate of growth through sound policies and procedures. Such growth depends on maximum sales of a kind and quality that will keep the company strong. Continuing research enables a company to be sensitive to shifts and changes in the economy and within the company itself that might adversely affect the realization of long-term goals.

The Planning Process

Generally, a life insurance company begins its planning process by gathering historical data. These data enable the company to identify its rate of growth in the past. This is generally broken down nationally, regionally and by individual sales areas. Such data as premium income, share of the market, profits and expenses should be calculated. All this information should then be compared with similar industry data.[1] These data, therefore, enable the company to evaluate its trends in relation to the industry.

Good research also reveals the markets penetrated by the company's sales force. Research may provide information relative to such items as: the proportions of insurance sold to the various age groups, to women as

---

[1] Such comparisons should be made with care. Because of different product mix or sales approach, comparisons from one company to another may lead to erroneous conclusions. Thus, when industry comparisons are made, management must be careful in selecting figures from companies in similar situations.

well as to men; the types of policies sold; the purposes for which the insurance was bought; the persistency rate of business placed by agents at various experience levels and in various markets; the recruiting rate of the company, its regions and individual sales offices; and the agent survival and average production rates at various experience levels.

This mass of facts affords a basis for establishing assumptions that can be used for forecasting future performance. If a projection based on past experience will not achieve desired production rates, planners can use the historical data to identify which aspects of past performance need to be improved and can measure the extent of the changes necessary to attain desired results.

The second step in the planning process is to project trends based upon these data. These trends should extend several years into the future and show just what results could be expected if current perfomance is maintained into the future. The third step is to set tentative goals, both short- and long-range. These hypotheses will serve as the foundation for establishing the final goals.

The fourth step involves a test to evaluate the feasibility of the goals. How do they measure against the projected trends? Is the difference realistic? Can it be reasonably attained? Can the company afford the growth—the cost of instituting new action programs, of opening new markets and the strain the contemplated new business will place on surplus? Based upon this evaluation, final goals should be established.

Finally, strategic planning takes place. In this step, action programs for bringing about the improvements needed to meet the goals are conceived. Alternative plans of action should be considered to meet the same goals. A final decision as to which action plans will be needed is then made and they are implemented and put into operation. It should be noted that, in a very real sense, a company has little control over production. It can only hope to influence changes in the behavior of the people who do generate production.

Decisions as to short- and long-term objectives will vary widely among companies. Some may set as a major objective maintaining or increasing their respective shares of the market; others may set a specific percentage gain in new volume or premiums; and others will establish a specified gain in net field sales manpower. Other objectives might involve reduction of expense ratios, increase in the persistency of business, increase in profits and so on.

Whatever the major and minor objectives may be, a company's sources of business must play a principal role in their achievement. Objectives involving such goals as share of the market, increases in new sales, better persistency, increases in net field sales manpower are almost entirely dependent upon the effectiveness of the sales organization. The type of agent, his competence in the sale and servicing of his business, the ability of the field management staff, the nature of the relationship between field and home office all need to be carefully evaluated during the process of setting realistic objectives and strategic planning.

RELATING THE AGENT TO CORPORATE PLANS

Thus far we have examined the types of agents, their capabilities, their interests, motivations and loyalties, and have reviewed in the most general terms a few of the problems and procedures involved in corporate planning. Next, it is appropriate to relate these elements in more specific terms.

Let us assume that a company has appraised its field organization, has researched the necessary data, and has set as its major short- and long-term objectives the development of new business in terms of volume at a growth rate that is 33-1/3 per cent higher than the average growth rate during the last ten years. As an illustration, assume that Company XYZ has been growing at the rate of 6 per cent a year on the basis of volume of new business sales for the past ten years. It has been decided that the company now wants to increase its rate of growth by 33-1/3 per cent, or a new growth rate of 8 per cent a year. This is the short-term and the long-term corporate goal.

Now that the company knows its main objective, the strategic planning begins. It looks at past performance and measures it against future objectives. It studies the net growth in sales-manpower to see if the annual increase, after the attrition caused by death, retirement, disability and turnover has been deleted, is sufficient to support the increased production demands. It studies the recruiting rate to see if the trend in numbers of new agents added each year is compatible with the growth demands. It studies the average production for full-time life agents of various lengths of experience to see if there is a trend upward or downward—since this, too, will have a strong positive or negative effect on attaining the main objective. Similar analyses are made of brokers and part-time agents. Ideally, all of these data should be analyzed not just on a national basis, but regionally and by individual sales offices as well.

The purpose of making such a study is to match current performance and apparent trends against the corporate goals. If planning has been challenging as well as realistic, current performance and projected goals rarely match. There will be a difference that can be offset only by future performance that is better than past performance. In other words, merely doing things in the future as they have been done in the past will not get the job done. Current programs and procedures must be improved. New programs that are creative and challenging must be planned.

Actually, where projected goals cannot be attained by a continuation of present performance, there are only three basic methods of improving performance to achieve higher goals. They are:

(1) Enlarge the size of the sales force by recruiting at a faster rate.
(2) Retain a larger proportion of the present sales force and of the additions to it.
(3) Improve the average production of agents, brokers and other sources of business.

For illustrative purposes, these three basic methods will be examined briefly, with specific reference to their relationship to full-time agents.

Increasing the Numbers of Recruits

The first method of improving production performance is enlargement of the size of the sales force by recruiting full-time life agents. If a company chooses this and *only this* method of making up the difference between current performance and the projected goals, it can apply existing survival and average production rates to arrive at the additional number of recruits needed to reach the projected goals.

For example, let us assume that a company's recruiting rate is 100 new agents a year and that the total volume produced by these agents for the *year in which they are recruited* is $10,000,000 or an average per agent of $100,000. Now, let us also assume that the company's goal for the first year is an additional $1,000,000 of volume above its current rate of production. If this is to be accomplished only by recruiting additional agents, it is readily apparent that this company now must recruit 110 agents during the first year instead of 100 ($1,000,000÷$100,000=10).

By using survival and average production rates of its agents, management can employ the same procedure to determine how many agents must be recruited in the second, third and subsequent years to achieve this corporate goal.

Although the mathematics of this is as simple as it is obvious, the real problem is the strategic planning involved in bringing about a 10 per cent improvement in recruiting results. A corporate decision alone will not accomplish this. It requires a close follow-through on these programs throughout the year. Nevertheless, if the $1,000,000 of additional volume is to be achieved by first-year men, the field management staff must accomplish it. Its confidence in its ability to do the job must be established through well-conceived, well-executed programs.

Improved Survival and Average Production

As far as the very early years are concerned, it is unlikely that a company would depend only on improved agent survival or on improved average production as the basis for producing an additional $1,000,000 of volume. Strategic plans for accomplishing improvements in agent survival or in average production are slower to mature. For example, if more effective training and supervision are an important part of one of the plans for improving agent survival, time is needed to educate and train the field management staff. Time then is also needed to carry out these plans with the agents themselves. The effectiveness of these programs could not be known for over a year or two at best.

Over a period of several years, however, significant improvements in these areas can be made. It is well known that certain companies enjoy agent survival and average production rates that are well above industry rates. To bring about these highly desirable results on a companywide basis requires creative, strategic planning, sound implementation of the plans and a consistent follow-through on the execution of those plans.

In the final analysis, however, reaching our fictitious company's sales goal depends on the company's sources of business. Its capability to produce the additional sales required to meet short-term corporate goals rests largely on its ability to recruit additional sources and on the willingness of these sources to accept the challenge . . . to be motivated, whether by a promotional campaign, a recognition program or out of sheer loyalty and pride. Long-term goals, however, can be favorably affected by adding other programs that are planned to improve agent competence and therefore agent survival and average production. As has been pointed out, more time is required to bring into sales-producing operation such strategic plans as: (1) new market penetration, (2) new products, and (3) additional education and training to equip the agents to new markets and to sell the new products.

In all probability, a typical company would not depend on only one but would use all three methods of improving performance to achieve its production goals. Therefore, a company would logically follow a three prong approach of (1) stepping up the rate of recruiting, (2) retaining a larger proportion of its sales force at all levels of experience and (3) bringing about better average production performance on the part of its sales force. By using a combination of all three methods, a company would more likely achieve its corporate goals.

OTHER CORPORATE OBJECTIVES INVOLVING THE AGENT

Growth in (1) volume of insurance sold, (2) new premiums and (3) sales manpower are goals that quite obviously involve the agent. There are other corporate goals, however, that also involve him. Let us consider a few of these.

Market Penetration

One of these additional goals might be market penetration. For example, assume that our fictious XYZ company has determined from research that, historically, it has confined its market penetration to the lower and middle income market (under $10,000), to the juvenile market and to the family plan market. Its sales methods have been largely of the single-need, one-interview type. It now desires to broaden its market penetration to include the higher income groups. To do this it must develop marketing techniques in programming, business insurance and estate protection areas. New products may be needed. New training courses will definitely be needed. The field management staff must develop competence in these new fields. Finally, the agents must be educated, trained and then led into these new markets if the desired penetration of these new markets is to be realized.

Quite obviously all of this takes an immense amount of creative work and a considerable period of time, and this calls for a substantial investment of funds. As has been pointed out earlier in this chapter, this investment is long term. The execution of action plans like these have long-range rather than short-range effects, and the profits from them will not be realized for many years.

Other examples of market penetration goals would be increasing sales to: the women's market, certain occupational groups (e.g., professions), the blue-collar market, the rural market, the annuity market, present policyholders, the military market, the business-insurance market and the salary-budget market. The penetration of any of these markets involves research and strategic planning such as that illustrated in the description of company XYZ's plan to increase its growth rate. The successful implementation of any of these decisions is dependent upon the agent.

It is not unusual for a company to decide to grow by penetrating new geographical areas. Sometimes this may involve entering another state or province and, sometimes, a foreign country. In any event such a decision should be preceded by extensive market research and analysis, which gives top management confidence that the long-term effect of the decision will be profitable.

Once the decision to enter a new geographical area has been made and the legal problems have been resolved, general agents or managers must be installed and agents (sources of business) must be recruited, trained and developed into productive sales personnel. Other programs must also be brought into action, such as advertising and promotional campaigns. Such a decision requires the investment of both time and money and, once again, it will be the agent who will be a major determinant of the ultimate success or failure of the decision.

The agent should also be the focal point when a life insurance company decides to accelerate its growth in peripheral lines, such as mutual funds, variable annuities, health insurance, group insurance, or general insurance lines. Any acceleration in marketing activity will require new capabilities on the part of the home office staff and special training for field management personnel, as well as for the agents. The entire plan must be backed by new sales procedures, sales promotional programs and materials, recognition programs and other ancillary programs.

It is not unusual for a life insurance company to use a small segment of its sales force to pre-test sales plans, new products or sales procedures that are being developed to support market penetration programs. Such field-testing not only helps to validate the item being tested, but also assists in gaining valuable field confidence and support for the new item when it is introduced field-wide.

Persistency

The saying, "business that stays is business that pays," is well known. It pays agent and company alike to sell contracts that stay in force. What is even more important is that it is also good for the policyowner. From the latter's viewpoint, the importance of persistency is painfully apparent: widows never collect on fully lapsed policies. Thus persistency is in the best interest to all concerned—to the agent, to the company and to the policyowner.

It is a common practice for a life insurance company to set as one of its corporate goals the improvement of its persistency rate and this, of course, makes the importance of the agent paramount once more. His market, his marketing methods and his service to his policyowners will virtually predetermine the persistency of his business. Poor persistency can be improved both by training and by directing an agent's sales and service activities into markets that will produce more persistent business.

The life insurance industry as a whole also has recognized the importance of persistency and has encouraged its increase through industry recognition of agents who write quality—high persistency-business. The National Quality Award has become a symbol of excellence that recognizes those agents whose business is of persistent quality.

Policyowner Service

The policyholder service department exists largely to serve those who bought life insurance from the company in the past. Most of the work of this department is received from the field offices and much of that is originated as the result of contacts between agent and policyowner. The most personal contact a company has with a policyowner is through the agent. The agent, therefore, is the company in the eyes of most policyowners.

Some policyowner services can be initiated from the home office by letters or premium notice enclosures, but the most effective services are those that are carried on by the face-to-face contacts of the agent. A competent agent can ask questions, analyze, clarify and advise his client. He often can speed the service being rendered because of the knowledge he has gained through his personal contact. An important role of the agent for himself, his client and the company is his role as advisor when a policyowner should be contemplating increases in his life insurance program.

In order to foster better policyowner service, some companies have organized formal programs for providing continuing service to policyowners. Typically, these are based on contacts by the agent with his own policyowners and with the so-called orphan policyowners who have moved out of the territory of their original agent or whose original agents are no longer active with the insurer. Here again the agent plays the principal role in achieving this corporate goal. His competence and his business philosophy, which have been heavily influenced by the company's education and training programs and by its sales philosophy, measure to a major extent the effectiveness of the formalized program.

Public Relations

The relationship of the agent to the public relations goals of a life insurance company is readily apparent. Few policyowners ever see the home office or the officials of a company in which they own life insurance. A few may visit a field office or they may have seen an advertisement in a magazine or on television. However, the typical policyowner's primary contact with the company has been the agent and to the policyowner the agent *is* the company. His way of doing business, his intelligence, his sincerity, the service he renders, the contact he maintains and his friendly, personal interest can build a strong, favorable feeling for the company. Unfortunately, the reverse is equally true.

The agent helps to build the company's image in other ways, too. His participation in fund-raising drives, his work on school boards, town councils, in P.T.A., service clubs, scouting and Y.M.C.A. mark him as public spirited and reflect favorably upon himself and his company. This is particularly true when this activity is not engaged in as an obvious means of making more sales. The agent is usually active in his church or temple and can be counted upon to give both his time and effort to its affairs.

The agent serves another important public relations function. His day-to-day contact with the public makes him sensitive to the reaction of the public to company programs. He hears the comments people make about the company's advertising or television programs and how it feels about the company's policy for settling claims. These and other public attitudes should be relayed to the home office and frequently are of great value in refining company programs or policies.

Market Evaluation

Closely related to the function described in the preceding paragraph is the role the agent plays in market evaluation. In this area it is his daily contact with the buying public, present policyowners and his competitors that enables him to act as a barometer of the company's posture in the market place. This sensitivity is of immense value to the company in adjusting strategic plans to fit interim changes in buyers' tastes and needs.

Buyers' interests do shift and, in fact, needs change constantly. Intensive national advertising programs that stress retirement income, for example, can cause a rise of interest in this form of insurance. An amendment to the Social Security Act can cause a change in the needs of the buying public. In both instances, the agents of a company test and evaluate the buyers' current interests and needs and their responses to various methods of satisfying them. This is a most effective way for a company to be sure that its strategic plans are in tune with the times.

The agent should also be alert to the buyers' reactions to his company's products. Frequently his ideas result in new products or in adjustments to present products that make them more salable.

A most valuable function performed by the agent is in evaluating the competitive position of his company. If the company's rates are out of line, if its underwriting policy is too strict, or if its product portfolio is inadequate to compete with other companies the agent is generally the first to know. Although this kind of information normally has a way of reaching the home office quickly, management should encourage its agents to communicate such data. It is important information for the company to have, and it often results in adjustments that might otherwise have been delayed for some time to the ultimate detriment of long-term goals.

Source of Manpower

Every short- or long-term goal is, to varying degrees, dependent upon new manpower. This is certainly true of corporate goals involving the agent. To achieve such goals not only are agents needed but field management staff is also needed. The agent force is a prime source from which management personnel can be drawn. Many of the greatest general agents and managers started their careers as agents. The agency departments of most life insurance companies also are heavily staffed by former agents.

Finally, agents are a source of manpower in yet another way: They are excellent sources of new recruits. Many companies have found their agents to be the best single source of new agents. The agent knows what the job requires and what type of person should be interested. He also meets a large number of people every week, and most of these people are new to him. He is in a unique position to recommend potential agents to his general agent or manager. This, too, is a real contribution to the achievement of corporate goals.

CONCLUSION

In this chapter we have examined many ways in which the agent is a vital factor in the achievement of the corporate goals of a life insurance company. We have examined him as a part of the business structure and as a person. We have sketched corporate goal setting and touched on strategic planning. At the foundation of all of these areas of consideration is a typically American desire for growth.

As the agent makes his plans for business growth and realizes that growth through his ability to motivate people to buy from him, so the corporation makes its plans and realizes its goals through its ability to organize and to motivate its agents to fulfill their part in this cooperative venture. It has been said that the character, image and prestige of a company are but the composite of those traits as they are found in its agents.

7

Significance of Sales Management to Total Corporate Operations

Darrell D. Eichhoff

The work of a life insurance company is extremely complex and requires a staff of highly competent people who possess a wide range of professional and technical skills. Although the number of individual activities performed in the operation of a life insurance company covers a wide range, in general, any one activity may be classified as falling into one of three major functional areas—sales, investments or administration.

The degree to which a life insurance company succeeds reflects the consolidated effort of all of the activities of the organization. Of the three major areas referred to above, sales is the largest in terms of both manpower requirements and costs. As the arm of the company that directly services its current policyowners as well as produces new policyowners and revenue, the sales department's role in contributing to a company's well-being is most vital. Thus, the need for effective sales management to provide an adequate volume of new business at a reasonable level of costs is obvious.

This chapter provides a discussion of some of the most important aspects of the sales management job and its relationships to other activities, of the company as well as to the organization as a whole.

INTERDEPENDENCE OF SALES MANAGEMENT OBJECTIVES AND OTHER COMPANY GOALS

Every company, consciously or instinctively, operates under a set of principles and towards recognizable objectives relating to its customers, employees, the public and owners. Although these objectives may or may not be in the form of written statements, they must be known, understood, and accepted by the entire management of the organization if such objectives are to be attained.

An example of one company's objectives, as set forth by its president and chief executive officer, are the following:[1]

1. To maintain the company's long-standing positions of general leadership in the life insurance business—leadership in the finest sense of that term—measured by the integrity of its ideals and of its people; by its stand on important public issues; by its service to its policyowners, to the institution of life insurance, and to our two nations; and by the great number of people who know the company and respect it.

2. To keep pace with the growth and development of the United States and Canada by providing the company's insurance and service to an ever-widening group of policyowners. A company that does not go forward goes backward. When a company stops growing, it starts to die.

3. To cover thoroughly all the markets for the company's various forms of coverage. Ever since the 1880's, the company's basic market has been the workingman. However, the workingman's economy, standard of living, and way of life have been undergoing almost revolutionary changes. The company must raise its sights to match the workingman and demonstrate to him his need for larger amounts of life insurance in his new circumstances. The company must be aggressively active not only in the workingman's blue-collar market, but the white-collar market and the so-called carriage-trade as well.

4. To improve continually the company's administrative, underwriting, and productive efficiency and economy of operation, so as to provide a full range of policies and prompt service of the highest quality to policyowners, prospects, and the field force, at reasonable cost.

5. To follow a sound investment policy determined by the highest qualities of stewardship, designed to produce, in the interest of our policyowners, the largest income compatible with safety of principal and consistent with the healthy economic growth and stability of the United States and Canada.

6. To be a good corporate citizen and encourage the company's

---

[1] These objectives are those of the Metropolitan Life Insurance Company.

people to be good individual citizens, interested in and participating in community affairs. The company believes that as a leader in its field its obligations go further—it must play its part in strengthening the private enterprise system that has made the United States and Canada great, and in fostering the personal and economic health of its policyowners and the general public.
7. To be a good employer. Since policies can be carried out and objectives accomplished only by people, the company must have a good "working climate," where people are fairly treated and fairly compensated—and know it.

Although the objectives in the above example are broad in scope, they are clearly an indication of the company's grand design. They are important, since they embrace the key goals of the company and provide management with a basis for derivative objectives within each of the integral operating units of the company. It should be observed that a number of the objectives relate directly to the company's marketing operations and provide a framework within which all selling and servicing activities must be focused.

The objectives of sales management, therefore, must not only be compatible with the overall company objectives but in addition must be designed to accomplish the missions that are to be fulfilled. Accordingly, the sales management objectives must include the development of strategic programs as well as plans for the implementation of such programs in keeping with company goals.

From a practical point of view it is desirable not to have too many formalized sales management objectives. It is preferable to limit them to the basic essentials. Too many objectives tend to minimize the importance of those objectives that are fundamental to sales management success and to direct attention from them. Furthermore, too great a number of objectives promotes a lack of flexibility of operations and requires centralization of authority to a degree that hampers an organization in adapting its operations in a rapidly changing socio-economic climate.

Where possible the sales management objectives should be stated quantitatively. The company noted above has four major sales management objectives that can be expressed quantitatively. One such objective is premium growth, i.e., the amount of premium placed less lapses (excluding terminations for death claims, matured endowments and paid-up policies). In addition, the qualitative corporate objectives relating to service, corporate citizenship and being a good employer are deeply ingrained throughout the entire sales organization, influencing not only the company's basic policy decisions but its day-to-day actions as well.

It is likely that many life insurance companies have objectives that differ substantially from the above goals used for illustrative purposes. A relatively new company, for example, may look for quite different results than those of an established company. There also might be differences because of company size, types of market covered, type of sales organization used, such as general agency or branch office, and many other factors. The basic principle remains the same, however: sales management objectives must be derived from overall company objectives if the organizational goals are to be achieved. It is essential, therefore, that the sales executive discuss tentative sales management objectives with the company's top management before implementation. It is only in this manner that goal congruence can be achieved with economy and effectiveness. Upon acceptance, sales management can then proceed with implementation of their plans, and top management has the right to expect full realization of the stated objectives.

INTERDEPENDENCE OF SALES MANAGEMENT AND OTHER COMPANY FUNCTIONS

Effective marketing is not the sole responsibility of the principal sales executive. Many of the factors that influence sales performance are beyond his direct control. For instance, the price of the policies being sold—and the extent to which they meet competition—is largely dependent on underwriting and investment practices, as well as the management of expense in both the home office and the field. Similarly, the effectiveness of marketing is dependent on the quality of service to policyowners and other manifestations of a public character that are generated by many outside the sales organization. Also, basic personnel policies, normally established at the corporate level, affect marketing operations because they influence the company's ability to attract and hold competent salesmen and middle management sales executives as well as home office personnel needed to support the field sales effort.

Sales management, therefore, does not operate in a vacuum of independence but rather has a wide variety of dependent relationships with the other operating units of the company. The nature and number of relationships with other departments is almost infinite since they encompass virtually every phase of a company's work. Some of the more important relationships are mentioned below.

Policy and Service Development

The development of new policies and services involves many considerations since such developments must be financially sound, competitive,

ట

legally acceptable and rewarding to the field force. Needs for new policies arise to satisfy markets that cannot be adequately covered under existing forms, for newly discovered insurance requirements, or for meeting competition. New policy plans and riders are developed primarily through the cooperation of the sales, actuarial and legal departments. The actual development requires, in addition to the above, the assistance of the medical department and those home office units that have the responsibility for administering policies when they are issued.[2]

Sales Promotion[3]

The preparation of sales promotional literature and other materials used by field representatives at the point of sale frequently involves several departments of a life insurance company. The rate book, for instance, is an integral part of the field representatives' sales kit and is normally developed jointly by the sales management department and the actuarial department. It must be developed so that it serves the needs of all who use it. Similarly, projections of future net costs have actuarial as well as legal considerations that involve participation by those departments.

Underwriting

In the area of underwriting, field representatives perform a vital role since they must be trained as to what constitutes good health, acceptable occupational risks, suitable moral conditions, ability to pay and insurable interest of beneficiaries. In effect, the agents are the underwriters for the company, since the home office underwriters can only accept or reject what is presented to them by the field force. Thus, because of the sales force's integral role in underwriting, the operations of the sales management departments and the underwriting and medical departments must be closely coordinated. Application forms must be developed jointly in order to provide the required information for home office underwriting as well as be consistent with the ability of the field force to use them properly.

Administration and Settlement

Once a policy is sold, the home office performs many of the principal record-keeping functions and assists in servicing a policy until final settlement is made. It is necessary that there be good working relations between the sales force and the home office units in order to develop and maintain optimum levels of service in terms of time, quality and economy. Efficient

---

[2] For a more detailed discussion of policy development, see Chapter 12.
[3] A more detailed discussion of sales promotion can be found in Chapter 19.

billing of premiums due, payment of death claims and maturities and the processing of policy loans, surrenders and changes give the company the opportunity to generate favorable impressions with policyowners and enhance the company's public character, thus facilitating future sales. Of course, in order for the home office units to do their jobs properly, the agency force must first do their share by providing needed information and complying with company practices and regulations. The achievement of desired goals in the servicing area is the joint responsibility of both the servicing and sales units and is brought about when there is a complete understanding of the requirements and capabilities of each.

Electronic Data Processing

The sales operations of many companies have felt the impact of technological development by the extension of electronic computers into areas affecting sales management. Electronic installations have taken over much of the routine work of record-keeping, commission calculations and payrolls for sales functions. In some companies they are being used to program a prospects' insurance needs.[4] A recent development is the periodic production of policy and policyowner data for field force use in conservation and policy review service activities, and in providing such information at the most propitious time for making additional sales. The high speed and accuracy of electronic data processing equipment make it ideally suited to life insurance work because of the vast amount of paper-handling that this business requires. Since present electronic programs cover only a small part of the work now being done, it can be expected that as time passes there will be an increasingly close relationship between sales management and electronics units.

Advertising and Market Research

Intimately associated with sales management are the company units that handle advertising and market research. If these are not under the direction of the principal sales executive, the need for coordination with sales management is most important. Advertising must be geared to support sales, either for particular policies or to enhance the public's knowledge of and confidence in the company.[5]

Market research performs a particularly important function in keeping the company abreast of economic developments and market conditions,

---

[4] For example, see "Hancock bets on postwar babies," *Business Week* (January 15, 1966), No. 1898, pp. 91–100.
[5] For a more detailed discussion on advertising see Chapter 19.

and is vital in the deployment of the company's manpower resources to areas where the greatest potential exists. It also assists in evaluation of the company's productivity in relation to its economic opportunities.[6]

Expense Management

Insurance sales executives are keenly aware of the importance of keeping policy costs at minimum levels as a matter of remaining competitive. The balance between a satisfactory operating cost and an acceptable volume of sales is not easily achieved, especially at the agency or branch office level. The need for this does exist, however, because the costs of operating the field organization, as stated previously, generally constitute the bulk of a company's expenses. The sales management department has the responsibility of evaluating expenses in terms of values gained (or risks avoided) and in keeping costs at optimum levels. The work relating to the control of expenses may involve the systems department of the company and budgetary authorities. They also may be involved with administrative or settlement units where procedural improvements can be effected.

Summary

There are many other relationships between the sales management department and other operating units that must be bridged between the field force and the home office. Some are nonrecurring, such as the development of a wire communication system between the home office and a branch office, and others are recurring, such as those activities discussed above. All relationships between the sales management department and other operational units, regardless of how frequent or rare, however, must be conducted in an atmosphere of mutuality of interest, with the well-being of the company as a whole and the attainment of primary objectives held superior to the interests or objectives of any one department.

TOP MANAGEMENT'S RESPONSIBILITY FOR SALES MANAGEMENT

The top management of a life insurance company bears the responsibility for the effectiveness of the organization's marketing operations. The decisions made at the highest level, typically the chairman of the board, the president, executive vice-president or executive committee, exert vital impacts on how the business is to be conducted and the extent to which

---

[6] For a more detailed discussion of market research at both the home office and agency level see Chapter 17.

it prospers. Top management has the responsibility for determining a number of basic policies in the sales area. Important among them are the kinds of markets to be reached, the type of organization to conduct the business, the amount of resources to be allocated for new business, and expansion and personnel policies.

The implementation of the policies established by top management is the job of the principal sales executive, as head of the sales department and the field force. The position is one of great importance to the company since it involves the direction of a substantial proportion of one of the company's principal resources—manpower. The job of chief sales executive is extremely broad in scope and involves both planning for the future and the responsibility for day-to-day effectiveness of the field organization.

The principal sales executive has the further obligation to top management of sensing the ever-changing requirements of the company's markets, both present and future, and making suitable recommendations based upon these requirements. Then, top management must evaluate these recommendations and accept or reject proposals that will modify or revise basic underlying philosophies or operating practices of the company.

Top management has a further role in sales management that is of vital importance. This is to ensure that the various parts of the marketing structure are brought together in a cohesive manner. Since many departments and people are involved in the total marketing operation, coordination of the marketing effort can only be achieved at the top level.

SALES RESPONSIBILITY OF THE AGENCY
DEPARTMENT AND THE FIELD

Sales management involves a myriad of activities. This fact is perhaps best illustrated by a study made by one research team that found that an agency manager's job embraced over 700 different actions necessary for successful fulfillment of his responsibilities. Although it is highly likely that the men making this study were overzealous in their efforts to be complete, the fact remains that all sales management positions in a life insurance company involve doing many things—all of which must be done with a high degree of professional competence.

The sales management hierarchy of a life insurance company includes a number of middle management positions that lie between the principal sales executive and the first-line supervisors of the field representatives. In a company operating over a wide geographical area, the number of middle management executives may be fairly large even when a reasonable span of control is maintained. If success is to be attained at all levels of management, therefore, adequate staff assistance must be available to handle the details of operating the business and to provide the research and development activities that must be maintained in a progressive, forward-looking organization. Even in a small company the principal sales executive must have the support of both competent line and staff people.

Although the duties of sales management are numerous, as shown above, they may be classified into six major areas of responsibility:

1. Developing and maintaining a sales program
2. Recruiting and selecting personnel
3. Training personnel
4. Motivating personnel
5. Directing administrative work
6. Developing and maintaining good public relations

These major areas of responsibility apply throughout the sales management hierarchy of a life insurance company. Although some positions may involve all six duties, other positions may be concerned with fewer. The duties are pervasive in that they apply equally well to the first-line supervisors of the sales personnel in the field as well as to the executive in charge of the entire sales operation and the line and staff positions between these two extremes.

Developing and Maintaining a Sales Program

The development and maintenance of a company sales program is the primary responsibility of the principal sales executive. The decisions made in this area and the recommendations made to the company's top executive provide the basis for all actions in the remaining five areas.

Foremost among these decisions is the type of market to be sought. A company can, for example, restrict its marketing to selected geographical areas, or it can be nationwide or even international in scope. It can decide on an urban operation or a rural one; it can concentrate on carriage trade, middle-income or low-income groups. Similarly, decisions must be made with respect to the product line as they relate to special policy features, such as term insurance riders, special purpose policies or the sale of group or health insurance.

Once decisions have been made regarding the market, fundamental decisions must be made regarding the type of marketing organization to be formed. Some life insurance companies choose to work through general agents, while others conduct their business through company-operated branch offices. Of equal importance is the question of the magnitude of a company's sales organization. If it is decided that the relative share-of-the-market position is to be maintained or increased, it may be necessary for the principal sales executive to develop and maintain programs for the horizontal expansion of the field force. On the other hand, if the organization's policy has been resolved to be one of increasing total sales by upgrading the capabilities of the present staff, a different set of programs for implementation must be formulated.

Too often the above questions are considered to have been settled in the past and are not currently pertinent to a going organization. In reality, this is not the case. The market—and the means by which it can be reached—is dynamic. The environment for life insurance marketing, both internally and externally is constantly changing. There have been many instances where life insurance companies have made major changes in their marketing philosophy. In many cases these have been brought about by internal changes in management thought and in other cases by the external environment in which the company must operate. Consider, for instance, the changes affecting the life insurance industry that have evolved as the result of social security legislation, and, most recently, medicare. Shifts in population from rural to urban areas, from the cities to the suburbs and from eastern to western states, also have materially affected the marketing programs of life insurance companies. For a combination company, the rapid extension of checking accounts, the fact that working wives form well over half of the employed females, the ability to save substantial proportions of income and other changes have had major impacts on the way of doing business. These changes are felt slowly, but they must be anticipated as early as possible for the maximum capitalization of opportunities for growth.

As time passes, the need for organizational change within the sales department must be appraised periodically to determine how it can function more effectively and be able to cope with the challenges of ever changing marketing conditions. This involves evaluation of the sales department's operations and territorial alignments, as well as the structure and responsibility given to key, intermediate management positions. In some instances the type of organization may be influenced by the capacity of particular individuals. It may be desirable, for instance, to change the organization structure in order to capitalize on the ability of one or more outstanding people, or, on the other hand, to make compensating adjustments when such persons pass from the scene.

To a considerable degree the sales operation is dependent on local economic conditions and the extent to which prospects have funds for the purchase of insurance. As population shifts occur and new marketing opportunities emerge, there must be a repositioning of agencies or branch offices as well as sales personnel. This process involves the creation of new agencies or the expansion of existing ones in growth areas and the elimination or consolidation of agencies where the sales potential is diminishing. The principal sales executive has the job of determining the basic framework and program within which the changes in field structure will occur.

An integral part of the development and maintenance of a sales program is the quantification of expected sales performances, based on a common understanding of the company's direction and a knowledge of long-range commitments to the chief executive. The principal sales executive's job in this area is to establish the company and territorial sales objectives. Finally, the marketing plan must provide a series of control reports to serve as signals and reminders to management at all levels to instigate corrective action when necessary.

The extent to which a company's sales programs are successful is dependent upon its agency or branch office management's ability to assess market potential and to develop quantity and quality sales manpower through which increased sales can be realized. At the local level, plans must be developed based upon an assessment of the capabilities of the agency's sales personnel, market opportunities, trends in population and economy and past performance. An effective marketing program, however, must be more than simply an estimation of the desired results; it must include plans for, as well as implementation of, the specific activities that are to be carried out in order to ensure that the desired objectives are attained. It includes action plans for training in specific areas and decisions on manpower growth, e.g., creation of additional sales positions, the consolidation of agencies, and recruiting plans for replacement or for additional people. All such manpower planning must take into consideration the strength of first-line supervisors and their capacity to train and direct the present and proposed staff of field representatives.

Since the agency manager's interests are completely oriented toward local conditions, the manager is expected to be alert to changes that are taking place and to propose changes that will take full advantage of the marketing opportunities that are available. Changes of this sort, however, must be reviewed carefully by the sales department, partly to evaluate the judgment and knowledge involved, but more particularly, to select from among the various alternatives those that offer the greatest prospects for the future within a framework of cost that can be reasonably supported.

Recruiting and Selecting Personnel[7]

The success of a company's sales operations depends primarily on the ability of the people in the various jobs throughout the entire sales structure. Success results when people have professional and technical competence and possess the will to do their work well. An important key to the success of a sales organization is its staffing with people who: (1) have the ability to absorb training, (2) use their knowledge in the performance of their work, (3) desire to improve their skills constantly, and (4) possess the motivational drive to achieve personal as well as company goals. The selection of the right person for a life insurance sales position is often considered to be one of the most difficult jobs of a general agent or manager.

The principal sales executive has the responsibility for providing the field organization with the tools and methods for maximizing the effectiveness of the recruiting and selecting efforts. To a degree these can be reduced to a series of proven techniques that can be furnished to agency or branch office management. These include methods of searching for men who come from desirable occupational sources and are predisposed towards life insurance as a career; procedures for preliminary interviewing; the use of psychological tests to indicate an individual's potential for success; the conduct of fact-finding, interviewing regarding education, background and other pertinent facts; or the use of references and preappointment training as a means of determining a candidate's willingness to work, his capacity to learn and his ability to fit into the organization.

The importance of having capable agency and branch office managers and first-line supervisors of field representatives cannot be overemphasized. It is the responsibility of the principal sales executive to have the means by which the right men for these key positions can be appointed. If the company's policy is to promote from within the organization, there must be ways by which latent managerial talent can be identified and developed so that recruiting and selecting will be facilitated. If management personnel are appointed from outside the ranks of company employees, the principal sales executive must set the guidelines and procedures through which candidates can be interviewed and selections made from among those that are the most qualified.

In the case of his key subordinates, it is the personal job of the principal sales executive to put together a team that will work harmoniously with

---

[7] See Chapters 21 and 22 for a more detailed discussion of recruiting and selection.

him, with each making his full contribution to the aims and objectives of the organization as a whole. The chief sales executive also has the personal job of providing support to key men in all major areas. This is essential to ensure continuity of operation and a logical sequence of personnel who have been trained to assume greater responsibility when they are needed.

At the agency or branch offices, each person in a managerial position must fully understand the need for the constant recruiting of new people who have the potential for success in selling. Recruiting must be carried on continually, but it must be done in an atmosphere that is devoid of haste. Thus, successful recruiting requires effective planning on the part of management. Such planning must begin with top management.

Training Personnel[8]

The life insurance business is entwined with legal considerations and social legislation; it is a highly sophisticated business because of its many facets; and finally it is a dynamic business that must meet the needs of changing economic conditions through the introduction of new and improved products and services. Accordingly, a person selling life insurance must have technical knowledge of insurance contracts and how they can serve his clients. The process of acquiring knowledge about life insurance and sales methods generally starts with the preappointment training and continues through home study, company and industry courses and on-the-job training throughout a person's entire career.

The training of both sales representatives and the management of agencies or branch offices is a primary responsibility of the principal sales executive with relatively little dependence on other company operations. Training, however, is expensive, and it is necessary that the various programs operate within a framework of cost that has the approval of top management.

The principal sales executive has a number of responsibilities that influence the training and development of the members of the company's sales force. The first of these is to organize and staff the agency or branch offices in order to provide skilled personnel capable of carrying on the training work. The second responsibility is the preparation of instructional material that will enhance the sales representatives' technical knowledge of insurance and strengthen their ability to prospect and sell. Once the tools and techniques have been provided by the home office, it is the responsibility of local management to train the sales representatives.

---

[8] See Chapters 24, 25 and 26 for discussion of education and training programs.

Motivating Personnel[9]

To achieve its objectives, a company must have a field organization that possesses more than expert knowledge and skill. It must have people who also have the will—the desire—to perform their duties well and to acquire new and improved skills. This can only be achieved through effective leadership.

The effectiveness of motivational efforts is perhaps the most important single factor in the success of a sales program. To a considerable degree the principal sales executive stands alone with the responsibility for providing the climate for proper motivation. His responsibility in this area involves: (1) directing agency or branch office operations in such a way that each person in a supervisory capacity will be stimulated to drive toward higher performance, (2) making sure that these people have the ability to motivate the sales force and (3) providing company-sponsored recognition plans.

The job of effectively motivating sales representatives rests heavily on the shoulders of the agency or branch office management. Motivation is not an activity that can be carried out sporadically—it is a day-in and day-out affair. Motivation of the sales staff is particularly challenging since these people have considerable latitude in scheduling their own time and are not continuously supervised. To perform their work under these conditions, sales staff members must possess enthusiasm to work consistently and conscientiously despite the many difficulties and disappointments that may be encountered. The creation and maintenance of this spirit are among the most vital tasks performed by first-line supervisory and managers of agencies or branch offices in the field.

Direct Administrative Work

The business of insurance is one of providing intangible services to its policyowners. This is accomplished through the receipt and disbursement of money, the completion of forms and correspondence or other means of communication. The magnitude of a life insurance company's operations and the numerous services that it provides result in a vast amount of paper work.

The principal sales executive has the responsibility for establishing a field organization capable of maintaining the necessary procedures for getting the work done. A system for handling the paper work routine must meet four primary tests: (1) provide service to policyowners with

---

[9] See Chapter 27 for a more detailed discussion of motivation.

reasonable speed and accuracy, (2) operate at desired levels of expense, (3) be compatible with home office requirements for policy issue, settlement or other action, and (4) not demand excessive time from the sales force to the serious detriment of the sales effort.

The increase in the cost of clerical employees and the effects on insurance costs have resulted in greater interest in an ever-growing list of technological developments for doing things faster, cheaper and better. Principal sales executives also have found it necessary to evaluate some of the actions that are being taken to determine that the benefits received are commensurate with the costs involved.

Management in agencies and branch offices has the responsibility to see that the practices being followed by both clerks and sales representatives are in accordance with established procedures. An important area of administration is the control and proper handling of company funds.

A key part of local management's administrative work is the maintenance of records and reports relating to the sales program, recruiting and selecting and training. Similarly, the maintenance of conservation controls is a vital step in keeping business on the books.

Since every member of the sales organization is concerned with his earnings, the development and maintenance of records relating to commissions and earnings is essential to company success. Thus, the sales manager must see that proper accounting records relating to agents' commissions are maintained.

Developing and Maintaining Good Public Relations[10]

The sale of a life insurance company's services depends upon many factors, among which is the public's opinion of insurance in general and of the individual company in particular. It is, therefore, a basic responsibility of every person in the company to make sure that the company benefits from the advantages that accrue from good public relations.

Good public relations start with the top management of the company. Because the key executives of a company may be nationally prominent, they exert a strong influence on shaping the public character of the company. Similarly, local managers, in their role as a company's principal representative in the communities they serve, also affect public opinion. The most frequent and continuous contact with the public, however, is made by the sales representatives in the course of their normal work, which means that their competence and sincerity in giving sound insurance advice are material factors in the public's opinion of the company.

_____
[10] See Chapter 18 for a more detailed discussion of public relations.

Thus, regardless of the public relations program provided by management, it is essential that a good public image is put forth by the sales force.

EFFECTS OF SALES MANAGEMENT ON LONG-TERM COMPANY GROWTH

Whatever goals and objectives a life insurance company may have, their achievement is primarily dependent on the success of the company's sales operation. If this program is not successful, eventually income will diminish and financial operations as well as all other functions performed by the company will wither away. Thus, no matter how well managed the other areas of the company may be, they cannot possibly succeed in the long-run if sales efforts fail to produce an adequate and constant stream of new business.

A life insurance company is in many respects like a human body. All of the parts must do their job if there is to be a healthy existence. Thus, the company is a system of mutually dependent elements. The heart of this system is the sales operation; when it stops, the other elements are no longer able to function properly. Unlike the human body, however, a life insurance company must develop the capacity for constant revitalization if it is to stay alive in an everchanging environment.

The job of producing the necessary ingredients for a successful life insurance sales operation is a difficult, demanding task; however, the job of maintaining it is even more difficult. The nature of the business obscures the fact that progress is not being maintained. The relatively large inflow of cash from premium payments and investments in excess of policy settlements and expense can be mistaken as a barometer of a company's growth. The effects of inflation and improvement in living standards may result in increasingly larger sales in terms of premium and amount of insurance; in reality, however, the long-term effect may be that the company is losing ground and real growth is not taking place in comparison with potential or with competition.

There is also the possibility that sales people at all levels may become complacent and be satisfied to do less than they are capable of doing. If this occurs, it is incumbent on top management to recognize the symptoms and to take appropriate corrective steps in spite of resistance to change. The principal sales executive must be alert to his responsibility for continued growth of the company. His is a key role that requires that his organization be kept up to date to supply the policies, tools and techniques needed to meet the challenges of ever changing market conditions in a dynamic economic environment. Of equal importance is the maintenance of an agency organization that is staffed with people who have the capacity to grow and develop in a highly competitive business.

Section III

FUNDAMENTAL PRINCIPLES

8

Basic Management Principles

Philip H. Dutter

COMMON DENOMINATORS FOR SUCCESS

The considerable differences among successful life insurance agency managers in their approach to agency management have led some to believe that there are no common denominators for success in life insurance agency management. In one successful agency, for example, the author has observed an agency manager who does not appear to *manage* his agents at all. They regard him as a friend and counselor whose closest approach to discipline is occasionally telling an agent a story containing a pertinent message. At the opposite extreme, the author has observed another equally successful agency where the manager and his agents appear to be at swords' points and the agents are motivated primarily by a keen, almost bitter, desire to outsell the manager.

"With two such divergent routes to success," one might think, "how can anyone generalize about what it takes to succeed in agency management?"

Many people who have watched life insurance agency managers in action would agree. Such radical differences in the ways successful agency managers operate have given rise to a common belief that managing a life insurance agency or agency force is more art than discipline, more a matter of native talent than of acquired skill, more a question of personality than of principle.

Thus, lip service is paid to the idea of developing agency managers,

113

but there is seldom much conviction behind it. So, even though most companies realize that the agency manager holds the key to their long-term success, few have made a determined, all-out effort to develop outstanding managers.

During the past 10 years I have worked with more than 200 agency managers in five different life insurance companies, as well as with managers in at least six other industries. This experience has convinced me that, despite the differences in leadership styles among successful agency managers—including both general agents and branch managers—common denominators can be found in the way they approach their jobs.

These common denominators are not peculiar to the life insurance industry; they can be found in the practices of successful managers in any industry. They are, in fact, common denominators of good management everywhere.

THE TWO FUNDAMENTAL AND UNIQUE TASKS OF MANAGEMENT

Managing, as a function, involves two fundamental tasks not found in other functions such as selling, or research, or providing technical service. These are (1) determining organizational (as opposed to individual) objectives; and (2) guiding people toward the successful achievement of those objectives. Unlike the agent, who is responsible only for his personal performance, the life insurance sales manager is responsible for the performance of others—a distinction frequently overlooked in evaluating agents as management candidates.

The common denominators for success among life insurance agency managers and among managers in other businesses have to do with the basic principles that they apply, in one way or another, in solving the two basic problems any manager faces:

1. What objectives should I establish for my organization?
2. What can I do to make sure these objectives are attained?

ESTABLISHING OBJECTIVES

In establishing agency objectives the manager is largely guided by his company and the products, service, training programs, and sales aids it makes available to him. Even so, he often has considerable latitude. He usually determines the kind of agents who are brought into the agency, the markets they seek to serve, the prospecting and selling methods they use, and the products they emphasize. It is, at least partly, his job to determine how fast he wants his agency to grow and what kind of agency he wants it to be.

Most successful agency managers, having formulated some vision of the agency they would like to have in 5 or 10 years, establish specific annual goals at the beginning of each year—goals designated to bring the agency closer to these long-term objectives. In setting such objectives, these managers apply two basic principles.

1. Objectives should be set in the light of available opportunities and reassessed whenever significant changes occur in the environment

Buggy whip manufacturers, chewing tobacco companies, and railroads are classic examples of failure to adapt to environmental changes. On the other hand, the Du Pont Company successfully converted itself from a munitions maker to a diversifield chemical company by anticipating the need for change before the end of World War I. Similarly, following World War II a number of leading aircraft companies managed to maintain their strong positions while undergoing the radical transformation brought on by the space age. Although life insurance markets and buying practices have undergone no such dramatic metamorphosis, life insurance marketing opportunities are changing at an accelerating rate. Consider, for example, the mushrooming suburban housing developments, the education explosion, the enactment of Medicare, changes in Social Security benefits, revisions to the Federal income tax law, as well as fluctuations in general economic conditions and interest rates. All of these have affected the life insurance market, and in some communities and some markets they have had a major impact.

While many of the problems and opportunities presented by these changes can be met simply by modifying products or selling approaches, others may have a bearing on such strategic issues as the kind of agent a manager should recruit, the kind of training he should be given, and the rate at which the manager should expect his agency to grow. An effective manager is sensitive to such changes. He takes them into account in periodically reassessing his long-term objectives, and considers them carefully in setting his short-term goals.

2. Objectives should be set in the light of available resources

Unlike other businesses, whose resources consist of plants, production equipment, and inventories, the key resource in the life insurance business is manpower—specifically, agents and staff personnel, including supervisors.

Over the long run, an agency manager may be able to recruit the kind of people he needs to achieve his long-term objectives. In the short-run, however, he must carefully assess the strengths and weaknesses of existing agents and staff personnel in order to set realistic short term sales goals and identify manpower needs to be met through recruiting and development so that the agency will grow at the desired rate over the long run.

ACHIEVING OBJECTIVES

No manager can achieve his long- and short-term objectives single-handed. He must work with and through other people. In doing so, most successful managers follow seven basic principles.

1. An effective manager sees to it that each member of his staff has a clear-cut job to do and the authority to get it done

Although some management theorists in recent years have tended to discount the worth of organization planning, my observation suggests that failure to establish an organization plan is an invitation to chaos, not cooperation. A clear-cut organization plan need not compel each person to operate independently within the narrow confines of his own particular responsibilities. If the plan is soundly conceived and communicated, however, it does require each person to understand his principal mission and how it relates to those of others. It tells him to whom he reports, and it defines his relationships with others in the organization. The plan may not be expressed in the form of an organization chart and job descriptions, but it should be clearly understood by everyone concerned. Lack of a plan, or failure to gain understanding of the plan, almost inevitably leads to confusion, frustration, duplication of effort, errors of omission, and conflict. Real teamwork is likely to result only when the role of each member of the team is clearly defined and understood.

A life insurance agency manager without a staff, of course, has no need for an organization plan. Typically, the agent's basic mission is well defined and understood. As soon as an agency manager acquires a single staff person, however, he needs to establish a clear division of responsibility. And this need increases as his staff grows.

2. An effective manager makes certain that each position is filled by a qualified person

The importance of having the right people in the organization cannot be overstated. Many of the most dramatic "turnarounds" in business history have been accomplished primarily by bringing in more effective people to fill key positions.

At the same time, it is important for a manager not to staff his organization with people who are overqualified for the positions they hold and ambitious out of all measure to the available opportunities. If a manager is realistic about the requirements of each position, he is likely to pick people with the right interests and temperament for the job, as well as the right knowledge and skills. Such a manager knows that a successful agent may not have the interest or temperament to become a successful manager, while a mediocre agent may have the makings of an outstanding instructor.

The principle of the right man for each job is simpler to state than to apply. It is perhaps the principle that is most frequently compromised in practice. Yet anyone with managerial experience will attest that it is probably the most critical to success.

3. An effective manager makes sure that each of his men is committed to specific objectives geared to the objectives of the organization

During the last 10 years the potential power of formal planning has become more widely recognized in management circles. In particular, the process of obtaining personal commitment to concrete objectives has been recognized as a dynamic means of motivating and directing people to achieve organizational goals. Companies of all types and sizes are currently struggling to make this planning process truly part of the corporate way of life. Their experience indicates that objectives should be both attainable and sufficiently demanding to "stretch" the abilities of individuals. Equally important, they should be consistent with the objectives of the total organization. In a sense, the objectives of the organization as a whole are the sum of the objectives of the individuals who make it up.

Even more important, perhaps, is the concept that goals should be agreed on by the individual and his manager. In the past, goals have typically consisted of either quotas dictated from the top or highly personal goals, known only to the individual concerned. The key to what has sometimes been called "participative management" lies in the ways goals are established. The manager's role is neither to dictate the goal nor to simply record whatever goal his subordinates propose. Rather, it is his task to stimulate and guide his subordinates to set goals that are realistic, demanding, and consistent with the objectives of the organization. This is a difficult balance to achieve, particularly for a manager who tends toward an extremely autocratic or permissive style. Yet it is a keystone of effective personnel development.

For years, effective agency managers found that getting an agent committed to producing a certain amount of business, winning a particular form of recognition, or earning a specified amount of income can be a powerful motivator. Now more agency managers have formalized this goal-setting process and related it to achieving agency goals. In addition, there is more stress on obtaining commitment from individual staff members to attain specific agent recruiting and development goals.

4. An effective manager makes sure each of his subordinates has an adequate plan for achieving his objectives

For most people there is a considerable gap between setting an objective and achieving it. This is particularly true of a "stretching" objective, one that requires a significant improvement over previous performance.

Recent experience has shown that the full power of the planning process is felt only when the steps needed to achieve key objectives are spelled out in written action plans. These may be simple statements of two or three key steps, or detailed descriptions of everything that must be done to achieve the desired end result, together with a timetable for each step. The degree of detail needed will vary with the situation and with the individual concerned. Typically, more detail is needed when precedents are lacking. In any case, an action plan is useless unless it provides both a meaningful guide for the individual and a basis for follow-up and evaluation of progress. Frequently, action plans need to be revised before the objective is achieved, either because they turn out not to be the best means of achieving the objective for the individual concerned or because of changing circumstances.

An illustration of the value of developing specific action plans can be found in the experience of life insurance agency managers in developing million-dollar producers. These agency managers have learned that a relatively new agent who wants to write a million dollars of life insurance during the coming year is much more likely to do it if he is persuaded to translate this objective into the number of sales he has to make and the number of people he has to see each week, and then into week-by-week prospecting plans for making the necessary contacts. Equally important, successful managers are finding that both they and their staffs can step up their own effectiveness in recruiting new agents and developing existing agents by spelling out the specific steps that each will take to meet the agency's objectives. In agency management, time can be used or misused in an infinite variety of ways. Planning a specific course of action in advance helps to focus the efforts of the agency manager and his staff on those activities that are most critical to success.

5. An effective manager follows up on progress to ensure appropriate action

While the term "training" suggests a classroom situation to most people, comprehensive studies of how job proficiency is actually developed have shown time and again that the most effective training takes place on the job. Furthermore, several depth studies have led to the conclusion that the best on-the-job training occurs when the learner has the benefit of a good coach in the early stages.

Such a coach, or manager, has a good sense not only of how much detailed instruction to give, but also of how closely to watch the learner's progress in order to correct his mistakes and make sure he takes the steps necessary to achieve the desired result. At the same time, he resists the temptation to step in and do the job for the learner, and he avoids encouraging the learner to depend on him for continuing close follow-up.

A frequently misunderstood principle of management is the idea that responsibility and authority should be delegated to the level where action is to be taken. There is a thin line between delegation of responsibility and abdication of managerial responsibility. A manager can delegate as much responsibility or authority as he likes, but he cannot escape accountability for results. Therefore, an effective manager will seek to delegate just as much responsibility as he believes the individual can handle, and he will usually risk delegating a little more than he *knows* the individual can handle. But, since he is personally accountable for the results achieved, he will tailor his follow-up activities to the individual and the situation so as to retain enough control to ensure the desired results.

In life insurance agency management, an effective manager soon learns the necessity of recognizing that brand new agents and successful, experienced agents differ widely in their need for follow-up. A new agent is likely to require detailed review of his previous day's activities and plans for the coming day at the beginning of each day, while a brief monthly checkup with an experienced agent may be all that is needed or desirable. Similarly, the needs of a supervisor or assistant manager for follow-up will vary greatly depending on his experience, the nature of his assignment, and the problems he is encountering. An effective manager will use control reports showing results achieved against the formalized plan to identify situations where more detailed follow-up is required to bring about corrective action.

6. An effective manager continually motivates his men through rewards and recognition

The problem of motivating people is of prime concern to any thoughtful manager and has been the subject of considerable research in recent years.

Effective managers in any business soon come to recognize that a high level of motivation is the product of a whole range of factors, many of them directly controllable. The simplest, most direct, and possibly most effective motivating tools available to the manager are the words of praise or blame by which he can instantly reward or penalize subordinates. Beyond this, most managers are in a position to exercise some influence on individual compensation and on recognition in the form of public commendation, improved status, or advancement.

Most life insurance agency managers are well ahead of managers in other businesses in the application of this principle. Perhaps because of the nature of the life insurance sales job—particularly the importance of developing and maintaining a strong drive to succeed—motivation through rewards and recognition is the "name of the game" for many agency managers. The approach an agency manager chooses will depend on his own personality and style as well as the background and the ambitions of his agents. Typically, the more perceptive and mature agency managers have learned to tailor their approach to the needs and temperament of both the entire group and the individuals who make up the group.

7. An effective manager establishes and enforces minimum performance standards

Any organization has a spirit or tone that reflects the characteristics and practices of its management. Perhaps the most important of these is the manager's demand for a high level of performance from each member of his organization, backed by a clear definition of what level of performance is expected. Without such definition, enforcement of the performance standards may seem completely arbitrary and ruthless, quickly demoralizing the staff. Beyond defining minimum performance standards, however, an effective manager acts decisively when those standards are not met.

In some of the most successful life insurance agencies, the performance standards—written or unwritten—are not confined to the amount of business an agent produces or the number of agents a staff member recruits. Standards are also set for the *kind* of business an agent writes, the way he conducts himself, and—where staff members are concerned—for the way they deal with agents, with each other, and with the public. While these standards differ from one agency to another, few agencies whose managers tolerate substandard performance are successful for long.

VARIATIONS IN APPLYING MANAGEMENT PRINCIPLES

Going back to the observation made at the beginning of this chapter that successful agency managers vary markedly in managerial style, it may seem to be stretching a point to claim that the principles discussed above are really common denominators for success.

One of the difficulties in pinning down the common denominators for success, of course, is the difficulty of distinguishing differences in personal leadership style from differences in basic approach to management. After observing a variety of agency managers who have proven their effectiveness by the sustained, outstanding growth of their agencies, I am convinced that the major differences that stand out are matters of personal leadership style, not fundamental principles. Just as there are wide differences in the personalities and, therefore, the styles of successful salesmen, so there are wide differences in the personalities and, therefore, the styles of successful managers. One successful manager will be extremely outgoing, enthusiastic, and blessed with a great facility for getting "close to his people." Another equally successful manager may be more inclined to be taciturn, "no-nonsense" in his manner, and difficult to know. One manager may appear to be impulsive, strictly intuitive in his thinking and incapable of discipline. On the other hand, another manager may be thoughtful, highly analytical, and meticulous in administrative detail.

These kinds of differences in personal makeup and capabilities clearly have a major influence on the way the basic principles discussed here are applied. In fact, the application of these principles will vary so greatly from one manager to another that it may be hard to recognize that they are, indeed, the same principles. For example, the apparently disorganized manager may really have given much more thought to the needs of the situation than one would expect. Similarly, the apparently aloof manager may have given considerably more attention to the motivation of his men than is evident on the surface.

At the same time, not all successful managers are equally effective in applying *all* of these basic management principles. The relative emphasis given each of the principles, as well as the manner of their application, is likely to be influenced by differences in personal style. Yet, few managers have built successful agencies without learning to become reasonably proficient in applying all of the basic management principles.

ROLE OF COMPANY MANAGEMENT

Although more is being learned about the art or science of managing every day, there is nothing very new in the basic management principles that have been discussed here. For the most part, they have been well-known for many years, both in the life insurance industry and in other industries.

The truly difficult problem is to find ways of stimulating and training more managers to apply these principles consistently. This is a particularly acute problem in the life insurance industry, where the success or failure of a large number of local managers is critical to the success of a company in building a large and capable agency force.

Until recently, the major thrust of most companies' efforts to encourage broader and more effective application of these basic principles has been limited to providing for agency managers to attend seminars and sending out reading material on the subject of management. While these efforts have been useful, they fail to recognize that the most effective training is on-the-job training with appropriate coaching. Moreover, they fail to capitalize on leverage that can be exerted in a large organization through an integrated management system.

In recent years, a number of companies have made important changes designed to go beyond the seminar and reading-material stage in stimulating more effective application of basic management principles throughout their field organizations. In preparing to do so, some of them have had to make fairly fundamental changes in agency department organization structures, compensation levels and in the roles played by key agency executives.

Any company that seriously attempts to apply these principles at all levels of its agency organization, however, faces a special problem. Just as the job of managing differs fundamentally from the job of selling or carrying out any activity as an individual performer, so the job of managing managers differs fundamentally from managing individual performers. An individual performer needs no authority over others in the organization in order to get his job done; a manager, on the other hand, needs authority to direct and motivate others. Thus, a manager of managers must constantly be aware of the need to match managerial authority to managerial responsibility.

He must also keep in mind how easily authority can be usurped, infringed upon, or diluted. Whenever an agency officer deals directly with an agent, he runs the risk of usurping the agency manager's authority. Whenever an agency officer "second guesses" a manager's decision, the officer runs the risk of infringing upon the manager's authority. Whenever an agency officer forces a manager to change his plans, he runs the risk of diluting the manager's authority.

Clearly, there are times when it is either necessary or worthwhile for an agency officer to do all of these things. Yet, an effective agency officer will exercise restraint and, in each case, will take care not to weaken the manager's position in the eyes of the manager's staff and agents.

An effective agency officer learns to make the distinction between man-

AN INTEGRATED MANAGEMENT SYSTEM
AIMED AT MULTIPLYING EFFECTIVE APPLICATION
OF BASIC MANAGEMENT PRINCIPLES

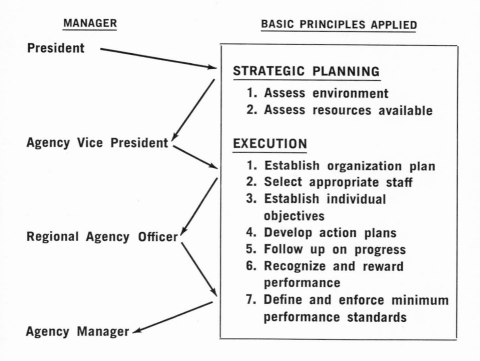

MANAGER   BASIC PRINCIPLES APPLIED

President

STRATEGIC PLANNING

1. Assess environment
2. Assess resources available

Agency Vice President

EXECUTION

1. Establish organization plan
2. Select appropriate staff
3. Establish individual objectives
4. Develop action plans
5. Follow up on progress
6. Recognize and reward performance
7. Define and enforce minimum performance standards

Regional Agency Officer

Agency Manager

aging a manager and managing *for* a manager. He disciplines himself to avoid the temptation to solve personally the problem which the agency faces. He views himself as being directly accountable for the *manager's* performance, both now and in the future, and indirectly accountable for the agency's performance. Therefore, he concentrates his attention on applying to the manager the same management principles that he would like the manager to apply to his staff and to his agents. Thus, the manager not only has the benefit of personal coaching, but also a management model to emulate.

Of course, an agency officer is most likely to apply these principles consistently if he sees that they are being applied in the way that he himself is managed. Thus, the full power of an integrated system of management in spreading the consistent application of sound management principles is realized only when the chief executive officer and chief agency officer apply these principles in the way they manage. The challenge of improving life insurance sales management effectiveness, therefore, is a personal challenge affecting thousands of people at all organizational levels in the life insurance industry.

9

Fundamental Principles of
Sales Management

William J. Stanton and Richard H. Buskirk

UNIVERSALITY OF MANAGEMENT PRINCIPLES IN
ADMINISTRATION OF HUMAN ACTIVITIES

Most human activities such as war, business, or sports are goal directed
—their participants are seeking to achieve something. Such behavior is
performed by groups of individuals who have joined together in the belief
that they have the same goals and that as a group they are more likely to
achieve those desired ends. Athletes subject themselves to the directions
and demands of their coaches because by doing so they will be more likely
to achieve their goals—wins, records, fame, money—than if they were to
try to reach the same goals by their own individual efforts. Similarly,
salesmen have goals and will respond to leadership only if the leader
demonstrates to them that he is indeed a manager—a leader of men. If
any semblance of efficiency and orderly progress toward achieving the
group's goals is to be realized, the group's activities must be managed, that
is, planned, organized, and controlled. It is this universality of management functions and principles that allows the administrator to transfer his
abilities from one job to another with ease. It is also the existence of management principles that makes administration a distinct skill separate from
technical abilities.

ADMINISTRATION IS A DISTINCT SKILL—
SELLING ABILITY NOT SUFFICIENT

Although many men of outstanding technical abilities do make good administrators, there is considerable evidence that the possession of technical talent does not necessarily mean that its owner would make a good manager of men. Witness the situation in the sports world where many successful coaches—administrators—were only average players. In the sales field, it is widely recognized that the best salesman may not make the best sales manager. An individual may be the greatest life insurance salesman who ever opened a rate book, but salesmanship alone will not equip him to be a successful manager of other life insurance salesmen.

The very factors that enable a man to become an outstanding salesman may be the ones that explain his failure as an administrator. Most highly successful sales representatives have in common a great liking for extensive personal contact with customers and the field work involved in selling. The successful sales manager, however, must attend to a considerable amount of paper work—planning and controlling—in the *office*. Also, many highly successful salesmen possess strongly aggressive personalities that can be a liability to the administrator who must work closely with his superiors, equals, and subordinates. Hence, in evaluating a person for an administrative position, one must make certain that a man's proficiency at a technical skill, such as selling, does not overly influence the evaluation of him as a possible administrator; they are two separate and distinct skills.

This is not to say that technical proficiency is not needed, for it most certainly is. It would be difficult to envision a successful sales manager without a knowledge of sales technique and considerably skill in selling. The administrator requires technical knowledge so that he can recognize undeveloped talent in his subordinates. It seems rather obvious that if a man plans to go bear hunting, he should know what a bear looks like. Similarly, if a sales manager is planning to hire a good salesman, he must first know what attributes to look for in the prospective recruit. The executive who lacks technical competency is continually at the mercy of his subordinates. He is unable to evaluate their technical competency and, hence, the soundness of their recommendations or methods of operation. In addition, it is critical to a sales manager's success that his men have confidence that he can lead them to success; without successful sales experience it is difficult for the manager to gain the confidence of the salesman. Finally, if a man is not a fairly successful salesman, he may never get the chance to become a sales manager no matter how good an administrator he may be. Unquestionably, his performance in the field affects his superiors' evaluation of him for a position in sales management.

The individual who has acquired administrative abilities is indeed fortunate, because he will find these talents useful in the management of any type of organization. The recent cross-migration of business and government administrators bears out this point. A relatively large number of military leaders, upon retirement, have been appointed to executive positions in business. It is widely recognized in the world of education that many successful college presidents have transferred with ease their administrative abilities from education to other activities, and many leaders from business and politics have successfully taken over college presidencies. The agile administrator, with proper orientation, can quickly put his talents to work in almost any managerial situation.

A PHILOSOPHY OF MANAGEMENT

A philosophy is a belief about ultimate reality, causes, and principles underlying being and thinking. Therefore, a philosophy of management is a belief in certain basic principles applicable to the management of men.

Just as most persons consciously or unconsciously have philosophies of life, most businessmen have philosophies on now best to manage men and organizations. Unfortunately, many of these executives allow their philosophies to lie unrecognized and uncrystalized and by doing so allow inconsistencies of managerial action to develop.

A life insurance sales manager, during his prior years as an agent, will have had considerable opportunity to serve some leaders while observing others—both successful and unsuccessful. By the time he becomes a manager he will normally have formulated his own notions about how best to manage life insurance salesmen. These ideas and beliefs represent his present philosophy of management. The desire of the company, as well as the manager, is that his philosophy be workable.

Need for Consistency

The ideas and beliefs constituting an executive's management philosophy must be consistent with each other and with the objectives and policies of the firm, or stresses will be created that will be detrimental to morale and achievement. For example, if the marketing vice president's philosophy was one that esteemed an authoritarian system of management as being ideal, but the company had corporatewide policies of decentralization, democratic leadership, and management by committee, the resultant conflicts between the marketing vice president and other members of the organization would be harmful to him, his subordinates, his peers and the company. Assume also that this executive held the philosophy that he should have only high quality, executive-caliber men as his subordinates.

With this assumption his philosophy is not only inconsistent with the policies of the firm but the two philosophies are inconsistent with each other. If this executive held onto his authoritarian philosophy of management, he would not be able to activate his second philosophy, since highly able men probably would not remain under his authoritarian leadership. A philosophy on personnel, which would be consistent with his leadership philosophy, would require the hiring of men who could take orders and carry them out efficiently but who had little desire for responsibility and authority.

Philosophy Must Be Workable

The possession of an unworkable philosophy renders the executive worse than useless. The sales manager who really believes in the philosophy that the salesman has no rights is living in the industrial dark ages. He might have been considered an acceptable executive fifty years ago, but today he would cause nothing but trouble for himself and the organization. He would be completely ineffective as a leader of men in the current business world.

Areas Affected by Managerial Philosophies

BUSINESS ORGANIZATION

Many problems of organization can be solved only after recognition of the executive's philosophy on the subject.

1. Centralization versus Decentralization of Authority and Operations. The extent to which control is vested in the top executives or in the field managers depends largely upon the philosophy held by management concerning the most efficient way of administering the situation at hand. Nevertheless, the personal attitude of executives toward the centralization of authority has a strong influence over the decision made regardless of the situation to which it is applied. Many executives who believe in decentralized operations will try to apply that philosophy to situations that might better be administered from one central post of authority.

2. Line versus Staff Relationships. The extent to which staff personnel is used and their role in the organization are greatly affected by the philosophy of the management. Some administrators dislike creating staff positions, preferring either to subcontract work of that nature to other organizations or to have line personnel take on the work as part of their regular duties. Other executives make great use of staff men, and at times the staff executives in such situations can have a great deal of power and tacit authority over line operations.

3. Supervision and Control. The closeness of supervision and the span of control depend in large part on the attitude of the chief administrator towards supervision. Some leaders have a philosophy that the man should be left alone unless he has given his superior some reason to believe that he requires close supervision, whereas other administrators adhere to a philosophy that their subordinates should be placed under close supervision. Of course, this decision cannot be made independently of others; it must be consistent with the philosophy on personnel, location of authority, and organizational structure.

4. Size of the Organization. Some administrators prefer to keep their organization as small as possible, relying on the frequent use of subcontractors, whereas other executives want large organizations and do everything they can to enlarge their domain. The reasons for these philosophies are many and complex. Some men prefer a close-knit relationship with their organization, which is impossible to realize when the group is large; others believe that their power and influence is enlarged as their organization grows; some executives feel that efficiency is lost as the structure increases in size, while others would disagree. The number of variations in attitudes toward this one small segment of organizational philosophy is almost infinite.

AUTHORITY

There are two views as to the source of authority. One school of thought, and it is the older and more recognized one, believes that authority stems from the rights of private property. This philosophy states that the owner of property has the right to dictate its usage and that persons who desire to use the property must follow the dictates of the owner or his representatives.

Unfortunately, this theory has some weaknesses. For instance, how can one explain authority in economic systems that do not have private property? Also, one encounters the problem of semantics: What is authority? Under the previous definition, authority means the right to control property. However, from a management viewpoint this is an inadequate definition. An executive can most certainly control property yet be an utter failure as an administrator. He could close down the plant or even go out of business when his employees went on strike against one of his edicts. However, he would not be achieving the goals of the organization. In fact, the administrator has moved the group even further away from its objectives. Administrative weapons of this type will be termed *Power*.

To have a useful meaning in this age of professional management, authority must mean *the ability to control or influence the efforts of a group of individuals.* The good leader, of course, is trying to control such efforts in a way that will move the group closer to its goals. Under such a definition, authority can be bestowed upon the administrator only by his subordinates. AUTHORITY FLOWS UPWARD FROM THE EMPLOYEES TO THE LEADERS. The leader has no more authority than his subordinates will allow him. If they refuse to follow an order, it is true that he can have them fired; however, this is not authority, but power, since he was still unable to move the group to action. Suppose a military officer ordered his men to capture a machine-gun nest and they refused. He could have them shot, but this still would not capture the gun emplacement; as a leader, he was ineffective. Granted that some subordinates will give the officer the authority out of fear of his power, nevertheless, they had to give it; the reason for giving it is beside the point in this instance. However, in business the reason for giving the authority is not beside the point; it vitally influences morale and efficiency.

A salesman will grant authority to the sales manager for at least two reasons. The first is that he does not want to risk losing his job—fear of power. The second, and by far the more important reason, is that the salesman is willing to follow the guidance of his manager because in so doing he believes he will come closer to reaching his own goals in life. This is known as the process of *integrating the interests of the man with the objectives of the organization.* Each person has certain personal goals he wants to achieve. Psychologists call this his "self-concept"—what he thinks he is and would like to be in this world. This self-concept is an extremely complex structure of wants, behavior traits, status symbols, and concepts of being in existence. Suppose that Joe is a salesman and has the following self-concept of what he is and what he wants to be. He feels that he is an excellent salesman, capable of selling life insurance in the individual as well as the group market. He believes that he is important to the agency and that he is a good employee. He has certain tangible goals in life. He wants to move into a new semi-mansion in the fashionable district of town; he would like to own a Lincoln-Continental or a Cadillac; he wants to be a good family man and father to his children; he wants his neighbors to realize how good a man he really is; and down deep he really feels that he would make an excellent agency manager if only his manager would recommend him.

Some of these goals conflict with one another. The desire for many material possessions conflicts with his desire to be with his family, and his thoughts about being an excellent salesman may run into trouble with his managerial aspirations. Now Joe will follow certain suggestions and directions with enthusiasm. If the agency manager suggests that the agents move into a more expensive price range in their clothing and automobile purchases, Joe will be the first in line. If the agency manager issues a directive for a special emphasis on selling juvenile policies and organizes an attractive contest, Joe probably will respond with vigor. But should the agency manager ask the men to take some refresher sales training, Joe would be only passive to that request. He might go through the motions, but little else. Or, if the agency manager were to start a system of close field supervision, Joe would probably resent that action, because of a feeling that he is good and that he is fully capable of managing his own efforts. Joe's reaction to direction is automatically screened through his self-concept. If the manager's request aids Joe in realizing his ideal self-concept, it is accepted and followed—the agency manager is given authority. If the request is in too much conflict with what Joe wants out of life, it is in serious danger of being ignored.

From the manager's point of view, it becomes obvious that before issuing instructions or requests for action, he should first ask himself whether the other party will respond favorably; few things are more embarrassing to a manager than to have a direct order disobeyed. If an order is disobeyed, the executive is immediately faced with having to do one of three things, all of which are undesirable: (1) he can punish the offender; (2) he can withdraw the order or (3) he can ignore the whole incident as if he were not aware of it. In any case, the executive loses considerable face among his subordinates and his effectiveness as a leader is impaired.

PERSONAL RELATIONSHIP WITH EQUALS, SUPERIORS, AND SUBORDINATES

The executive can take one of two basic attitudes toward his relationship with each level of authority in the organizational structure. He can attempt to maintain a distinct status differential or he can look upon his organization as one big happy family. Each has its place and use, depending upon the circumstances.

ON CONTROL—ITS ADMINISTRATION, DEGREE, AND ENFORCEMENT

Control of organization efforts can be likened to a scale. At one end is the executive who lets his organization run as it will without any leash on it whatsoever; at the other end is the executive who insists on controlling every little detail of the operation. At either of the extremes, management is likely to encounter difficulty; most leaders find it advisable to follow courses of action falling in the middle. Exactly which side of the middle the executive should choose depends upon several things: (1) the caliber of men in the organization; (2) the nature of the job being done; (3) the span of control existing in the organizational structure; (4) the capabilities of the leader himself; (5) the duties required of the leader; and (6) the importance which the controlled activity bears to the over-all success of the organization.

1. Caliber of Men. Good salesmen require less control and resent excessive supervision more than do poor ones. The good man feels he is able to control himself properly with a minimum of supervision from the manager. It is sound executive training to allow management trainees as much freedom in their operations as is feasible under existing conditions, too much freedom, however, may be harmful.

2. Nature of Job. Some sales jobs almost defy close control; they are of such a nonroutine nature and so far removed from home or branch office supervision that close control becomes difficult and unwise. On the other hand, some sales positions are such that the salesman is working with the manager every day. In these cases, close control over the salesman's activities is not only easy but can be extremely helpful to him.

3. Span of Control. The more men the supervisor must administer, the less time he can spend supervising and controlling any one of them. The span of control is established by the organization philosophy of the company and is not usually determined by the supervisor. If there are but a few salesman under him, the supervisor is able to keep closer control over them than otherwise would be the case.[1]

4. Capabilities of the Leader. A highly able leader is capable of maintaining closer control over his organization, if he so desires, than is an administrator who finds himself bogged down in the details of his job other than control. Also, the capable leader is able to devise control systems which meet the requirements of the job, yet require little of his time to operate.

5. Duties Required of Administrator. The job of some managers is far more complex and time consuming than that of others. Executives who are strictly managers of sales forces will have far more time to control their men than will persons who have been given the responsibility for all marketing activities. The fact is simple but inescapable—the more duties given a man, the less time he has to perform each one.

6. Importance of Activity Controlled. There comes a time when the costs of controlling an activity outweigh the advantages to be gained by instituting the control mechanism. If an activity is not of importance to the achievement of the goals set forth, the validity of instituting rigorous controls over the activity may be questioned.

---

[1] Some writers use the term "span of executive control" to denote the number of managerial personnel reporting to one administrator and the term "unit of supervision" to denote the number of workers reporting to one supervisor. The term "span of control" is used here to encompass both concepts; it is the number of people reporting to one person at any level in the organization.

THE FUNDAMENTAL RESPONSIBILITY OF THE ADMINISTRATOR IS TO STAFF HIS ORGANIZATION WITH THE RIGHT MEN

If the authors have any one basic philosophy toward the problem of managing men, it is this one. Above all else, the administrator's basic duty and function in an organization is to staff it properly.

If he has hired the right men, even bad plans may be successful. But more importantly, the right men will not make bad plans. The right men eliminate or considerably lessen most of the manager's problems. With highly competent men, training becomes easier and more effective, compensation plans will work as intended, a minimum of supervision and stimulation will be required, and control of efforts will pose fewer problems. In short, once competent men are hired, life becomes easier for the manager.

The reason this is particularly important in sales management is that marketing is an art of execution. The success of most marketing plans rests not so much with the plan as it does with the aptness with which it is carried out. Actually, the devising of proper marketing strategies is not at all difficult. Most of the time the necessary actions are quite obvious. But the success of the entire endeavor depends upon the execution of the plans.

MARKETING MANAGEMENT AND ITS EVOLUTION

Although this handbook is devoted largely to the management of a sales organization, a sales executive should understand where his field fits into the total system of marketing. Managers of sales organizations increasingly will have to plan and coordinate their activities with other phases of a company's total marketing program.

The Marketing Concept

As executives have come to realize marketing's importance to a company's success and as they understand that a company is a marketing organization, a new way of business thinking is evolving. The so-called *marketing concept* has developed as production- and engineering-oriented firms have evolved into marketing-oriented structures. Two fundamental ideas epitomize the marketing concept. First is the idea that the company should be customer oriented in all aspects of its management and operations. The second basic thought is that with this orientation management should strive for *profitable* sales volume.

Possibly the most important aspect of the marketing concept is that it is an entirely new way of thinking—it is a *philosophy* and not merely a reshuffling of the corporate organization in which a new department is established to be responsible for a wider variety and range of activities. The essence of this philosophy is that customers' want-satisfaction is the economic and social justification for a firm's existence; *customers* are what make the economic system function. Therefore, all business effort in production and finance, as well as in marketing, must be devoted toward determining the customers' needs and wants and then satisfying them while still making a reasonable profit.

As one of the marketing management executives at General Electric so ably summarized the concept:

> ... we feel that marketing is a fundamental business philosophy. This definition recognizes marketing's functions and methods of organizational structuring as *only the implementation* of the philosophy. These things are not, in themselves, the philosophy.
> ... fundamental to this philosophy is the recognition and acceptance of a customer-oriented way of doing business. Under marketing the customer becomes the fulcrum, the pivot point about which the business moves in operating for the balanced best interests of all concerned ...
> The second fundamental on which the marketing philosophy rests is that it is rooted in the profit concept, not the volume concept. (I am not eliminating the use of volume as a rewarding way of obtaining profits from the efficiency of the service rendered; rather, I am referring to the profitless volume or volume-for-the-sake-of-volume-alone concept.)[2]

Another writer defined the marketing concept as "a corporate state of mind that insists on the integration and coordination of all marketing functions which, in turn, are welded with all other corporate functions, for the basic objective of producing maximum long-range corporate profits."[3]

A significant difference exists between the marketing concept and marketing itself. The marketing concept is a philosophy, a state of mind, or a way of business *thinking*; marketing is a process, a system, or a course of business *action*. Naturally, the way of thinking determines the course of action. That is, the action system (marketing) is based upon the philosophical concept.

---

[2] Fred J. Borch, "The Marketing Philosophy As a Way of Business Life," in *The Marketing Concept: Its Meaning to Management* (New York: The American Management Association, 1957), Marketing Series, No. 99, pp. 3–5.

[3] Arthur P. Felton, "Making the Marketing Concept Work," *Harvard Business Review* (July-August, 1959), p. 55. The author stated that the *important ingredients* in the concept are (1) a proper state of mind, (2) the actual coordination of all marketing functions, and (3) the use of professional and executive skill of a high order. *Common pitfalls* in implementing the concept are (1) inexperienced executives, (2) unsound organizational structures, (3) incomplete integration traceable to personality clashes, lack of executive teamwork, or one-man domination.

Marketing Management—The Application of the Marketing Concept

For a business enterprise to realize the full benefits of the marketing concept, the philosophy must be translated into practice. This means that (a) the marketing activities in a firm must be better organized, coordinated, and managed, and (b) the marketing executive must be accorded a more important role in total company planning and policy making than generally has been true in the past. Thus the idea of marketing management is seen emerging in American business. *Marketing management is the marketing concept in action.*

IMPORTANCE OF MANAGEMENT OF THE SALES ORGANIZATION

With the increasing attention being devoted to marketing management and with businesses showing some trend toward an adoption of the marketing concept in their organizational structures, some managerial activities need to be set in their proper perspective. Accepting the concept of marketing management in no way negates the importance of sales force management within a company. In fact, caution must be exercised by top administrators lest they neglect the management of their sales forces in their preoccupation with the growth of marketing management. Certainly a direct relationship exists between company profits and the management of salesmen.

In a corporate structure which features marketing management, much executive attention is devoted to sales and market planning. Such emphasis is well placed, but no company administrator should overlook the fact that ordinarily it takes the salesmen in the field to carry out the sales plan. No plan is of much value until it is executed properly. A jet airliner may be soundly planned on a drawing board and a prototype may even be constructed. Until the airplane is air tested and is in mass production, however, the dreams on the drawing board will not have been realized.

A sales force is in a crucial position in the marketing program of most companies. If the men cannot successfully sell their product because they are improperly selected, trained, compensated, or supervised, the excellent efforts devoted to product planning, sales planning, market forecasting, and other functions will be of little value. About the only exceptions are firms that do not rely on salesmen but instead primarily use advertising or agent middlemen, such as brokers, to move the products. Therefore, if the salesmen are critical to the success of a concern's marketing venture obviously the sound management of these representatives is of paramount importance. The increasing demand for a higher standard of living in America makes it essential that business have an effective, well-managed group of salesmen, because this group will be responsible in the final analysis, for delivering this standard of living.

Another major reason proper management of the salesmen is so important is that the cost of managing and operating a sales force typically is the largest single marketing expense for most companies. Public attention is often directed toward advertising and a question is raised about the huge amounts of money spent by a given firm for its television or magazine advertisements. At the same time, the critical public group may not know whether the company even has a sales force, much less knowing what it costs. Yet, this firm's total advertising expenditures may be only 3 or 4 percent of net sales, while the total expenses related to the salespeople may be 15 or 20 percent of net sales.

Sales force management is also important in most companies because it still is far from perfection. Sales administrators openly and honestly admit their policies and procedures in selection, training, motivation, compensation, and several other areas leave much to be desired.

Management of the sales force is tremendously important in the administration picture because so many echelons of management are involved. When a firm speaks of a sales manager, it may be talking about any one of several men, such as the top marketing executive, the head of the field sales force, a divisional sales manager responsible for several districts, the manager of any one of those districts, an administrator in charge of the men who sell only one of the company's product lines, or some other type or level of sales manager. In contrast, when a person speaks of executives in the advertising, marketing research, or some other division within the marketing structure, he is speaking of a relatively few people.

Section IV

ORGANIZING FOR
LIFE INSURANCE SALES

10

Organization of the Marketing Department

Paul A. Norton*

A. THE PURPOSE AND NATURE OF ORGANIZATION

1. The Unity and Hierarchy of Purposes

An organization exists solely to fulfill an active purpose, whether to govern a people, to manufacture a product, or to sell a service. Without a common purpose, an organization's members would have no goals. Without goals for what members do, consistent with this overall purpose, the organization would have no clients or customers. Success of an organization is proportional to accomplishment of its purpose, and failure is apt to begin with loss or irrelevance of purpose before it shows in lack of achievement.

Achieving specific objectives, as contrasted with general purposes, is important to any organization. These must be reviewed and rescheduled from time to time to preserve a sense of mission and accomplishment. However, "achievements" may follow from simply doing the same thing year after year. Unless the *purpose* of activity is continually reviewed, mere momentum can conceal an organization's decreasing significance in a world which provides the reason for its existence.

* With the assistance of Charles J. Dexter, Research Associate at New York Life and past chairman of the Organization Development Council, New York City.

In this context, "purpose" should be broadly rather than narrowly conceived, and refer to actions and results in *qualitative* terms, whereas "goals" are more *quantitative* in nature. An organization which has a hierarchy of members should have parallel purposes. The purpose of one level can be analyzed or "quantified" in terms of the goals of the level below it. These goals, in turn, can be synthesized or "qualified" as a purpose which helps to interpret the goals of still lower levels.

For example, the purpose of a marketing department may be to render qualities of insurance services of various types to selected markets in the United States. These can be quantified in terms of regional objectives and goals for each agency, as well as individual agents. Since these areas and levels may differ as to both manpower and markets, each aspect of the purpose and means of achieving it must be periodically reconsidered in terms of current capacities and methods to be used to improve them.

2. Motivational and Social Values of Purpose

The overall unity of purpose of the organization as a whole should be expressed in terms that every member can understand. This purpose can be so general, however, that it appears eternal, like *mother love,* and thus beyond either evaluation or evolution. Too broadly stated, or interpreted only as goals for the total organization, a purpose loses its motivational power. Once lost, this power can best be regained as the hierarchy of purposes is made more specific and put in terms of goals which are appropriate for each level and unit of organization.

An organization's purpose and those of its subdivisions must be consistent with the social and economic goals of the society of which it is a part. Whenever an organization loses this perspective, and essentially exploits rather than serves society, it can be punished directly by penalty or indirectly by neglect as people seek other sources or forms of the offered service. Since social values are subject to continued change, organizational purposes should be frequently re-evaluated in terms of current and even future social and economic environments. As the means to certain ends change, purposes should also be reviewed in the light of the question— what can be accomplished today that was impossible yesterday, and will be needed tomorrow?

As a major area of response to this question, electronic data processing techniques are providing many new means of fulfilling old purposes.

3. The Human Nature of Organization

"Purpose" is a human concept which may be considered a flexible extension of the less adaptable instincts or drives of animal life. Thus, purpose pulls where instinct pushes. Purpose permits a variety of imaginative adjustments, where drives tend only to succeed or fail. Species can blindly adapt to changing conditions by survival of the fittest in successive generations—which is far too slow for individuals or organizations.

Any organization is a society in miniature; its members have the same basic characteristics as other members of society at large. Just as an apiary must conform to the nature of bees, an organization must conform to human nature, or lose both members and customers alike.

Consistently with nature in general and human nature in particular, society and its organizations tend toward both singularity and plurality. We have only one United States government, but many state, county and municipal governments. Any area may have a single public utility where services must be uniform; but should have many businesses when services can be varied in quantity and quality while competing for consumer dollars.

Managing through objectives requires organizational purposes which individuals who have an even wider range of purposes can readily identify as part of their own. The popularity of this style of managing suggests its competitive value.

In the long run, the survival of any industry, company or smaller unit of organization depends on its competitive adaptation not only to human nature, but to the individual natures of its own humans.

4. Efficiency and Effectiveness in Organization

The viability of an organization in a competitive world is determined by its efficiency and effectiveness. It must be both efficient in terms of its internal operations and effective in terms of its external services.

To the extent that an organization exists to serve others, "effectiveness" has the more direct and obvious value of supporting survival. "Efficiency" is also valuable, since waste reduces rewards which are divided between producers and consumers alike, and greater rewards elsewhere tend to cause a loss of both to any organization. However, for an organization to give efficiency a higher priority than effectiveness is to run the danger of having no one to serve.

In brief, an organization must provide for itself the means of monitoring its external effects in relation to its opportunities, and its internal efficiency in terms of its problems. The result of the monitoring process should affect periodic appraisals of purposes and goals, and new plans for organizational progress. For the insurance industry to fail to improve in line with its opportunities might simply mean that other businesses would get insurance dollars.

The essential nature of insurance does not assure the survival of any given company, much less its success. An efficient and effective expression of this nature in human terms is necessary to fulfillment of the purposes of insurance.

5. The Success of Organizations

The success of organizations is determined in large part by their ability to improve and sustain individual performance. This performance must be guided by purposes and goals, as well as the more objective requirements of efficiency and effectiveness, as already indicated. Since members of organizations do not work alone, almost by definition, their relationships with others can significantly modify the performance intended to fulfill organizational purposes. These relationships are formally identified as "structure" in organization.

As Peter F. Drucker has said:

> Good organization structure does not by itself produce good performance—just as a good constitution does not guarantee great presidents or good laws a moral society. But poor organization makes good performance impossible, no matter how good individual managers may be.
> To improve organization structure . . . will therefore always improve performance. It will make it possible for good men, heretofore stifled, to do a good job effectively. It will make better performers out of mediocre men by raising their sights and the demands on them. It will identify the poor performers and make possible their replacement by better men.[1]

Thus, purposes and goals as well as efficiency and effectiveness of an organization are significantly affected by its structure. The importance of structure, then, should be emphasized not only because of its effect on members, but also because a more appropriate structure is one of the factors which give an organization a competitive edge over its rivals.

B. THE STRUCTURES OF ORGANIZATION

1. Organization Relationships and Structures

Key relationships between people in an organization must be struc-

---

[1] From P. F. Drucker, *The Practice of Management*, Harper & Brothers, 1954; pp. 225–26.

turally designed to facilitate the attainment of fundamental purposes. However, the structures outlined in organization analyses, descriptions and charts are progressive simplifications of complex relationships. Such structures are not intended to outline all relationships, and temporary exceptions even to those indicated may be useful in advancing organization purposes, if undertaken with the approval of persons principally concerned.

An organization chart is not an organization, any more than a map is a road. The chart depicts a limited number of formal relationships, and not the many pathways of communication and contact necessary to get work done. The general purpose of organizing as a phase of managing is to direct human resources toward economic results. This direction is planned or designed under very general criteria, using conventional organizational concepts for the sake of convenience.

2. Criteria for Organizational Design

Criteria for the design of organization structures are not as accurate as those used in building a bridge, perhaps for roughly the same reasons that managing is not engineering. A few structural requirements can be listed, however, as suggestions which could be variously interpreted and expanded almost indefinitely. Organizational structures should be designed:

> —so manpower and other resources can together accomplish expected results at each unit and level of organization (i.e. recruiting, supervision and training for production in agencies);
> —so supervisory and managerial planning and control can be centrally directed for decentralized execution;
> —so men and their abilities can be developed to yield increasing satisfaction through individual and group progress.

3. Concepts of Organization Structure

The following outline mentions only the basic meaning of very general terms, and does not discuss the subtleties with which they are sometimes endowed.

a. Organization dimensions include *height* or number of levels in direct reporting relationships, *breadth* or number of units of people grouped to perform activities at each level, and *span* or number of persons at the lower level of each unit.

b. The *shape* of an organization is usually conceived as an overall triangle or pyramid, in which each unit's triangle is linked to the one above it as its "superior" (in two-dimensional terms) is a "subordinate" in the higher unit. The shape may also be considered as circular, with concentric circles of units equally distant from the chief executive at its center.

c. In other types of organization charting, the shape may also be depicted as a square. Key positions are shown across the top and major repeated actions or programs in a left column, with types of responsibility for the program coded at the intersection of columns and rows. (Linear Responsibility Charts)

d. For savings of time and space, particularly in the case of changes, organizations are increasingly outlined in a vertical format capable of data processing machine tabulation. Lists of positions and persons are shown successively under common heads, indicating different levels by the extent of indentation. Vertical lines may be drawn or lightly pre-printed to show the grouping of positions, with short horizontal lines from each position to the appropriate vertical line. (Organization Directories)

e. In small groups, leadership-following situations may be indicated by multiple lines leading to the peak of a triangle, to the apex of a pyramid, or the center of a wheel. Various other relationships may be shown by multi-sided figures with interconnected lines. Engineers particularly like spirals and three-dimensional or other shapes which show power centers in "proper" perspective.

f. No matter what device is used to illustrate interpersonal relationships in organization, it should be understood that reality is only partially represented. No one has yet devised a chart for showing the value systems of individuals which permit some relationships to be more, and others less constructive. Yet these value systems often are the reason that some organizations, particularly in face-to-face groups, are both more effective and efficient than others.

g. The conventional box-and-line chart reflects only one type of reporting relationship. This is one of the most significant dimensions of organization, however, since its appropriate use can strengthen the effect of all other relationships.

4. Types of Large-Scale Structure

The larger scale of organization structure, as distinct from personal relationships, is intended to facilitate the coordination of groups of specialists. These are not necessarily groups specializing in a skill or profession, but include all positions identified with various products, processes, projects, areas, markets, or channels of distribution. The following summary does not describe types of organization for a company as a whole, but types of structure which may be found in any organization. In each case, the simplest definitions are used in order to avoid unnecessary complication of a complex situation.

a. *Line*—the most direct relationship between the peak or center of an organization and its foot or cutting edge. The structure of this relationship is necessarily the strongest in its own field, because it creates basic economic values—as in the case of insurance marketing.

b. *Staff*—any individual or group of men who provide collateral support for the "line". This support may be in the form of assistance, service, information, advice, and planning or other assigned functions. The relationship of staff and line in terms of leadership or dominance with respect to any given program is usually decided by senior levels of management. Where "staff" has a close support or service function, it may be held jointly responsible with the "line" for particular results.

c. *Product*—individual ordinary, industrial or health coverages; group life and health coverages; individual or group fixed or variable annuities; and various property-casualty coverages, as well as equity funds are all considered product lines in an insurance company. The extent to which these lines should be handled by the same sales organization is a structural type of decision. A "product manager" or group sometimes initi·ates and coordinates special activities in relation to each line when several are sold by the same organization.

d. *Process*—organizations sometimes center on a particular process or service, such as training managers and agents, issuing contracts, collecting data, or promoting sales in a marketing department.

e. *Projects*—task forces may be set up for specific purposes in any organization, and usually act as a separate group only until the purpose is accomplished—such as the development and introduction of a new product.

f. *Areas*—as an insurance company grows in size, it usually spreads geographically. The basic geographic unit is normally the individual agency, or a subdivision such as districts. A large company may have found it advantageous to group contiguous areas into divisions, and a still larger one may combine adjoining divisions into regions. Structuring by area serves a number of purposes: providing centers of expansion, communicating ideas to and from the field, reducing the span of management, and decentralizing such services and processes as training and advanced underwriting. The division of powers and functions on a geographic basis is a major structural aspect of organizational decisions.

g. *Markets*—although "markets" sometimes refers to geographic areas as outlined above, in the insurance business this term is often used to indicate cross-sections of the buying public. These may include markets identified with: farmers, women, youth, small or large companies, types of business organization (partnerships, corporations), types of employees (blue or white collar, keymen), or professional associations, and sometimes ethnic or national characteristics. This sense of "markets" should be recognized at the agency level of organization, but has only a few structural implications (i.e. special assistance provided for business markets).

h. *Distribution*—in terms of channels of distribution, insurance may be sold through a general agency or branch office organization, and by agents or brokers. To the extent that general agents appoint, train and supervise agents on their own, the general agency organization may require less centralized service and control. These may be more important in a branch office company, as its managers are nominally more dependent on the company for assistance. However, such differences are more of degree than category, and are reducing in structural implications. A brokerage distribution structure can be smaller, since less supervision and training may be needed, but may require greater emphasis on sales promotion and services. (Distribution of insurance by mail, coupon advertising and machines at airports offers a minimum of structural problems.)

i. *Committees*—small groups of individuals who usually represent one or more process or product viewpoints. Committees may aid communication and coordination, but when used to advise or even direct, may also reduce both innovation and action. Although committees are frequently criticized for wasting time, they are found as temporary or permanent features of most insurance marketing structures.

A single organization may have all of the foregoing structural features. Every insurance marketing organization has a *line* from the chief agency officer through regional and possibly divisional vice presidents, general agents or managers and assistant managers, district managers or supervisors, to individual agents. The chief agency officer also has a *line* to individual clerks in agencies or branch offices, as well as the home office, through such equivalent positions as vice presidents, directors, managers, and assistant managers or supervisors. The home office "line" from the chief marketing officer to the clerk is usually considered *staff* with respect to the field organization.

The field organization is always divided on an *area* basis, and may include *market* specialists such as agents who sell primarily to doctors, farmers or businessmen. The home office organization is usually divided on a *process* basis, such as training or sales promotion; and may include product specialists, such as health insurance sales managers. Many marketing organizations set up temporary *projects,* or ad hoc and permanent *committees* which have members from several units. In addition, most insurance companies *distribute* products and services through brokers as well as their own agents.

5. An Example of Marketing Organization

The following outline reflects typical reporting relationships in an insurance marketing organization, shown in a "directory" format. Many variations of these relationships are possible, notably in agencies organized on a Unit, or on a Staff-Line basis (see following chapter on *Agency Organizing: A Case Example*). Titles and divisional breakdowns would depend partly on the size of the organization, and partly on the functions covered under "Marketing" (i.e. including or excluding Premium Collections, and Industrial and Group, as well as Ordinary and Health Insurance Sales).

DIRECTORY OF AN INSURANCE MARKETING ORGANIZATION*

Chief Marketing Officer
    Field Organization
  Regional Vice Presidents (Major Geographic Divisions)
    Regional Staff (Administration, Development)
    General Manager (Recruiting, Training, Administration)
      New and Experienced Agents
      Assistant Managers (Recruiting, Training)
      New Agents
      Production Assistant (Advanced Underwriting, Campaigns)
      Office Manager (Clerical Services)
    Home Office Organization
  Marketing Committee (Present Coordination)
  Compensation Committee (Personnel and Salary)
  Planning Committee (Future and Corporate Coordination)
Vice-President—Administration
  Manager—Field Relations and Contracts
  Manager—Compensation and Reports
  Manager—Controls and Adjustments
Vice President—Sales Promotion
  Manager—Life, Health and Special Sales
  Manager—Promotional Material
  Manager—Creative Services
Vice President—Development
  Manager—Management Training
  Manager—Sales and Advanced Underwriting Training
  Manager—Marketing Research

* In an Organization Directory, vertical lines reflect reporting relationships, and common indentations show similar levels or organization. This directory emphasizes major functional divisions, but omits supervisory and clerical specialization.

Variations and simplifications or elaborations of the *structural* features outlined above come into being through the *process* of organizing as reviewed in the following section.[2] Limitations of this article prevent analyses of "mega-organization" structures through which an insurance company divides itself into multiple home offices, and of "extra-organizational" relationships which include all "stakeholders" of a given company.

C. THE PROCESSES OF ORGANIZATION

1. Growth as a Basis for the Process of Organizing

Organizations normally start small and grow larger, while evolving from simple to complex structures. Organizations of similar size and purpose may have different structures, however, because of variations which have occurred in the continuous process of organizing.

Growth usually involves the acquisition of additional human, financial and material resources. This accumulation is often accompanied by diversification of products, evolution in methods of production and distribution, and broadening of markets by both type and location, as well as the introduction of *new* products, methods and markets.

In order to secure the advantages of specialization with expansion, growing organizations tend to divide and combine old units while adding new ones. This requires more means of *coordination* as each specialist works at only part of what is necessary to accomplish a given purpose. Simultaneously, more care must be given to *integrating* the roles of people as individuals and as members of both the company and their own "team".

As an organization grows, face-to-face contacts show even more need for coordinative and integrative attention. New styles and methods of managing become necessary, however, as an organization develops greater

---

[2] For life insurance marketing organization structures showing historical developments, see the following:

J. B. Lunger, on "Office Organization in Life Insurance" and "Organization of Agencies", in *Yale Insurance Lectures, Volume I,* Tuttle, Morehouse & Taylor Press 1904, pages 113–143. J. Owen Stalson, *Marketing Life Insurance—Its History in America,* Harvard University Press, Cambridge, 1942; discussion of sales organization of various companies.

Agency Department Organization, Life Insurance Sales Research Bureau (Life Insurance Agency Management Assn.), Hartford, 1944; and *Agency Department Organization Charts—A Compilation of Charts of 46 Companies,* L.I.A.M.A., Hartford, 1955.

Harry J. Volk and Thomas Allsopp, *Life Insurance Company Organization,* American College of Life Underwriters, Philadelphia, 1955. R. Werner Lederer, *Home Office and Field Agency Organization—Life,* Life Office Management Assn., New York, 1966. Coy G. Eklund, C.L.U., *Agency Organizing: A Case Example,* American College of Life Underwriters, Bryn Mawr, 1969. Dan M. McGill, Editor, *Life Insurance Sales Management,* Richard D. Irwin, Homewood, 1957; Chapters 2 and 3, "The Role of the Agency Department," and "Field Organization and Management."

height and breadth, both through more levels and more units at each level. Some styles of managing are better adapted than others to increasing the spans of supervision within each unit, making fewer levels and units a desirable possibility.

2. Processes of Organizing and Managing

Organizational growth gives rise to processes of *adding, dividing* and *combining* units of activity, *specializing* and *coordinating* work to be done, and *integrating* people in terms of individual and team purposes. If an appropriate process of *managing* is also developed for the growing organization, its structure can be simplified—irrespective of size—for greater efficiency and effectiveness. (Although the subject of "managing" is not covered in this chapter, a few comments about its effect on structure are necessary.)

Certain aspects of managing have a substantial bearing on organizational structure. In particular, the structure must be relatively tall and narrow if the head of each unit keeps part of operational work, and fails to give subordinates "complete" jobs to do, with an opportunity to observe their results in the light of goals and purposes created or accepted as their own.

On the other hand, a relatively low-profiled and broad structure can be developed, if its members have motives and incentives for growth, and the head of each unit gives each member objective standards of performance and individual or team-oriented stimuli, depending on the nature of work to be done.

As organizations grow in size, their efficiency and effectiveness increasingly depend on decentralized operation and centralized control. Properly conceived and designed, the mechanism of control may be decentralized while operational standards and long-range plans are given strong central support.

3. Decentralization and Functionalization

During the process of growth or perhaps simply while improving its structure, a company may both decentralize and functionalize its organization. In general terms, "decentralizing" may include: (a) the assignment of activities previously carried out in the home office as a responsibility of regional offices or agencies, or (b) the increase of levels of responsibility of regional offices or agencies for activities which may continue to involve the home office. A reversal of this process, or return of certain types or levels of responsibility to "headquarters," is called "recentralizing."

"Functionalizing" is a process of establishing central guidance and control for field activities, and may occur with or after decentralization. However, an organization may decentralize an operation without functionalizing it, simply by moving it into the field from the home office.

Examples of decentralization and functionalization which may occur in marketing departments suggest that, in practice, these terms are not as distinct as in theory.

a. *Licenses*: An agent must be licensed by the state where he sells insurance. A home office may decentralize the required operations by making agencies responsible for securing or renewing licenses. In this case, the state exercises primary control, so "functionalization" is not involved.

b. *Selection*: An agent must have a signed contract in order to represent a company. A home office may authorize its general agents or managers to approve the contracts of agents meeting minimum standards. If the home office reviews all contracts and changes standards which prove inappropriate, it retains a form of functional control over selection.

c. *Training*: Agents may receive training in business and estate insurance, in part by attending advanced underwriting seminars. The compay may decentralize the scheduling of seminars and increase agent consultations by placing advanced underwriting personnel on regional staffs. The home office retains functional control by approving both seminar leaders and training courses, although the daily activities of such men are given general direction by regional executives.

The term "divisionalization" sometimes used with "decentralization" normally means that responsibility for "profit" is also decentralized. Although this idea is conceptually appealing, it implies a degree of control over costs and investment in growth for which adequate insurance accounting techniques have not been fully developed. To the extent that decentralization of management moves toward independence of planning and control, as well as execution, it also approaches divisionalization of organization.

An adequately divisionalized organization establishes centers for further decentralization, subject to the minimum reserved power of the central structure.

4.   Home Office Processes and Structures[3]

The Life Insurance Agency Management Association once outlined the functions and duties of a chief agency officer under about 150 captions. These can be retained, or delegated and combined, or further subdivided in many different ways, partly depending on the size of company. In a later analysis of the actual distribution of work, some 121 different agency

---

[3] See: *Chart of Functions & Duties of the Chief Agency Officer of a Life Insurance Company* (1955), and *Responsibilities and Functional Activities of the Agency Department* (1963); Life Insurance Agency Management Assn., Hartford, Conn.

department activities were found under 33 subheadings, outlining the details of 12 major functions.

Key marketing responsibilities included planning, organizing and controlling the following functions: (1) market development, (2) agency department organization, (3) building field organization, (4) training field organization, (5) supervising field organization, (6) motivating field organization, (7) advertising and sales promotion, (8) field compensation and costs, (9) improving persistency, (10) policyowner service, (11) product development and introduction, and (12) internal and external relations.

Carrying out the duties entailed in these functions may require a home office agency department of only a few to several thousand men and women, depending largely on company size. Decentralization of some of these functions may involve up to a score or more persons in regional offices. In some companies, parallel field organizations may handle clerical operations, or the sale of major product lines such as group life, and property-casualty insurance.

A study of the degree of centralization of responsibility for organization planning showed that:

a. Compared to other companies, insurance firms were far more likely to reserve organization planning to top management, and assigned such responsibilities to existing rather than separate departments, when relinquished.

b. Insurance executives were less likely than officers in other companies to share or delegate such responsibilities to divisional or departmental management.

Responsibility for Organizational Matters Assigned to:	Type of Company[4]	
	Insurance	Other
Separate Department	0%	10%
Existing Department	21	15
Specific Individual or Group	15	14
Reserved by Top Management	43	27
Shared with Divisional or Departmental Management	17	25
Delegated to Divisional or Departmental Management	4	9
Total Percentage Distribution	100%	100%

J. K. Bailey, *The Responsibility for the Organizational Planning Function*, Journal of Risk and Insurance, March, 1965, pages 91–102. (Replies from 48 insurance. and 591 other companies among the 750 surveyed, from *Fortune's* largest companies.)

----

[4] The "size" of companies in the annual report by *Fortune* (see July and August 1969 issues) is based on assets, whereas organization subjects should be considered in the light of complexity of functions and number of personnel. Banks and insurance company organization practices might be better compared with smaller companies than indicated by their asset size. Thus, the study quoted, although it does not make this point, should not be considered critical, but merely descriptive of insurance and other organizational practices.

Considering all of the other subjects for which chief agency officers are responsible, it would seem unreasonable to include more than major structural and functional alignments of the marketing department among their personal duties. However, this carries a correspondingly greater responsibility for divisional and department managers. Each of them must carry the balance of *other* organizational duties within his own area.

5. Agency-Building Processes and Structures

The incentives of the agency system theoretically lead toward a low-profile, minimum-cost type of field organization. A general agent or manager who can develop a large number of independent and effective agents should thereafter have a low-profile organization structure. To the extent that agents know how to prospect and sell on their own with a minimum of supervision, commission incentives and high production goals should assure low costs per unit of sales.

The opportunity for excellence in agency work lies in the fact that building agent manpower is a slow and continuous process. It requires investment of years of agency men's valuable time, yielding many agent failures. Abilities used to recruit men are not necessarily those needed to train them. Agents who are good salesmen are not always at their best in analytic preparation for advanced underwriting. Unless more new agents are ready to replace those who fail or retire, and continuing agents are adequately supervised, an agency has no place to go except downhill.

A good agency head not only can use assistants, but can become a center of growth by developing them. Some assistants thus duplicate his work on a smaller scale while others may act as staff specialists—perhaps combining training and analysis. Until an agency grows large enough to support a special staff, or unless the company desires to cover their cost as an investment in agency growth, staff services may be provided for a number of agencies by regional headquarters.

Agency and regional offices are becoming increasingly involved in new electronic data processing and communication techniques. These have organizational implications which are not yet fully explored, but point toward higher levels of public service from more sophisticated methods of administration.

In some companies, managers and assistants continue to sell insurance, in combination with their recruiting and supervisory duties. This arrangement requires less initial company investment, but suggests that non-selling activities are likely to remain problems. In such a combination, the agency is apt to have a relatively high profile, as the span of supervision remains narrower than it could be, if agency men used all of their time and skill in developing agents.

Both coordination of field with home office organization, and integration of critical viewpoints of all personnel are essential to marketing success. If the structures and processes of organization-building are guided by common purposes and objectives, agency growth needs to recognize few limitations.

D. THE PRINCIPLES OF ORGANIZATION

1. Organizational and Psychological Principles

Organization principles are guides to be considered in outlining the structures and processes of organization. Principles of this type are normally derived from experience which includes many specific organizations, each of which may differ in important respects. The common elements summarized from experience were applicable to old organizations only in the most general terms, and should thus be applied with due concern to particular situations in new organizations.

"Principles of organization" normally do not include psychological principles applicable to leadership or to personal conduct in face-to-face situations. These may be profitably studied with respect to the behavior of people in organization settings. However, the principles of organization are significant to the extent that they affect behavior and direct it toward not only organizational purposes, but also personal purposes which can be achieved through organization.

In this sense, organizational principles must be interpreted in ways which are consistent with sound psychological principles. The two are not the same, however, any more than ecology is the same as physiology.

Although organization principles require an individual to have authority with respect to others, psychological principles must be followed to make it a constructive relationship from which satisfaction can be mutually attained.

2. Definitions Underlying Principles

Common terms in organization include "authority", "accountability", "responsibility," "delegation" and "function." Linking these in one sentence: Since a president carries ultimate *responsibility* for results no matter how many *functions* are required to achieve them, he *delegates authority* downward and requires *accountability* upward throughout the organization.
a. *Authority* may be defined as the right, power and freedom to take an action which will affect a result. Its limits may be intrinsic to those required by the situation, or extrinsic as defined either by a superior or by common codes. When authority involves other people, its effect is

modified by their degree of acceptance of the leadership of the person exercising the authority.

Conflicts of authority in relation to practical problems should be recognized as a possibility, both between relative equals, and superiors and subordinates. Valid issues can be compromised, or one view suppressed at the expense of result. Thus, organizational means should be developed for the resolution or integration, rather than abolition of conflict.

b. *Accountability* is the obligation to produce results in line with given purposes and objectives. Accountability is frequently expressed in reports which compare goals and production. However, since broader purposes may also be affected, the total results of exercising authority are often as significant as reaching a specific goal, and should also be evaluated.

Accountability is less strictly construed with respect to method than results, unless certain techniques are absolutely prescribed. Thus, if the objective is much more important than the method, freedom in selecting the means used is a proper exercise of authority in attaining given ends.

c. *Responsibility* is a concept which encompasses both authority and accountability. An individual or an organization unit which is responsible for a function, has both sufficient authority for reaching it and accountability for the net results. ("Duty" is a narrow phase of "responsibility.")

Responsibility may be jointly held, if provided in a particular program. Thus, a staff function may cut across several lines of authority (i.e. in personnel matters); or two lines of authority may be responsible for a joint result (i.e. both group and ordinary, or ordinary and industrial departments for agent sales). In this case, goals and results should be spelled out in sufficient scope to satisfy all requirements of authority and accountability.

d. *Delegation* is the passage of part of a senior's authorities to a subordinate. It may be included in the process of establishing a position. However, delegation may be incomplete or temporary in the sense that the authority may be withdrawn or the supervisor may intervene in its execution. Delegation does not even occur if the subordinate's proposal requires approval before action.

Delegation is not the sole source of authority, since the establishment of a new product or process may require the exercise of previously nonexistent authority. Authority may be established without specific delegation, as in the case of structural redesign of positions. However, "delegation" is sometimes used to describe the total process of distributing authority.

e. *Functions* are related activities which are conducted for a common purpose. Their subdivision usually defines the major structure of an organization in which all activities have a unified objective. However, a function may also cut across an organization structure, again to carry out a single purpose.

The "marketing" function is thus carried out by a marketing department, each element of which directly or indirectly supports selling activities. It excludes activities with other purposes—such as actuarial or legal functions. On the other hand, a "personnel" function may conduct activities which cut across all organizational lines, but have common purposes relating to employees. The context in which "function" is used determines the purposes to which it refers.

The definitions of organization terms outlined above are here given fairly specific interpretation. Each may be broadened or narrowed according to the circumstances of their use. The meaning of "authority" of a supervisor over a clerk would differ from that of a manager over an agent, for example, more because of their roles than their relationships.

3. Useful Principles of Organization

Literature on organization provides anywhere from three to twenty-five "principles," as various authors use different criteria for generalizing what they have seen or believe true of organizations.

Some lists of principles, including those quoted by the American Management Association and the National Industrial Conference Board, find a middle ground in ten to twelve—with both duplications and differences. The following discussion assumes knowledge of the conceptions and terms outlined above, particularly with reference to the meaning, structures and processes of organization.

a. The objectives of the enterprise and each of its component elements should be clearly defined in writing. (The preparation and revision of written objectives requires analysis and communication which should encourage simplicity and flexibility within an organization.)

b. Functions should be assigned to organizational units on the basis of homogeneity of objectives for purposes of efficiency and effectiveness in operations. (These purposes are common to all elements of organization; other purposes should be identified with each objective.)

c. Responsibilities of every position should center on a single leading function. (The functions of all positions should be integrated as the function of their unit of the organization.)

d. Clear-cut lines of authority should run from top to bottom, and of accountability from bottom to top of the organization. (These "lines" determine the vertical structure of organization.)

e. The responsibilities of each position should be defined in writing for the interest of all concerned. (Authentication of the position and its powers should be clear to both its incumbent and any others affected, particularly in the case of change.)

f. Accountability should be coupled with equivalent authority. (Anyone subject to account for quantity or quality of results should have the appropriate data; and assistants should not be critics of those they assist.)

g. The number of levels of organization should be kept to a minimum. (This criterion facilitates upward and downward communication, and requires relatively broader spans of organization with generally less supervisory expense.)

h. The number of persons under a single supervisor should be as large as his capacities and as small as their needs, consistently with the nature of the work to be done. (This principle of organization is substantially affected by methods of management.)

i. Authority to act should be located as close to the scene of action as possible. (Delegation and decentralization can go as far as individuals can adequately plan and observe results, subject to requirements of integration and coordination.)

j. Every individual should have a single principal reporting relationship. (Although his work may be guided by others, each man should expect substantial reward or criticism only from his "line" superior.)

k. The responsibility of a superior for the acts of a subordinate is absolute. (This imposes an obligation on a subordinate to act consistently with the interests of his superior.)

If all of the foregoing principles were applied constantly, the process of reorganization would be continuous. Objectives should change with external conditions, and the means for pursuing them should make internal progress. Thus, each higher stage of organization becomes the foundation for further evolution—as long as the world changes and an understanding of organization progresses.[5]

[5] For additional insight into organizational aspects of managing, see:
Samuel P. Hayes, Jr., *Relating Behavior Research to the Problems of Organization,* (Pamphlet extract from "Some Applications of Behavioral Research"), UNESCO; a report on the Foundation for Research in Human Behavior, University of Michigan, founded in 1952. John B. Miner, *The Management of Ineffective Performance,* McGraw-Hill, 1963. L. P. Bradford, J. R. Gibbs, K. D. Benne, Editors, *T-Group Theory and Laboratory Methods,* John Wiley, New York, 1964. Leonard R. Sayles, *Managerial Behavior—Administration in Complex Organizations,* McGraw-Hill, 1964. Bernard M. Bass, *Organizational Psychology,* Allyn and Bacon, Boston, 1965. Philip B. Applewhite, *Organizational Behavior,* Prentice-Hall, Englewood Cliffs, 1965. Charles D. Flory, Editor, *Managing Through Insight,* World, New York, 1968. Paul Hersey and Kenneth Blanchard, *Management of Organizational Behavior,* Prentice-Hall, 1969.

11

Agency Organizing:
A Case Example*

Coy G. Eklund

PRINCIPLES OF ORGANIZING

Introduction

Organizing is the basic and decisive function of management. The same aggregate of people will perform effectively or ineptly, depending upon the character and quality of the way in which they are organized for action and upon the way in which that organization is managed.

One outstanding author on the subject, General Henry S. Aurant (U.S. Army, Retired), has gone beyond this to state: "The rate of progress of the human race is probably more dependent upon the art of organization than on any other art or science."

Organizing effort focuses on evolving a living structure of people called an "organization" so qualified, equipped, arranged and programmed as to provide, in the aggregate, a capacity for attaining efficiently the objectives of the enterprise. Organizing thus deals with tasks and with the people and technology to perform them. The better the "organization," the better the performance. In turn, the quality of the organizing effort depends on the top manager. Management comes first and organization is its off-spring. Organizing is as important to life insurance sales management as it is to any other kind of enterprise. Without exception a successful agency is traceable to the successful organizing efforts of a manager.

It is doubtful that any two agencies are organized exactly alike. Agencies are too much the personal creation of an individual manager for this to be true. It should therefore be evident that the specific forms of agency-organizing described in this chapter cannot be adopted in every detail in every agency. Rather, this account is intended to stimulate the reader to create his own form of organization, as he relates it to his own identifiable needs and available resources. The three general considerations involved in organizing an agency for successful performance are: (1) the agency objective; (2) the agency structure; and (3) the agency program.

The Agency Objective

The objective is the beginning. Organizing an agency is predicated on knowing what you intend to accomplish. Setting objectives or goals is the orderly place to start. This must begin with a vision of the future that stirs the individual manager. Goals and objectives are sure to be permeated by his ideals, standards, and basic philosophy. Succcessful agencies are those that move toward what the manager conceives to be important, inspiring, and worthwhile goals. They are, moreover, goals which are clearly stated (in writing) and thoroughly communicated throughout the organization so as to be thoroughly understood. Yet it is probably true that only a few agency managers[1] have clearly established their ultimate, and even inter-mediate goals in specific terms and in written form.

Basically, the manager's personal objective is to succeed in building and operating his agency. He must make good. As a sales manager, his performance is readily measurable; almost everyone can see the results. Sales management must add; there is little use for any other kind of result. As long as a man holds his job as a manager, he will be expected to provide a directive force that results in ever-increasing production from an ever-improving productive resource—the sales force.

The productive resource of an agency is sales manpower. In considering agency objectives, the primacy of manpower must not be mistaken or overlooked. The recruitment, development and advancement of an ex-panding sales force is the way to success as an agency manager. Increased production is the essential goal but improved manpower is the essential

---

[1] The term "agency manager" is used generically to include all heads of life insur-ance field agency organization, no matter what the various titles or types of operations may be.

means to attainment of that goal. To state the long-term objective of an agency then in terms of development of sales manpower may be more precise and more effective in evoking the appropriate effort than by stating only the obvious objectives of production. Indeed, the foremost objective of agency management must be the expansion and development of manpower. That is what the job requires. This is not a requirement imposed by the company or the agency vice president or the director of agencies, it is just what the job requires, it is what "succeeding" requires.

The major agency objectives can best be stated in terms of increasing numbers of productive and steadfast manpower; such a sales force surely achieves ever-increasing amounts of production year by year.

Agency objectives must be established first. Only then can the manager organize structure and program to get the job done.

Organizing the Agency Structure

> Good organization structure does not by itself produce good performance—just as a good constitution does not guarantee great presidents, or good laws, or a moral society. But a poor organization structure makes good performance impossible no matter how good the individual managers may be. To improve organization structure . . . will therefore always improve performance.[2]

Business organizations have both formal and informal structures. The formal structure (with which we are concerned here) sets forth organizational positions and prescribes definite relationships among the people occupying those positions. As we all know, there are three principal types of formal organization structure: line, staff, and line-staff-functional.[3]

1. LINE ORGANIZATION

In its simplest form, the line insurance agency is purely a "line" organization with the manager of a group of agents constituting the first echelon of line management. (See Figure 1.) He is the manager on the "firing-line." He is responsible for directing and controlling every aspect of the organization and its performance. In him is centered true "unity of command." He is the sole organizational connection between his people and his superior, and so comprises the "channel" to higher authority for his subordinates. Viewed from above, he serves as a link in the "chain of command." Within the limits of policy, the higher organizational level

---

[2] Peter F. Drucker, *The Practice of Management* (New York, N. Y.: Harper and Brothers, 1954), pp. 225–226.

[3] For a review of these major types of organization structure the reader is referred to the American College brochure, "Life Insurance Company Organization" by Harry J. Volk and Thomas Allsopp.

FIGURE 1
LINE ORGANIZATION

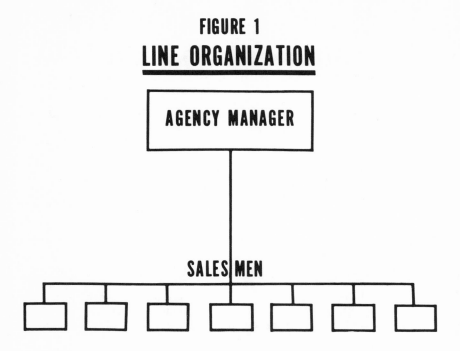

has assigned the job full responsibility and commensurate authority. This is in keeping with the principle of management that authority should be delegated downward to a position in the structure that is as close as possible to the action which it will control. The agency manager who directs and controls an organization of life underwriters holds the basic, first-echelon line management job in the company's sales operation. All other managers placed higher in the company's organization seek to provide those things that support and enhance the performance achieved by this first-echelon.

In a special sense, the agency manager does not manage "workers." Instead, he manages "managers." For agents act in a dual-capacity, as workers *and* as managers. Quite uniquely, agents must plan their own work, organize their own methods, direct their own activity and evaluate their own results. These are clearly management functions. To a significant degree, an agency manager manages more than work and workers; he manages managers too.

2. THREE-ECHELON AGENCY ORGANIZATION

As a general rule, an effective organization will be structured with a minimum number of "layers of management authority." It would at first seem that "layering," as a problem of organizational structure, need not concern

FIGURE 2
3-ECHELON LINE ORGANIZATION

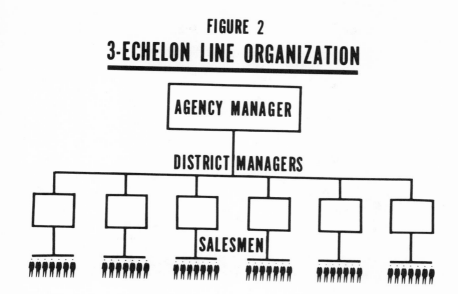

the typical agency manager because of the relatively small organization that he heads.

Nevertheless, an agency organization may be deliberately structured for considerable manpower expansion by adding another echelon of management. (See Figure 2.) Some life insurance companies have employed this plan of organization for years and it seems to be gaining in popularity. As indicated in Figure 2, "District Managers" are each responsible for a group of life underwriters. Through this plan, the ability of a particular agency manager may be utilized to a greater degree. It might be thought of as a grouping of two or more separate agencies under a second echelon of line management. By this arrangement he truly operates as a manager of managers, directing a considerably larger organization and focusing his efforts mainly on bringing about the most effective performance on the part of his immediate managerial subordinates.

3. LINE-STAFF

Although the simple line organizations described above are common, many agency organizations are elaborated somewhat to achieve a "line-staff" arrangement. This is a line organization to which are added "staff people" who "advise, counsel and assist" the top man in some specialized areas of their competence and responsibility. The staff member does not have operating or line authority, nor does the staff constitute, in itself, an echelon of management. However, a staff man may be given almost any kind of an assignment by his "chief" and, in effect, carry it out for him, in his name. It is not unusual in larger agencies to employ staff people to assist the agency manager in such specialized matters as administration, training or recruiting. Where such an arrangement exists, it may be called a "line-staff" organization. (See Figure 3.)

4. SPAN OF CONTROL

Ordinarily, the "span of control" in organizations is thought to be a consideration only in large enterprises. In fact, it is an inescapable factor in agency management as well. Moreover, it is an organizational gremlin which lurks ubiquitously about, whether the head of the organization recognizes it or not.

Span of control concerns arise out of the fact that the head of an organization can direct and control effectively only a limited number of people. While no exact number can be set by formula, the limit is generally sensed by the manager himself as his "span of control" is extended. As he strains to encompass all his immediate associates in a satisfying work relationship, he begins to feel the effects of "spreading himself too thin." When this happens, it is a sign that he may have exceeded the limits of his span of control. As we know, several variables affect the number of people an executive can effectively supervise and coordinate. Of considerable importance is the capacity and experience of the higher executive and of the individuals he supervises.[4] All possess varying degrees of energy, intelligence, education, training, experience, judgment and leadership. If the executive is above average in these respects, he can absorb the extra pressures and deal effectively with a broader "span of control." So, too, when associates possess a high degree of competence, the "span of control" can be extended beyond the usual limit.

Of almost equal importance is the nature of the work of the organization. Managers responsible for people whose work is similar (or identical) in nature can effectively relate to and supervise a number larger than otherwise.

The limit on the "span of control" is not fixed or specified. But it is a limit that effectively asserts itself when it is ignored—and, once exceeded, it can prevent effective or satisfying organizational performance. When the agency manager of a growing group of agents begins exceeding a reasonable "span of control," it may be time to consider staff assistance, or the

---

[4] William H. Newman, Charles E. Summer, and E. Kirby Warren, *The Process of Management*, Second Edition (Englewood Cliffs, N. J.: Prentice-Hall, Inc., 1967), pp. 132–136.

FIGURE 3
LINE-STAFF ORGANIZATION
(3 Echelon)

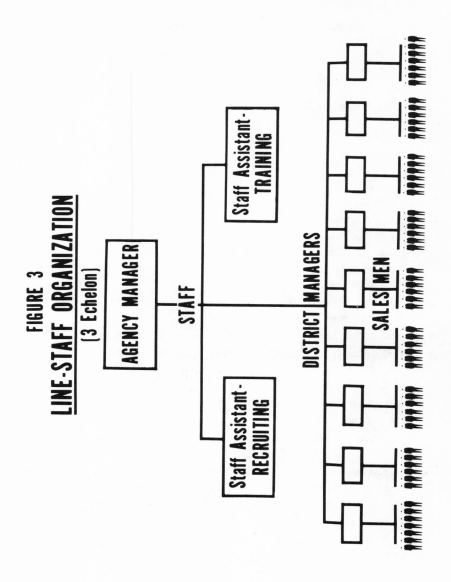

creation of a subordinate level of line management.

At some stage of growth, the successful agency manager must be prepared to counter the span of control limitation and to stave off its stagnating effect on manpower expansion. While the agency manager can effectively supervise only a limited number of life underwriters personally, he can, by appointing a subordinate level of "line managers," greatly augment the manpower potential. The imaginative manager might also consider the counter move of adding "staff" to his organization structure. Such staff people, by enlarging the manager's effectiveness, can significantly extend his span of control.

The Agency Program

Organizing the agency program is a matter of determining in detail the procedures, practices and policies which will prevail in the agency, and establishing the format or pattern of all operations essential to achieve the objectives. The agency program is the determined course of action which will be pursued. It channels, directs, and governs the individual and combined activities of the organization personnel—both agents and management. The agency structure is the skeletal framework; the agency program is the musculation.

In preparation for achieving the objectives set for the agency, the manager must develop a considerable body of policy and procedure which is, for the most part, an outgrowth of his own individuality, his own principles, his own ideals and purposes. These are shaped into clearcut decisions, expressed in writing. They comprise the rules and guidelines essential to systematic, efficient and satisfying organizational performance.

As the manager foresees or experiences major problems and difficulties relating to his several organizational responsibilities, he must create for each a satisfactory solution which can be readily applied in the future. His recorded decisions about such things enter into the agency program. They are the distinguishing feature of "his" agency. When he has formulated a broad range of integrated decisions relating to major responsibilities and has systematically put them in readily available, understandable, communicable written form, he has created an agency program that is his hallmark, his chosen pathway to success.

Organizing the agency program is a never-ending process, because it relates to people and to circumstances which will continually change. The program itself must continuously evolve. But it should evolve, not as submissive accommodation to changing environment, but as an aggressive adjustment for achieving agency objectives within it.

A CASE EXAMPLE

The Agency Objectives

When I have said so far is in general terms of organization and management theory. All this can perhaps be better communicated and specified by outlining the program, organization and management developed in a specific agency operation, taken as a case example.

The objective of agency management is, of course, the production goal. That is the end result we must achieve—a quantity and quality of production satisfying to the enterprise. The production goal is understandably scheduled as ever-increasing. Implicit in such a goal, and essential to it, is ever-improving manpower. The productive resource must be created, maintained, and—importantly—enhanced. The quantity, quality, and, of course, the performance of the organization, must be continuously upgraded. Increased production is the goal, but improved manpower is the means. Therefore, this agency manager's "means mission" is to conceive, create, and forever improve an organization, consisting of manpower skilled, thinking right, supplied with tools, and directed toward achievement of the production goals. (See Figure 4.) Consider, then, how such a program might be organized in this specific agency.

1. MANPOWER SKILLED ("SIFT")

Selection, Indoctrination, Financing, and Training (SIFT) are the key words describing the manager's responsibilities under his broad area of concern with manpower. "SIFT" embraces all matters relating to the problem of discovering, attracting, screening, and hiring, then developing, retaining, advancing and establishing personnel for the purpose of replacing and expanding manpower.

Recruitment is, of course, primary but it is important to think of it in relation to its purpose ("Replacement and Expansion") rather than as mere ongoing activity. Recruitment usually suffers until its critical essentiality for enhancement of the basic productive resource (and consequently, for growth of production) is clearly understood.

The purpose of recruiting is twofold. First, there must be a replacement of manpower that is continuously "going off the books" due to natural causes such as death, disability, and retirement, and, of course, due to "failure," promotion, transfer and other forms of manpower subtraction. Second, there must be recruitment for expansion (numerical growth) beyond the replacement level in order to achieve an ever-increasing production through an ever-improving productive resource.

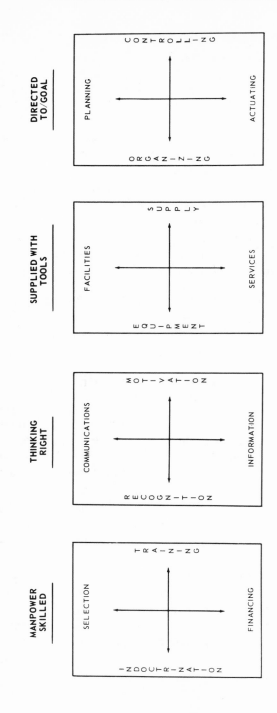

FIGURE 4

INCREASED PRODUCTION IS THE GOAL . . .

IMPROVED MANPOWER IS THE MEANS . . .

MAIN MISSION: To Conceive, Create, and Forever Improve

A SUPERIOR SALES FORCE

consisting of

DIRECTED TO/GOAL

CONTROLLING

PLANNING — ACTUATING

ORGANIZING

SUPPLIED WITH TOOLS

SUPPLY

FACILITIES — SERVICES

EQUIPMENT

THINKING RIGHT

MOTIVATION

COMMUNICATIONS — INFORMATION

RECOGNITION

MANPOWER SKILLED

TRAINING

SELECTION — FINANCING

INDOCTRINATION

Figure 5 indicates how an agency head might think of recruitment as he strives to achieve numerical growth.

Selection, Indoctrination, Financing, and Training embrace far more than a concern for increasing numerical strength. In the SIFT area we house concern for the items of sustenance in the lives of agents. Financing (special compensation arrangements for newer agents) is one of those essential elements.

Indoctrination and Training play an equally important part in giving him confidence and viability. Knowledge and skills are obviously necessary, but steadfast conviction and unshakable belief are vital too. We must remember the selling environment is generally cool if not hostile, and even a successful life underwriter fails to succeed 50 to 80 percent of the time!

The purpose of Indoctrination and Training is to enhance retention and productivity—to achieve manpower development.

In the SIFT area, the manager identifies and consolidates his manpower development responsibilities into an organized unity that keeps them ever in clear focus.

2. THINKING RIGHT ("CRIM")

The second area of responsibility for this agency manager includes everything that relates to the need of people for understanding. This connotes the substance with four words Communication, Recognition, Information, Motivation (CRIM). We mean to embrace all stimuli that produce good morale, all things that elevate the spirit of an organization that have to do with judgments, attitudes, feelings, assumptions and expectations, that elicit a more wholehearted productive performance.

CRIM embraces all the psychological considerations and devices which help the life underwriter shape a positive frame of mind and a desire to perform at his very best. Aristotle wrote "Man by nature wants to know." Thomas Carlyle stated "It's the spiritual always that determines the material." Peter F. Drucker stressed "It is the spirit that motivates, that calls upon a man's reserves of dedication and effort, that decides whether he will give his best, or do just enough to get by." "Surely, the will must accompany the skill."

One of America's large corporations, in an important study of manpower development, learned that basically "all development is self-development." We really teach men nothing—we improve them not at all—until something happens within them that sparks their desire to improve. Only then do men develop, and then they virtually develop themselves. It is this "hot button" that the manager must find. And this is not easy, because it is different for different men.

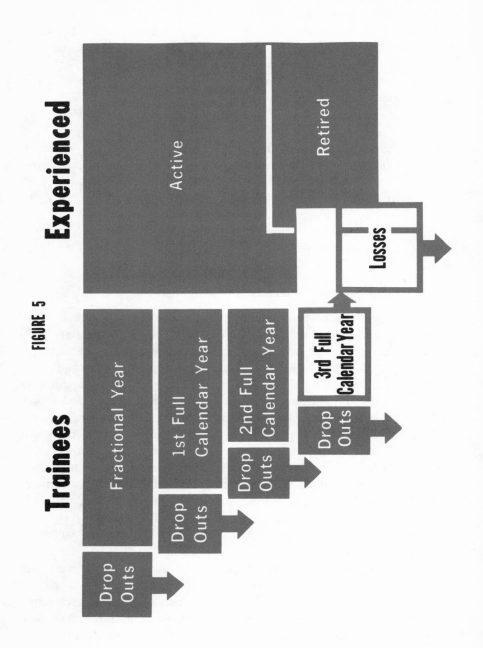

FIGURE 5

The succcessful agency manager creates a broad structure of recognition and motivation effort plus a continuous two-way flow of information and expression that in the aggregate will elevate the spirit of the individual and will effectively power the organization as a whole.

3. SUPPLIED WITH TOOLS ("FESS")

The third area includes concern for Facilities, Equipment, Services, and Supply. These embrace all the physical or material resources—company and agency—that stand behind the life underwriter in the field, that support him, and that furnish him the means to get the job done efficiently and effectively.

It is not difficult to picture an agent's normal requirements for the "means" of performing his work successfully. He needs office space, desk, office supplies, files, secretarial service, mail and telephone service, sales literature, sales materials, programming service, a "lead" system, and medical examiner services, just to name some of the most obvious. The increasing array of computerized services and support facilities surely play an important part in the more successful performance of life underwriters. FESS focuses attention on the need to provide assistance and working accommodations that will enhance productivity and efficiency.

4. DIRECTED TOWARD THE GOAL ("POAC")

Responsibility for the management functions of Planning, Organizing, Actuating, and Controlling are housed in this area.[5] Here the manager looks at the basic elements of his job. Here he expresses his management concern for his management functions. Here he focuses on "all the things he does about all things he is concerned about."

For example, the manager-leader must plan, organize, actuate, and control his SIFT responsibilities; he must plan, organize, actuate, and control his CRIM and FESS responsibilities and finally, but with no less logic, he must plan, organize, actuate, and control his POAC responsibilities for, if you stop to think about it, planning and organizing activities must themselves be *planned* and *organized,* actuated and controlled. And like a play within a play, activating and controlling actions must also be planned, organized, actuated, and controlled!

Figure 6 gives a partial breakdown for each of the four areas of responsibility, but of course it should be considered as only a starting list. The

---

[5] George R. Terry, *Principles of Management,* Fifth Edition (Homewood, Illinois: Richard D. Irwin, Inc., 1968), pp. 129–133.

FIGURE 6

Illustrative Breakdown of Considerations Within Each Area. (Not All-Inclusive)

SIFT

Selection - Indoctrination
Financing - Training

STRENGTH RECORDS
  Rosters
  Directories

APPOINTMENTS
  Terminations
  Promotions

FINANCING

TRAINING, EDUCATION
  Reference Library
  CLU Extension
  Institutes
  Schools, Clinics

ASSOCIATION AFFAIRS

CRIM

Communications - Recognition
Information - Motivation

PUBLICITY
  Publications

SPECIAL EVENTS

SPECIAL RECOGNITION

SPECIAL GROUPS

PERSONAL AFFAIRS
  Life Insurance & Wills
  Health
  Improvement (Knowledge et al)
  Finances

AGENCY MEETINGS
  Conferences

SALES CAMPAIGNS

"FOSTER PARENT" PROJECT

FESS

Facilities - Equipment
Services - Supplies

OFFICE SPACE

SECRETARIAL STAFF

MEDICAL EXAMINERS

LEAD AND SERVICE SYSTEM

MAIL

TELEPHONES

EXPEDITING

PROGRAMMING

SUPPLY AND EQUIPMENT

CASHIER'S SERVICES

GOLD STAMPING

POAC

Planning - Organizing
Actuating - Controlling

GOALS AND PRINCIPLES

PLANS, PRACTICES

PROCEDURES AND POLICIES

UNIT MANAGEMENT-STAFF
  Appointment
  Development
  Performance
  Promotion

RECORD AND REPORT SYSTEM

INFORMATION DISSEMINATION

COORDINATION
  Agency Calendar

BUDGET AND EXPENSE

PERSISTENCY AND CONSERVATION

agency manager can expand each of these by adding items he considers important in his own agency.

THE AGENCY PROGRAM

Each of these four areas of responsibility is vital and of comparable importance in the formulation of the agency objectives. But merely to identify and enumerate these areas of concern is only to provide an outline of the program that must be formulated as the plan of action. How good a job of agency management he does depends critically on how the manager conceives and shapes a full-blown and well-balanced program for all four constituent parts of his agency objectives.

It should be stressed that although these four areas have separate identity with few interstices, there is, nevertheless, a close interdependence among them. It is just as with the four tires on a car. If three of them are properly inflated, and just one is flat, forward progress will be difficult, if not impossible. If the agency is to progress, each element of the program must be fully developed and in balance with the others.

To take a specific example, an agency might be enjoying a fine CRIM program as developed by a resourceful manager who possesses exceptional talent for inspiring and elevating the spirit of his people. But unless this strong element of the operation can be complemented and reinforced by an equally good "lead system" (as part of the FESS Program) that is considered fair and just by all members of the agency, the desirable effect of the first may be largely eroded by the deficiency in the second.

Plans, Practices, Procedures, and Policies

In this specific case example, organizing the agency program means developing a body of plans, practices, procedures, and policies relating to SIFT, CRIM, FESS and POAC. The manager must confront each problem within these four areas with a resolution to formulate decisions which become a coordinated pattern of success. Problems, opportunities, and challenges are transformed into successful work patterns through wise decision-making. The decision-made end-product consists of an array of spelled-out "Plans, Practices, Procedures, and Policies." These constitute the agency program.

Major decisions dealing with these general behavior patterns or guidelines should be in writing. Change within organizations requires adjustments enough without compounding the problem through hazy or inaccurate recollection of what had once been decided. Unless major plans and policies

FIGURE 7

No-Proselyting Policy

#404.4

Under no circumstances will we contract or hire anyone as an Agent who is, or has been in the past 12 months, engaged in the Life Insurance business on a full-time basis with any other legal-reserve Life Insurance company.

We value highly the clean reputation we have acquired of "developing our own people" and we intend always to maintain it no matter how attractive the shortcuts may appear.

Our conscience dictates that we cannot attempt to make gains out of other people's losses! Moreover, "enlightened self-interest" makes clear that our own people can maintain greater pride in their organization and higher confidence in their leaders through our adherence to this policy which then redounds to our selfish advantage in the form of greater loyalty within our Agency.

We believe that organizations which are hard to join are hard to leave.

Similarly, all promotions to managerial positions will always be made from the ranks of our own Agents.

are put in written form, there is little chance that an organized feeling about the agency program will ever be experienced. (See Figure 7 for an example of a written statement of an agency policy.)

As the manager formulates the mosaic of such decisions for all the major tasks that challenge him within each of the four "areas of responsibility," he approaches the point of having a well formulated agency program.

While basic decisions will endure for a long time, it should not be assumed that it is possible to evolve permanent programs in every detail. People change; circumstances change. Both create new situations, and generally "the situation is the boss." An ever-present danger in formulating an agency program is the set feeling that may develop once the manager has things "well organized." No agency program that remains fixed and unchanging in detail will likely continue to produce long-term satasfactory results. The manager must be ready to adjust, revise, refine. He constantly seeks "the better way."

An "Agency Program" Manual

As the number of decisions or written plans, practices, procedures, and policies expanded, it was found that an organized filing system could be helpful for quick reference. The manager established a simple loose-leaf (three-ring binder) serially numbered filing system, based on the four major subdivisions, (1) SIFT, (2) CRIM, (3) FESS, and (4) POAC.

To illustrate, SIFT was assigned the 100 series; for example, the "Agency Recruiting Plan" was numbered #101, the "Training and Education Program" #102, the "Agent Financing Procedure" #103, etc. CRIM subjects were assigned the 200 series; for example #201 identified "The Agency Leaders Club Plan," and #202 the "Publicity Program." Similarly, the 300 and 400 series were used for FESS and POAC, respectively.

As additions were made to the original treatment of a major subject, they were given decimal identification. For example, where an addition was made to the established Agency Financing Procedure it was designated #103.1. A second addition would be designated #103.2, thus keeping the system flexible and easily expandable.

This loose-leaf binder of "Plans, Practices, Procedures, and Policies," was maintained scrupulously up to date and made available to each member of the agency. Obviously, for guidelines or policies to be effective, the people affected must know and understand them.[6]

---

[6] Figure 8 suggests subjects for development as components in the Agency Program; the many other subjects requiring such treatment will occur to the reader as he reflects on his own operation and challenges.

FIGURE 8

SIFT
Selection, Indoctrination, Financing, Training

101   - Man Plan (Agency Recruiting Plan)

101.1 - Sidlexam Procedure (State Insurance Department License Examination)

101.8 - Non-Medical Privilege Procedure

103   - Agent Financing Administration

103.1 - Fifth Week Validation Report

103.2 - Procedure for "Release of Financing Checks"

104   - Training and Education Program

104.1 - Basic Induction Plan

104.2 - Initial Training Period

104.3 - Agency Library

106   - NALU Membership Policy

CRIM
Communications, Recognition, Information, Motivation

201 - The Agency Leaders Club

202 - Field Suggestion Program

203 - Krystina Program (Foster Parent Project)

204 - Special Recognition Program

205 - Joint Promotional Fund

207 - Junior Associate Round Table

208 - Agency Key Men

209 - Publicity Program

210 - Man of the Year and Man of the Month

211 - Agency Meetings and Conferences

212 - Publications (Agency)

FESS
Facilities, Equipment, Services, Supplies

301   - Cashier's Services

302   - Office Staff (Secretarial Services)

302.1 - Special Secretarial Services

303   - Office Space

303.1 - Private and Semi-Private Offices

303.2 - Space Allocations, Revisions

303.4 - Name on Corridor Doors

304   - Furniture and Equipment Control

306   - Lead and Service System

307   - Stamp Fund

POAC
Planning, Organizing, Actuating, Controlling

401   - Management Staff Performance

402   - Unit Administration Policy

404   - Agency Goal and Principles

404.1 - Minimum Standard of Success

404.2 - Full-Time Representation Policy

404.3 - Professional Courtesy Policy

404.4 - No-Proselyting Policy

405   - Objectives

405.1 - Expense Budget (Current Year)

409   - Unit Manager Appointment Policy

The Organization Structure

The organization chart depicting the manner in which the agency under discussion was structured at one stage of its growth is presented in Figure 9. It can be described as a line-staff organization.

The line authority in this agency extended from the agency manager directly to the district manager, each of whom assumed full responsibility for several agents assigned. The district managers comprised management on the "firing line." They constituted the first echelon of line management. Since their authority was truly "line" in the full meaning of the term, they should not be confused with those management assistants usually designated as "supervisors," to whom can be delegated only special or limited authority. (Supervisors are normally "special staff" people. Special staff will ordinarily perform certain delegated functions in an operating sense; this contrasts sharply with "general staff" which normally would not have any operating authority.)

The diagrams (Figure 9) may be somewhat misleading if they are taken to mean that the general staff and special staff each constitute a separate echelon of management. This, of course, is not true. Staff by itself never constitutes a level of management; staff ties to the line management echelon it serves. For this reason, general and special staff combined are referred to as "agency headquarters staff" and support the agency manager, who constitutes the second echelon of line management. The advantages of staff in a large agency are quite obvious. However, a staff costs money and as with many attractive ideas, budget considerations may dictate some improvisation.

General staff. The agency being described had ten operating or "district" managers. The agency manager designated four of them to perform in dual capacity as his general staff. Responsibility for SIFT, CRIM, FESS and POAC was assumed by each respectively. Their staff job was to think and to recommend, to focus on all of the considerations that fell within their respective areas and to formulate proposals for an improved program. They consulted with the agency manager individually and as a group about their ideas for improving each element of the agency operation. They occasionally presented their completed thinking to him in the form of written recommendations. Thus he had capable thinking partners with whom he could continuously interact in regard to each area of his overall responsibility. As a group, the four served as General Staff Chiefs for the agency.

It could be alleged that these four people constituted only a pseudo-staff, for each of them had the all-encompassing line responsibility for an

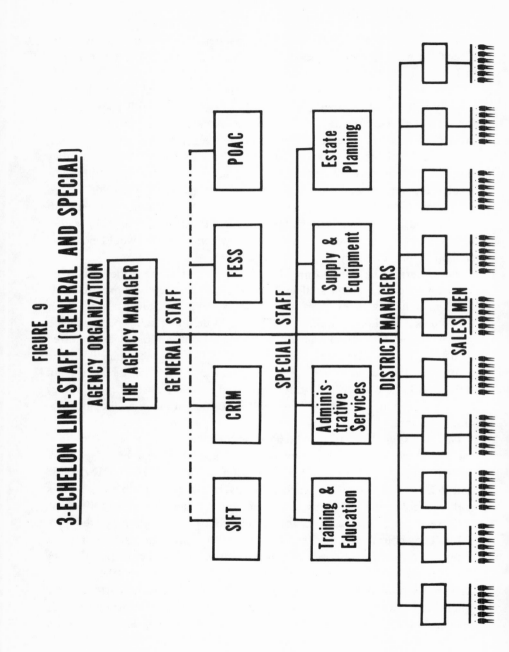

FIGURE 9

3-ECHELON LINE-STAFF (GENERAL AND SPECIAL)

assigned group of salesmen and could devote relatively little time to the staff role. Yet, the fact is that each found time to think and to make suggestions in a manner that proved helpful, both to the agency and to their personal development. The creation and use of a staff involves the purposeful employment of diversified talents in a business enterprise without dissipating the single authority (unity of command) and ultimate accountability reposing inescapably in the "head man." Through a staff operation, it becomes possible to muster better ideas and more of them. It is almost a literal multiplying of one's self.

But because it involves more people in the formulation of the decision, the decision-making process may be slowed. This may be considered a disadvantage, but it is not only that. On the plus side, the more thoroughly considered decision generally meets with better acceptance and more whole-hearted implementation. And the success of an organization generally depends more on the effective application of the decision than on the swift formulation of it.

All general staff work is advisory in nature. It always takes the form of proposals or recommendations. The ideas and schemes so generated are binding on no one until approved and put into line operation by the "head man." He is, of course, free to approve, modify or reject the recommendation. Although the power to recommend is a significant force in an organization, the general staff can never serve to constrict or direct the line chief, nor to relieve him of ultimate responsibility. No matter who proposed the idea, the decision to use it is solely his, and while good leadership may require that he take none of the credit, he must always be ready to take all of the blame.

Special Staff. A special staff differs from a general staff in that definite functional responsibilities and authorities may be delegated to it. Generally these functions are aimed at supporting the subordinate line elements of the organization.

In our Case Example, the special staff performed specific functions of genuine value to subordinate line managers in the specialized areas of (a) Training and Education, (b) Administrative Services, (c) Supply and Equipment, and (d) Advanced Underwriting. While it can be argued that responsibility for each of these functions inherently rests with the "firing-line" manager, it was felt that these services could be better performed if centralized at the agency level, on a standard basis, in support of those managers. This was in keeping with the principle that higher levels of management should general perform only those functions the lower line manager cannot perform (as well) for himself.

Because of the specialized nature of their assignments, they were called "special staff." These full-time salaried people advised and counseled the agency manager with respect to their specific areas of interest.

The detailed responsibilities of the four special staff members were as follows:

1. DIRECTOR OF TRAINING AND EDUCATION

The Director of Training and Education planned, structured and conducted the standardized elements of the Agency Training Program (on a class instruction basis) with emphasis on two extremes—elementary "induction training" and the more complicated "advanced training." This program was mounted only after the "firing-line" district managers had participated in formulating it and had been fully coordinated with regard to it. The key word for all staff people is "coordination;" in addition to "advising" a course of action, they should smooth the way by obtaining the advance concurrence of all interested or affected management people during the planning and organizing phase.

2. DIRECTOR OF ADMINISTRATIVE SERVICES

The Director of Administrative Services maintained day-by-day record of all necessary production information as well as facts relating to the agent-financing operation. These data were made available to line managers periodically and as special situations required. Centralization (with standardization) led to increased efficiency, accuracy, and service. Although this function was obviously a responsibility rightfully vested in the several operating (district) managers, there appeared to be great advantages in using a special staff man at the agency level for this purpose, in support of, and as a service to, those operating managers. This procedure was in keeping with the principle that special staff should seek to serve the next lower level of line management, thereby serving best the line manager who is their "boss."

3. SUPERVISOR OF THE SUPPLY AND EQUIPMENT OFFICE

The Supervisor of the Supply and Equipment Office had full charge of the agency stock room, handled the stamp fund, and operated the "wallet and gold-stamping service." Maintaining supplies of sales literature and promotional materials above the critical level is an important agency responsibility not generally discharged to the complete satisfaction of agent needs. Centralizing this operation and delegating full responsibility to a specific person authorized to act in all necessary respects (selecting, requisitioning, stocking, distributing, and controlling) provided a reasonably satisfactory supply facility for all agency personnel.

This Supervisor had agency-wide responsibility for inventory control for all furniture and equipment, shifting and purchasing such items in accordance with the established "basis of distribution" policy.

Certain miscellaneous functions were also included in his duties, such as the preparation and maintenance of special visual materials: charts, graphs, posters, scoreboards, directories and photo-display boards, the various items of equipment essential to the agency CRIM program.

4. MANAGER OF ADVANCED UNDERWRITING SERVICE

The Manager of the Advanced Underwriting Service had responsibility for providing both full-blown "estate planning" assistance and tailored consultation service for those agents who had moved into the field of advanced underwriting. This assignment required professional qualifications of a higher order.

To develop interest in and competence for advanced underwriting among agents, the Manager of the Advanced Underwriting Service was often called upon as a resource person for certain portions of the training and education program. In addition, this key person had the special responsibility of maintaining the agency relationships with many attorneys, accountants, and trust officers. Normal routine also included occasional joint field work with agents on "programming," "business" or "estate planning" cases.

While all these functions inhere organizationally in the first echelon line manager, it was possible to provide them on a more highly specialized and component basis, at the agency level, as a valuable assist to him.

SUMMARY

Organizing an agency is a dynamic, ever-continuing and ever-challenging process. Essentially a creative function, it is motivated by a ceaseless drive toward finding "the better way." Those managers possessing a strong desire for orderliness and system are likely to be able organizers, particularly if they have the imagination to spark the creative process.

Organizing an agency starts with designation of objectives, and establishment of the organizational structure. But it is the Agency Program that truly distinguishes and identifies an agency as the unique creation of a particular manager. Setting the objectives and fixing the structure may be easily accomplished; creating the program (devising satisfying and effective plans, practices, procedures, and policies) will always constitute the greater challenge—and the more fulfilling accomplishment.

Section V

MARKET PLANNING
FOR LIFE INSURANCE SALES

12

Product Planning

Fredrick E. Rathgeber

The sound planning of the product line to be sold and continuous attention to the updating of these products are essential to the success of any life insurance company. The purpose of this chapter is to describe the principal management functions that must be performed in achieving successful product planning.

BASIC CONSIDERATIONS IN PLANNING THE PORTFOLIO

Before a portfolio of products can be designed, some rather fundamental questions must be answered. Management must determine how broadly it conceives the business in which it is engaged (life insurance in the narrow sense or the providing of financial services in a broad sense), the type of field organization to be employed, and the markets to be served.

Branch of Business to be Included

First, management must decide what classes of business it is going to write. Is the company going to write only ordinary business, only debit, or both debit and ordinary? This decision is an important one for product planning. Products sold on a debit basis are usually limited as to maximum face amount, maximum premium, variety of plans, and mode of premium payment. Policies written on an ordinary basis, on the other hand, may offer a much greater variety as to plan, amount and special features. Of course, it is perfectly feasible for a company to offer both debit and ordinary lines. This may be done through a separate series of policies— one series for debit business and one or more series for the ordinary lines.

Another question that must be answered is whether management desires to write group insurance as well as individual insurance contracts. Product planning in the group area normally involves many considerations quite different from those of individual insurance. These differences will be described in Chapter 15, "Market Planning for Group Sales" and little attention will be given to product planning in group insurance in this chapter except for the most general of principles.

Is the company going to sell individual health insurance? It is quite possible for a life insurance company to sell both individual life insurance and health insurance (hospital and surgical expense, major medical and income protection). In fact, most companies in the United States today do sell both lines of insurance. Agents can be trained to sell and service both lines of insurance, and each line tends to supplement the other by furnishing sales leads and providing a complete family security program. The main disadvantages are the complexity of the portfolio and the attendant problems of training and administration.

If the company is a stock company, its management must decide if it is going to offer participating contracts. Here again an affirmative answer will necessitate management's confrontation with the problems of portfolio complexity, training and administration. Many stock companies, however, feel that it is quite important to offer participating as well as non-participating insurance contracts.

Finally, the company must determine to what extent it will broaden its concept of its business. It will need to answer the question of whether the company will attempt to accommodate the public's increased predilection for equity investments or will continue to offer only the conventional contracts. In answering this question management will logically discuss the appropriateness of marketing mutual funds, variable annuities and newly designed products whose reserves are tied to equity type investments.

Type of Field Organization

A basic question to be answered by the management of a new life insurance company is: Will the company operate with branch managers, general agents, or both? This question generally is not of great significance to the planning of the product line. However, the type of agency management system used does affect the incidence of costs and the latter are reflected in the year-by-year price of the company's products. A company using a branch manager system is normally faced with higher initial expenses, whereas under a general agency system some of the expense money going to general agents can be deferred. Therefore, a company using a branch manager system might prefer to emphasize long-term life insurance contracts so that the company can recapture this initial high acquisition expense over the longer period of time.

Is the company going to accept and/or actively seek brokerage business? This is a more important question than the previous one because an affirmative answer has a direct influence on product planning. A company expecting to do an active brokerage business must have a wide variety of products to offer and the pricing of its contracts must be competitive, especially for those contracts whose average face values are high. Usually, where brokerage business is sought, it is not too important that there be facilities available for offering policies that typically have low average face values.

Thus, the type of field organization employed as well as the source of business will be significant factors for the company to consider in the planning of its product portfolio.

Markets to be Covered

Perhaps one of the most important areas of decision making for company management, as it affects product planning, is the determination of the markets to be served. A company must determine the geographical areas it desires to serve, the age groups, income levels, and any special groups it desires to reach.

First, management must determine in what countries and states does it desire the company to operate. Product planning for an organization that intends to do business in many countries is a subject beyond the scope of this chapter. The complexities caused by differences in currencies, languages, customs, mortality rates and legal requirements are manifold. Even for a company selling business in Canada there are many complications. Most United States companies operating in Canada have found it necessary to develop separate product portfolios in order to recognize the differences in the principal factors affecting the cost of insurance, particularly the levels of expense and investment income that can be expected in our neighbor country.

Even the states in which a company operates can have a direct bearing on the product line since there are wide variations in state laws and regulations concerning policy forms. Some states will permit the inclusion of policy benefits that others may not. All of these nuances must be given consideration in product planning.

What will be the income levels of the families among whom the company will attempt to develop its principal market? Products for the lower and lower-middle income markets should be simple in design, with emphasis on the permanent forms. As the market progresses up the income scale the emphasis generally switches to term plans and term riders on basic permanent policies. Long-term endowments and income endowments are also quite popular in the middle-income market. In the upper-income market the two biggest sellers are level term and whole life contracts. These contracts do not need to be complicated, but their pricing must stand up well in competition. Some companies establish "band" breaks at fairly high levels, such as $50,000, and use preferred risk underwriting in order to achieve every possible advantage in pricing. Others use a policy fee that has the effect of reducing the premium per unit as the amount of insurance increases. For the large amount whole life contract there is also a demand for high early cash values. Part of this demand has been created in order to meet the requirements of "minimum deposit," "bank loans," or "split dollar" agreements. This demand has diminished, however, because of recent unfavorable tax rulings. Some corporate purchasers like the high early cash values in order to keep ledger costs as low as possible.

The management of a company must decide whether it should aim at any special age level. Much of what has been said in the preceding paragraph also would apply here to the extent that incomes normally are correlated positively with age level. It might be useful, however, to add some comments concerning the various age markets. Insurance on the very young can take the form of basic burial coverage, which can be supplied through standard contracts, or it can be in the form of policies especially designed for young people. One popular type has been the so called "estate builder" or "jumping juvenile" policy that, for example, may be a small amount policy up until age 21 when the amount quintuples but the premium remains level throughout. Another popular feature of juvenile insurance is the option to purchase additional insurance. This method of "insuring the insurability" of a young person is quite inexpensive and is quite logical from a selling standpoint.

For middle aged persons with adequate insurance protection, there is a need for retirement annuities that will guarantee supplementary retirement income. Thus, emphasis on product planning for this group tends to be in annuities rather than life insurance contracts.

At the upper end of the age scale, the question of product planning becomes quite different. Although many senior citizens are cutting back on their privately purchased health insurance programs because of "Medicare" there are still some who have a real need to purchase additional life insurance. For these people a company needs to provide a few whole life and limited payment life contracts and it is almost essential to have some substandard health classifications. There is also a need for single premium annuities at the advanced ages to provide the maximum possible life income from accumulated capital.

Does the company plan to concentrate on any special markets? Some types of special markets have been mentioned in the preceding paragraphs. There are other types of special markets, however, that might be considered.

a. *The market composed of persons eligible for Individual Policy Tax-Qualified Retirement Plans.* Federal laws currently provide income tax relief under special conditions for funds set aside to provide supplementary retirement income. There are many funding arrangements that can be used to take advantage of these provisions. Individual retirement annuity and income endowment contracts provide an efficient way of doing it when the number of people to be covered is relatively small. There are three broad categories that can qualify for this current tax relief. Employees of public schools and many non-profit organizations can elect to have their salaries reduced, within limits, and the amount of the reduction used to purchase an individual policy. No income tax is payable on the amount used to purchase this annuity until the annuity payments or the cash value are received. Self-employed persons under the so-called Keogh legislation may also buy annuities or income endowments and receive a current tax deduction. Purchases must be made in accordance with a plan that, among other things, provides for coverage of all the firm's employees with three years or more of service. Small corporations may similarly establish a pension or profit sharing plan. Although much greater flexibility is permitted in these plans, the work involved in complying with Federal tax requirements is correspondingly greater. To service this field, insurance and annuity contracts that meet Federal requirements are needed, along with careful instruction of the agency force as to the conditions that must be met. Because of the complexity of this business, provision must also be made for additional legal and administrative staff in the home office.

b. *Small Business Organizations.* Small business organizations will usually need life and health insurance coverage before they are prepared to undertake any type of retirement plan. For their insurance needs it is possible to design what might be called "small group" plans with various combinations of life and health benefits. These plans can be marketed successfully for "groups" as small as two. Actually, this form of insurance is much more akin to individual insurance than it is to group insofar as its selling, underwriting and servicing are concerned. These products may be fitted into a debit system of operation.

c. *Larger Business Organizations.* If a company plans to sell to business organizations that are larger than those mentioned above, it
must carefully appraise its marketing and operational strength to
establish what types of services it is capable of rendering in the
face of intense and continuing competition. Group insurance and
group annuity products require substantial specialized staffs in
order to meet the competition provided by continuous development in coverages and other techniques being made by both competitors in the insurance field and those companies advocating
self-insured arrangements. Individual policy qualified pension
plans for corporations using ordinary life insurance contracts
rather than endowment policies may be developed in conjunction
with supplementary funds that require actuarial services similar
to those needed for a group annuity deposit administration contract or a separate trust fund. All of the above arrangements involve heavy expense both in the development of products and in
the training of the field organization. Another question that must
be answered in selling to larger business organizations is that of
guaranteed issue. This is more of an underwriting question than
one of product design but it has implications in the latter area
because guaranteed issue on any sort of liberal basis is bound to
have an effect on prices and commissions. There are many possibilities for furnishing special services to help develop sales to
business organizations, large or small. An example of such a service is the development of specimen agreements that may be
needed for deferred compensation and keyman insurance plans.
In all of these cases, the problem is to compare the cost of preparing for and handling the additional types of business, including the training of the field personnel that is involved, to the margins available from the additional premium income that results
from being able to write the additional types of business.

d. *Military.* Although the introduction of Servicemen's Group Life
Insurance (SGLI) has reduced somewhat the market for sales to
military personnel, there is still a need for individual life insurance, especially among career military personnel. The problems
to be faced here are primarily of an underwriting nature. From
a product standpoint it is necessary to have both a complete range
of policies suitable to the income level involved and protective
devices for the company in the form of war and aviation clauses.

e. *Female.* In recent years, with more women working, the female
market has become an important segment for life insurance sales.
Of special importance in the female market are products stressing retirement income and income protection. A company hop-
ing to write a large proportion of its business on female lives
must consider the desirability of having separate premium rates
for males and females. Since female mortality is better than that
of males, it is possible to design products with lower premium

rates for females. Many companies use the same products but simply rate down the age of females for premium purposes—three years being the most typical reduction. Of course, just the opposite effect is seen in annuities and it is quite appropriate, therefore, to charge higher rates for annuities on the lives of females.

RESPONSIBILITY FOR PRODUCT PLANNING

Since product planning is so important, the responsibility and authority for this function should be clearly delineated. Although there are many possible approaches for achieving this, it should be understood that sufficient actuarial and legal assistance must be provided. One approach is to give the actuarial department the responsibility, with support provided from both the agency department and legal department. Another approach is to establish a new products department. Finally, the responsibility could be placed in a task force or high level committee with representatives from all the interested departments. If a committee is chosen, however, responsibility for decision making and results should be assigned to one person so that someone is directly accountable for results. A small or newly formed company may need to rely upon a consulting actuary to be its product developer.

It should be clear from the above discussion, however, that a company doing its own product planning must consider the requirements of several departments. Its success in finding an organizational mechanism for smoothly assessing many different requirements and translating this assessment into up-to-date product lines will, to a great extent, be related to the company's overall prosperity. In many cases, however, product planning has failed because no one has been given direct responsibility for it. Thus, regardless of the interdepartmental nature of product planning, to be successful someone in management must be designated as responsible for this important function.

SOURCES OF PRODUCT IDEAS

Although the responsibility for product development should be assigned to a single department head or committee, the originating sources of new product ideas should not be limited in any respect. It should be made clear to every member of the company, in the field and home office alike, that new product suggestions are welcome and procedures should be established for promptly handling these suggestions as they are submitted. Ultimately, acceptable suggestions will reach the product development stage and it may be desirable, therefore, that the organizational unit, established for product development, also be charged with the responsibility for assessing new product ideas. If the company is a large one, however, it may be desirable to send the suggested product ideas through a screening process before reaching the development stage. A logical place to perform the screening process is in the agency department.

A source of product ideas that must not be neglected is the steady stream of new product announcements by other companies. Following the lead of other companies has certain advantages. First, it saves development costs and provides a wide variety of products. Also, it furnishes a pretesting mechanism. Finally, it can be good for field morale in that they feel that their company is in step with the industry. On the other hand, there are distinct disadvantages to a system that relies too heavily on copying what other companies have done. Many of the products being copied may not be well suited to your own requirements and your portfolio may soon be cluttered with such items. Perhaps the biggest danger is that the lack of initiative on the part of a company soon becomes apparent to its field force and they may lose some confidence in management.

The general public occasionally will submit ideas for new products. Although most of these will generally turn out to be not as new as the contributor believes, they must all be handled politely and expeditiously. If a company receives a suggestion that it believes has merit for further exploration, it is well advised to seek legal counsel as it proceeds since most people submitting suggestions of products are motivated to do so for reasons other than altruism. Therefore, the interests of the company, as well as the interests of the contributors of the idea should be clearly defined from the outset.

Product ideas are frequently an outgrowth of legislative and regulatory developments. New laws or changes in existing ones often create new product needs. For example:

    a. The Keogh legislation of 1963, with its tax deferred provisions for the self-employed, generated a need for insurance and annuity products that would qualify under the act.

    b. The addition of Medicare to Social Security virtually forced portfolio changes in the health portfolios of insurance companies. Although many products being sold had to be withdrawn or drastically modified, an opportunity was created to design new products that could be sold to supplement the governmental plans.

    c. Changes in the regulations of New York State on such matters as pricing by size opened up many doors for product innovation.

    d. On a more general basis, any time there is a revision in the standard nonforfeiture laws, such as that which required the use of the 1958 CSO table for regular ordinary issues after January 1, 1966, an opportunity arises for making many product revisions. The mere fact that the entire portfolio has to be reworked allows the introduction of many minor improvements that might not be practical otherwise because of the heavy expense involved.

In summary, there are many ways in which ideas for new products may arise. A company is well advised to be alert to all these sources and to establish means for their rapid appraisal. This is particularly true in these days when rapid advances in computer technology have made operations feasible that were not previously practical.

NEW PRODUCT CONSIDERATIONS

The preceding discussion has described some of the general principles of product planning. This section will discuss some of the specific considerations, questions and problems that must be faced up to by a company in the development of new products.

A primary consideration in the assessment of any new product is its saleability. Questions that should be asked concerning a proposed product are: Will it be attractive to the buying public? Is it priced competitively? Will it be acceptable to the field force and will the latter, with proper training and instruction, be able to market the product successfully? Does it meet a real demand in the marketplace?

The next question concerns the actuarial soundness of the proposed product and its pricing. This is of equal importance to the question of saleability since no company should knowingly embark on the sale of a product that cannot be self-supporting. Loss leaders have no rightful place in the portfolio of life insurance companies that expect to experience long-term prosperity.

Another question is whether the new policy will be approved in the states in which it is going to be filed. It is most desirable in designing new products to keep in mind the approval standards of all the states involved. The process of filing new forms is a lengthy one at best. Delays caused by refiling in order to correct technical deficiencies that might have been foreseen can be most frustrating, especially when the new product is eagerly awaited and a time schedule for the introduction has been established.

The administrative problems created by a new product should be carefully weighed before the product design is finally determined. In many cases, simple changes in the product can transform it from an administrative nightmare to an additional product that can be added to the portfolio without difficulty.

A final question that should always be asked when considering changes in the product line is that of timing. There is no doubt that the agency organization requires an occasional infusion of new products to sell as a stimulation and as evidence that the company is alert to the changing needs of the marketplace. Likewise, there is no doubt that a portfolio that changes and expands too rapidly will end up by confusing the agency forces and much of the benefit of innovation will be lost. The company must, therefore, exercise a fine balance between these two extremes.

MECHANICS OF PRODUCT PLANNING

Some of the steps involved in product planning have already been covered. It might be useful, however, to trace through a complete cycle in the development of a new product.

The first steps in the planning of new products are the submission or development of new product suggestions, the screening and preliminary evaluation of these suggestions, and the further development of promising suggestions. It has already been mentioned that the responsibility for new products can be assigned in many different ways. Regardless of the assignment of responsibility, it is essential that a number of departments have an opportunity to comment on any proposal. These should include at least the agency, actuarial, legal, administrative and sales promotion departments. Let us assume that all of the departments agree on what might be called the rough sketch of the product and that the necessary executive approval to move ahead on the product has been obtained.

The next step is the policy drafting and filing. Because of the time required to secure the necessary state approval it is most advisable to file the proposed policy form just as quickly as possible. This filing requires a calculation of rates and values for the age shown in the filed form.

Following the drafting and filing of the policy, preparation of rate book material can begin. This will entail:

a. Calculation of rates and values for all ages and premium frequencies.
b. Preparation of illustrative dividends.
c. Writing of descriptive text for the rate book. This should include a technical description of the new policy, its special features, and instructions to the field concerning its underwriting and issue requirements.

While the rate book material is being prepared, others can be involved in preparation of sales promotional material, development of training material, preparation of administrative procedures, and the drafting of an announcement letter. These steps can be carried out simultaneously and should be in order to reduce the total development time.

The final step is the introduction of the new product to the field and the public.

All through the process there is a great need for close communication among the many departments involved. The actuaries and lawyers should have an opportunity to review the sales promotional and training material and, naturally, the agency and sales promotional personnel must have ready access to the rate book material as it is prepared by the actuaries.

A question that frequently arises is that of the advisability of field testing of a new product before it is generally introduced. The arguments for doing so are:

a. *The saving in time and dollars.* There is no doubt that a test group can be prepared and trained to market a new product much faster and at much less expense than the whole field organization can be prepared and trained. This procedure can get the product on the testing line quickly and the dollars saved can be significant if the product turns out to be a failure.

b. *The ability to make modifications and adjustments in the test product.* There is no doubt that a field tested product can be easily modified and adjusted if such steps appear to be advisable before introduction of the new product to the whole field organization.

On the other hand, there are distinct disadvantages to field testing:

a. *The delay in introduction to the entire field force.* Most agents have a natural desire to have the opportunity to sell anything new at the earliest possible moment. Seeing fellow agents selling a product that is barred to them is bound to lead to complaints. If the product being tested is particularly attractive, there is also the danger that competitors will duplicate it before the innovating company has a chance to extend its marketing effort to a broader market.

b. *The difficulty in appraising early results.* If the sales in the test group are good there is no particular problem except to explain why the test was necessary. If the results are mediocre or poor, then a number of questions must be answered: Should the product be revised, completely reworked or abandoned? Was the test an adequate one? Would a different segment of the field force do a better marketing job? Would the product be more enthusiastically received in another part of the market? Only if the test is a complete failure can a company really be glad that it took the field testing approach. In such an event, the company might be well advised to reexamine the qualifications of the group charged with the initial appraisal and later development of the product. It should be kept in mind that the company will still have to administer for many years to come the few policies sold during the field testing period.

FOLLOW THROUGH

It is sound policy to follow up a new product's introduction with an analysis of the results obtained. It is not especially difficult to review and evaluate sales results with respect to such items as geographical area, type of marketing organization and income level of the purchasers. It is much more difficult to assess, however, the net increase in sales brought about by a new product. The amount of additional sales made because of the new product is a subjective question that should include an assessment of the increased sales efforts of the agency organization in marketing all of the company's products because of the stimulus and door-opening potentialities offered by the new product itself.

A companion function of the appraisal of new product results should be the periodic evaluation of the existing portfolio. As the needs of the marketplace and the demands of the public change with time, some products become outmoded and obsolete. A life insurance company that desires continued success should have a procedure, therefore, for weeding out such products and preventing the company's portfolio from becoming too unwieldy.

SUMMARY

Although the function of product planning, if properly pursued, can be costly and demanding on the time of many people, it is essential to company success. Someone in management must be given the responsibility and authority for product planning. This person must then see that new product suggestions are developed, analyzed, and where feasible, brought to fruition. Because of its importance in a dynamic marketing environment, product planning must be given top-level executive attention and support.

13

Market Planning for Individual Life Sales

Thomas C. Simons

THE NATURE OF PLANNING

Planning is the orderly structuring of action to achieve organizational goals. The organizational units doing the planning may be the corporation as a whole, one division, one department, one agency or even one agent. Whatever the size of the organizational unit, the process of planning should be the same—the rational arranging of organizational activities to achieve the objectives of the organization. "Planning is deciding in advance what to do, how to do it, when to do it and who is to do it."[1]

Planning Implies a Time Schedule

A time schedule is implied in our definition of planning. If organization action is to be structured to achieve organizational goals, presumably this means that the goals are to be achieved in accordance with a time schedule. This suggests that each phase of organizational action must conform to a rational sequence. Otherwise, the ultimate organizational goals will not be achieved in accordance with management's projected expectations. Thus, short-term objectives must be established and achieved in accordance with

---

[1] Koontz, Harold and O'Donnell, Cyril, *Principles of Management*, McGraw-Hill Book Co., New York, 1964. p. 71.

a time schedule that will contribute to the achievement of long-term objectives. Adherence to a time schedule also implies an establishment of a schedule of priorities for objectives. This schedule of priorities is sometimes referred to as a hierarchy of objectives. Whatever terminology is used the concept is the same. Certain objectives should be given greater attention than others.

Planning Affected by Change

Change intensifies the need for planning. A business that operates in an environment that is insulated from change will have a minimum need for planning. The life insurance business, for example, had less need to emphasize planning fifty years ago than it does today. However, today the life insurance business environment abounds in dynamic forces that are accelerating changes and that are pressuring the life insurance companies to change. The demographic changes, the social changes and the economic changes described in Chapter 1 all have a significant impact on the need for planning. The dynamic role of government will continue to be an important factor affecting the need for planning.

Planning Affected by Existence of Alternative Courses of Action

The existence of alternative courses of action also intensifies the need for planning. This principle is substantiated by the facts in present day life insurance company operations. An intensified need for planning exists today because of the alternative courses of action available in (1) selecting products (mutual funds, variable annuities, Major Medical expense policies, disability income policies and property and liability policies), (2) selecting channels of distribution, (3) selecting advertising media and other sales promotion techniques, (4) selecting broader markets including the international market and (5) selecting the appropriate operational structure to maximize the sales effort. In former years there was not the same necessity for planning because the companies did not have as many alternatives confronting them.

Planning Must be Responsive to Changing Needs and Wants

It is fatal for a life insurance company to assume that the future will be an extrapolation of the past. It is vitally important, if a company is to be responsive to future trends in the marketplace, to know what that marketplace will be demanding. To a far greater extent than ever before, life insurance companies must attempt to become "customer oriented."

This requires careful study and analysis of changing customer wants and needs and adjustment to them—not just adjustment to what the buyer of the future wants, but in addition, adjustment to what today's buyer will want and need in customer service.

If a life insurance company is to capitalize on its strengths, management must first identify these strengths. Long-term decisions should then be made to enable the company to take advantage of these strengths. These decisions must be subject, of course, to periodic review and revision (which will be discussed later in this chapter). Certain definitive decisions, however, must be made before meaningful market planning can take place.

DEVELOPMENT OF BASIC OBJECTIVES

Among the definitive decisions that management must make is the defining of both its long-term and short-term objectives. In addition it must make sure that the attainment of short-term objectives contributes to the achievement of long-term objectives. The first step in planning is the establishment of the long-term and the short-term objectives to be achieved by the organization.

Interrelationship Between Product Planning and Market Planning

The same long-term objectives that management establishes to assist it in product planning, as described in Chapter 12, will provide guidelines for market planning for individual life sales. Therefore, we can assume that the company has already done considerable thinking in regard to its basic objectives relative to (1) the products and services to be marketed, (2) the channels of distribution that will be used, and (3) the markets that will be served. In fact, product planning and market planning involve practically the same questions and any discussion of one will almost inevitably involve questions of significance to the other. It is hard to imagine a discussion of product planning without reference to the markets in which those products will be marketed. Likewise, any discussion of market plans must give consideration to products currently available and products to be developed in the future. The close interrelationship between product planning and market planning therefore suggests that the two will be conducted on an integrated basis.

In addition to long-term product planning described in Chapter 12, a life insurance company will wish to determine long-term objectives for (1) the future public image of the company and (2) the extent the company will compete in the whole national market.

Image of the Company

Management must decide the kind of company, or image, it desires to have. Does it want to be known as a low-price, low-service company? Is business to be attracted (1) through emphasis on savings associated with careful underwriting, (2) through low-cost operation, (3) through high service, or (4) through exceptional field personnel? Which one of these, or which combination of these will the company emphasize?

Unless the company takes a long-term approach in each of these areas, and adheres to its established objectives with a high degree of consistency, the various departments of the company can quickly become disjointed. For example, a field force built on a product price approach does not easily convert to a high-service, middle-price philosophy. Such a change might create great discomfort. Thus, all departments must be in agreement as to the type of company desired. The impetus for this, of course, must come from top management.

Market Coverage

Does management desire to be a national company, a regional company, a big-city company, a rural company, a company directed to high income markets, or a company directed to low income markets? Which or what combination of these will the company adopt? Each of these market alternatives must be investigated in the light of the resources and strengths of the company. For example, what are the advantages of being a national company and, on the other hand, what are the disadvantages, if any?

SPECIFIC LONG-TERM OBJECTIVES

Once the company's basic objectives have been identified and decisions reached, management must next address itself to the specific objectives to be attained over the long run in the marketing of individual life insurance.

Profit Objectives

What is the amount of gain or profit that will be satisfactory for a five-, ten-, or fifteen-year forward run on new life insurance issues? Management must be extremely careful not to be deluded by gains on older insurance in force, but must concentrate it's profit objectives on the business that is currently being written. Profit, or gain from operations, whether the company be a stock company or a mutual company, provides the basic measurement as to whether all of the cost factors of the marketing operation are in proper balance. Profit is a necessary discipline for any corporation offering products or services to the public. Needless to say, gain from operations also depends to a large extent on other factors, such as expense levels, development costs, investment levels, mortality levels, and product price.

Sales Objectives

The sales objectives of a company must be expressed in the most meaningful terms that can be found and can be monitored. For example, total *volume* of new life insurance provides an unsatisfactory measurement of sales results as there are too many variations in types of business possible. For example, $500,000,000 of term insurance may produce quite different results than $500,000,000 of whole life and endowment contracts. Premiums, or commissions are a better measure of sales, especially if the commissions reflect the desirability of a particular type of business to the company. Sometimes, sales objectives may be expressed by product line. They also, of course, may be expressed in terms of market share in order to reflect the company's progress relative to other companies.

A long-range sales objective should be defined for each major division of the company's business, and it should be expressed in the most meaningful terms feasible. This objective should then be broken down into the annual increments necessary for the company to attain its long-term objective.

Manpower Development

Manpower development objectives must be refined to the greatest extent possible in order to emphasize the type of manpower development desired and to evaluate the results of current manpower development efforts. For example, an objective expressed in terms of the "gross number of agent personnel by a certain date" is nowhere near as valuable as an objective expressed in terms of the number of mature, quality agent personnel needed by the company to achieve its sales objectives. A long-term objective, therefore, should be established in terms of the number of trainees, agents, and managerial personnel needed to fulfill the company's growth plans. This must follow, of course, from a decision as to the channels of distribution to be employed, the type of business to be sold and other such factors related to manpower requirements. Once the objectives have been established, methods must be provided to measure performance, retention rates and quality of the manpower.

Branch Offices or General Agencies Needed

In addition to the above specific objectives, management must establish an objective for the number of distribution outlets desired and the quality of these outlets. The decision as to the number of distribution outlets will depend to a large extent upon the geographical coverage the company desires. The decision concerning the quality of these outlets will depend upon the size and sophistication of the market and the quality of service desired. Management must look at least five years ahead and maintain a continuing search for suitable locations for new offices.

SHORT-TERM OBJECTIVES

Short-term objectives should provide for the implementation and attainment of long-range objectives. Thus, they should represent long-range objectives broken down for the immediate future, or some controlled segment of time. Usually one year is selected. Short run objectives should reflect the state of progress towards the long run objectives as of now and the current strengths and weaknesses of the organization in attaining these objectives. Any external economic or market conditions that would affect progress must be considered. For example:

1. How much of each kind of life or health insurance did we sell this year? Is there a need to correct imbalances? Is there a particular acceptance or rejection of individual product lines? How does the competitive picture look—are prices in line with the price objective?

2. How many men should be hired this year? What is the capacity to find and train the recruits and how pressed are our training facilities? Should there be concentration in particular marketing areas—both geographic or by type of marketing division?

3. What will be the growth in the various classes of producers from first year men to mature producers in numbers and in production levels? This presupposes data in all these areas from previous years' activities, but is vital for establishing meaningful manpower targets. Is retention of personnel to be especially stressed and if so, how?

4. What expense levels do we forecast this next year to support this program? Can "development" costs be segregated from costs to support current production? What profit will be generated from this year's business?

5. What development do we expect in particular types of markets like salary allotment, the business market, pensions and so forth. What product promotions and staffing will be necessary in this next year to support this strategy?

6. What office openings do we plan for this next year? Do we have personnel available? How many terminations or resignations can we

expect in our manager or general agent strength this next year?

7. What research programs should be definitely planned for the coming year to position us for better knowledge and data in the years ahead?

8. What advertising plans should be considered? What will be stressed? To whom, and where will the message be beamed?

9. What additional home office personnel will be needed to execute the plans and to train for the execution of future plans?

10. What types of training schools will be carried out next year to bolster areas that are weak?

11. Will there be any change in the meetings program to carry out the objectives of the marketing organization and to move further toward achieving the company's long-range plans? All conventions and meetings should be structured and executed to accomplish a particular corporate purpose.

12. What travel plans should personnel consider? The total marketting plan will affect management's answer to this question.

Once these questions have been answered, management must establish the year's objectives in the light of the answers developed.

The short-term objectives should vary from year to year based upon how results of previous years are moving the company toward or away from its long run goals. If short run objectives are not varying from one year to the next, then management is probably not giving adequate attention to results or management has no long-range objectives in mind.

COORDINATION OF MARKET OBJECTIVES WITH OTHER CORPORATE OBJECTIVES

It is vitally important that marketing management establish its long-term and short-term objectives in concert with the top management of the company.

The marketing activities in a life insurance company normally represent the largest single area of expense. Therefore, unless top management is committed to the long and short range plans of the marketing department, the latter will most likely be engaged in a continual hassle with top management in reconciling expense results attained. The sales objectives of the marketing department must also be in concert with the long-term corporate profit objectives so that the marketing department will understand the part it is to play in the total company profit objective. From this, the marketing department will know what is expected of it but will have the freedom to operate within the known guidelines.

There is usually a long time between effort and result in the life insurance business. For example, there is typically a three year interval between the hiring of agent manpower and the full speed production that that manpower ultimately generates. Furthermore, the profit on the business that the new agent manpower will develop may be delayed an additional 5–10 years or more. Manpower development programs, therefore, whether they are successful or unsuccessful, have an impact on profit only after many years. Thus, it is absolutely essential that management recognizes these facts as well as the costs incidental to such development. Many of the best laid plans for manpower development have been defeated by a lack of recognition of this point. Therefore, unless top management subscribes to and is supportive of the long-term objectives of the marketing division, such as the type of marketing operations planned, the image desired, the price philosophy to be followed and the types of markets to be developed, the organization is liable to go in several directions.

Furthermore, the other departments of the company must plan in unison, particularly with respect to coordinating operational functions. Departments, for example, such as underwriting must be capable of expanding as the marketing organization plans for an expansion of new business is written. The investment department also must understand what flow of investable funds will be available in the future so as to be able to plan its staff requirements and to determine funds that will be available for forward commitments. Departments concerned with such activities as office planning, communications, printing, accounting, data processing, policyowner and field services, and payment of benefits must have a clear idea of the long-term objectives and the short-term objectives of the marketing department.

These plans must be fully discussed, comments communicated, objections voiced and priorities determined.

Management should recognize the stake that all the other departments have in the company's attempt to attain the long-term marketing plans and the positive effect on progress that can be created if all departments feel that they have an important part to play in the marketing department's plans for sales expansion.

MARKET PLANNING ASSUMPTIONS

Assumptions are the premises on which market plans are based. Assumptions are either based on studies of historical data or are hypotheses that management believes are realistic. Basically, market planning assumptions fall into two categories: external and internal.

External Assumptions

External assumptions are based upon factors and circumstances outside the organization. Some examples of external factors that are significant to market planning are: (1) population growth, (2) population shifts, (3) gross national product and national income, (4) changes in income distribution, (5) consumer attitudes, (6) competitive products, (7) competitive government, and (8) state and federal legislation. Market planning based on some external assumptions can have long-term effects. Market planning based on other external assumptions will have effects that will be of shorter duration. In other words, certain assumptions will be valid for only a short period of time. Other assumptions can be expected to be reasonably valid for a longer period of time. In formulating its market plans a company must recognize that such plans are only as realistic as the assumptions on which they are based and are valid only for the period of time for which the assumptions can be expected to be valid. It is also important that management examine its external assumptions periodically and test their validity whenever this is feasible.

1. MARKET AND SALES POTENTIAL

In formulating its market plans management must have a realistic approximation of the market potential and its own sales potential for its products. In approximating the market potential for life insurance for the market in which it operates the company will make use of available studies relative to the number of family units in the market area, the buying power of these family units, income levels, home and automobile ownership, and other data helpful in determining market potential.

2. DEMOGRAPHIC AND INCOME CHARACTERISTICS

Another important area of managerial assumptions in planning are the demographic characteristics of the market the company desires to serve. What are the shifts in income levels and disposable dollar levels now and in the future? Will there be a larger supply of discretionary income available and to what groups of the population? Where will the major groups of people with buying power reside: rural, urban, East, West, North, South, what cities, and in what states? The answers to all of these questions will provide important data for decisions in market planning.

3. CONSUMER ATTITUDES

A basic determination for a life company to make as a part of its market planning is the future role of life insurance in family financial planning, the public's attitude toward life insurance and the public's preference for equity based products. The company must be aware of the other forms of savings and investments and risk sharing that are in demand in the marketplace and determine what will be the future for these other products as contrasted with present lines of coverage offered by the company. With specific reference to the types of insurance, management must make some assumption as to demand. Will the demand in the marketplace be for term, permanent, retirement income, endowment, or other forms? Although a life insurance company can play an important role in determining what forms of insurance the market desires, in many cases the forms demanded will be affected by external factors, such as government programs and economic variables.

Management must also have some way of determining the attitudes of consumers, both current owners of the company's products as well as prospective purchasers. What are buyer attitudes relative to savings, to education of children, to retirement, and to life insurance versus other forms of savings? How are these attitudes likely to change over time?

4. FUTURE ROLE OF GOVERNMENT

A major external variable in any planning in business today is the role of the government. This is particularly so in the life insurance business because of the government's direct involvement in the provision of security. What will be the government's role in providing welfare benefits in the future—will it level off or increase? What will be the government's role in providing insurance coverages? What will be the tax and regulatory situation, one, five, ten, twenty years from now? Will state regulations remain or will the Federal Government become the regulator of insurance? For a more detailed discussion of the significance of the increasing involvement of the federal government in providing economic security the reader is referred to Chapter 14, "Market Planning for Individual Health Insurance Sales."

5. BEST METHODS TO REACH THE MARKET

Management must decide what will be the best manner of reaching the people who need the company's services. What will be the distribution channels through which to reach the buying public in the future? For example, what will be the role in the future of the general insurance broker? Will his role expand or contract as a force in the marketplace? What will be the role of mass coverages? To what degree will mass coverages affect the amount of individual coverage desired? What will be the role of banks, credit card companies, and mutual funds in the sale of life insurance and the providing of family financial security? Finally, what will be the role of the employer in the employee's life insurance and financial security decisions? For example, it may be easier to reach the market for life insurance through the employer on a payroll deduction basis.

6. SERVICE AND PRICE

What will be the attitude of the public, or segments of the public, on such questions as service, price, and tailoring of the product to meet special needs? For example, will people be interested in a supermarket approach where they can obtain a wide variety of services from one company, or will they prefer the small specialty store approach where a company sells a limited number of products but perhaps with higher quality and more personal service than the supermarket? Also, what about one-stop shopping? Will people prefer to obtain a complete security package from one salesman because of the convenience?

7. COMPETITION

Management must determine who their competitors will be, and what will be the response of this competition to the dynamic marketing environment of the future. Management must then determine how the response of its competition will affect the company's market position. Thus, market planning must be made in the light of the expected actions of others.

Internal Assumptions

Internal assumptions should be based on a careful analysis of all of the company's capital and human resources and an evaluation of them in terms of meeting the company's goals. Management must in particular measure the company's current potential for growth and its ability to attract new resources.

1. HIRING CAPACITY

What is the capacity of the company to recruit and train sales manpower? By how much can the company's manpower be increased in any one year? A severe limitation can be placed on the attainment of sales objectives, if a company does not have the ability to expand its manpower, both in its field sales activities as well as in its home office operations. Also, management should continually be inquiring into the possibilities for manpower reduction in some departments.

2. RETENTION

What assumptions can the company make concerning the retention of existing personnel and personnel to be hired in the future? Can improvements in retention be made over past results?

3. PRODUCTION

What assumptions can the company make concerning sales production per man and what increases in sales production can be projected for each level of maturity and experience for the men in the sales organization? Is it practical to assume an improvement in these sales production assumptions? If production per man cannot be increased, then sales growth must come from adding additional men.

4. COSTS

Management must be able to determine the development costs it can incur in the development of new agents and new sales offices. Management should also conduct a continuing analysis of existing sales units and their effectiveness in achieving sales goals. The following specific areas should be reviewed:

> a. What assumptions will be made in terms of levels of initial financing of new agents and net levels of financing after production credits for each year of producer growth?
> b. What housing will be provided the sales force and what will be the rent, clerical, and equipment costs to meet these requirements?
> c. What production will be achieved per office? What is a satisfactory cost/production relationship?
> d. What will be the cost of providing the required training?

5. PROFIT AND GROWTH BY CLASSES OF BUSINESS

Assumptions must be made about the growth in specific lines of business, and a determination made of the gains that will be realized by each line as the company grows. These assumptions will be derived from the external assumptions described in the preceding section.

6. LAPSE AND MORTALITY ASSUMPTIONS

Management must forecast the expected lapse and mortality levels and determine how they will be affected by future market plans. For example, in an organization composed of many new producers, one is likely to find poorer lapse and mortality experience than in a seasoned and mature organization where quality business will be a larger percentage of the total business produced.

7. MANAGEMENT DEVELOPMENT

The sales management needs of the future must be assessed. What will be the management maturity rate? Will this provide enough staff in the development process to provide adequate training and supervision for producers? What will be the cost per man and the total cost of management development? What are the desired ratios of producers to staff and management personnel?

8. NEW SALES OFFICES

At what rate can new sales offices be established? What effect will this have on agent recruiting patterns and marketing costs? What production can be expected for new offices or break-off offices?

9. CONFERENCES

Management should attempt to determine the cost per attendee for the various schools, conferences and conventions. Once determined, it must decide the benefits received from such conferences, weighed against their costs. What should be the plans for future conferences?

10. TECHNOLOGY

What will be the effect on all the above factors of new technologies available for (1) training, (2) communications, (3) data transmission, and (4) information gathering? What will be the costs of implementing such new technologies and will they be feasible for the specific company's operations? What criteria should be employed in evaluating the merits of new ideas and proposals that emanate from meetings, conferences, conventions and trade publications?

ORGANIZATIONAL RESPONSIBILITIES FOR MARKET PLANNING

Importance of Broad Corporate Involvement

There are a number of different levels of planning and unless planning involves the entire organization, it becomes difficult to implement. The corporate aspects of a marketing department's operations must be in concert with the corporate design and with the cycling of total corporate planning. Further, the general objectives of the company and the expression of those objectives in the market plan must be arrived at by top marketing management in conjunction with other top company management responsible for corporate policy making and with responsibilities for implementation. The establishment of general policy and the determination of the general direction of future growth should come from all segments of the corporate organization.

An intensive effort should be made by top management to discuss long-range corporate objectives with as many levels of marketing management as possible so that the chief marketing officer brings to corporate policy-setting decisions the ideas and thoughts of as many people as possible. This will assure that when corporate policy has been established it will be understood by as broad a representation of the organization as possible.

Function of Research Units

Research units within a company should be continually collecting, sifting and analyzing data to test assumptions, progress, and engage in new research. There is an advantage in having these research units separated from the direct operating areas so that they are not influenced by the operators too directly and therefore can take detached views of operations.

Planning Specialists at the Company Level

On the company level there may be planning specialists who are studying the technology of planning itself. They may also coordinate the study of company goals, the development of planning cycles and the dissemination of planning data. There should also be a market research organization on the corporate level. This can keep the corporation "marketing" oriented and also can engage the talent of additional specialists as needed in this type of research.

Planning Specialists in the Marketing Department

Within the marketing department there should be a planning officer in charge of a unit that collects data, analyzes results, evaluates results in terms of expectation and constructs models for future courses of action of a shorter term nature. The function of planning is becoming increasingly a field for experts. It is the role of this unit to provide performance data for line operations.

Planning Responsibilities of Line Officers in Agency Departments

Managers responsible for line operations, such as directors of agencies, should build their plans within the general framework of corporate and departmental objectives. The assumption data can be supplied by the corporate or agency department planning units. The parameters that guide a particular operation must be supplied by the senior marketing officer. Deviation from or modification of the assumptions can be made by the individual operating officers, but their overall planning must be in concert with the broader corporate and departmental objectives.

Planning Responsibility of Field Management

Field managers must build their plans within the same context. They should be furnished with planning assumptions, data and objectives from their director of agencies. They also should be provided information on the results that they are achieving in order to adjust their activities and see that changes are made when necessary. These results should be provided on a periodic basis and not simply at the year's end.

Other sales support departments or divisions within the agency department also must operate to support the marketing plan. They should develop personnel needs, training, or support programs in conjunction with departmental plans and the plans of the operating units.

IMPLEMENTING THE MARKET PLAN

Market planning should continually involve the operating people. If planning is merely an exercise of a group of personnel who do not have any understanding of the sales process or do not have any relationship with the people who must make the plans work, planning becomes a waste of money, time, effort and energy. If the ideas and the needs of the operating people are not considered in developing the plans, they are equally worthless. Therefore, the assumptions used and the plans developed must be communicated to and understood by all people who will be involved in implementing the plans. The operating people must feel a part of the success of the planning. They must recognize the role that their unit plays in the total corporate plan.

Each production agency should have a plan based on cycling that is similar to the cycling of the corporate plan. The agency's market planning must be revised periodically to reflect changes in the market and sales potential.

There are many advantages in having as many people as practical involved in the planning process. It exposes all participants to the problems top management experiences in establishing priorities of effort. It demonstrates the role of expenditures in pricing, in development rates, and in profits. It allows top management to obtain new ideas for the accomplishment of objectives, ideas that any thoughtful member of the organization may have, but that may not come forth without stimulation in a planning context. It allows top management to obtain feedback concerning the validity of its assumptions. In short, all the factors that go into success or failure are debated in the planning cycle and the more people who participate in this activity, the more understood will be the direction, purpose and result.

The more carefully planning is done and the more completely it is carried out will determine the degree to which each person understands what job he is supposed to do. "Standards of Performance" become virtually irrelevant if planning is well done. Each person knows what he has done well and what he has done poorly and he understands what remains to be done.

Definite review dates should be established during the year to provide management with an opportunity to take overall looks at progress on current strategies. Most importantly, information systems must be established to gather data on all results that bear on the plan. Some data must be assembled daily, monthly, quarterly, annually, or less frequently, but in all cases, the plan cannot be implemented without ways to check progress. Electronic data processing has made this information gathering more feasible for the sophisticated enterprise and continual effort must be made to get information promptly into hands that can use it. Information must be carefully screened for its relevancy, as too much data, or data that does not affect decision-making, can defeat an otherwise good system.

CONCLUSION

This chapter has placed market planning in a framework that perhaps makes planning sound easy. In reality, however, planning produces major changes of direction slowly. Most going concerns are more or less committed, explicitly or implicitly, to certain basic ways that can be redirected only over the long-run. But the planning effort is still worth the price. Planning makes an enterprise pull together. Everyone knows what others are doing, and all departments and individuals are doing things together as a part of an understood program of action.

Planning also brings about the shaping of the future of the enterprise so that results can occur. Planning removes uncertainty and protects the corporate entity from being tossed about on waters and in winds over which the enterprise has no control.

14

Market Planning for Individual Health Insurance Sales

Robert W. Carey

FEATURES IN COMMON WITH INDIVIDUAL LIFE INSURANCE SALES

Market planning for individual health insurance sales is basically similar to that required for individual life insurance sales. Therefore, companies that are marketing both types of coverage are increasingly integrating the market planning for individual health insurance sales with their market planning for individual life sales. There are several reasons why market planning for the two products are similar.

Products Have Similar Economic Bases

First, from an economic point of view the two products are similar. Both provide protection against financial loss that arises out of an impairment to the economic value of a human life. In the case of life insurance, the coverage is for a loss arising out of an impairment that is complete. The economic value of the human life is obliterated by death. In the case of health insurance, the coverage is for a loss to the human life value that is less complete and comes in two forms. The first type of loss is the loss of income that occurs when the injured or sick person is not able to work. The second type of loss is the loss of family assets and income that must be diverted from family economic needs to meet the expenses of medical care. The similarity in the economic benefits provided by the two products endow them with qualities that make them attractive to meet the needs of the same families.

Similar Sales Efforts for Developing Sales Volume

Second, to develop a volume of sales for life and health products, the same form of sales effort must be initiated. The volume of sales will be directly related to the amount of sales promotional effort the marketing department gives to the health insurance product. However, one of the most effective means of increasing sales volume is by increasing the average size of policies sold. This may be achieved to some extent by special sales efforts promoting the sale of larger size policies. However, the income level of the families solicited usually will determine the average size of policies sold. Therefore, a company will attempt to increase the average size of policies sold for both products by increasing its marketing efforts in the middle income and the higher income markets. It is sound economics for the insurer to spread its marketing costs over both products when the same marketing effort can be beneficial to both products.

Similar Marketing Techniques

Third, since the two products are both intangibles, they both require the same marketing techniques to motivate and arouse consumer interest to purchase. Sales promotion materials are frequently prepared to emphasize the substantial economic value that is lost whenever there is any impairment to the human life value. Sales promotion ideas that are effective in emphasizing the intangible service performed by one contract will be equally effective in emphasizing the service performed by the other contract.

Purchase Reluctance Has Similar Basis

Fourth, the purchaser of both life insurance and health insurance must be persuaded to make an immediate sacrifice in the form of a premium payment to obtain the right to a benefit that may be long deferred. Particularly with respect to life insurance and disability income protection, the premium payer may be reluctant to forego color television now so that his family can have guaranteed income in the event that he dies or becomes disabled. Hospital expense insurance does not pose a problem of similar magnitude because the premium payer has either observed the frequency with which his neighbors and friends, if not his own family, have made use of hospital services. Due to the recognized receptivity of the public to the purchase of hospital policies, the sales force often utilizes this product as a door opener to the sale of life insurance and disability income products. However, insuring one's income against death and disability frequently appears like a purchase that can be deferred until a later time. The overcoming of this purchase reluctance requires marketing expertise that is similar for both products.

Similar Planning for Manpower Development

Fifth, to a large extent persons who possess the qualifications to market one product will be successful in the marketing of the other product. Thus, market planning for manpower development will be similar for both products. This point should be clear from a reading of Chapters 13 and 20.

Similar Training Programs

Sixth, the life training courses for agents are readily adaptable and parallel the training necessary for the education of agents to sell health coverages. More emphasis is now being given to the programming of disability benefits similar to the techniques which have been incorporated for many years in the life insurance training courses.

Similar Creative Thinking for Product Development and Market Planning

Seventh, the same type of creative thinking that is required for formulating market plans is required for both products. Thus, there can be considerable cross fertilization of ideas in formulating market plans for the two products on an integrated basis.

SIGNIFICANCE OF COMPANY PHILOSOPHY TO MARKET PLANNING

An important aspect of market planning for health insurance sales is deciding the extent to which the company intends to become involved in the health insurance business. There are several possible approaches. Some insurers decide to offer only those coverages that replace income lost because of accident or sickness on the theory that this is a logical extension of life insurance protection of the human life value. Other companies prefer to specialize in coverages that protect the insured against hospital and medical expense. A few highly specialized insurers are interested only in protecting against accident risks associated with travel or other limited risks.

Another approach is to build upon the broadest possible base. This marketing philosophy, stated simply, is to offer a complete line of personal health insurance, and to make it available to as many people as possible. Under this philosophy, when the agent walks into a home, he can be sure that regardless of the type of prospect he encounters he has a useful health insurance coverage to offer and one that the prospect is usually able to buy.

GOVERNMENT REGULATIONS

Health insurance, because it is endowed with a public interest and because of the technical nature of the business, is subject to a high degree of governmental regulation. Currently, each state has a department of insurance that is vested with the right, power, and responsibility to regulate the business of insurance in that state. Nearly every phase of the insurance business is regulated by these departments. Although sometimes cumbersome and restrictive, these regulations have resulted in a growing public confidence in insurance products. The state regulatory system has promoted the stability of the insurance business, prevented unfair competition and encouraged reasonable competition.

Today, the insurance business in the United States probably is more closely regulated than any other business with the possible exception of banking. Moreover, there have been increased efforts in the past few years to further this control by centralizing a regulatory department on the national level.

In addition to government regulation, most companies have within their own organizations a "watch-dog" department for purposes of self-control. The control that companies exercise over their own affairs helps to relieve the pressures sometimes placed on a state insurance department by outside forces and should, it is hoped, reduce the need for additional regulatory systems.

In recent years, there has been increased interest expressed and numerous articles written concerning the relative merits of federal regulation of insurance. In addition, the health insurance companies are confronted with the real possibility of increased competition from the federal government with respect to medical expense insurance provided for all families under an expanded Social Security program or some form of national health program.

GOVERNMENT SECURITY PROGRAMS

A problem that is unique to market planning for individual health insurance sales is the increasing importance of federal and state legislation relative to economic security. Chapter 1, "The Life Insurance Marketing Environment," has described some of the recent federal legislation that has been of significance to life and health insurance marketing. The present chapter expands on the introductory material presented in Chapter 1 and attempts to show the significance to health insurance marketing of these legislative changes.

State Disability Benefit Plans

The first government health legislation which had a major effect on health insurance coverages being marketed and administrative practices was the passage in 1942 of a compulsory cash disability insurance law in the State of Rhode Island. This law provided for payment of 50% of salary up to a stated maximum for a period of six months. During the period 1942 to 1950, similar laws, providing what is commonly referred to as "Cash Sickness Benefits," were adopted in California, New Jersey and New York. Although laws providing similar benefits have been proposed in a number of states since 1950, no laws of this type were passed until in 1969, when first Puerto Rico and then Hawaii approved compulsory disability benefit laws. The availability of benefits in states with such laws has to be taken into account when designing disability income products and particularly in the establishment of underwriting rules concerning the amount of benefits for which a person will be considered.

Medicare

One of the most publicized forms of legislation in this country became the law of the land in 1965. Public Law 89–97, better known as Medicare, provided for entrance of the Federal Government into health care insurance. The program may require many years, however, before its full impact on the voluntary health insurance business is known. As the most significant piece of federal legislation to affect the health insurance industry, the act has naturally created more concern than other previous legislation. The loss of the senior citizen market was disturbing to the health insurance industry but of more concern was the threat that this was only a foot in the door type of legislation, with this plan or a similar program being eventually extended to persons under age 65. This concern of the health insurance companies would appear justified in view of the Nixon Administration's interest in proposals for a national health insurance program for most, if not all, Americans.[1] Also, Governor Rockefeller, in

---

[1] *New York Times,* September 19, 1969.

a speech at the 1969 National Governors' Conference in Colorado Springs, proposed the financing of universal health insurance through contributions from employers, employees, and general Federal revenues. The proposals for a national health insurance program advanced by Walter Reuther before his death, and recently introduced in Congress by Senator Kennedy, are indicative of the substantial public support for a federal program of health care. With both political parties vying with each other in their proposals for liberalizing Medicare, health insurers may, in the not too distant future, see more extensive intrusion upon their market.

Disability Income Benefits Under Social Security

One of the earliest pieces of federal legislation that has had a significant effect on the general environment of the health insurance industry was passed in 1956. During the 84th Congress, an amendment to Public Law 880 added cash disability benefits to the Social Security laws. This marked the first time that health insurance type benefits were included under Social Security. This amendment provided disability income benefits at age 50. In 1960, through Public Law 778 of the 86th Congress, the age limit for paying these disability benefits was lowered to age 24. In 1968, Public Law 89–97, which contained the Medicare Act, had a section (Section 303) replacing the existing total and permanent disability insurance program of the Social Security Act by liberalizing the definition of total disability so as to provide, in effect, a temporary disability program.

Medicaid

In addition to the above, another type of legislation appeared on the scene during the 86th Congress. The Kerr-Mills Act was passed to provide a federal government solution to the problem of those who could not pay for medical care. Based on need, the program seemed on its way to providing assistance through state agencies. Under a section of the Social Security Amendments passed by Congress in 1965, however, a program, now called "Medicaid" was passed that replaced the Kerr-Mills Program. Known as Title XIX, this section attempted to liberalize and bring together under one administrative roof a federal-state sharing program that would provide medical assistance to a variety of needy people. New York State turned the spotlight on Medicaid by showing just how generous a state could make its Title XIX Program. Although other states are not expected to have programs with such liberal provisions, the entire program is one that could seriously affect the future of private health insurance. The substantial cost to the tax payers of the Medicaid program may be a deterrent to future expansion. In fiscal year ending June 30, 1969, the federal government spent $2.4 billion on Medicaid. Several states have sharply curtailed Medicaid services and tightened eligibility requirements to save money.[2]

Future Developments

The future of the health insurance industry as a private enterprise will depend to a large extent upon the ability of the companies to meet the constantly changing insurance needs of the public. These changes are significant to the insurance business. To the extent that the health industry fails to provide for the ever changing needs of the public, political strategists will see that government action provides programs that will care for these needs.

Most companies, however, are confident that the health insurance business can survive and succeed despite the increasing extent that government is making health insurance coverage available. Insurance companies have the capacity to change and are demonstrating a will to change. Increasingly the companies are broadening available coverages and liberalizing benefits. The public is responding to these changes by purchasing increasing amounts of health insurance protection.

It can be expected, of course, that in today's complex society, the scope of public welfare programs—both state and national—will increase. It follows that one of the principal challenges to the health insurance business, therefore, is to assist the government in making these programs economical and efficient in operation and at the same time to preserve for the health insurance companies those markets that can be served best through the initiative of the private health insurance companies.

The health insurance industry will be asked to an increasing extent in the future to provide important services to the government as the latter expands its welfare programs. In several respects the health insurance industry has already made available its offices and its expertise to assist the federal government. For example, the United States Government in 1956 passed the Dependent's Medical Care Act. Since the passage of the Act, companies in the industry have served as fiscal agents and have administered health claims. Medicare has also opened an area where private enterprise is also providing assistance. Assignments as fiscal intermediaries are being accepted by many companies as an additional responsibility that they can perform effectively while continuing to provide health insurance protection to persons of all ages.

---

[2] *New York Times,* September 19, 1969.

PRODUCT DEVELOPMENT

Over the years health insurance policies have been developed that cover a wide spectrum of family needs. As new needs develop, however, new coverages must be designed to fit them. The new coverages of the future will be available through both individual and group plans.

The product portfolio of most health insurers includes three general types of accident and health insurance coverages. (1) Disability income plans provide weekly or monthly payments to disabled persons to replace income lost while the individual is unable to work. Policies are available for both short-term and long-term protection and the benefit periods may vary from as short as six months to as long as lifetime. (2) Basic hospital-surgical plans provide coverage for costs of hospital confinement and surgical operations. Policies in this classification may be designed to provide benefits on a reimbursement basis or on the basis of a fixed amount per day of hospital confinement without regard to the actual hospital bill (surgical fees are typically paid on the basis of a schedule included in the policy). (3) Major medical plans protect against catastrophic hospital and medical expenses with deductibles of usually $500, $750 and $1,000. The same type of major medical coverage is sometimes available with a $50 or $100 deductible and then is usually referred to as comprehensive medical expense coverage.

People's needs for health insurance protection are constantly changing. Therefore, to stay abreast of these needs a company must periodically modify its existing policies and in some cases, design entirely new policies. This is the nature of the market.

Impact of Medical Science and Types of Care on Product Development

As medical and hospital science achieve new progress and implement new types of care, health insurance companies must be alert to such innovations so that adequate coverage is available for the public to realize optimum use of these new developments. Examples of how the health insurance industry has responded to changes in medical care is the inclusion in many current policies of coverage for persons when they are confined in nursing or convalescent homes and intensive care facilities.

Impact of Government Benefits on Product Development

The introduction of Medicare resulted in most companies revising their policies which provided medical benefits so that benefits on covered persons would terminate at age 65 when they became eligible for Medicare. Some companies restructured their plans and offered products for persons over 65 to supplement the Medicare benefits. Taking cognizance of the short term benefits being provided in some states under their cash sickness laws and the long-term disability benefits available under Social Security, many companies have designed special supplementary income benefits to integrate with the state and federal plans.

Impact of Inflation on Product Development

The same inflationary forces that have characterized our economy in general during recent years have had a similar impact on the cost of medical care. According to the Consumer Price Index during the period of 1948 to 1968 medical costs increased faster than any other major category of personal expenses. The ability to control the rapid rise in medical and hospital costs does not appear to be within the grasp of the health insurance business despite its willingness to share its expertise in any efforts to effect some control. It is important, therefore, that the benefits available under medical expense insurance contracts keep pace with these rising medical costs. It is equally important that the health insurance companies increase the benefits available under replacement of income policies as inflationary forces result in increased average family incomes. Likewise, the company's sales representatives should be oriented to emphasize in their sales presentations the need for higher benefit levels. More frequent reviews by agents of existing policyholders' coverages should be encouraged to assure that benefit levels are commensurate with the increased need for benefits associated with an inflationary economy.

Impact of Higher Living Standards on Product Development

An important economic and social development of recent years that is significant for health insurance product planning and market planning is the higher standard of living of American families. This development has had an important impact on the demand for higher quality medical care facilities that in many cases approach luxury suites in the newer hospitals.

People have more leisure time and in most cases enough money to enjoy it. This pattern of living has generated an increase in the need for specialized health insurance coverages. For example, the vacationer wants to be covered while he is boating, skiing and driving to and from the lake or mountains. The hunter wants coverage while he is in the duck blind or in the field looking for pheasants. In addition, people want extra protection for accidental death and dismemberment or medical cost reimbursement related to these various activities.

Impact of Business Needs on Product Development

Specialized needs for health insurance protection are demanded in the business world. In a manner similar to earlier developments in life insurance, health insurance marketing people are directing their attention to designing products that can be offered in the business insurance field. Disability income plans can be used by sole proprietors to fund salary continuation agreements with their key personnel. Partnerships and closed corporations can use disability income coverage to fund buy and sell agreements to assure the continuation of the business. Special disability policies have been created to provide reimbursement for continuing business or overhead expenses when a proprietor or partner is disabled.

Impact of Persistency on Product Development

One of the major problems within the health insurance business is the high lapse rate of individual policies. This is particularly true with respect to hospital policies as apparently they often are purchased as stop-gap coverage when persons are temporarily not eligible for group insurance. It also has been demonstrated that there is a high lapse rate following payment of a maternity claim on hospital policies which provide maternity benefits. This experience has prompted many companies to de-emphasize the maternity benefit and in some cases the benefit has been withdrawn from the market. Major medical and disability income policies, especially contracts providing long-term benefits, have better persistency than hospital policies.

Impact on Product Development of the Increasing Emphasis on Dental Care

A more recent development in health insurance has been the development of dental care insurance to provide benefits in this important area of health care. This is another example of the importance of the health insurance companies being alert to new ideas and the ever changing family needs for health insurance coverage.

The Four Procedural Steps in Product Development

The function of product development usually encompasses four general steps: (1) product research, (2) product development, (3) product approval, and (4) implementation of sales plans.

1. PRODUCT RESEARCH

Product research is the systematic study and evaluation of consumer needs and wants relative to the products the health insurance industry is currently marketing and has the capability for marketing in the future. Thus product research is concerned with market acceptability of existing products as well as with market potential for new products. With specific reference to the health insurance product, product research is concerned with the collecting of information on (a) company claim and lapse experience, and sales volume on current products; (b) changes and trends in medical services and health care facilities; (c) insurance legislation as this affects the supply and demand for private health insurance; and (d) the needs and the wants of the insurance buying public. As described in Chapter 12, "Product Planning," there are many sources of information available to a company to help it determine the changing needs and wants of the insurance buying public. A company's sales personnel can often serve as an excellent source of information to help the home office keep abreast of changing market conditions. Whenever possible it is advisable, before mass marketing a product, to field test it to determine its saleability. However, in most cases this approach is not feasible due to the cost and time necessary to draft policies, develop premiums and file policies with the state insurance departments. Therefore, it is certainly advisable to carefully review the outline of specifications for a new product with a representative group of the sales force before introducing a new coverage.

2. PRODUCT DEVELOPMENT

Development of new coverages, as well as modification of existing plans, may be under the direction of the marketing director, the product coordinator, or someone given any of a variety of titles. The mechanics of policy development normally require some type of policy form committee, and probably also a research committee that analyzes suggestions for changes in old products or development of new products. For details relative to the mechanics of policy development the reader is referred to Chapter 12, "Product Planning."

Special attention should be directed to the preparation of sales material, such as sales proposals outlining policy benefits, to avoid misunderstanding on the part of the purchaser as to the coverage being provided. Consumer sales material must conform to the NAIC Advertising Rules. At least one state, Georgia, requires that sales proposals used in the solicitation of health insurance business must be filed with the insurance department and approved before being used.

3. PRODUCT APPROVAL

The final responsibility for securing approval of a new policy by the various state insurance departments usually rests with a director of policy forms or some person responsible for the filing of policies. Following notification of approval of the policies, the product coordinator will advise all interested departments concerned with introducing the new product to the field force.

4. PRODUCT IMPLEMENTATION

Implementation consists of introduction of the product, training of agents in the marketing of the new product, and providing the sales force with the necessary merchandising tools and methods for maximizing sales results.

Sales Promotion and Advertising Activity

The same form of sales promotion efforts used to generate life sales may be employed to promote health insurance. The frequent motivation of the field force with special health insurance sales promotion campaigns is especially important in companies selling both life and health insurance, but which have been primarily oriented to the sales of life products. In the preparation of the advertising material designed for the health insurance product, emphasis should be given to significant benefits provided in the policies. If the company is offering a unique type of coverage, it is especially important to highlight this benefit. While the cost of a health product is certainly of significance, apparently the benefits offered in the health package develop a greater interest on the part of the consumer. Many companies have found that there is a better response, judged on the basis of coupon mail returns, to advertisements for health insurance products than life insurance coverage.

Importance of Commissions and Production Recognition

To develop effectively a volume of quality health insurance business, it is necessary to compensate adequately the agents for selling the product. Most companies use a graded commission scale with high first year commissions scaled down in the second and succeeding years. Recognizing that a greater sales effort is generally necessary to sell disability income and major medical policies, higher first year commissions than for hospital policies are usually paid on these contracts.

In addition to paying commissions for producing health insurance, it is also important to provide the usual other sales incentives for the agents. This should include appropriate awards for sales leaders and, on the basis of volume and quality of business produced, an opportunity to qualify to attend company leaders' meetings. If the company is marketing both life and health products and the carrier wishes to produce a reasonable volume of health insurance, the sale of health insurance should be given sufficient production credits when establishing the qualification requirements for attendance at leaders' meetings.

Competition With Other Companies and Organizations Selling Health Plans

Among the companies marketing individual medical policies, the main competitive consideration is the amount and types of benefits provided in the contracts. Since the coverages under the medical policies, hospital and major medical, vary to such a great extent among companies, it is difficult to compare costs for these products and therefore, the price of the product does not usually become a primary factor from the standpoint of competition. It is not as difficult to make benefit comparisons on individual disability income policies, although even these products are by no means standardized. However, cost certainly is more of a factor in competition with respect to disability income products than for medical expense policies.

It is a somewhat different situation when the competition is with a group plan, whether the coverage is being sold by an insurance company or a Blue Cross-Blue Shield organization. The agent has to be realistic and recognize that in most cases for the same type of coverage, the cost to the consumer will be less when the benefits are purchased under a group plan as compared to under an individual contract. Although group insurance may be in force, there is still a market for the individual health product. Often, the group benefits are not adequate or all forms of coverage may not be provided under the group plan. Therefore, an individual medical or disability income contract frequently may be sold to supplement benefits provided under a group plan.

MANPOWER DEVELOPMENT

Sales Manpower

An important part of market planning relative to any product is the planning for recruiting, training and future development of sales manpower and sales management personnel. In the early days of the health insurance business the prerequisites for a sales position were simple and unsophisticated because the policies and rates at that time were uncomplicated. This is another area where changes in the product and the marketing environment have necessitated changes to conform to the changed conditions in the marketplace. To meet the requirements of today's knowledgeable buyer, the successful life and health insurance agent must be highly conversant with a complete, personal insurance line that typically includes both health and life insurance protection.

The development of sales manpower for health insurance sales requires management's attention to all of these areas that are also important to the development of sales manpower for life insurance sales. This is increasingly apparent as a company broadens its marketing concept to include the sale of both life and health insurance policies by all agents. Therefore, companies that have accepted the broadened marketing concept no longer are recruiting sales manpower for a monoline market. They are recruiting men for the company's entire product line. This policy is intensely practical because there is little distinction between a life insurance policy and a health insurance policy from an economic point of view. A person who can sell one can learn to sell the other. It is true that a person initially embarking on a sales career in selling hospital expense coverage is not equipped to do estate planning. But neither is that same person equipped to sell disability income policies to fund a partnership buy-out agreement.

In the same way that manpower recruiting requires the same attention of management for health insurance sales as for life sales, so also does the performance of the other functions of sales management require the careful attention of management whether the product is life or health insurance. Thus, sales management must be vigilant in its selection of manpower, its education and training of that manpower and its continued supervision of sales manpower.

The financing of new agents is similar for both life and health insurance. To attract capable men today most companies are finding that they must finance them. The financing system may be a guarantee against commissions, a drawing account, or some type of outright subsidy. Any financing system is normally based on a validation scale, which makes continued financing contingent on the meeting of validation requirements.

Brokerage Business

The brokerage market is a fertile area for the production of health insurance. Brokers will generally produce higher average size disability income cases and sell primarily to persons in the professional, executive and managerial group. Through this clientele, they also will produce a sizeable volume of major medical and in some cases business overhead disability policies. Business produced by brokers usually has a better than average rate of persistency.

CONCLUSIONS

Market planning for individual health insurance sales is typically integrated with market planning for individual life insurance sales. This is inevitably true for the increasing number of companies that market both individual life insurance and individual health insurance. The integration of market planning for both products is logical for the several reasons set forth in the first part of this chapter.

Market planning for health insurance requires that management give considerable attention to the effect on supply and demand for health insurance resulting from the continued expansion of government activities in providing family security. It is true that both death benefits and retirement benefits are an integral part of the Social Security program. However, these benefits are not as significant to life insurance as the impact on health insurance of state short-term and Social Security long-term disability benefits and Medicare. Therefore, market planning for individual health insurance sales requires continued attention to the significance of developments in government programs. This is a unique aspect of market planning for individual health insurance sales.

The marketing of individual health insurance coverage will continually require insurers to adapt their coverages and their marketing plans to the dynamic changes taking place in the marketing environment. The whole company must be responsive to these changes. But probably the greatest flexibility, adaptability and responsiveness to change must be preserved in product planning and market planning. No one can be exactly certain what the future has in store for private health insurance, so the capacity to adapt to the dynamic changes taking place is mandatory for continued success. Flexibility can only be maintained by having the right men, the right machines and the right attitude. For the company that is prepared with flexible marketing plans, the future is one of considerable promise.

15

Market Planning for Group Sales

Kenneth C. Nichols

The basic principles of market planning discussed in Chapter 13, "Market Planning For Individual Life Sales" and in Chapter 14, "Market Planning For Individual Health Insurance Sales" are equally applicable to market planning for group sales. This chapter assumes that the reader is already aware of the nature and purpose of market planning, in general, and the steps to be followed in the preparation of market plans. Therefore, Chapter 15 begins with a discussion of the first steps in market planning—the establishment of objectives—for the group department. We have attempted to keep to a minimum repetition of concepts and principles described in the two previous chapters. A certain amount of duplication is inevitable, because the procedures and practices for market planning have a great deal in common. The differences are basically differences in the nature of the products and the marketing processes employed.

Development of Long-Term Objectives

Long-term objectives, which reflect an attention to the events and changes on the business horizon, are essential if a company's group operations are to meet effectively the opportunities in the market place. In this presentation, it is assumed that the company's institutional purpose is clearly defined and supported by official and publicized policy and operational principles. The availability of such guidelines is necessary for the effective performance of all business activities and a prerequisite for the purposeful implementation of the group sales planning function.

What is the Market—Actual and Potential

A realistic appraisal of the market as it exists today and more importantly as it will evolve in the future is the essential raw material for the formulation of objectives.

Importance of Market Analysis

The products to be sold and the market channels through which they will be distributed will reflect a response to this evaluation of the future market. If, for example, an analysis of the trade association business reveals that virtually all such organizations have already established group plans, the development of special sales, administrative and enrollment techniques necessary to underwrite and administer such business may not be warranted for the sales volume potential involved. Obviously, there are very practical time and expense limitations governing the depth of any such analysis. The more cursorily the customer potential is examined, however, the greater the chance that product clutter or misdirected marketing aims will result.

Significant Information to be Acquired

First in the acquisition sequence is the identification of the potential customers in the market. Group customers can be classified broadly as follows:

(a) *Employer–employee groups.* These are single employer groups and they comprise the largest segment of the group market.

(b) *Multiple employer groups.* Trade associations or groups of employers in the same industry make up the vast majority of such group customers. A recent and growing phenomenon, however, has been the writing of Associations of Employers not in the same industry.

(c) *Union–management groups.* These groups usually involve more than one employer also but they are jointly managed by labor and management representatives.

(d) *Associations of individuals.* This type of group is sub-divided on an occupational basis into homogeneous and heterogeneous classifications. *Homogeneous,* as used here, refers to a common occupation and *heterogeneous* refers to more loosely structured associations whose employment characteristics are not considered in the formation of the organization.

(e) *Labor unions.* This is a somewhat limited market as compared to the union–management groups referred to above. The Taft-Hartley Act prohibits employers from making contributions directly to labor unions, and, therefore, coverage for such groups is restricted because it must be on a member-pay-all basis or paid for by the union treasury.

(f) *Savings and investment groups.* Bank customers. These groups include participants of mutual fund plans, depositors of banks, and shareholders of credit unions, and bank credit card holders. Although the number of such groups is large, the amounts of insurance carried by them are usually quite small.

(g) *Creditor groups.* Creditors' insurance is purchased to reduce or to extinguish the obligations borrowers or purchasers have with banks, finance companies, retail establishments, credit unions, savings and loan organizations and small loan companies.

(h) *Student Groups.* This is a relatively new and expanding market. Although health insurance is usually the only coverage involved, there is growing interest in life insurance.

Measuring the relative size of these market segments is somewhat difficult because of the lack of up-to-date statistics. The Institute of Life Insurance published a study in 1970, which reflected the distribution of business of life insurance companies having 77% of the total master policies and 89% of the total amount of group life insurance in force. Results of this survey are shown in Table 15:1.

A logical by-product of the identification of the market is the *geographical locations of the potential customers.* In the United States and Canada, the interdependence of population centers, with their manifold industrial, financial and legislative activities, tends to emphasize specific locations where group customers are concentrated and where marketing activities should be directed.

A significant question to be asked in this information gathering process is "What, if any, are the *unfulfilled needs* within the range of existing or potential insurance company service?" The answer to this question should reflect an open mind with respect to the expansion and flexibility of group marketing services.

Part of this evaluation of unfulfilled customer needs is the *consideration of existing competition.* Numerous examples can be cited either of companies that entered the group business, or where growth of a static group organization was accelerated, by capitalizing on a product or type of customer that offered exceptional competitive opportunity.

A final item of significant information to be acquired is the *prediction and analysis of trends.* In establishing objectives for future group sales it is important to analyze the social and economic changes that are occurring today and to appraise the effects these changes will have on tomorrow's market for group insurance. Two good examples of the historical reaction of the insurance industry to broad environmental changes are: (1) the

TABLE 15 : 1

GROUP LIFE INSURANCE IN FORCE BY TYPE AND BY SIZE OF INSURED GROUP—1968

(Excluding dependent coverage, group credit life, Federal Employees Group Life, and Servicemen's Group Life)

| | Master Polices | | Number | Insurance in Force | | Average Amount |
	Number	% of Total	of Members*	Amount	% of total	of Insurance per Member
TYPE OF GROUP						
1. Related to Employment or Occupation						
A. Employer-Employee	239,820	87.5%	34,636,000	$298,481,000,000	83.9%	$8,618
B. Union and Joint Employer-Union	5,060	1.9	6,205,000	22,447,000,000	6.3	3,618
C. Professional Society	670	.2	614,000	7,669,000,000	2.2	12,490
D. Employer Association	1,690	.6	1,547,000	10,840,000,000	3.0	7,007
E. Other						
(1) Related to Employee Benefit Program	1,340	.5	435,000	3,431,000,000	1.0	7,887
(2) Not Related to Employee Benefit Program	210	.1	215.000	1,547,000,000	.4	7,197
Total	248,790	90.8	43,652,000	$344,415,000,000	96.8%	7,890
2. Not Related to Employment or Occupation						
A. Fraternal Society	50	**	82,000	$241,000.000	.1%	2,939
B. Savings or Investment Group	23,890	8.7%	18,212,000	8,421,000,000	2.4	462
C. Other	1,260	.5	842,000	2,486,000,000	.7	2,952
Total	25,200	9.2%	19,136,000	$11,148,000,000	3.2%	583
TOTAL	273,990	100.0%	62,788,000	$355,563,000,000	100.0%	$5,663

* Includes duplication where individuals are included as members of more than one group.

** Less than 0.05%.

Source: Institute of Life Insurance, "Analysis of Group Life Insurance in Force—1968." The Tally of Life Insurance Statistics, Feb., 1970.

development of the variable annuity as a solution to the shrinkage of retirement benefits due to inflation and (2) the tremendous growth of group creditor life and disability coverages in the last decade which capitalized on the explosive expansion of consumer debt.

Sources of Information

No discussion of market analysis would be complete without suggesting where information necessary to the analytical process can be obtained. Among the more important sources are the following:

 a. *Roster publications.* There are available from both governmental and private sources many lists of businesses and non-business organizations. Some are on a national basis (e.g., government publications of all existing labor unions and another of all known trade associations) and others on a state, regional or city basis (e.g., manufacturers' directories or chamber of commerce listings of local employers).
 b. *Employee benefit publications.* There is a variety of publications dealing with employee benefits which include services helpful to understanding the group market.
 c. *Industry publications.* The life insurance industry, through its various trade associations, publishes a wealth of material on the the extent and growth of group insurance and group annuities.
 d. *Special services.* Organizations like Commerce Clearing House and Dun and Bradstreet can be excellent sources of information on customer potential.
 e. *Personal interviews.* A great deal can be learned by discussing the group market with those who are intimately associated with it, e.g., officials of group writing companies, independent employee benefit consultants and labor officials.

Group market analysis is a painstaking, thought-provoking process whereby current and future market potential are evaluated for both existing products and those still on the drawing board. Insufficient detail, unjustified assumptions or the absence of imagination may lead to conclusions with a high probability of marketing failure.

Determining a Role in the Market

Underlying all types of sales planning is the objective of competitive success. The effect of market analysis upon the achievement of competitive success has been discussed above. Another factor of vital significance to this success is the company's determination of its role in the market.

1. BASIC APPROACH—RIFLE OR SHOTGUN

The group market is one which, for the most part, has demanded a multiple coverage underwriting capability by insurance companies. The cost reducing trend of combining group coverages (life, medical expense and disability income) under one policy has encouraged companies to underwrite diverse coverages not originally contemplated. For a company to stimulate an agency force to market group coverages or to gain recognition by brokers as a competitive force in the group business, the company should underwrite most kinds of groups and have available a complete portfolio of group coverages. This does not preclude a "rifle" approach using one or a very limited number of coverages or by narrowly defining the kind of case that the company wants to underwrite. It is significant, however, to note that today's trend in group product availability is toward the "shotgun" approach.

2. PRODUCT CONSIDERATION

The products to be sold today and in the future receive never ending attention in the group business. Product consideration not only involves the important concept of innovation but also includes a continuing critical assessment of the existing product lines and services. It has been said that a main cause of the difficulties facing the nation's railroads has been their self-identification with the railroad business instead of with the transportation business. In an analogous sense, it is important to remember that the real business of life insurance companies is to provide financial security for people. An illustration of this expanded frame of reference is the origin of group creditor insurance. Had group writing companies not originally expanded beyond the employer-employee concept, the public would have been deprived of insurance protection for consumer debt. Agents and brokers would have been denied an important source of business, and the insurance companies themselves would have lost a profitable coverage line. Still worse for the insurance industry, banks and other financial institutions might well have resorted to self-insurance or some other form of coverage to fill the growing need. Another example of the fluidity of the group market is the trend toward Survivor Benefits. Traditionally, plans provide group term life insurance in amounts of 1, 2, 3 times annual earnings, with the highest amounts coming to an employee in his later years when his needs are less. Survivor Benefits, on the other hand, provide a percent of annual income, such as 30% or 40%, of an employee's predeath earnings in the form of monthly payments to the surviving spouse and children. Many contend that this approach better fits the needs concept of group life insurance. Diversification should always be an important factor in product consideration for an insurer's group department.

3. DEFINING THE GROUPS TO BE SOLD

There are three basic ways to classify eligible groups: (a) size, (b) type and (c) by the products to be marketed.

a. *Size.* Historically the determination of the size of groups eligible for coverage has been based on the number of employee lives to be insured. In determining the limits on size, a number of factors must be considered. If a basic purpose of selling group products is to provide a source of earnings for a company's *agency force,* then the company must market a broad line of coverages to small groups. The company's *administrative capability* must also be considered. The administration of many small group cases will necessitate a larger administration unit (for all home office functions including payments of claims) than will a lesser number of large cases. The company's *earnings* (profit) *objectives* will influence the size of groups to be written. The earnings on small cases are less predictible, and are more difficult to attain bcause of the higher lapse rates associated with such business. The company's *individual and franchise product lines* will help determine the minimum size group. For example, if a company has a successful individual policy pension trust product, it might limit the minimum size group annuity plan to 25 lives.

The size bands which have evolved and their relative importance in the group market are shown in Table 15:2.

b. *Type of Group.* In defining the types of cases to be sold, the factors the insurance company will normally consider are its existing product and policyholder mix, current or expected underwriting expense, relative profitability, effects on the company's agency force and whether, in fact, a competitive product and marketing system are possible within the company's basic philosophy.

In most situations, single employer groups will constitute the customer base of the group department's operations. Frequently, however, a company will be confronted with an opportunity to underwrite a new kind of case. If the case in question is particularly attractive, an aggressive effort may be made to close the case. The first cases of this kind that are written are frequently classified as experimental. If they prove satisfactory, the company will place more emphasis on them in the future.

c. *Products to be Marketed.* A very obvious limit on the groups to be sold may be imposed by a limited product line and an unwillingness to broaden it.

TABLE 15 : 2

GROUP LIFE INSURANCE IN FORCE BY TYPE OF GROUPS—1968

(Excluding dependent coverage, group credit life, and Federal Employees group life)

SIZE OF GROUP	Master Policies		No. of Members*	Insurance In Force		Average Amount of insurance per member
	Number	% of Total		Amount	% of Total	
1. Fewer than 25 Members	146,950	53.6%	1,403,000	$8,535,000,000	2.4%	$6,083
2. 25-99 Members	70,710	25.8	2,795,000	15,031,000,000	4.2	5,378
3. 100-499 Members	36,650	13.4	6,872,000	28,959,000,000	8.2	4,214
4. 500 or More Members	19,680	7.2	51,718,000	303,038,000,000	8.2	5,859
TOTAL	278,890	100.0%	$62,788,000	$355,563,000,000	100.0%	$5,663

* Includes duplication where individuals are included as members of more than one group.

Source: Institute of Life Insurance, "Analysis of Group Life Insurance in Force—1968", The Tally of Life Insurance Statistics, Feb., 1970. This survey excludes dependents' coverage, creditor group life, federal employees group life, reinsurance assumed, and insurance outside the United States.

4. PRESENT AND POTENTIAL SALES FORCE

The term "sales force" is defined to include group representatives, agency representatives, brokers, and consultants.

Group Representatives. If a company is to make an impact on the market place, it is essential that it furnish the sales, service, and technical functions typically provided by group representatives. The composition and extent of the group sales field force play a major part in determining an insurer's role in the market place. Also, the size of the market has a direct influence on the composition and the size of the group field organization. Most companies market their group products with both agents and brokers. It normally takes the combined efforts of the agent or broker and the group representative to successfully market group products. Usually, group representatives are housed in separate field group offices. This tends to avoid any conflict of interest which may arise in the mind of the broker when the group representative is housed within an agency location. However, some companies have housed their group representatives in agency offices and have apparently been successful with this approach.

Agency Representatives. The existence of an agency force and its attitudes toward group insurance will have a significant influence on a company's market role. If group insurance is to be marketed by a company's agents, the company must make available the kind of product that will fit its agents' markets—typically, the small employer of less than 100 lives. The sale of creditors' mortgage insurance, dependents' life insurance, high amounts of group life, and group cases such as professional and trade associations are sometimes opposed by agents who feel such business invades and restricts their market for individual insurance.

Brokers and Consultants. If an insurance company is to capitalize on large case business, it must utilize the services of brokers and consultants who dominate the market involving groups of more than 100 lives. Developing group brokers may be a natural offshoot of the existing solicitation of brokerage business in the individual and/or general insurance lines. Because brokers and consultants generally represent more sophisticated buyers, the company which solicits their business must be prepared to provide all the technical skills, services, and capabilities required in this highly competitive larger case market.

5. INTERNAL RESTRAINTS

Development of long-term objectives will be influenced and controlled by a number of internal restraints. Some of these can be modified, extended, or even temporarily overlooked, but in the long-run they cannot be ignored.

a. *Expenses.* How much money a company can allocate to the development of group sales governs such key functions as the rate of staff growth, the improvement of administrative capabilities, the quality and extent of sales promotion and advertising, and the development of new or improved products and services. A company newly entering the group market has unique problems, as it will probably be many years before the initial expenses can be recouped. The established company, therefore, may be better able to allocate funds for the development of new ideas, technique, and products.

b. *Risk Consideration.* Allied to the factor of expense limitation is the question of the degree of risk a company is willing and able to take in underwriting a new line of group products, a new coverage or a new type of business. A company may, for a limited period, knowingly underwrite business at marginal premiums in order to gain a foothold in a market. Group coverages such as Major Medical and Long-Term Disability when first introduced were often sold at rates of questionable adequacy due to competition and the lack of refined knowledge of expected claim experience.

c. *Availability of Adequately Trained Personnel.* The group business requires skilled and well-trained personnel in its sales, service, administration, and claim paying functions. The product is a complex one which is ever-changing. Its inherent flexibility demands a high degree of judgment skills in its underwriting. Its multi-coverage features and the inclusion of different employee classes and plans under one policy complicate its administration. Due to such characteristics, the recruitment and training of personnel is a time consuming process which should be fully appreciated when the company develops plans involving the growth or expansion of group sales.

d. *Influence of Agency Opinion.* Group writing companies that sell other products through the agency system often find themselves with internal conflicts related to the development of certain kinds of group coverage or expansion into new markets. The development of new products or markets through the group planning function may have to be modified in consideration of the ultimate effect upon the company's agency sales staff.

6. EXTERNAL RESTRAINTS

A realistic appraisal of limiting factors largely beyond the company's control is important. The following are sufficiently beyond the control of the individual company to merit classification as external restraints.

a. *Legal Environment.* Although some aspects of group coverage are governed by federal law, the basic body of insurance law is at the state level. While many of the group laws follow a pattern, there are considerable variations from state to state. This fact, together with the fact that many group cases, especially the large ones, are "tailor made," leads to many questions of legal interpretation. Also, there are many contacts with insurance departments concerning the legality of the forms filed and the provisions in regulations proposed by departments concerning group coverage. Two recent examples of federal enactments or rulings which provide obvious external restraints are (1) the ruling which subjected the sale of variable annuities to the jurisdiction of the Securities and Exchange Commission and (2) Section 79 of the Internal Revenue Regulations which deals with the taxation of Group Life Insurance.

b. *Existing Competition.* How well entrenched the competition is or how well saturated a given market is may be considered as possible limiting factors. The amount of future business expected and the "price" necessary to gain an entry into the market represent very practical considerations.

c. *Government as a Competitor.* Competition with the federal and the state governments is not new to the insurance industry, but in recent years an acceleration of this activity at the federal level in the form of Medicare, Title XIX plans and other liberalized Social Security benefits has occurred. Many of the new programs, however, have included a role for insurance companies either in a risk bearing capacity (Federal Employees Group Life Insurance and Health Insurance and Servicemens Group Life Insurance) or in performing an administrative function (Medicare).

The spectre of spiraling medical care costs dramatically illustrated in large rate increase requests by insurance companies, the Blue Cross organizations, and the Medicare program is intensifying the growing pressure for a National Health Insurance plan. Wide support for this idea has been given by influential Senators and Representatives as well as a volunteer "Committee of 100" comprised of prominent Americans from many fields.

The future role of government in providing security will obviously influence to a great degree the insurance company's role in the employee benefit field.

d. *Socio-economic Developments.* Our environment is a rapidly changing one. In order to have timely understanding of these changes, continuing study must be devoted to their identification and interpretation. The changes in our social and economic structure normally present great opportunities for growth and success to those companies that can anticipate and capitalize on such developments.

The Scope of Long-Term Group Department Objectives

Long-range objectives identify those organizational targets upon which strategic planning activities should be focused. In most Group Departments such long-range objectives will include realistic yet challenging goals in each of the following areas:

Production
In Force Persistency
Expenses
Underwriting
Service
Earnings or profit, for the majority of firms. (All of these objectives really boil down to maximized earnings, consistent with ethical practices).
Manpower development
Share of the Market

It is readily apparent from the foregoing that such objectives are, in most cases, interdependent. For example, good service is the keystone of persistency of inforce business, and satisfactory earnings are dependent on quality underwriting and low unit expenses.

COMMUNICATION OF OBJECTIVES

The communication of the Group Department's long-term objectives to all its personnel is essential for their understanding the "big picture," as people at all levels work better when they can relate their own activities to the purposes of the organization. The ultimate determination of the broad long-range objectives of the department must rest with the senior officer, and once established, they should be stated in written form and disseminated at all levels of activity.

Summary of Development of Long-Term Objectives

The development of long-term objectives is a very basic part of the market planning process. They provide an encompassing framework within which planning will be more purposeful. Defining these objectives in the group marketing area should not be a haphazard or superficial process. Realistic and meaningful long-range goals should be based on (1) an analysis of the market and (2) determination of the company's role in that market. The communication of objectives to all levels of activity is essential. Periodic reconsideration of the long-range goals should be an integral part of the objective formulating process. Changes in the market and in the socio-economic environment in which the sale of group products takes place do not permit inflexible objectives. From time to time, new ones must be added and some of the present ones modified or perhaps discarded altogether. The pattern of change in group products is dramatic and the marketing process ever fluid—the guidelines established for direction must recognize this.

CURRENT PLANNING AND SHORT-TERM OBJECTIVES

The terms "current" and "short-term" as used herein are defined in time as one year or less. These two functions are inseparably related and are therefore discussed under this combined heading. It must also be emphasized that short-term goals represent milestones of achievement in keeping with the longer term objectives. At any point of time, current aims will represent the necessary and desirable progression toward the longer term objectives. A brief definition of planning is "deciding in advance what is to be done; that is, a plan is a projected course of action."[1] Current planning, therefore, is deciding what must be done to meet short-term objectives. Short-term objectives in turn, are the goals of the group organization that the latter hopes to accomplish within the next year.

Communication

There is little value in establishing short-range goals unless management makes clear to all group personnel that for objectives to serve a meaningful purpose, due emphasis must and will be placed upon their attainment.

A few of the ways short-term objectives can be communicated are:

1. Periodic (weekly, monthly, quarterly, etc.) performance or production reports related to goals for the period. This "on-schedule" measurement device lends itself to a continuing process of transmitting not only the goals themselves but also the progress being made in attaining them.
2. Staff meetings are particularly appropriate in communicating short-term goals at the beginning of a measurement period, since they provide an opportunity for detailed discussion of both plans and individual roles.
3. Individual performance analyses between managers and subordinates are yet another way to stress the importance and understanding of short-range objectives. This also provides an opportunity

---

[1] William H. Newman, *Administrative Action* (3rd ed.; Englewood Cliffs, N. J.: Prentice-Hall, Inc. 1963), p. 15.

to measure performance of a prior period against the objectives. From such discussions and interviews emerges an acceptable standard of performance.

Participation in Setting Objectives

The group insurance business is highly technical and complex. It demands of those involved in its marketing activities: intelligence, continuous training, ingenuity, industry and the ability to adjust to continually changing conditions. Therefore, it is important that the person whose performance is to be judged should have an opportunity to participate in the setting of his objectives.

Higher management must, however, have the prerogative to approve or disapprove these goals, since higher management must ultimately assume the responsibility for the performance of subordinates.

Variables to Be Considered

A number of factors unique to group operations can occasion significant fluctuations in those standards of performance considered appropriate. Normally, these occurrences are beyond the control of both the group representatives and the company executives. The major ones are:

1. The significance of the *large case scale*. The existence of large components of business results in a group sales graph of peaks and valleys. Predicting which large prospects will place their business with one's company and at what time intervals is among the most challenging of prognostications A discrepancy of one or two sales can occasion final results so markedly different from the objectives that the casual observer would be inclined to dismiss the whole process as poor market planning.
2. *Labor negotiations.* Particularly in the large industrial unions, (e.g., steel and auto workers), labor negotiations play a significant part in group production. While the timing of contract negotiations is known, the latter represents a variable because the inclusion of new or increased employee benefits is often unpredictable.
3. *State of the economy.* In times of economic downturn or recession, fringe benefits are among the first items employers look at in curtailing expenditures. A reluctance to increase present employer contributions for additional group coverages can have a marked effect on final sales results.
4. *Changes in law.* Every year a number of laws are passed which were either unexpected or unpredictable in terms of their final form. For example, there are laws in force in many states which limit the amount of group life insurance that may be provided.

Agents favor such limitations but employers are feeling ever increasing pressure to provide greater benefits for their employees. Depending upon the relative strength of the opposing forces in the state legislature there may be an outright repeal, an increase in the permissible amount, or no change at all.

Other legal uncertainties arise from an inability to predict when a state legislature will pass legislation that affects the product to be sold. An example of this is the field of Group Annuities: the Variable Annuity which is based in part on common stock performance required approval by the Securities and Exchange Commission. Approval was also required in most states and the uncertainity of if, and when, individual states would pass enabling legislation and settle jurisdictional questions made market planning very difficult.

Recognition of these variables does not diminish the importance to be placed on setting objectives in the group sales planning process. It does, however, suggest more flexible and more frequent reconsideration of objectives throughout the measurement period.

SOME TYPICAL SHORT-TERM GROUP SALES OBJECTIVES

The following include most of the short-range goals of the typical group sales organization. Obviously, most of them will be expressed in numbers and will be established on the basis of the previous year's results, the market climate, and the company's long-term objectives.

1. New Premium
2. New Group Life Insurance Volume
3. Number of New Policyholders
4. Inforce Premium[2]
5. Inforce Group Life Volume[2]
   Sub-classifications under items 1–5 are normally included to reflect the results attributable to new cases or increases on existing policies and the different kinds of coverage sold (i.e., Life, Health, Annuities).
6. Lapse Rate. This may be expressed in some form of weighted index to give recognition to type, size and duration of a company's inforce.
7. Agent compensation attributable to group sales.
8. Expense rate. A rate obtained by comparing expenses to productivity is one way to improve the validity of expense measurement.
9. New coverage lines sold. The sale of new group coverages may be identified as a short-term objective for a year or two in their early marketing stages.

---

[2] There is a valid argument that inforce figures are the *result* of the attainment of other objectives and as such are not proper objectives in themselves.

238

IMPLEMENTING PLANS

The establishment of objectives defines the job to be done. The implementation of plans is the process by which activities are organized and initiated in order to attain those objectives.

The Importance of Flexibility

The ever changing nature of group products and the manner in which they are marketed makes flexibility in planning a cardinal principle. All plans, both those in operation and those being implemented, must allow for modification to reflect changing circumstances and/or to incorporate new and creative ideas. As an illustration, the group health insurance business today is at a planning crossroads. Existing products and forms of marketing need to be imaginatively updated as a viable alternative to a government sponsored national health plan. For example, pre-paid group practice plans like the Harvard Medical School Plan and the Columbia, Maryland plan have a great deal to offer. Pre-paid medical plans generally involve a medical clinic and its doctors who agree to provide certain medical services within fairly broad limits for a pre-paid monthly or annual premium for each member or family. Insurance companies can play a key role in the planning, administrative, and underwriting areas. It is likely that both present and future plans for the marketing of group health insurance will continue to undergo a metamorphosis to adjust to the role insurance companies must play if they are to continue to be the primary purveyors of group health insurance for those under age 65.

The Planning Function Process

The planning function commences with a clear understanding of the objectives and provides the means to "bridge the gap" between the current and desired standard of performance.

No decision should be made to implement a course of action without knowing the *purpose* to be served. Unfortunately, decisions are sometimes made to enter a market, or increase the share of a market, because "competition demands it" instead of because "there is a need for it and our present and potential customers will look to us to fill it."

Timing and *strategy* are important considerations in the group planning function. The continuing evolution of new group products poses some very difficult decisions on whether or not to pioneer. There are rewards for those who innovate and first venture into the relative unknown. There are also pitfalls, including potential losses which have to be made up from other profitable product lines. When is the right time—the time to gain some of the pioneering advantages but with a minimum of guesswork? The timing of increases in health rate levels, changes in agent compensation, or significant group underwriting modifications are other examples of the importance of when things are to be done.

Motivation

Group sales results are dependent on the positive action of a number of people. Some people can be controlled quite directly (home office employees); others (contract agents), having a status somewhat similar to individual entrepreneurs, are quite independent of company control. In either case, the degree of effective motivation for the implementation of the market planning process will have a far-reaching effect on the achievement of the organization's objectives.

The success of most group organizations is largely dependent on three kinds of salesmen: the group representative, the company agent, and the broker or consultant. The desire for financial income, status, and prestige are the primary factors that motivate these market specialists to achieve optimum results.

1. FINANCIAL INCOME

While the ratio of commissions to premium is lower for group than for individual coverages, the substantially higher premiums in the former offset this difference to a large degree. The form of payment is also important. On small cases, the graded scale (high first year commissions and low 9 year renewals) is often used to stimulate agency and broker interest. On the other hand, the level scale (same commission scale for each of 10 years) contributes to case persistency and rate stability and enhances the profitability of business written.

A recent trend has been to "potentialize" the high first year commission and make one large payment (75% or 80%) with an adjustment at year end to balance the actual first year commission due. This is a particularly effective incentive for agents.

Overriding compensation to agency management is essential if they are to encourage their agents and brokers to actively solicit group business.

Financial incentives beyond salary for the group representative have been adopted by most carriers. Most such compensation plans provide a significant part of the successful representative's income. Commissions and group representative compensation are frequently weighted to reflect the company's desire to sell a given product or coverage line.

Consultant fees are normally mutually agreed upon by the consultant and the policyholder, even in those situations where the insurance company makes payment.

2. STATUS AND PRESTIGE

There is a certain amount of prestige attendant to selling in the group market. This results from the demand for technical proficiency, the ability to deal with key executives and the magnitude of the typical group sale contrasted to the average individual policy sale. The group sales organization should continually recognize such factors in its communications with these salesmen.

The group representative's job is usually in itself a prestigious one. Companies often give recognition to its importance by providing first class group office quarters, financial assistance for club memberships and yearly sales conferences. Home office administrative personnel should be made to feel that, they too, are an integral part of this respected group marketing organization by frequent acknowledgment of the positive part they are playing in the sales accomplishments.

THE GROUP DEPARTMENT ORGANIZATION
IN MARKET PLANNING

No discussion of group sales market planning would be complete without some observations on the organizational form and structure within which it takes place and through which it is implemented. The most appropriate group organization will be influenced by a number of considerations.

Approach to Organizational Design

1. *Company purpose and objectives.* What the role of the group department is within the purpose and objectives of the company will certainly affect its organizational design.
2. *Organization of the company itself.* This will directly affect how the group department is structured. A very large, dominant agency department might warrant inclusion of the group sales organization as part of the agency operation. Whether or not a company is decentralized will also influence departmental functions and location.
3. *Extent of existing business.* The base of inforce will tend to govern the size of the department. From this emanates a far different organization for an established group organization in contrast to a newer department. The degree of job specialization is of course greater in the former than in the latter.

4. *The size and geographic spread of the agency force and the number of inforce cases* will substantially determine how the field group sales force is organized. Whether market plans contemplate the aggressive solicitation of brokerage business also influences the number and location of group representatives.

5. *Relationship of Group Insurance and Group Annuities.* Most companies combine the marketing of these two group products under one sales organization. However, the dissimilar characteristics of the two coverages frequently result in a distinction in terms of staff organization and responsibility and in some situations they are completely divorced. The increasing complexity of both products, and the pressures for a divergence in marketing methods, will probably result in more companies giving consideration to a departmental division of these two areas.

Determination of Department Responsibilities

How department responsibilities are allocated will depend on how well integrated are the three major functions of (1) sales and service, (2) administration, and (3) actuarial and technical services. When all three functions are separated from any comparable individual insurance activity, the specific determination of responsibility is more direct and easily accomplished. The overlapping of some areas of group activity with other departments (e.g., actuarial or claims) can reduce effectiveness because of the dual subordination which results. The integration of responsibilities is typical of group marketing because of the rapid evolution of products, services and marketing methods and the complex changes which naturally emerge.

Staffing

Management should arrange for the staffing of the group sales department only after it has established the department's organizational design. The following should be considered by management to assure proper staffing of the group sales department.

1. *Recruitment.* A newly formed group sales organization will probably find it necessary to go outside the company and recruit people with group experience for both field and home office jobs. An existing group department will normally have the depth which permits the integration of inexperienced personnel without eroding its effectiveness.

2. *Training.* The amount and form of specialized training will also tend to vary with the scope and maturity of the group organization. The dynamic changes characteristic of the group business do make one

thing quite clear—continuing education and training are essential to the success of both the individual and the organization.

3. *Placement.* The importance of integrated activity previously mentioned emphasizes the procedural principle of placing people in the right job.

Major Group Department Areas and Their Roles

The following chart shows the major operational areas of a group sales organization and lists their respective roles.

GROUP ORGANIZATION

Sales and Service	Administration	Actuarial and Technical Services
1. Forward planning and objectives.	1. Forward planning and objectives.	1. Forward planning and objectives.
2. Supervision of group field staff.	2. New and renewal case underwriting.	2. Premium rate determination.
3. Supervision of policyholder service.	3. Policy issue and amendment.	3. Dividend or experience refund procedures.
4. Account case relations.	4. Premium accounting.	4. Valuation and annual statement preparation.
5. Specialized broker and consultant relations.	5. Commission accounting.	5. Contract development and filing.
6. Agency relations.	6. Dividend or experience refund calculations.	6. New and renewal case underwriting.
*7. Advertising and sales promotion.	*7. Claim administrations.	7. Product development.
8. Product development.	8. Methods and system procedures.	
	9. Product development.	

* Frequently these functions may be assigned to a separate department as part of a company-wide function.

SOURCE: Eilers, Robert D., and Crowe, Robert M., *Group Insurance Handbook*, Richard D. Irwin, Inc., Homewood, Illinois, 1965, p. 514.

This particular structure is fully integrated with no major functions assigned to non-group areas.

Supportive Areas

The expansive and changing nature of group sales requires close and expert support from a number of departments whose functions are usually company-wide.

1. MAJOR AREAS OF SUPPORT

a. *Claims.* This is the single most important supportive area, which is sometimes integrated into the group operation itself. Claim specialists have a favorable insight into policyholder needs and a good feel for coverage effectiveness. Close liaison with claim personnel improves overall policyholder service, aids product design, improves the quality of underwriting, and frequently assists in securing new business.

b. *Law.* The extent of state regulation and the increasing impact of Federal legislation require close liaison between the group department and company counsel. Changing times bring changing laws and changing interpretations of existing laws. The company's counsel should keep in close touch with this situation so that he can render effective advice and service to the group department. Of course this has a very significant impact on the sales planning process.

c. *Advertising and Sales Promotion.* In most situations these functions are more closely involved in the promotion of individual coverage lines due to the differences of the group sales process. Activity in the group area is normally centered around sales pieces (brochures, mail-outs, etc.) and proposal design. Very little in the way of media advertising is usually done.

2. OTHER AREAS OF SUPPORT

a. *Individual Underwriting.* The process of some individual applications for coverage (e.g., late entrants) requires the submission of acceptable medical evidence, which is often referred to the individual underwriting department because of its greater skill and experience in appraising such risks.

b. *Planning.* Many companies have established separate planning units in order to coordinate the planning activity of all the company's departments.

c. *Financial.* In the group annuity business the help of financial specialists and economists can be invaluable in projecting interest rates; administering variable unit contracts, etc.

EVALUATION AS PART OF THE PLANNING PROCESS

Group sales market planning is not simply a schedule of activities—it is a style of supervision, a state of mind. Because it involves the future effect of present decisions, regular evaluation of results, in relation to the plans which produced them, is essential.

Periodic Reconsideration of Objectives

Because objectives are so vital to future performance and results (both short-term and long-range), they must be continually re-examined in the light of three broad influences.

1. *Changing environmental conditions.* The group business exists in its present form as the result of adjusting to the changing environment over the past 50 years. The inclusion of group benefits in labor contracts, enactment of the changes in the Social Security Act, Federal Government imposition of wage freezes during World War II and the Korean war, and a general trend of rising costs since the Depression are examples of environmental changes which have shaped group marketing.
2. *Changing internal conditions.* Changes occur from time to time within the broad realm of the company, or even within the group department, which require re-examination of present goals. Increasing company expenses or reduced profits may require significant operational changes in order to reverse such trends.
3. *Changes in company policy.* Significant directional trends, such as the extension of mass marketing concepts, will prompt re-evaluation of current company policy. The principles of the company as expressed in its policy must be reflected in the group sales operations. It follows that when such policy changes, group department objectives must be re-examined.

Measuring Results in the Light of Objectives

A fundamental purpose of establishing objectives is the standard of measurement they represent. The measurement process should be continuous during the entire period(s) in question. Short-range objectives are, by their very nature, more easily evaluated than are the less specific long range goals. As previously discussed, the nature of the group business is such that conditions affecting performance can change materially after initial objectives are set. Not all of these situations will lend themselves to a timely reconsideration process as described under the preceding heading. However, where valid, these aberrations should be noted.

Tools for Analyzing Results

Measuring and analyzing results are done through a variety of systems, reports or procedures grouped here under the heading of "tools." A broad classification of analytical tools is (1) personal observation (including interviews), (2) computerized systems, and (3) written reports. Each of these affords a different insight into results attained.

1. *Personal observation.* In many areas there is simply no acceptable substitute for evaluating results by direct observation and personal contact. Key people in the group management organization need to know how products, procedures, and service are accepted by policyholders, agents, brokers, and consultants. A different, more expansive personal view of sales results will develop a better understanding than the most exhaustive written reports. As an internal home office device, direct contact with subordinate areas of the group operation can assist management in understanding how administrative changes might help the group operation achieve its goals.

2. *Computerized systems.* The capabilities of electronic data processing equipment provide group sales management a tremendous array of measurement tools. Detailed production results, analyses of the kinds of business being sold, earnings reports, expense analyses, and claim studies are but a few of the capabilities computers offer.

3. *Written reports.* Members of the group management team may find written reports to be an excellent device for analyzing results. Statistical results will frequently require amplification or interpretation in order to become meaningful information.

Modification of Plans in the Light of Results Obtained

The essence of proper planning is the ability to adjust plans at any time to fit changing circumstances. Newman has defined the necessary corrective action in changing plans as some combination of the following steps:

    a. Adjust physical and external situations.
    b. Review the direction, training and selection of subordinates.
    c. Improve motivation.
    d. Modify plans where necessary.[3]

Physical and external situations would include such things as the number and location of group sales offices. The review of direction, training and selection of subordinates is self-explanatory. Improvement of motivation should concern itself with not only group department personnel but also with brokers and consultants who are so vital to group sales results. The modification of plans would evolve as a broader response which would include the three previous steps if appropriate.

Irrespective of the kind of plan changes contemplated, consideration

---

[3] William H. Newman, *Administrative Action* (3rd ed.; Englewood Cliffs, N. J.: Prentice-Hall, Inc. 1963), p. 437.

must be given to the time lag between inauguration of the activity and its effect on results.

Summary and Conclusion

Market planning for Group Sales involves the development of long-term objectives and the organization of the Group Department to attain maximum results. Short-term objectives should be part of the current planning that leads to the actual implementation of plans. The importance of flexibility in the whole planning process cannot be overemphasized. Continuing evaluation must be part of the overall planning process.

Market planning in the group area should not be viewed as an end in itself, but rather as a vehicle for getting the total job done.

16

Sales Planning for
the Life Insurance Agency*

Wm. Eugene Hays

PLANNING—THE BASIS FOR ORDERLY PROGRESS

As with any human endeavor the success of a life insurance agency depends, in large part, on a sound plan. Agency sales planning is the process of designing a course of action for the accomplishment of definite sales objectives. The first step in the planning process is the setting of reasonable and clearly defined objectives. Beyond this it is necessary to assign priorities among various activities necessary to implement these objectives, and to establish appropriate long range and short range plans. Agency sales planning also includes the development of a series of planned activities through which plans can be better effectuated and orderly progress can be made toward the achievement of objectives. In addition to this, the time period for long range plans and the annual nature of short range plans provide a schedule for reaching sales objectives.

It is virtually impossible to successfully manage an agency without a plan. This serves as a road map for the entire agency force. The agency manager, the life underwriters on the agency sales force, agency staff personnel who advise and service the manager and sales force, and the clerical staff all need an agency plan to guide them in their daily activities and to serve as a standard by which performance can be measured.

DEVELOPMENT OF AGENCY OBJECTIVES

Planning—A Team Project

Planning is a team project. The members of the team are the manager or general agent and the agency department of his company. The extent to which each participates in the planning process varies among companies. In some companies most of the planning is done by the home office. Agency managers are furnished a complete blueprint of company expectations, which provides each agency manager with considerable assistance in developing his sales planning. At the other end of the spectrum are companies that delegate a substantial part of the responsibility for planning to their individual agency managers. Company policy on the centralization of sales operations will usually govern the extent to which it participates in agency planning.

Ideally, any agency plan of operation should be formulated by both members of the planning team (company and agency) working in close cooperation with each other. Agency departments usually have a wide range of technical competence and experience in this area, and possess market information not generally available to an agency manager. A few companies are beginning to use computers to aid in the development of sales plans. However, the whole task of sales planning cannot be effectively done at the home office. Since agency managers are responsible for the execution of agency plans, they must play a primary role in establishing the agency objectives and selecting the sales and manpower development activities required to achieve those objectives. In addition, the manager, if he has been assigned for several years to the territory for which he is currently responsible, and especially if he has been a member of the agency he heads, should have a better understanding of the local markets and the capabilities of his agents than the agency department does. This article will refer to the planner as "the manager" simply to avoid confusion and repetition, with the full understanding that he seldom has the sole responsibility for the sales planning function.

Qualitative and Quantitative Objectives

When considering agency objectives, most managers think in terms of volume of sales, millions of insurance in force, number of new agents to be hired, and other quantitative goals. The student of management, however, understands that the attainment of qualitative objectives most always carries with it the desired sales and manpower results.

A number of successful business leaders establish qualitative objectives for their companies. At a recent annual meeting, the president of a giant corporation reviewed the five objectives which its management had established. They were:

> 1. We would like to be looked upon as a respectable company among American corporations. To earn this sobriquet, we must earn at least 11% on our stockholders' investment.
> 2. We would like to be a growth company. To qualify for this characterization, we believe our sales and earnings should increase every year by not less than 10%.
> 3. We want this company to be a stable company. Our earnings mix should be from enough sources so that the setbacks from one geographic production area or from one product line will not be seriously damaging to our earnings progress.
> 4. We want this company to be a progressive company. Our people policies—that is the body of practices that deal with personnel, labor and industrial relations, management development, and compensation—should be up to date and progressive.
> 5. We want this company to be an intelligently diversified company. However, in our opinion, the diversification that we should engage in should be a rationale and not a hodgepodge. It should be easily understood by company executives, by our employees, by our stockholders, and by the investment world outside. It should make sense.

The time schedule for the realization of the above objectives, as expressed by this business leader, covered a period of several years. Of the given objectives, the last three are plainly qualitative, but their attainment would inevitably result in the production of profits.

In establishing his objectives, the life insurance agency manager also must give thought to those qualitative objectives that would lead to the attainment of his quantitative goals.

The qualitative objectives of an agency manager might include such matters as the goal of being recognized in his territory as the best equipped agency for the advanced uses of life insurance in estate planning, employee benefits, and the funding of business requirements. To have adequate representation in every segment of his community; to have the greatest ratio of C.L.U.s to sales personnel of any agency in the territory; to earn the reputation for having the most effective training program of any agency in the community; and to be known by the excellence of its service to policyowners are additional examples of qualitative agency objectives. It is clear that the attainment of these objectives will be accompanied by an improvement in the volume of sales.

Quantitative objectives generally refer to desired sales or manpower results in numerical terms. To double the number of agents, to increase sales volume forty percent within the next year, or to increase insurance in force twenty percent are all appropriate examples. To avoid disappointment and frustration in setting and reaching quantitative objectives, this type of goal should be broken into segments and each sub-division assigned a target date for attainment. For example, a manager who has a sales staff of twenty agents decides that he must have a total of forty agents to realize his territorial sales potential. It is obvious that to double his organization will take time. He should, therefore, estimate his growth capacity for each year and then establish annual net manpower quotas, until he reaches his objective. The same process can be followed for new sales, insurance in force, and other quantitative objectives.

THE NEED FOR PRIORITIES IN THE IMPLEMENTATION OF OBJECTIVES

Few managers have a set of reasonable objectives and a well-formulated plan of action when they are first appointed to head an agency. An evolutionary process usually takes place, with a good many false starts and much wasted effort before the manager settles down to a workable plan of action that puts him on the road toward the attainment of his goals. Much of this confusion is caused by an absence of priorities assigned with care and intelligence to the activities that are necessary to implement his initial plans.

For example, a manager is told that to progress, the agency must have more manpower. This may be true but, most likely, there are other activities that should have higher, more immediate priority than recruiting. A study of the experienced agents might disclose a great need for improving their productivity and their morale. Until this is accomplished, it could be a waste of effort to bring new, inexperienced men into an agency environment that might retard their progress. There might not be a well-defined new agent training program in effect in the agency. Again, bringing new men into the business without a well formulated training program could be a waste of time and manpower. Unless priorities are assigned, a manager might also be tempted to recruit and train men in cities separated from agency headquarters by many miles when space and training facilities are readily available in the agency's city.

These few examples reflect how doing the right things in the wrong sequence can retard sound progress. They also emphasize the necessity for the assignment of priorities based on the particular circumstances surrounding the agency, the territory, the supervisory staff, and all the other factors in the agency picture.

MAJOR FACTORS THAT REGULATE AGENCY PLANNING AND GROWTH

It is an oversimplification to assume that to reach production and other objectives, the manager must just recruit a sufficient number of new agents who, at an assumed rate, will provide the desired volume of sales and other results. This is not to say that recruiting is not vital to an agency's activity. However, as an agency manager plans for growth, he must give attention to all the factors that regulate the establishment of agency objectives.

The major factors that regulate agency planning and growth are: (1) Company policy as it relates to manpower development, (2) Company and agency image in the community, (3) Composition of product mix, (4) Manager's technical competence, (5) Capability of training and supervisory staff, (6) Territorial characteristics, and (7) Financial resources available for expansion.

Company Policy as it Relates to Manpower Development

Life insurance companies provide agency managers with statements of policies related to agency operations. This, of course, includes policies covering sales planning activities. However, every company policy is not always clearly defined. A manager must often look to company custom and tradition, examine speeches made by company officers and review discussions he has had with members of his agency department to learn company policy in certain areas of his operation. Company policy on new manpower development is sometimes a good example of this type of situation.

In these days of manpower shortages, there is seldom any question about the need for new manpower in any company. The extent of company participation in new agent financing often indicates the degree of its determination to add field manpower. This also usually governs company standards for selection of prospective agents submitted by managers for contract approval. No company will logically participate extensively in agent financing unless it has assurances that the investment is reasonably safe and has good possibilities of becoming profitable. A manager's standards of selection should be at least as high as those of his company. He should carefully examine the selection standards of his company to avoid wasting efforts in recruiting men that the home office will not accept.

Company and Agency Image in the Community

It is axiomatic that the more favorable the company and agency are regarded in a community, the higher the quality of the agents who are attracted to the agency. Research shows that a large majority of new agents recruited have been referred to the particular agency by its agents or centers of influence who have a favorable impression of the company, the agency, or both. Many men who are considering life insurance selling as a career seek the advice of those whose opinions they respect. Often they are advised to interview with more than one agency. Their advisor, who has their interests at heart, usually names one or more companies or agencies which he believes to be superior. Company and agency image does influence the quality of recruits, and a manager should give careful attention to this factor.

Composition of Product Mix

The range of policies and, to a degree, the competitive position of a company are related to the type of recruit that a manager should seek. For example, some companies have well developed facilities for the sale and servicing of employee benefit plans, including pension trusts. This would seem to indicate that mature men with a broad background of business experience located in urban centers could successfully be attracted to an agency of such a company. Other companies do not issue health policies, or are not equipped to offer group contracts. Factors such as this most certainly must be considered by an agency manager in his recruiting, and total sales planning.

The Manager's Technical Competence

A manager must critically appraise his own performance and capabilities in order to adjust his recruiting level to his technical capacity to manage. If his sales experience is centered around personal programming, he should initially attempt to hire men who will most likely succeed in this phase of selling. The same care should be taken with regard to such things as age. An older maanger is not always atuned with the concepts of younger men. Conversely, a young manager with limited selling experience may have difficulty gaining the respect of a new agent who is several years his senior and who has a broad business background.

This is not to say that an agency should be static. An agency manager should strive to attain a sales force that is dynamic. Generally, as young managers grow in managerial and technical competence, they will gradually attract and successfully induct new agents whose capabilities and personal situations cover a wide range.

Capability of Training and Supervisory Staff

A careful appraisal of the capacities of the training and supervisory staff is a necessary planning function. The strengths and limitations of these staffs are determining factors in manpower growth.

There is a tendency in life insurance to recruit a larger number of new agents than the training staff can handle adequately. While there is no general agreement as to the limitations of the span of control, it obviously is wasteful to neglect the close supervision of an agent who is partially trained and only a few man-hours of supervision short of becoming self-sustaining, in order to use the time to train a new recruit. It is also important to assign new agents to trainers and supervisors in an organized manner. The technical competence of these assistants should be matched with the capabilities and interests of the agents assigned to them.

Territorial Characteristics

It is obvious that the characteristics of the territory should be a major factor in agency sales planning. The development plans of an agency in Vermont must differ in many ways from those of an agency in New York City. The concentration of buying power within communities in the territory is also a consideration when deciding the number of agents to appoint in a given area.

Distance from agency headquarters should influence the priorities assigned for the development of various areas. It usually is more profitable to first develop the communities closest to the agency city, and thereafter to radiate gradually outward to the more distant cities and towns.

Financial Resources Available for Expansion

Financial resources available for manpower development will, of course, influence agency growth. Practices differ among companies regarding the amount of new agent financing the home office will underwrite and the amount that must be provided by the manager himself. If the company furnishes none of the capital, the manager's development plans are likely to be more modest unless he has considerable personal resources. The same principle applies to the availability of capital for supervisory staff expansion.

There are many other factors that affect agency planning and growth. However, these seven are considered to be the major factors an agency manager must consider in establishing agency objectives. Consequently, they are of great importance in agency sales planning.

LONG RANGE SALES PLANNING FOR THE AGENCY

With clearly defined agency objectives established and with each assigned a priority, long range planning becomes the next logical step.

In our existing system for the distribution and servicing of life insurance, the individual agent is the unit of production. There are very few agencies that concentrate their entire efforts on the general insurance broker with most or all of their sales volume coming from this source. For these few agencies, the insurance broker is the unit of production. For the purposes of this discussion, however, we will devote attention to the sales organizations that are composed of full-time agents who spend all or most of their time in the sale and servicing of contracts issued by their companies.

With the agent as the production unit, all planning revolves around him, his welfare, and the development of his skills as a life underwriter. The expansion of agency sales will occur only by improving the capacity of existing sales personnel and/or the adding of new, well trained, and supervised agents.

Planning Tools

An agency manager needs a sound understanding of the principles of management which cover planning, organizing, leading, and measuring and controlling. An agency planner must also be in possession of certain facts about the agency to assist him in his planning.

If a manager has been appointed to head an established agency, the improvement of the sales effectiveness and morale of experienced agents will probably be objectives of high priority. If a manager has been appointed from within the agency, his former position as a co-worker with those he is now to lead undergoes considerable change. He has a new role to play. What once was a casual acquaintanceship now becomes a more vital relationship. He must know more intimately the attitudes and skills of each of the agents, in order to determine what, if any, corrective procedure to apply. The agents' relationships to the new manager also undergo a change. They must be shown by word and deed that the new manager has the ability and the desire to help each man improve his sales effectiveness and earning power.

Thus it is vital for a new manager to become fully acquainted with the agency and its environment. In order to attain success he must become intimately acquainted with each agent and his sales record. A new agency manager must also be familiar with the sales potential of the agency. Two important planning tools, therefore, are a complete analysis of all experienced sales personnel and an agency market analysis.

Analysis of Experienced Sales Personnel

A complete analysis of each experienced man in the agency should be made in some detail and put into writing for future reference and comparison. There are two general divisions of such analysis: The first part may be obtained from the agency and company records. The second, and perhaps more important part of the analysis, generally requires a personal interview with every agent, and also a self-analysis by each agent.

The analysis of each agent should include the following facts, and these probably can be obtained from existing records:

1. Age and marital status
2. Sales production results over the past five years
3. Quality of sales and trend in quality for the past five years, average size sale, average premium per thousand, frequency of premium collection and persistency of business.
4. Type of market in which he is operating as represented by the occupation and financial condition of his most important policyholders.

Additional information necessary for a complete analysis of each agent might be available in the files. In many instances, however, it can only be obtained from a personal interview with every man and a subjective analysis by each agent of his own performance. The added information needed includes the following:

1. Types of markets in which he has sold most successfully.[1]

---

[1] For example, are his sales concentrated in the professional market or is he most successful in sales for business uses or employee benefit plans? If he has no clearly-defined markets, this should be an important piece of information to the manager. If it is possible to obtain, a self-analysis of his market by each agent would be of great value. This should be accompanied by a list of recent sales, including the source of his prospects and their occupations. Is he satisfied that he is getting the maximum results in the markets in which he is operating? Does he have the background knowledge and temperament to sell in the markets he would like to reach? These are intangible factors and often are not recognized by the individual unless an intelligent analysis is made of sales results versus work input.

The following is an actual example of how a manager can misinterpret marketing activities and results of an agent unless a careful analysis of the facts accompanies his observation. An agent with ten years of better than average experience sincerely considered himself a specialist in the business insurance field, and so informed his new manager. His early experience had been with doctors in hospitals. An analysis of his performance for the past year disclosed that even though eighty-five percent of his time had been spent in soliciting business insurance, eighty percent of his sales had been repeat business from the medical policyholders and their referrals. This information gave the manager a factual basis for counseling with the agent.

2. Agent's personal characteristics
   (a) physical condition
   (b) work habits
   (c) aspiration level—what does he want for himself and his family?
   (d) attitudes toward the service that life insurance performs. It is also valuable to learn his wife's attitudes towards her husband's business, if this can be ascertained.
3. The agent's financial condition and sources of income from other than life insurance sales.

The interviews with the agents would be more meaningful if each would furnish a self-analysis prior to the discussion. The results of this interviewing process, which is time-consuming if properly done, provide a sound basis for long range planning, in that it gives a measurement of the production potential of existing sales personnel. A second important result is that this process provides the planner with a basis for his program of training and development. The end-result of this survey will probably be a decision to terminate the contracts of those who do not have the present capacity or the potential to become productive members of a successful agency team.

Market Analysis

A realistic evaluation of the potential sales for his territory is a vital sales tool for the planner. Many companies furnish their managers with a market analysis. These generally consist of a traditional study of family units, buying power, income levels, home and automobile ownership, and other data from which market potential may be determined. There is marked variance between the *market potential* of a given territory and the *sales potential* of an agency operating within that territory. Market potential is the expected total level of life insurance sales in a given territory during a specified period of time. The sales potential of an agency is measured by reference to such factors as: (1) the quantity and quality of the agency's sales personnel, (2) the degree of coverage of major markets within the territory, (3) the training capacity of the agency, (4) the leadership ability of the agency's management, and (5) the number and composition of the policyholders of the agency. All of these indications of sales potential are just as important to the agency in its sales planning as the measurement of the potential buying power of the marketing area.

Market potential emphasizes the amount of effective demand for life insurance in a territory during a definite period of time. Sales potential emphasizes the share of that market potential that an agency can realistically gain. It is based on the capacity of an agency to take advantage of the existing market potential.

SECONDARY SOURCES OF MARKET DATA

It has been stressed that agency managers have a major responsibility for sales planning. Accordingly, an agency manager must gather appropriate external data if he is to appraise his market potential intelligently. Fortunately, there are sufficient, up-to-date data available to him. This secondary data may be obtained from a number of sources. The local chambers of commerce usually provide such data for their members, Sales Management magazine's annual "Survey of Buying Power" is an accurate breakdown of consumer spending units by county and city, and the Federal Reserve's "Survey of Consumer Finances" is useful to the planner.

PERSONAL MARKET SURVEY

No survey of market potential is complete without a personal investigation and appraisal by the manager. He must understand that markets are of no value to him unless he has men who can successfully work in those markets or unless he can recruit men who will tap those markets for sales. This premise of marketing depends on a concept that is growing in its application by life insurance management. This concept has evolved from the observation that successful agents tend to concentrate their prospecting within homogeneous groups that have common occupations, ethnic backgrounds, educational experiences, or a strong community of interest. Agents find that it is easier to establish a favorable reputation within these groups. Also, prospects are referred more readily, and the agents' contact is stronger when there is a common bond between the client and prospect.

In some instances an agent can base his entire sales efforts on one large "market group." Other agents develop a satisfactory clientele in two or more such homogeneous groups. When using this approach to conduct a market survey, the manager must identify the major professional groups, industrial and commercial corporations, alumni associations of major universities, ethnical groupings, and other areas in which there is a strong community of interest. He must determine which of these markets his agents are now adequately reaching, and which are not being solicited but have representation within the agency's policyholder body. If the latter situation exists, he must then appraise his existing sales personnel to determine if any can be pointed toward these markets. If there is no possible coverage within the agency, the manager must make a part of his planning the acquisition of one or more new men to develop these markets. There is no substitute for this type of personalized market appraisal.

The Need for Flexibility in Long Range Planning

The very term "long range planning" connotes a plan of activity that will take several years to mature. It obviously is impractical to believe that every piece of the plan will fall into place exactly as it was originally envisioned. There are many circumstances that might dictate an adjustment in the plan or that might cause a change in the assigned priorities. The manager must recognize this fact and provide for flexibility in his long range plan. More important, he must be flexible in adjusting his plan to meet changing conditions.

SHORT RANGE PLANNING

Short range planning should be done within the framework of long range agency plans. Objectives that were broadly expressed as long range plans are more specifically stated and are assigned target dates for their achievement in short range plans. The manager usually does his short range planning around the year-end. This is the time to appraise the agency sales results in relation to its sales potential; time to take stock of agency strengths and weaknesses; and time to again lay short range plans for the improvement of agency performance in the forthcoming year.

Establishing Quotas

Inasmuch as the agent is the production unit whose aggregate output constitutes agency sales, he is central to short range planning, as well as long range planning. The principal purpose of an agency's existence is sales. Thus in planning, the greatest emphasis should be placed on the agents and on sales.

It is customary for an agency to have an annual sales quota. This is generally established by the agency department of the company in cooperation with the agency manager. In establishing a sales quota, many factors are considered, including economic conditions, market potential, established manpower, new manpower to be recruited during the year, and other circumstances that have an influence on the agency's sales potential. In addition to an agency sales quota, every agent has a sales quota set. The sum of these individual quotas is equal to the total agency quota.

Use of Personal Interviews in Setting Quotas

Ideally the setting of a quota for an agency begins with the establishment of individual quotas for the agents. This provides an occasion for a contructive conference between each agent and his manager or supervisor. All agents should be requested to prepare for the conference by compiling a record of their sales for the current year and their sources, in advance of the interview. This interview should be scheduled with plenty of uninterrupted time to allow a complete planning job to be done. If quotas are established in this manner, they are most likely to be realistic and to form the foundation for subsequent progress interviews between the agents and the manager throughout the year. This is a necessary supervisory function that is of value to both the agents and the agency manager.

Use of Plan Books in Setting Quotas

Another method of setting quotas is through the use of "Plan Books." Generally, at the close of business in December, each agent is supplied with a Plan Book together with instructions for its use. The completed Plan Books and signed accompanying quota cards are returned to the manager by the first week in the new year. These Plan Books are so arranged that each agent will review his performance for the year just past, establish a finincial budget based on his family needs, and project his expected renewal and deferred commission income for the new year. The budget deficit that is inevitable must then be met by commissions from new sales. By applying his average commission per sales unit to this deficit, the agent arrives at the number of new sales units needed to balance his budget. If an agent has ambitions beyond his basic needs, he adds enough additional sales units to his quota to permit him to achieve his idealized financial objectives.

These are the steps which the agent takes, theoretically, in arriving at his quota unassisted. However, agents, being salesmen, are typically deficient in their planning. Usually only a few do an adequate planning job without the aid of the agency manager.

After these individual quotas have been satisfactorily completed, the agency manager develops an agency sales quota for the ensuing year. He must consider the quotas of the agents and all other pertinent factors in setting the agency sales quota.

This is a less desirable method for setting sales quotas because its programmed nature does not encourage agents to realistically consider their situation and potential, and voluntarily make a personal commitment for improvement. The fact that this method does not specifically provide for an interview of each agent with the manager is another shortcoming. Only a naive manager would total his agents' quotas and take this total as his agency quota. At the very least, staff supervisors should participate personally with each agent in establishing the quotas. Agents who are allowed to develop their own sales quotas may be overly optimistic and take quotas well beyond reasonable expectation of their accomplishment. In other words, they set quotas which they hope to reach and which often do not correlate with reality. Others may underestimate their needs, abilities, and sales potential, and set quotas below reasonable and realistic levels.

Use of Forecasts in Setting Quotas

The development of an agency sales forecast is a more logical approach to setting agency quotas than the Plan Book method. Under this technique the agency manager and his assistants first assemble all the facts concerning each agent. These would include:

1. Sales performance for the year just past, stated in terms of cases sold, average premium and other quantitative measuring rods
2. Markets reached and degree of penetration
3. Age and condition of health
4. Growth potential for the short term
5. Special needs such as new car, private school and other personal matters
6. Response to motivation, or the manager's ability to motivate the agent this year

Armed with this information, the manager is then able to forecast, with some degree of accuracy, the probable sales production of his established agents. He will need to discount the totals, thus reached, for possible agent terminations during the year. This is a more realistic method for establishing sales quotas because the personal situation of every agent is fully considered, as well as the current level of accomplishment and potential for growth of each agent.

New Manpower Quota

In addition to individual agent sales quotas and an overall agency sales quota, it is also necessary to establish a realistic objective for new agent appointments for the coming year. If the manager has developed sound long range planning, he will have certain priorities established for the development of new areas within his territory. He must consider these in relation to the capacity of his supervisory staff, and the extent to which they are loaded with trainees who are not yet self-sufficient. Moreover, a manager may have to appoint and train a new supervisor before he feels safe in hiring the planned number of new agents. If this is the case, it will, necessarily, limit the new agents to be hired while the supervisor is in training.

At agency headquarters there is another factor that would tend to limit the number of agents to be hired. This is the availability of office space.

An agency office is often tight on office space because an unoccupied desk is a non-productive expense. A manager usually has only one or two unoccupied desks at any one time. Thus in the process of planning his appointments for the coming year an agency manager must consider this factor. In order to have private space for the new recruits that the manager has determined he must have, he is sometimes forced to reach a final decision to terminate one or more of the agents who have not satisfactorily contributed to the success of the agency.

Estimate of Sales from New Manpower and Other Additional Sources

After deciding how many new agents he plans to appoint, the manager must then estimate the volume of sales he will receive from them. Inasmuch as these new agents are to be appointed throughout the year, it is well to estimate that the group will be in production an average of six months.[2] The forecast of sales expected from new agents is made in accordance with this formula. Having arrived at the expected production from established agents and also from expected new agents, the manager now has the forecast for his full-time organization.

If the manager is a personal producer, his own estimated sales should be added. If he accepts brokerage business, he must estimate as carefully as possible the volume of sales from this source. Since brokerage production is usually erratic, it is well to be conservative in estimating brokerage business. Finally, there is usually a small volume of production to be expected from miscellaneous sources, such as superannuated agents who are not considered full-time members of the office staff.

The addition of expected sales from all of these carefully considered sources should result in a realistic sales quota.

THE BUDGET AS A PLANNING TOOL

The manager who is obliged to prepare his own income and expense budget has an excellent additional planning tool available. Forecasting income to be derived from the sale of new business, when this revenue must form a substantial part of the cash flow for the payment of operating overhead, permits little wishful thinking. Estimates of the performance of established agents and the projection of sales for newly-acquired agents

---

[2] An alternate method is to decide in which months throughout the entire year the manager will get his recruits (to keep him recruiting constantly) and then the manager determines a monthly production quota for each new recruit. The approach may be used but it should be recognized that it has shortcomings with respect to the accuracy of predicting.

must be starkly realistic, if the manager expects to balance his budget and make a reasonable profit.

It is likely that the agency manager will tend toward conservatism in his estimates of new sales when he is preparing his budget estimates of expected agency income. Ideally the manager should go through the process of arriving at a quota twice: first, he should prepare a forecast of the expected sales from all sources and, secondly, for budgeting purposes he should prepare a "rock bottom" estimate of what each production unit will deliver. The latter will inevitably be more conservative than the former. Then he should take the two forecasts that have been independently established and adjust where, in his judgment, he might be in error.

The manager whose home office sets the agency budget does not have the advantage of this planning tool. However, this can be a useful aid for short range planning for a general agent whose very survival depends on sound financial operation. Even the branch manager who has no responsibility for budget making would be well advised to go through the process. He should recognize that his agency must be a profitable operation for the company if it is to continue in existence.

PLANS FOR AGENCY ACTIVITIES

The process of short range planning also encompasses the many qualitative adjustments necessary to achieve quantitative goals. It is impossible to arrive at a sound sales quota without taking a thoughtful look at the various components of the production machine. The most logical time to institute corrective measures and to adopt new projects is at the beginning of the calendar year. At such time then, an agency manager should plan his sales and office staff changes, and review the sales facilities of the agency.

Planning Sales and Office Staff Changes

The most vital production component is the sales management staff. Each supervisor's performance should be reviewed, his strengths and weaknesses analyzed. If he is to be retained, plans for the improvement of his performance should be made. This usually takes place as a part of the manager's interview with the supervisor when the agents under his supervision are appraised. Any corrective procedures and plans for improvement must have the enthusiastic endorsement of the supervisor before they are adopted. He must also be an active participant in any decision affecting the agents under his supervision.

In this year-end planning process, the manager should appraise the supervisor's capacity to absorb new trainees. If he does have the ability to supervise one or more new men, a commitment should be made, and an approximate target date for their induction should be set. It is the author's concept that the recruitment of new agents is a team project and each individual supervisor should not be perfunctorily allotted a specific number of recruits to bring into the agency. The concept of recruiting as a team effort involves a balanced judgment on the part of the agency manager regarding the values of the contributions made by his various supervisors. Some men are natural recruiters, others are more effective as trainers. If the recruiting function is considered to be a team effort, a new recruit will be assigned to a supervisor who has the time to train him adequately, and this may not be the supervisor who introduced him to the agency. The recruiting supervisor may already be overloaded with trainees, and therefore, will not be able to do an adequate job of effective training. Moreover, when a supervisor spends too much time recruiting he does not have sufficient time to perform the crucial function of bringing the current trainees into successful, self-sustaining production. The record of agencies that overemphasize recruiting will disclose an abnormal new agents' failure ratio with a resulting necessity to recruit replacements for the agents who have failed.

Occasionally a supervisor just isn't equipped to do the job required of him. The year-end review of his agents' individual performances provides the basis for a frank discussion of his aptitudes and the logical time to suggest that he return to personal production.

The need for appointing or acquiring additional supervisory staff will often be suggested as a result of the year-end planning process. An added supervisor may be required at agency headquarters if the objective is to appoint several new agents and the existing training supervisors are already operating at capacity. A part of the short range plan, then, will be the appointment of this new staff member and his training in preparation for the assignment of a complement of new agents to his unit. Usually, it is best that the newly appointed supervisor have only one or two trainees at first. A new supervisor must be given sufficient time to learn the job. He should not be overwhelmed with a large number of new agents for whom he is responsible.

If a high priority objective of the agency is the development of a sales organization in a section of the territory not now adequately covered, the manager is faced with a decision of how to meet the supervisory staff requirements at the new location. When the undeveloped section of the territory is a community with a large potential market and the community is some distance from the agency's headquarters, the manager should find a supervisor to place in charge of the new office before he begins to recruit for it. As previously stated, an agency manager would be well advised to build his sales organization outward from his agency city, considering his headquarters as a hub and saving peripheral areas for later development. In this automobile age, initial training is more effectively done in agency headquarters. The supervisor can then conduct field training in the trainee's community.

The year-end planning session is also the logical time to review the efficiency of the office staff and to consider changes or additions that may be necessary. This is an important segment of an agency. Agents and manager need the supporting efforts of an efficient staff in order to run a successful agency.

A Review of Agency's Sales Facilities

Other qualitative components of the agency's productive process should be examined thoroughly. These other qualitative components include the following: (1) New agent training program, (2) Continued training for established agents, (3) Agency sales meetings, (4) Sales Contests, (5) Morale-building activities, (6) Special agency services, (7) Agency public relations programs, (8) Agency advertising, and (9) Seminars for centers of influence.

NEW AGENT TRAINING PROGRAM

The manager should determine if the newly appointed agents have performed as expected. If not, has the quality of their training been a factor in their failure to achieve a satisfactory level of production? By "training," we mean the entire process of preparing the new agent to become a permanent and successful member of the agency's sales organization. Therefore, "training" in this broad sense includes office education and training as well as training in the field. Perhaps the deficiency is due to a lack of aptitude on the part of those responsible for new agent training, or perhaps the training program itself is inadequate. These are questions that should be resolved at the year-end planning sessions and, if it is necessary, corrective procedures adopted. Here again the manager cannot usually make decisions alone. Certainly, he must have the cooperation of his training supervisors in the formulation of any new training procedures.

CONTINUED TRAINING FOR ESTABLISHED AGENTS

Training is often thought to be confined to the development of sales skills in the new agents. This is a mistake. All agents, no matter how experienced, should follow a program of continuing education and training. Much of this type of training and self-improvement may be provided through outside organizations, such as life underwriter meetings and sales conferences, or institutional courses, such as LUTC and CLU. The wise agency manager, however, will have a full program of continuing education and training operating within his agency. He must be conscious of the need to have a person to serve as a catalyst within the agency. This person should focus the attention of the other agency personnel on the advanced uses of life insurance and interpret these uses in terms of the skills necessary to capitalize on them. The "catalyst" may be a senior supervisor or even a knowledgeable senior agent who is willing to share this "know-how" with his associates. The purpose of year-end planning in this context is to determine the most important advanced underwriting areas to be covered by agency seminars and sales clinics and the times and dates for such training activities. Participation by all segments of agency management is necessary to effect a successful program.

AGENCY SALES MEETINGS

The average agency is composed of agents in many stages of their development. Agents in initial training need drill on selling skills. Sophisticated agents have developed sales skills but demand more technical information about the uses of life insurance that are usually beyond the comprehension of new agents. To provide a series of agency sales meetings that would be meaningful to all segments of the sales staff requires careful planning and much ingenuity on the part of the agency manager.

Year-end planning should be used to determine the types of meetings that would likely be of the greatest value to the largest number of agency members. After the decision has been made concerning the general theme for agency sales meetings over the next several months, it is then easier to fill in the topical assignments. Often it will be desirable to invite speakers from outside the agency. It is important then to set dates and commit as many of these speakers as practicable. Agency sales meetings planned in advance are certain to be more productive than those set up on the spur of the moment.

SALES CONTESTS

Some managers question the permanent value of sales contests. Others find that their agents respond positively to the challenge of a sales contest. This seems to be a matter that varies with the composition of the agency group and the attitude of its management.

If sales contests are to be conducted, their careful planning will pay off. Timing is an important ingredient in the success of a sales contest. Further, if the company conducts traditional sales drives, the manager should conduct his agency contests in conjunction with the company effort. As nearly as possible, all sales contests for the year should be planned and synchronized at the year-end planning session.

MORALE-BUILDING ACTIVITIES

Many day-to-day activities are designed to build agency morale. These should be reviewed to be sure that they are accomplishing the desired purposes.

All agency affairs might be placed under this heading. The extent of such activities depends on the degree of compatability of the agency membership and their families, as well as the manager's attitude toward the morale value of extra agency socialization. Fortunate is the manager whose agents and office staff like to work together and play together. He will most likely experience a team response and a ready acceptance of agency objectives as they apply to individuals within the agency.

All formal agency social activities for the year should be planned at the beginning of the year and a date set for each event. It is helpful to agency morale if committees representative of each segment of the agency are assigned the various responsibilities involved in arranging these social activities.

SPECIAL AGENCY ACTIVITIES

The beginning of the calendar year is the customary time to introduce any special agency services designed to improve sales. The details of such services must be planned well in advance, so that they will become productive as soon as possible after their installation. Such services might include providing leads obtained from responses to advertising and direct mail, or from contacts with policyholders. A cooperative advertising program wherein the agency shares in an agent's advertising costs is sometimes used. Estate planning facilities and pension planning facilities can be established to provide technical back-up to agents who work in either of these advanced areas. This should also include service and an annual review to determine additions and increases to pension plans already installed. An agency might also establish a policyholder service department to provide field service for those policyholders who do not have an active agent assigned to them.

AGENCY PUBLIC RELATIONS PROGRAM

It is vital to the realization of the agency's long range objectives that it have a favorable image among the various publics with which it deals. Agents who are known to represent a successful organization, one which is staffed with technically competent people, are usually accepted more readily by top level prospects. Moreover, agents who recognize their agency has a favorable image in the community will approach their prospects with greater confidence.

Furthermore, when an agency views recruiting as a team project, it is highly important that the agency be well and favorably known, and it must have a reputation for developing successful personnel. It has been noted that many prospective agents seek the advice of one or more men whose opinion they value. By having a favorable image with the leading business and professional men in the community, an agency will have a sizeable proportion of these prospective agents referred to it. Also, it is not unusual for an agent in one agency to refer a prospective agent to another agency because he believes it to possess a superior training plan or more effective facilities for assisting its agents than his own agency. Thus, the insurance community is an important public for the agency to reach. Policyowners, centers of influence in the community, and brokers from whom the agency accepts business also are important publics. Of course, the personal friends and acquaintances of the manager, life underwriters, and agency personnel are significant publics too.

An agency's primary public relations objective is to establish a reputation for having a group of well informed, successful representatives, especially among the "opinion makers" in the agency territory. To implement this objective, an agency manager must develop specific plans to reach the agency's various publics. Such plans should be integrated into a carefully designed public relations program. Such a program is long range in its effects, since impressions are not quickly made, but the program should be reviewed frequently and checked against its basic purposes. Agency advertising and the use of agency seminars for centers of influence are two activities that are closely associated with an agency public relations program.

AGENCY ADVERTISING

Although advertising can become a costly and time consuming project in a big city, agency advertising also can be designed for special audiences with a minimum of cost. Paid advertising should be accompanied by interesting and judiciously timed news releases. To get the full value from advertising, the agency must first isolate the most important publics that the agency must reach, and then design a public relations program for the greatest impact on each of these important publics.

A. INSURANCE TRADE PAPERS

If the company advertises in the local trade papers, the manager can get his agency's message in front of the readers with a minimum of advertising outlay. These papers are usually glad to print articles and news items of real value to their readers. To accomplish this will tax the ingenuity of the manager but, with some imagination, he can turn out articles from time to time that will be of interest to the local insurance community. Readers tire of continuous statements of agency sales records, but will read stories with a human interest angle.

Advertising in these papers should emphasize the high level of success enjoyed by the agency members, such as membership in Million Dollar Round Table, company honor clubs, newly designated C.L.U.s and other similar achievements by the members of the agency. The agency advertising might also emphasize unusual agency facilities, such as an estate planning or a pension planning department.

B. LIFE UNDERWRITERS ASSOCIATION NEWSLETTER

The large life underwriters associations usually publish monthly newsletters. If they are good, these letters are read carefully by the members. The same type of advertising and news releases used in insurance trade papers are appropriate for the monthly publication of the life underwriters association.

C. PROFESSIONAL JOURNALS

Among the most important opinion makers who influence the large life insurance buyers are the professional advisors. This group, then, is most important for the agency to reach. If the agency is equipped to work in the advanced underwriting field, a comparatively small sum spent in advertising the agency's facilities for assisting in the solution of business, estate and employee welfare problems, will pay handsome dividends. Bar association journals and CPA association journals have a limited circulation and a moderate lineage cost, but the audience they reach is highly select. If the agency is active in the medical market, a modest advertisement in the publication of the local medical association should prove worthwhile.

D. COMMUNITY NEWSPAPERS

Recognition of an agent's superior performance by an advertisement in his community newspaper is a comparatively inexpensive form of advertising that has a positive impact on agency morale. These often are weekly papers and welcome news releases that are newsworthy. A double impact may be gained by running the advertisement and news release in different issues.

SEMINARS FOR CENTERS OF INFLUENCE

Successful agents obtain a considerable amount of their new sales from prospects referred to them. Some of these prospects are referred by satisfied clients, but a considerable number of the larger cases are referred by persons who are advisors to substantial business owners and professional men. Even though there may not be any direct referrals from these lawyers, accountants and others who are in an advisory capacity, their good will is a most valuable asset to agents and the agency. More important than good will is the respect of these professional men for the technical competence as a life underwriter and the fact that an agency has the staff and other facilities to competently handle complex cases.

For these reasons, the agency must prove its competence to this important group of centers of influence. In addition to an advertising program as an important and effective public relations project, an agency should endeavor to present a series of seminars on the use of life insurance in solving complex business and estate planning problems. To make a seminar worthwhile to the professional advisor, it must cover, in depth, an area in which he might have a number of applicable cases. Furthermore, the information provided to him must be such that is not readily available from other sources, or that might otherwise require considerable research to obtain. It goes without saying that lawyers and accountants are extremely busy people and unless they are persuaded that they can get value received for time expended at such seminars, they just will not attend. Unless the agency can furnish an authoritative seminar leader, it would be better not to attempt such a project.

An ideal leader or speaker for a seminar is someone from the home office, a lawyer or other specialist in the subject matter to be discussed at the meeting. However, this is not always possible. A team consisting of a lawyer, accountant or other well-qualified individual and the agency manager or some other representative from the agency will likely do a very acceptable job. It is well to keep in mind that a specialist from another city is frequently more impressive than a local man with equal ability.

The invitation list to such seminars should be considered carefully. Certainly each agent who works in the advanced field should be asked to invite one guest. Usually, the most manageable number is twelve guests and their agent hosts. If there are not enough acceptances to make up this number, the manager may invite one or more guests who would be classed as centers of influence of the agency. It is not feasible to invite guests who are not professional advisors. The general discussion, that is a valuable part of these seminars, might be restrained if clients and prospective clients were also present. If it were thought to be practicable, the manager could set up a separate seminar for prospective buyers. However, the success of a seminar that is highly technical is of questionable value in promoting public relations with clients and prospective clients.

The topics to be presented at a seminar for the professional advisors would logically include one or more of the following:

> Pension and profit sharing planning
> Estate planning for minimizing death expenses
> Deferred compensation plans for the business executive
> The effect of HR-10 on the professional man's estate
> Tax-sheltered annuities under Section 109-c(3)
> Funding methods for partnership buy-and-sell agreements
>   (cross purchase vs. entity purchase)
> Split-dollar arrangements under today's tax laws

If the agency is large enough or if the participating agents have sufficient professional centers of influence, the same subject could be repeated several times.

Following the formal program, a general, informal discussion of the subject should be encouraged. It is even advisable to have one or two questions planted in advance, in order to get things underway. This informal discussion period often brings out questions that have bothered the guests but are questions they have hesitated to ask.

An important by-product of the advanced underwriting seminar is the continuing education effect the seminar has on the agents who are present as joint hosts. A review of a complicated subject, accompanied by a general discussion by well-informed practitioners, sharpens an agent's knowledge and gives him confidence to use it more frequently in his sales work.

Managers who operate in large cities might be inclined to believe that the type of seminar described above might not work for them because of the sophistication of the professional advisors in their community and the multitude of facilities, such as tax institutes, available to them. It is reasonable that the seminars would attract a greater acceptance in the smaller cities, but it is also true that seminars for professional advisors have been conducted successfully in New York, Boston, and other major cities.

COMMUNICATION OF AGENCY PLANS

The objective every thoughtful life insurance agency manager is to develop an organization in which each component, management, office staff and agents, work together as a coordinated team toward common objectives.

In order to accomplish this, the agency's objectives and plans to achieve them must be communicated to all personnel in the agency. An individual who is a member of an organization will not work actively for a group objective unless he understands that the attainment of the objective will personally benefit him. This does not mean that the benefit to be gained must be financial; it may well be that a psychic reward is a stronger motivator, under certain circumstances, then a monetary reward. Agency objectives should be established after careful consideration is given to their effect. The objectives should then be interpreted to the agency members in a manner that will assure their cooperation. An enlightened manager recognizes that every agency achievement that benefits the members of the agency will also be a personal benefit for the manager.

The communication to the members of the agency should be in writing and in a form that may be frequently used for reference. Objectives should be of permanent or long-term nature so that the organization is always working toward their attainment or toward their perpetuation once they are attained. Frequent repetition of agency objectives helps to make them a part of the continued thinking of the members of the agency. The announcement of agency short range plans is always more effective and thus more likely to get organizational acceptance and support if the announcement is made within the framework of the agency's long range objectives.

It is advantageous for an agency manager to communicate his objectives to the agency department of his company. The same is also true of his long range plans. This will provide him with an opportunity to get a critical appraisal and some meaningful suggestions. It should also increase the level of mutual understanding and agreement between the parties regarding matters that are basic to agency management, and enable an agency manager to better coordinate his daily activities with agency plans.

An agency's short range plans are usually shared with the home office agency department. This is especially true of sales quotas and manpower quotas. These quotas will be more meaningful to the home office agency department if the planning steps used to reach them are also communicated. Progress can then be checked by the company against goals at intervals throughout the year and helpful suggestions for improvement may be made in areas where deficiencies are occurring.

There is considerable value to the manager in communicating his objectives and the results of his planning to everyone who might participate in the agency's progress. The management of a sales organization is often a lonely operation and all possible assistance from every source is needed to bring the organization to its optimum potential.

17

Life Insurance Marketing Research[*]

Brent Baxter and William Kashnig

Marketing research relates to the whole marketing process. It involves the study and evaluation of all the activities that are significant to the marketing of a product or service. This broad concept suggests that life insurance marketing research contributes knowledge about 1) the demand for the various products of the life insurance industry, 2) product planning to meet market demands, 3) determining and measuring market potential, 4) determining and measuring sales potential, 5) advertising and sales promotion, 6) conservation of business, 7) expense analysis and 8) the various activities of the agency including recruiting, selection, training, prospecting, interviewing and closing.

PURPOSE OF MARKETING RESEARCH

Marketing research is designed to provide a better understanding of the process and results of marketing life insurance. It is achieved through developing and analyzing information that will be helpful to management in achieving its marketing objectives. Since marketing research is designed to provide significant information for management, marketing research people should be both marketing oriented and management oriented.

The information to be generated should be 1) relevant, 2) significant, 3) reliable and 4) feasible from a budgetary point of view. Unless the information meets this four-fold criteria, management would normally not undertake the research. In other words, before embarking upon any marketing research project, management should know 1) will the information obtained be reliable and, therefore, helpful in solving a significant marketing problem and 2) will the cost be reasonable relative to the benefits achieved (increase of income, reduction of expenses or achievement of other goals).

In general, it may be said that the purpose of marketing research is to provide relevant information to make the marketing of a product or service a more efficient operation. At any level of research (agent, agency, company or industry) the purpose is to provide the necessary information so that intelligent decisions can be made relative to improving the efficiency of the marketing process of any given producing unit. Marketing research is thus the intelligence arm, in the military sense, of each sales executive.

SCOPE OF LIFE INSURANCE MARKETING RESEARCH

The scope of marketing research is broadly conceived to embrace all aspects of and the various interrelationships which exist in the entire marketing process. This includes research on markets, research on all aspects of the distribution process and research on products. Furthermore, since life insurance is a continuous payment product, the scope of marketing research commonly includes research on maintaining the sale, or research on conservation and lapse. Installment sales of consumer durables involve some of the same problems of continuity of periodic payment, but typically this is considered to be a problem of the finance company and not a problem of the marketing department.

IMPORTANCE OF MARKETING RESEARCH

Since the purpose of marketing research is to improve the efficiency of the marketing process, its importance can best be underlined by specific illustrations of how it can achieve that purpose in different aspects of the marketing process.

Developing Markets

For every agent, agency and company, there is usually a market or markets for which a particular style of operation and product line is best suited. Marketing research, aimed at identifying the value of various markets, can point the way for a given productive unit to identify and locate its best markets. With this information, the agent, agency or company is in a position to take necessary steps to assure that its sales effort is being expended in proper proportion to the market. Also, once it knows the total size of the particular market and where it is located, the agency or company is in a position to determine how many productive units are needed and where these should be placed. Judgments can be made regarding the rate of growth needed to assure coverage of the market within a specified period of time.

Measuring Consumer Preferences

Often, when a company develops a new product, or seeks to increase the sale of old products, it has preformed judgments about the markets for which the particular products are best suited. Research on markets can be used to confirm or reject management's preformed judgments. Marketing research can be used to measure consumer preferences for products and identify consumer attitudes toward other aspects of the marketing process:

1) Through a program of pre-testing advertisements, management can evaluate public reactions of proposed ads and determine which ads will have the most favorable impact and thus pave the way for a more favorable reception for the agent. This information can be used effectively in designing copy for advertisements and in more efficiently spending the advertising dollar.

2) Marketing research can determine the prospecting methods to which the public reacts most favorably. For example, the researcher might investigate the relative response of consumers to different types of direct mail pieces.

Improving Recruiting and Selection

There are many ways in which research can be beneficial in improving recruiting and selection. For example, assume that an assistant manager of an agency spends his time in the following manner:

Average Weekly Time Distribution

Activity	No. of Hours	Percent
Recruiting	13	29
Training—In Office	10	22
Training—Joint Field Work	9	20
Administration	13	29
Total	45	100

Assume now that as a result of better selection techniques developed through marketing research, the agent turnover rate is reduced so that no longer does he have to spend 29% of his time on recruiting plus another 22% on in-office training. Only a small reduction in the amount of time needed for these two activities would be extremely beneficial. For example, if the assistant manager needed to spend only 25% and 20%, respectively on recruiting and in-office training, he would be able to spend this additional 6% of his time on joint field work, thus increasing his time spent in this important area from 20% to 26% or an increase of 30%. The ability to make this kind of a time adjustment through only a small improvement in recruiting and selection activity would have the effect of making the job more satisfying to the assistant manager, and result in higher production from his present agents, thus achieving increased earnings for both him and his men.

Evaluating Training Activity

Research can be helpful in evaluating the relative effectiveness of different approaches, techniques and materials used in agency education and training. An agency frequently has the choice between group and individual training, field office and home office instruction, training by field personnel and home office personnel, tutored and self-instruction or some combination of these. Only through a study and evaluation of the ultimate sales effectiveness of the various techniques can a company make intelligent decisions affecting the overall efficiency of its marketing process. Furthermore, life companies are expanding their product lines and are increasing the uses of existing products to provide for more complex business and personal needs. Therefore, the problem of how to train agents quickly and effectively in these specialized areas is of prime importance.

METHODOLOGY IN MARKETING RESEARCH[1]

Research should begin with a careful statement of the problem to be solved. The easiest way to waste research time is to wander around with only a vague idea of what one is looking for. Or the problem may be stated so generally that it is difficult to know where to begin. For example, if the problem is one of low production in an agency, the agency manager should pinpoint whether the problem is with the new agents, the longer

---

[1] A more complete treatment of experimental design, statistical methodology and sources of data can be found in Baxter and Kashnig, *Life Insurance Market Research* published in 1962 by The American College of Life Underwriters.

service agents, the agents under a particular supervisor, or whether the problem is a seasonal one. The old cliché makes a great deal of sense: an accurate statement of the problem means a long step toward its solution.

Researchers too often get themselves involved in a study of symptoms and forget to direct their attention to causes of the real problem underlying the surface. For example, many studies relative to the cause of lapse concern themselves with the size of the policy. Size of policy, however, is usually only a symptom of the quality of the original sale. The real cause of the lapse is the failure of the agent and the underwriting department to make sure there was an appropriate relationship between the insured's income and the amount of the annual premium.

In marketing research, it is more difficult to control the variables that may exist in a problem or opportunity situation, but the researcher still strives for that design. Thus, he develops groups or sets of conditions in which all the variables, except one, are as similar as possible. Then by changing that one variable, and mating the consequences of that change, the classical cause-effect understanding is obtained.

For example: 1) How do changes in the age of the agent (causal variable) affect the degree of agent's success (effect variable)? 2) How does the kind of sales presentation (causal variable) affect the persistence or length of survival of the policy (effect variable)? 3) How does the number of churches in a town (causal variable) affect the sales potential in that town (effect variable)? Professionals in marketing research identify the causal variable as "independent" and the effect variable as "dependent."

RESEARCH ON MARKETS

The word "markets" means many things to many people. Often it is used loosely to mean 1) a given geographic territory, 2) a selected income group, 3) the undefined people who might be likely to buy a given type of policy, 4) a group of people who have been prospected in a certain way, (such as the referred lead market) or by the need which prompted the insurance relationship, (such as the mortgage market). Several other definitions of markets used by various members of the insurance industry may be found. Thus, in any discussion of either the market for life insurance or of research on markets it will be necessary to define exactly which concept of markets is being examined.

Types of Research on Markets

Generally speaking, the various types of research on markets can be classified broadly into three major areas: 1) quantitative market analysis, 2) qualitative market analysis and 3) consumer motivation research.

QUANTITATIVE MARKET ANALYSIS

Quantitative market analysis generally tries to answer the question: "How big is the market, however it is defined?" In this general area fall the various studies of sales potentials, sales quotas, size and location of agencies, staffing needs in an area, and market penetration studies.

QUALITATIVE MARKET ANALYSIS

Qualitative market analysis attempts to answer the question: "How good is the market?" Included in this general area are the studies which are and can be conducted in the field of demographic characteristics of buyers and non-buyers, the ratio of calls to interviews to sales achieved among prospects developed by different prospecting techniques, and lastly, qualitative analysis of various geographic markets.

MOTIVATION RESEARCH

Lastly, but becoming more important in the competition for the public's savings and security expenditure, is the area of motivation research. Research in this area seeks to answer many aspects of the question: "Why?" Why do people of certain economic characteristics buy more life insurance than others? What needs are they satisfying? In what ways can the life insurance companies, including their agencies and agents, best motivate the consumer to buy? Why is it that a prospect will turn down an agent from one company and then a month later, buy from a different agent of the same company or a different company? How does the public look upon the life insurance salesmen? The questions, of course, go on and on; but they are all pointed to getting an understanding of the potential buyer's attitude towards life insurance and an understanding of why the buyer behaves as he does in the life insurance sales situation.

Agent Research on Markets

From the standpoint of the individual salesmen, perhaps the most critical question for investigation is: "In which markets do my product line and my sales techniques make me the most effective?" For each salesman's method of operation and products there is probably one group of people with whom he can operate most successfully. If, through researching markets, an agent can identify this group, he is well on his way to directing his activities most efficiently. Correlated to this finding is, of course, market research to determine where these particular types of people can be found.

CASE STUDY—TED JOHNSON

These points can best be illustrated by a case study. Ted Johnson, full time salesman for the Stock Life Insurance Company, has consistently sold about 50 policies a year for the past five years and an average total volume of about $300,000. This amount of business, even with renewals, gives Ted an inadequate income. He has tried to increase it by several different methods in recent years, but with no success. All his attempts still yield approximately 50 cases a year with a production volume of about $300,-000. Ted has just about given up trying new methods of operating and has resigned himself to the fact that $300,000 a year seems to be his "natural" level. Ted's manager, however, suggested some research on Ted's occupational market as a means of getting further insight into the problem. Together, they tabulated the occupations of Ted's adult male buyers in the last full year and found the following distribution:

Occupation Distribution of Johnson's Sales

Occupation Group	No. of Policies Sold	Volume	Average Policy Size
Professional Man	10	$60,000	$6,000
Managers and Executives	5	20,000	4,000
White Collar Workers	10	40,000	4,000
Blue Collar Workers	20	160,000	8,000
Others	5	20,000	4,000
Total	50	$300,000	$6,000

This analysis proved to be quite revealing both to Ted and to his manager. First, it showed that Ted's most lucrative market, in terms of average policy size, was the blue collar market. Every policy Ted sold in this market was worth 1/3 more than the average. Thus, if Ted had sold all his 50 policies in the blue collar market, his level of activity (50 sales) would have yielded a production volume of $400,000 rather than the $300,000 which he actually did write. Ted also found out, that for him, the white collar, and managers and executive groups were not as lucrative as the other markets. The professional market for Ted was just average.

Perhaps the most crucial part of this study lay in correlating these findings with Ted's plan of activity. Ted, in searching out a way to increase his sales, had read the market research material published by his company and by LIAMA.[2] Both of these studies had shown that the average size policy was highest in the professional, managers and executive market— just the reverse of what Ted found. As a result, Ted had been systematically trying to approach more men in the professional, managers and executive class and, as it turns out, had actually been working against himself.

As a result of this analysis, Ted resolved to work more in the blue collar market. With his curiosity piqued, however, he asked himself a further question which could make a big difference in what markets he planned to operate. "Maybe it is true that when I sell a policy, I sell a larger sized policy to the blue collar market. However, what about my effectiveness in each of these markets? Maybe I can sell two policies to the managers group at the same time I sell only one to the blue collar class."

Again Ted and his manager mulled over the problem and decided that the best way they could equate effort spent in the various occupational groups was to see how many calls, and then interviews, and finally sales were made in each of Ted's occupational markets. Fortunately, Ted's records were adequate to handle the inquiry (most agents' files are not) and Ted tabulated calls first, then interviews, and finally, sales in each market category.

Calls, Interviews and Sales Data—Ted Johnson

Occupation Group	No. of Calls	No. of Interviews	No. of Sales
Professional	110	22	10
Managers & Executives	60	15	5
White Collar	108	18	10
Blue Collar	114	38	20
Others	14	7	5
Total	406	100	50

Looking at these figures, Ted determined he was spending approximately equal time in the professional, white collar and blue collar markets. However, he noticed from the sales column that he was not getting equal results, and he decided to turn the above table into more meaningful ratios and developed the table shown on the following page.

Now Ted felt he had all the information he needed to find out what his best market was, and in what market he operated most effectively. Looking at the table, he saw first of all that it took 4.1 calls to get an inter-

---

[2] The LIAMA prepares an annual Buyers Study which presents demographic information on life insurance buyers.

Occupational Market Effectiveness—Ted Johnson

Occupation Group	Calls Per Interview	Interviews Per Sale	Calls Per Sale	Average Size Policy
Professional	5.0	2.2	11.0	$6,000
Managers & Executives	4.0	3.0	12.0	4,000
White Collar	6.0	1.8	10.8	4,000
Blue Collar	3.0	1.9	5.7	8,000
Others	2.0	1.4	2.8	4,000
Average	4.1	2.0	8.1	$6,000

view. He did the poorest in terms of getting interviews in the white collar market and the best in the "others" group. (Upon further investigation these turned out to be special situations and Ted could not capitalize on them in planning his work.) On the other hand, Ted found that once he had obtained the interview, he could count on a sale about every other time and did better in the white collar group than in any other class (excluding the "others" category). He did the poorest in the managers group.

Putting these two together, Ted found it took, on the average, 8.1 calls to make a sale and in the blue collar group only 5.7 calls for a sale. Overall, he was almost twice as effective in terms of calls per sale among the blue collar workers as among the professional, managers and executives and white collar workers. When he combined this information with the fact that his average size policy was 1/3 higher than average in the blue collar group, Ted was sure that he had found his natural market—the market in which his methods of operation and his product line yielded the best results.

Ted studied the results of his research and came to the conclusion that if he had made all 406 calls to blue collar workers and sold an $8,000 policy for every 5.7 calls, he would have sold 71 policies for a total volume of $568,000. And he would not have worked any harder than usual—just smarter.

Ted resolved then and there to concentrate primarily in the blue collar market, and his next question was, "Where can I find these blue collar workers, and how many of them are there in my geographic market area?"

This led him naturally to a *qualitative* occupational analysis of his market. Ted's prime market area consisted of a city of 20,000. His next task was to obtain an occupational distribution of the adult male workers in that market. Several possibilities existed for Ted:

1) The 1970 census statistics were available and he could check for the detailed occupational statistics with the nearest Department of Commerce Field Office.

2) The State Employment Bureau also had an office in town, and
they frequently prepared releases on the occupational characteristics of Ted's market area.

Ted found that the State Employment Service provided monthly statistics
on the occupational classifications of the male adult labor force. He told
them what figures he was interested in and together they were able to
summarize the following information:

Employed Adult Male Workers

Occupation Group	No. of Workers	Percent
Professional	1,000	17%
Managers & Executives	500	8
White Collar	2,000	33
Blue Collar	2,000	33
Others	500	8
	6,000	99%*

* Does not add to 100% because of "rounding error."

Thus, Ted could see at a glance that in his market area, on the basis
of 400 calls a year he could make 5 years of calls on his "quality market,"
the blue collar worker, without even calling back on the same man twice.
After that time, or even before that, Ted felt that he would have built
a good clientele of repeat business in this market so that he would not
be confronted with the problem of running out of a market. Or, as another
possibility, if this did not prove successful, Ted reasoned that he could
work the blue collar market in another industrial city, only 20 miles away.
It was probably fortunate for Ted that his "quality" occupational market
did not turn out to be the managers and executive group, since there were
only 500 men that fell into this class in the whole city. Had he tried to
concentrate on this market, he would very quickly have run out of a market. In addition, with several other agents and brokers in town, the competition would be stiff.

Ted realized that as a practical matter he would not limit himself to the
blue collar occupational market, for his natural and normal prospecting
methods would lead him to other occupational groups as well. Since he
did much of his prospecting on a geographic basis, he decided that the
best way to organize his prospecting was to determine which sections of
the city had the highest percent of blue collar workers living in them, and
choose these areas as the ones in which he would spend most of his time.

His next question, therefore, was "What is my best quality area in which to work?" or "How good are each of the subdivisions of the city for my prospecting purposes?"

Ted called the United States Department of Commerce Field Office and found that detailed occupational data by census tracts were available. Since Ted reasoned he had five years of prime market in the city, he divided the city into five equal population segments and studied the occupational characteristics of each of the segments.

Population Characteristics in Five Market Areas

Market Area	Total Population	Employed Adult Males	Adult Males Classified as Blue Collar	
			No.	Percent
A	4,200	1,400	560	40%
B	3,900	1,300	260	20
C	3,900	1,100	660	60
D	3,800	1,100	330	30
E	4,200	1,300	290	22
Total	20,000	6,200*	2,100*	34%

* Figures differ slightly from those supplied by the State Employment Service because of a different date and different methods of gathering the data.

Looking at the table above, Ted found that Area C not only had the highest number of blue collar workers of the five geographic market areas, but also had the highest percent of blue collar workers in the adult male market. As a matter of fact, by concentrating in Area C as opposed to Area B, Ted could be assured of hitting three times as many of his prime market units—the blue collar worker. He would be able to hit 60% as compared to 20%.

Thus, as a result of the total research that Ted had done, he now had the key to increasing his production and his earnings, and using his time most effectively, both in terms of the geographic market area in which he planned to prospect, and the occupation group on which he wanted to concentrate. He had done a good quantitative and qualitative analysis of his occupation market.

The one thing that still bothered Ted, however, was the fact that he knew what, where and how big, but he did not know why. Although he and his manager had had frequent discussions trying to understand why Ted was as effective as he was in selling the blue collar market, they still could not pinpoint the real reason. They still needed to do *motivation* research to determine "why" he was more effective in the blue collar markets.

Finally, Ted said to himself, "Instead of puzzling over this problem, why don't I ask the people who know. I'll take a small sample of the people who bought from me and another sample of those who didn't buy and I'll ask those who bought why they bought and I'll ask those who didn't buy why they didn't buy their policies from me."

So Ted again went to his files and selected at random a sample of 20 buyers and 20 non-buyers during the past 6 months. He asked all of them the following three questions:

1. Did you buy any life insurance in the past twelve months? (He worded the question slightly differently when he asked the men who bought from him).
2. What caused you to buy a policy from the particular company that you did? (Asked of buyers only).
3. What was it about the (insert cause given as answer to question 2) that influenced you the most in your decision to buy insurance?

Tabulating the results to the first question, Ted found this situation:

Question 1: Did you buy any life insurance policies in the past twelve months?

Answer	Ted's Buyers	Ted's Non-Buyers
Yes	20	10
No	0	10
Total	20	20

Looking at these data, Ted decided that if he were to get anything out of his second and third questions, he would have to compare the answers given by those who bought from him with the other buyers who bought from somebody else. So he tabulated his 20 buyers and the other 10 buyers. The answers to question 2 looked like this:

Question 2: What caused you to buy a policy from the particular company that you did?

Answer	Ted's Buyers		Other Buyers	
	No.	Percent	No.	Percent
Former Policyholder	4	20%	2	20%
Co. Advertising	1	5	1	10
The Agent	14	70	6	60
No Specific Reason	1	5	1	10
Total	20	100%	10	100%

Looking at these responses, Ted was a bit disappointed. Both his buyers and the other buyers gave roughly the same pattern of responses, and it did not look at though his research would be very productive. But he did notice that in both instances, the agent was the dominating influence in the decision to buy from that particular company. So he decided to sort down those replies to see what responses he got to question number three. He received a variety of responses, but he was able to classify the responses into several general categories.

Question 3: What was it about (the agent) that influenced you the most in your decision to buy insurance?

Answer	Ted's Buyers		Other Buyers	
	No.	Percent	No.	Percent
He knew his business	1	7%	1	17%
Understood my problem	3	22	—	—
We had something in common	8	57	3	50
Miscellaneous reasons	2	14	2	33
Total	14	100%	6	100%

Again, there was not too much difference between the reasons Ted's buyers gave and the reasons the other buyers gave. What did stand out, however, was the fact that the buyer felt he had something in common with the agent in over 50% of the cases.

Now, thinking back over his own background and his hobbies, Ted realized that his previous job in the office of a contractor enabled him to easily discuss work connected problems with the blue collar workers he prospected. As a result, he quickly established himself as a salesman who could understand the problems of the blue collar market, but found it difficult to do so when talking with other occupational groups. He was now satisfied that he had found the answer to the "Why" question and resolved to do some reading on the work practices of other occupational groups so he could be more effective when working in these occupational markets.

Summary

The above case history illustrates how a combination of quantitative, qualitative and motivation research at the agent level helped to solve a marketing problem. In illustrating this, only one type of market was examined—the occupational market. It would be a rare instance when the solution to the marketing problem through research on markets would come so quickly or neatly. In most instances, studies similar to the above would have to be done on other markets that the agent operated in, such as the age market, the education market, the income market, and perhaps others, before positive results would be obtained. In some instances, research on markets may not prove to be productive at all, because the problem is not a markets problem, but a distribution or product problem.

Agency and Company Research on Markets

In many respects, research on markets at the agency level is similar to that at the agent level. Again the general problem is one of defining and measuring the best market for the particular agency. In doing so, however, the average agent's skills, rather than a particular agent's skills, and the whole product line rather than a specialized line for each agent has to be taken into consideration.

For example, in the previous discussion of Ted Johnson's case, we concluded that the blue collar occupational market was the best market for Ted. Does it necessarily follow that all the agents in the agency should concentrate in the blue collar market? The answer obviously, is "No." For the agency as a whole a similar type of analysis would have to be undertaken. But instead of working with a sample of Ted's policies, a sample of the agency's policies would have to be analyzed. The answers which would be obtained would then be applicable to the agency as a whole and not to any particular agent. This is what is meant by the statement that the average agent's skills must be taken into consideration.

USE OF AGENCY AND COMPANY DATA

Because a manager cannot work with an average agent nor can a company work with an average agency, of what use are analyses such as these? The answer is, "considerable." After determining what markets are best to operate in, and where these markets are concentrated most heavily in the total territory assigned to him, the agency manager is in a position to recruit and train agents in the specific territories which contain his most profitable markets.

Similarly, a company in expanding its agency structure or in realigning its present agencies, after an analysis such as the above, is in a position to grow or concentrate in a manner most profitable to it.

Sales Potentials

No discussion of research on markets would be complete without some mention of the research that is done and can be done in the area of sales potentials. For the most part, this type of market analysis is conducted by company or industry research groups because of its complexity.

It would be well to differentiate between sales potentials and sales quotas at this point. These terms are often used interchangeably in the industry, although, they are, in fact, two separate and distinct concepts. Sales potentials can be defined as that portion of the total industry's sales which can be sold by any one company; while sales quotas are sales goals usually set for a specific productive unit and a certain period of time.

TYPES OF ANALYSIS

In general, sales potential research can be classified into two broad areas:

1) Studies which attempt to determine how much insurance in dollar amounts can or should be sold in any given area.
2) Studies which attempt to determine what percent of the total sales potential should be sold in any given area.

The former by far constitutes the more difficult of the two tasks, since the dollar amount of insurance sales obtained in any territory is a result of a myriad of forces, including market factors, a company's product line, the aggressiveness of its sales force, the quality of salesmen's training, and other factors.

In both instances, however, the approach to sales potential research is much the same, usually following these lines:

1) Determining market factors which are related to actual sales results.
2) Identifying these market factors in various geographic segments of the company's territory.
3) Evaluating actual results against the sales potential, usually by means of a percentage comparison.

DETERMINING THE MARKET FACTORS

In determining the market factors related to sales results, there are two general lines of approach:

1) A statistical study can be made which relates the volume of sales in any given territory to various market factors such as population, income, age distribution of the population, average size of families, amount of life insurance in force and other items.
2) On the basis of company or agency objectives and goals, a decision may be made to sell primarily to a selected, well-defined market. For example, the determination of sales potential for a company or an agency specializing in sales to college students would probably be based on the college student population in an area.

In both approaches, however, the end result is the same—a determination will have been made as to which market factors are important in influencing the sales of insurance of a particular company. In the case of an agency, this same determination can be made.

IDENTIFYING MARKET FACTORS BY AREA

Once the determination has been made of the important market factors, the next step is to measure them (either on an absolute amount or a percentage basis) in the various geographic segments of the company's or agency's territory. This information is usually available from the United States Department of Commerce Census Bureau reports or state or local government sources.

EVALUATING RESULTS

When the researcher has determined (1) a percentage distribution or (2) the absolute amounts of potential sales by geographic area, the final step is to compare "actual" sales results against the potential. On this basis, the researcher can identify (1) the areas of greatest sales potential, and (2) the areas of greatest penetration and successful sales performance.

RESEARCH ON THE DISTRIBUTION SYSTEM

The distribution system at the local level in the life insurance business consists of a personnel structure which usually includes an agency manager, one or more assistant managers, a staff of salesmen, and a group of clerks to handle the clerical processing of new business and inforce policies. In addition there is a procedural structure covering selection, training, prospecting, closing and the other parts of the sales and service functions of the agency. As such, the area of marketing research on the distribution system encompasses the broadest segment of the marketing process in the life insurance industry.

No attempt will be made here to outline completely all of the possible facets of the distribution system on which research can or has been conducted. Instead, only three of the many possible areas will be covered in order to give the reader some indication of the scope of the area, the problems involved in conducting studies and some insight into methods of procedure. The three areas which will be briefly described are:

(1) Training research
(2) Prospecting research
(3) Activity analysis

Training Research

An area of great importance to success in agency management is the area of agent and management training. Yet, as one reviews the literature about marketing research in the life insurance business, he finds a dearth of material on the evaluation of the variety of training methods and techniques which are available to life insurance personnel. It would seem that here is a very important part of the distribution system, and the overall marketing process, which should be further studied and in which considerable experimentation should be done.

At present in the life insurance business, there are a variety of training methods employed by the various companies, and even by different agencies within the same companies.

Yet, only intuitively does sales management know what is best, recommend changes or develop new programs. For example, some companies spend as little as a week on in-office training before sending new men out on sales calls; others might spend as much as a month performing the same function. Some companies send new men into the home office for an intensified course conducted by specialists; still others rely entirely on field management to perform the training function. Still others might hold training schools in various population centers in the field, but conducted by home office men. Some companies believe in and utilize precontract training; others do not.

These differences concern only the time and place aspects of the training process. In addition, and perhaps even more important, are the many unresolved questions regarding course content and methods of instruction. Should the emphasis on new agent training be on product knowledge or sales techniques? Which would yield the best immediate and long range results? Is it best to try to teach facility of use of a product kit or a regimented, canned sales talk? Is it best to try to teach one product and approach, then practice it in field interviews before proceeding to another product, with all this prior to teaching programming? Or can the best results be achieved by teaching programming right at the outset of the training course? At what point in time should field demonstrations of techniques and principles be undertaken?

These are not all of the questions which could and should be asked about training, of course; there are many more. They are, however, typical of the kinds of questions which effective marketing research on the distribution process is designed to answer.

RESEARCH DESIGN

Theoretically, it would be possible to set up one grand study which would answer all of the questions posed above. However, it would be monumental and very long in its experimental stages. From a practical standpoint, it is wiser to take one or two specific questions and attempt to get definite answers to them and then proceed to another question or set of questions. In this way, gains in training knowledge can be achieved in a much shorter time, and would be more readily understood by those responsible for making decisions involved in the training process.

Prospecting Research

It is widely recognized and accepted today that one of the most difficult parts of the life insurance salesman's job is prospecting. Some authorities contend that success or failure in life insurance selling depends on prospecting ability. Yet in spite of the importance of prospecting, it is surprising how little is known and how few studies are actually carried on in this area. Research in this area could be designed to answer questions such as:

1) How many cold-canvass calls can be made in an hour?
2) How many interviews and subsequent sales can an agent expect to obtain from an hour's cold-canvassing?
3) Which prospecting method provides the most efficient use of an agent's time?
4) Are there certain markets for which certain prospecting methods are particularly effective?
5) Within each of the specific prospecting methods (cold-canvass, direct mail, telephoning, and so on) what specific technique should be used to increase the likelihood of securing an interview?
6) What appeals should the agent use in prospecting, regardless of which method of prospecting he is using?

These are, of course, only sample questions which could be asked in the general area of prospecting which could be answered through marketing research. Probably one of the reasons more work has not been done in this area is because of the lack of readily available records with which to make analyses, and secondly, the difficulties of accumulating records for a large enough number of agents and calls so that a meaningful analysis could be prepared. To obtain accurate data both time and activity records should be maintained over a long period of time. Agents would have to cooperate in conducting some portion of their work in line with the specified conditions of the experiment. In spite of these drawbacks, however, it would seem that the possible gains to be realized in sales efficiency through conducting research in this area would make such research well worthwhile.

DIRECT MAIL PROSPECTING

One of the frequently used tools in prospecting in the life insurance industry is direct mail. For the agency manager, research in this area, particularly if the agency does considerable direct mail prospecting, can be very rewarding in terms of increasing the efficiency of this part of the sales process.

In the general area of direct mail, there are many possibilities for different types of studies to be done. For example, an analysis could be made of the "pulling power" measured in terms of returns and subsequent sales resulting from the various direct mail pieces which are used by an agency. Analysis of these same pieces by type of prospect also could be made to determine which pieces should be sent to which type of prospect.

Also of interest to both home office and fieldmen are answers to questions regarding the technical details of direct mail. For example, because of cost considerations, it would be well to know whether first or third class mail yeilds the greater probability of reasons, or alternatively, whether a post card reply would yield as many returns as an envelope reply. The experiment described below is a test of these two items. The test was conducted by six eastern agencies in one life insurance company. The results enabled the company to save money on their postage costs.

Over a two month test period, over 5,500 test letters of two types were sent out, equally divided between first class mail and third class mail. Each of these groups was again split. Half of the letters provided for replies using return envelopes and half contained return post cards. The following table summarizes the experience with first class mail versus third class mail. The results parallel those of the actual study.

Direct Mail Results, by Type of Mailing

	Type of Mailing		Combined
	First Class	Third Class	
Total Letters Mailed	2755	2752	5507
Total Replies Received	180	188	368
Per Cent Replying	6.53%	6.83%	6.68%

An approximately equal number of letters were mailed by each mailing method, and overall 6.68% replied to the mailing. While this figure is low, it is not unusual for a direct mail letter of the type used. The important thing learned was that the third class mailing brought essentially the same percentage of returns as did the first class mail. On the basis of this test, it was found that considerable money could be saved in the mailing process without affecting the rate of returns.

The other test which was conducted simultaneously was the test of results obtained by providing different types of mail pieces for the respondents. The following table shows the results obtained.

Direct Mail Results, by Type of Reply

	Type of Reply		Combined
	Post Card	Envelope	
Total Letters Mailed	2754	2753	5507
Total Replies Received	152	216	368
Per Cent Replying	5.51%	7.80	6.68%

As was mentioned previously, the overall rate of return was 6.68%. However, when envelopes were provided 7.80% of the mailings brought responses, as compared to 5.51% responding when post cards were provided. In this case the additional printing costs of the envelope over the post card were negligible and the additional return mail cost was only one cent. In terms of cost the envelope provided 42% more replies for only 17% more postage outlay (the card replies cost $.06 while the envelope cost $.07). On the basis of this, the additional cost (this assumes that an overall rate of return of 7.80% as satisfactory) was felt to be justified. Further follow-up studies would have to be made to learn the sales results if the criterion for selection of the appropriate direct mail program was sales rather than replies received.

Activity Analysis

A study area about which not too much exact information is known, but which also could prove to be quite fruitful on an agent and agency basis, is an analysis of the activity of agents. It would improve our understanding of the work habits and the patterns of successful and failing agents. Typical of the type of research in this area is a study made of the amount and quality of activity of high and low producers in one mid-western region of a large life company.

The results of the first 40 weeks of activity were summarized from the available training records of the agents, and are presented below.

It is readily apparent that the high producers had a higher level of activity than the low producers in every phase of the sales process that was measured.

On the average, the high producers made 6.5 more face calls per week, had 1.4 more interviews, conducted .7 more closing interviews and made 1.0 more sales. Assuming the same ratio of face calls to final sales as the

Average Amount of Activity, for High and Low Producers

Activity	High Producers	Low Producers	Difference
Face Calls	39.7	33.2	6.5
Total Interviews	8.9	7.5	1.4
Closing Interviews	6.5	5.8	.7
Sales	2.2	1.2	1.0

low producers evidence above, this analysis shows that the low producers simply by raising their face call level of activity to the same level as the high producers (from 33.2 to 39.7), could have increased their weekly sales 17% from 1.2 to 1.4. This is not spectacular, but it does emphasize how it is possible to increase life insurance production by simply increasing total activity. Similar types of analysis in different areas or agencies would probably yield different results and remedial action would have to be taken accordingly.

As the second step in this study, an analysis of the quality of activity was undertaken. The following table summarizes results in this area.

Quality of Activity Analysis, for High and Low Producers

	Activity Ratios	
	High Producers	Low Producers
Ratio of Face Calls to Total Interviews	4.5	4.4
Ratio of Total Interviews to Closing Interviews	1.4	1.3
Ratio of Closing Interviews to Sales	2.9	4.8

This type of analysis is designed to pin-point the activity area in which the low producers are deficient. It should be noted that not much difference exists in the first two items listed above. The low producers were almost equally efficient as the high producers in obtaining interviews and also in obtaining subsequent closing interviews, after allowing for differences in amount of activity. The big difference existed in the ratios of closing interviews to sales. It would seem likely that the remedial action needed to improve this ratio for the low producer would be refresher courses in sales techniques as well as additional knowledge training and increased joint call work with the management staff or perhaps with successful agents. Or another possibility at this point would be to conduct further research to determine why the high producers were more effective in closing than the low producers.

EVALUATING RESEARCH REPORTS

Probably most of the readers of this handbook will not actually be conducting research themselves but will be in the position of reviewing and evaluating the results of research for possible application in their day to day activities of life insurance sales management. Therefore we will conclude this chapter with a discussion of some major points to consider when reviewing and evaluating research reports.

A Major Pitfall

One of the greatest dangers in reading a research report is placing too much reliance on the summary and conclusion section. To save time we are prone to skip over the details of procedures and results and rely entirely on the author's interpretations. In many cases we are not in a position to evaluate his conclusions nor are we likely to understand fully his hypotheses and terminology. For example, a summary may state: Total needs sales made by experienced agents are subject to high lapse. This seems like a straightforward statement not subject to much misinterpretation. But note that before a clear understanding can be obtained, several points must be clarified.

1. How did the author define "total-needs sale?" Is it what you mean by this term?
2. What length of service did the "experienced" agents have? Would it be better to remember this conclusion in terms of the number of years service, e.g., over 5 years' service?
3. What is meant by high lapse? A rate that is high under one condition is judged to be low under another set of conditions. We need to know the rates and the conditions.
4. The statement is vague as to whether the relation holds true for all experienced agents, for all their sales, for the average experienced agent or for their average sale. We do not know if tests of significance have been applied to see if the results could have arisen through chance.

Thus, it should be clear that there is considerable risk in relying exclusively on a reading of the conclusions. One's understanding of the report can be greatly enhanced by reading the entire report. A logical reason, of course, for reading the summary first is to see if the subject is of interest and to prepare one's self for studying the complete article.

Specific Guidelines

The following is a list of specific points for one to consider in reading a research report. They will prove helpful as guidelines for accepting or rejecting as well as understanding the conclusions.

1. Look to see if there is a clear and accurate statement of the problem. Was the question explicitly and clearly posed or was a problem area only vaguely described?
2. Decide whether or not the answer is prejudged in the way the question is stated. (e.g., Why is method A the best method of training new agents?—this is hardly an open-minded approach to the value of method A!).
3. Note how the statement of the problem is translated in specific agency operations. For example, was method A fully described? Were agent length of service, high production, low lapse, kind of policy, and so on, explicitly spelled out?
4. Identify the assumptions made in the definitions. Will they apply to your operation? For example, the author may define successful new agents as those staying with the company six months and producing at company average. Would you call all such men successful? Similarly, would you "buy" the definition: "A quality agent is one who year after year produces at least a half million dollars of sales"? Or does "quality" imply to you additional aspects of performance (e.g., persistency, needs-selling, higher income markets)?
5. Determine whether or not the steps in the study were carefully planned. So often when data are on hand on a given topic, someone will suggest that it be used to "shed light" on the subject. Such data are usually useless. To get crisp answers, it is likely necessary to collect facts in a manner specially related to the problem.
6. Examine the quality of the sample. Of what group is it a sample? How was the sample chosen? Were volunteers used? Were those agents willing to cooperate?
7. Identify the dependent variable(s), the independent variable(s). Were there any other controlled variables? Did the latter "over-control" or restrict the study unduly?
8. See if a control group was used. Was it formulated properly? Were groups that were compared comparable in all respects except for the independent variable?
9. Look to see if the design considers equal time periods, seasonal effects, and delayed effects.
10. Examine the use of the dependent variables. Were important effects of the independent variable overlooked? For example, a direct mail letter might pull a high percentage of replies, but the leads might produce either few sales or poor persistency business.
11. Judge whether or not the handling of the dependent variable justifies any degree of generalizing. For example, a study may compare advertisements with and without coupons. If a single pair of "ads" is used, our conclusions should be limited to the particular ad. On the other hand, if a wide variety of ads were used with and without coupons, a better basis of generalizing is present. In other studies this concept might also apply to the

range of agents used, the variety of direct mail letters, the kinds of prospects, the length of the sales presentation, and so on.

12. If data were used from some outside public source, did the author define the terms in the same manner as the original source? If the data are shown for several years, make sure that the measures were defined in the same way during the entire period. For example, if industry sales results are shown over a period of years, fluctuations may arise solely from changes in classifications of business that major companies make. If certain kinds of debit business are modified slightly and now are called ordinary business, the trend in industry ordinary life sales will have a jump the year the change is made. Do not be fooled by other explanations that may be rationalized.

13. Beware the use of base years. A report may compare results of today with those of ten years ago. This leads to certain conclusions. But if nine years or eleven years were taken, the results might be quite different. Unless there is some very important reason for the comparison with a certain year (e.g., a new policy was issued in that year), test out the hypothesis on several other periods.

14. Was the sample large enough to permit a small though practical difference to be judged significant? Remember, it is equally dangerous to decide a real effect is unimportant as it is to decide an irrelevant factor has a real impact. To illustrate, a study may conclude that a particular form of training has no effect greater than chance. If this study has involved training 10 to 20 agents, only a very major training factor would have any hope of showing statistical significance.

These are some of the major points to consider when reading research reports and evaluating their possible use and application to a specific situation. It is hoped that by referring to them before taking any action, agency management will be in a better position to use and apply only those findings that will have a real bearing on their operations.

Section VI

PUBLIC RELATIONS

AND SALES PROMOTION

18

Public Relations
and Prestige Building

Solomon Huber

THE NATURE OF PUBLIC RELATIONS

Public relations for a life insurance agency is the continuous process of creating attitudes among its various publics that are favorable to the accomplishment of the agency's marketing objectives. Certain key-concepts implicit in this definition should be emphasized. First, public relations is a "continuing process." Once a year newspaper advertising might be a part of a long-term and carefully developed public relations program. However, the one-shot advertisement cannot be dignified as a "public relations program." Second, the continuing process of building favorable attitudes among the agency's publics requires thoughtful long-term planning.

The agency will obviously have certain short-term goals and objectives but public relations' accomplishments should be viewed as distinctly long-term. Building the desired image of the agency in the eyes of all the various publics of the agency is not accomplished over-night. It is a slow evolutionary process.

Emphasis should also be placed on the fact that public relations is a process in which all personnel in the agency participate. Public relations activities are not the pleasant prerogative of the agency manager. The latter's memberships in Kiwanis, the Chamber of Commerce and the Estate Planning Council are all important. However, the arrogance of a clerk in her personal relationships with policyowners may destroy the benefits of six months of the manager's regular attendance at Kiwanis. In other words, the whole agency should be public relations oriented and should consciously practice the amiable amenities of courteous service to the agency's "marketing" publics. The principles of sound public relations should be recognized by each employee and put into practice at every conceivable opportunity.

The basic objective of a public relations program for any organization is the creation of favorable attitudes among its specific publics. A favorable attitude among the buying public means a disposition to approach the agency with a feeling of pleasant expectation, to view kindly the people in the agency and to receive members of the agency graciously when visited or telephoned. This highly social concept of "favorable attitude," however, should not be overemphasized. The agency also must have professional dignity and respectability among its prospects and clients. The agency is not a social institution. It is a professional partnership. Therefore, the agency should build among its publics in its marketing area an attitude of respect as well as a feeling of friendliness and social compatability.

Public Relations and Publicity

In defining public relations we should be careful to distinguish public relations from publicity. Publicity is only one phase or aspect of a public relations program. However, a specific publicity campaign may be integrated into the agency's overall public relations program. In fact, the overall strategy for a publicity campaign should be determined with due regard for the long-term objectives and plans formulated for the continuing public relations program. It is probably over-emphasizing the obvious to suggest that all publicity is not necessarily good publicity or good public relations.

Internal Public Relations

Public relations usually implies activities designed to improve relationships with external publics. However, in identifying the agency's important publics the agency manager should remember that building prestige and favorable relationships is like charity—it should begin at home. A life insurance agency's primary "public" is within. If the agents and other employees are not enthusiastic about the agency and its sales activities the agency's external publics cannot be expected to warmly embrace the agency. By what he is, and what he does, the alert manager will strive to establish the right attitudes in his cashier or office manager, agency employees, supervisors or unit managers, and agents. This forms the foundation of any public relations effort, and the agency manager cannot sidestep this basic fact. A properly implemented internal public relations program will build an atmosphere within the organization that not only will contribute to internal efficiency but will also win external friendships. The casual visitor to an agency that is practicing good internal public relations will observe this "camaraderie" and will react favorably to this pleasant and comfortable environment.

A life insurance agency's basic objective is the marketing of its products. However, the accomplishment of this objective requires the accomplishment of several other objectives which contribute to the principal objective. Important among these secondary objectives is the recruiting of capable agency manpower. An effective agency public relations program can be of tremendous help in manpower recruiting and we will have more to say on this point later in the chapter.

Effective Communications as an Instrument of Public Relations

Before discussing specific what-to-do procedures, it might be helpful to pause to take a look at the central subject of our public relations endeavors—the human animal. At the same time we should examine some of the problems of communicating with homo sapiens.

Although effective public relations must be established by deeds as well as by words, a substantial part of effective public relations is accomplished through effectively communicating with our publics. Since the public relations message must be communicated to people it is important that when we undertake to communicate for public relations purposes that we keep constantly in mind certain important characteristics of people:

(1) People have basic needs—the need to feel economically secure, the need for social recognition, the need for a feeling of accomplishment, the need for personal security, the need for adventure and recreation. In general, people admit into their consciousness those ideas that interest them and those ideas that they believe will provide a benefit to them. Ideas that are related to the above human needs are more likely to be accepted than those that are unrelated.

(2) People have a profound desire to be treated as human beings. They will receive more favorably any communication that emphasizes human dignity and respect for the individual.

(3) People are interested primarily in themselves. After that, they are interested in other people, then in things, and as a general rule, finally, in ideas.

(4) Most people believe they are right. The agency's messages to

be communicated to its various publics, therefore, should be prepared in such a way that the majority of the readers will find the
opening sections consistent with their own views.

(5) What people expect may be as important as what they receive.

(6) People believe what they want to believe. For this reason, a
reader or listener will often read into a message what he wishes to
believe. This means he will often completely misconstrue the original meaning.

(7) The majority of people are middle-of-the-road thinkers.

If we take into account these basic points concerning why people behave
as people—which we sometimes tend to resist—it is little wonder that so
many of us have the experience of being sure we have communicated with
crystal clarity only to discover that our listener has not received the message the way we intended to communicate it. We know what we were
saying—it was plain enough *to us*. But somehow the other fellow gave
a different meaning to our words. A brief investigation of the psychology
of communication will not eliminate all our errors in communicating, but
it will go a long way toward enabling us to put our efforts in harness.
Here are eight basic checking points that can be helpful in improving
the agency's communications:

(1) We should think a moment about our aim—what are we trying to do? We usually communicate because we want a result; what
is this result explicitly? It will be helpful to walk around our purpose
and fence it in before we speak or write.

(2) Our listeners carry a headful of problems that are more important than anything else, to them. They are naturally I-centered
and wrapped up in their own problems. Therefore, we should not
antagonize our listeners by presenting opposing views. Rather, their
problems should provide us with an opportunity to emphasize advantages to them. We should put them in the center and talk about
advantages to them.

(3) It is helpful to know how much our listeners know. On the
subject of our communication, the listeners' knowledge is probably
less than we think. So we should start at their level, and use words
they will interpret as we intended. The pay-off in communicating is
not on what we think we are saying, but on what they think we are
saying.

(4) To get the most out of people, we should keep them informed. People have a deep instinctive need to know what is going
on, where they fit in, how they are doing. They rate the satisfaction
of "belonging" higher than many other satisfactions. It is a prime
sin of communications to be too secretive.

(5) We are communicating all the time. A frown, as well as a
wink or a smile, communicates. Our silence or absence may commu-

nicate ideas that would surprise us. To those around us, our manner, our gestures, and the tone of our voice are broadcasting messages and feelings all day.

(6) We should remember that people want to stick a label on us, based on our position, their experiences with us, or what they have heard about us. So they have a strong tendency to resist our "ax to grind" or hear what they expect to hear instead of what we mean to say.

(7) We should not be too sure. When we are categorically cocksure, we think we are making the sale. But normal people have a powerful urge to contradict. In their minds they fight back when the bulldozing technique is used.

(8) It is helpful to watch carefully the way people read and listen and understand. We should learn all we can about the receiving process in communication—how people filter our words through their own experiences. We should remember that we are not really communicating unless our listeners "get" our message as we intended.

DOES PERFORMANCE PRECEDE PUBLICITY?

A medical society in a western state a few years ago employed a public relations counsel. He quickly saw that they expected him to pour out an avalanche of laudatory publicity, and said to them, "When you've been kicking the customers around, it doesn't do any good to tell them through newspapers and radio how wonderful you are. First stop kicking them around." It is a common precept of public relations that performance must come first—that goodwill and prestige have to be earned. To a degree, this is a sound rule. Yet a moment's informed reflection on some of the laws of human behavior will remind us of this vital fact: that a person lives up to the picture carried in his mind. Our actions and beliefs conform almost inexorably to a concept or image lying often in a deep layer of our subconsciousness. On this premise, why doesn't it make sense to try to paint a picture in the minds of ourselves and our co-workers so we will tend to live up to it? If we say we are good, we are likely to find ourselves being magnetized to live up to the promise.

A realization that the performance-versus-reputation idea really works both ways is a good starting point for the construction of a public relations plan for an agency. Such a reminder is a provocative example of the wisdom of giving thought to the question of how a rule of thumb applies to one's own individual situation. To what extent does one place the performance before the talking about it? Wherein can one utilize the main idea that he live up to, or down to, his reputation?

BUILDING THE AGENCY'S OWN PLAN

An agency's public relations program should be conceived as a positive instrument for the implementation of marketing plans and the achievement of marketing objectives. Some writers in the field of public relations refer to the so-called "bank account" approach which emphasizes the positive by recommending "regular and sizable deposits in the Bank of Public Goodwill." When practiced as it should be this approach assures an adequate "bank account" for continuous daily operations as well as for the "emergency problem."

It is unfortunately true that too often an organization does not set up a public relations program until it has a problem to solve—a real emergency problem. This approach is basically defensive. An agency's public relations program should be neither preventive or curative. The program should be building prestige and goodwill as a living cash value. When an organization waits for trouble to erupt and goes around figuratively putting out small fires, it never seems to be in control. It is axiomatic in public relations, for example, that the truth rarely catches up with a rumor. The real trick, of course is to forestall the rumor through imaginative foresight and continual emphasis of the positive.

In simple outline, a workable procedure for initiating an agency prestige building and public relations plan consists of four basic steps:

A. *Identifying or defining the agency's publics.* Like any organization that endeavors to cultivate favorable attitudes toward itself, a life insurance agency has numerous "publics" that must be understood and reached. These groups or "audiences" are characterized by substantial differences in age, income, family status, type of home and neighborhood, occupation, and what is more important, great diversity in schooling, ideas, beliefs, prejudices, mental ability, habits and so on. There is no standard way to sort out an agency's publics, but the following are the most important: (1) policyowners; (2) prospective buyers of life and health insurance; (3) business firms; (4) centers of influence; (5) professional groups; (6) property and casualty insurance agents; (7) life and health insurance agents of other companies; (8) editors; (9) radio and television stations; and (10) all of the office staff and agency staff that would be identified as the agency's internal public.

B. *Learning as much as possible about what the agency's publics think and feel now.* Anyone in the business of selling or mixing with people has the beginnings of a pretty good idea about what is on the minds of these people. But usually it is possible to go a good deal further in probing the mental and emotional workings of these audiences that are important to the agency. It is a good idea to meet as many new persons in the particular groups as possible. It is helpful also to talk with other persons concerning what they think about the ideas and feelings of particular groups that comprise our marketing community. What the manager needs at this stage, however, is not suggestions and critical comments; he is striving merely to gather all the information he can—no punches pulled—about those people's background of ideas and information, their beliefs and prejudices, what they read, their attitudes, and of course what they think about life insurance, life insurance agents, the company, and the members of the agency. This is the firm foundation the manager will build on, and this step is critically important. It should not be treated lightly or shortchanged.

C. *Determining or defining the objectives to be accomplished by the agency's public relations program.* On the basis of the knowledge and attitudes possessed by the target group or groups, and the "relations" that currently exist between them and the agency, the agency manager is prepared to take the third step. The third step sounds deceptively simple, but an unhurried and thoughtful application of the manager's best efforts to determine what he wants will pay off handsomely. "Define" means clarify and fence in. The agency must say in detail what it wants the relationship to be—what it wants the various publics to know and feel about the agency. Defining is hard work. But it almost always pays to spend considerable time and work to define—to picture—to walk around and pin down what is wanted. In fact, to paraphrase a famous saying, "well defined is half done."

Two fundamental hints are in order when we define the desired end product of our efforts. First, the agency should hitch onto as many of the specific public's existing ideas and feelings as possible. It takes a fortune to change people more than an inch. It frequently is necessary to go more than half way to meet people rather than asking them to adapt to our ideas. So, we need to picture the way we want people to be, ideally, but we must still realize that we must build largely upon what is already in their minds and hearts.

The second point is this. We want people to look up to us and the members of our agency with respect. We want them to be impressed with our knowledge, experience, and competence. The agency's marketing publics must gain profound confidence in the technical competency of the sales organization. And this goal of a public relations program is the primary one to be emphasized. However, a secondary objective and an extremely practical objective is that we want people to LIKE us. Not long ago a policyholder who was vice president of a corporation in Massachusetts wrote a letter to his life insurance company citing five reasons why he gave his business to Agent J. The final reason, underlined, was: "I have learned to like him." A successful salesman or sales manager realizes this principle almost instinctively. But when we pause to formulate concrete plans of action, we are apt to forget the overriding importance of this emotional magnetism. That is why a public relations official, when asked if he could define public relations in one sentence, said: "I can define it in two words—making friends."

D. *Determining how to reach the individuals in the public or publics the agency plans to influence.* If the manager has carefully selected the group to go to work on first, second, third, and so on, then he is ready to select his channels of communication. What do these publics read? Can they be reached by letter? Where do they gather to eat or talk? What conventions do they attend? Who exerts an influence over them? The agency manager should ask these and other questions; he should ask them seriously and he should keep asking them. The manager should then compile a list of media or avenues of approach. Some managers call these media pipelines connecting with the desired audiences.

These channels or pipelines should be written down and judged for their availability to the agency and their suitability for reaching the people the manager has in mind. The primary channels are newspapers, including local and specialized ones such as the legal periodicals, magazines and so-called "organs" published for special groups. In using newspapers the manager should take advantage of the newspapers' special departments—financial, legal, social and other specific departments. With a little effort the agency manager can discover the names of a number of influential trade journals that reach his marketing community as well as small publications put out for certain groups in his community or certain occupations in his community. The manager should not overlook the many magazines or house organs published by big companies for their employees and for their customers and friends. In using radio and television, the manager should resist the temptation to think in terms of the broad appeal, and consider the use of such programs as might appeal to the audiences the agency wishes to work with.

Vehicles to Convey the Agency's Message

The list of materials and means for communicating the agency's messages is almost without end. It would include letters of all kinds, envelope inserts, newsletters and various periodicals, special or regular bulletins, descriptive booklets, publicity for newspapers and magazines, the use of the telephone, speeches, "open house" in the agency, meetings and seminars, signs and billboards, various kinds of displays and exhibits, slides and moving pictures. Perhaps such a list fails to include one of the most decisive, but overlooked, means of influencing people—everyday informal contacts. Suppose we take a look at several of the most significant of these communication vehicles.

DAY-TO-DAY CONTACTS AND FORMAL CONVERSATION

The way we say "Good morning" in the office, and the manner of "passing the time of day" on the street or at the club, communicate a great deal about us. Our casual conversation, and even our expression and manner without words, gives people ideas about the kind of person we are—rightly or wrongly—and provide a clue by which they formulate definite feelings and attitudes toward us. The face we wear, literally and figuratively, can make us or break us in our public relations endeavors. Even our absences and silences, according to management experts, can have a deleterious effect on the way people react to us. The boss who seems to be always away or who refuses to mix with his men, the secretary who will barely answer questions with no extra words to lubricate good feelings, the manager who proclaims the "open door" policy but contrives to make his employees feel uneasy when they drop in: All these are committing cardinal errors that damage the agency's efforts to establish goodwill and favorable feelings in the minds of any group of people. To build good relationships, we must be willing to be friendly, be accessible, talk, listen, take people seriously, hide our own headaches and think about the headaches of others.

THE TELEPHONE

The way we and our employees use the telephone is a vital building block in the structure of prestige and right relationships with many publics. A good telephone personality comes naturally to very few of us; we must cultivate it. The listener cannot see us to get the effect of our manner, our facial expression, the atmosphere of our office. So we must train ourselves to plant in his mind the feeling that we are friendly and ready to be of service. We can do a lot just in developing a good voice—one that is sincere and friendly, and at the same time clear and businesslike. Here are eight salient hints for improving telephone communications:

> (1) Materials and needed equipment should be kept beside the telephone. Pencil and paper should always be within reach. For some people special items such as reference material should be handy.
> (2) When the telephone rings, it should be answered immediately if possible. If the person himself cannot answer, then someone else should answer it.

(3) The person answering should sound friendly. One's voice should say that we are receptive and ready to listen, just as we would if a friend called at our home.

(4) It is important to speak distinctly, especially at the beginning. It takes a moment for the other fellow to tune in on our voice.

(5) Good enunciation is developed from practice. We should remember that the telephone transmits vowel sounds (a, e, i, o, u) well, but the listener has to guess at most consonant sounds by context. Therefore, we should speak slowly and clearly like a good actor.

(6) We should be patient. What we are saying, and the way we are saying it, may be all Greek to our listener. We should be willing to concede that maybe we have not been clear in explaining things.

(7) When we are away from the office, word should be left as to where we will be or when we will be back. The other people in the office should be encouraged to do likewise. Neglect of this habit causes tremendous losses in time and efficiency, and creates irritation.

(8) When the person called is not in, the person receiving the call should be constructive in arranging a contact. It may be possible to relay a message, or have the person call back. The function of the person receiving the call is to bring the two parties together.

CORRESPONDENCE AND DIRECT MAIL

The letters the agency manager and his personnel write are instrumental in building the image the manager seeks for his organization, and this paramount fact is too often neglected in the press of daily details. To the recipient of a letter, whoever he is, the letter-writer represents the agency. Every letter is important—whether it is a missive handling the serious complaint of a large policyholder or a direct mail "bait" letter. A letter is usually intended to produce some specific kind of result, usually tangible, and should be designed around that aim. But a letter—every letter—also carries overtones and leaves an impression about the agency, a taste in the mouth. Unconsciously, the recipient reads "between the lines" and forms ideas and attitudes about the agency, the agent, the agency's products and its way of doing business. This is the tone or "personality" of a letter and is just as important as the personality of an agent in the living room of a prospect or the girl on the telephone switchboard. So among the plethora of rules on letter writing presented in many books, these two should lead the rest:

(1) Before we write (or dictate) and while we are writing, we should think hard and explicitly about the purpose of the letter. Why are we writing? What do we want the reader to do? It makes an amazing difference in the effectiveness of a letter to keep the purpose of the letter before the writer's eyes.

(2) We should feel friendly and helpful. We should think of

things from the reader's viewpoint, and show that we are interested in him. We should try to make him like us. Any mature person who is reasonably social-minded knows, without thinking, the rules for being liked. But most of us stiffen up when we sit down to write a letter, and we forget those rules. So we must consciously bring them up and put them to work in our letters.

Among checking points for letters that contribute to an agency's public relations progress are these: "Set up" the letter to look neat and readable, without erasures. Use short paragraphs. Write short sentences, or vary the length with one idea to a sentence. Come to the point quickly. Check for clarity (to the reader); can he surely understand you? If seeking to influence the reader, talk in terms of advantages to him. Design your message around the reader instead of yourself and your problems. Be brief when you can, but take your reader's problem seriously, which sometimes requires a long answer. If you are replying to a request, read your letter over and ask "Have I really answered him?"

Most life insurance companies provide a direct mail service which is essentially a work organization device. Even so, every letter sent out is still important. Every letter leaves a taste, however small, and adds to or subtracts from the attitude the author is trying to cultivate in his publics. If the agency manager means business in his public relations program, he will want to choose letters and plans that help his efforts, and he should reject those that damage.

PUBLICITY

Almost everybody, it seems, wants publicity, and almost nobody knows how to get it. Loud are the lamentations when the publicity chairman sends in a three-page report and the editor prints three lines—or nothing. Then a publicity expert is hired and he is exhorted to "get something in the paper." Someone may suggest that all you have to do is know the editor. Most of these ideas about publicity are based on fallacious thinking or inadequate knowledge of the subject. Editors want news; they appreciate getting it. The problem is that most editors are hounded by people and organizations who are trying to "use" the editor for their own selfish interests. Some department editors of big newspapers receive thousands of "releases" every day when they have space for a dozen or fewer.

To get results with publicity, then, the first requisite is to think from the viewpoint of the editor. Is it really newsworthy? Will he feel that it is something that will interest his readers? The field of publicity is strewn with DON'Ts. Here are a few "DON'Ts" for the agency manager:

Don't try to force something on an editor or tell him how to run his business; ask him what he wants and how he wants it. Don't try to write your story in newspaper style unless you are trained and experienced in news work; instead supply full facts and accurate information (including exact names, with titles or identification, of people). Don't assume that you should see him personally; he is busy and it probably won't help. Talk with him on the phone or send your material in the mail. Don't even think of using newspaper publicity unless you are sure it is what you want; if you do, consider using the departments (to reach specific audiences) rather than the general news columns. Study your local newspapers for a week to see what special sections appear.

In general, the best way for the agency to get in the news is to do news-worthy things. The agency can manufacture its own news by making significant speeches, conducting forums or seminars for policyholders, attorneys, and other professional groups, joining hands with other important groups in the community, setting up a retirement workshop for men nearing retirement age, organizing an advisory group to work with schools or other organizations, and so on. An important rule is to "keep editors informed and build a reputation for reliability."

SIGNIFICANT SPEECHES

When the agency manager or members of his agency make a speech, the speaker has the opportunity to build good public relationships in two ways —the effect of the speech itself on the audience, and the result of having something about the speech appear in the newspapers. Both of these effects, of course, depend upon making speeches that contribute something significant to the thinking of the community. There is obviously no way to write a set of rules useful for all individuals in all communities, so this chapter will not undertake to do so. Libraries are filled with books and articles on the subject. The agency manager's own bookshelves probably contain a number of helpful volumes. Persons experienced in working with speech-makers, however, probably rate as the most important of all precepts for speechmaking, the crucial matter of preparation. Very few speeches given by busy men are well prepared. Preparation calls for time and hard work, but it produces self-confidence in the speaker—and makes a very substantial difference in effectiveness on the listeners. If you feel your speech should be written, or partly written, try in every way you can to avoid giving the impression that you are reading a manuscript. Reading is almost inevitably dull and sleep-producing. If you must read, practice till you are familiar enough with your material so eyes will not be glued to the paper. Visual material of various kinds—graphic demonstrations, physical objects, and flip-charts—help enormously to hold attention and make your point.

PRINTED LITERATURE AND ADVERTISING

Most of the agency's sales promotion material probably will originate in the home office, but that fact hardly relieves the agency manager from making his voice heard to keep influencing the home office creative staff never to overlook good public relations techniques. Every piece can be scrutinized for its presumed effect on people's attitudes, particularly how the items make people in the agency's own community feel about the life insurance business and about the agency.

The agency manager's major task, nevertheless, is that of riding herd on printed material, aside from letters and memos, that originate in the agency. This "printed material" would include not only material for prospects, policy-holders, and other outside publics; but also material addressed to agents and agency personnel. The agency manager must remember that public relations begins at home. And the printed word and the shape it takes can exert a powerful effect on the motions as well as the brain to set up favorable or unfavorable attitudes toward the agency and its management. As a reminder, the manager should jot down a simple list of some of the printed things that move around inside the agency—bulletins, notices and instructions to agents, periodical sheets perhaps with standings, items for the bulletin board, and special proposal forms. As in the case of letters, two important yardsticks ought to be applied to all this material: (a) Is the material prepared and written so it will produce the intended result (as opposed to a mere expression of the writer's problem)?—and (b) Will the material contribute to the cementing of friendly feelings and a favorable image in the mind of the reader? A little constructive thought along these lines can make giant differences in an area of primary importance, the agency's own immediate family.

These are some of the vehicles that convey the agency's communications to one or more of its publics, always with the hope that the results will contribute to the successful achievement of the agency's marketing objectives. But whatever he does to shape his communicating devices to the proper purpose, the agency head would do well to remind himself of the comment made by Ralph Waldo Emerson: "What you are ... thunders so, I cannot hear what you say." It is difficult to fool anybody who knows you, because what you are shows through. And it's almost as hard to deceive a stranger for long. Your character and reputation are undeniable facts, and no public relations expert can cover them up with a coat of paint. No matter how unceasingly you work at forging a program of prestige-building, something —call it integrity—deep within you will insist on doing its own communicating.

Constructive Suggestions for Implementing an Agency Public Relations Program

To assist him in implementing the foregoing precepts and ideas, the agency manager will find the following specific public relations suggestions to be applicable to the various agency publics, internal and external.

AGENCY SALES FORCE

In designing his over-all public relations program, the agency manager must give appropriate attention to his sales force. The agents should be continually courted and not taken for granted. Direct supervision should not give way after two or three years to mere greetings or occasional discussion of cases. Activities for the agents should be scheduled as far ahead as possible. The agent must feel wanted, needed, appreciated. Some ways of doing this are: Noting his birthday, his contract date, wedding anniversary, attainment of 60th and 65th birthdays and retirement date. Other ideas that have been used successfully include group meetings of advanced men, top producers and supervisors; room hopping meetings where expert associates and outsiders can preside—this is feasible for even a small agency; and installing a Big Brother plan where Big Brother is confidant, adviser and friend to new men. A Boston agency has developed a series of seminars to which the agency has invited attorneys and accountants who are centers of influence of its salesmen. This device obviously builds public relations in two directions. The program includes pension and profit-sharing plans, deferred compensation plans, estate planning, and other advanced uses for life insurance. Another agency is planning to conduct an afternoon meeting at which a recognized authority on economics and finance will speak. Members of the agency will invite centers of influence, policyholders, and key prospects.

The time-honored agency bulletin board should be divided into two sections. One should deal with matters personal to the agent such as production, standings, earnings, volume and contest winners, and this board should never be displayed in the reception or waiting room or public area, since these matters are private to the agent. A board which lists standings of agents may be a hazard to a sale when quarters are so arranged that a client or would-be buyer must pass or confront it in order to get to an agent's office. A second board, however, may be located away from the inner sanctum, to deal with matters of public interest—company and agency standings, client endorsement letters, clippings and items dealing with awards won, and similar matters.

Some managers recognize agents' accomplishments publicly by means of letters to influential persons, clients, prospective clients, and by means of releases to local newspapers. This, too, has a dual public relations effect.

Finally, hardly any act of the manager can be more effective in producing that feeling of goodwill in his own men than merely writing a personal letter to the agent. No matter how a man is honored through the public prints, direct mail or agency circulars, a hand written or a specially dictated note from the boss is always treasured.

POLICYHOLDERS

If public relations begins within and spreads outward in concentric circles, then the agency's policyholders comprise a public of considerable importance. This is true because a great part of the new sales of many agencies comes from policyholders who are adding to their programs, or from prospects to whom members of the agency have been referred by their existing policyholders. It would be a sad day indeed if much ill will resided in the hearts of many of the agency's current policyholders. It is worth a good deal of planning and hard work to build the right kind of favorable feelings in policyholders—partly because there are so many kinds of policyholders.

In planning a schedule of public relations activities for policyholders, the agency manager might make good use of the following check list of public relations tools:

—Agency periodical newsletter or mailing piece on taxation or other subjects of interest and value to the client.
—Periodic insurance review system.
—Welcome letter to new policyholder.
—Second letter upon purchase of another policy.
—Special agency premium enclosures.
—Invitation to attend a forum.
—Invitation to visit offices.
—Personal type letter asking for ideas and suggestions.
—Greetings on birthdays, anniversaries, and holidays.
—Special functions for owners of $50,000 of insurance.
—Offer of reprints of significant articles, speeches, etc.

Other ideas will occur to the manager who takes seriously the task of cultivating prestige among that very important audience—policyholders.

ORPHAN POLICYHOLDERS

In a surprising number of life insurance agencies there is a sort of no-man's land where persons who own policies in the company have been virtually forgotten. Because of the pressure of many activities, too many agencies must plead guilty to this neglect. The alert agency manager, however, will frequently find it quite profitable to develop a plan by which orphan policyholders are made to feel they are a part of the family and well taken care of. If a routine plan does not exist for handling this problem, it should probably be undertaken as a definite project without delay. Names should be distributed to agents on some basis such as geographic location or amount of insurance owned. This should be done on an assignment basis, in most cases, with the definite expectation that a report will be rendered to the agency head. In many cases, of course, a friendly letter or telephone call can precede a personal visit. No one likes to feel abandoned, and even though the policyholder may protest that he doesn't want to see a salesman, he will feel much better in his heart toward the agency and its manager if he knows that the agency is thinking about him and offering to provide the service he is entitled to.

PROSPECTIVE CLIENTS

This particular public, if properly qualified, can be profitably conditioned for the visit of the agent, and this is not always the task exclusively of the agent himself. Pre-approach material sent by mail can introduce the salesman, his company, and his agency in a favorable light. A monthly mailing piece or newsletter can be used with good effect. But in terms of influence, nothing can ever take the place of a letter which appears to be personally addressed to the prospect. There is no limit to the good effect that a well designed letter can produce in paving the way for a profitable meeting betwen agent and prospect. Such pre-approach material is often followed up with a telephone call aimed to make an appointment. The correct use of such material can predispose the prospect through its dignity and quality. Any literature used should be of impressive quality, and agents should rehearse telephone procedures carefully. The agency head should have a hand in all this, and should teach the things he has learned so well.

CLERICAL AND OFFICE STAFF

The most important objective of making the clerical and office staff an integral part of the agency's overall public relations program is to orient the office staff toward the concept that they are an important part of the agency team and that their many contacts with the "publics" which deal with the agency will have a significant bearing on the agency's progress. It is good business to imbue the agency's office employees with favorable attitudes toward the agency's management, and it is good business to take advantage of the tremendous influence that those employees have over their friends and neighbors. The agency's staff knows literally hundreds of people. By means of the things this staff does and says, the agency's reputation will precede the field man in many homes. These homes should learn about the agency's accomplishments and the way it does business. Clerical employees should participate in most agency events, and special courses should be made available to them on agency time, not their time. In these courses, homework should be assigned but completed assignments should not be insisted on. Accomplishment always should be praised and rewarded. In general, the office staff should be accorded the same respect and consideration that is accorded field men. They are important in building a successful agency.

SUPERVISORS

The supervisory personnel, agency's middle management, usually comprise the company's future general agents and managers. The agency head should meet and plan with them regularly. They should be encouraged to do original and creative thinking. The manager should use their ideas when he can, and reject them when he must, but in an appreciative tone. Since someone somewhere will want to hire one of the agency's supervisors, the manager will want to bind them to the agency with hoops of steel. A management principle of fundamental importance must operate here: The manager should take his supervisory staff into his confidence and keep them informed in every way. A supervisor, who hears about new plans from an agent first, is a public relations liability. Nothing can be more detrimental to morale. Supervisors, of course, should be encouraged to discuss their problems freely with the manager. In these ways, supervisors will be made to feel that they are an integral part of the agency mechanism. They will be better recruiters, better supervisors, and they will do a superb job of projecting the desired agency image.

PRESS REPRESENTATIVES

One of the most effective means of spreading a blanket of favorable attitudes toward the agency is that of developing harmonious relations with editors and representatives of institutional and non-institutional publications. The manager can well afford to get acquainted with various publication people and attempt to learn about their needs and fancies. As previously pointed out in this chapter, the manager should try not to use pressure with the representatives of the press, but he should learn to provide material in the way the editors like it. Personal acquaintanceship is not always essential for getting good results in the press, but where it seems appropriate and where there is no intent to pressure the editor, then an occasional meeting or even a small luncheon affair can be planned with good results.

TRADE ASSOCIATION RELATIONSHIPS

One of the most productive and lasting ways for the members of the agency to enhance their stature and reputation and that of their agency is to be intimately involved in the various programs of the industry's trade associations. Such participation builds good relations with other life insurance people in the community whose goodwill can be extremely valuable when clients ask other members of the life insurance business for their evaluation of the agency or some particular agent. The members of the agency should be encouraged to take part in the national, state, and local trade association activities and qualify for the institutional awards that symbolize excellence of performance. Such activities result in favorable publicity, usually by the local or national organization and this type of third-party influence can be valuable.

GOOD HOUSEKEEPING

An attractively decorated and furnished agency office can be an effective public relations instrument. It is amazing what is communicated by appearance. We judge people—often erroneously—by their appearance. Likewise the agency's publics that visit the office, will judge the agency by its physical appearance. Giving adequate attention to office appearance does not necessarily suggest expensive furniture, drapes and floral displays. However, few agencies are so isolated from their various publics that they can afford to ignore the fundamentals of good housekeeping. The agency image is projected to a large extent by its appearance. Included under the category of "good housekeeping" are such important items as ease of accessibility to the agency's office, ease of identifying location of the office, adequacy of parking space, adequacy and comfort of the reception area and the graciousness and hospitality of the receptionist.

Final Reminders

Upon the solid rock of good straight thinking and using as building materials the specific ideas enumerated on the preceding pages, adapted to the agency's particular situation, the manager can construct a successful public relations program. Success means that the important people in the community's variegated population mix will know about the agency, respect it, understand its objectives and come to like the members of the agency. And this in turn means they will tend to want to do business with the agency's representatives, or be glad to influence others to do so. Getting the right people to have favorable attitudes toward the agency is an important step in achieving the agency's objective of being a profitable business operation.

Public relations efforts should not take the form of an occasional spurt or special drive. Little good will accrue from a Monday meeting in which the manager waxes eloquently about the benefit of good relationships, unless his convictions are forged into a continuous program thoughtfully and appropriately developed to suit community and agency circumstances.

The advantages of putting public relations on a program basis are many. It will forestall the mistake made by numbers of life insurance men—getting into too many community activities instead of concentrating on a few. It will permit the comprehensive view so that various elements can be kept in balance. It will lend itself to timetabling; human nature being what it is, most of us accomplish little unless we are pushed by a "time tag." An organized program will assure that the subject is kept continually in a primary position in our consciousness. And it will help get everyone into the act— an extremely important consideration. The agency's own family of agents and employees must be the first recipients of the manager's efforts to build goodwill and favorable relationships; they must also become the agency's partners in active work to influence all the external publics.

19

Sales Promotion

Robert A. Adams

THE DIMENSIONS OF SALES PROMOTION

Sales promotion, in modern marketing parlance, includes all those functions which enhance the personal selling efforts of the agent to make himself and his product more readily acceptable to the prospect. Beyond this, it enables the agent to provide continuity of acceptance once the prospect has become a client.

The functions of sales promotion, varied and compelling, take many forms. Perhaps, however, they can be divided into two operative procedures: (1) *Advertising*, which brings the customer to an awareness of the product; and (2) those many other forms such as direct mail, leaflets and proposals, or special exhibits, all of which move the product to the prospect. In both of these procedures, prospect and product are brought face to face in that miracle of marketing called the sales interview.

COMPANY STRUCTURING

The degree to which sales promotion is brought into play depends entirely upon the management philosophy within a company. In most small companies operating with limited numbers of personnel, the functions of sales promotion will be locked into the sales department. In medium or large scale companies, the organization structure is quite varied. One organization chart indicates that the sales promotion manager, the director of sales and the manager of research are on the same level in a marketing team;

another splits the sales promotion responsibility and adds an advertising manager to the team. Still another chart shows the sales promotion group directly responsible to an official outside of the direct sales organization. And yet a fourth calls for the sales promotion team to be split, with an advertising manager answering to a key executive and the rest of promotion a part of the sales department.

It would be interesting to speculate on the best structure, but there is not sufficient space in this whole handbook to do so. Suffice it to say that there seems to be a growing trend toward the marketing team type of organization.

OBJECTIVES OF A SALES PROMOTION DEPARTMENT

Most sales promotion departments have grown because the public has become more sophisticated in its interests and selective in product acceptance. It must be a basic objective for a department to grasp new advances in graphics and combine them with old reliable formulas.

In addition, it must be a solid premise that sales promotion is there to help the agent in his selling endeavor. To this end, the objective must be to present the product with the utmost clarity.

Still a third objective is to enhance the prestige of the agent and his company in order to create a favorable attitude for his interview.

There are other objectives—(1) providing sustained interest in the company on the part of present clients; (2) helping the agent and broker to feel that they are receiving the backing of the company; (3) developing sales aids which, in a decreasing manpower situation, will enable the agent to conserve his preparation time.

RESPONSIBILITY

Specially trained and competent sales promotion personnel are the key to successful operations. No longer can a life company (if it ever could) indulge in the luxury of staffing its department with rejects from the field force or from elsewhere in the company. In organizing the department there are a number of questions to be resolved: (1) the *operational level* of the department must be determined. To whom will the director or manager report? Does his responsibility embrace promotion for all divisions—ordinary, group, and brokerage? Limits of responsibility should be clarified, for many a well-conceived marketing plan has been watered down because of inter-departmental squabbles. (2) *Number of personnel* hired depends in large measure upon the output required. Usually, a young company employs a small staff of two or three people with consulting services purchased for peak loads. (3) *Job descriptions* are necessary because they help to fix responsibility and encourage creative activity. When an individual knows the framework within which he may operate, it frees his mind from trivia. (4) *Responsibility* must be delegated and respected. Ordinarily, a company requires its sales promotion force to secure approval of copy at the law and actuarial level. This is a very acceptable safeguard, but the responsibility of such departments is to point out problem areas and not to attempt to rewrite.

STRUCTURE

Organization usually follows basic company philosophy. *The Roster* of the Life Insurance Advertisers Association clearly indicates the wide spectrum of job titles and responsibilities within a sales promotion department. Usually, there is a department head and reporting to him are the heads of various functional sections or units, such as direct mail, publications, and sales aids. Many larger departments have found it to their advantage to hire people to handle production work—printing, artwork, type specifications, billing.

FUNCTIONS OF SALES PROMOTION

As stated earlier, there are two objectives for the functions of sales promotion—the first one is to move the product to the prospect. There are many means to accomplish this:

Direct Mail

A method of prospecting known as direct mail uses the mails as a means of obtaining appointments for sales interviews. There are three basic forms of direct mail within most life companies.

> *Reply-Type* letters are individually addressed to a prospect. Such letters offer a gift to encourage inquiry and are processed at the home office from a selected list prepared by the agent. In most companies, this type of letter is a must. It creates a compulsive and consistent pattern for agent follow-up. And it pays off handsomely. In one company, for every dollar an agent spends for such services, he receives a return of $10 in sales commissions.
> *Pre-Approach* letters are usually sent by the agent in advance of the interview. By a personal and direct appeal, he hopes to prepare the prospect for his call.
> *Post-Approach* letters are sent after an agent (1) has found no one there when he called, or (2) has called and wants to remind his prospect or client of his visit.

Leaflets

Another principal ingredient to prospecting is the leaflet. Brief, and to the point, the copy in such sales aids presents the reasons for receiving a more complete explanation; this way the prospect is placed in a receptive frame of mind for the agent's call.

Leaflets and booklets are used in many ways. Some agents mail a leaflet to a prospect following a telephone call for an appointment. The mailing serves a twofold purpose: as a reminder of the interview, and to provide some information concerning the subject to be discussed.

There are also times when the agent wants to keep his client aware of the coverage he owns; the periodic mailing of a leaflet concerning such benefits helps to keep the business in force.

Another situation where leaflets are useful is when the agent has made his call and either has been unable to see the prospect or has made no sale. Often the agent dispatches a leaflet with a covering note expressing regret and leaving the door open to a future appointment.

Proposals

Proposals are used during the sales interview and portray, in concise, step-by-step fashion, the actual benefits and pertinent terms of the policy. The copy attempts to reduce technical contract phrases to those of everyday use; in doing so, the agent's time is saved and the client forms a stronger concept of his benefits. Many times, too, the proposal becomes a "track" to guide the inexperienced agent during the interview.

Some proposals are extremely simple, composed of an outline for filling in very basic facts. This type may cover an 8½" × 11" page and pertain to a single need for insurance, such as mortgage protection or education. Other proposals are quite formidable in their aspects and combine many factors involved in estate analysis. For instance, a client's full program can run for 15 or 20 pages and be presented in a beautifully bound, personalized format.

Displays and Exhibits

Other mediums by which an agent can develop a favorable sales climate are the display spaces in his own community, or the booth spaces at periodic business, industrial, or agricultural shows.

Too often overlooked, this form of public presentation, when worked out on a cost-per-lead basis, can prove to be quite rewarding. Very often a community bank or retail store may seek to build good will by featuring local business. Agencies or individual agents should be able to secure suggestions from promotion departments in the home office. Such ideas would include crowd-stopping devices which help to accumulate a large number of productive leads.

If home office help is not available, there are firms which specialize in this type of service. A bit of ingenuity and a rented motion device can produce some very satisfying results.

These points also apply to trade shows where the major outlay for a small-town exhibition is for booth rental fees. Such space, manned by a team of agents, provides a forum for on-the-spot discussion and the gathering of sales leads.

Publications

Generally, life insurance company publications may be classified in three categories: (1) field-oriented news periodicals; (2) production reports; (3) public-oriented periodicals.

Publications for field men vary from newsletter editions, printed by standard duplication methods, to the 64-page journals which are run on letter-press. There are also some companies which use a newspaper format and publish four to sixteen pages in tabloid size. Publication dates vary widely; some companies publish weekly, others distribute on a monthly basis. There is no relationship between the size of a company and the size and circulation of publication.

Most publications for field men serve a threefold purpose: (1) to encourage a fine *esprit de corps,* build morale, strengthen feelings of pride of occupation; (2) to continue sales education by presenting typical sales case studies; (3) to report company and general business developments.

Sales records of agents, whether computed monthly, quarterly, or otherwise, are generally reported by separate bulletin, though some companies include production figures in the field publication. The main purpose for production reports, other than to verify sales statistics, is to provide a competitive spirit within the organization.

Public-oriented periodicals run the gamut from the company's published annual report to the policyowners magazine, which may be small enough to be inserted with premium notices. Perhaps the greatest variety of publications is found in this group. There are special newsletters for brokerage development, others for an agent to mail to his clients over his logotype (these are still further divided according to markets, such as doctors, lawyers or engineers). Some agencies issue special reports to their clientele; companies mail special recruiting material to key nominators. Others prepare special publications for group clients to distribute to their employees. This list is almost endless!

Audio-Visuals

A newer form of sales romotion is the audio-visual aid, a product of the Electronic Age. Audio-visuals have seen increasing use in life companies, particularly in the recruiting and training sectors of the company operations. Moreover, a growing number of companies use audio-visuals for providing new agents with a professional approach to the sales interview. By having a concise, graphic review of major points at his fingertips, the agent approaches his clients with poise and confidence.

On the other hand, most experienced agents feel that such a device tends to separate them from their clients. To some degree, they feel relegated to a secondary role by the smooth operations of the audio-visual equipment. Additionally, they question whether it is not too limiting for the many conditions which exist in an estate-planning interview.

Undoubtedly, these latter questions will be resolved as new improvements and applications evolve in the electronics field.

ADVERTISING

The second of the two objectives for the functions of sales promotion is to bring the customer to a greater awareness of the product. This objective is fulfilled by planned programs using the various media of advertising, including newspapers, radio, television, consumer magazines, billboards, insurance journals, and car cards.

Company policies regarding expense and sales philosophy have a direct bearing upon advertising campaigns. Before any department proceeds, it must have full comprehension of these two factors. The best campaign in the business will fail because of insufficient budget or because its theme is at odds with accepted sales procedures.

Planning an advertising campaign is a job for the experts. The type of campaign, the choice of media, the copy appeal, layout, and artwork are all intricately tied together and dependent upon market research.

In the medium-to-large companies, such planning may be done by the advertising sales promotion staff, often with advertising agency cooperation; in small companies, an advertising agency is usually the most practical and effective solution.

KEEPING THE AGENT INFORMED

One of the basic problems of all sales promotion departments is that of keeping the sales aids from piling up on the stockroom shelves. Too often a promotion man will hear an agent lament "Why don't we have an

XYZ presentation?" When in actuality, he not only has an XYZ presentation, but one that has been honored in a national competition!

Presenting New Materials

Imagination seems to be the key to the problem. One of the chief gripes of a field man is the constant flood of letters from the home office. Therefore, it becomes necessary to find different ways to merchandise new (and established) materials.

Some promotion departments issue to the agents a newsletter which announces new materials. Each issue is numbered, dated, and mailed at regular periods. Very often a cross index to the subjects contained in the newsletter is mailed, say at six-month intervals. This helps the agent to locate a reference to a new leaflet or proposal he may want to use.

Another device is a special bulletin board distributed to each agency or field office of the company. Materials for display on the special board are mailed to the agencies at certain intervals. Perhaps one month all of the sales aids relate to mortgage insurance, the next month's packet contains sales materials for a theme on juvenile insurance. Included are ideas on how and when to use these promotional aids.

Agents' magazines are also a fine merchandising medium for sales aids. Editors often build a feature article around some new visual aid or a new sales promotion kit. In such instances, the materials are pictured and ordering procedures, outlined. Sometimes there is a special insert prepared for the magazine, which includes a special tear-off order form.

There are instances when an agent-authored article includes references to certain of the company sales aids. Usually, the editor inserts the proper name and form number of those materials mentioned.

Filing Systems

Once the agent is made aware of the existence of new materials, it is axiomatic that it be made easy for him to find them.

Most sales promotion departments provide a special file for use in the agency. Such a file can take many forms: a set of loose-leaf books with pasted-in samples, a series of reference files containing separators and sample items, a special inventory file system containing room not only for samples but for actual supplies as well.

Some companies provide their full-time men with a special file box for cards, filed by form number, referring to each major sales aid in stock. Periodically, an index is issued by which the fieldmen may bring their references up to date.

Another method is to provide the agent with a couple of large containers in which are complete package kits. The typical kit contains a leaflet, a sample direct mail letter, a proposal, a sales track including answers to objections, and perhaps an application or some rate information. Each kit relates to a specific coverage—mortgage, juvenile, etc. It is the duty of the agent to keep them up to date, though it is current practice to mail replacement material when newly introduced.

USING SALES AIDS

Unquestionably, the agent must have some fundamental concepts of the value and use of sales aids. Because of this, he receives considerable information during his early training periods.

During sales meetings or special training seminars very often it is general practice for the sales promotion people to have a part in the program. At this time, they can explain to a broader degree, perhaps, the relationship of promotion functions—what to use, when, and where. Special visual demonstrations and reference materials are often made available in order to demonstrate the value of sales promotion more dramatically.

Interestingly, it is during one of these meetings that an agent suddenly becomes aware of the objective of a certain program of advertising or a sales aid; and his enthusiasm communicates itself to others in such fashion as to greatly increase the use of that item.

PREPARING THE BUDGET

There are many methods for developing the appropriation for sales promotion functions; *Printers' Ink* once published eleven. The two most common seem to be the budget system and the task method.

Systems

In the budgetary system, an appropriation is devised as the result of examining past expense, making adjustments as determined by the department head. Under the task method, the objectives are examined in the light of minimum expense for accomplishment and that figure is the projection.

Some company promotion heads refer to the expenditures of their competitors for guidance (line 5.2 of exhibit 5—General Expense of the Annual Statement). This is not the most dependable procedure, since each company puts its own interpretation on definitions and may have different objectives.

Other sales promotion departments base their overall costs on a percentage of new premium. From this figure they work out allotments for each function.

The bases are varied and the implementation is just as much so. Once assembled, the appropriation request often has a final screening through an approval or budget committee consisting of some members of the executive branch and the controller.

Controls

Production and budget control are interlocking. If some sort of system is established to check on the whereabouts of jobs, it is comparatively simple to add a budget check as well. For instance, a system of file folders is set up. In each folder is the original approved manuscript, a few printed samples, carbons of art, type, and printing bills. The folder then is marked with the stock number of the piece it contains. Thus, typical cost information is always accessible for quick estimate.

For a guide on budget, a ledger book is prepared and divided by functional accounts. Each time a new folder is filed, the production costs are entered on the proper account sheet in the ledger book. At any specified interval, the pages for each account are totaled, and in this way a full accounting becomes readily available.

Subsidy

Of course, subsidy has a direct bearing upon the budget and can be quite helpful in financing added services. A large number of companies underwrite the complete cost of promotion materials on the philosophy that these are sales aids that should be given the agent to help him sell. Some promotion departments charge a very small amount to encourage thrifty use of materials. This is usually done through a special formula. There is no charge for art and the agents are assessed one-half of the printing cost.

Advertising is often entered into cooperatively. The agent pays half of the space costs and the company absorbs the remaining costs. Some companies pay all the production costs and ask the agent to pay for the newspaper space.

COMPANY COMMUNICATION

Home Office

It is of paramount importance for the sales promotion people to keep open the lines of contact with other departments. This will provide them a means for proper appraisal of promotion objectives and the opportunity to see and evaluate actual materials in the light of the objectives. Such understanding has a twofold benefit: better objectivity at budget review time; easier acceptance by management of new campaigns and programs.

One of the means used to accomplish these ends is the distribution of announcement material. Each time a letter and its samples are dispatched to the field men, the promotion people also route a set to key executives in the home office. Some departments issue a special bulletin to home office personnel which contains the samples as well as actual background material on how or why such pieces were selected.

Field

Good communication with agents is extremely important. Methods have been discussed earlier, but the importance of service to the agent cannot be over-emphasized. Communications is a two-way street, and many a fine sales promotion idea had its inception in the bright mind of an agent. And because he knew there was a sympathetic reception there, he sent it on for development by the sales promotion department.

SUMMARY

The many types of sales aids readily available for use by the fieldman and the many different advertising campaigns which are displayed year after year, all have helped greatly in improving the status of the life under-writer. Of course, all of this has required the intelligent application and the creativity of the sales promotion technician to sort out practical, but exciting, means for arousing the prospect's interest. In combination, this team has brought into being a tremendous and ever-growing acceptance of the role of life insurance and the life insurance counselor.

Section VII

MANPOWER DEVELOPMENT

20

The Development
and Growth of Manpower

Edward B. Bates

THE NEED FOR MANPOWER

The fact that Americans now own more than a trillion dollars of life insurance protection is a tribute to their character, their sense of responsibility and their desire to provide for themselves and their families.

It is also a tribute to the agent. The life insurance agent has not only helped people to understand their responsibilities; he also has persuaded them to act on these responsibilities. History has shown that although many people readily acknowledge the value and unique advantages of life insurance, they do not normally buy on their own initiative nor do they buy in adequate amounts. They do buy when a competent agent identifies their problem and offers a solution with the matchless guarantees of life insurance.

The Manpower Problem

If the key to marketing life insurance is the agent, then the key to successful sales management is the development and growth of adequate agent manpower. This is easier said that done. Why is manpower such a problem? In the first place, the job of selling life insurance is a difficult one, sometime referred to as "the best paid hard work in the world." Because of a lack of high career prestige, relatively few men seek out a career in life insurance selling. The manpower problem also has been compounded in recent years by an unusually tight market for skilled manpower—a situation that gives promise of continuing into the foreseeable future.

If life insurance and the life insurance business as a whole are even to hold their own in competition for people's security and investment dollars, they must increase their sales power. The approach is dual in nature:

1. Add new manpower at a better net rate than heretofore.
2. Improve the effectiveness of present manpower.

It is important to the future of individual life insurance companies, and the life insurance business overall, that both of the above approaches be undertaken—and undertaken well. Alone, neither approach can provide a long-run solution to the manpower problem. For example, it does little good to hire new men if they are not given superior training and supervision so that they may develop to their full potential. On the other hand, if no new men are hired, then the agency force eventually dies, no matter how effective it may have been in the meantime.

The Life Insurance Market

Most signs point to a continuing great potential market for life insurance. The population is not only going to continue to grow, but people are going to have increasingly higher standards of living to protect, with more and more real disposable income to provide for protection. More specifically, the age group that includes the ideal buyers of life insurance (ages 25–34) is now growing at a faster rate than other age groups in the population.

If the life insurance business is to capitalize fully on the expanding market potentials of today and tomorrow, however, sales management people at all levels must give top priority to the development and growth of manpower.

Manpower and the Company Objectives

Just as the acquisition of adequate sales manpower is a continuing challenge for the life insurance business as a whole, it should be likewise a high priority objective for any life insurance company wishing to maintain its relative position in the industry. This holds true whether a company specializes in individual policies, group insurance or credit life insurance. Although all three require a sound sales organization, the emphasis in this chapter will be on a sales organization for the marketing of individual policies.

If a company desires stable growth and profitable operations, it can hardly expect to achieve these objectives without *its own* sales organization. The economies of size and the need to provide expanding opportunities for employees and agents virtually dictate that growth be an objective of every life insurance company. Growth, in turn, calls for increasing sales results. These, in turn, call for more and more effective field manpower. No company has reached a position of significance in the market place except from the foundation of its own sales organization.

Equally as important as an established field organization is the need for a continuing flow of new sales manpower. A sales organization soon loses both its numbers and its impact if there is not a steady infusion ot new manpower. In most established field organizations, about one half of the field force can be classified as established and experienced. The other half consists largely of agents in their early years, with the balance in their retirement years.

No company can afford to lose the momentum of new manpower development. Not only would it lose the flow of business from new agents, but, perhaps more importantly, it would lose the example of successful new agents who serve as magnets in the recruiting and development process. Further, the company that adds no new manpower loses its flow of candidates for future field management posts.

Equally as important, although perhaps slightly more difficult to measure precisely, is the effect of new manpower on the total growth and vitality of a life insurance company. A steady flow of new and able sales manpower into an agency and a company is an all-important ingredient in assuring enthusiasm, esprit de corps, morale and challenge. Successful new men stimulate each other. They also serve, in many cases, as a powerful stimulus to improved performance by established men in the same organization. Of the many actions that the management of a life insurance company can initiate, therefore, none will contribute more to the long-range growth and health of the company than consistent emphasis on the right kind of manpower growth and development.

ESSENTIALS FOR MANPOWER DEVELOPMENT AND GROWTH

Field manpower development and growth succeed or fail—occur or do not occur—almost entirely at the field level. Home office efforts in direct recruiting and development are a minor factor in most companies. At the same time, however, the success of field efforts is influenced in a major way by home office decisions and home office support. It is important, therefore, to delineate clearly the basic responsibilities of home office from the field and their relationships.

A successful program of manpower development and growth should include each of the following essentials:

1. Clearly defined company objectives.
2. Adequate program of field management development.
3. Adequate and competent home office agency department staff.
4. Home office support of field efforts in manpower development.

Company Objectives

The first step in manpower development has been taken when a company has clearly thought out its objectives, developed policies and procedures to support these objectives, and defined a program that will lead to their attainment. Management must then communicate these plans to all who are involved in the manpower development activity. Nothing can be more important than clearly defined objectives, the establishment of individual responsibilities, and the definition of the necessary relationships. Each of these, of course, are not attained until they are communicated effectively. This process begins with the definition of total corporate objectives as they apply to the philosophy for agency growth and development, the pattern of this growth, and the assurance that the objectives and the programs will have the necessary degree of permanence. Without objectives and the necessary follow-through, a company can hardly expect any degree of continuity from its field management.

Manpower objectives must be specific—both for the company as a whole and for each agency. The total responsibilities of manpower development also must be clearly defined. Recruiting is only one step, although an important one, in the total process. Selection, training, and supervision in the initial years and continuous programs for upgrading established agents are also important parts of the manpower development process.

Field Management Support

Any discussion of manpower development must include field management. The development of field management can never be separated from the total manpower development process. The development of future field management personnel may even commence before a general agent or manager is aware that a particular man is managerial caliber.

The field manager must clearly understand the company's total corporate objectives, his own specific manpower objectives, and the tools that the company will provide to assist him in attaining his objectives. Of course, he must have confidence in these objectives and in the support being provided.

Another important ingredient, and one frequently neglected, is a clearly defined program of financial support for field management together with a clear delineation of whatever limitations are necessary. If the company is to provide financial assistance through an agent's training allowance plan, or if the company is to provide certain home office training schools, these programs should be realistic in light of the prevailing conditions. In view of the competition for manpower and the extensive financial assistance and training offered by all industry today, it is unrealistic for life insurance company management to expect superior or even adequate results from its field management with inadequate home office financial support. Such support must be on a continuous basis, not a sporadic nor transitory basis.

The Home Office Agency Department

The caliber and organizational structure of the home office agency department staff must be adequate for the task and results expected. Continuous liaison between the field manager and his home office agency department is important, both for practical and morale reasons. Just as the agent needs his general agent, or manager, for frequent communication and support, the general agent or manager needs his home office agency department. Many times this will be for psychological reasons alone. So there must be open lines of communication both ways, confidence both ways, and a program that insures periodic review of plans, programs, and progress for agency manpower development.

The home office agency department fills another vital role—that of providing sales and training assistance. As the need for quality training has increased, more and more home office agency departments have found it necessary to step up their training efforts. The activities of the home office agency department in all areas of sales support can directly contribute to an agent's total development. For example, training sessions for both field managers and agents can provide a needed link between agent and company, in addition to satisfying a basic training and development need.

Development of Field Management

To parallel the over-all program for agent development and to assure continuous growth of the company through field manpower growth, it is important to have an ongoing program for developing field management. Good field management will not just happen. Men who have not been successful as agents can seldom qualify for field management. Those who have been successful as agents frequently hesitate to leave one successful career path for another. The reasons why many men leave a salaried career in industry for life insurance selling are the same reasons that they sometimes do not desire to enter field management. There is a certain paradox in recruiting a man to the independence and financial opportunity of life insurance selling and then a few years later suggesting that he give up some of that independence for a management opportunity, either in the field or home office!

What about the company that has a surplus of well-qualified people seeking field management opportunities? First, this may not always be a desirable situation! It may suggest that too many men in the company view the agent's career with less than enthusiasm. At the same time, a goal of company growth demands growth and expansion in the company's field management. Thus, it is necessary to have a certain "backlog" of prospective managers. Along with this goes the need for intelligent selection and outstanding training. When a company puts a qualified man into field management, it takes on a responsibility to make certain that the man has an ample opportunity to develop and progress in management—or, if things don't work out—to return to personal selling with the least possible disruption. Since manpower results depend, in the final analysis, on what field management does, the responsibility for developing competent field management should be given top priority in terms of action, resources, and support.

Total Home Office Support

Increasingly, home offices are accelerating and expanding their activities in direct support of manpower development programs. Of course, "manpower development" is a broad term. It includes recruitment of the agent and extends through his total career development. Few agency managers or general agents can develop an organization that is sufficiently large and financially able to provide all of the training and sales support requisite for agent success today. Thus, support from the home office is required. This support from the home office should complement—not substitute for —what is provided at the agency level.

Today, home office departments are active in many areas of agent development. For example, home office activity in direct recruiting, especially at the college level, is increasing. Early agent training, at the home office or with home office support on a regional basis, is also becoming more important. Such training makes possible the use of a variety of training techniques that would be impractical at the agency level. The prospect for the future is for increasing home office support in training, especially in the more complex sales areas, such as business insurance and pension and profit-sharing plans.

In some cases, manpower development and growth have been less than satisfactory because the program has been fragmented. It is most important that there be a *total* definition and understanding of manpower development and growth, and that there be a *total* program to bring about desired results. Both definition and program need to be continually enlarged. Each new technique of training and sales help enlarges the definition of total development of the agent. In turn, this means an enlargement of the program for accomplishing this development. Periodic assessment of the ingredients and relationships of the manpower development program is essential to the success of that program.

MANPOWER PLANNING

Every aspect of a company's long-range planning is related, in varying degrees, to the quantity and quality of its field manpower. At the same time, planning by the agency department carries a high degree of accountability, not only to the executive management of the company, but to all other operating functions.

Manpower Audit[1]

The place to begin in agency department planning is with a total and cross-sectional inventory of field manpower, as it stands currently and as it may reasonably be projected into the future. The foundation for all company forecasting and planning is an accurate and well-structured audit of existing manpower—including all levels of field management, as well as a realistic cross-section of all sales manpower. A good audit will serve as a road map to progress.

To be useful, any manpower audit must be kept up to date. It must consider manpower from a number of standpoints and on the basis of a number of criteria. For example, the chief executive of the company and the head of the agency department need to know whether the agency department table of organization is properly staffed. But this is not all. They want to know the age of each individual together with an assessment of performance, capabilities, future senior management possibilities, and potential for advancement.

Audit of Field Management

An important part of the audit will be concerned with the top level of

---

[1] For an example of a manpower audit form, see Appendix A at the end of this chapter.

field management. The aim is to have on tap an always-current evaluation of general agents or managers. Among the factors that should be included are: (1) years to retirement; (2) years in the job; (3) a performance level evaluation for each year in the job; (4) potential transfers to larger responsibilities; (5) potential transfers to home office; and (6) potential terminations for reasons other than retirement.

Once the audit is constructed it must be analyzed and evaluated. The evaluation of the audit is not a one time affair, but instead must be done periodically. For the agency vice president, the evaluation should be completed perhaps even quarterly. From these evaluations will come answers to the following as well as other important questions:

1. What changes are occurring in our over-all inventory of field management?
2. Is the number of potential retirees increasing or decreasing?
3. Is the number of potential terminators increasing or decreasing?
4. How many potential transfers to greater responsibility can we accurately identify?
5. What has been the trend of terminators in recent years?

The next audit to construct is for staff management—assistant general agents, assistant managers, supervisors or whatever they may be termed in a given company. Again, there are a number of measurements to be taken on a regular basis to provide for an always-current appraisal of this highly important segment of the management team.

It is necessary for management to be alert to dangers of both underdevelopment as well as occasionally to dangers of oversupply. Keeping this group of field management people in balance, from the standpoint of their needs and opportunities, is a major responsibility for the agency department head. When this responsibility is carried out well, the usual result is high morale among the entire field management staff. Frequent assessment of the progress and potential of each member of the staff management group should be a major responsibility, not of just the agency vice president, but of all those with field management responsibilities.

As competition for field management accelerates, it becomes increasingly important for a company to try to develop enough field management for its own needs. It is equally important to encourage each individual to develop to the peak of his own capability. An always sensitive question is when to move a man into a larger assignment. This is ideally done just as soon as the man is ready—but not before. Whose responsibility is it to make the selection? Normally, it is a joint decision between the general agent, or manager, and his corresponding home office associate. Hopefully, they will be able to make the right selections at the right time.

It is obvious that the larger the group, the more difficult it is to maintain an accurate, meaningful manpower audit. An agency vice president who has 100 general agents, or managers, might be able to rely to some degree on his own "feel" for the status of his first-line field management. If this group has, as its companion, 250 staff managers of various levels of experience and responsibility, the vice president will be less certain of the overall composition of that group. Additionally, if there are some 1250 life underwriters to consider, he will be in dire need of an accurate manpower audit. This audit should tell him a number of important things about his sales force. For example:

1. The number who are over age 65.
2. The number who have less than 12 months of completed service.
3. The number who have more than 12 but less than 24 months of completed service.
4. The number who are producing less than a reasonable production minimum. This can be further indexed by years of service, age, and number of sales.
5. The over-all educational and training achievements, again cross-indexed by years of service and age.
6. The various production and income levels, again indexed by years of service, age, and number of sales per year.

Application of Audit Findings

Once this cross section of the entire field organization has been properly structured, and maintained over a reasonable period of time, the agency department head and his associates will have a valuable tool for evaluating the present and controlling the future.

From a study of audits of the three groups—field management first-line, field staff management, and agents—a nucleus of competent people should emerge in each group. These will be the people who meet the criteria of performance, reasonable years of experience, and age.

Depending on the manner in which standards are set, a company might find that little more than one-half of each of the three groups could be classified as above-average manpower with good potential. When a company can identify barely one-half of its general agents or managers in the "above-average productivity" category—a problem exists. For example, it is unrealistic to think that even as many as one-half of the sales manpower personnel in each of those below-average agencies will meet any reasonable standard of performance. It is also unrealistic to expect much growth in those agencies.

When is management ready to make realistic projections and plans? Only after the manpower audit at all levels has been made and firmly documented! Even then, it is important to continue to observe the pattern or trend in each of the three groups over a reasonable period of time. At some point in time the effect of management decisions in the area of recruiting, training, and over-all manpower development at various levels will be measurable.

How can management go about building permanent manpower? There is no certain way. Obviously, it cannot be done simply by accelerating the recruiting rate. Most likely there is some level of recruiting new manpower that will yield the best "rate of delivery" to an experienced sales manpower group.

If the manpower audit reveals a level of production among the experienced group that is unrealistically low, this may suggest a need for a certain type of training or supervision. Of course, it will be possible to evaluate the effect of these moves through a continual examination of the manpower audit.

Another question that must be answered by management is: How fast should agency offices be expanded? Whatever rate is chosen, it should be closely geared to the total inventory of field management. For example, a company that has been "liquidating" its inventory of potential agency managers would use poor judgment if it attempted, in the face of this fact, to accelerate the rate of agency expansion. Yet, without a manpower audit, such information would be lacking on which to base a sound decision.

The manpower audit can also be valuable in reaching decisions about training allowance plans for new agents, projecting new premium income, projecting costs under group insurance and retirement plans for agents, and many other programs that have a major effect on total company expenses and operating results.

Careful evaluation of the manpower audit over a period of years will also enable the company to make accurate projections and assessments of its training needs—for both field management and sales manpower.

An effective manpower audit can also be used as a point of reference by individual agency managers. Their own plans and performance have much more meaning when first related to the cross section of the company as a whole, and then to the cross section of the superior agencies of the company. So, the manpower audit can serve not only as a management tool for home office management, but as a management guide and motivator for field management.

To carry this one step further: The company that has developed a well integrated market research program will be able to relate certain sales and market findings to the various segments of the manpower audit. Are there characteristics of manpower that seem to go hand in hand with top-flight sales results? What knowledge can be gained and what techniques can be learned from these cross relationships? Which techniques might be transferable?

The uses of a well structured and frequently updated manpower audit are virtually infinite. Undoubtedly, the longer an audit is maintained and carefully studied by those in authority, the more uses will be developed and the broader will be their application. But if there were no other values from a manpower audit, this alone would make it worthwhile: *To stimulate intelligent management thinking and management planning!*

The audit, therefore, becomes the launching pad for projecting the company's manpower requirements for both the long- and the short-range. As experience is gained with the audit, it will be easier to predict the amount of time needed to bring various levels of field management to maturity. The recruiting rate and the attrition rate, together with productivity and training requirements, will be easier to define, to document, and to develop into reasonably reliable projections.

Matching Manpower with Market Objectives

The next step in manpower planning is to match manpower to the company's market objectives. Although this planning may not be as reliable as if scientific management procedures were used, nevertheless, the validity of the projections will be directly related to the validity of the manpower audit.

A sound manpower audit enables management to control its manpower planning. It enables management to implement its manpower planning. Of course, these goals will not be achieved unless there is widespread understanding of, and agreement on, company objectives and agency objectives. There must be effective communication in all directions. Such communication rests largely on the documentation of results that come from a manpower audit. General agents or managers will best understand what is expected of them when they can view in detail the manpower results of the company and of individual general agents or managers.

Personal commitment toward the over-all goals of the company will be in direct proportion to the effectiveness of this communication and the documentation on which it is based. Commitment also will be stronger if results are accurately analyzed and related to other results throughout the company. It is important that home office management not only be able to define precisely what is expected, but also be able to show exactly what has happened. There is no question but what the effectiveness of manpower planning and evaluation of results will rest in large part on the reliability, believability, and acceptance of the manpower audit and related reports.

Total performance of the sales organization must be under continuous evaluation. It is important that the standard of performance for each individual, whether in management or in sales, be clearly defined and carefully communicated. Training and other aspects of over-all development must be geared closely to predetermined standards of performance. Careful measurements of that performance must be frequent and well communicated throughout the company.

Finally, there must be a termination policy in keeping with the standards of performance and the actual performance. Commitment to levels of performance will be diluted considerably if those who fail to meet the standards are allowed to continue with the company indefinitely. In other words, if a man fails to measure up over a reasonable period of time, he should be terminated or given a different opportunity.

Manpower planning must be continuous and ongoing. There must be sound, carefully structured measurements to document both expectations and performance. There must be good communications. There must be personal commitment. Finally, there must be management discipline at all levels—an important dimension in the performance-commitment-performance cycle.

THE INTERACTION OF ALL FORCES
IN MANPOWER DEVELOPMENT

To achieve sound manpower development, many forces need to act and interact. They are ingredients of the whole manpower development process. The way they interact can result in the success or failure of the company's entire marketing effort. So they are both contributor to, and product of, manpower development. Although these forces may be separately identified, they are so interrelated that it is difficult to evaluate the precise dimension of any one force by itself.

The following are the forces that must not only be present, but must mesh in proper relationship if a company is to achieve sound manpower development:

1. Company vitality.
2. Management opportunities and development.
3. Levels of achievement for individual agencies and agents.
4. Sales results and their pattern.
5. Morale of the entire company and more specifically, morale of the sales organization.

Company Vitality

This highly important, admittedly elusive, quality is probably the best over-all measurement of the effectiveness of company management and over-all company effort. Company vitality is in a large part the end-result of superior sales results, exceptional levels of achievement by individuals, a high degree of morale, and a proper balance between management development and management opportunity. Company vitality affects manpower development in no small degree. It has a direct bearing on sales results, on individual levels of achievement, on morale, and the entire process of field management development.

Management Opportunities and Development

In assessing each of these ingredients and interacting forces, some become more specifically traceable to the manpower development process than others. The happy condition of having adequate and competent field management can provide a basic and direct key to the recruitment and development of field manpower. Obviously there must be competent field management at all levels, as well as adequate opportunities for those who are qualified and who desire field management opportunity. At the same time, there must be an adequate supply of competent field management people to meet the expansion objectives of the company.

A competent field management team is perhaps the biggest, single, positive factor in the development of field manpower. It is responsible for first identifying and then attracting prospective agents to the company. It is responsible for their training and supervision in the early years, and for their broader development and advancement in the continuing career years.

Manpower development also depends on what kind of opportunities exist for new people to join the management team and to grow with it. Without these opportunities and without the example of men moving successfully into field management, many prospective agents simply will not be attracted to the career.

Levels of Achievement for Individual Agencies and Agents

The next major force that is both a factor in manpower development and an end result of good manpower development is the individual level of achievement for the agency force. Next to the direct activity and influence of the general agent or manager in the recruiting and total development of an agent is the example that an agent sees in others. Also important is the contribution he in turn makes to the level of achievement that establishes the example.

Prospective agents are attracted to a life insurance career, and to a specific agency, by individual patterns of success and methods of operation that they can relate to their own ambitions. Individual levels of achievement and, in turn, company sales results, are measurably influenced by the achievement levels of company and agency leaders. It is up to both company and agency management to establish realistic yet ambitious objectives. It is up to these management teams to help all individuals meet their set objectives.

Those who join an agency aspire to a given production level as they are influenced by the example of others both in their agency and throughout the company. Production levels required for company convention requirements, attendance at schools, and other recognitions can also be great motivators.

New agents, who reach high levels of achievement early in their careers, are likely to have a salutary effect on longer-established associates in an agency. If a general agent, or manager, can relate various achievement levels from the very beginning of an agent's career, and continually upgrade objectives for each member of his organization, he will be playing a vital part in the over-all manpower development process.

In challenging an agent with specific goals of achievement, it is important that the manager set only goals that are meaningful and realistic for that man. Although the manager will want to present the full dimensions of opportunity, he will also want to be open about the pitfalls as well as the rewards. He cannot afford to raise hopes that may be beyond a particular agent's reach at a particular point in time. In other words, although the manager wants the agent to enjoy great expectations, he can and must save him from becoming the victim of over-expectations.

How should the manager view the agent and the agent's career? Hopefully, he will realize that his foremost consideration should be for the agent's career. For the agent is the ultimate source of business. Therefore, the agent's career must always be uppermost in the plans and priorities of field management, as well as home office management. Of course, no agent need be coddled or spoiled but every agent's career must remain the priority of concern of his manager.

Sales Results and Their Pattern

Total sales results of the company are both a contributor to and a product of manpower development. It is important to try for the direct involvement of all members of the sales organization in the accomplishment of the company's sales objectives. It is important to try to mold the total sales organization into a team that will strive for new levels of agency and company sales. It is important to encourage members of the established team to help other members achieve results commensurate with their capabilities.

Morale

Morale is both an important measure of conditions in a company and/or an agency, as well as a contributor to those conditions. When there is high morale in a company or an agency, the established agents are more likely to bring new men to the company, and to work individually with them to help assure their success. On the contrary, when there is low morale, established agents are not going to go out of their way to help one another nor are they likely to recommend new candidates. In fact, if morale is too low, the current agents themselves will likely leave the organization. This is particularly true where opportunities are present elsewhere. Low morale will act as the "push" to another company.

SUMMARY

Thus, there are five forces that must be present and must interact effectively *if* there is to be effective manpower development. But is there one catalyst guaranteed to bring about this desired interaction? There is! It is the catalyst of a deep-seated, company-wide philosophy based on belief in the individual. It is the philosophy that encourages the individual to develop to the maximum of his abilities. In this climate each individual is motivated to do no less than his best—for his own sake, for the sake of his clients, and for the sake of the organization.

All of this revolves around management in both home office and field. If management would stimulate the continued personal growth of staff and associates, members of management must continue to improve their own skills, their own knowledge, and to grow as individuals. If management's growth and development begins to plateau, associates must look elsewhere for leadership and inspiration or they will soon be afflicted with the same disease.

The agent, in turn, who allows his personal horizons to shrink will soon become less than inspiring and less than convincing to his clients.

Basic to sound manpower development, then, is an emphasis on development of the individual. The individual can do some of this on his own. At the same time, he is not likely to make much progress unless the climate is right, unless the attitude of both peers and superiors is one of encouragement, inspiration, and helpfulness.

Another way to say this is that the road to success is traveled by those who regularly set and meet continually rising goals in life. This applies as much to the man in management as it does to the agent. In reality, it applies more to the man in management for it is the responsibility of management at all levels to help and encourage the agent to develop and grow to his maximum potential. These are the basic principles on which all sound development and growth of manpower must be built.

APPENDIX A

Manpower Audit Clairvoyant Life
FULL TIME AGENTS
19__ Volume Breakdown By Length of Service
(Survivors as of 12/31/19__)

	Under $250,000	etc...etc...etc...	$2 mill. +	Total No.	Percent
Less 1 year	120	. . . . . .	1	200	17%
1 to 4 years	55	. . . . . .	5	. . .	. . .
etc...etc...					
40+ years	30	. . . . . .	0	40	3.5%
TOTALS	344	etc...etc...etc...	39	. . .	. . .
PERCENT	32%	etc...etc...etc...	4%	. . .	. . .

Some other areas for making a Manpower Audit:
- Supervisors—Volume Breakdown by Length Service
- Full Time Agents and Supervisors—Cases by Length of Service and Volume Groups
- Full Time Agents—Volume Breakdown by Age
- Supervisors—Volume Breakdown by Age

21

Finding Agency Manpower

Maurice L. Stewart

IMPORTANCE OF MANPOWER

Manpower is the indispensable element in a profitable business, a victorious army, a widely diffused religion and a successful life insurance agency. Mr. Carnegie was willing to give up his ships, his factories and his steel mills but not his manpower. Napoleon left his prison island of Elba with neither sword nor cannon. However, the loyal attachment of his former troops to his mission nearly gave Napoleon his desired victory. And the great religions of the world have achieved success because of the dedicated allegiance of faithful manpower.

One need be neither scholar nor charlatan to recognize that a life insurance agency achieves its success because of productive manpower. The continued health and future growth of a life insurance company and its agencies depend on continuous manpower development. This continuous process of development requires that considerable attention be given to education, training, supervision, motivation and general personnel administration. However, if no new manpower is brought to the agency's doors, the other important functions of agency management are useless. If there is no manpower to educate, train, supervise and motivate the whole process comes to a grinding halt. An agency can linger on for several years, nourished by the strength of the manpower recruited in previous year; but a dynamic, vigorous, virile, and vibrant organization remains healthy and successful only if new manpower is coming in the front door.

Any organization composed of people needs new blood to assure continued good health. Aging is an imperceptible process but none the less inexorable. Chiang Kai-shek's army on Formosa cannot long remain an effective fighting force if denied the opportunity to recruit. The Senate of the United States would hardly retain its national or international prestige if all senators were elected for the duration of their lives. A life insurance agency will not maintain its prestige and its wholesome image in its marketing community if its personnel is not strengthened by the periodic infusion of new talent. Furthermore, everyone likes a winner and an agency that is growing looks like a winner. An agency that is aging looks like a loser.

Reasons for Planned Recruiting

The above suggests two basic reasons for a well planned agency recruiting program: (1) it provides the new blood for the maintenance of a healthy dynamic organization and (2) it helps to build and maintain a favorable image for the agency in the eyes of its marketing community. In addition there are several other reasons why an agency must give adequate attention to recruiting manpower. First, an agency can expect a normal amount of attrition to occur as a result of retirements, disabilities, deaths, transfers to other agencies, and transfers to management. If the latter transfer is to a management position within the agency, the person is not lost to the agency, but he must be replaced if the agency is to maintain the same number of salesmen who are devoting their full time to selling. Second, from time to time the agency undertakes to expand its operations into new markets. Such expansion requires additional manpower. Third, the agency will also undertake the marketing of new products or new uses for the conventional products. The marketing of group insurance, health insurance, and pensions are all examples of an additional need for new manpower that has prevailed since World War II.

Finally, new manpower is desirable because it brings to the agency refreshing new ideas and new entrées to different types of markets. Each new recruit is a unique combination of personality and exposure to markets. A new broom sweeps clean and a new personality in the agency makes a contribution to the "group dynamics" that can be an inspiration to the whole organization. Enthusiasm is a quality that abounds in young men. It is also contagious and can be transmitted throughout an agency that is adding new blood each year. The vibrant enthusiasm of youth buoys up the flagging interest of the older men. When the older agent observes a new young agent producing more new sales than himself, the older man will be motivated to extend himself a little more. There is something in a man that exhorts him to extra effort when youth's performance sets a challenging pace.

Of course, the older men in the agency are a tremendous help to the new agent. The maturity, experience and knowledge possessed by the older members of the agency lend strength and stability to the new recruits. What has been called a "beneficient reciprocity" evolves out of this relationship between the newly recruited youth and the "stalwart strength of the sages." Youth contributes its enthusiasm. Maturity contributes its knowledge and experience. The greatest combination in the world is an agency team composed of: (1) young, energetic and enthusiastic recruits and (2) experienced, mature and knowledgeable pros. Each of the two groups reenforces the other. It is interesting to observe an "old pro" taking pride in a new agent's accomplishments. It is equally inspiring to observe a new recruit's enthusiasm transcending and permeating the whole organization. The older men feel it, and they responsively embrace it. A rekindling of desire to emulate the enthusiasm of the new recruits diffuses throughout the agency.

A Case Example of the Significance of Effective Recruiting

A brief summary of the actual experience of a large and long established life insurance agency will perhaps illustrate more eloquently the significance of new manpower to agency growth. In 1960 the agency had forty-three men who wrote $30 million of new life insurance. This was an average of approximately $700,000 per man. During the next six years the agency revitalized itself by (1) carefully planning, (2) effectively organizing, (3) enthusiastically implementing, and (4) rigorously controlling a comprehensive program for manpower development. The results of this program are impressive. In six years the agency grew from 43 men to 78 men and production increased from $30 million to $67 million. The new men who were recruited after 1960 were responsible for $39 million of the total $67 million of new life sales. The older men who had joined the agency prior to 1960 produced $28 million. In other words, if the agency had failed to recruit in those six years it would have declined from a $30 million agency to a $28 million agency and if the motivational effect of the new men on the older men is taken into consideration the decline would have been even greater. With proper attention to the important function of recruiting, the agency in 1966 was doing 240 percent of the sales volume it would have been doing if there had been no recruiting after 1960. It is also interesting to observe that although the production of the older agents declined, the average production for the agency increased from $700,000 per man to approximately $860,000 per man.

This achievement is more impressive when one recognizes that much of the total production came from men who had been with the agency only one, two and three years. Truly, recruiting has contributed life blood to this agency.

This same agency has projected the expected results of its manpower development program to 1975. At that time it is anticipated that there will be 75 men in the agency producing an annual volume of $115 million of new life sales. Of this $115 million of new life sales, $100 million is the expected production of those agents recruited since 1960. Only $15 million of life production is expected from those agents that were recruited prior to 1960. With respect to this latter group it is interesting to observe that only 14 of these men will be under age 65 in 1970. Aging is an inevitable phenomenon in every agency. The only effective antidote to this phenomenon of attrition is recruiting.

THE PLANNING FUNCTION IN THE MANAGEMENT OF RECRUITING

The management of recruiting requires adamant attention to those same indispensable functions of management that must be emphasized whatever the particular phase of the operation of a business or a life insurance agency is being considered. This means that recruiting must be planned, organized, implemented and controlled. The following discussion will treat each of these management functions as it applies to recruiting.

The planning of recruiting must be based on both long range and short range plans. Quite logically the home office agency department will be interested and can be extremely helpful to the agency manager in developing long range marketing plans for the agency. Chapter 16 "Sales Planning for the Life Insurance Agency" presents a detailed analysis of the planning tools that will be helpful to the agency manager in his long range planning. The chapter emphasizes the importance of a market analysis for the measurement of the market potential of the area and the sales potential for the agency. The chapter also points out the importance of a measurement of market potential to the formation of the agency's long range recruiting plans. The agency manager must understand that potential markets are of little value to him unless he has the manpower that can successfully exploit those markets or unless the manager can recruit men who can tap those markets for sales.

Long Range Plans

Long range recruiting plans for the agency suggest a program of manpower development that will require several years to mature to the optimum in accomplishment. Long range plans extend up to five or ten years. For example, an agency manager may have developed a five year plan to increase the size of his agency from ten agents to thirty agents. At the present time he may have only one assistant manager to assist him in training and supervision. There may be no one in the agency who is specializing and concentrating his sales activities in the increasingly important area of pension planning. There may be only one or two men in the agency devoting a significant amount of time to business insurance. The agency manager's long range plans must consider the problem of developing sales in both pensions and business insurance. Among the ten men in the agency will be some who will do very well in these two markets. In fact, the sales talent for developing business insurance and pension clients is more likely to be found among existing personnel of the agency than among the new recruits. However, to some extent the long range plans for recruiting of new manpower should give consideration to recruiting men with specialized talents for specialized markets. In other words, long range recruiting plans should be qualitative as well as quantitative. Obtaining management talent to assist the agency manager in training and supervision is another important consideration in the long range growth plans of the agency. Some of this talent can come from within the agency. However, to some extent the recruiting plans of the agency manager will require the recruiting of men who have the potential for becoming future supervisors and assistant managers.

Circumstances will inevitably arise that will require modification of original long range recruiting plans. The alert agency manager will recognize this fact and will provide for flexibility in his long range plans. The agency manager must be flexible in adjusting his plans to meet changing conditions.

Short Range Plans

Short range recruiting plans must be coordinated with the agency's overall short range plans. For example, if the agency manager in our preceding example decides to implement his long range plan to develop a thirty man agency, he may decide on a short range objective of adding five new men during the next twelve months.

Assuming that the manager's long range plans have been soundly conceived, certain priorities will have been established for the development of new marketing areas. The manager's short range plan to add five new men should include some qualitative objectives with respect to specific markets for which the manager is recruiting new agents. The manager should formulate his recruiting plans with due consideration of the overall capacity of the agency's training and supervisory staff. It will only frustrate the training and supervisory staff to be required to accept a number of new recruits if the staff is already loaded with trainees who are not yet self-sufficient. The solution may be to appoint and train new staff members to perform the required supervisory and training functions. Certainly, the manager should not add new agents to his organization until adequate provision has been made to properly train and supervise them.

Another factor that will place practical limitations on recruiting new agents is the office space available. The efficient manager is always tight on office space, since an unoccupied agent's desk is a non-productive expense. Therefore, the decision has to be made whether to block the future growth of the agency or provide the necessary office space to accommodate the new recruits. The needed office space may be provided by incurring additional expense or by terminating some of the tired blood.

This matter of the proper planning of training, supervision and office space must be kept in proper perspective. Certainly these items should not be used as an excuse for not recruiting. Furthermore, it is doubtful that office space in particular is a serious bottleneck to recruiting in most agencies. If the new manpower can be found, it does not require great ingenuity on the part of a resourceful agency manager to find desk space and office space for the new manpower.

The recruiting of new manpower is so vitally important to the success of a life insurance agency that extra effort and even inconvenience are a small price to pay for new talent. Reference to the matter of planning is included in this chapter only to emphasize that new manpower is assimilated more readily and effectively if adequate planning is completed relative to those functions that must be performed as a result of the recruiting of the new manpower.

Both long range and short range planning for recruiting requires that the manager consider several basic questions. The answering of most of these questions is the articulating of the obvious. However, management planning for most business is to a large extent merely the formal consideration of the obvious. But it is surprising how often the obvious is overlooked. The following questions are basic to the formulation of sound recruiting plans.

1. What Type of Person Is the Agency Looking For?

Chapter 22 discusses the important problem of selecting agency manpower and provides some answers to this question. This present chapter concentrates its attention on recruiting or the finding of desirable manpower. However, it should be obvious that unless the person responsible for recruiting has some knowledge of the personal characteristics that help to identify this "desirable manpower," he cannot initiate a search for manpower. The recruiter cannot look for something, if he does not know what he is looking for. Therefore, the recruiter must be oriented at least in a broad way to the type of person the agency is seeking.

Some agency managers emphasize the "key man concept" in identifying prospective successful agents. The principal characteristic of the so-called "key-man" is his identification with a market but he also possesses certain personality traits that give him a high potential for success. "A key-man is a man with a following. He is probably a native of the area, has his degree, is colorful, persuasive and successful. But always he is well and favorably known. He has the following. That's what makes him a key-man. . . ."[1] Other agency managers place more emphasis on personality traits. These managers acknowledge the importance of favorable association with a market but they believe that sales talent is the most important factor. "Does he have the guts to stay with this business during the difficult early days. Is he persistent, tenacious, and does he have that shark or killer instinct we look for in the strong salesman."[2]

During the first interview the agency manager is to some extent selling himself, selling the agency, selling the company and also selling the career opportunity in life insurance sales work. At the same time that he is doing all of this, the manager is also "screening" and "selecting." All of these functions become imperceptibly merged during the first interview with the prospective agent. However, the more formal selection tests are typically administered after the first interview, and if possible on the same day. The first interview should establish whether the prospective agent has enough potential to warrant administering to him the formal selection tests.

The second interview can be scheduled to coincide with the availability of the results of the selection tests. Many agency managers use the results of the selection tests to persuade the prospective agent of his potential success in life insurance selling. It must be remembered that one of the important reasons deterring many potential successes in life insurance selling from embarking upon a life insurance sales career is the uncertainty in their own mind as to whether they can sell. The results of the selection tests may be used to allay these anxieties and suspend apprehensions. The tests are powerful persuaders as well as erudite estimators.

Thus, the recruiting process must be viewed as involving the integrated functions of (1) finding or discovering manpower, (2) selecting from among applicants and (3) persuading acceptance of the career.

[1] Jack C. Kinder and Garry D. Kinder, Managers of Equitable Society at Akron and Detroit in a presentation before the life agency management meeting of the General Agents and Managers Conference at Atlanta, cited March 18, 1967 issue of the National Underwriter.
[2] David Mark, Jr., General Agent at New York City for New England Life, Ibid.

2. When Does the Agency Recruit?

Recruiting must be a continuous process. It is not done only in the spring or the fall. Recruiting is not a seasonal activity. Neither is it a part time activity to which the agency manager turns his attention when there is nothing else particularly pressing in the office.

The answer to the question of the timing of recruiting is to some extent dependent upon the coordination of those activities in the agency that are affected by an influx of new manpower. We have emphasized previously the importance of coordinating recruiting activities with the training and supervisory capacity of the agency. Recruiting plans must also be integrated with the agency's overall market planning. Perhaps a better way of stating this principle is to say that the manager must make sure that all of the agency's activities that will be affected by an influx of new manpower will be coordinated to assist in the smooth assimilation of the new manpower.

3. Where Does the Agency Recruit?

The answer to this question depends to a large extent upon the answer to question one: "What type of person is the agency looking for?" For example, the market planning of the agency may indicate that the recently established General Electric plant in the city's suburbs can become a potentially lucrative market for life insurance sales. The next question is: "What person or type of person would have the best entrée to this market?" An analysis stemming from this question would quickly disqualify a person who had not finished high school or who would be overwhelmed and overawed by an electrical engineer who talks to every life insurance agent while fidgeting with a slide-rule. In addition to having the usually expected personality qualifications, an agent working in the General Electric market should be comfortable while trying to provide leadership to an electrical engineer to establish a sound estate plan. The president of the company would probably meet these qualifications. So also would the president of a similar company. But since probably neither of these men would be available, some compromises can be expected. However, finding a personable former engineer who would be comfortable in the presence of a slide rule would be one approach to the problem. If this former engineer has the necessary qualifications and zeal, he will probably double his income within five years. It is doubtful that he would do that well with his current employer.

The quest for talent must be conducted ubiquitously. The recruiter must carry his search to wherever potential sales manpower may be imprisoned by jealous employers. During every working hour the recruiter must be obsessed by the driving exhortation to find capable new people. In all instances the recruiter will not have a specific market for which he is recruiting. However, sound recruiting practices can be implemented by seeking agents who will be "general practitioners" rather than estate planners in a specific market.

FINDING MANPOWER HIDDEN IN OTHER INDUSTRIES

It is perhaps an exaggeration to paint a picture of potentially successful life insurance salesmen hidden in the vast labor force of our country. But there is a certain realism to this picture. The average person changes his employment several times during his working life. Therefore, recruiting manpower for the life insurance industry should not be thought of as the pirating or proselyting of manpower from other industries to the detriment of our economy as a whole. On the contrary, the economy as a whole benefits when a man increases his productivity by transferring from one industry to another. The economist tells us that mobility of labor should be encouraged because labor's marginal productivity may be higher in one industry than in another. The facts will establish that tremendous opportunities are available in life insurance sales work for many engineers, accountants, administrators, bank cashiers, teachers, coaches and sales representatives of other industries. Furthermore, society benefits when greater productivity is unleashed by the transfer of economically disturbed people who are predisposed to leave one industry to become effective producers in another. This does not suggest that the life insurance agency recruiter should seek prospects from among the malcontents and derelicts of other industries. It means that many men have not yet found their most productive and creative place in our economy. Life insurance could well be that opportunity for maximum release of their potential.

Salesmen communicate more effectively with some groups than they do with others. This is partly attributable to the fact that people have a greater affinity for particular people than for others. Agency recruiting for specific markets will respect this basic principle of social relationships: we all feel more comfortable in the company of those with whom we have the most in common. In recognition of this principle, life insurance agencies have recruited: (1) engineers to handle the market composed of technical and scientific people, (2) sons of doctors to sell in the medical market, (3) former businessmen and CPA's to call on members of the business community and to sell business insurance, (4) high school principals and superintendents to sell to their former students and (5) former army and navy officers to develop the military market. These men have a background that will enable them to understand the problems and motivations of their prospects. They oftentimes have an established personal acquaintance with their prospects. Many men can attain success in almost any market, but for most agents, having a previous orientation to a given market will make the probability of success much greater. One of the inspiring and intriguing aspects of the life insurance business is the different types of persons who are successful and through their success provide so much good in helping families establish sound financial plans. Life insurance enables a man to capitalize on his previous background, experience and business orientation to achieve professional status in a growing and dynamic industry. Very few industries can offer the opportunity for professional service to such a broad spectrum of people in other types of work.

FINDING MANPOWER ON THE COLLEGE CAMPUS

The agency's policy concerning age limits for new recruits will affect the recruiting markets in which manpower is sought. Some agencies have a rigorous policy of accepting only agents twenty-five years of age or older. Such agencies obvious will not recruit on the college campus. Other agencies have had success in recruiting on the college campus and depend on this source of manpower for a substantial part of their annual new-manpower requirements. One company has attained success with its campus-agency arrangement whereby undergraduates are recruited for life insurance sales during the latter part of their college careers and join an agency on a full-time basis after graduation. Summer time employment and training are combined to develop a well oriented career salesman by the time the student is graduated from college. The young college man is most successful in selling to men approximately his same age. A man in his early twenties will sell most effectively in the young man's market with the package and simple programming approaches. As the knowledge, confidence and experience of these young college men increase, they can logically move into the more advanced programming areas and ultimately into business insurance and estate planning. However, experience demonstrates that it is wise in most cases not to push these young college men too fast toward the business insurance and estate planning markets.

FINDING MANPOWER MADE AVAILABLE BY BUSINESS MERGERS

Business mergers can oftentimes make manpower available for other employment. First, mergers involve transfer of personnel from one location to another. Many families are reluctant to make this change. Therefore, alternative employment in the same geographical area may be attractive. Second, mergers may involve the actual release of personnel because of termination of position, combining of functions or actual personality clashes at the upper management levels. In all of these situations there is a man who is "economically disturbed." Whatever his motive or his employer's motive for termination of employment, such a man is a good prospect for new employment. Life insurance could be that new employment.

FINDING MANPOWER THROUGH THE EFFORTS OF THE AGENCY'S OWN PERSONNEL

Perhaps one of the best sources of names of possible recruits is the personnel in the agency. There are several reasons why the agency's personnel can be very helpful in finding manpower.

First, the agency force has a good idea of the type of person being sought and can do a better job of identifying the type of person wanted.

Second, the agency staff can do a better job of screening and preselecting the potential recruits so that the recruiter or the manager does not have to spend time with poor recommendations.

Third, it is easier for an agency associate to communicate information concerning a potential recruit than it is for a center of influence who is blocks or miles away.

Fourth, the members of the agency staff have at least a modicum of interest in assisting in the performance of the recruiting function as compared to other persons whose primary interests push the agency's needs into the background. For example, the president of the local bank can hardly be expected to be keenly interested in the future growth of the XYZ agency. On the other hand, most agents like to see their agency growing and achieving recognition in the community.

Fifth, the members of the agency realize that helping the manager with his job can be recognized in various ways by the manager. Sixth, the members of an agency enjoying high morale will take pride in their agency and will wish to see it become an even better agency.

The agency manager can do a great deal to encourage the members of the agency to be on the look out for new recruits. This encouragement does not necessarily have to be financial in nature. As indicated above, a thoughtful manager can find many ways to express his appreciation to his agency associates for their interest in bringing new men to the agency. The members of the agency should be reminded periodically of the agency's need for manpower and why it will be beneficial to themselves, their company, their agency and the new man who accepts the opportunity. In addition, it is wise to review with the members of the agency from time to time the objectives of the agency's recruiting program, the selection procedures, the training schedules and the supervision procedures. These periodic communications can help to remind the members of the agency that the organization has recruiting needs. Eventually, each agent will have this matter on his mind at the time of fact finding and closing interviews. Usually, each member of the agency will be willing to help the cause of recruiting if: (1) he is reminded periodically of how he may help, (2) he is instructed as to any specific agency needs, and (3) his assistance is appreciated by the manager and the company.

The agency personnel must be shown they will benefit from suggesting the names of outstanding people who subsequently become successful salesmen in the agency. The tendency among agents is to recommend persons they think are not as good as themselves. They fear competition from new agents. They must be convinced that if they are responsible for bringing in an outstanding new agent it will be a definite advantage to them. The following are some of the advantages that can be emphasized. The new agent will have a favorable attitude toward the agent who recommends him. This favorable attitude can be reflected in many ways: (1) sharing business on a joint basis, (2) telling clients and office associates about the man who was responsible for his coming into the business, (3) telling centers of influence in the community about his sponsor and (4) friendly camaraderie in the office since the new agent will have a warm and friendly attitude toward his sponsor. An agent who has been with the agency should recognize that he is going to be number one on the new agent's list of office friends. This can only result in benefits to the older agent.

We should comment briefly on the obvious problem that may arise when a potential recruit is recommended by a member of the agency and then is turned down after being interviewed and tested. In such a situation, there will obviously be good reasons for the decision and these reasons must be communicated to the recommending agent. This must be done in such a way as not to cast aspersions on the recommending agent's judgment. If this is not done carefully the agent will recommend no other persons and furthermore may be offended to the extent that the relationship becomes strained between the recommending agent and the manager. This latter result can be prevented if the manager discusses the whole matter with the recommending agent in objective terms and keeps the whole discussion on an impersonal basis.

FINDING MANPOWER THROUGH NEWSPAPER ADVERTISING

Newspaper advertising as a recruiting medium presents a rather unique challenge because there is no built in screening mechanism as is available, for example, when agency associates are assisting in recruiting. Therefore, potential recruits must be interviewed under some organized system for preliminary screening and selection. Research studies indicate that approximately fifty men answering a newspaper recruiting advertisement must be interviewed in order to find one that will meet the agency's selection standards. Furthermore, the retention rate is very poor for agents placed under contract as a result of their responding to a newspaper recruiting advertisement. Nevertheless, many of the top producers in the life insurance business today were recruited through the medium of the newspaper advertisement.

There are two types of newspaper recruiting advertisements that may be used. The first is known as the "open ad" and indicates that the opportunity is in sales and is in the life insurance business. The second is known as the "closed ad" and does not indicate either the fact that the opportunity is in sales or the fact that the employer is a life insurance agency. Both types of advertisements can produce satisfactory results. However, the "closed" type of advertisement will produce responses from many persons who, at the time of responding, did not have a specific interest in life insurance selling. But the "closed ad" may produce responses from persons who appear to be good candidates. The fact that they are looking for employment provides them with at least one credential that may be significant. On the other hand, the "closed ad" does produce responses from many who obviously would not be qualified and who would probably have disqualified themselves if the advertisement had been of the "open ad" type.

FINDING MANPOWER THROUGH MISCELLANEOUS SOURCES

Some of the more obvious sources of new names of potential recruits not previously mentioned are: (1) centers of influence in the community, (2) policyowners, (3) prospects who may or may not be interested in life insurance at that particular time, (4) the clergyman at one's own and other churches, (5) bank officers, (6) the mayor or other municipal officials and (7) those many friends and business acquaintances with whom the manager and his staff can communicate. This list could be expanded. The agency manager will want to consider all of these sources and will give specific attention to them in accordance with the strength of his own and his agency's unique association with the particular source.

4. Who in the Agency Is Responsible for Recruiting?

The agency manager is ultimately responsible for all management functions. This principle of ultimate responsibility remains valid even though some other staff member is asked by the manager to become the "recruiter" for the agency. In our previous discussion we have not identified this person we have referred to as the "recruiter." In the small agency the manager may be the person who performs the functions of recruiting, training, supervision, and office manager. Thus, in the small agency the manager is typically the recruiter. In the larger agency an assistant manager or some other staff man may be designated to perform those activities usually associated with the operation of an agency recruiting program. However, whoever is serving as the recruiting specialist will attempt to orient each member of the agency concerning the agency's recruiting objectives and will attempt to enlist the assistance of each staff member in accomplishing those objectives.

Delegating responsibility for recruiting to an associate does not mean that the manager gives up his ultimate responsibility. The manager must (1) consult frequently with the staff member serving as "recruiter," (2) review procedures being followed, (3) make suggestions where appropriate, (4) continually demonstrate a keen interest in the recruiting program and (5) generally motivate the staff member to the greater accomplishments that are required to achieve the overall marketing objectives of the agency.

SELLING THE OPPORTUNITY

The most important phase in the recruiting process is the persuasive presentation to the prospective agent of the attractive opportunities in life insurance selling. This presentation is the final capstone to the whole recruiting process. The recruiting function has been successfully completed when the prospective agent says, "Yes, I'd like to join your agency." The agency has really found a "recruit" only when the prospect says, "Yes."

Obviously, the recruiting process in each instance is not divided neatly into the same specific steps. However, in whatever order the recruiting steps have been organized with respect to (1) contacting, (2) interviewing and (3) administering selection tests, the final all important step in recruiting is the presentation of the opportunity with enthusiasm but also with sincerity. We have indicated previously that there must be an enthusiastic presentation of the opportunities in life insurance selling at the very first interview. The prospective recruit must have his interest aroused. He must be informed concerning some of the interesting aspects of the career. However, the hard sell and the dynamic presentation of the career will be an important part of the closing interview.

The career opportunity must not be misrepresented. The hard work that is required must be properly described. Furthermore, the prospective agent should not be led to believe that he is being hired to open a consulting office relative to estate planning and pension planning. But neither should these future opportunities be concealed.

There are opportunities for every life insurance agent, who has the required aptitude, to work in the areas of estate planning, advanced life underwriting, pension planning and management. These fields appear often-times to the prospective recruit as being more glamorous than making ten prospecting calls and having two closing interviews each day. It is the glamour in any business that makes it attractive. In presenting the life insurance career there is no reason why the glamour should be concealed. But the prospective recruit should realize that there is much hard work that can be interesting, challenging and rewarding, but it may not be glamorous. Furthermore, the prospective recruit should be made to realize that some of the more glamorous aspects of life insurance sales work come after a few years of successful work in some of the less glamorous aspects but none the less challenging and profitable aspects of the career.

The most effective presentation of the career will be built around the career objectives of the prospective recruit. The latter wants answers that he can integrate with his evaluation of life insurance selling as meeting his objectives. The recruiter should emphasize those aspects of the career that are of greatest significance to the prospect only when he has had an opportunity to visit with the prospect and get an insight into his motivations, needs, wants and objectives. Chapter 22, "Selecting Agency Manpower," describes the fundamentals of interviewing and therefore this chapter will not devote attention to the interviewing process. However, it should be pointed out that there are differences in emphasis between a selection interview and a career presentation interview. In the latter case, the assumption is that this is the man we want. We have previously enquired concerning the man's ambitions, his goals and objectives. We have enquired concerning his prospect list and his "shark killing" propensities and now whether he is a "shark killer" or only a "sail fish killer," we have decided we want him. Therefore, we want to be as persuasive as possible in convincing this prospective agent what a great opportunity awaits him.

It is essential that the manager have a well organized plan or outline to follow in presenting the career opportunity. The manager should not attempt to talk off the top of his head. If the agency manager insists that each agent must have a well organized life insurance sales talk because experience has proven this to be desirable, the same logic should convince the manager that the career sales talk should be even more carefully prepared. If the presentation of the career opportunity is to be well done, it must be carefully prepared, conscientiously rehearsed and enthusiastically presented. The competition of other industries for competent sales talent demands that life insurance present its career opportunities as eloquently and as persuasively as possible.

Emphasizing the Strong Points of the Agency

Every agency has virtues that are unique and attractive. These virtues should be stressed. If the agency has been established for a long time its permanence and status in the community are attractive features. If important persons in the business community are policyholders in the agency, they may be willing to have this fact told to prospective recruits. There are many features of an agency that can be persuasive: the location of the agency, plans for a new suite of offices, the education and training program, the number of C.L.U.'s, the number of MDRT members, the supervisory assistance, the prospecting help and many other features that can be pointed out to the new agent.

For the newly established agency there will not be a record of successes with which to impress the prospective agent. However, the new agency has hopes and expectations. These can be inspiring. A well prepared training manual can also be available in even the newest agency. An attractively prepared training manual can be a strong recruiting tool.

Pre-contract training is used in some agencies as an integrated part of their manpower development programs. Not only is pre-contract training a method for orienting a prospective recruit and giving him some preliminary training, but it can also be used as an effective instrument for recruiting. The man may not be sold completely on the life insurance business and may be reluctant to give up his current employment. The prospective agent may agree, however, to participate for a few weeks in a pre-contract training program. The man is willing to go part-way toward accepting life insurance as a career. If the pre-contract training period may be used by the agency manager to measure the sales capacity of the prospective recruit and if this measurement is favorable, the manager can intensify his efforts to get the man.

One successful agency manager emphasizes the intensive thinking and careful planning that must go into all aspects of organizing an agency for successfully selling itself to prospective agents in these words: "It may take an agency head six months to pick his spots and organize his supporting material. But since successful recruiting is the heart of his job, it is well worth it. How effectively he performs in talking to prospective agents may well represent the difference between building an agency and losing his franchise."[3]

ORGANIZING, IMPLEMENTING AND CONTROLLING RECRUITING

In the previous discussion of planning agency recruiting we have touched upon some aspects of organizing, implementing and controlling recruiting. For example, we have pointed out that the ultimate responsibility for recruiting rests with the agency manager. He cannot divest himself of this ultimate responsibility. However, in accordance with sound organization principles, the agency manager will frequently delegate responsibility for recruiting to a specific staff member. The agency manager will consult with this staff member from time to time but his responsibility will be ultimate rather than continuously attuned to the operation of the program. Since Chapter 11 deals extensively with agency organization the reader is referred to this chapter for a more detailed treatment.

The implementation of a recruiting program for the agency should follow the same sound principles of motivation and leadership that are discussed in Chapter 27. It need only be emphasized here that, like any other important agency activity, an agency recruiting program must be provided continuous leadership and direction. In the first part of this chapter we emphasized the disastrous results that occur when an agency manager fails to provide the indispensable leadership and guiding direction to bringing new manpower into the agency. The strength of this leadership must be felt throughout the whole agency so that each staff member will be alive and alert to the agency's recruiting objectives. Quite naturally, the staff member assigned the responsibility for recruiting will be the person who is most acutely aware of the importance of continuous recruiting activity. However, the implementation of the program and the motivating leadership of the program by the manager must be felt by the whole organization.

The function of management control over recruiting should be performed in accordance with the four fold requirements emphasized by management experts. The first requirement is for the establishment of a standard of expected accomplishment. For a life insurance agency this may be a flexible standard depending upon the agency's long range and short range marketing objectives. The second requirement is for a periodic measurement of accomplishment with respect to recruiting. To fulfill this requirement the agency manager should maintain accurate records of interviews held, tests administered, and new agents hired. The third requirement is

---

[3] Josephson, Halsey D., "Josephson on Agency Management", Probe, Inc. New York, N. Y. 1964 p. 14–15.

the comparison of the measured accomplishment with the standard of expected accomplishment set forth under the first requirement. The fourth requirement is the taking of remedial action to correct any deviation of actual accomplishment from the recruiting accomplishments expected and specifically prescribed by the established standard.

CONCLUSIONS

This chapter has emphasized the tremendous importance of recruiting to the continued good health of a life insurance agency. However, recruiting is only the first domino in a long series of important dominos. Even if the recruiting activities of the agency meet the highest standard expected, the row of standing dominos will collapse if there faulty selection, inadequate training, incompetent supervision or poor leadership with respect to other important agency activities. Thus, the interrelationship of all these functions is emphasized.

Chapter 22, "Selecting Agency Manpower," stresses the importance of having an adequate number of new recruits so that the selection tools can work the most effectively. If there are only two men who have indicated an interest in joining the agency and the agency feels obligated to add two men, the selection tools might just as well be discarded. However, if the recruiting activity of the agency can provide a substantial number of applicants, the selection tools then have an opportunity to pick and choose. This process will inevitably provide the agency with more competent sales manpower than will result if each man expressing an interest automatically is hired as an agent.

22

Selecting Agency Manpower

Jack C. Keir

Selection problems are not unique to life insurance. From the cradle to the grave we are involved in selecting our associates. Consciously or unconsciously we select our friends, our luncheon companions, our golf partners, our bridge opponents, and most important—our spouses. Our lack of success in selecting our spouses is eloquently described by the annual statistics of the divorce courts. From Hollywood comes further evidence of selection problems in the biographical exposés of our favorite stars. The life insurance industry is understandably concerned about high agent turnover. Nor should this concern be diminished by our observing the discomfort of other industries wrestling with the same problem. This complex and esoteric problem of predicting the future performance of people has defied the analytical acumen of the world's great leaders from the dawn of history.

In determining the appropriate content for a chapter on the selection of life insurance agents, we have recognized that for many agencies finding manpower is a much more critical problem than is selection. In recent years many life insurance agency managers have achieved improved selection through use of validated procedures prescribed by their companies and the Life Insurance Agency Management Association. This chapter is not designed either to set forth a new testing procedure or to prescribe a new testing program. The purpose of this chapter is to increase the agency manager's depth and breadth of understanding of some of the basic principles of selecting personnel. This knowledge of principles will provide

361

a background of knowledge to which the agency manager can relate his current selection practices.

THE SELECTION PROCESS

Basically there are three steps involved in selecting personnel: (1) determining the qualifications required for the successful performance of the specific job (job description), (2) finding persons who appear to possess these qualifications, (3) using reliable measuring devices to determine as accurately as possible if those persons do meet the established minimum qualification standards for the specific job.

The difficulty of implementing a successful selection program in a life insurance agency arises from the complexities associated with each of the three steps. The first step requires a knowledge of the personal characteristics associated with an aptitude for life insurance selling. Aptitude itself is a complex quality composed of intelligence, interest, personality, attitude and special abilities. Each of these several aspects of aptitude is complex in itself. There is considerable disagreement among life insurance sales executives as to the characteristics that are most important to success in life insurance selling.[1] There is, also, considerable disagreement as to the degree of importance of each of the various characteristics. Unfortunately, those characteristics most important for success in life insurance selling are the characteristics most difficult to measure in an individual. For example, if we arrayed personal characteristics in the order of the accuracy with which they can be measured, they would fall into the order shown in Table A. Note that those human characteristics arrayed in Column 4 are measured with the least accuracy. Many of the characteristics in Column 4 are those considered important to success in life insurance selling.

It is interesting to observe different types of personalities successful in life insurance selling. However, these different personalities do not use the same sales procedures nor work in the same markets. The premed student who dropped out of college to get married is now successful in selling life insurance in a market composed largely of medical practitioners. The former officer in the merchant marine is successful in selling

---

[1] It is interesting to observe that Mayer and Greenberg concluded that two personality traits make a good salesman: (1) empathy and (2) ego drive. The empathetic salesman supposedly senses what the customer is feeling, and makes whatever creative modification is necessary in his sales presentation to close the sale. For the salesman with high "ego drive" each failure to close a sale must act as a motivator to greater effort which will assure success in the next interview and will thus bring about the ego enhancement the salesman seeks.—Mayer, David and Greenberg, Herbert M., "What Makes A Good Salesman," Harvard Business Review, July-August 1964, pp. 119–125.

Table A
Measuring Accurately Human Characteristics

1. Physical Characteristics	2. Abilities and Skills
(a) Height	(a) Dexterity
(b) Weight	(b) Mathematical ability
(c) Visual acuity	(c) Verbal ability
(d) Hearing	(d) Intelligence
(e) Condition of health	(e) Clerical skills
	(f) Mechanical aptitudes
3. Interests	4. Personality Traits
(a) Mechanical	(a) Industry
(b) Scientific	(b) Initiative
(c) Economic	(c) Sociability
(d) Cultural	(d) Dominance
	(e) Cooperativeness
	(f) Tolerance
	(g) Emotional stability

to navy yard employees living around Boston. The former President of the Chamber of Commerce appears to have success in a broader market, which suggests perhaps that some personalities can operate as "generalists" rather than as specialists. However, for the majority of life insurance salesmen it may be as much a problem of selecting the market for the man as a problem of selecting the man for the market. Certainly, it is a fallacy to believe that a "good salesman" can sell anything in any and every market.

THE SELECTION RATIO

If the recruiting sources available to the agency manager produced a wealth of prospective new agents, and the manager needed only to select five percent of those persons available, the manager would no doubt do a commendable job of selection. Using psychological tests under the same conditions, the agency manager would likewise achieve gratifying results. In technical terms, the test expert would say that the lower the selection ratio the greater the predictive value of psychological tests. By the term "selection ratio" the test expert refers to the ratio of the number of applicants to be selected to the number being tested. Selecting five salesmen from 100 being tested is a selection ratio of 5/100.

If the agency manager is under pressure to place new agents under contract as soon as possible, he may be pressured into placing under contract persons who rate low on selection tests. Thus, when the selection ratio must be high, the predictive efficiency of any selection device will be worsened.

SELECTION DEVICES

The principal selection tools which are used by life insurance agency managers are basically the same as those used in other businesses and industries. These include: (1) the application blank, (2) personal referances, (3) psychological testing and (4) the interview. When tempered by sound judgment, these four selection tools can be extremely helpful to the agency manager. But they are not infallible.

THE APPLICATION BLANK

Although widely used for personnel selection in business and in industry, the application blank is too frequently used ineffectively. Useless information is sometimes requested thereby irritating the applicant and confusing the selector. Valuable data about the applicant's past work record may not be requested in the application blank, and must be obtained in the later selection interview at considerably greater expense in terms of time and money. The purpose of the application blank ought to be that of screening out those applicants whose records do not include the activities and abilities that are important in the sale of life insurance. The application blank may be thought of as a wide mesh screen that sifts out the obvious rejections.

Application blanks may vary in length from a single page to a more detailed eight page form. The following information is typically requested in application blanks: Family Information; General Health Information; Military Service Records; Educational Experiences (High School, College and Post Graduate Work); Business Experiences; Recreational Activities; Organizational Activities; Personal Financial Information; and other general information concerning community activities, fund raising experiences, and similar activities. Factual information concerning experiences that are matters of record rather than of subjective opinion ought to be obtained through the application blank, rather than through the more expensive interviewing process. The interview itself can be more effectively used in clarifying information obtained in the application blank and in obtaining information that may be subject to individual interpretation.

A long and detailed application blank may at first seem dismaying to the applicant, but the length and completeness of the application blank can be used to stimulate the interest of the applicant in the position. Most applicants are likely to be motivated to join a firm which seems intent on making a sound selection based on as many objective facts as possible.

Of the information listed above, perhaps previous business experience is the most useful and pertinent to the selection of life insurance agents. The application form can request the name of the previous company, the kind of business that it is, where it is located, and the dates of employment. The applicant should also be asked to describe his specific duties in the various positions he has held, the person to whom he reported, and some information regarding individuals he may have supervised. The applicant can be asked the number of hours a week he worked, the initial training, and later training or educational experiences he had. For previous sales positions, the applicant can be asked to specify his product or service, the territory he covered, the sources of prospects or leads, the types of customers he serviced, and the method and extent of his compensation. The applicant can be asked for the names of his immediate supervisors and also, whether the applicant will agree to the employer contacting his previous supervisors for further information.

Depending on the information obtained in the application blank, additional questions will occur to the selector. The questions which occur to the selector as he scans the information blank should be written down so that they are not forgotten by the time of the selection interview.

While it is tempting to analyze application blank information to discover the applicant's personality traits, this procedure is risky for most laymen. For example, we cannot be certain that because an applicant has been graduated from a college or university, he, therefore, possesses superior intelligence. While the great bulk of college graduates would have a mean I.Q. of more than one standard deviation above the general population mean, individuals of average or even below average intelligence can obtain degrees from accredited institutions of higher education. The applicant's rank in his class does little to make our guess of his basic intelligence any more precise. His rank position in his class depends on the measured intelligence of the entire group, and group intelligence can vary widely from school to school and from state to state. Some selectors, in noticing that the applicant did not complete his college work, may jump to the conclusion that the applicant lacks stability and perseverance. Many factors can contribute to an individual's interrupting his education, and one should be very cautious in assuming personality traits based on such information.

The question of requiring a photograph of the applicant is frequently debated. Some selectors feel that they can judge the character of the applicant from his photograph. Carefully controlled studies by psychologists have demonstrated that the average observer, for example, cannot successfully discriminate between photographs of convicted felons and photographs of bank presidents. The attempt to analyze an applicant's personality from a photograph increases the probability that the selector's own biases and prejudices will be projected into that photograph. The request of a photograph may also run afoul of new employment restrictions against discrimination.

Membership and participation in organizations and other social activities does, of course, tell us about the applicant's involvement in groups. We cannot tell from evidence of membership, however, whether he is an extrovert or introvert. Even holding offices in social or civic organizations is not necessarily indicative of leadership qualities. While we want to obtain such information in our selection interview so that we can follow up the full implications of such memberships, we must be very cautious about the assumptions we make based only on the application blank information.

In looking over the information supplied in the application blank, one should be alert to inconsistencies of data reported. For example, one may find that the applicant has listed his employment dates with a firm as being from, say, February, 1942, to March of 1949. One might note elsewhere in the application blank that the applicant lists military service from June, 1943, to December, 1945. We must, of course, then realize that the amount of time he indicates that he was with the firm is inaccurate. It is important, also, to be alert to omissions, particularly in the time the applicant indicates for business experiences. Large amounts of time between periods of employment should be investigated.

By noting that during a particular period of time an individual held a full time job, was also going to school, and perhaps even held positions of authority in various organizations, the selector may obtain a picture of hard work and accomplishment. The validity of this impression can be examined more carefully during the selection interview.

PERSONAL REFERENCES

References supplied by the applicant can provide useful information. It is doubtful that we can learn much regarding the applicant's personality traits, but we certainly can make an attempt to verify the factual data which is presented in the applicant's application blank. It is difficult to obtain valid information from references regarding the applicant's personality traits because of the very nature of the words the reference uses to describe such personality traits. The reference, who describes the applicant as being "friendly," "dominant," "aggressive," and "mature," may not be defining those words in his own mind in the same way that we, the readers

SELECTING AGENCY MANPOWER

of the application blank, would define them. The method of contacting such business and personal references determines to a great extent the amount of useful information that can be obtained. Probably, a face to face interview with the reference will result in more useful information being obtained than either the telephone interview or the even less personal letter which may be sent. Telephone contact of a reference is next best to a personal face to face interview with a reference. The enthusiasm (or lack of it), inflexion of voice, hesitancy in answering questions, and other verbal and non-verbal communications by the reference may convey significant information. Use of the telephone saves time and also may enlist frank answers to specific questions because the element of surprise disarms the reference without providing an opportunity for him to plan and weigh his answers.

Preparing for the interview with the reference by having specific questions in mind increases the effectiveness of this interview. Specific questions which relate to the applicant's demonstrated behavior patterns while in the employ of the reference are preferred over general questions regarding the former employer's subjective impressions of the applicant. For a number of reasons, a former employer or other personal reference may want either to be of a great deal of help to the applicant, or perhaps even to harm the applicant in his future job seeking activities. It is difficult to know what motivates a reference when he is reporting on the applicant. It is probably better to restrict questions to those areas and activities which can be quantified. In this way, we can confirm the data which the applicant has already supplied in his application blank. Questions such as: "How did the applicant react to refusals for a sales interview?"; "What were his hours of work?"; "How many new accounts did he open?" are better questions than "Is he eligible for rehire?" and "Did he get along with other people?"

While the applicant will supply the names of some persons to whom the selector may talk, other individuals who know of the work experiences of the applicant may also be contacted. The applicant should have the right, however, to request that his present employer or other individuals connected with his present employment not be contacted during the initial stages of the selection process.

While it cannot be claimed that an individual's past is a certain predictor of his future behavior, it may be one of the best predictors available. If the applicant is expected to call on people as a life underwriter and is expected to work hard, engage in competitive activities, handle details of his work accurately, then perhaps we should look for these kinds of behavior in his immediate past experiences. In using both the application blank and the

personal references as sources of information it is, perhaps, safer for the
selector to rely on numerical or quantitative data regarding the applicant's
previous performance, rather than on the personal opinion or subjective
impressions of the applicant by either the reference or the selector himself.

PSYCHOLOGICAL TESTING

In recent years psychological testing has been much talked about and
much written about. Despite its popularity in business and industry, psychological testing has been criticized and in some cases ridiculed by various
writers. Martin L. Gross in his acid analysis of personality testing has said:
"Many psychologists, most of them a reasonable academic distance removed from the testing marketplace, have gratuitously expressed the
opinion that there is more sell than science in personality testing, and that
much of the work being done today is unsound (and dangerous) as pre-
Repeal aged-in-the-bathtub gin."[2] *The New York Times Book Review*
congratulated Mr. Gross for his timely exposé by writing: "The American
public has been in need of a blast against the use of invalid personality
tests. . . . "

Another critic of psychological testing, Frank Barron, research psychologist, University of California, has written as follows concerning one of
the widely used personality tests: "Judging from the literature on the Ed-
wards Personal Preference Schedule at this date the verdict of caution
should be that the test is not yet ready for use in counseling or personnel
selection."

In view of these criticisms of personality tests, it is amusing to recall
that Harvard psychologist, Professor Truman Lee Kelley, co-author of
The Stanford Achievement Battery, made headlines by bequeathing a small
fortune to his sons provided the women they selected for their wives first
passed a series of mental and personality tests. Probably the conclusion of
Albright, Glennon and Smith is closer to the truth than either the belief
of some psychological test administrators or the disdain of their critics.
They write " . . . there is nothing inherently good or bad about tests. As
with any tool, it is the degree of skill with which tests are used that determines the quality of the results."[3]

---

[2] Gross, Martin L., *The Brain Watchers,* Random House, New York, 1962, p.
204–205.
[3] Albright, Lewis E., Glennon, J. R., and Smith, Wallace J., "The Use of Psychological Tests in Industry," Howard Allen, Inc., Cleveland, 1963, p. 17. It should
be pointed out that the quality of results in testing depend, also, on the adequacy
of the criteria used to validate the test and the thoroughness with which the test
itself is validated, both concurrently and on a predictive level.

What Are Psychological Tests ?

The term "psychological tests" is used to refer to all of those types of tests that are designed to measure the many different aspects of human behavior, e.g., mental ability, clerical ability, sales ability, personality, interest and other kinds of behavior. Thus, the term "psychological testing" is the broad generic term that refers to the many different methods of sampling behavior for the purpose of predicting future behavior or performance. Other terms are used when reference is made to specific types of psychological tests. A mechanical aptitude test is a type of psychological test. Personality tests and vocational interest tests are all examples of psychological tests.

It should be recognized that much of psychological testing is, and will likely remain, at a relatively low level of precision. Any psychological test score should be treated as a "tentative hypothesis rather than as an established conclusion."[4] The advice of two experts in psychological testing is persuasive: "The more elegant procedures of formal tests and measurements must be supplemented by the cruder procedures of informal observation, anecdotal description, and rating if we are to obtain a description of the individual that is usefully complete and comprehensive."[5] Admitting that psychological measurement procedures are incomplete does not mean they should be ignored. Better measurement procedures should be developed, but in the meantime, those concerned with personnel selection should gain greater understanding of the strengths and weaknesses of existing procedures so that they may use the existing procedures with greater wisdom.

Aptitude Tests

There is no general agreement among experts in psychological testing or life insurance sales management concerning the relative importance of the various components of aptitude for life insurance selling. However, there appears to be general agreement that intelligence, interests, personality and attitude are all important factors or components of aptitude for life insurance selling. Although there is general agreement that all four of these factors are important, there is considerable difference of opinion as to their relative importance. Furthermore, there is considerable question as to how accurately one can measure these four factors.

---

[4] Thorndike, R. L., and Hagen, Elizabeth, *Measurement and Evaluation in Psychology and Education,* John Wiley and Sons, 1955, p. 14.

[5] Ibid., p. 14.

INTEREST INVENTORIES

If a person has extensive interest in a given activity it is reasonable to assume that he will have greater motivation toward participation in that activity. Furthermore, we know that the greater a person's motivation toward participation in a specific activity or business the greater is the probability that the person will be successful in that activity or business. However, specific measuring rods for gauging a person's motivation for purpose of predicting employment success are virtually unknown. The next best measuring rod for motivation appears to be a measuring rod for interest.

Interest may be thought of as a propensity to *participate* in a *specific* activity. In other words, interest is an inclination or a predisposition to do something without being prodded by economic rewards or threats of punishment if one does not do it. The key words in the concept of interest are: "participate" and "specific." A teenager may enjoy going to school dances. However, it would not be accurate for his parents to infer that the teenager has an interest in dancing. He may enjoy the camaraderie of his buddies. He may find the school dance the only parentally approved opportunity for him to spend two hours in a parked car with his girl friend. Only if the teenager demonstrates the specific behavior of dancing while attending the dance can it be inferred that he has an interest in dancing. Neither will reading about dancing or talking about dancing be an adequate indication of a real interest in participating.

Psychologists believe that the best measure of the intensity of a person's interest is obtained by the use of inventories of interests or preferences.[6] Inventories differ from tests in that the former have no right or wrong answers. The answers to inventory questions are descriptive of a person's preferences, interests, personality or attitude. Such descriptions, if honest, are always right. There are no wrong answers.

A systematic approach is mandatory if accurate measurements are to be made of such intangibles as interest or activity preferences. The typical interview does not provide such a systematic approach. This does not mean that the interview cannot be conducted systematically. But typically it is not so conducted. Furthermore, there is considerable opportunity for distractions and confusion to occur in an interview. First, there is the confusion that is inherent in any oral communication. This problem is virtually eliminated in a standardized inventory such as the Kuder Preference Record. The printed page is usually more lucid and comprehensible than the

---

6 Gekoski, Norman, "Psychological Testing," Charles C. Thomas, Springfield, Illinois, 1964, p. 131.

spoken word. Second, in an interview there is great difficulty in determining whether an interviewee indicates a sincere interest in an activity or whether the interviewee expresses an interest bcause he believes the activity should be viewed favorably. For example, the individual may feel golf is a mark of respectability while fishing is for the indolent and the poor. However, by inspecting the responses on the Kuder Preference or the Strong Vocational Interest Blank, it is possible to observe whether a profession of interest is because of the social desirability ascribed to an activity or if an activity interest actually exists.

There are several interest inventories available. However, those of Kuder and Strong are the most widely used. Research on and validation of these two tests have been impressive. Both tests have demonstrated high reliability coefficients. Follow-up studies of the Strong VIB have indicated considerable correspondence between initial interests scores and ultimate occupation choice.[7] Although there have been follow-up studies for the Kuder inventory it still lacks the systematic evidence for empirical validity which is available for the Strong VIB.[8]

MEASURING PERSONALITY TRAITS

It should be obvious that personality traits per se are not observed. It is a person's behavior that is observed; his personality traits are inferred from the observed behavior. The term "trait indicator" is used by psychologists to refer to this observed behavior that provides the basis for inferences concerning the existence and strength of personality traits. For example, if we observe a new life insurance salesman making 25 calls before he makes his first sale, we can infer that he has the trait of persistence to a considerable degree.

Some personnel psychologists interested in the assessment of the personalities of job applicants have recommended that the emotional reaction of the interviewer be used as an indication concerning the traits of the applicant.[9] In situations of this kind the interviewer examines his own feelings and his own reactions to the applicant. The interviewer then describes the applicant in accordance with the personal reaction of the interviewer to the applicant. It is claimed that the impressions of the interviewer are helpful in determining the effect that the applicant would have on other persons with whom he would meet in a business or social situation. The assumption is that the applicant will affect other persons in much the same way that he

---

[7] Anastasi, Anne, *Psychological Testing,* The Macmillan Company, New York, 1961, p. 571.

[8] *Ibid.,* p. 575.

[9] Guilford, J. P., *Personality,* McGraw-Hill Book Co., Inc., New York, 1959, p. 54.

affects the interviewer. However, there are a number of reasons to suggest that the reaction of an interviewer is not dependable. First, other persons are not necessarily affected in the same way by the particular person. Second, persons differ in the extent to which they like or dislike the behavior and traits of other persons. Finally, the reaction of the interviewer to the applicant may reveal more about the interviewer than about the applicant.[10]

There are three sources of information which may be used in assessing the strength of specific personality traits in an applicant. The first source is the person himself, the second is other persons who have observed the applicant and the third source would be an objective test that would be as free as possible from personal biases. There are, of course, limitations on the accuracy of a test since the person to whom the test is administered may inject considerable subjectivity and thereby bias the results. Most personality test results can be faked by a sophisticated subject. It should be emphasized again that the observing and measuring of personality traits is far from being an exact science. Even highly trained professional psychologists find it difficult to agree on the personality traits of an individual whom all have had an opportunity to observe and test.

1. Information from Person Himself

Self-Rating Approach—When a person rates himself with respect to a given trait he is actually inferring his own "trait position" on the basis of his own observation of his own behavior over his lifetime. To the extent that he relies upon remembered past observations of himself, the process is not as good as if he were using more current observations. Errors of memory may distort the picture he has of himself. However, there is a compensating advantage in that his lifetime gives him a larger number of observations than would be available on only one occasion.

Personality-Inventory Approach—Probably the most widely used personality inventory is the Bernreuter and some success has been reported in its use in measuring self-confidence and sociability. But no general claim can be made for its success in screening salesmen. However, psychologists have greater confidence in the personality-inventory approach to assessing personality traits than in either the self-rating of personality traits or ratings made from observations by other persons. One reason for this is that the personality-inventory approach calls for relatively less inference. In the personality-inventory approach the person is asked specific questions regarding his interests, habits and attitudes. The person is not asked to measure his gregariousness but rather to indicate his interest in reading,

[10] *Ibid.,* p. 56.

painting, hiking, club membership, public speaking, and community activities. In responding to such questions the person is not required to indicate his relative position on a rating scale but rather to respond "yes" or "no." The existence of a specific habit has to be inferred to some extent. However, the extent of the inference required is not as great as determining a single rating for a person for a general personality trait. Psychologists emphasize that there should be less error involved in obtaining a score by summing several specific and direct inferences to measure a general personality trait than if a person supplies a single rating for the personality trait.

2. Information from Other Persons

It should be reemphasized that if the person being rated wishes to influence the results he may conceal habits, interests and attitudes from the observer. He can do this likewise in making his self-report. However, it is unlikely that a person can conceal a great deal from another person who has had an opportunity to observe him over an extended period of time. Therefore, obtaining information from reliable references can be very helpful. References and other persons who have had an opportunity to observe the applicant are the second source of information for assessing the strength of specific personality traits of an applicant.

One agency carefully observes a few college students during the summer between their junior and senior years.[11] These students do no selling. Their job is to call on business men to enquire concerning the latter's opinion relative to the ownership of life insurance. The situation to which the student is exposed in conducting the summer survey is very close to an actual sales interview. Feed-back from the business men interviewed as well as the observance of the other agency staff can be helpful in evaluating the students' performance under "simulated sales conditions."

3. Projective Tests

The third source of information for assessing the strength of specific personality traits is the projective test. The projective technique is based on the principle that an individual will respond to an "unstructured" stimulus by giving responses influenced by his needs, motives, fears, expectations, and attitudes. In other words, a person is expected to project his personality and attitudes as he is exposed to a stimulus.

---

[11] Robbins, Walter S., The National Underwriter—Life and Health, March 30, 1968, p. 16. Report of talk before 1968 insurance conference sponsored by Ohio State University in cooperation with Griffith Foundation for Insurance Education.

Probably the most widely used projective technique in industry testing is the Rorschach. The person taking the test is presented with ten cards, each of which has a bilaterally symmetrical ink blot. Five of the ink blot cards are made in shades of black and gray. Two of the ink blot cards have bright patches of red in addition to shades of gray. The other three cards have various colors. They are all ambiguous in shape, shading, and form. The examinee is asked to describe what he sees. In addition to keeping a verbatim record of the responses of the examinee to each card, the examiner keeps notes as to the time of responses, position or positions in which the cards are held, spontaneous remarks, emotional expressions, and other incidental behavior of the subject during the test session. After the examinee has had a chance to view all ten cards, the questioner then systematically examines the subject regarding the various parts and aspects of each blot to which the examinee had previously responded. The scoring of the Rorschach test obviously requires a highly trained and experienced psychologist. For this reason the Rorschach cannot be used for selection purposes by most life insurance agency managers.

Another type of projective test is the word association test. A list of words are read to the examinee one at a time. He is asked to give the first word that comes to his mind immediately after hearing the word that is read. A technique which is similar to word association is incomplete sentences. The examinee is requested to write a response or to complete a group of sentences. The sentences are structured so that the examiner can acquire information about the applicant relative to different subject areas. Again, it should be emphasized that the word association test and other projective tests must be interpreted by a professionally trained psychologist or psychiatrist, and cannot be used meaningfully by the typical agency manager himself.

The main advantages of the sentence completion technique are (1) the freedom of response which is encouraged may disclose significant aspects of personality which would not be obtained in a forced-choice personality inventory; (2) no special training is generally needed for administration of the test; (3) less time is required to administer the test than for most tests using the projective technique; (4) substantial flexibility is provided in that new sentence beginnings may be tailor made for specific applications.

There are two major disadvantages of this type of projective technique for use by life insurance agency managers for selection purposes: (1) other projective methods, principally the ink blot test, provide greater disguise of the purpose of the test; (2) interpretation depends to a large extent upon the examiner's specific training and knowledge of personality analysis.

Conclusion Concerning Psychological Testing

The highly realistic conclusion of a respected authority in psychological testing should be carefully considered in evaluating psychological tests as selection procedures.

> From the bewildering diversity of techniques or potential techniques which have been considered, one impression should be clear: the field of personality testing is still in a formative stage. Few if any available instruments have as yet proved their value empirically to the same extent as have aptitude or achievement tests. Consequently, the tester in this field must proceed warily—at his own risk. Personality testing today offers a real challenge, both to the creative ingenuity of the test constructor and to the scientific vigilance of the test user. Even more than in other branches of psychological testing, the fullest utilization of personality tests requires the ability to recognize promise, without accepting unsupported claims—to be receptive toward that which is new, without being credulous toward that which is unverified.[13]

THE SELECTION INTERVIEW

The pre-contract interview is another tool which can be helpful in the selection process. Like any tool, its efficiency depends upon the degree of competence with which it is used. Some psychologists, however, emphasize certain shortcomings of the interview as a selection device. They point out that the efficiency of the interview in assessing the personal characteristics of the interviewee is rather limited. Gekoski indicates that "by and large, tests are far superior to the interview in predicting job success. . . . The few studies on the interview which have been done reflect very little predictive usefulness."[14] One of the reasons that psychologists have greater confidence in psychological testing than in interviewing is that tests have been subjected to careful scrutiny as to their validity and reliability. The results of an interview produce no measurements that can be checked for their validity and reliability. Since tests can be validated relatively easily there are a greater number of test validation studies reported in the testing literature.

Some agency managers are intuitively more skillful interviewers than others. They appear to have an innate ability to ask appropriate questions. They obtain the desired information from the interviewee as naturally and effortlessly as two neighbors conversing about the weather. Other agency managers do not appear to have a natural aptitude for interviewing. How-

[13] Anastasi, Anne, *Op. Cit.* p. 660–661.
[14] Gekoski, Norman, *Op. Cit.,* p. 9.

ever, interviewing skills can be developed and probably even the best of us
can improve our capacity for maximizing the benefits of the interview.

Objectives of Interviewing

The interview should supplement and not merely duplicate the application blank, references and psychological tests. Therefore, the primary
objective of the selection interview should be to obtain as much additional
information as possible that cannot be obtained from other media. If,
as often happens, the interviewer asks for the same information that the
applicant has already supplied in the application blank, this is very likely
to give the applicant the feeling that the interviewer is not really interested
in him. But in addition to this, it is much more expensive for the interviewer to obtain factual data during the interview than to have this data
supplied by the applicant on the application blank prior to the expensive
and time consuming selection interview.

The interviewer should make use of the information revealed by the
application blank, references and psychological tests to probe deeper in
specific areas to obtain greater knowledge and understanding of the applicant. First, the interview can be used to confirm certain information provided in the written application blank or biographical profile. However, a
minimum amount of time should be devoted to this since this can become
a mere duplication of the other media. A more beneficial use of interviewing time would result from having the interviewee expand upon
some specific aspects of his previous education and experience which
is particularly relevant to his interest in or aptitude for life insurance
selling. For example, perhaps at some time the applicant sold Fuller
Brushes or soap flakes or men's clothing. It would be extremely beneficial
to explore with the interviewee such questions as: (1) How did you happen to enter that particular sales work? (2) What did you like most in that
work? (3) What kinds of people did you come in contact with in this
work? (4) What were some of the unpleasant aspects of this type of work?
(5) How successful were you in this work? (6) What could you have done
to have been more successful in this type of work? (7) Why did you give
up this type of work?

The types of questions to ask should be suggested by the objective of
the interview. The objective is to obtain all possible additional information
that will assist the agency manager in making an important decision: Does
this person possess what it takes to make a success in life insurance selling?
To answer that question and to make that decision the agency manager
wants to know as much as possible about the interviewee's (1) past experi-

ence, (2) personality traits, (3) likes and dislikes relative to work activities, (4) interest in making money and (5) strength of self-motivation.

Probably the most important principle to keep in mind in the whole selection process is the old axiom that the previous job performance of a person is the best predictor of future job performance. Leopards do not change their spots. Persons with success patterns in previous employments are better bets than those who have not established a success pattern. This generalization should be interpreted carefully. A person with a success pattern in architecture or engineering or, even, law is not necessarily a good candidate for life insurance sales. It should be emphasized that in selecting salesmen the life insurance agency manager should look for success patterns in previous employments that are very similar in nature to that of life insurance sales. The less similar the previous activity to life insurance selling, the less a previous success pattern really means. Naturally, extenuating circumstances should be considered. But the eagerness for new agents should not pressure the manager into rationalizing that he can help this good-looking man make a success. Losing the one possible success will probably be no great loss since the training and supervision time that would be required to save him would be gross extravagance with agency and company resources.

Conducting the Interview

1. PREPARATION

The selection interview that is well planned is well started. What the agency manager does the day before or the night before he interviews a new recruit can be as important as the actual interview itself. Inadequate preparation can be a serious handicap.

As a minimum, the agency manager should review the application blank and the biographical profile. He should be familiar with the applicant's previous background and experience. This knowledge will save valuable time during the interview by eliminating the need to spend time traversing this ground a second time. In addition, familiarity with the applicant's background will suggest possible strengths and weaknesses in character and personality. This information will indicate specific topics for further exploration during the interview. Rather than having to begin his questioning from ignorance, the agency manager can start with a well organized sequence of questioning based on knowledge and a well organized plan for covering relevant topics.

In addition to planning the topics to be covered during the interview the agency manager should plan his time for the occasion. He should be ready to greet the applicant at the appointed time. He should not keep the applicant waiting. Waiting may make the applicant feel he is being given the brush-off. In any event, it will not assist in getting the interview off to a good start. Furthermore, it is not good human relations.

2. APPROPRIATE INTERVIEWING CONDITIONS

The circumstances and the physical conditions for conducting a selection interview should be as pleasant and comfortable as possible. The room should be well ventilated, properly lighted and equipped with appropriate furnishings.

After the interview is underway there should be no interruptions to receive telephone calls or conduct other business. The manager's secretary should be alerted to the fact that no interruptions should occur. Adequate planning can assure that other agency matters can be taken care of either before or after the scheduled time for the interview. If the preliminary interview and the other screening of the applicant suggest that he may make a successful life insurance salesman, he may become an important addition to the agency. Treat him and the time allotted to interviewing him as being important.

3. BEGINNING THE INTERVIEW

The interviewer should be as anxious to make a good impression at the beginning of the interview as the person to be interviewed. The agency manager may not know at the beginning of the interview how anxious he will be ultimately to add the interviewee to his agency staff. Thus the agency manager should be as gracious and hospitable in his first greeting of the interviewee as he would in greeting his new agency vice president for the first time. Making a good first impression will assist the agency manager in gaining the applicant's confidence. The agency manager's demonstration of sincere interest in the applicant will help to establish the necessary rapport. The manager must "reach the applicant" if the latter is to speak freely and openly about himself and his previous background. This does not mean that the manager needs to take off his coat, roll up his sleeves and swap racy stories for 30 minutes. To establish a pleasant relationship does not require that the manager abdicate either his position or his dignity. In fact, it should be emphasized that the interviewer should maintain his position of authority throughout the interview. This does not mean that he should be authoritarian, but it does mean that he should be the leader and in control of the interview throughout. The applicant wants to respect the interviewer. He wants to feel that his listener is a superior person and that he is privileged to have this opportunity to describe his previous experience to the interviewer.

We all like to be treated with respect. The applicant will be more relaxed and more willing to communicate if he feels that he is being accepted by the interviewer. He wants to feel that the interviewer has a sincere regard for him. Personnel psychologists suggest that the interviewer should show empathy for the applicant but not sympathy. The projection of one's own consciousness into another person does not mean one has to sympathize with that person. But in demonstrating empathy the interviewer comes close to feeling what the applicant feels. When empathy is demonstrated the applicant feels he is being understood. Balinsky has emphasized that empathy is important as an enhancement of one's ability to pick up the talker's feelings and respond in appropriate terms. "It gives the candidate the feeling that you perceive him correctly, which results in an easier flow of conversation. It is a quality that can readily be described as a lubricant to interviewing."[15]

4. COMMON ERRORS TO BE AVOIDED

The following are some of the more common errors to be avoided by the successful interviewer in his interview questioning.

1. Asking questions that require merely "yes" or "no" as an answer.

2. Asking questions that lead the interviewee to the expected or proper answer.

3. Asking conventional stereotyped questions which the interviewee has been coached to answer properly.

4. Asking questions which serve no useful purpose. We have discussed the importance of cordially greeting the applicant, putting him at ease and assuring him that the interviewer is keenly interested in having this opportunity to visit with him. But once the interview is under way the questioning should be purposeful.

5. Asking questions relative to factual information that can be obtained from the application blank or biographical profile unless the interviewer is trying to confirm or resolve discrepancies in factual information obtained from other sources.

6. Asking questions in an attempt to measure the applicant's intelligence or knowledge of technical aspects of the life insurance business. Other methods are more reliable and more appropriate for obtaining such measurements.

[15] Balinsky, Benjamin, "The Selection Interview: Essentials for Management," Martin M. Bruce, New York, 1962, p. 21.

Magee has suggested four important areas for interview questioning which should be kept in mind by the agency manager to aid him in successful interviewing.[16] Magee suggests having the applicant describe (1) how he feels about his present employment, (2) how he feels about people, (3) what his job objectives are and finally, (4) how the applicant regards himself. These areas of questioning give the interviewer an opportunity to probe deeply and find out considerably more about the applicant's personality than could be learned in any other way.

Importance of Objectivity

The good interviewer tries to be objective in planning and conducting each interview. This is sometimes difficult. All of us have preconceived ideas, prejudices and biases. Some of these are known to us. Others are not recognized.

During a selection interview the interviewer is evaluating, measuring and judging. He must listen and view objectively so as not to misinterpret the interviewee's responses. Misinterpretation occurs when the interviewer's own personality, prejudices and biases destroy objectivity. The interviewer should be aware of these limitations so that he can try to correct them. At the very least he should allow for them in making a final judgment.

The interviewer makes his final judgment on the basis of observations and inferences from what was observed. Objectivity should be preserved in the observation process. The successful use of the interview is almost wholly dependent upon the accuracy and reliability of the observations of the interviewer. To standardize the evaluation process interviewers have developed different types of rating scales such as numerical, graphic, checklist, and forced-choice. All of these, however, involve various sources of error. First, it is generally recognized that some raters are more lenient than others. Other raters may be severe in their ratings. A third group of raters may "play it safe" by giving mainly average ratings. In general, it has been found that raters have a consistent error with respect to their severity or leniency of rating.

Psychologists use the phrase "halo effect" in referring to the rating error that occurs when a particular person tends to rate another similarly on all traits. If the rater has a generally favorable impression of a particular person the rater attaches a "halo" to the person and the ratings he submits on all traits are likely to be favorable.

Another source of error in judging personality traits is the so-called

---

[16] Magee, Richard H., "The Employment Interview—Techniques of Questioning," *Personnel Journal,* May 1962, pp. 242–243.

"contrast error." This error occurs because of a tendency for some persons who possess a given trait to a large degree to rate down others rather severely who may be lacking in a given characteristic. On the other hand, there is evidence that some interviewers will rate down interviewees who possess to a small degree unfavorable characteristics that the interviewer possesses to a greater degree. For example, a person who is rather nervous will attribute this same characteristic to others. Apparently we tend to attribute to others the faults that we disown in ourselves.

Another error in rating is the tendency to rate similarly traits that seem to the person doing the rating to be similar or related. For example, the quiet, reticent person may erroneously be rated as also being studious. To a large extent such errors in rating may be caused by the failure of the person doing the rating to discriminate clearly as to the precise meaning of the given trait concept being measured. Another source of error may be the fact that the person doing the rating has a poor conception concerning the structure of personality. As indicated earlier, human behavior and personality structure are extremely complex. It is a serious error to over-simplify or to generalize too quickly in evaluating others.

Reliability of Interview Measurements

Measurements are most reliable and accurate when the person being measured is not disturbed by chance external factors. The selection interview frequently does not satisfy this criterion. Both the interviewee and the interviewer can be affected by chance external factors. Either one or both can have indigestion. They both could have spent sleepless nights. They both could have home problems. They both could have their attention distracted by innumerable possible circumstances. All of these factors affect both the performance of the interviewee and the interpretation of that performance by the interviewer.

A great deal can be done to improve the reliability of measurements taken by the interviewer. First, reliability of the measurements taken depend upon the understanding by the interviewer of what he is looking for. Such understanding is enhanced by making more precise the definition of the behavior to be observed.[17] Second, the simpler the behavior to be observed the more reliable will be the interviewer's interpretation and the recording of his observations. This would suggest that the interviewer should try to break up complex behavior patterns into as simple responses as possible. Third, the more overt and the less covert are the responses

---

[17] Thorndike, R. L., *Personnel Selection: Test and Measurement Techniques,* John Wiley & Sons, Inc., New York, 1949, p. 129.

of the person being interviewed, the more reliable are the observations of
the interviewer. On the other hand, if the interviewee restrains himself
and restricts his responses, the observations of the interviewer will have
considerably less reliability. Fourth, the greater the extent to which use
is made of standardized procedures and planned questioning the more
reliable will be the observations of the interviewer.

EVALUATION OF SELECTION PROCEDURES

The evaluation of the merits of any selection procedure requires consideration of two important questions. First, is the procedure valid? Second,
is the procedure reliable? Test experts emphasize that the former is the
more important. Therefore, we turn our attention first to the question of
validity. The following discussion is concerned primarily with psychological
testing. However, a consideration of the validity and reliability of other
selection procedures is equally important. The reader should recognize
that the principles of validity and reliability are as applicable to the other
selection procedures, including the interview, as to psychological testing.

Confusion sometimes arises because test experts use the word "validity"
to refer to slightly different concepts. We will be concerned with only two
types of validity. (1) Content validity and (2) predictive validity.

Content Validity

Content validity refers to the accuracy with which a test measures what
it is supposed to measure. For a selection test to have content validity, it
must sample adequately the behavior characteristic to be measured. For
example, a life insurance selling aptitude test must obtain samples of
specific individual behavior which has some relationship to a person's
ability to be persuasive in the marketing of life insurance. (It is generally
believed that to be successful in life insurance selling the person should be
socially poised, confident in own ability, reasonably extrovertive, persuasive
in personal contacts, an effective leader, reasonably aggressive and socially
ascendant, fluent and articulate, well established in one's community and
having strong cultural and social ties to the community.) At this stage in
the development of tests to measure aptitude for life insurance selling
there is no clearly documented experimental evidence to what extent the
above enumerated characteristics are necessary in life insurance selling.
However, they are generally accepted as being the characteristics that
are possessed by many successful life insurance salesmen. To have content
validity in accordance with the above assumptions, a test of a person's

aptitude for life insurance selling should determine the extent to which the person possesses the above characteristics.

It is important to emphasize that the content area to be tested must be analyzed systematically to make certain that all major aspects are adequately covered by the test items, and in the correct proportions. For example, a test to measure a person's aptitude for life insurance selling might become overloaded with those aspects of selling having to do with aggressiveness and persuasive leadership. A person who would be extremely successful in estate planning, business insurance and pension sales might possess these specific characteristics only to a limited extent. Such a person might compensate for only average aggressiveness and persuasive leadership by having strong motivation to succeed and an outstanding ability to analyze business needs and a capacity to present these in a logical form. In fact, some men are persuasive as leaders who are not particularly aggressive or socially ascendant. Persuasiveness may be strong in some persons who are not emphatically extroverted. It is axiomatic that the content area under consideration should be described fully in advance before preparation of the items making up the test to sample individual behavior. Content validity requires a relationship between individual test responses and the behavior area under consideration.

Items in a test to measure word fluency would be another example of a test having content validity but not necessarily having predictive validity. The test might be very valid for measuring word fluency. However, it has yet to be proved that word fluency is as important a characteristic for assuring success in life insurance selling as confidence and aggressiveness. The extreme case of the shy and reticent yet very articulate Mr. Chips who teaches English Literature at Collosal College illustrates the point.

Prediction Validity

For our purposes we are not as much interested in validity in the sense of measuring what we intend to measure as we are in determining the validity of a test as a predictor of future performance. Rather than being directly concerned with measuring a person's social ascendancy and word fluency, we are interested primarily in determining the prevalence of the overall kind of behavior that will specifically assist a person in life insurance selling. We want to know if the person's overall behavior pattern is appropriate for the job duties. The statistician has developed a way to determine this. The statistician can compute a relationship between two variables. For example, if there is a close statistical relationship between the scores on a selection test and subsequent job performance the statistician says that the test has predictive validity.

An illustration should clarify the point. As each one of 100 life insurance salesmen are placed under contract, arrangements are made for them to take the LIAMA selection test known as the *Aptitude Index Battery*.[19] A record is kept of each man's results on the test. All of the 100 men are given similar training in life insurance selling. Several months later the production for each man is determined. The results of the *Aptitude Index Battery* (the independent or "X" variable) and the production volume (the dependent or "Y" variable) are matched with each other to facilitate the calculation of the "validity coefficient or correlation."

Reliability of Selection Procedures

Establishing the validity of a selection device is of primary importance, but a second important requirement is its reliability. A measuring device or a testing procedure is said to be reliable if it produces consistent results. A yardstick is a reliable measuring device because it can be used by a tailor to measure 36 inches of cloth as accurately for the 90th suit as for the first. A piece of string possessing some elasticity would not produce the same consistency of results. Reliability in a measuring device is thus a matter of degree. Even the yardstick will not yield absolute consistency. The human eye will vary in its alignment. The stick may be moved accidentally. The marking intervals on the yardstick will require interpretation which may produce human errors. The amount of chance error will vary but it will always be present to some extent.

In measuring specific characteristics of people there is an additional element of chance variation which does not exist when we are measuring cloth with a yardstick. People are not consistent in their portrayal of specific characteristics or personality traits. Cloth will not change much from day to day. But people vary from day to day in their portrayal of such characteristics as confidence, nervousness, alertness, happiness, enthusiasm and many other characteristics too numerous to mention.

SUMMARY

The application of sound selection procedures is indispensable to the sound growth of a life insurance agency. This chapter has described the principal selection tools that are available to the life insurance agency manager. However, selection procedures are only effective when used in conjunction with effective management in each of the other important

---

[19] For a full and complete description and analysis of the *Aptitude Index Battery*, see Chapter 23, "Research on Agency Selection, Survival and Productivity."

SELECTING AGENCY MANPOWER 385

operational areas of a life insurance agency. The unique dependence of successful selection upon successful performance of the other agency management functions is cogently emphasized by a company executive's statement that success in selecting life insurance agents is usually attributable to six factors:

1. Providing financial incentive for the agency manager to do a careful job of selecting.
2. Selecting only a small proportion of those men who apply. This means, of course, that there must be effective recruiting procedures used so that the agencies may enjoy the luxury of a low selection ratio.
3. Careful attention to the basic rules of good selection procedure.
4. Refusing to take any man unless he has a clearly discernible success pattern in his previous employment.
5. Intelligent use of pre-contract training.
6. Following through with the new men in the application of sound training and supervision after the pre-contract training period is over.

A company-wide program that gave adequate recognition to each of these six factors would no doubt go a long way toward improving agent retention. But there is no escaping the importance of the fact that success in agent retention starts with adequate and careful attention to selection.

23

Research on Agency Selection, Survival, and Productivity

Donald Bramley

SELECTION

Introduction

One of the most valuable and sought-after skills in management is the ability to select new personnel and to select present employees for promotion. Putting the right man in the right job is a process which has fascinated management of all businesses for many years—no less the life insurance business. The obvious results of poor selection, in terms of excessive turnover and waste of time, effort, and money, make this true. Similarly, the unfortunate image that our business can gain by putting unqualified agents before the public adds to the concern. To a large extent, the image of a job is determined by the quality of its incumbents. The degree of skill they bring to the performance of the job will have a great deal to do with its status. If they perform poorly or unethically, then they drag down the job and make it more difficult to attract qualified applicants in the future. If, on the other hand, they achieve success in the job within the bounds of public interest, they enhance the likelihood of better selection in the future.

The years have seemed to demonstrate this principle in the life insurance business. The acceptance of life insurance today as compared with fifty years ago is surely a function of our increasing attention to the agent. While we are hardly satisfied with our results in agent selection and development today, our efforts stand in vivid contrast to the situation prevailing around the turn of the century. One has only to leaf through the pages of J. Owen Stalson's classic *Marketing Life Insurance* to get a flavor of those times: agents contracted without regard to qualification, sent into the field without training, returned to the general population without regret. The emphasis was on getting as much business as possible without too much concern for the method or for the agent involved in getting it.

Today the situation is vastly different. We are concerned with hiring better agents. We are concerned with equipping them to deal with family and business financial problems. We are concerned about our turnover rate. We are concerned with what the public thinks of our agents. And we are constantly seeking better ways of making it possible for men and women to achieve rewarding careers in selling life insurance.

This chapter will deal with the selection aspect of that process, though it is by no means the only part of it. It is vital, however, that the people we hire have the potential for succeeding. The extent to which we have been able to identify that potential will be discussed here.

The Meaning of Selection

It's a sad fact that in almost any job you can think of, failure is a good deal more likely than success. If we define success as meeting some performance standard (a definitional problem in itself) *and* staying in the business, then success depends on a number of factors. It may involve the possession of unique physical skills. It may involve an inordinate amount of drudgery and perseverance. It may require the ability to overcome boredom. It may depend heavily on the amount and kind of training given. It will almost certainly be affected by factors external to the individual, such as the general manpower market, economic conditions, quality of management, consumer attitudes, and other similar factors.

All of these factors are in some degree operative in our business and therefore have their effect on selection. Some of them are difficult or impossible to allow for. For example, in an economy where good jobs are plentiful, how can one take into account in a selection procedure the possibility of a good agent leaving the business to become sales manager of the Widget Company? Yet this must be included in our measurement of the selection system if one part of the success definition is staying in the business.

It's easy to see that on the basis of unpredictable factors alone, it is easier to predict "failure" than it is to predict success. In addition, qualities such as ability to do the job and the kind of training given to an agent are highly variable from applicant to applicant and from agency to agency. Therefore, the process of selection becomes largely a matter of rejecting the unfit.

Statistics gathered by the Life Insurance Agency Management Association bear this out. Over the years, the one-year agent survival rate in ordinary companies has hovered around 40 percent. In this instance, survival means survival in the agent's original company, not survival in the business. Since a certain amount of company switching takes place in the first year, the industry rate would be somewhat higher. But using company survival as a definition of success, half again as many men fail to meet the standard as the number who do. If we make the definition more stringent (and more realistic) by adding a performance qualification such as some minimum level of production, we cut our successes even further. Once again, from the standpoint of making predictions alone, we could do a lot better predicting failure than success.

However, we have to do more than stand on the sidelines and make bets. We have to hire men. This means developing a system which will distinguish between potential successes and failures with as much accuracy as possible. And since it is easier to identify potential failures, our system must rely heavily on weeding these people out first, in order to leave a group in which there is a higher percentage of potential successes than would be found in the general population. We can never hope to do a perfect job of selection, there being too many unpredictable factors. The job of identifying with perfect accuracy either successes or failures is beyond our present knowledge and ability, if it ever will be possible. Therefore, our best course of action is to reduce the population to more manageable proportions: to eliminate as many potential failures as possible without at the same time eliminating an undue number of potential successes. If we can do this, we will be left with a group from which we have a better chance of picking potential successes, because they are in higher proportion.

To a considerable extent, then, our selection process is really a rejection process and would be more descriptive if it were so named. The more of the unfit we can identify and eliminate, the more likely we are to be left with the fit to choose from. As stated previously, the unfit are easier to identify. Even so, the process is far from perfect, and the degree to which it deviates from perfection gives rise to certain costs.

Over and above the administrative costs of any selection procedure, there are also the costs incurred in rejecting men who would have succeeded and accepting men who fail. For example, consider a device which rejects 50% of the average run of agent applicants. Also suppose that 35% of those accepted survive through one year under contract and validate the company financing plan. If a company hires 200 men in a year and uses this device, its results will look like this:

Number of men examined	400
Number hired	200
Number performing acceptably	70
Number rejected	200

What is the cost of this device? For one thing, the company hired 130 men who did not perform acceptably, which represents a real cost in terms of both time and money. But another cost, possibly bigger, is the number rejected who might have performed acceptably. How many of the 200 eliminated might have succeeded?

Under certain conditions, this might not be too important to us. If, for example, men were begging for the chance to be life insurance agents on straight commissions, without office space, training or supervision, it really wouldn't worry us. Or at the other extreme, if men were so hard to get that we'd take anyone who would come in, then we might as well forget about selection entirely.

But the real conditions are somewhere in between these extremes. We are never so desperate as to take anybody. Neither are we close enough to the perfect recruiting situation not to regret passing up good men. Hence, these costs become important to us.

Suppose, for example, we found that 70 of the men rejected with this selection device would have performed acceptably. Has the device done any good? No, because the results would have been the same if we had accepted the men the device rejected and rejected those it accepted. Has the device done any harm? Yes, it has, because it has caused us to turn down 200 men and increased our recruiting problem without increasing the proportion who justify our investment. In other words, it has reduced the population from which we select *without* increasing the proportion of potential successes. One hundred and forty successes out of 400 is the same proportion (35%) as 70 out of 200.

If, on the other hand, every one of the 200 rejected men would have failed, then the device has done us an enormous amount of good by reducing the population and increasing the proportion of successes. Seventy out of 200 is, of course, twice the proportion of 70 out of 400. In actuality, we cannot hope for this good a job from any selection device. There will always be a few potential successes among the rejectees under the best of circumstances.

Validity

The degree to which a device or test rejects a high proportion of potential failures and a low proportion of potential successes is a measure of its validity. The more potential failures and fewer potential success it rejects, the higher its validity. Conversely, the more potential failures it accepts and more potential successes it rejects, the lower its validity.

In terms of cost, it can be seen that the validity of a selection instrument is extremely important. As noted above, the greatest costs associated with a selection procedure are those incurred by accepting failures and rejecting successes—far greater than the cost of administering the procedure itself. Therefore, any test which purports to select men for a given position should be examined very carefully as to its validity.

Such an examination is a straightforward process in theory but a complex and difficult one in practice. One common method is to administer the test to men currently on the job who have previously been classified as successful and unsuccessful according to some agreed upon standard. The degree to which the test differentiates between these two groups is called its concurrent validity. This method is known as concurrent validation because it compares a current measure of performance with a current measure of potential. Having established such validity, however, does not mean that we can use the test to differentiate between applicants for the job. Identification of performance of experienced people on a particular job is not the same thing as predicting the performance of inexperienced people not yet on the job. To know that good producers score better on a test than low producers may tell us something about how production experience changes test scores. But it tells us considerably less about how to separate potential failures with test scores at the time of hiring.

The correct procedure for checking the predictive validity of a test follows six basic steps:

1. Administer the test to a group of applicants (at least 500).
2. Hire all applicants before the tests are scored.
3. Define a criterion of performance by which the men will be measured or classified.
4. Score the tests, but do not release the scores of the men to their managers.
5. After a reasonable period of time (one or two years), order or classify the men on the criterion of performance.
6. Determine the relationship between test score and criterion classification.

The Aptitude Index Battery

An example of a selection device which has been put to this rigorous validity check is the *Aptitude Index Battery,* prepared by the Life Insurance Agency Management Association. When the test was first published in 1937 (then known as the *Aptitude Index*), it had been validated by the above procedure and had shown a significant relationship between the applicant's score and his subsequent performance. Through the intervening years, it has been periodically rechecked and updated in order to maintain a level of validity consonant with reasonable cost in terms of potential failures rejected and potential successes accepted. In fact, up until 1965, six revisions of the *Aptitude Index* had been made based on these continuous validation studies. In 1965, the *Aptitude Index Battery,* Form I, was introduced incorporating a personality test which had been found to improve the validity of the *Aptitude Index.*

The *Aptitude Index* is no exception to the rule that potential failures are easier to identify than potential successes. It is indeed a rejection test, in that its primary function is to screen out applicants whose potential for success is so low that they would represent a cost far in excess of their worth to a company.

This fact creates a problem in validating the *Aptitude Index.* As long as it is being used—and used properly—very few low scoring men are hired into the business. Thus, for the low scoring men, the great majority of whom are never hired, it is impossible to tell what their performance would have been had they been given a chance. Item number 2 in the six-step validation procedure above is therefore violated.

Fortunately for research purposes, *some* low scoring men are hired, and though it takes a long time, enough data can be accumulated to make a meaningful comparison with the high scorers. This method has been the basis of the studies made of the *Aptitude Index* leading to the six revisions. The results of such a study with Form 7 (the sixth revision) are shown below. The scores range from a low of 20 to a high of 39. The agents were inexperienced, financed men, contracted by ordinary companies in 1961

TABLE 1

Form 7 Rating	Success Rate
37–39	42%
33–36	31
29–32	28
25–28	24
20–24	11

and the first quarter of 1962. "Success" is defined as survival in their companies for six months and production at or above their companies' median for six-month survivors.

These figures demonstrate that the test works: that there is a larger proportion of high scorers who meet the success definition than low scorers. They also seem to demonstrate that the wisest course of action in using the test would be to eliminate everyone who did not score at least 37. However, only 3 percent of the agents contracted scored that high, so that such a course of action would involve knocking out 97 percent of the applicants. And while it would eliminate 97 percent of the failures, it would also knock out 95 percent of the successes. What cost is a company or an agency willing to pay in its search for good men? Hardly that high.

But there is another question that these figures raise. Except at the very high and very low scores, there doesn't seem to be much differentiation between success rates. It would appear that the difference in success rate between the scores of 29 and 36 is only a matter of three percentage points. (The actual difference is greater when the scores are listed individually rather than grouped.) This apparent low level of differentiation is again caused by the fact that the validation study is carried on while the test is being used. Only if we could conduct the "classic" validation according to the six-step procedure would we know the true validity of the test.

In 1965, LIAMA was able to do this with one of its member companies. This company was concerned about the value of the *Aptitude Index,* and agreed to take it out of use for the purpose of a classic study. This involved having its managers continue to give the test to applicants, but instead of receiving the scores back from LIAMA headquarters as usual, these scores were withheld. Applicants were contracted or rejected without the assistance of an *Aptitude Index* score. Here is a comparison of the success rates from the "in-use" study quoted above and the company classic study. (The scores are grouped differently from Table 1.)

TABLE 2
Success Rates

Score	In-Use Study	Classic Study
32–39	30.7%	54.2%
29–31	27.0	34.2
27–28	24.8	17.9
25–26	22.1	15.0
20–24	11.4	5.6

Both tables show that the *Aptitude Index* is valid, but the company data show a much stronger relationship of test score with success than the industry data. The reason for this apparent lessening of test validity when the test is being used may lie in several areas:

1. There may be something unusual about the men who are hired in spite of their low score, which makes them better bets than low-scoring men in general.
2. The manager's selection and training procedures may be affected by knowledge of the test score. With high-scoring applicants, he may relax his other selection standards. With a low-scoring man, he may work harder to bring him through and vindicate his judgment. Conversely with the high-scorer, he may feel that intensive training is unnecessary.
3. To the extent that some managers "help" the applicant take the test, this may alter the score in either direction. In any event, it is not a true score.

Whatever the reasons, the fact is that use of a test can result in an apparent validity which is quite different from its true validity. It is important to note, however, that even in use, the *Aptitude Index* does show validity. Its real validity is strong enough so that the factors mentioned above do not obliterate it entirely. It would be easy to use one or more of those factors to justify a test which showed no validity at all. This kind of excuse can only be suspect, because a selection device must operate and show results in the world as it is—not in a laboratory world.

Through the years, LIAMA has examined about 25 different tests in its quest for improvement of selection of agents. In every case, the validity of these tests as determined by the procedure outlined was either nonexistent or was so low that its use would not justify its administrative cost.

Then in 1962, a personality test developed by Dr. David Merrill of Denver, Colorado, showed enough promise to justify a validation study for life insurance agents. The results were positive and the test was incorporated with the *Aptitude Index Battery*. The validity at the *AIB* has since been established by both an in-use study and a classic study as described above.

The Combination Inventory

Fairly early in the history of the *Aptitude Index,* it became apparent that its validity for the combination or debit agent was not nearly as high as that for ordinary agents. It became increasingly apparent that for most combination companies, the *Aptitude Index* was not doing a good selection job in terms of screening out potential failures. The reasons for this are subject to conjecture, but they all revolve around the nature of the combination agent's job and more particularly his assigned territorial account or debit.

It should be noted here that this is one of the best illustrations of why a selection device should be put to rigorous checks before assuming its validity for any group. One might reasonably assume that since the *Aptitude Index* helps identify potential life insurance salesmen, it can do this regardless of how they sell or whatever other duties their job involves. Experience with combination agents proves this to be an incorrect assumption. It demonstrates that a test which is useful for one purpose may have no validity, or even negative validity, for another purpose even within the same occupation.

As a result of this finding, LIAMA developed a different device for combination agents known as the *Combination Inventory*. It consists of five parts:

1. Arithmetic
2. General knowledge
3. Interest
4. Reactions
5. Personal history

The arithmetic section is designed to determine whether the applicant will have trouble handling debit accounting. The general knowledge section provides an indication of mental alertness and, therefore, ability to learn. The interest section gives an indication of the similarity of the applicant's interests to those of successful agents. The reactions section is designed to indicate the degree to which the applicant "puts his best foot forward" in answering test questions. And the personal history section provides biographical information, with emphasis on the applicant's economic progress compared to others of his age.

These all sound like worthy objectives, but we are interested in predictive validity. To what extent do they relate to the applicant's subsequent performance on the job as a combination agent?

Unlike the *Aptitude Index Battery* which combines the individual scores of its sections into one predictive score, the *Combination Inventory* sections are scored separately. On the basis of the number of sections passed or failed a management decision is made as to whether to continue the selection procedure or drop the applicant from further consideration.

The effectiveness of the first two sections of the *Combination Inventory* is borne out by actual experience. High scoring applicants are less likely to have trouble with accounts and with learning new material than are low scoring applicants. These results are based on managerial ratings. The same difficulty arises here, however, as with the *Aptitude Index,* but in a little different way. The validity of the first two sections is affected by the fact that they are timed tests—15 minutes each. The score distributions would indicate that these times are not always rigidly adhered to by the person administering the test, which has a serious effect on any attempt to measure validity. Suppose two men achieve identical scores on the arithmetic test, but one has taken 15 minutes and the other has taken 30. The scores are obviously *not* the same, nor would they distinguish between any future differences in ability with accounts. In spite of this defect, the tests do show validity, though probably not as high as it would be under ideal conditions.

The other three sections of the test—interest, reactions, and personal history— all turn out to be related to first-year production. In other words, more applicants who score above average on these sections become above average producers than those who score below average. In developing a suitable standard of performance against which to measure test scores, production had to be corrected for debit size, since the size of an agent's debit is a significant factor in the amount of business he produces. Generally, the larger the debit, the greater the production. Hence, averages were developed for various debit sizes, and to be considered successful an agent had to have above average production for his debit size.

The Agent's Job and Selection

As indicated above, it is not safe to assume that the validity of a test is transferable from one kind of agent to another. The structure of his job and the products he sells may have an effect on that validity, as we have seen with the combination agent.

The same could be said for the agent who sells both life and health insurance. Is there enough difference in the methods used to sell health insurance to have an effect on a test designed to predict life sales? This question was investigated by LIAMA in a validity study of the *Aptitude Index* with a group of applicants whose sales would include varying proportions of life and health insurance. The study showed a positive relationship between test scores and combined life and health production. The evidence further indicated that the relative proportions of life and health insurance in the total made no difference.

It is possible that further refinements in agent job descriptions will have implications for better test validity determination. There are a number of different ways of being successful as an insurance agent. For example, one may be strictly a package salesman, or one may be an estate analyst, or one may specialize in a particular market. Also, there are different ways of prospecting, approaching, making sales presentations, and other sales activities. The term "life insurance agent" may in fact cover a multitude of different jobs. These different jobs may require different sets of skills in order to perform them successfully. The identification and classification of the different jobs and skills is an enormous job, but worth doing. If the skills can be measured and related to test scores, it could mean a vast improvement in our ability to select the right man for the right job. Such a project is currently going on at LIAMA.

Other Selection Procedures

With the great emphasis given to selection testing, it might seem as if the test was the most important element of the selection procedure. However, this emphasis does not stem from the importance of the test, but rather from the fact that most of the research has been carried on in the testing area. Also, general misconceptions about tests—what they can do, how they work, etc.—have caused more time to be devoted to their explanation.

It should be categorically stated here that no test will select life insurance agents. That is the job of management, on the basis of experience, judgment and proper use of the tools available. The test is simply one of those tools. There are a number of other tools available also, some of which have a basis in research and some of which don't. For a number of them research would be inappropriate. Take the inspection report, for example. One of its purposes is to give an estimate of the character of the applicant. To subject this to a validation study against performance would be irrelevant. If a company does not wish to hire men with criminal records, to take an extreme, it doesn't really care how well they might produce. Similar standards might pertain in other areas irrespective of predicted performance on the job.

For most areas, however, we are concerned with how they relate to performance. Does the picture we can get of an individual add up to potential success in selling life insurance, or doesn't it? One of the best ways of determining this is through the "work sample" technique, which *does* have a basis in research.

WORK SAMPLE

As the name implies, work sample involves giving the applicant a sample of the job to do in order to determine his ability and willingness to do it. The technique is used in many industries for many different kinds of jobs, as well as in the Armed Forces. One of the best examples is the Link Trainer used by the Air Force to train pilots in instrument flying. Anyone who went through pilot training in World War II remembers the hours spent simulating cross country flights on instruments in the Link Trainer.

In the life insurance business, the vehicle for a work sample is precontract orientation. Its purpose is to put the applicant in situations as closely approximating the actual job as possible, before he actually contracts to do the job. These situations include prospecting assignments, simulated selling interviews, telephone approaches, and planning work schedules. If the applicant is either unable or unwilling to carry out these assignments, he will presumably be a failure on the job.

Such a procedure is costly in terms of time spent with applicants. Also, as with selection tests, if it did not weed out the unworthy or if it eliminated too many potential successes, it would be even more costly. What evidence is there that it is a valid procedure?

The most recent study of precontract orientation compared the survival rates of two groups of agents, one with precontract orientation and the other without. The one-year retention of the precontract group was 38 percent higher than the nonprecontract group. An even greater difference existed in the attainment of high production standards, in favor of the precontract group.

This study points to one conclusion: precontract orientation is effective in creating turnover before contract, resulting in both better survival and better production. Its primary benefit is better selection—by the manager and by the man. While some benefit seems to come from giving the survivors of precontract orientation a headstart on their training program, the greater part of the results derive from the elimination of men who can't or won't do the job.

In terms of cost, precontract orientation is a worthwhile procedure. In this study, no analysis was made of the actual time spent by management in precontract activity. But the results would certainly justify the assumption that this was time well spent.

JOB CONCEPT

One of the reasons the work sample procedure works is because it gives the applicant a realistic picture of the job he's to undertake. Prior to the research done in precontract orientation, it had already been determined that the kind of expectations an agent had of his job when he was contracted is directly related to his subsequent survival or termination. Separate studies of both ordinary and combination agents bear this out.

In both studies (conducted by LIAMA), booklets were prepared for the prospective agent giving a realistic description of the job. In the first study, the booklet stated in terms of hours how much time would be spent in various activities. These hour estimates had been obtained from questionnaires sent to the company's existing agents, who probably tended to overestimate the amount of time they spent on the job. In the second study, the opportunities and challenges of the job were combined into a coherent picture, with emphasis on the need for training, night work and the frustrations involved in selling.

In both studies, the agencies were divided into two equal groups. In the first study, only the prospective recruits of one group of agencies received the booklet; in the second study, prospective agents of one group received the new booklet, while candidates in the other group received a booklet previously in use, which was considerably less objective. The improvement in survival in both studies was quite startling. In the first study, six-month terminations were 30 percent lower for the "booklet" recruits. In the second study, the six-month survival rate was 71 percent for the new booklet recruits and 57 percent for old booklet recruits.

In neither study did the use of the "realistic" booklet have an adverse effect on the number of recruits contracted. Thus, the improvement in survival was not attained at the cost of fewer recruits being brought into the business.

THE SELECTION INTERVIEW

The selection interview is probably the most widely used selection method, and yet less is known about its effectiveness than any other part of the selection procedure. A review of the literature reveals a great many articles on selection interviewing and a considerable number of rules on how to do it. But there is little evidence that the suggested methods, do's and don'ts, etc., are backed up by much more than "best guesses" and opinion.

A long term study of interviewing is now being undertaken by LIAMA with its primary focus on the decision-making process. A knowledge of how this process operates in the selection interview is a first step toward the ultimate goal of making appropriate changes in interviewing methodology in order to obtain improved reliability and validity.

The first phases in this study have led to the following conclusions:

1. There is a great deal of disagreement among managers as to the favorability of a large number of individual items of information. When confronted with identical characteristics of applicants, different managers come to different conclusions as to whether those characteristics are likely to be associated with success.

2. Managers give more weight to negative information than to positive information in reaching a final decision.
3. Managers differ as to how many applicants they consider as being favorably suited for the job of a life insurance agent. They do not hold an identical picture of the ideal applicant. While there seem to be certain characteristics on which most managers share agreement, there are particular characteristics on which they disagree to the extent of precluding any broad stereotype.

These conclusions are based on paper and pencil tests carried out in a "clinical" atmosphere. Whether they will hold up when this research moves into "live" situations, remains to be seen.

Other research in the area of interviewing has demonstrated that a structured interview is useful in the selection interview. Since the objective of this interview is to get specific information about an applicant, it is best conducted with a planned procedure, including specific goals, a guide to follow, questions planned in advance and a method of evaluating the information received. This kind of approach is in contrast to the unstructured, or nondirective interview such as the psychoanalyst might use. For the manager, who is distinctly not a psychoanalyst, it is well established that the structured type of interview is best.

On the basis of research thus far completed, LIAMA has produced for its member companies a procedure known as the Agent Selection Kit. While it covers all the selection steps in logical order, heavy emphasis is placed on building skills in interviewing the applicant. Specially constructed interview guides assist the manager in eliciting the information he needs to make rational predictions about the applicant's probable behavior on the job.

SURVIVAL AND PRODUCTIVITY

Earlier in this chapter, it was pointed out that the real measure of a selection device is its relationship to subsequent performance on the job. For this and a number of other reasons, we need yardsticks of performance which can tell us how an agent is doing relative to other agents or to some predetermined standard.

A long list of possible measures could be drawn up, all of which are used for one purpose or another:

1. Volume production
2. Premium production
3. Number of policies sold
4. Commission earnings
5. Persistency

6. Activity, in terms of calls, closing interviews, etc.
7. Training courses completed
8. Survival

Some of these are used in constructing financing validation schedules, some are used in agent supervision, some are used to determine whether the agent's contract should be continued, some are used for honor club qualification, and so on.

Industry research is also concerned with measuring agent performance —for test validation as already mentioned, but also for keeping track of the general level of performance and providing that information to companies. The two most commonly used criteria of performance for this purpose are volume production and survival. The use of these measures in research does not mean that they are necessarily the best measures of agent performance. However, they do have two important attributes: first, they are the most easily obtainable statistics on a consistent basis; and second, they are almost universally acceptable as terms which everyone understands.

They do, of course, have defects. Survival, for example, doesn't always mean success, nor does termination necessarily mean failure. A number of agents somehow manage to survive on what would be regarded as below-subsistence production. Many high volume producers leave the business because they don't like it or because they like something else better, or for whatever reason.

Volume production as a measure suffers from the fact of varying premium per thousand, due to differences in policies and the general decline of premium rates over the past ten or fifteen years. Thus, $100,000 of production can mean a number of different levels of performance in terms of premium.

In spite of these defects, survival and production in combination have proven to be useful measures of job performance. Let's look at some trend figures, based on a representative group of large ordinary companies.

Survival and Production

In 1950, the average one-year survival rate (contract year) of inexperienced financed agents was 42 percent. During the next six years, that figure remained fairly constant. In 1957, it began a decline which took it to a low of 34 percent in 1961. By 1963, it had returned to 40 percent. The latest figures indicate a swing back to about 38%. In looking at this survival record, one is tempted to reach the conclusion that not much progress has been made in retention of agents. As pointed out earlier, however, so many factors affect turnover that it is hazardous to use it as a criterion alone. As an example, to what extent have tightened validation requirements and stricter postselection standards increased early turnover? No one knows for sure, but in an era of rising costs, including agent financing, it is certainly a factor.

Survival alone is not a good measure of performance. When we examine the production of those who survive, we see quite a different picture. In 1950, the average production of first-year survivors was $181,000. In 1963, that figure had increased to $353,000, an increase of 90 percent. More recently it had increased to $425,000. The rise has been steady throughout the years.

Two factors must be taken into consideration in evaluating the production increase between 1950 and 1963. One is the rising price index which made 1963 dollars worth about 78 percent of 1950 dollars. When this is applied to the 1963 production of $353,000, it "deflates" it to $277,000. In other words, one might expect the surviving agent to sell more business in 1963 than he did in 1950 just on the basis of inflation alone. And so he did. But he not only kept pace with 1950 in terms of constant dollars, he exceeded it by a respectable margin.

The other factor to consider is the change in premium per thousand. While the average premium per thousand for the industry as a whole has declined substantially during the period in question, the figure is not available for first-year agents alone. It would be hazardous to use the industry figures for a comparison of first-year survivors, because there is good reason to believe that they differ markedly. If it is true, for example, that most new agents start out selling savings plans, then their average premium could well be higher than the industry average. Or it might be lower for market reasons. This points up the need for more information on more dimensions of agent performance, a subject which will be referred to again below.

Number of Policies

A recent LIAMA study of first-contract-year survivors in 16 large U.S. companies showed that the median number of policies sold was 29. In other words, half of the agents sold less than 29 policies in their first-contract-year and half sold more. Perhaps it is startling that so many agents survive for a year without reaching a level much beyond two policies per month.

This statistic again demonstrates the inadequacy of survival alone as a standard of performance. When we look at a group of *successful* survivors, the picture is quite different. A successful survivor is defined in this study as one who was financed at $400 or more and is still on the financing plan at the end of his first contract year. The following table shows the result:

TABLE 3
Agents Classified by Number of Cases per Month

	Less than 1 case	1 case but less than 2	2 cases but less than 3	3 cases or more	All groups combined
	Percent Successful in Each Group				
Best Company	0	15%	44%	73%	31%
Median Company	0	9	23	65	20
Poorest Company	0	0	5	29	7

In the "best" company, 31 percent of the survivors were successful (see column headed "All groups combined"). The "poorest" company only had 7 percent of its survivors as successes, while the "median" company had 20 percent. All other companies fell somewhere in between.

In all three of these companies, by far the greatest percentage of successes came from agents producing three or more policies per month. In the best company, 73 percent of the agents producing three or more cases were successful, more than double the company's overall success rate. Even in the poorest company, whose 29 percent is much lower than the others, it is four times its own success rate. The success rate drops drastically for production levels less than three cases. It would appear then that the number of cases produced is closely related to successful survival, and is therefore a pretty good measure of agent performance.

Long-Range Performance

First-year survival and production is one measure of how well the business is doing in inducting new recruits. Early measures of performance are indispensable to the evaluation of selection procedures, because too many other factors enter the picture to obscure the effect of selection as an agent gains experience.

Longer term measures of agent performance are more appropriate to an evaluation of agency or company growth. To what extent are agents surviving the difficult early years and becoming established as career agents? Available data from LIAMA show the following retention based on inexperienced financed agents hired in 1955:*

* Because of data collection difficulties, long-term performance figures were not collected after 1955.

TABLE 4

Contract year	Number surviving out of each 100 originally contracted
1	42
2	26
3	22
4	16
5	13
6	12

The average and median production of the six-year survivors in each of the six years is given below:

TABLE 5

Contract year	Production in thousands	
	Average	Median
1	$360	$320
2	494	390
3	499	460
4	476	400
5	474	350
6	417	320

These figures would indicate that the average surviving agent reaches a plateau quite early in his career and remains at that level at least through his sixth year. Subsequent evidence, though based on shorter term experience, would bear out this contention. The amount that an agent produces in his first six months generally sets the pace for what he will produce in his first few years.

A New Approach to Performance Evaluation

A more recent method of analyzing agent performance and the growth of the field force involves dividing agents into calendar year "classes." Up to this point, we have dealt with the contract year as the basic unit of measurement in time. Since the contract year rarely coincides with the calendar year, survival and production statistics based on the contract year become rather clumsy to use in making projections of future growth. For planning purposes, the calendar year is much more appropriate because most records are kept on this basis.

To convert contract year to calendar year, it is first assumed that the year in which the agent is recruited is his first calendar year, regardless of when he was recruited during that year. Thus, both the agent recruited in January of 1969 and the agent recruited in December of 1969 have the same first calendar year, even though they differ in length of service by as much as eleven months.

The second assumption is that the agent enters his second calendar year on January 1 of the year following his year of recruitment, regardless of when he was hired during that year. The two agents above would both enter their second calendar year on January 1, 1970. Subsequently, each new calendar year becomes a new calendar year for the agent. In this way, every agent can be assigned to a calendar year class—one, two, three, etc., or numbered by years.

For each calendar year class, survival and production figures can be developed, so that with enough experience, a reliable set of statistics can be established for each calendar year class. It will further develop that beyond a certain number of years, the figures are so similar that all classes can be lumped together. It is probable that retention rates beyond the fifth or sixth calendar years are so constant that it is needless to calculate them for each year.

The most recent retention rates calculated by LIAMA show the following calendar year rates for a sample of ordinary companies:

TABLE 6

1st calendar year........	63%
2nd // //	55
3rd // //	62
4th // //	67
5th and subsequent......	92

Note that the second calendar year rate is lower than the first. This is because the first is not a full year's exposure for all agents, since they are hired throughout the year.

The major advantage of this system is its application to planning for future recruiting needs. It also provides a method of expressing in more realistic terms the induction of agents into the business. One company, for example, designates the first four calendar years A, B, C, and D, and the fifth and over group is called ESF. These letters stand for: Appointment year, Base year, Commitment year, Delivery year, and Experienced Sales Force. With a set of production and survival figures for each year, the company can predict with considerable accuracy how many agents will be delivered into the established sales force with how much production. It can also predict how many agents must be appointed this year to deliver X agents four years hence.

If data were collected on this basis regularly from a representative group of companies, a valuable body of information would become available:

1. It would provide benchmarks with which individual companies could compare their own figures.
2. It would give greater insight into the dynamics of the agency field force—its composition, how it grows, and how it changes over time.
3. It would provide an opportunity to examine some of the other measures of agent performance referred to earlier.

In the fall of 1966, LIAMA embarked on such a survey with the ultimate objective of providing these data to its member companies. *The Manpower and Production Survey,* as it is called, seeks to collect data from a large number of companies on retention and production on a calendar year basis. The initial request asked for data on full time agents appointed in each of five previous years, plus all those contracted prior to that time lumped together. In order to achieve a broad sampling through time, it asked that this process be repeated for each of the three years prior to 1966.

In addition, the survey asked for information on producers other than full time agents, for premiums, commissions, paid-for policies, and several other breakdowns. The result, hopefully, will be better measurement of agent performance, beyond the traditional survival and volume production criteria.

Postselection

A final item relevant to research in survival and productivity is postselection. Repeated studies have shown that an agent's early production is a guide to his future success. The level of an agent's production in his first six months is highly predictive of whether he will reach a reasonable production level in his second year.

The concept of postselection was developed when financing, at least at the company level, was not an important factor. As financing increased, however, periodic performance requirements were formalized so that, theoretically at least, financed agents are automatically terminated when they do not meet their validation schedules. Termination through validation schedules, however, differs from the concept of postselection in a number of ways. Probably the most important difference is that validation requirements are usually proportionate to the level of an agent's financing income, whereas the postselection concept is to apply one postselection standard and one minimum success criterion to all agents. Postselection appears to answer the question, "Does the agent have the potential to sell life insurance?", not, "Does he have the potential to sell enough life insurance to earn $300, $400, or $500 per month?"

In a study of financing validation and postselection, LIAMA found that for all levels of financing grouped together, for agents who have completed six months, the odds against surviving for two years and producing at least $350,000 in the second year are almost 4 to 1. The range varies from 5 to 1 in the lowest financed group (less than $280 per month) to 3 to 1 for the highest ($400 per month or more). If these agents are divided into two groups, those who produced at least $100,000 in their first six months and those who produced less than that, the odds become sharply different. For those who produced $100,000, the odds against "success" drop to 2 to 1, with very little difference among the financing groups. For those with less than $100,000, the odds rise to almost 23 to 1, with a range of 14.5 to 1 for the high financed group to 100 to 0 for the low financed group.

Thus, it would appear that the elimination of all agents who did not produce at least $100,000 in their first six months would leave a group among whom there are almost twice as many potential successes. This elimination would amount to about 40 percent of those who complete six months. The same question can be raised here as should be raised about selection tests: What is the cost of such a procedure in terms of potential successes eliminated and potential failures retained. In this study, the results showed that terminating those who had not produced at least $100,-000 in their first six months would have eliminated 49 percent of the potential failures and only 8 percent of the potential successes. The cost of 8 percent of potential successes does not seem excessive in view of the advantages to be gained in money, time, and morale by eliminating half of the potential failures.

It should be emphasized here that the $100,000 production figures should not be regarded as a standard. It is the result of our study involving several companies. The right figure for any particular company must be determined by that company on the basis of the success criterion it wants to use and on the basis of the cost in terms of failures retained and successes eliminated. The major point to be made is that failure to achieve a satisfactory production level is predictable—early in the new agent's career.

24

Basic Education and Training

Edmund L. Zalinski

Chapter 1 of this handbook has emphasized the important significance of the changes taking place in the life insurance marketing environment. No phase of life insurance sales management is more acutely affected by these changes than life insurance education and training. The more complex and more sophisticated life insurance marketing environment of today demands a more highly educated and a more carefully trained agent. The proper and adequate education and training of two or three decades ago is now no more than an introduction to the knowledge and skills required today.

We have heard that half of man's knowledge today was not in existence ten years ago. The transition through the next ten years will undoubtedly more than double today's knowledge. Adequate education contributes substantially to man's capacity to survive in this changing environment by supplying the important ability to understand and adapt to that environment.

THE PURPOSE OF EDUCATION AND TRAINING

The degree to which life underwriters are accepted as professional advisers will materially condition the extent to which their message is accepted by the American people. Today, life underwriters serve an enlightened public that is better informed, better educated than ever before, and in many respects more knowledgeable in the uses of life insurance than were many of our life agents of a few decades ago. It is neither practical nor wise to preach the doctrine of professional service and then fail to give it. The only way that the life insurance agent can be equipped to render professional service is through adequate training and education and farsighted leadership on the part of company management. Putting the case rather bluntly, if the great growth in American life insurance that has come about since the turn of the century, and particularly in the past decade, is to continue, the industry will find it necessary to step up the quality of its training to meet the competition of other products and to interest even more promising men in a sales career.

It is obvious that proper training not only lowers selling costs to the company through reduced turnover, but results in increased earnings for the agent. Well trained people know their jobs and gain the satisfaction that comes from doing their work well. Finally, the continuous training and education of both agents and field management result in better service to the insurance buying public; thus bringing about an improvement in acceptance of life insurance and the particular company that they represent.

A PROCESS OF PERSONAL DEVELOPMENT

In the broad sense, society is the chief beneficiary of improved education and training. Such improvements as are accomplished, however, must necessarily have a positive impact on those who receive the "new" education and training. They are the ones who receive the benefit directly, and the individual participating in the development program necessarily becomes involved in a deeply personal way in his own development.

The central aspect of this impact should be the perspective it will give those who aspire to rendering services that can be considered "professional" in nature. Because he can expect that "change" will be the rule rather than the exception, every aspirant to professional status must expect that his informational working capital will become obsolete not once but many times during his career. With such a perspective of his chosen career, he must plan for and he must commit himself to, a continuing education program if he is merely to maintain his position relative to that of his colleagues, let alone improve that position.

Personal development of the life underwriter, then, is a continual process. The objective of personal development for the life underwriter should be nothing less than a continual improvement in sales performance and service to policyholders. But an objective of this kind is too broad and must be reduced to more simple components before a meaningful program of education and training can be developed. Let us define those personal characteristics of a life underwriter that determine his performance and which we seek to improve in the process of personal development.

Attitude

The first, and by far the most important, is that of attitude. Many agency executives believe that the prime objective of both education and training is the development of constructive attitudes as well as skills. There are two divisions of education and training intimately related to this question of attitude. First, there is indoctrination and orientation, and second, sales training. The former should undertake to give the agent the attitude that he is embarking on a great career in earning a living and living a life. It should give him an understanding of the importance of the agent, the value of his product, the importance of life insurance in the economy, and his opportunity for personal development. He should also learn that his results will be judged solely on the basis of his performance, and that his following the sales procedures recommended as part of his training will significantly affect the size of his income and the degree of his success.

Work Habits

The second performance determining personal characteristic is "work habits." Certain habits are not conducive to satisfactory performance; others are absolutely essential to sales success. These habits may be recognized in others almost as readily as a characteristic gait or a peculiar manner of speaking. These habits are in the process of formation day in and day out; yet, too rarely does management stop to think that the formation of habits can be controlled through the supervision of personal development. Habits are the actions that men take to avoid the necessity for continually making decisions. If, in the development process, they can be made to recognize this, an important step will have been taken toward correcting the habits that are impeding their progress. The groundwork has been established for those habits that will result in sales success.

Skills

The third personal characteristic is skill. Sales are made through a combination of the salesman's personality, his insight into the prospect's wants, his ability to present his product, and the extent of the buyer's ability to buy. No sales presentation, however skillfully presented, can guarantee a sale every time. The realization of this hard, cold fact is basic to anyone who presumes to direct the personal development of a salesman. The skills related to the sales presentation can be grouped or examined from several aspects: locating the person to talk to; developing the facts necessary to understand his needs; presenting the solution; and the close. These four areas seem to be logical ones on which to concentrate attention in the development of skill in the life underwriter. Others may be added if the definition of sales performance includes more of the service activities than have been mentioned here.

Knowledge

The fourth personal characteristic is knowledge. Of course, there is no limit to the knowledge that the life underwriter can profitably absorb about people, their financial problems and the underwriter's own reason for being. There are some things that he must know before he even has the right to call himself a life underwriter. These are the things that management must see that he has engraved on his memory. First, and probably most important, the life underwriter must know his job: not all the details and ramifications of it—it will take him his entire career to find all those, and then he will not be satisfied—but the basic concepts and ideas behind his relationship to his company, his policyholders and prospects, and his associates. He must know what is expected of him and what he can expect of other people. Then, he must know his product and its relation to society: the death benefits and living benefits that people buy when they trust him with their premium dollars, and how they should be used to meet the financial needs of the family. He should know why life insurance is one of the best investments any man can make, particularly today when there is such great competition for the savings dollar.

And so the big job of personal development and the continual improvement in sales performance can be broken down into four smaller jobs. Improvement in each of these areas will bring about advancement in the others. For example, an improvement in knowledge or skill will usually result in an improvement in attitude and perhaps work habits as well. The continual improvement we seek relates directly to the self confidence and morale of the life underwriter, and gives him the courage of his convictions as he comes face-to-face with the public he aspires to serve.

In addition, the process of personal development must permit consideration of individual differences. It would be unrealistic to expect every man to improve at the same rate. Then, too, a rate of improvement that seems realistic today may appear in future years entirely too slow. Education and training plans should not only be geared to bring the average agent up to an acceptable level; ideally they should also be flexible enough to handle the exceptional man, the brilliant producer who will not respond to the routine pace. There are no boundaries, no artificial limits that can contain the character and personality of a human being. Thus, education and training present to management both an opportunity and a great challenge.

THE DISTINCTION BETWEEN EDUCATION AND TRAINING

Education and Training Defined

The distinction between "education" and "training" has caused much discussion in business and industry. The two terms are essentially two aspects of the teaching process which has as its ultimate goal a modification in individual behavior. The distinction, as it relates to life insurance selling and sales management, is reasonably clear. Education usually involves the imparting of the knowledge and understanding described earlier, while training is the development of the techniques or skills (along with attitude and work habits) which result in sales. Education provides important background knowledge; training deals with the application of this knowledge in specific situations. In simple terms, education is concerned with the "what" and the "why," and training with the "how."

A Partnership of Learning

The importance of training in preparing the new agent (or the experienced one for that matter) to overcome the obstacles he faces is unquestioned. Furthermore, training is generally effective when a job is as well structured as the job of the life underwriter and when the objectives are equally as clear cut. From the company's point of view the investment in training is recoverable almost immediately in terms of increased sales. No doubt this is the motivating factor behind the considerable emphasis companies place upon training—sometimes to the extent of overlooking the importance of education.

If the expense of training is identified as an investment in the present, then education can be described as an investment in the future. Education creates an environment within which the individual achieves personal growth. An important function of education is to encourage self-improvement and to encourage an attitude of continuous learning. Education permits the individual to develop personal yardsticks to identify that which is valuable to his personal achievement. Through education, the individual recognizes the continuity of his efforts, eliminating to a large extent the inefficiency of trial and error. Particularly during periods of change (either personal or social and economic), an emphasis on knowledge and under-standing gives the individual an ability to adapt to that changing situation without the continual necessity for retraining. Finally, education enables him to learn, keep on learning, and train himself to meet broader objectives and greater responsibilities.

In life insurance selling, neither education nor training can be effective without the other. A life underwriter could be well educated in the principles and technicalities of life insurance or sales management and still fail through lack of skill in their practical application. It would be equally unsatisfactory for a life underwriter to undertake the various phases of the sales process by rote without understanding why each step was being taken, what each step was supposed to accomplish, and how it related to the overall objective. Thus, the interests of both the individual life underwriter and the company are best served by a well balanced program of education and training.

THE LEARNING PROCESS

The achievement of management's objectives with respect to the attitudes, work habits, skills, and knowledge of the agent depends to a great extent upon an understanding of the way in which people learn. Too often training and education are undertaken without sufficient insight into the learning process, and the results are, therefore, disappointing. A detailed review of the learning process is not contemplated here, but a few points should be emphasized.

A Clear Picture of Objectives for the Student

Most trainers agree they get their points across much better in their training activities if their presentation pattern is clearly understood by the agent; and the latter will learn more readily if his whole background and self are utilized. The agent can often solve problems or train himself if he sees his objectives clearly, and if he sees also how the attainment of his objectives will affect him. The most direct way to get agents to see these organized patterns is by relating the instructional subject matter to the experiences, interests, and aspiration of each agent. More emphasis should, therefore, be placed on individualized instruction. However, if this is impossible, agents should at least be given an opportunity to help in deciding the objectives of their own training pattern and perhaps some of the methods of achieving those objectives. Stimulating the agent to think by asking him to select from among alternatives, giving reasons why each is good or bad, is a useful technique for involving the agent in his own training program. It is not sufficient to provide merely the opportunity for learning. There must also be the motivation for learning. The student may have a high level of ability and still fail to learn unless we identify and communicate to him the personal benefit he will receive. The encouragement of active participation on the part of the student leads to a personal involvement that contributes to the motivation we seek.

The Importance of Method

The management of learning clearly requires special knowledge and skills. It is much more than a matter of giving instructions and demonstrations of how to do something. While demonstration and instruction are certainly the heart of training, much preparatory work must be done if that instrument is to be effective. This includes determining what knowledge and skills are needed; planning to meet these needs; evaluating the agent's progress; and determining the proper methods of instruction. There obviously exists a multitude of specific methods, ranging from the trial-and-error method to the carefully designed training experiences in the home office. Lectures, group discussions, on-the-job training, role playing, all are used effectively, particularly those that involve the active participation of the student. However, there is little evidence that any one technique of training is clearly superior to another. Different subject matter can usually be programed into learning best by using a variety of methods or techniques. The most important conclusion, which can be substantiated by results, is that organized and planned training is superior to unorganized and haphazard training.

Measurement of Results

Letting the agent know how well he is doing is essential to the learning process. An act which receives praise is likely to recur, and conversely, a response that receives criticism tends to disappear. The student must know whether or not he is performing correctly if he is to improve his performance. In addition, informing agents of how well they are learning tends to motivate them to greater achievement as the learning process develops.

PLANNING THE EDUCATION AND TRAINING PROGRAM

Sources of Training

Viewed in the broadest perspective, formalized training is only one of many techniques employed by management to improve the performance of the new agent. Other opportunities to influence the agent include personal contacts with agency and home office personnel, association meetings, conventions, field meetings, conferences, company publications and advertising, and many others. All play an important role in the training process. Many of these influences are difficult to control, but their effect can be taken into consideration when designing the overall company training program. The important consideration, as we have discussed earlier, is that planning take place, and that the overall training program be consistent with company objectives and company policy. Thus, the many sources of education and training will fit into an overall pattern of development for the agent.

Home Office Versus Field Office Training

Persons charged with the responsibility for training frequently debate the merits of home office versus field training. Actually, they have oversimplified the issue. The home office provides field trainers who prepare courses and conduct home office schools. Frequently, they also put on intensive training sessions in the field, regionally or in individual branch offices. These home office trainers also undertake to aid field management in the solution of their local training problems and to provide them with the skills and tools that are needed to make training effective on a local level.

More and more individual personal security is being provided through group insurance and pension plans. Therefore, it becomes increasingly important for companies to equip their agents so they can successfully sell group insurance, pension plans and business insurance. The specialized knowledge required for this kind of selling makes it necessary to have available specialists who can provide the agent with assistance. It is difficult for the agency manager, without assistance, to provide such advanced training at the local level. With its skilled personnel, the home office can initiate and conduct conferences, schools, and meetings that will keep field management and agents alike informed and up-to-date in these areas.

Home office schools should offer uniform high-quality instruction, superior props, and good training materials—as well as exposure to company philosophy, officials and operations. They can attain great effectiveness in the area of "attitude" training. However, the costs involved, and the fact that such schools take the agent out of the field, persuade some companies to take the training to the agents. This is done through traveling field programs rather than by bringing agents to headquarters. Thus, more important than the actual location of the training, is the uniform quality that results from careful planning.

Correspondence Courses

Correspondence courses are sometimes necessary where distances make it impossible for agents to attend agency meetings. Many correspondence courses of excellent quality are available through the life insurance industry (or the company may prefer to design its own) that cover all areas from the fundamentals of life insurance to the most complex areas of advanced underwriting. They lack, however, the inspiration of group contacts and the personal guidance of an instructor. It is frequently difficult for the agent to apply what he has learned, and sufficient incentive is sometimes lacking to insure that the assignments are completed properly and on time. Where correspondence courses must be used, it is wise to supplement them with periodic meetings and frequent contacts by letter and by telephone. It is essential to make the student agents aware of the importance of the material and of the knowledge gained through this medium.

Institutional Training and Other Sources

Most companies have made a strong effort to integrate their own training programs with those offered by LIAMA, the American College of Life Underwriters, the Institute of Life Insurance Marketing, and the Life Underwriter Training Council. In addition, many colleges and universities are expanding the number of insurance courses offered to students. The extent to which these programs are used depends upon their availability and upon company objectives plus the adequacy of company training. Timing is also an important factor. Generally speaking, fieldmen should not be enrolled in institutional training programs until they have completed company training and are thoroughly established in their jobs. Most companies provide scholarship programs and thereby encourage their men to enroll at the proper time.

Institutional training has a broadening effect in that it exposes fieldmen to new people, new ideas, and different philosophies. One of the great strengths of the life insurance business has been the ability of the companies and fieldmen alike to work together in formulating and supporting such programs; however, they are not in any sense a substitute for company training. Their value is enhanced when companies and agency heads follow through in helping their agents to integrate and apply what they have learned.

Magazines, industry services, and company bulletins can be helpful to the training program as valuable sources of ideas and information, but they are not training in the formal sense. Home offices and agency heads not only use house organs as a channel of communication and ego recognition but they frequently call articles of special significance to the attention of their agents. Home office magazines that are distributed to the field force often contain articles by fieldmen on sales subjects, announcements, advanced underwriting topics, sales promotion materials, advertising, and other subjects. "Life Association News," "The Insurance Salesman," and a host of other trade magazines also supply a continuous stream of ideas on selling life insurance. Services such as the Diamond Life Bulletins "Agents Service" and the Research and Review Service "Advanced Underwriting Service" provide monthly information on the latest developments and double as reference manuals on sales problems.

Factors Influencing the Program

COMPANY OBJECTIVES

The quantity and quality of the training given to fieldmen is determined by (1) a company's sales objectives that implement general policy, (2) the share of the market that the company desires to command, (3) the amount of money the company is willing and able to invest in training, and (4) the way in which it wishes to spend this money. To what extent does management want (and is it practical) to increase the production of the present agency force, and will this be done through further training, better supervision, or sales promotion? Does the company wish to add new outlets and additional agents? If so, it may decide to concentrate on the training of additional managers and supervisors. As new agents are recruited, the company may emphasize training of new agents instead of upgrading present agents. Perhaps the company may decide to make its products more competitive as a means of increasing sales instead of investing money in training.

COMPANY SIZE

The size of a company will influence its training program considerably. If it is new or small, its training budget is likely to be limited. Geographic considerations will also be important. If the company's operations are concentrated in a single state or in a small area, all training might be done at the Home Office. This would not be as practical for a company with a large agency force functioning on a national or worldwide basis.

How much assistance the home office can give its agency heads in training also depends in part on the size of the agency department, its organization, and its budget. The agency vice president with a small staff may be able to provide only limited training aid and materials. In such instances, heavy reliance is usually placed on publishers such as Research & Review Service and Diamond Life Bulletins as well as institutional courses such as LUTC. A large company, on the other hand, may have a staff of training experts in the home office and a group of field vice presidents or superintendents of agencies responsible for seeing that the company's training program is carried out in each agency. These field officers, in some instances, also have special training assistants, concerned entirely with training in the agencies under their supervision.

AGENCY OPERATION AND TYPE OF FIELD FORCE

The company's training program will be further influenced by whether it uses the managerial or general agency system of operation. Under the managerial system, the manager is an employee and the agents' contracts are with the company which, therefore, has the right to communicate directly with them. The general agent, on the other hand, is an independent entrepreneur with a contract from the company which empowers him to make contracts with sub-agents who do not have the same direct legal relationship with the company. Each general agent may have his own ideas as to how his agents should be trained and will accept only that portion of a company's training program that happens to fit in with his plans.

The type of field force will affect the training program considerably, depending upon whether the company sells through ordinary agents, combination agents, brokers or part time agents. Ordinary agents and combination agents, for example, are normally more closely associated with the company and can more easily be persuaded to accept a company training program than a broker, who, at the other extreme, represents no company and will accept training only if he is convinced that it is worth the time. It is also questionable how much money a company should invest in training brokers from whom no permanent allegiance can be expected. When a company's field force includes several types of agents, the training needs of each may be considered, but the training program should be designed to meet the needs of those producing the major part of the company's business.

TYPE OF MARKET AND PRODUCT LINES

The market a company wishes to serve affects not only the training program but the product lines offered. A company that is selling primarily to farmers in rural areas may have a different approach to product lines and sales methods than one whose agencies are located in large cities. While it is true that the fundamentals of salesmenship are quite similar regardless of the market, the company that sells conventional ordinary life insurance will typically have a relatively simpler training program than the company engaged in the sale of pension trusts, group annuities, group life insurance and group health contracts, not to mention property and liability insurance. One company may be interested in producing package sales in the large market whereas another might beam its sales efforts at business coverages or the upper income groups. Even where the product line has been designed to cover all markets in the low income to the highest income groups, the question remains which lines should the new agent be trained to sell first. The amount of knowledge required to sell the various product lines can vary considerably, and there is a substantial difference in the manner in which each line is sold.

EDUCATION AND TRAINING DEPARTMENT

The organization of the company's education and training department is itself an important factor in determining the success of the program. It is necessary to have a properly qualified staff with demonstrated training ability and field experience. It must be acceptable to both the home office agency department and the representatives of field management. There should be an understanding as to what phases of training are to be done at the home office level and what will be conducted in the agencies. The training department's duties and responsibilities must be clearly spelled out, including its relationship to the line organization. And finally, those charged with the training responsibility are entitled to have the physical means, the necessary time, and the required personnel to carry out those duties and responsibilities.

ORGANIZING THE EDUCATION AND TRAINING PROGRAM

We have already stated that perhaps the most important conclusion about any training program is that organized and planned training is superior to unorganized and haphazard training. Thus, the first step in designing a training program is to agree on objectives and define what the learner must learn in order to perform his job satisfactorily. We must also answer the questions: Who is to instruct the agent? Where is the instruction to take place? What techniques are to be used? At what time will each phase of the training program take place? A great deal of planning is required. Unfortunately, it is altogether too common that in the rush to get something done a great deal of the preparatory work of the training program is by-passed.

Clearly, the main purpose behind the training for the agent is to teach him to produce sales in the shortest possible time and to eliminate the uncertainties and delays of the trial-and-error method. Although there can be a multitude of pathways to reach this objective, the organizational effort to get there will contain a number of common principles. One of the foremost of these common principles is to assign qualified personnel to the training program whether it be in the home office or in the field. We must ask: Does the trainer know how to train others? Do we select the men to be given this training responsibility primarily on the basis of their ability to train or their ability to sell? If we place too much emphasis on the latter in selecting field trainers and assistant managers, we may find them selling substantial amounts of business for their men without accomplishing the more immediate objective of transferring their skills. In practice, both criteria must be considered, for men expect to be led by those with proven ability and a successful background in the skills and material to be mastered.

Another common principle is that the material and techniques to be mastered must be clearly identified and should be broken down and grouped into practical units. The organization of these units should also be sufficiently flexible so that their timing can keep pace with the ability of the agent to be trained. The "small bites" offered in this way are more easily digested and retained, and in addition, give the student the motivating reward of success along the way. The objectives set forth must be realistic and attainable, since few things are more harmful to morale than an objective that is too ambitious and obviously cannot be attained. However, the objectives must present a challenge somewhat in the manner of the mechanical rabbit at the dog track—apparently attainable but sufficiently ahead to encourage that "extra" effort. But without question, the trainee must have a clear picture of what it is he is expected to learn, how he will reach this objective, and what criteria will be used in measuring his success.

Content of the Training Program

The content of the company training program will, of course, depend to a large extent upon the company's objectives. Generally speaking, it should include: text materials designed to provide background information; case studies to illustrate how each phase of the job should be done; projects requiring that the material and skills learned be applied successfully in the field; and skull practice sessions designed to increase knowledge of such subjects as settlement options, buy and sell agreements, and other technical matters. For example, when mortgage insurance is being studied, the text should treat the need and the solution to that need. A case study should be used to show how mortgage insurance is sold and how some agents have successfully made mortgage insurance their major market. A project should be assigned which will require the agent to make actual solicitations for mortgage insurance and report back within a certain period of time. Skull practice exercises should be used to make certain that agents understand which of the company's policies are best for mortgage protection purposes. And finally, the agents should be shown how to attain the most value from the company's sales promotion pieces and direct mail program which have been prepared to help in selling mortgage insurance. The company's sales promotion literature and sales tools should be tied in closely with the training program. Other subjects, or sales "packages" covering different needs, will be handled in the same fashion as the mortgage insurance unit. But in adding new sales skills, care must be exercised to relate the "new" sales procedures to those already mastered. The content of the training program should be designed so that selling is taught on a step-by-step basis, each innovation being added to that which has already been established and mastered, rather than developed as a series of unrelated blocks.

There has been a natural tendency in developing training programs to classify sales training on the same basis as academic education. Kindergarten, grade school, high school, and college have been paraphrased as preinduction, basic, intermediate, and advanced. Those labels have their value, but mistakes have sometimes been made in classifying some subjects arbitrarily as advanced and introducing them to the agent only after he has been in the business for several years. It may be somewhat extreme to say that, "the only thing advanced about advanced underwriting is getting to the prospect in advance of the other agent." Yet, a subject such as business insurance can be presented simply and possibly should be introduced reasonably early in an agent's career. Otherwise, he may never become adept at selling insurance for business purposes, or at the very least he may defer a potentially profitable market in fear of its complexities. There is no necessity in the beginning to introduce the new agent to the complexities of buy and sell agreements or other technicalities. He can learn to sell the various business insurance needs gradually in the same manner that he becomes familiar with the personal needs for life insurance. For example, the concept of juvenile insurance is simple and is usually included early in the agent's career, but it can also become exceedingly complex when it gets into the area of taxes and estate planning.

Specific Training Techniques

There are a number of specific training techniques which can be used equally well in the training of field personnel. They include LECTURES;

AUDIENCE REPRESENTATION PANELS, in which groups of trainees explore an assigned topic and report back to the group; CONFERENCES, which offer considerable value in the sharing of facts and ideas; ROLE-PLAYING CLINICS, or supervised practice; MULTIPLE ROLE-PLAYING, which involves several people in the group simultaneously playing the same part; DIAGNOSTIC TRAINING, which is similar to role-playing with the added element of categorizing prospect types into typical groups; so-called BUZZ SESSIONS; the CASE METHOD, in which participants study and discuss an actual situation taken from real life involving the actions and interactions of people; VIDEO and AUDIO AIDS; and EVALUATION TECHNIQUES, which are used primarily to test the validity of the training techniques used. Two relative newcomers in training techniques as used by industry are SENSITIVITY TRAINING, which is based on the assumption that people can learn to improve both their understanding of others and their interpersonal skills; and BUSINESS GAMES or GAMESMANSHIP, in which "games" are developed to simulate most phases of business or industrial management.

In selecting the appropriate technique for a specific purpose, we should discount the claims of satisfied users and select the technique on the basis of what it is to accomplish. We can apply such tests as: Does the technique provide motivation? Does the technique require active participation? Is active participation desirable? Does the technique provide for individual differences? Does the technique provide an opportunity for evaluation of the student? Is the cost of the training technique consistent with other methods that are available?

Those charged with the responsibility for training should carefully review the ideas they wish to transmit to the learner. Then, in the light of the learner's background and stage of development, management should choose the technique in which communication will be most effective. A great deal of time and effort is wasted when the message does not get across because insufficient thought has been given to the selection of the proper transmission vehicle.

It should be emphasized that good training involves two-way communication and that people learn only to the extent that they participate. The so-called "feed back" from the learner to the trainer indicates the degree to which the message has been understood and accepted. "Feed back" is the heart of the time tested "D. O. C." method: Demonstrate; Observe; Correct.

Agency Training

In the so-called one man agency where one person must perform all management functions, only limited formal training can be provided. In the large agency, on the other hand, there may be a variety of specialists to assist the agency manager in the training, administration, and sales promotion, or he may be aided by the assistant or unit managers. Although agency size does not have an inevitable effect on quality, we may safely conclude that the training in a large agency can be more comprehensive and intensive than in a one-man shop.

The new agent's market or markets should be clearly defined before he is hired. His trainer should be in a position to teach the agent what he needs to know and do to sell effectively in that market. The agent should learn as much as he can about the people who compose that market and their life insurance requirements. This knowledge will determine the type of sales talk the agent must learn and the promotional material needed. It will influence what he is taught about life insurance and the order in which it is learned. The agent's experience, education, intelligence, personality, business contacts, social position and other factors will also enter into the decision as to what he should sell and to whom he should sell.

The training objectives of each agency manager will vary, depending upon the extent and nature of his territory, the markets he wishes to serve, and the assistance and the money available to him. The nature and extent of his training will depend upon whether the agency manager wishes to emphasize brokerage, new full-time agency building, or the production of established agents. The agency manager's plans for agency building and training should have the approval of his agency vice president or super-intendent of agencies in order to dovetail with company goals. If a comprehensive company training program is available, utilizing it will save a good deal of time, and guard against training omissions. The company's agency department usually is able to produce a better training program than can be formulated locally, and the field manager will still have plenty to do with job coaching and supervisory duties. A further advantage of following a company training program is that it reduces a substantial part of the training job to an organized routine that is done the same way time after time. The company training program should, of course, be sufficiently flexible to meet some variations in training needs caused by local conditions. However, when an agency manager has found what he considers a better method of performing some particular phase of the training, it should be brought to the attention of the agency department with the reasons for its adoption.

Home Office Schools

At some point in the career for the life insurance agent, many companies arrange for some training to take place in the home office itself. This step in a training program can overcome many of the problems that exist in training the agent in a small agency. In addition to the advantages of consistent quality of instruction and the certainty that all material will be covered, both agent and company benefit from the more personal relationship that can thus be developed. The timing of this phase of the training program is certainly important, particularly in the case of a new agent. Some companies begin the new agent's training by bringing him to a school in the home office as the first training he receives. This is done primarily with the view to achieving the best quality of instruction at the very beginning. Most companies feel, however, with some eye to the expense factor, that the agent should be tested to some extent in the field before he receives home office training. A delay of a number of months prior to attending a home office school will not only screen out those who are found to be unsuited to the life insurance business early in their career, but also has the benefit of making the training more meaningful for those who do attend. The agent with several months exposure to prospecting, making calls, holding sales interviews, and closing will generally benefit more from the school through having been exposed to the typical problems that he is to face. His greater appreciation of the problems also tends to increase his motivation to learn and substantially increases the contribution he may make in the exchange of ideas with others in his class.

IMPLEMENTING THE PROGRAM

Preparation and Acceptance

The success of a company training program depends upon the extent to which it has the approval of every responsible person in the company from top management to the newest agent. If top management is not 100% behind the program, it will be difficult to secure the necessary budget, and it probably will not be accepted by the field. Even with the support of top management, it is important for the company's general agents and managers to play a part in determining the content and administration of the program. Participation will lead to understanding and acceptance. In every company, there are agency heads doing outstanding jobs in various phases of training who can make practical comments and valuable suggestions. The training program itself is likely to be less academic, more specific, and more realistic because it will reflect actual field conditions. Everyone will be talking the same language, as opposed to the opposite extreme in which each agency head goes off on his own particular tangent. Refinements that otherwise would not be thought of are possible because everyone is trying to perfect or improve the same system of training. Initiative is not stifled but rather is expanded because, having a well formulated training program as a basis, field management men devote their energies to other facets of the training program and spend more time in personal supervision and coaching on the job.

The appointment of a training committee from among the company's general agents or managers can be extremely valuable both to the acceptance of the training program and to its initial development. Those selected for membership on these committees should be general agents who are doing a superior job in training their agents and in running their agencies. Agreement should be obtained as to the training tools needed by the field and the scope and content of the training program. Furthermore, an outline should be prepared covering both content and administration. As parts of the training course are prepared, they should be submitted to members of the committee for criticism and suggestions. Members of these training committees and others should be asked to supply the home office with specific examples that can be used to illustrate important points. By rotating committee membership, it is possible not only to obtain the views of a large number of general agents but also to keep training materials up-to-date and "to educate" some general agents or managers in the philosophy and objectives behind the company training program. Such committees can also be called upon to assist in selling the program to the field.

Launching

Even when all these things have been done, the program must be launched with care, and continuous promotion will be required to see that it is used with maximum effectiveness. No training program will be perfect regardless of the care that has been used in its preparation. It will require constant revision in order to adapt it to changing markets, changes in laws, company practices, and policy forms. Such changes not only require adjustments to keep the training up-to-date for the new agent but also suggest the need for retraining the present agency force. Yet, changes and innovations in the training program, should be introduced only after careful consideration. It is frequently better to continue an accepted satisfactory procedure rather than to introduce a new and superior method which will not produce as good results for some time because it has not been sold to and accepted by the field organization.

Administration

The content of the training program, important though it may be, is second in importance to its administration. Procedures should be established that will require the trainer and trainee alike to check frequently the results of their training. The best ideas in the world are powerless when stored in books. Only when understood and applied do they produce results. Everything possible should be done to make it easy for field management to use the company's program in terms of text, visual aids, sales promotion, training outlines, guides, incentives, and assistance from the home office training department.

The home office may wish to help its general agents or managers follow through at a local level by requiring that payment be withheld under the company's training allowance program unless training assignments are properly completed and received on time. This strengthens the trainer's hand and tends to establish proper work habits from the beginning. Such measures, of course, are not nearly as necessary with advanced training. Agents can be hand picked for advanced courses and are frequently eager and willing to spend the time and bear a part of the cost because they recognize that these activities will increase their sales.

CONTROLLING THE PROGRAM

Evaluation of Results

To be successful, a training program should include other methods of evaluation in addition to that of production results. Sales are not a completely reliable guide to the effectiveness of training because they are influenced by other factors such as personality, willingness to work, market, and previous experience. This is where supervision comes in. To decide what training is needed, it is necessary to know well the man to be trained, the sales methods in which he is to be trained, the market he will serve, the products he will sell, as well as the agent's knowledge of the job, his attitude towards it, his skill in performing it, and the work habits he has formulated. Neither the agent nor those in positions of greater responsibility can be trained in a vacuum; training must be based upon an evaluation of performance under field conditions. Therefore, performance must be continually recorded in various ways and measured periodically against definite standards to determine the areas in which training is needed and what type of training should be given.

Good training is based upon a knowledge of the man and the job he is doing. Management should be able to prove to the trainee, based on his performance, that a particular type of training is needed and such proof must be based on facts and not opinion. Certain aspects of training evaluation must be in terms of specific rather than generalities. Too often trainers talk in complimentary or critical generalities but fail to relate their recommendations to the trainee's pattern of operation in terms of specific activities. There is, for example, a vast difference between telling an agent he must see more people as compared to specifically working out a program in terms of his market and his activity pattern which will result in his spending more time in front of qualified prospects. It bears repeating that letting the learner know how he is doing is essential to his progress. He should be aware of what he is doing right; and if he is making errors, he needs to know what they are in order to correct them. The learner must have knowledge of whether he is performing correctly if he is to improve.

Need for Continual Reappraisal

The evaluation of results is not only important to the improvement of the trainee, but it is an essential ingredient to the improvement of the training program itself. Training programs can become outmoded and inefficient. In the same way that we observe the agent to detect those danger signs which indicate a slowing of performance, we must also continually review the training program. We must be constantly alert to possible improvements in the methods of preparing the new agent for the demanding assignment he has. We must be ever alert to the retraining needs of the experienced agent whose sales techniques may lose their sharp edge and whose storehouse of knowledge may become obsolete. Only in this way can we be sure that the principles which were followed in developing the training program are still effective. Only in this way can the training program keep pace with the development of the company and the needs of its agents.

25

Agency Training

Walter L. Downing

OBJECTIVES OF AGENCY TRAINING

Training will take place in a life insurance agency, planned or un-planned. If the agency manager recognizes this inevitability, he will quickly see the great advantages of planned training over unplanned training. The rationale of planned training lies in the reduction of wasteful trial and error learning efforts and a more efficient development of the trainee to full potential. Planned training makes the following basic assumptions, (1) that the behavior of successful agents differs from that of unsuccessful agents, (2) that specific behavior can be developed through a formal pro-cess called training, and (3) that the expense to be incurred is worth the results to be achieved.

Precisely what is planned training? What has taken place when one is said to have been trained? The training process for a life insurance sales-man is first and foremost the development of selling skills to a level predic-tive of meeting prescribed performance standards. Inherent in any skill development program is the transfer concept. As applied to life insurance selling, the critical element in the transfer process is the development of the capacity to express an idea, however abstract, with such power and persuasive clarity as to motivate the listener to the desired action. This is a process which, if repeated frequently, creates patterns of idea expres-sion which lead to habit. Once the habit is established, the salesman has acquired the ability to convert almost any abstract idea in the same manner into a motivating presentation which leads to sales action. When this has been accomplished, the agent is said to have been "trained." At this point the salesman needs only additional ideas or knowledge which he processes or converts into the desired presentation. The ability to transfer an idea into sales action requires endless hours of systematic practice and application. Implementation of this skill development process is the unique challenge of planned training—a challenge which is the exclusive prerogative of the agency. The remainder of this chapter attempts to describe the nature of the training process which creates and implements the critical skill-building activity.

Planned training requires objectives. Such objectives become more meaningful and have more promise of fulfillment if coordinated with company objectives, agency objectives, trainer objectives and trainee objectives. A brief look at the possibilities for coordinating the objectives of each of these four groups will be helpful in setting the stage for any discussion of the procedural and substantive aspects of life insurance agency training.

Coordination with Company Objectives and Facilities

Company marketing policy can exert recognizable influence on agency training objectives. If company product design and facilities are beamed to the advanced fields, agency markets and training are materially reinforced if directed toward the same areas. An agency threatens to circumscribe its growth potential if the training activity is directed toward development in markets in which the company product design and facilities are not competitive or well developed. Furthermore, home office training courses which reinforce agency training provide added leverage to both and further the development of agent potential.

Coordination of Training with Agency Objectives

Agency training objectives must relate to all agency objectives. If agency facilities are primed to well-defined market areas, the training process gains in support and effectiveness. A statistical department operating in the single needs and programming field will often conflict with a training program designed to turn out an underwriter trained to operate in the more sophisticated markets. A brokerage manager's contribution to the other agency departments is limited if the brokerage services are not coordinated with those of other agency departments. Brokerage specialists tapping markets established by agency objectives can reinforce training through specialized know-how in underwriting and sales services. At the same time, other agency facilities, geared to the same markets, can support brokerage services. Office staff facilities operating under coordinated agency objectives will reinforce the sales efforts of both trainees and established graduates of training programs.

Frequently, a training department fails in its attempt to develop superior agents, not because of what it does, but because of conflict and misunderstanding between departments operating under contradictory objectives. The result is a general wavering and uncertainty in organizational attitudes and climate.

The problems of coordination are as important, if not as challenging, in the small agency as in the large agency equipped with specialized departments.

Coordination of agency objectives among departments also serves to strengthen an agency's public image which reinforces the trainees' efforts in the field.

Coordination with Trainer's Objectives

It is axiomatic that those responsible for training relate the company, agency, and agency training department objectives to their own. An imported trainer, for example, must clearly adapt to the training objectives, methods, and procedures of his newly-affiliated agency in order to implement that agency's objectives. His capacities must coincide with the requirements of the job dictated by the training objectives. Clearly, the imported trainer runs the gamut of inner conflict in making the transition to another training orientation. The trainer who is the product of the training system he administers has at least minimized this important coordination problem.

Coordination with Trainees' Objectives

The wise agency manager solves many future problems in advance by confining his selection of trainees to those capable of adapting to the agency's broad objectives and training department objectives. His concern should be to make sure that the capacity of the trainees by both background and experience will make them comfortable with the market objectives to which agency training is directed. Further, the ability of the trainee to reach the required knowledge and skill levels of agency training may be a critical problem. Finally, the trainees' ability to identify personal needs and motives with agency and company objectives will be a determinant of possible conflicts with objectives.

The main point is that agency training objectives have an increasing chance for fulfillment if designed to coordinate with agency and company planning. Ideally, if all production factors in both the agency and the company reinforce training objectives, the leverage for successful agent development to full potential increases accordingly.

The by-products of coordination are endless. They include increased motivation of training staff and trainees, improved communications at all levels, and a more effective working team of office staff, agents, and agency manager.

Training Goals

The setting of training goals, both long and short range, commits the agency manager to a number of vital considerations. The following are the primary considerations to which the agency manager must give his attention as he attempts to develop the agency's long and short range training goals.

1. Analysis and selection of the markets to be solicited.
2. Description of the trainee who is best qualified to develop those markets.
3. Content of training most adaptable to those markets and to the trainees' capacity levels.
4. Evaluation system to measure progress.

Once the objectives are established and coordinated, the question of organizing the training staff arises.

ORGANIZATION OF THE TRAINING FUNCTION

There are several systems of organization by which training can be administered.

1. Staff or functional system utilizing specialists to perform the varied tasks of the training job. The prime advantage of this system is the deployment of training personnel according to their strengths. In addition, the system offers flexibility and depth by interchanging personnel and rotating the jobs which have been carefully defined and segmented.
2. The unit manager system. Here the emphasis is on line responsibility for the development of the trainee by a unit manager performing most, if not all, the training jobs. The essential difference between the staff and unit manager system lies in the shared responsibilities of the former and the exclusive responsibility of the latter for manpower development.
3. Combination of both staff-supervisory system, and unit manager system in which a central training staff performs the in-office training job and a supervisor or unit manager is responsible for the trainees' performance.

4. Senior-junior or apprenticeship system, in which the trainee is assigned an established agent for the purpose of understudying the senior agent's sales techniques and methods. The apprentice or junior agent eventually is weaned into independence.

The variations of the above are many but, nevertheless, have a common objective—the organization of training for the purpose of transferring to the trainee the requisite knowledge, work habits, and motivation to achieve agency training goals. The selection of the most appropriate system depends upon the philosophy of the agency manager, the complexity of the training job, and the size of the agency.

There are also financial factors which influence the choice of the organization system for the administration of agency training. For many agencies the choice has already been made, if the agency manager represents a managerial company. The general agent, however, in most instances, will be influenced by the amount of capital available and the nature of his compensation system and the incentive the compensation system provides for developing new men.

SELECTION AND TRAINING OF THE TRAINER

There is little scientific evidence to demonstrate conclusively what the characteristics are of a good trainer. Experience has taught that a good sales performer is not necessarily a good trainer. Oftentimes, the good salesman lacks the ability to transfer what it is that he does well. Most attempts to define the qualities of an able instructor and match them with the candidate have severe shortcomings. The science of teaching has yet to validate those factors which are predictive of the ability to train. Experience, however, does indicate several helpful guidelines for the selection of a trainer.

1. At least a satisfactory level of sales performance, preferably within the agency in which the trainer is to train.
2. A demonstrated capacity for leadership as evidenced by a leadership record both before and after entering the agency.
3. A demonstrated ability to respond to and support the agency training system.
4. A capacity to absorb the training content and material at all levels of complexity.
5. A predisposition on the part of the candidate's associates, particularly trainees, to seek the candidate's counsel and help.
6. A capacity to analyze personal strengths and weaknesses and adapt accordingly.

The extent to which a potential trainer possesses the above requirements is usually observable by the agency manager if he has the luxury
of an opportunity to evaluate the candidate for the position of trainer
while the candidate is within the same agency. To attempt the same evaluation of a stranger is a difficult process at best. Certainly, a choice from
within the organization reinforces the continuation and the uniformity of
training and its adaptation to all agency objectives.

There are two basic questions concerning the selection of a trainer which
remain and can best be answered by on-the-job experience. The first concerns the prospective trainer's ability to help the trainee adjust to the critical
strains and stresses of development. The trainer's reaction to the pressures
of his own job is vital. By definition the trainer is in an insecure position
until his future is determined. Oftentimes, the job of instilling confidence
in trainees is left to the trainer who lacks that quality himself. A wise
agency manager profitably asks himself, "If the job of finding a trainer
with these qualifications is difficult within my own agency, is it made any
easier by looking outside and judging a stranger for the same characteristics?"

On occasion, the above guidelines can be qualified if the requirements
of the trainer's job are narrowed or specialized. If a trainer is a joint field
work specialist with no ambitions to become a field manager, then the
ability to transfer his sales techniques becomes the primary qualification.
If the trainer requirements are structured to an in-office training specialist,
then technical competence will be a primary consideration.

Training the Trainer

The selection of a trainer by the agency manager does not terminate
the agency manager's responsibility for the results of training. Presumably,
the new responsibility of the agency manager is to train the trainer. The
assumption here is that the trainer has to learn how to train. As in the
case of the trainee, the trainer can either train himself or be trained. The
agency manager who believes that his responsibility for training ends at
the time of the appointment of the trainer is engaging in dangerous self-
deception.

The first step in training the trainer is to define the tasks of the job and
periodically evaluate the trainer's performance of those tasks. An effective
managerial tool for such evaluation is the staff meeting held at regular
intervals. The major premise of any discussion at the staff meeting is "If
the trainee has not learned, the trainer has not taught."

The staff meeting becomes a periodic learning experience for the trainer. The trainer discusses and reviews his trainees' problems and learns from the agency manager how to apply the principles of training to specific training problems.

In the development of a trainer there are several important guidelines to be followed in furthering his growth.

First, rarely if ever should the agency manager load the trainer with more trainees than his ability to train.

Second, the agency manager may hire a trainee whose capacity levels may exceed those of the trainee's supervisor. This situation may be a source of considerable conflict, and may impair the growth of the trainee if not properly handled.

Third, the agency manager should refrain from interceding between the trainer and the trainee. Such action erodes control and breaks down the morale of the trainer.

Fourth, the agency manager should constantly seek ways and means to provide his trainers with recognition. A sound program of trainer development may well include varied forms of rewards and recognition to motivate the trainer. This can well result in increased trainee performance.

The agency manager who is not prepared to develop a trainer rarely can afford the luxury of hiring one.

TRAINING METHODS AND TECHNIQUES

In general, there are three types of trainees.

1. The new agent who has had extensive sales experience and also life insurance sales experience.
2. The new agent who has had extensive sales experience, but no life insurance sales experience.
3. The new agent who has limited or no sales experience and no life insurance sales experience.

Our discussion shall be limited to the third category—the novice trainee. The other two are exposed to vitally different development programs.

The job of training the novice is primary a job of integration. The process of integration concerns the transfer of requisite skills and knowledge to the trainee in such a manner that the trainee converts them into habit patterns. Essentially, the job is to change the behavior of the trainee. There are several methods by which this process may be accomplished.

The first method is the skill development process. There are three primary training tools that may be used for the development of skills:

    1. Clinics or sales meetings in which role playing and interview drilling predominate.
    2. Coaching on the job.
    3. Case consultation.

Training clinics are essentially sales clinics in which the trainee follows a prescribed sales procedure and practices the sales interview by actual drill. If the interview is segmented and structured into a number of defined steps, the drill process increases the trainee's effectiveness. The steps are practiced over and over again until the trainee builds a well-rehearsed interview habit pattern. Accordingly, the trainee, by the principle of over-learning and constant repetition, refines the skill of conducting a sales interview. The closer the sales clinic represents field conditions, the more the learning experience will be reinforced when applied to actual interview conditions. Criticism of the interview concentrates on what the trainee did well and what he could do to improve. The result is a habit-forming process in which the concept of a sales interview is transferred to the trainee and integrated by feedback through criticism by the trainer. When clinics are conducted in small groups, a trainee is afforded increased opportunity to measure progress by comparison and competition.

Intensive and continuous clinic training helps the trainee to develop sales skills by additional techniques:

    1. Demonstration by a skilled trainer in which the trainer attempts to closely duplicate actual field conditions. The demonstration follows a prescribed sales track applicable to all subsequent demonstrations.
    2. Step-by-step drill of the trainee rehearsing the demonstration of the supervisor.
    3. Criticism of the drill by other trainees in the clinic.
    4. Summary of the criticism by trainer.
    5. Repetition of the process.

The clinic format is repeated over and over with emphasis on maximum participation by the trainees in both the interview drill and the criticism of the drill.

Skill development, in summary, is the repetition by role playing of small sequential steps into habit-forming processes.

Coaching on the Job

A second major training technique for building skills is joint field work or coaching on the job, often considered the most valuable skill building technique of all. Effective joint work technique may be described as follows:

1. *The preparation phase*—Before the field interview itself, the trainee and his trainer carefully review all aspects of the case and agree upon the strategy to be used in the interview.
2. *The execution phase*—During the interview, the trainee conducts the interview along the lines agreed upon, under the observation of his training supervisor.
3. *The evaluation phase*—At the termination of the interview the supervisor reviews each step and points out possible improvements. The supervisor is under restraint not to take over the interview unless the trainee gets over his depth. Learning under this technique takes place rapidly. Retention is high because the skill-building efforts of the supervisor take place immediately after the actual experience in which the trainee does most if not all of the interviewing. In addition, if a sale is made, this training technique immediately relates the skill to the sale and reinforces the learning experience with what has been learned. This technique has further validity because it is on-the-job training which checks the actual transfer of training and determines whether the transfer has actually taken place. Sales are not always a reliable measure of the transfer process. It is possible in the short run to be making sales without acquiring the requisite selling skills.

Mere participation in joint work with the trainee is not enough. The most effective supervisors are those who not only have sensitive powers of appraisal but also have mastered the art of criticism. The most effective criticism usually contains these factors:

1. *Immediacy*—Delivered immediately after the interview, when the appetite for learning is at its height and mutual recognition of interview details is easy.
2. *Relevance*—Each comment should have an example extracted from the interview itself followed by another example of how the interview could be improved.
3. *Impartiality*—The improvement of the trainee should be the only consideration.
4. *Constructiveness*—Adverse criticism will rarely be accepted unless a way to perform more effectively is pointed out.
5. *Clarity*—Criticism should never be directed to an area not yet exposed to the trainee through previous drill or a previous interview.
6. *Encouragement*—Acceptance of criticism increases with the knowledge that improvement has taken place. Pointing out what has been done well first serves as a stimulant to ensuring correction of weaknesses.

To the trainer skilled in the art of criticism lies the open door to the skill development process. His trainee will respond freely and of his own will to the challenge of a joint interview because of the anticipated richness of the learning experience in selling. Indeed, participation on the firing line with the trainee is the beginning of the leadership role for the training supervisor. In summary, the skill-building process is essential to the training of an agent. Its primary technique is the repetition of small steps through role playing with accent on participation by the trainee and immediate positive feedback from the trainer.

Case Consultation

The case consultation device is a combination briefing session and dress rehearsal of the actual case itself. The briefing session includes:

1. An examination of the facts of the case by both trainer and trainee jointly.
2. A joint discussion of the problems which these facts suggest.
3. A selection of the most adequate solution or solutions.
4. The development of an interview strategy designed to sell the case.

The dress rehearsal represents an attempt by the trainee to simulate actual interview conditions by role-playing the sales interview based on the strategy developed in the briefing session. The final step in the case consultation method is the critique of the dress rehearsal, with the trainer applying the techniques of criticism mentioned above.

The case consultation method is a powerful ally of the joint field technique. One reinforces the other. Case consultation practiced in this manner applies training in the preparation phase of the sale to build the trainee's skills and confidence and a high level of expectancy immediately prior to the sales interview itself. If followed by the trainer's observation of the actual sales interview, the opportunity to transfer selling skills increases dramatically.

BUILDING TECHNICAL COMPETENCE

Also essential in modifying the behavior of the trainee is the acquisition of knowledge and the build-up of technical competence. The life insurance industry is rich in knowledge sources, both from the company and institutional sources mentioned in a previous chapter. The problem is how to integrate knowledge into the skill-building process for effective use and high retention. Knowledge when immediately converted to sales application is retained. Knowledge merely stored without application is lost quickly. Knowledge is limited in its ability to change behavior unless utilized. Unless sales skills have been prepared to a point where the trainee has a built-in converter which knowledge fuels into sales action, the transfer process breaks down. Knowledge unapplied at the time of acquisition is not training, because it is not job-related. Technical competence, however, may serve another function even if not immediately applied. It is helpful behaviorally in building confidence into the uncertain trainee. Competence fibers the trainee's style, providing him with a mounting reservoir of ammunition from which to draw and thereby drains off interview tension.

The Use of Programmed Instruction

As in the case of skill building, knowledge must be taken in small steps and related to practice before the transfer is effective. The lecture technique for imparting knowledge has been for years the main instrument. The difficulty here is restricted feedback and limited participation by the trainee. Seminar techniques relieve the lecture system of some of its difficulties by allowing extensive trainee feedback. A more recent development promises much in increasing the trainee's ability to learn more factual material in less time. This method is commonly referred to as "programmed instruction," a major discovery of the behavioral scientist. This modern technique attempts to structure factual material into small sequential steps with an opportunity by the trainee to participate actively after each step by completing a blank or answering a question. Under this discipline, the student participates in a self-learning exercise continuously throughout the learning process. The reward of a correct answer is repeated throughout, thereby telling the student that he is "getting it" as he goes along. Further, the student by this technique is able to set his own pace for learning—an advantage rarely achieved in the lecture system. More recent attempts by the behavioral scientist in the programmed instruction field represent efforts to structure a skill-building process using the same principles. A by-product of the programmed instruction method is the release of the trainer's time from a task not often executed as well by the trainer using the instruction method.

In summary, programmed instruction by its structuring process boils down the vital facts and separates the irrelevant, rewards the correct answer immediately, standardizes the content so that the content never varies and the student always gets the same facts in the same way.

Integrating the Overall Training Program

The role of company training courses has been discussed elsewhere in this book. Therefore, it is enough in this chapter only to emphasize that agency training and company training courses must be coordinated, integrated and have relevancy to the trainee's improvement of performance.

ORGANIZATION OF TRAINEE'S WORK HABITS

In addition to the development of selling skills and knowledge, a sound agency training program should make provision for the organization of a trainee's work habits. The objective is to transfer to the trainee the performance of those activities necessary to perform the selling function and create an orderly flow of calls and interviews. As in the case of skill-building in the sales interview, the job of building interview activity must be structured in small steps and repeated frequently until the process becomes a habit.

To integrate knowledge, skills, and work habits into a meaningful pattern for the trainee requires at the very least a healthy relationship between trainer and trainee. Wide variations in training results among agencies using similar sales materials and methods, strongly suggest that the critical factor is the nature of the trainer-trainee relationship. Successful trainers largely by instinct have created with their trainees an environment of acceptance and reward highly predictive of trainee success. The same methods and materials used in different agencies can produce remarkably different results. This observation inevitably leads to the conclusion that training is both an art and a science. The facts are that the behavioral sciences have more to learn about group and individual motivation, about the influence of agency environment on agency training and the factors which make up agency environment and how such factors are perceived by the trainees. The ability of the trainer to arouse and stimulate the trainee to performance depends not so much on training methods and materials, agency rules and procedures, as on the nature of his relationship with the trainee.

Successful agencies frequently can be distinguished by the presence of trainers who have mastered several arts. The following three abilities are often the proud possession of successful trainers.

1. The ability to perceive the needs of the trainee in relation to the requirements of the job.
2. The ability to translate those needs into satisfactions by smoothing over the critical stresses often encountered by the trainee in his development to maturity.
3. The ability to relate the agency environment to the needs satisfaction of the trainee.

The above process may be described as the adjustment process through which every trainee must pass before his ultimate development of habit patterns that are predictive of successful growth. How is this accomplished? Research in this area largely conducted by the behavioral scientist has scarcely begun. Improvement in manpower retention awaits more learning from the behavioral scientist. It is suggested here that major breakthroughs in the techniques of improving agent performance will come from the discoveries of the behavioral scientist.

Advanced Training Programs

Developments since World War II have innovated the use of the specialist in advanced underwriting. Changes in the tax code and increasing consumer affluence have combined to signal the development of the sophisticated life underwriter to solve the complex needs of those who have accumulated wealth or ascended into the higher tax brackets.

The response of the companies to the challenge to adapt their training facilities to meet these demands has taken many directions. Many companies have created special departments staffed by experts in the fields of business insurance, employee benefits and estate analysis. Trade associations have been created to keep fieldmen abreast the fast changing developments and represent in Washington the interests of those committed to this selling function. Sharp increases in student enrollment in the challenging courses of study offered by the American College of Life Underwriters reflect the increased interest of the life underwriter in advanced education. The growth of new Certificate Courses offered by the American College in the fields of group insurance, pensions, estate analysis and personal investments indicates another response to the inexorable demand for continuing life underwriter education. The net effect of this knowledge revolution has been a broadening of its spectrum from the convenient and traditional pigeonholes of single needs selling and programming techniques to new horizons of complexity subject to constant change.

The impact of these developments on agency training has produced new challenges. Agencies have seen the inevitable need for a new group of specialists to tap the sophisticated markets. An agency head's decision to meet this demand requires new thinking in both the organization and type of training. Numerous approaches have been attempted. The following methods serve to emphasize the variation in agency training systems in the advanced areas:

1. The appointment of a staff expert whose training function may be organized as follows:
   (a) Holding sales seminars to build technical competence in advanced areas.
   (b) Discussion and briefing by these specialists in the complicated aspects of specific cases.

    (c) Sales assistance in the field.
2. Informal teaming up of the expert agent and the novice in joint field work.
3. Appointment of a staff department to guide and direct the agent in all steps in the advanced underwriting area, including
    (a) Calculation of funding requirements for employee benefit plans.
    (b) Processing and administration. (The continuity of administration of employee benefit plans requires specialists whose administrative skills release the agent from a job which he neither has the time nor the skill to perform. Delegation of the administrative work to a quasi permanent staff also assures continuity of administration.)
    (c) Reporting. (The use of specialists to provide the information needed by the accountant and lawyer for making the required IRS filings makes it possible for the agent to devote his time to building sales competence.)
    (d) Calculation and preparation of adequate briefs for the prospect's consideration in complex estate or business insurance cases.
4. Creation of a marketing team of highly competent sales specialists within the agency. The learning experience under this system is derived largely from the case method, combining the staff specialist and the sales specialist. The ability of the trainee to learn from both specialists by actual case observation is critical to the trainee's development of a satisfactory level of technical competence.

Suffice it to say that the need for continuous training, especially in the advanced underwriting fields is paramount and critical in the development of the agent whose background and talents show promise of reaching the markets which require this special skill.

26

Continuing Education and Training

Leland T. Waggoner

"The things taught in colleges and schools are not an education, but the means of education." This is Ralph Waldo Emerson's exhortation to all of us to continue our education after formal schooling.

The essayist was right. If life insurance agency and home office marketing personnel are to achieve the goals set for them, continuing education and training programs are vital. Today's highly specialized markets demand that the life insurance industry constantly raise the levels of knowledge and skill of its marketing personnel to meet the unrelenting competition for the consumer dollar.

This chapter describes how a continuing education program may be directed toward leading field management to increasing levels of knowledge and skill for the achievement of agency and individual growth and development. Continuous sales management development is essential to progress and growth.

The field underwriter, once he is past his initial training, must be directed into a continuing education program that guides him to a fuller understanding of life insurance as property and its varied uses in the more advanced and complex situations he finds today and will face increasingly in the years ahead.

It is equally important to train each field underwriter to develop the sales skills necessary to transmit ideas clearly and understandably—skills that also aid in building client confidence in the salesman's professional competence and his ability to perform in the client's best interests.

In our present dynamic economy, with new markets developing at an accelerated pace, management at both home office and field levels, together with an alert, educated, and skillful field sales organization, must be prepared to serve these markets intelligently—to render service far beyond the sale and purchase of life insurance.

Management must continuously upgrade the managers' and field underwriters' education and training and help them grow in the ever-expanding markets of estate planning, business insurance, pensions and profit sharing, for example. This is particularly true in view of the fact that while certain markets are expanding others are shrinking.

UNDERWRITER EDUCATION AND TRAINING BEYOND THE BASICS

Recent industry studies make us acutely aware of the importance of training beyond the early stages. Some time ago the Committee on Sales Manpower appointed by LIAMA reported:

> Too often there is a great difference between training and supervisory programs as envisioned by life insurance companies and as executed in the field. Training and supervisory time for agents may be too sparse. Supervision is often relaxed too soon in their early careers. Close supervision should continue until a new agent has achieved a satisfactory level of performance.
>
> The fact that training time for a new agent is often sharply reduced after the early months may be a reason why many agents reach production plateaus at the end of the first six months. More time for training and supervising have caused those agents who have plateaued to seek and reach new levels of accomplishment.[1]

There are numerous stimuli to the field underwriter, assistant manager and manager to broaden their knowledge. One example is the prediction that by 1975 there will be an explosive growth in the discretionary spending ability of "middle income" families. The Bureau of Labor Statistics considers income above $7,000 per year as available to a family to spend as it will. In the immediate past, this discretionary income amounted to approximately $150 billion. By 1975, the total of such income is expected to be $300 billion—two-fifths of all disposable income in the country.

---

[1] Committee consisting of nine leading chief executive officers under the chairmanship of Roger Hull conducted one of the most intensive studies ever undertaken on the development of sales manpower that included training and supervision.

Another factor focusing on the importance and need for continuing education and training is the phenomenal increase in understanding of and appreciation for our product on the part of the public. During recent years, as the result of institutional information, company advertising, cultivation of clients by individual field men, and, most importantly, the actual performance of real service by qualified field men, the buying public has been educated to the fact that its interest will be served best by well-trained, educated, skillful, professional life insurance salesmen.

THE OBJECTIVES OF CONTINUING EDUCATION AND TRAINING

The objectives of continuing education and training embrace the overall growth and development of the company, including field management and field underwriters. In order best to accomplish this, there should be a well-organized program for continuing education and training that flows from the sales department to field management and to field underwriters.

These objectives of continuing education and training can be specifically enumerated as follows:

(1) To build upon the basic education and training already developed from company and institutional sources. An important principle is that the various facets of a company's overall educational program should be integrated and coordinated to avoid uneconomical duplication as well as undesirable gaps in training. Anyone who has completed an adequate course in the "basics" should find particular stimulus and satisfaction in continuing to more advanced areas. The old adage that, "Good men seek knowledge and training," is still true. In addition to sharpening the skills already attained, this will result in progress toward some of the other objectives listed below.

(2) To provide refresher work in the basic knowledge and skills so the fundamental principles and skills will become increasingly ingrained, thereby making it easier to expand further knowledge.

(3) To provide advanced education and training that carries the sales force beyond their previous mastery of fundamentals.

(4) To provide continuing motivation for excellence. Without such motivation the sales force may lose sight of their objectives, with a subsequent deterioration of skills and objectives.

(5) To provide specialized work in such new areas as political, economic and social changes dictate.

(6) To coordinate education and training programs with agency supervisory objectives—with resultant far-reaching effects on the size, type and caliber of an agency.

(7) To provide a tool for morale building for all members of the

organization and to make more effective use of all personnel directly or indirectly concerned with sales. Thus, the improved recruiting, retention, morale, and sales results brought about through a program of continuing education will indirectly improve the morale and efficiency of the entire organization.

(8) To coordinate with other agency objectives, thereby having most effective results. For example, this would include an agency program for improving the quality of business, reaching specific production goals, and planning entry into specific markets.

(9) To provide a strong force for recruiting additional high-caliber manpower. Industry and company studies have shown that prospective recruits are attracted to companies or agencies that have good training programs not just for the basics but for continuing education and training as well.

(10) To assist in the retention of manpower. Few if any activities have a more far reaching effect than this important facet of the life insurance business.

(11) To be responsive to changes in overall company objectives and policies. If, for example, a company has decided to develop a new product or go into a new field, its training and education facilities must be ready to prepare company personnel for the new development.

The necessity for developing these objectives is aptly portrayed by an authority on the application of continuing education:

> Much of the technical knowledge and the application of principles which we have learned today will be obsolete in five years, and almost non-existent ten years from now. For example, in the field of medicine, 70 of our 100 chemical tools we use today were not even in existence ten years ago. One-half of the medical knowledge being used today did not exist ten years ago. Furthermore, one-half of what a medical student learns today will be of no value whatever ten years from now because it will be outdated, and half of what he must know ten years from now has not yet been brought to our attention.
>
> This "knowledge explosion" is taking place in every field of applied science. It is particularly true in the behavioral sciences which, in part, encompass the practitioner in the field of life insurance.
>
> To avoid losing his present competence and further to meet the challenge of the immediate future, any professional man should, by every means at his command, devote a regular and consistent time each day to assimilating new information and ideas and developing new skills and techniques.[2]

---

[2] Annis, Dr. Edward R., Past President American Medical Association and Consultant for Home Life Insurance Company.

PLANNING AND IMPLEMENTING THE PROGRAM

The success of a continuing education and training program requires effective performance of the following basic management functions with respect to the program:

1. Planning

This involves determining a program to accomplish the objectives that have been set. It also includes scheduling actual education and training sessions and coordinating these sessions with other agency activities, sales efforts, and home office programs.

2. Organizing

Who assumes responsibility for sales education and training? When are sessions scheduled? Where are they held? Who presents the various materials? What methods are to be used—lectures, discussions, case methods, or a combination? Should outside talent, agency talent, or both be used? To what extent should institutional material or courses be used?

3. Implementation

This requires assurance that the program will be accepted and that there will be cooperation from agency and field personnel. This can only come through adequate demonstration of the practical value of the program.

4. Control

The success of the program requires periodic evaluation of results through setting standards, measuring achievements, comparing these standards originally set, and taking any indicated remedial action.

THE SALES DEPARTMENT

A major objective of the sales or agency department of a life insurance company—indeed, *the* major objective in the area of continuing education and training—is the planning of a program that will bring superior management at the agency level and, in turn, a progressive, skilled field organization. This combination will insure continued progress and growth for the company as a whole.

In implementing the above, the sales department's responsibilities are threefold:

(1) To organize and implement a program for the continuing education and training of field management.
(2) To organize and implement a program for field underwriters leading to management positions as they qualify for such positions.
(3) To organize and implement a program for the continuing education of field underwriters.

In addition, there is the overall obligation for growth. LIAMA has reported, "One of the major changes facing member companies in recent years has been to expand their sales forces and to keep pace with expanding markets."

Therefore, since the development and maintenance of qualified field management is a prerequisite for growth, a continuing education and training program must be focused not only on present field management for its further development but also on present and future field underwriters as a source of new managers. A total program should be directed to managers, assistant managers, and field underwriters. This should be administered by the sales department with the director of agencies responsible for its implementation, with, of course, the complete cooperation of the agency managers.

CONTINUING EDUCATION OF FIELD MANAGEMENT

In order to build successful managers whose skills will, in turn, be directed to the building of successful field underwriters, an important objective is to organize and emphasize a program for continuing education and training of *field* management. The assumption here is that all agency managers are beyond the indoctrination stage. Also, it should be recognized that until they are fully established and successful, most managers require (and the better ones will seek out) continuing sources of knowledge as well as further skill refinement in salesmanship. Any program for additional growth and development, regardless of the degree of individual success, should emphasize this fact.

Therefore, the sales department's objectives and responsibility with regard to continuing education and training of field management tend to fall in three areas.

(1) The total or overall job of management
(2) The skillful execution of the manager's individual program in relation to the company's total objectives and, in particular, to what will be expected from his territory
(3) The specific areas of continuing education and training that will result in a constantly expanding group of management trainees and successful field underwriters.

Further, while it is the sales department's function to provide a program for continuing education and skill development in management, an equal responsibility falls on field management to undertake a collateral program for self-development. In any case, the fact remains that the responsibility for final implementation of their part of the program rests with the managers.

Study of Agency Manager's Job

The overall job of management requires a study of the functions and primary objectives of the agency manager's job. These functions and objectives would seem to be:

(1) The manager must function successfully not only as a business manager but as a sales manager as well. The two roles are dependent upon one another and his knowledge and skill in the interrelated roles do much to decide his management success.

(2) As a businessman, the manager must have the know-how to produce and conserve an increasing volume of business commensurate with the market potential of his territory.

(3) The manager must be able to produce a growing volume of business at a decreasing unit cost for profitable agency operation.

(4) As a sales manager, he must have the capacity and ability to attract, select, and train men who will acquire the knowledge, perfect the skills, and develop the morale that makes for individual success.

The manager's continuing education and training never end. Just as in the case of field underwriters, continuing training has as its ultimate purpose the lifting of men to higher earning and achievement levels. The same relationship should exist between the company's sales department and field management as between field management and the field underwriters. The same sense of responsibility for an individual's success must exist. The proper discharge of this responsibility is one of the most important contributions a sales department can make to field management and, as a result, to its field force.

Suggested Steps In Management Training

Reference to the objectives and functions of field management has been made. Now let us cover some of the other specific steps by which continuing education for field management may be achieved. This assumes that courses such as L.U.T.C. and C.L.U. and, as desired, American College Certificate courses have been or are in the process of completion. The order of importance will vary by company. The steps include, but are not limited to, the following:

(1) Complete and continuous participation in the company's organized training plan for growth and development which covers all of the steps in building a successful agency.

(2) Attendance at LIAMA's two-week management schools and its graduate courses.

(3) Completion of the American College of Life Underwriters' Certificate Course in Agency Management.

(4) Participation in institutional and university courses dealing with sales, estate planning, and business insurance.

(5) Attendance at company managers' meetings that disseminate information, provide inspiration, and serve as background for testing and demonstrating sales management skills and as a sounding board for the exchange of ideas.

(6) Attendance at periodic CLU Institutes.

(7) Participation in management courses offered by publishing houses that are active in promoting sales and management courses for life insurance personnel.

(8) Participation in university courses in specialized life insurance subjects and management such as those offered by Purdue and Southern Methodist Universities.

(9) Active participation in various courses of GAMC.

SELECTING AND TRAINING ASSISTANT MANAGERS

The second phase of continuing education and training applies to secondary management—a source of future management. For any company to grow and prosper, a part of its continuing education and training must be a planned training program for embryonic managers.

When an assistant manager, supervisor, or field underwriter indicates, after thorough evaluation, that he does have management potential, the company then should launch him on a specific program for further education and training in the field of management. His final entry into full-fledged field management naturally comes only after he has performed satisfactorily in various assigned areas.

Both the sales department and field management, working as a team, will be responsible for this program leading qualified individuals to management. The program in the initial stages should place emphasis on particulars rather than on all the steps leading to management.

Each man should undertake a program tailored especially for the individual and based on his previous experience, results, and management objectives. As an illustration, an assistant manager's program should include an understanding of the home office's responsibility to him, the agency manager's part in his training and education, and the individual's responsibility to the company, agency and self. The program would establish both short- and long-range objectives.

It would not be our objective to transfer a field underwriter immediately into full management. Rather, there should be a gradual process that would, in essence, be tied to the following program that is planned and organized by the sales department and would be implemented by field management with the cooperation and direction of the agency director.

(1) The candidate would have a minimum objective, say no less than two men in his unit by the end of the first year. Therefore, under the guidance of his manager, he would learn and execute the steps in recruiting and selection—the areas which, in the final analysis, are the difference between success and failure in agency management.

(2) He would be expected, in addition to becoming skillful in using company materials in recruiting and selection, to be able to demonstrate that he can bring qualified field underwriters "through to success" by proper use and application of the training and development program with the field underwriters in his unit. This will entail joint work, on-the-job coaching, in-the-office training, and individual and group motivation and supervision.

(3) Naturally, his work and the development and progress of his unit would be under the close supervision and direction of his manager and director of agencies at all times. However, he will soon realize that he will have to use his initiative and ingenuity in many ways as each new day poses new challenges.

(4) In addition to this work with his individual unit, the candidate will be expected to be a "team player" and participate in the overall development of the agency as well. Perhaps one of the greatest differences in the attitude required of a man in management and that of an individual field underwriter is that *his success depends upon the success of others* and the success of the agency undertaking comes before personal consideration.

After a reasonable period, the candidate's progress would be measured. If it is satisfactory, and after additional evaluation, full management would be recommended for him, and a program of continuing education and training would be drawn up for him leading to full management responsibility.

A suggested program might follow wholly or in part the following steps:

(1) Attendance at the LIAMA Management Orientation School where the emphasis is on the *how* of agency building.

(2) Where practicable, this would be followed by a home office conducted managers' school. The advantage, of course, is that there the newly appointed managers receive identical training

prior to assuming agencies of their own. Here the general principles of agency management are explored and applied to specific operations, as well as providing background for the company's management philosophy. Some specific topics that might be covered are:

> —The Company Organizational Structure
> —Product and Services — Review
> —Recruiting and Selection — Test for Skill
> —Training and Direction — Test for Skill
> —Public Relations
> —Agency Office Management

(3) Continuing assistance and home office guidance would be provided by the director of agencies who is assigned responsibility for the agency.

Once the decision is made that the individual will assume full management responsibility, a program for his future development must be tailored to both company and individual objectives. It would follow generally what has previously been outlined for established managers.

FIELD UNDERWRITER CONTINUING EDUCATION

The third phase of a program for continuing education and training would apply directly to field underwriters through a program designed for participation in and implementation by the director of agencies, field managers, and field underwriters. Direct participation through demonstration, coaching, and evaluation would be required of each manager as well as execution on the part of each field underwriter.

The field underwriter's objective would be to reach a high level of effectiveness and personal achievement as the result of involvement in an organized process of continuing education and training. As a member of a dynamic organization, he has, in addition to participation in company programs, a responsibility for his own development and continuing education outside of programs specifically provided by the company. For instance, it is his responsibility to:

(1) Expand his business sources and markets through skillful use of company and agency educational material and training opportunities.

(2) Undertake aggressively a well-organized personal program that will have as its major objective the creating of an image in the community of a professionally competent life underwriter.

(3) Personally subscribe to business and tax services that will add to his knowledge and broaden his capacity to perform effectively and profitably for policyowners and clients.

(4) Enroll in LUTC, CLU, and special courses in trusts, wills and taxation for further education and training.

The final leg of the success triangle is the need for continuing education and training for the field where, in the final analysis, the effectiveness of field management programs for continuing education and training will be determined. Implementation and creative expansion is dependent on and a part of continuing education and training flowing from the sales department to field management and thus to the field men.

The entire program for continuing education and training has its beginning in the sales department where it is organized and designed by the director of training to meet the company's overall objectives. Where possible, the director of advanced underwriting will participate in developing the program, and it will be his function to stimulate continuing education among managers and field underwriters alike. Everyone agrees that the acquisition of knowledge and the refinement of skills require action on the part of those involved. However, an organized plan to generate that action is needed.

The only way the effectiveness of the program may be evaluated is by the performance of the participants. In the case of field underwriters, it is the "playback"—their response—their results through application of skills. Unless there is total participation in a program for furthering education and continuing training by sales department director, manager, and field underwriter, especially the training-for-skills aspect, the effort will fall far short of the predetermined objectives.

Teaching and Coaching

To be effective, the program must follow the sound principles involved in the teaching and coaching process. For that reason, the continuing education and training plans should be designed:

—to build the field underwriter's convictions
—to establish basic habits for self-development
—to increase technical knowledge
—to develop selling skills
—to increase his enthusiasm and advance his progress

With so many calls on a manager's time, an organized program such as we propose is intended to conserve his time and organize his efforts for maximum results. One illustration of such a program is a complete advanced underwriting program to build a productive plan of action.

The plan for continuing education and training of field underwriters calls for joint participation of the sales department director, field manager and field underwriter, and is the responsibility of all three. However, the home office would be responsible for establishing and directing a program for continuing education and training as well as the physical means for its implementation.

Advanced Underwriting

The advanced underwriting and pension divisions, whether organized as a division with one head or as two separate divisions, would provide the guidance and supervision and the physical means and program to be followed by field management and field underwriters. The home office can provide, assist, counsel and direct the process of continuing education and training, but in the final analysis, the success of any program rests on the degree of efficient execution by agency managers and field men.

The advanced underwriting division and the pension division would provide complete manuals covering all aspects of business insurance, pensions and profit sharing, including the approach and sales ideas that would apply in particular situations.

With the program designed and organized for use in the field, the managers must follow through with each qualified field underwriter to—

(1) Implement acquired knowledge through in-office and field training for the purpose of polishing skills in the sale of life insurance to solve business and corporate problems.

(2) To encourage and, if necessary, participate with the field underwriter in courses outside the company and agency that will add to knowledge and strengthen skills in the more advanced areas.

(3) Encourage entry into:
(a) NALU Sales Seminars
(b) CLU Courses
(c) LUTC Sessions

The result of such a program would tend to build both field management and underwriters to a point where, through attainment of knowledge and sales skills in the more advanced fields of life insurance sales, each will profit to the maximum.

Additional opportunities for continuing education and training are provided by:

(1) Company schools either at the home office or on a regional basis.

(2) Company programs at conventions or through regional conferences.

(3) Conferences attended by honor men—million-dollar producers.

Company Schools

To supplement training given in the agencies and elsewhere, home office schools would be held at intervals for field men who have qualified for attendance by virtue of (a) time under contract, (b) being fully validated, (c) having acquired knowledge in the advanced underwriting category and at least limited sales results in advanced areas, and (d) being recommended for attendance by their agency manager or others.

There could well be both an intermediate knowledge training school and still another at a later date for the more experienced and productive salesmen. The intermediate school would be a follow-up on the field training program as well as an introduction to specific advanced sales areas. Later, these same men, together with others who may qualify, would return to the home office for still further training in more advanced sales techniques. On the other hand, a home office team plus qualified field men could conduct regional seminars when practicable.

The subjects covered might fall into the advanced underwriting areas, with greatest emphasis placed on acquiring knowledge and developing sales skill. The conferences would be conducted mainly by competent and experienced men. For instance, field managers and field men with known records of achievements and results in the more sophisticated markets would:

> (a) teach
> (b) demonstrate
> (c) hold question-and-answer periods

Experience teaches that in conferences of this type the greatest benefit comes from having successful salesmen not only instruct but demonstrate how they apply their ideas. Home office participation might best be limited to men who are known and accepted by the field as advanced underwriting experts. In addition to home office and field instructors, there is much to be said for bringing in recognized outside authorities to conduct sessions on particular subjects, such as, for example, estate planning. It is wise to give the expert enough time to develop his subject in depth—which in many cases means a half or a full day. In any event, whether it be a company-conducted school for the purpose of continuing education and training, a regional conference, or company convention, a detailed pre-timed agenda must be prepared as a prerequisite to a successful meeting.

One additional activity that provides an important background and source of continuing education and training is attendance at company conventions and conferences which are limited to a group that has performed exceptionally—such as million-dollar producers or other groups of outstanding leaders. These provide a source of continuing education both through the formal programs and through the interchange of ideas among those in attendance. Neither conventions nor conferences can be covered in detail here, but they both offer real opportunities to expose large numbers to the educational and training processes.

CONCLUSION

In conclusion, it would seem that we should travel every possible avenue in our process of continuing education and training for the sales department, field management and field underwriters. However, we must also be realistic and recognize that education—as valuable as it is in itself—means little in the context of this discussion unless translated into meaningful action, i.e. solving problems through life insurance. Learning must be transformed into increased effectiveness on the job. The ultimate objective of continuing education and training is to design and executive a program that will encourage, lead and motivate the greatest possible number of field men to ever higher levels of professional competence and performance in the widening and changing markets of our present economy.

Section VIII

MOTIVATION, SUPERVISION
AND RETENTION OF MANPOWER

27

Creating a Motivational Work Environment

Stanley S. Watts
and William T. Earls

"I know not what course others may take, but as for me, give me liberty or give me death!" These words, spoken by Patrick Henry on March 23, 1775, ended his impassioned speech before the Virginia Provincial Convention. The colonial patriot's oratory and logic inspired and motivated the colonies to begin the fight for American independence.

Patrick Henry dedicated his life to the cause of freedom. The "Orator of American Independence" was motivated by his love of liberty. By voicing his feelings and beliefs he inspired others to action and helped make America great.

Companies, like countries, need motivated men! Successful life insurance managers, like successful athletic coaches, inspire their staffs to great heights of personal performance. High individual performance will depend, to some extent, on the capacity of the manager or coach to evoke it!

MOTIVATIONAL WORK ENVIRONMENT

Orators like Patrick Henry, as well as agency managers, must accomplish objectives through the efforts of other people. Whether the manager's function is called leading, actuating, or persuading, his success depends to a large extent upon providing a motivational work environment.

MOTIVATING THE SALES FORCE

What is meant by the phrase "motivational work environment?" A motivational work environment is one that encourages an individual, or group, to maximum effort—this is the essence of motivation and also the essence of management. However, we should be careful not to oversimplify this matter of motivation. Actually, motivation is a complex psychological phenomenon, and there is wide disagreement among psychologists as to the real nature of motivation.

Most psychologists use the term motivation to refer to "the inner control of human behavior as it is affected by bodily conditions, learned interests, values, mental attitudes, and recognized or unrecognized goals or aspirations."[1]

This definition emphasizes that human behavior is largely controlled by inner forces. The secret to motivation is the energizing or activating of those inner forces so that human behavior is unleashed and channeled into productive economic and social activities. The above definition of motivation acknowledges that human behavior can be controlled by physical force or restraint. However, this negative approach to controlling human behavior is mainly effective in determining and preventing specific activity and does not serve to release the vast reservoirs of potential energy that await the activating impulse of effective positive leadership. The former Secretary of Health, Education and Welfare, John Gardner has said, "Motivation is a powerful ingredient in performance. Talent without motivation is inert and of little use to the world."[2] The challenge and the opportunity for the life insurance agency manager is helping men grow. This idea is best expressed in a quotation from Goethe, "If we take men as they are, we make them worse, but if we take them as they should be, we promote them to what they can become."

The manager must provide a working environment that will permit the maximum motivational forces to become effective within each agent and each office employee in the agency. However, "human motivation is not a push-button operation."[3] The subject of "motivation is so complex and the behavior of people is so unpredictable that an attempt to apply generalized rules of human behavior in a mechanical fashion simply does not work."[4] Human behavior is moved by a myriad of forces. Many of these forces are incomprehensible. Of course, the agency manager should not, and cannot become either a professional psychologist or a magician. But in the majority of cases, people respond in a predictable manner, in accordance with certain fundamental principles of motivation.

---

[1] Russell, G. Hugh and Black, Kenneth, Jr., *Human Behavior and Life Insurance* (Englewood Cliffs, New Jersey: Prentice-Hall, Inc., 1963), p. 166.
[2] Gardner, John W., *Excellence* (New York, N. Y.: Harper & Row, 1961).
[3] Russell, G. Hugh and Black, Kenneth, Jr., *Op Cit.*, p. 169.
[4] *Ibid.*, p. 169.

The psychologist's definition of motivation emphasizes that a motive is an inner control that moves behavior toward recognized or unrecognized goals. The goal is the end result desired. The intensity of the behavior activity generally varies directly with the intensity of the desire for attainment of the goal. A dog deprived of food for three days will make a more courageous fight for a scrap of meat than the dog that has been fed recently. Some life insurance agents continuously have a more intense desire to make the Million Dollar Round Table than do other agents. Paraphrasing H. D. Thoreau, "Every man listens to a different drummer." Some agents continuously seek the honor and prestige of being the highest producer in their agency. All men have goals. Some have higher goals than others. Some men have different kinds of goals. The significance of all this for the life insurance agency manager is that he should help each agent in the agency to establish individual goals that will activate each agent's most productive performance for the benefit of himself and his agency.

The manager's responsibility is to develop an agency of maximum productivity and stability. This can only be accomplished by a highly motivated agency sales force that is continuously aspiring to attain higher production goals and greater manpower development. Chapter 28, "Supervision," indicates the great advantage to the agency in having each agent establish target goals. The several dimensions of the motivational forces within the agent then spur him on to reach these target goals.

Although psychologists do not agree as to the specific nature of motivation or as to its significance in determining human behavior, there are many aspects of motivation about which there is general agreement. The following paragraphs set forth some of the applications to life insurance agency management of the generally accepted fundamentals of motivation theory.

FUNDAMENTALS OF MOTIVATION THEORY

Reward versus Punishment

In most situations in a life insurance agency and for most people in the agency, more effective motivation is achieved by rewarding behavior that is approved rather than by punishing behavior that is disapproved. Many parents, supervisors, and agency managers too often make the mistake of believing that punishment is the most effective means of motivating others. This negative approach has the effect of saying to the person, "What you are doing is wrong." Punishment does not explicitly tell the person what he should be doing. On the other hand, rewarding a person for approved behavior tells the person, "This specific bit of behavior that you have been doing is what is correct." The person is able to continue the behavior without having to cast his eyes about to find more suitable forms of behavior. This is in contrast to punishment which does not have this strictly informational effect.

What if an agent is not engaging in the kinds of behavior desired? For example, the agent may have established a sales schedule for himself of $20,000 of new business a week. However, during the last three months he has only averaged $8,000 of new business a week. It would seem at this point that there is very little that can be rewarded. However, the principle of *shaping* would be applicable. Shaping implies that the person in authority rewards behavior that gets closer and closer to the goal desired. Thus, while the agent has not been performing in complete accordance with his target goals, some of the things he has been doing are deserving of praise and commendation. Furthermore, when the agent does have a good week, this achievement should be singled out and rewarded. No man's performance can be so bad that there is not some aspect of it that can be praised. The concept of shaping implies that the behavior is potentially there in the person and it is up to the environment with its reinforcements to bring out such behavior. Individuals differ in their ultimate potential but in most instances their daily achievement is far from their real potential. The potential is there, but it is not being fully realized. In the use of *reinforcement,* a term which is used synonomously with reward, the manager or the supervisor can help the person come closer to achieving his potential. This concept is sometimes referred to as the *law of effect* which holds that behavior that is rewarded tends to be repeated.

Since punishment is such a universal form of behavioral control, we should discuss some of the reasons why it is often inappropriate. First, the person who is punished may not necessarily change his behavior. This is ironic since the change is specifically the effect desired by the punisher. Second, what often happens as a result of punishment is that the punished party feels that he is not liked by the person who administered the punishment or that he is not a worthy individual. In either case, the punished person may change his behavior or his self-concept, but he does not necessarily change his behavior in accord with what the punishing party desires. Thus, punishment, aside from not necessarily being effective may also have the harmful consequence of changing areas of behavior that the punishing party did not wish to have changed.

An additional complication inherent in the use of punishment to mold behavior is the fact that a person sometimes deliberately engages in "undesirable" behavior because he wants (usually unconsciously) to be punished. It may seem to him that being punished is better, at least, than being ignored. The relative merits of positive and negative leadership are discussed in a later section of this chapter.

Types of Rewards

If rewards are so important, what are the most effective types of rewards which can be used? Perhaps the first to come to most people's minds is financial reward and it must certainly be realized that in our capitalistic economic system, financial inducements are very important and can have a strong rewarding effect. However, it should also be realized that what the person is working for may not be the financial reward itself in terms of purchasing power that the dollar brings, but rather he may be working for the implied prestige associated with the financial rewards. Thus, the mistake should not be made of thinking that a person works solely for the financial gain. He may be strongly motivated by a financial reward but it may be because the financial reward symbolizes something that he values.

Need for Achievement

Research by Dr. David C. McClelland, Professor of Psychology at Harvard University, and his associates on what they call "need for achievement," discloses that the person with high need for achievement is not primarily motivated by financial reward, but rather he is motivated more by the demands of the task.[5] Many life insurance agents are not so much concerned with gaining the approval or the money that others will bestow upon them as they are concerned with meeting a particular challenge, and in being successful in it. Obviously, such qualities are highly desirable in agents. Such men do not need others to tell them what to do but are sufficiently challenged by the sales task to go out and get the job done.

It would be helpful for us at this point to look at some of the characteristics associated with people with high need for achievement and observe the significance of these human characteristics to the problem of providing a motivational work environment. First, the person with high need for achievement typically is one who has an extremely autonomous way of life. This is not to say that the individual with a high need for achievement is a beatnik or is overtly very non-conforming. It is to say, however, that the agent with a high need for achievement typically is more independent than the majority of his fellow workers. Here then exists a possible source of strain because it may be that the agent who would be the best salesman is the one who superficially does not live up to the images, does not verbalize what the other salesmen say and is not a "yes-man" in his relationship with the manager. The agency manager should not be misled by this, however, because it may be merely a reflection of the independence of this particular type of individual that will pay off in increased sales effectiveness.

5 McClelland, D. C., Atkinson, J. W., Clark, R. A. and Lowell, E. L., *The Achievement Motive* (New York, N. Y.: Appleton-Century-Crofts, 1953).

The second characteristic of people with high need for achievement is their task orientation as opposed to what the psychologist calls a *social-emotional orientation*. Bales has shown there are usually two kinds of leaders who emerge in any group.[6] One is the task leader who asks the most relevant questions and is similarly concerned with getting the task done. The second kind of leader is the social-emotional leader who is concerned with having people get along with each other, having the group feel good, and so forth. Both of the above are necessarily there for the smooth integration and functioning of a given group, and one should not be valued over the other. However, for the purposes of our present discussion, the person with high need for achievement is likely to be a task leader rather than a social-emotional leader although this does not mean that he is socially inert. The person with the task orientation will ask questions about technical matters in an attempt to obtain information relating to the job to be done and in general will be highly oriented toward the specific business at hand. The task oriented person, however, is primarily a doer and an achiever not a student in quest of knowledge for knowledge's sake.

The third characteristic of the person with high need for achievement is his intense commitment to what he is doing. This almost follows from the above emphasis on the task orientation. A person who does not have high need for achievement may attend to the task simply because he feels he should. On the other hand, intense commitment to the task comes from basic personality characteristics within the individual and is a highly valued asset as far as achievement is concerned. This commitment is likely to allow the person to enjoy his work and not to see it as just a job or merely something he has to do. When a man makes a personal commitment to someone he admires and respects, then this commitment can be the strongest possible motivation for fulfillment—the intense desire not to disappoint will oftentimes propel the individual to a success otherwise unattainable.

McClelland succinctly summarizes the character of the person with a high need for achievement by describing him as a man who is more self-confident, enjoys taking carefully calculated risks, researches his environment actively and is very much interested in concrete measures of how well he is doing. A high achiever, however, does not seem to galvanize his activities by the prospect of profit. People with low achievement needs require money incentives, but people with high achievement needs work hard anyway, provided there is an opportunity for achieving something significant.[7]

---

[6] Bales, R. and Slater, P. "Role Differentiation in Small Decision-Making Groups," in Parsons, T., Bales, R., et al., *Family Socialization and Interaction Process* (Glencoe, Ill.: Free Press, 1955).

[7] McClelland, David C., "Business Drive and National Achievement," *Harvard Business Review,* July-August, 1962.

Motivation in Selection and Training

Coaches of nationally-ranked football, basketball and other athletic teams have admitted that recruiting has contributed greatly to the success of other teams. Recruiting is equally important in successful agency building.

John Gardner emphasizes the importance of selecting highly motivated manpower. "Just as selection for talent produces a group with high aptitude, so selection for high motivation produces a group with vigor, spirit, and morale . . . [8] eager and ambitious individuals will drive themselves to achieve, and the apathetic ones will not drive themselves in any case. The man who struggles from lowly beginnings to the top of the heap is fiercely motivated."[9] "Surmounting of hardships strengthens character—difficulty is the nurse of greatness."[10]

Duffy Daugherty, Michigan State's famed football coach says, "There are three kinds of athletes. Ten percent are winners, and you can leave them alone. Ten percent are losers, and you might as well leave them alone, too. The other 80 percent are shoulder-shruggers—you ask them if they can do anything and they shrug their shoulders. They are the ones on whom you have to do all your coaching."

In *The Incomparable Salesmen* Perrin Stryker states that the two most dominant characteristics of members of the Million Dollar Round Table are persuasive ability and achievement drive. Men with these qualities should be sought out by agency managers, for they have the attributes that can be motivated to outstanding production performance.[11]

Prestige

The desire for prestige is recognized as an important motivational factor. In terms of our internal-external continuum we are on tricky ground, for while the motive may be strongly within a particular person, and thus be internalized, the specific form of prestige is always something external, i.e., something "out there" in the environment. Prestige implies social recognition by others, and thus the individual who is motivated by the desire for prestige is in marked contrast to the individual who has a great personal need for achievement. While agents with a high need for achievement may be a boon to any agency or company, those agents motivated by prestige are going to be numerically greater in number.

---

[8] Gardner, John W., *Op. Cit.,* p. 97.
[9] *Ibid.,* p. 96.
[10] *Ibid.,* p. 98.
[11] Stryker, Perrin, *The Incomparable Salesman*, (New York, N. Y.: McGraw-Hill, Inc., 1967).

Why are people motivated by prestige? In attempting to answer this question of prestige, we may gain a better understanding of what prestige is and why it is significant to a life insurance agency.

The acquisition of wealth and the attainment of power provide a person with material gain, and also with the ability to manipulate resources. However, they may not provide a person with respect from either his peers or his superiors, and it is this social recognition that is strongly implied when we say that a position, or a person, has prestige. Thus, to be associated with a good company or a good agency may have high prestige value because it signifies to others and to oneself that one is worthy. The desire to become a member of the Million Dollar Round Table is an example of motivation associated with prestige. The agent feels that he has attained respectability in his career when he has demonstrated his capacity to qualify for membership in the Million Dollar Round Table. The prestige associated with the attainment of this objective may be even more motivational than the desire to increase income.

Some agents will be motivated by prestige, others by financial inducements, and others by a challenging task. Many agents will be motivated by a mixture of these motives, some motives being more applicable in a given situation for a particular agent while another agent may tend to be motivated primarily at all times by one type of motive. Therefore, an important part of the job of agency management is to discover the objectives of each unique agent—finding that "button" that will inspire a man to perform to his fullest capabilities. This process will naturally involve some *shaping* of the agent's objectives to harmonize with the agency's overall objectives.

MOTIVATION AND PERSONAL HARMONY

What has been discussed above relates primarily to ways in which the life insurance agency manager can apply principles of motivation in helping agents increase their sales. However, it should be recognized that increased sales is only one way of looking at the problem of motivating the sales force. For example, all the excellent principles of motivation may be ineffective if there is disharmony in the group, if an agent would like to be interested in his job but cannot for personal reasons, or if the agent perceives the job itself, including his peers and superiors, as placing obstacles in his way.

It is thus extremely important that the agent working in the agency environment find himself doing something that is compatible with his conception of himself. While such a conception may not be overtly verbalized by the agent, it is important that he not, for example, have to do work which he considers immoral or beneath him. Radical departure from what one feels is the proper form of conduct will lead to either (a) a final cessation of that behavior which leads one away from his standards, or (b) some kind of rationalization in which the person concludes that his behavior is consistent with his standards. The maintenance of imbalance will surely be personally harmful to the individual and will be reflected in all kinds of symptoms, some of them having a direct and deleterious effect on his job performance.

Group Cohesiveness

How can the work environment bring out the best in the individual? One of the most potent variables is group cohesiveness. Numerous studies have shown the effects of the cohesiveness, or lack of it, of the group on a variety of tasks. In terms of the individual member's perception, a noncohesive group is one which does not really function like a group, which does not demand his attendance, or, if it does, does not inspire him to engage in behavior in accordance with group goals. Additionally, a noncohesive group may obtain lip service from members with regard to group goals, but such a group is not likely to encourage a spirited or effectual utilization of members' efforts on behalf of the group. Cohesiveness refers to how well the group hangs together. An impregnable group is certainly a cohesive group, although such extreme solidarity in the face of outside influence may mean that the group is insensitive to change, and therefore unable to recognize its own inadequacies.

Why is the effect of the cohesive group so strong in motivating individual behavior? For one thing, a cohesive group has a tremendous reinforcing potential, by which is meant that the cohesive group can dispense rewards and punishment. Note that anyone in power can dispense rewards and punishment; what makes the cohesive group different is that its judgment is valued by its members, i.e., its judgments or at least its goals have been strongly internalized. Thus, for the group to approve or disapprove is a very strong motivating force. The person who is out of line with the group may seek to change his behavior, and the person who is rewarded by a cohesive group will particularly value the reinforcement.

Group cohesiveness is an effective motivational factor in a life insurance agency when the whole agency enthusiastically embraces the philosophy of personal growth through greater sales achievement. In an agency in which each member is imbued with the philosophy and is actively striving to make the Million Dollar Round Table, a new agent will find this kind of an attitude contagious. If the new agent has been carefully selected, and adequately trained, it is expected that he will be encouraged to emulate the production goals of his peers. The negative aspect of group cohesiveness is that the new agent may feel frustrated if his production does not conform to the standard of the group. However, if the man has been properly selected and adequately trained he will usually respond positively to the standards of the cohesive group. A negative response may be indicative of the man's unsuitability for life insurance selling.

John Gardner describes his wife's experience in asking a Dutchwoman why children and adults in Holland showed such an extraordinary high incidence of language skills. The answer was: "We expect it of children. We think it important." Gardner goes on to say, "More and more we are coming to see that high performance, particularly where children are concerned, takes place in a framework of expectation."[12] The degree of motivation is very much affected by what is expected, or demanded of a life insurance agent.

This is not to say that new agents are like children, but that children provide a clear and simple example of how people react. We are all subject to environmental influences in similar ways. In many cases, substantially better production results will be achieved if the manager and the cohesive group make it apparent that it is expected and it is important.

The cohesive group may not always be the best kind of group for the outsider. From his standpoint, group cohesiveness may manifest itself in opposition to something he says or does, and he may merely think of the group as argumentative or strongheaded. This is due to the different perspectives: the outsider views the group in terms of what it does to or for him, while we are looking at the group in a more detached manner, and asking what are the conditions necessary.

It is essential that every agent in an agency feel and believe that he is wanted and needed. This helps to build esprit de corps, team effort and unity of purposes. Quite often an associate can do more to motivate a fellow agent than his manager. When this team spirit prevails, the morale of the team and each agent spurs them on to performing beyond their normal capacity. Loyalty to a company and to an agency brings out the best in men!

PLEASURE IN SELLING

The life insurance business provides a tremendous opportunity for those persons endowed with certain qualities. Among these qualities is the capac-

---

[12] Gardner, John W., *Op. Cit.*, p. 101.

ity to derive pleasure and satisfaction in selling life insurance—a liking for the job. If a person is going to be motivated to sell life insurance, it helps if he possesses a basic liking for those activities that are associated with life insurance selling. We have all observed children learning to swim. However, the child that initially is afraid to go in the water, is going to learn to swim with greater difficulty. Furthermore, a child may have his fear of the water accentuated by a terrifying ducking by a thoughtless or impatient parent. A liking for water or swimming will be much longer delayed by such thoughtless tactics. Likewise, in starting a man in a career in life insurance selling, it is far better that the man's first few experiences be pleasant rather than terrifying. Psychologists tell us that to a large extent, we learn our anxieties and fears. Once fear of making calls is learned, it takes a lot of unlearning to remove the fear and anxiety.

A teacher was recently quoted as referring to one of his pupils as being "endowed with extraordinary gifts but too lazy to open up the packages." Far too often in management we are inclined to accept this teacher's reason to brush off an agent's low performance with the label of being lazy. In many cases it is fear rather than laziness that keeps salesmen from working regularly, and it is the manager's job and training responsibility to see that the seemingly "lazy" agents will have the confidence to do the things they *can do* that will make them successful.

An ingredient in high performance is morale—or confidence. Those who achieve excellence must have a hard core of conviction and self-trust that makes their achievement possible—this contributes to the proper mental attitude which is so essential to continued success. Good leadership promotes and motivates the proper mental attitude. Responsibility for learning and growth rests finally with the individual—as agency managers, we can stimulate and challenge but in the last analysis, the individual must foster his own development. The chief resource must be the individual's own interest, drive and enthusiasm for self-fulfillment. Managers can help him raise his sights and recognize his own abilities.

SIGNIFICANCE OF AGENT'S HIERARCHY OF NEEDS*

All of us have certain needs that we try to satisfy by our daily activities. Psychologists speak of the *hierarchy of needs* and distinguish between primary, or physical needs, and secondary needs. The satisfaction of primary needs is essential to our survival or physical well-being and includes such needs as hunger, thirst, warmth, pain-avoidance and mating. Most people today are attaining adequate satisfaction of their primary

---

* See Chapter 28 for detailed discussion of agent's hierarchy of needs.

needs and therefore are devoting an increasing attention and emphasis to the satisfactions of their secondary needs. Important among the secondary needs of most people are: security, a chance for economic and career advancement, a working environment in which employees are treated like human beings, the respect of one's associates and independence.

It is important that the agency manager realize that each agent has his own hierarchy of needs and objectives. The challenge for the agency manager is to discover the needs and objectives of his agents and to show them how they can realize these through their contribution to the attainment of the agency's objectives. The important point is that the agent's primary needs are usually adequately provided for, therefore, it is the quest for satisfaction of his secondary needs that should be harnessed or coordinated with the agency's objectives.

"The best kept secret in America today is that people would rather work hard for something they believe in than enjoy a pampered idleness. They would rather give up their comfort for an honored objective than bask in extravagant leisure. It is a mistake to speak of dedication as a sacrifice. Every man knows that there is exhilaration in intense effort applied toward a meaningful end. . . .

"Ask the physician at the height of his power whether he would trade his life, with its 18-hour days, its midnight calls, its pressures and anxieties, for a life of idleness in tranquil surroundings. Ask the retired man whether he would trade his leisure for a job in which he could apply his full powers toward something he believed in. . . .

"We fall into the error of thinking that happiness necessarily involves ease, diversion, tranquility—a state in which all of one's wishes are satisfied. For more peple, happiness is not to be found in this vegetative state but in *striving toward meaningful goals*. The dedicated person has not achieved all of his goals. His life is the endless *pursuit of goals, some of them unattainable*. He may often be tense, worried, fatigued. He has little of the leisure one associates with the storybook conception of happiness. But he has found a more meaningful happiness. It appears that happiness in the sense of total gratification is not a state to which man meaningfully can aspire."[13]

THE MOTIVATION PROCESS

If the manager follows the "need-satisfaction" approach in providing a motivational work environment, he will provide opportunities for the agency personnel to achieve satisfaction of their higher-order needs. Davis

---

[13] *Ibid.,* pp. 148–149.

sets forth six specific steps that a manager should follow in the motivation process as he attempts to coordinate the agency's objectives with the higher-order needs of the agents.

Applied to a life insurance agency the six steps in the motivation process are as follows:[14]

(1) The manager must first determine his objective or purpose. The agency manager cannot attempt to motivate the members of the agency in a specific direction until the manager himself has determined the objective he seeks to attain.

(2) The manager must empathize, i.e., he must try to see the situation as the agent sees it and to feel about it as the agent feels.

(3) The manager must communicate his ideas and allow for feedback from the agent.

(4) The manager must attempt to integrate interests, i.e., he must relate the agency's purpose to the agent's needs-wants-goals complex.

(5) The manager must provide the necessary auxiliary conditions.

(6) The manager must develop teamwork, i.e., he must integrate each agent's goal seeking with the actions of other agents so that there is both a coordinated and cooperative group effort.

An illustration of the use of these six steps might be an agency manager attempting to increase the activity of the members of the sales force in the pension market. In step one, the manager clearly identifies his specific objective. Next, he tries to see the situation in terms of the agents' need-satisfactions. Some of the agents are presently very successful in estate planning and are obtaining referred leads that are providing them with an excellent clientele. They are reluctant to spend the necessary time to become familiar with pensions or to develop leads in the industrial market. The agency manager needs to empathize with his agents. Perhaps his empathizing will give the agency manager an insight into some possibilities for developing pension business through contacts made by those agents who are presently devoting most of their time to estate planning.

Communicating his ideas effectively requires great skill on the part of the manager and the successful performance of this step is probably the key to the success of the whole motivation process. There are several possible ways the manager might present his plans for expanding pension sales. He might present his ideas in a carefully planned agency meeting. Perhaps he should call upon the more active agents in the pension field to assist him in the presentation. The meeting should stress such things as the potential,

---

[14] The following discussion of the motivation process is developed from the excellent treatment of this topic by Keith Davis in *Human Relations at Work* (New York, N. Y.: McGraw-Hill, Inc., 1962), pp. 32-33.

the rewards for the agents, and the services the agency plans to make available to those interested in developing pension business. The agency manager might then hold an office conference with each agent for the purpose of learning the agent's personal reactions and feelings about the ideas presented at the meeting. The ultimate objective of the conference should be to assist the agent in defining his own markets for pensions, setting his own goals, and formulating his plan of operation with respect to these markets. The manager should arrange to publicize accomplishments within this area, plan a number of future agency meetings for the purpose of discussing the kinds of problems the agents actually encounter in selling pensions and the actions the manager and the agency might take to assist in their solution. He could then arrange for follow-up office conferences with each agent for the purpose of letting each agent evaluate his own progress toward the goal he has set for himself.

LEADERSHIP AND MOTIVATION

A motivational work environment requires the use of positive leadership rather than negative leadership. President Eisenhower succinctly expressed it this way:

"Now, look, I happen to know a little about leadership and I tell you this. You do not *lead* by hitting people over the head. Any damn fool can do that, but it's usually called 'assault'—not 'leadership' . . . I'll tell you what leadership is. It's *persuasion*—and *conciliation*—and *education*—and *patience*. It's long, slow, tough work. That's the only kind of leadership I know—or believe in—or will practice."

Positive leadership refers to the skill of the leader to motivate people by increasing their satisfaction. Such leadership gets the employees to want to do something rather than threatening them with a decrease in need satisfaction. The manager exercising positive leadership does not merely issue orders but interprets them, makes sure that his personnel have suitable skills to carry them out, and delegates authority to carry out these orders. He explains carefully why a job must be done and assigns a fair workload to each employee. Implicit in positive leadership is the manager's selection, development and trust of his personnel. The positive leader takes the viewpoint that people naturally want to do good work if given the opportunity and proper incentive.

Negative leadership, on the other hand, is accomplished by imposing on the employee a feeling of fear and insecurity through threats of decreasing satisfaction. Penalties, reprimands, threats of demotion and firing, and the like, are used to frighten the employees into productivity. This manager becomes the boss, not the leader. Generally, his viewpoint is that people need to be forced to be cooperative and productive because they do not naturally want to do so. This type of leadership may result in the employees spending more time in tasks involved with pleasing the boss's personal wishes than in the actual production within the agency. Thus, much time is spent in "covering" one's self.

Positive leadership gets additional values into an organization by adding the energies of the employees to the energy of the leader to accomplish the agency's goals. Because of this, positive leadership is more desirable and its effects are longer-lasting.

The most important quality in the success of an individual is discipline —and not discipline imposed by the agency manager, but self-discipline. "No one can ever truly be disciplined by another. We may persuade another to engage in disciplined activities, but this discipline is always self-discipline."[15] The best way to persuade another to engage in disciplined activities is for the agency manager to set the proper example.

COMMUNICATIONS AND MOTIVATION

We have emphasized throughout this chapter that motivation is the process by which the agency manager helps create and maintain the desire of his agents to achieve planned objectives. We should emphasize now the significance of communications to motivation. Communications is the means by which the manager activates the motivational process. If the manager is to play an effective part in the motivational process he must use various media of communication. To be motivational the manager must somehow reach the agent with a word, phrase, smile, pat on the back, invitation to lunch, memoranda, telephone call, personal interview, and other similar media for communicating.

Although language is not the only form of man-to-man communication, it is the most frequently used. Through the use of language, the manager transmits images from his own mind to that of the agent. The transmissions can be received as stimulating and electrifying images or they can depress and embitter the receiver. The manager need not be an orator or a spellbinder. He need be only sincerely interested in the career success of the agents. However, effective use of language can make his written and spoken communications more motivational.

Language can result in garbled communication that results in a lowering of morale and presenting obstacles to the motivational process. Many

[15] Johnson, Marietta, *Youth in a World of Men* (New York: N. Y.: John Day Company, 1929), p. 237.

examples could be cited in which a manager confidently related an idea, only to find that a key word or phrase was interpreted differently from what he expected. The reality of a message is what the receiver hears, rather than what the sender says. Furthermore, what the recipient wants to hear is affected by what motivates him at the time the communication is received.

In many agency offices, bulletins, memoranda, reports and home office communications are circulated rather frequently. Research indicates that after a period of exposure to a given communication medium, some people reject the medium and stereotype it unfavorably. In doing this, they accept or reject totally that medium rather than make specific judgments concerning individual items within it.

For example, certain employees whose employer issues a house organ may reject it entirely and not bother to analyze its contents for specific items. No matter what content management included in this house organ, it would be rejected by these employees. By limiting the number of media the employees simplify the problem of receiving information from the environment.

When communications have become routine and stereotyped, they are likely to be judged in terms of the kind of information usually conveyed. It may become almost useless for transmitting information of any other kind. The lesson to be learned by the agency manager is that any method of formal or routine communication is in need of continuous evaluation and analysis. Feedback is continuously necessary in order to determine the effect of formal communications on those to whom it is directed.

In many life insurance agencies, the Monday morning meeting may become a routine and formalized medium of communication. In most agencies, the managers take the view that the meeting will be held only if there are worthwhile topics to be discussed. However, in some agencies the meeting is held regardless of whether or not there are important topics to be discussed or pertinent information to be conveyed. Implicit is the hope that an important topic may be developed during the meeting. Unfortunately, this frequently leads to a complete rejection of the Monday morning meeting by the agents as a vehicle for conveying useful information. Thus, the agents by their lack of attendance, reject the entire contents of these meetings, regardless of the fact that occasionally important, useful information is presented.

THE MOTIVATIONAL EFFECT OF SALES CAMPAIGNS

On either a national or agency level, sales campaigns can be the agency manager's finest hour to motivate the sales force. Agents typically respond to a sales contest like deer hunters on the first day of the hunting season. Although it is true that agents defer some production in order to qualify it for the contest and they probably have some let-down after the contest closes, total production for the agency is generally greater than it would have been if there had been no contest. There are a number of important direct and indirect benefits that accrue to the agency from having well planned and properly administered sales campaigns.

Sales campaigns create an air of excitement. Even the secretaries seem to be swept along by the spirit and enthusiasm that inevitably develop during sales campaigns. In national campaigns every man in the agency should have instilled in himself the burning desire to be a national winner. These national campaigns promote a team effort, since not only are agents competing against agents, but agencies are also competing against other agencies. The desire to be a part of the team effort is contagious. The spirited competition conjures up dormant energies, stimulates latent potential and encourages the reticent. Agents are stimulated to perform above and beyond their normal pattern.

Agents' commission income may be substantially increased through a sales campaign. A well-run campaign will typically encourage greater production and therefore greater commission income for all agents for the year as compared to the production that they would have achieved if there had been no campaign.

Sales campaigns provide another incentive for the sales force in addition to the commission incentive. This second incentive is the desire for the recognition that is given for the salesman's achievement during the contest. Agents will take great pride in their contest performance. This pride exists because performance is recognized. The possibility of receiving the personal congratulations of his company president will inspire considerable extra effort. To a lesser degree, but also of importance, the recognition of his manager, his supervisor and his fellow underwriters is a source of inspiration for greater achievement.

A medium for ego satisfaction is also provided through a sales campaign. It is a source of great personal satisfaction to an agent to receive the coveted prize, award, club membership, group fishing trip, golfing weekend or other form of special treatment accorded him for his contest achievement. This ego satisfaction can have continuing effects that are beneficial for the agent's attitude and morale for some time after the contest is over.

Sales campaigns can have a favorable effect on group spirit, attitudes and morale. The beneficial effects do not necessarily accrue only to the winners. There is a friendly "camaraderie" that usually is associated with a well-run contest as the agents vie with each other in their effort to excel personally and the agents collectively try to place the agency at the top in the national rankings. This heightened morale and "esprit de corps" can be carried over to the continued activities of the agency long after the contest has ended.

A little extra pressure is added to the sales force by a sales campaign. All of us are capable of doing just a little bit better than we are doing. The sales campaign is a social device for applying the kind of gentle pressure that will bring out a little extra effort on the part of each member of the agency.

It should also be noted that sales campaigns can have a favorable effect on the agency's overall education and training program. For example, some agents will realize that they could have done better in the contest if their knowledge and skills had been just a little bit better. This realization may provide the appropriate incentive to sharpen their knowledge and skills in anticipation of the next contest.

Frequently interest is generated on the part of the agent's family in a sales campaign. The whole family may become so interested in dad's effort to win the contest that they become prospect conscious at school, church, and neighborhood gatherings. If the campaign provides a prize that is coveted by the whole family, there is all the more reason for an interest in the campaign on the part of the whole family. All of this interest is motivational and encouraging to the agent.

A sales campaign can also be helpful in eliminating off-season slumps. For example, there is a tendency for many life underwriters to produce less near the end of the summer in anticipation of a post-Labor Day campaign. Several agencies that have run campaigns immediately preceding Labor Day have been singularly successful in preventing this seasonal slump from occurring.

Sales campaigns generate business that oftentimes is not consummated until months after the campagin ends—and perhaps the prospect would never have been contacted if it had not been for the motivation of the agent wanting to make an excellent showing in the campaign.

People are given the opportunity of buying insurance who possibly would not have been contacted by the agent if it were not for the excitement of the campaign.

Sales campaigns are not endorsed unanimously by life insurance agency managers. Those agency managers who are lukewarm concerning the merits of sales campaigns point out the possibility of the several negative effects from agency sales campaigns. The sudden spurts and stops that inevitably are associated with sales campaigns are not as beneficial to an agency's overall production achievement as a uniform, well-planned, steady application of energies to the fundamental tasks that must be performed regularly throughout the year. The agency that has a rhythmical pattern to its prospecting, fact finding, interviewing, and closing interviewing will do a better overall job of selling than the agency that relies on contests to provide needed incentives. After a contest is over there is usually a decline in sales. The agents will exhaust their list of prospects during the contest and time is required to build up a new prospect list. Furthermore, prospect lists are "used up" under conditions that are not the most favorable for sales. During the contest the underwriter may not devote as careful and thorough attention to making the best presentation for each prospect. The pressure of the contest will frequently result in the underwriter conducting a hasty fact-finding interview, an inadequate analysis of needs and a poor final presentation. The emphasis on sales within the short period of time may thus encourage short-cuts which detract from the most effective selling effort.

The emphasis on making sales during the campaign may be contrary to the high ideals of the professional approach in life underwriting. Furthermore, this abandonment of adherence to the principles and practices of professionalism in life underwriting will detract from the dignified image and professional appearance that the agency is trying to project in the community.

High pressure selling oftentimes is the result of the pressure that all underwriters feel and work under during a sales contest. Business that is sold by pressure tactics frequently shows a poor persistency.

Sales campaigns may result in a large volume of easily written, but poor quality business. This poor quality business could take the form of temporary, low-cost insurance or such types of policies as the manager has found to be expensive to service.

Agency expenses per $1000 of sales may increase as a result of a campaign. The emphasis on sales volume and the pressure to excel during the campaign may result in an almost complete disregard of expenses incurred to achieve the higher volume of sales. The same volume of sales spread over a whole year would be achieved at less cost to the agency.

Sales campaigns may result in temporary abandonment of or inadequate attention to the longer-term objectives of the agency. When the whole agency is zealously geared to the immediate goal of excelling during the contest, there may be scant attention paid to recruiting manpower for future growth, education and training programs to build sales excellence for tomorrow or public relations activities that will have long-term significance for the agency.

During the period immediately preceding a campaign, most agents postpone some production that appears about ready in order to qualify the production for the contest. This "postponing" may actually take the form of reduced activity in the days before the contest starts. This natural tendency to coast in anticipation of the intensified production activity of the campaign can result in an overall reduction in annual sales.

Difficulty of Designing Equitable Campaigns

It is difficult to construct a sales campaign that will be fair to all participants. In fact, this is often mentioned as another criticism of sales campaigns. For example, how can the new agent hope to compete against the well-established million dollar producer. The following are some of the possible approaches that the agency manager might use to equalize the opportunities so that every agent will have a fair chance to win one of the prizes.

First, prizes may be awarded on a daily or weekly basis. If prizes are awarded on this basis, more interest will be maintained throughout the campaign than if all prizes are awarded at its conclusion, and more agents will have an opportunity to win a prize.

Second, a quota may be set for each agent on any or several of the following bases: number of applications, written volume, and volume of business in which the agent receives cash or a check. The quota also could be based on past performance or other specific bases might be used. This sets up a fair handicap in which the novice competes fairly with the experienced agent. The agency manager could then have each agent compete against himself. The winners would be the agents who exceeded their own quotas by the greatest percentage.

Third, a multiplicity of prizes could be offered. This technique could be utilized by setting more than one quota for each agent. The agency manager could then establish a winner for each category. The winner would be the agent who exceeded his quota for that particular category by the greatest percentage. A winner also could be designated as anyone who exceeded his own quota by some margin such as 10 or 20 percent.

The agency manager also might divide his agents into homogeneous competing groups based on factors such as years of experience, for example. Each group could have a winner or the winning group could be established as the one which exceeded its quota by the greatest percentage. The agency manager also could divide his agents according to their ability. This technique would require the establishment of teams made up of high and low producers. The winning group would be the one which exceeded its quota by the greatest percentage.

Finally, a sliding scale for scoring could be used. A sliding scale of prizes may be offered through which agents are rewarded more generously for each successful attainment above a basic quota.

SUMMARY

To sum up this discussion of motivating the sales force, it can be said that the agency manager literally cannot motivate his agents. At best he can only provide the kind of atmosphere or work environment in which it is easy for his agents to respond to their own inner motives. It is the agents' perception of goals with which the manager must work. It is the agents' needs, not the manager's, that move the agent toward the sources of satisfaction of these needs.

Indeed, the manager's main task as a motivational influence must be to perceive accurately the agent as he is and help that agent maximize the use of his own unique talents. The manager who skillfully translates for the agent the meaning and significance of the life insurance business in general and the meaning and importance of the necessary work activities underlying success in life insurance selling, specifically, can truly call himself a motivating manager of men.

To be truly successful, an agency manager must always set the proper example for his associates to emulate—and this applies to transferable sales ideas as well as to financial management. Dr. G. Hugh Russell spoke these inspirational words to an annual Million Dollar Round Table meeting, "Be careful how you live as life insurance managers and builders of men—you may be the only bible on motivation that your associates will ever read."

28

Supervision

James Gatza

"To be a leader of men, one must turn one's back on men." Oh, that life were as simple as pictured by the obscure scholar who spoke those glib words! But no, that part of the manager's day that is occupied by the process of personal supervision brings many of us our most exciting challenges and our greatest rewards. We wouldn't want to turn our backs on such a task.

COMMON NOTIONS CONCERNING SUPERVISION

Supervision has always been a bit mystifying. It is anything but easy to become really good at directing the work of others. We all know individuals who have been outstanding performers yet fail miserably as managers. The skills of the supervisor are not the same as the skills of the individuals doing the actual job. Supervision is a highly complex process. In trying to understand it, we have oversimplified it all too often. Indeed, there are three common notions of what makes an effective supervisor—each of them popular but inadequate. Let us take a look at each of these three notions— "inspiration," "perspiration," and "manipulation."

"Inspiration"—Many people feel that a supervisor is effective because he can inspire his subordinates. They feel that men cooperate with a manager because of what he is, because of his personality and strength of character. They feel that good supervisors are born and certainly not made. (They would feel that a management training program is not worthless, but

that training works by removing the obstacles so that the leader's natural abilities are turned loose.) If the ability to supervise is essentially the ability to inspire others, how then can we improve supervision within an agency? Those who see supervision in terms of personal magic and the inspiring of subordinates would answer by emphasizing the selection of managers. They are still searching for a list of character traits to serve as a checklist of the qualities of the good supervisor.

In short, some people think of the good supervisor as one who can inspire his subordinates and make them willing followers. Within the past few years the word *charisma* has sprung into popularity: it refers to the compelling, almost magical aura about the leader. Its popularity reflects once more the notion that the ability to influence others comes from the special inner qualities of the leader that inspire men.

"Perspiration"—The second popular concept of good supervision is the myth of "perspiration." The idea here is that the good supervisor knows more and can do more than his followers. In fact, that is precisely why they follow his lead. In this school of thought, initiative, dedication, drive, and industry are the hallmarks of the manager. Hard work and experience are the stepping-stones to the top. Rather than stressing management selection, those who lean toward the "perspiration" approach place their stress on job rotation and other forms of management training. To them, a person qualifies for promotion because of the positions he has held rather than because of the qualities he possesses.

"Manipulation"—The third school of thought is that of "manipulation." Its advocates believe that the important skills of the supervisor are those that have to do with dealing with others. Indeed, a manager is defined as one who gets things done through others rather than in terms of the unique functions he performs within an organization. *Human relations* is a favorite phrase of those who see supervision as the manipulation of subordinates. (In fact, they would probably resent the idea of *manipulating others* as a label for the approaches they take.) Management training is all-important in this school of thought. The training places almost exclusive emphasis upon the ability to influence others, and puts communications skills in the forefront, with participation and non-directive interviewing only slightly behind.

We have obviously exaggerated in describing these three approaches toward supervision. There is more than a smattering of truth in each of these three ways of looking at what goes on between supervisor and subordinate. Yet, as we have tried to suggest, each can be carried too far. None is a very complete picture of the supervisory relationship. Yet one of the three is often found as the central theme in a company's management selection program or in a management training course. Supervision is much too complex to be described by such simple models! We need a better picture of the supervisory relationship. This chapter is an attempt to paint such a picture.

SUPERVISION AS THE PROCESS OF INTEGRATING THE SUBORDINATE, THE SITUATION AND THE SUPERVISOR

First, supervision is a process of influencing one's subordinates. The supervision is good if the subordinate succeeds in his duties. Effective supervision, then, lies in the ability to help a subordinate achieve top performance. The effective supervisor integrates three elements—the subordinate, the situation, and himself. That is, he combines an understanding of the subordinate with an understanding of the situation and comes up with specific leadership acts that help the subordinate meet the demands of the situation.

To be an effective supervisor, an agency manager or assistant manager must be responsive. This is asking more than it might seem at first glance. We are too used to the search for "the best way"—we tend to approach supervision the same way, as a search for the best technique or the right style. Instead of this, it is being suggested that the effective supervisor has no "one best way," no time-tested techniques for instructing, coaching, or evaluating subordinates that he relies upon again and again. The ability to achieve the agency's goals through his subordinates' efforts over an extended period of time is much the same as the ability of the agency manager to keep his own behavior flexible. He must adapt to the slightest changes in the three elements—the situation, the subordinate, and himself. In his dealings with his subordinates, the effective supervisor is responsive rather than rigid; he is flexible rather than fixed in his approach to the problems of the agency. He is searching, not satisfied with today's answers.

Does this mean that the secret of supervision is to have the personality trait responsiveness? Does this mean, like the "inspiration" approach, that leaders are born not made? Quite the contrary—and the answer is the key point of this chapter. We can improve our abilities as supervisors by increasing our skills in understanding the three elements—the situation, the subordinates, and the supervisor. We can improve as supervisors by sharpening our abilities to "read" developments in each of these three areas and by deepening our skills in communicating these developments to our subordinates, and by building a varied repertoire of supervisory patterns.

To sum up our picture of effectiveness is supervision: the truly good supervisor is *adaptive*. He *devises* appropriate action (or supervisory practices) in response to three ever-changing elements: the situation, the subordinates, and himself.

This is a hopeful way to look at supervision in that one can improve as a supervisor by becoming better at gathering and interpreting information about the three elements. Let us now consider how as agency managers (or other supervisors within a life insurance agency) we can improve our ability to understand the situation, our subordinates, and ourselves.

UNDERSTANDING THE ENVIRONMENT

Success—over the long haul—in any competitive business requires success in what we might call "reading" the environment. Except for the one top man in an organization, each employee has only a portion of the total job. Except for the agency manager, each employee in an agency is concerned with only a part of the mission of the agency. Each employee sees less than the total picture of agency goals and operations. Yet the fullest measure of performance in the employee's job requires that he coordinate his efforts with the efforts of others in the agency. The agent (whose crucial activities usually take place outside of the office) can contribute more to the goals of the agency, if he is "tuned in" to the efforts of the manager, for example, in sales planning or policyholders services. In short, the jobs in a modern life insurance agency are *interdependent*—so much so that success in any one position cannot be complete unless there has been the closest coordination with the whole range of agency activities.

Because of this interdependence of jobs, each member of the agency must be fed information about anything that affects his job or is affected by it. This includes changes in the industry, the client population, the economy of the nation and of the region, and even broad developments in society itself. To do his job well, the agency member must be informed of the developments that he does not observe by himself in the normal course of his duties. The task of information-providing is the task of his supervisor. The normal top-downward flow of instructions in an organization underscores the fact that the supervisor typically has a fund of knowledge to pass on to his people. Unfortunately, all too often a supervisor pictures his role as that of merely passing instructions downward, and he fails to grasp the broader responsibility of seeing to it that his subordinates receive all the information relevant to their jobs.

In a nutshell—*the supervisor can help his subordinates to do a better job by helping them "read" the environment*. In turn, this means that the agent and his supervisor must develop procedures to keep themselves up-to-date on all of the environmental factors that have a bearing upon agency operations. Since changes in human affairs tend to be subtle and gradual, keeping well informed is no easy task!

Chapter 1 discussed the external marketing environment and suggested some of the factors that the agency manager and his supervisors should explore jointly with their subordinates. It might also be useful if we itemize some of the sources that the manager and his supervisor can use to keep watch on developments outside the agency.

Market forces and customers can be observed through the reports of agents, examining doctors, brokers, policyholders, and through the manager's participation in conventions, workshops, conferences, community affairs, charity drives, school functions, sports activities, and social affairs. General and specialized magazines, journals, and newspapers provide information not only in their articles but also in their advertising pages. Census, employment, business and other data provided by the government can be quite useful but require interpretation before they can be brought to bear upon a specific agency problem.

The activities of competitors can be watched through these channels: agent reports, analysis of customers' present policies, company surveys, social contacts with other agents, attendance at industry conferences, government publications, and study of competitive advertising.

Economic and social forces must also be monitored. Sources of data are: news and general magazines, company and government publications, newspapers, books, conferences, and general entertainment media. Interpretative studies of activities in the stock market and reports on real estate transactions can be particularly useful to an agency manager or staff member.

Several of these sources of information are currently used in many progressive agencies. Therefore, it might seem that we are belaboring the obvious in stressing the information-providing role of the supervisor. The true weight of these responsibilities, however, will become clearer shortly when we discuss the role of the subordinate and his needs.

Turning now to the internal side of the work situation, there are many factors—strong and subtle—that affect the work of subordinates. Indeed, it is probably more difficult to sense the delicate shifts of relationships within the agency. In this regard, an agency manager would be well advised to take a course in organizational behavior and to do occasional reading in what is called the *informal organization*. While we cannot possibly paint the picture with rich detail, we can sketch some of the highlights of an understanding of the informal organization.

THE AGENCY AS A SOCIAL SYSTEM

First of all, the life insurance agency should be viewed as a *social system,* a small society. This means that it contains not only members, but established relationships among these members. It also means that a change imposed on one part of the system is likely to disturb or be felt throughout the system. Seeing the relationships is as important as recognizing the members of the agency. There will be relationships of friendship, respect, and mutual interest. There will also be relationships of dislike, distrust, and competition for power. These relationships exert tremendous influence upon a person's approach to his job and the way in which he tries to blend his efforts with the efforts of others in the agency. These relationships have a great deal to do with his output, his satisfaction, and his growth over time.

An agency has a *social structure* that probably bears litle resemblance to the formal structure as depicted by the agency organization chart. Agency members form groups, large and small, stable and temporary, helpful and sometimes harmful to the agency's objectives. It is impossible to predict the way in which people will cluster into social groups. In one agency of twenty people there may be four groups of relatively equal size. In another agency of the same size there may be only two large groups and some individuals may be excluded from both groups. In addition to the number and size of the social groups, the *social structure* of the agency refers to the various *membership roles* held by agency members. There are leaders and "regulars" within groups; there are also "isolates" denied membership in any group and "deviants" who are not totally isolated but are still treated cooly because they do not accept dominant group values.

Every informal organization contains many *shared values.* Feelings, beliefs, opinions, attitudes, and perceptions become collective or group properties. So too, goals become group phenomena although individual differences still remain. To illustrate, every salesman in an agency may work hard trying to do well in a sales contest. However, the informal organization is likely to define the importance of winning. Also, the social system is likely to determine the kinds of selling procedures that are appropriate and the techniques that are "out of line" in trying to win the contest.

A social system has a built-in tendency to remain rather stable. The shared values will be preserved and protected, partly because people associate them (psychologically, at least) with the friendships and pleasant activities that led to these values. These things are all interrelated and not easily dislodged. Trying to impose a new goal or a new activity upon a group is likely to disturb the values of the group and threaten the interpersonal relationships that supported these values.

How can the agency manager or other supervisor within a life insurance agency gain insight into the informal side of the agency? It is, of course, difficult to picture the forest when standing amidst the trees. Here is a list of suggestions that can be helpful in "reading" the internal environment of the agency:

(1) Identify the number and membership of social groups
(2) Identify the group leaders
(3) Identify other persons who have a special status or role in a group
(4) Identify the non-members and determine the extent to which they are being ostracized by group members
(5) Listen for shared values—remember that the leader often voices the opinions and values of the entire group
(6) Watch for non-required activities, in particular helping and sharing
(7) Observe the non-required interactions: at lunch, coffee breaks, off the job meetings, joking, and other similar activities

It is important that the manager learn to accept the informal organization as it exists and not as he would like it to be. A particular secretary might have high social status and exert considerable influence over the agents. This might be "wrong" according to the organization chart, but the manager must accept it as social fact. He must learn to see what exists rather than what is supposed to exist. He must do this in order to *use* the informal organization—by recognizing the informal leaders, consulting them, or perhaps even supporting their leadership by giving them advance information, and using them as upward channels of communication.

Before turning to the next section, let us sum up briefly. To succeed as a supervisor, the manager must help his subordinates achieve operational success in their duties. The manager must develop skill in understanding the external and internal environment in order to keep his own behavior *responsive* to the forces that influence agency success. In addition, he must help each subordinate in "reading" the external environment and the agency social system. The essence of this task is not to pass information downward; instead it is to help the subordinate develop his own skill in seeing and interpreting the many forces that can influence his job or are influenced by it.

UNDERSTANDING THE SUBORDINATE

Insight into the position of each subordinate in the agency social system will certainly enhance the manager's ability to supervise him and help him to understand his immediate environment. But this is not enough. The manager or the supervisor should also have an appreciation of the nature of man and of his relationship with his work. Social scientists have added greatly to our knowledge of these matters in recent years. We will draw upon some recent contributions of behavioral scientists in the paragraphs that follow. It is interesting to observe that many business organizations have put these behavioral insights into operation by revamping jobs and revising supervisory practices. The results have been nothing short of remarkable—substantial increases in productivity and in personal satisfaction or morale.

What are man's basic needs? Psychologists today emphasize a *hierarchy of needs*. Needs are arranged as a ladder, with man moving from one rung to the next higher one.

At the bottom are the physiological needs—the need for food, shelter, clothing, and maintenance of a proper temperature, and the like. These needs are basic or primary in the sense that if they are not satisfied, man will give up his other activities in order to satisfy them.

In a level above the physiological needs are man's safety needs or assurance needs. This refers to the feeling that the basic physical needs will continue to be satisfied in the future. It also refers to the feeling that one's life will remain as it is without major disturbance. One's safety needs are met if he feels that his job, his home, his family, and his daily routine will go on tomorrow as they are today.

Above the assurance needs are the social needs. This phrase refers to man's desire to be with others. He wants to be part of a group. He wants to belong, to have a part in the social life of the agency and of the neighborhood. He wants a chance to communicate with others: to share his thoughts big and small. He wants to know what the people around him are thinking.

On the next higher level are the needs for recognition. This means recognition and respect from those around us. It also means self-respect and self-esteem. The previous category of social needs include belonging to a group. Man usually wants to do more than merely belong. In the category of recognition needs are man's needs to be accepted as the individual he really is. He wants to be himself, to reveal the full range of his ideas, beliefs, and wishes. Then he wants to be accepted by others for what he is. He also wants to feel good about himself. He wants to feel that he is a valuable member of society, church, agency, and neighborhood.

Finally, the highest level of needs has been called self-actualization or self-fulfillment. Not everyone reaches this highest rung from which man reaches for perfection. This does not mean absolute perfection; instead it means being the best person that one is capable of being. It means doing the best possible job, being the best possible citizen, being a good father. It means continued growth toward greater skills, greater knowledge, greater competence on the job and in life.

Why are these categories of needs arranged in a hierarchy? Why are the physical needs on the bottom, then safety, social, recognition and finally self-actualization at the top? The idea is that a person must meet most of his needs at one level before he will move up to the next level. This means that a person will not strive for recognition until he feels accepted in the social system. The all-important general pattern is that of upward movement. Most normal adults show a tendency to move upward on the ladder of needs. To verify this, observe a newly hired employee. At first he is usually preoccupied with learning the job and geting feedback so that he feels he is out of danger of losing the job. As he begins to feel more secure in the job, more and more of his time will be diverted to finding a place in the social system of the agency.

There is another significant implication in the need hierarchy. A satisfied need no longer serves to motivate behavior. If the personnel in an agency are already meeting their social needs, the manager may be wasting energies with programs aimed at building teamwork and agency spirit. Instead, the manager should be looking for ways in which the agents and other personnel can express themselves as individuals and receive personal recognition.

From time to time the manager may meet an individual who seems to be stuck at one level on the need hierarchy. The person may, for example, be a conformist whose need for acceptance is so strong that he never goes against the group's opinion or desires. There may have been more of these "stuck" individuals in generations past, but our society today offers relatively greater mobility, flexibility, and reward. Despite an occasional exception, the general pattern is that the person strives to move upward on the need hierarchy. In a very real sense, man is never satisfied—he is always trying to grow as a person.

It follows from this that the most satisfying work experiences are those that allow personal growth and achievement. The work experiences most meaningful in our lives are those in which we sense personal growth and earn recognition. Recognition here does not mean mere praise. It means earned recognition both from one's self and from others. It means recognition for achievement in a full sense: a tough and important job completed with success. The job itself must have meaning. It must be important to the success of the organization. And it must be difficult. It must have challenge and a chance of failure. Success in such tasks provides the deeply meaningful experience of achievement. Success in a progression of more and more challenging tasks provides the deeply meaningful experience of psychological growth.

Earned recognition, achievement in a difficult and meaningful task, becoming more and more competent, and growth as a person—these things have a double effect. They are both a reward and a source of motivation. No motivation is as strong as that flowing from the opportunity to develop greater total competence within the organization and thereby achieve growth as a person.

This approach is still new and hard for many people to accept. For many years the management texts have glorified specialization and stand-ardization. They have preached—and we have believed—that job descriptions should be firm and unchanging. The manager's emphasis has been directed to the process of organizing—of defining jobs, eliminating overlap between jobs, and fitting the jobs into a neat structure then called "the organization." Although no one would deny that any job changes gradually over time, attention in the past has been riveted on the impossible goal of achieving the perfect organization chart, with all conceivable tasks distrib-uted to the proper recipient and without ambiguity or overlap among job descriptions. It now looks as if we have gone too far in trying to build perfect organization structures. We have made jobs too restrictive, too con-fining. Supervisors are now finding that the performance pay-off lies not in clarifying job relationships, but in motivating people.

PROVIDING A MOTIVATIONAL WORK ENVIRONMENT

How can the agency manager make sure that his subordinates receive the greatest possible motivation in their jobs? The first step is to make the jobs *open-ended*. The manager can make the jobs flexible rather than rigid. This does not mean that the manager should throw away the organization chart and the job descriptions. It does mean that the manager should actively seek ways in which all agency personnel can push out the bound-aries of their jobs. It means that the manager should allow the job to grow as the person grows. This concept of providing opportunity for growth is as applicable to the agent and his marketing activities as it is to the office personnel and their administrative duties. For example, the young agents in their early twenties will usually sell most effectively in the young men's market with the package and simple programming approaches. As the knowledge, confidence and experience of the younger men increase, they can logically be encouraged to move into the more advanced programming areas and ultimately into business insurance and estate planning. At all times the majority of the agency sales organization has unrealized potential for future growth in terms of sales volume, more sophisticated markets or the marketing of new products in the form of pension plans or business insurance.

Providing a motivational environment also means remembering that increases in income and promotions are not the only rewards for achievement in the agency. And it means that the manager must expend his own energies in helping subordinates see the opportunities for challenge. He must point the way for them to learn more and more about life insurance, about the agency, and about themselves so that they can discover the paths toward personal growth.

Let us now sum up what we have said about the subordinate. His most important characteristic is that he seeks growth and challenge in his work. He strives to climb upward on the need hierarchy. He strives for achievement in his job and for deserved recognition. The most potent motivational force the manager can provide each person in the agency is the opportunity to achieve personal growth through growth in competence and achievement in his job. The supervisor must learn where *each* subordinate is on the need hierarchy, and see to it that he can satisfy those needs that are active at each point of time.

UNDERSTANDING ONE'S SELF

It was said earlier that effective supervision resides in applying three kinds of knowledge: knowledge about the situation, about the subordinate, and about one's self. What was said earlier about the subordinate must certainly apply to the manager or the supervisor. The manager and the supervisor are also seeking recognition, meaningful achievement, and progressive growth through their positions in the agency. They also seek challenge in their work, so much so that they may neglect some duties simply because they find greater challenge in other areas. The trick, then, is for the manager and his supervisors to be aware of their own needs for recognition and self-fulfillment, and to seek out way to obtain these satisfactions through their supervisory duties.

We learn early in life to idolize and copy the great leaders of the past. All too often the popular stories of famous men fit the "inspiration" mold (George Washington, General Douglas MacArthur) or the "perspiration" mold (Abraham Lincoln, Thomas Edison). Unfortunately, we are given the impression that each great man has a certain style, approach, or customary way about him that accounts for his success. As a result, we are accustomed to look at supervisors and leaders with the expectation that they will stay the same over time. We are led to expect that each leader succeeds because of something about him or perhaps because of something he does. In either case, we expect that something to be rather permanent —a life-long tool. This is misleading.

Our point here is that the effective supervisor is *not* constant or uniform in handling managerial problems. He does not have an approach or a technique or a style. Instead, he has many. He tailors his tactics and his own behavior to meet the needs of each situation. His skill lies not in having a well-defined approach, but in the capacity to determine the best approach for the circumstances at hand.

Clearly this also applies to the kind of relationship the manager or supervisors build with their subordinates. The successful supervisor does not try to develop one authority relationship with his juniors. On the contrary, he allows the subordinate and the situation to influence authority relationships. Sometimes he is strict, controlling, and depends heavily upon his formal authority. At other times he is friendly, informal, and permissive. He selects the amount and kind of influence to direct toward each subordinate as he works on a particular agency objective. In so doing, he draws heavily upon his skills in "reading" the environment and in understanding the subordinate. He also works hard at understanding himself and "reading" his own emotions, biases, and current needs.

Are we simply saying that the effective supervisor is *responsive?* The word *responsive* does capture the idea, but it oversimplifies the task. Most supervisors think of themselves as flexible already. (It would be pretty hard to find a supervisor who admits to being rigid.) The problem is that the typical supervisor tends to underestimate the extent to which he must interpret and respond to the forces at play in each instance. One reason is that as supervisors we are victims of the law of reward. We repeat the behavior that has previously proven to be successful. We copy the techniques and answers that have worked for us in the past. We copy yesterday's answers and apply them to today's problems. This is a very normal and efficient tendency. We could hardly cope with today's problems without making use of our past experiences.

To succeed in his managerial responsibilities, however, the agency manager frequently must go against this normal tendency to repeat the actions that have worked in the past. In reality, no two organizational problems are ever identical. Even situations that crop up often may not be as similar as we are prone to believe. Different persons may be involved, or different customers, or slightly different circumstances. If nothing else, the time that it occurs makes each problem unique. Problems may be *similar,* but never *identical.* (We overemphasize the similarities to past events. We tend not to see the slight differences. We have these natural tendencies because they normally simplify our tasks and make new situations easier to understand. This does not suggest that the agency manager should spend lavish amounts of time on unimportant routine problems. Instead, the above concept of responsiveness in supervision suggests that the manager must recognize his own tendency to see the ways in which a current problem resembles a past problem and his tendency to ignore the ways in which it departs from his previous experience.) In effect, the manager must be on his guard against his own efficiency-seeking inclinations.

ENHANCING RESPONSIVENESS

What can the agency manager do to enhance his ability to be *responsive* rather than *repetitive?* First, the manager can ask for feedback on his decisions. He can obtain some feedback through formal accounting and control procedures. He can also get feedback by soliciting reports on specific activities or projects. Informal leaders, assistant managers, and other key persons in the agency can be consulted often so that they gradually assume the responsibility of keeping the manager informed on the results of his actions.

Second, the manager can verify his perceptions even before key decisions are made. No one sees things with perfect objectivity. Our needs, values, and past experiences strongly influence our perceptions. We tend to see that which can satisfy our needs. We tend to block out signals that are unpleasant or threaten our self-image. (We will not ignore real danger signals, however.) The manager's past experiences as an agent or as a supervisor exert a profound influence upon his perception of agency activities. The manager's needs and background affect his ability to pick some signals out from the background clutter. His needs and background also provide him with the equipment (ideas, relationships, and ways of categorizing facts) used in interpreting what he sees.

Assuming that the manager's perception is no more perfect than that of the next man, how can he verify his perception on a more or less regular basis? One way is to develop his skills in conducting and participating at meetings. Keeping silent when a new topic is introduced will allow him to hear the perceptions of others before they are influenced by the manager's own views. People commonly hold their statements in check until they can find out what the boss is thinking. As a result, the manager's listening skills become more important as his prestige rises.

Routine meetings are not enough to provide a sufficient check on a manager's own perceptions. Special problem-solving sessions and "brainstorming" sessions will encourage agency members to voice their thoughts with fewer inhibitions. The new manager can also test some of his views by asking for reports and recommendations from others before taking action.

One of the best of all procedures for gaining insight into one's own perceptions is the role-playing technique. However, successful role-playing sessions require extensive preparation of materials and not all agency problems lend themselves to role-playing.

SUMMING UP: WHAT IS GOOD SUPERVISION?

We can now restate the main theme of this chapter. The effective supervisor is responsive and adaptive. Rather than having a single approach to an agency problem, he custom-tailors his behavior to meet the dictates of each specific situation and the needs of each subordinate. The foundation stone in this view is the fact that each subordinate seeks greater competence and personal growth. The effective agency manager can earn the greatest pay-off as a supervisor not by improving his order-giving technique, but by unleashing the motivation of his subordinates.

It follows from this that the manager's role centers on helping each subordinate make good his own inner drive toward greater performance. In turn, this makes information-gathering and information-providing paramount supervisory functions. The manager's ability to help each subordinate depends in part upon his ability to see each agent or other subordinate as an individual; it also depends upon his own self-awareness. The manager must gain insight into his own perceptions, preferences, and goals. He must counteract his own human tendency to repeat yesterday's answers. The greater his self-awareness, the greater his ability to "tune in" to the needs of the members of his agency as he attempts to make good his own striving for personal growth through his management job.

MANAGEMENT BY OBJECTIVES

So far we have discussed "how to be a good supervisor" in rather theoretical terms. This theory has been necessary to facilitate understanding of all that is included in the more practical suggestions that follow. Let us now apply what we have talked about by establishing concrete steps that an agency manager may take to help his agents and other agency personnel to achieve greater results. First, in summary form:

Step one: each agent establishes a set of performance targets.[1]
Step two: the manager meets with each agent to discuss the tar-

---

[1] The following discussion of management by objectives is oriented toward the supervision of agents. However, the principles set forth and the procedures recommended are equally valid and appropriate for the supervision of all personnel in the agency.

gets established in step one and to discuss also the factors bearing upon the achievement of those goals.

Step three: the agent revises his target goals as a result of the discussion recommended in step two.

Step four: after the elapse of an agreed-upon period of time, each agent evaluates his results.

Step five: the agency manager meets with each agent and jointly they explore the results achieved and the problems encountered in trying to reach the targets established in step three.

1. Establishing Performance Targets

Step one is conducted by the agent himself. He selects a program of performance targets for his sales work in the months ahead. There should be general agreement between the manager and the agent as to the most important responsibilities that must be fulfilled by the agent—prospecting, fact-finding interviews, closing interviews and the other sales related responsibilities that are so important to the achievement of ultimate sales goals. (Should this mutual understanding be missing, the manager must take time out, meet with the agent and exchange ideas until there is a meeting of the minds with respect to the responsibilities and priorities of the agent's job.)

It is vital that the agent formulate his own target goals first before there is any discussion with the manager. The targets established must be the agent's goals—not the manager's. They must be the agent's own objectives —not those suggested to him by his boss. He must be committed to the goals. He must feel that they are sensible, important, and attainable. They must represent his choices of what are essential from among dozens or even hundreds of possible objectives.

The word *targets* is the best one for these personal performance objectives. Targets should be specific; they should be precise. "To increase sales twelve percent" *is* a real target. The agent will know if he has achieved this specific goal and he will know when he has achieved it.

In drawing up a list of targets for his future efforts, the agent should exercise care to see that the list is not too long or unattainable. He should express his targets in the order of their importance. The list should include some goals that have to do with his own self-development. In fact, one of the major benefits of the target-setting approach is that it helps bring into balance the individual's efforts within the strict boundaries of his job and his efforts to acquire the knowledge and skill needed for continued growth and self-development.

The following hypothetical list of target objectives will illustrate how an agent might establish a target program for his efforts for a calendar year:

1) To increase my total sales volume by 22%
2) To increase my sales of disability income policies by 15%
3) To secure at least five clients in a new housing subdivision
4) To make "repeat" sales to at least 12% of last year's purchasers of life insurance
5) To pass Courses 3 and 4 of the C.L.U. examination program
6) To read three books in the subject areas of business finance, accounting and budgetary control

2. Supervisor Discusses Performance Targets with Agent

Step two is the meeting at which the manager discusses the preliminary performance targets with the agent. The object of this meeting is to explore all aspects of the agent's target program: obstacles, costs, advantages, resources needed, implications for other members of the agency, and the like. During this discussion the manager will be required to play the role of information-provider. The manager's function is to help the agent see all of the problems associated with the achievement of the targets he has chosen. The manager performs this function not only by providing the agent with information, but also by artful questioning to assist the agent to recognize the various problems.

As the meeting draws to a close, the agent will usually make a revised target program for his future performance that appears to be appropriate and realistic in the light of the manager's discussion with the agent. The manager must exercise extreme care to avoid any semblance of the use of his authority. The agent's final targets must be *his* targets, not the manager's. The agent must feel free to make the final choices even if they appear to run counter to the manager's own preferences and inclinations. It is not easy to preserve this freedom, since subordinates everywhere are accustomed to accepting their superior's suggestions as outright commands. *The manager must give the agent the right to make mistakes* if he is to reach his full potential.

This meeting will surely take some time. In fact, it may take a few hours or even stretch out over a period of days. The agency manager who sees this meeting as a waste of time simply is not a manager. The agency manager or supervisor who says that his other duties are more important is running away from *supervising*. To be sure, the manager bears a risk in supervising through the target-setting process as described. But if the agent is shielded from the full risk of failure, how much can he learn?

3. Agent Commits Himself to Achieve Revised Targets

Step three takes place at the conclusion of the conference. The agent makes a commitment to achieve his targets. In taking step three, the agent makes a written record of the targets he has finally selected. The written document can be highly informal—its chief purpose is to avoid misunderstanding or faulty memory later. The written list will also minimize the disruption in the event that a supervisor or assistant manager is subsequently appointed to assist the manager in the more effective performance of the supervision function. Two copies of the revised target program should be prepared—one for the agent and one for the manager.

It is helpful to specify for each target the exact means to be used in measuring results. For example, assume that the target goal has been established as a twelve percent increase in annual sales. Does this mean twelve percent of the previous year's sales or twelve percent of average sales for the last few years? The year immediately preceding the current year may have been an unusually good year or an unusually poor year. Does the target mean a twelve percent increase in life sales without distinguishing term insurance from permanent insurance? Does the target mean a twelve percent increase in life sales, including or excluding group life insurance? Does the target mean a twelve percent to be applied to overall sales including individual health insurance, group health insurance, group life insurance, group deferred annuities and deposit administration group annuities? If health insurance is to be included in the overall twelve percent increase, what conversion factor is to be used to convert health insurance premiums to $1,000 of life insurance? These and other similar questions should be resolved so that results can be measured by a meaningful yardstick. The other non-production target goals also require a means of measurement of results so that it can be determined if the agent is attaining his target goals.

4. Agent Evaluates Results

Step four takes place after an agreed-upon time period has elapsed. A year is the time period typically used in those businesses in which the seasonality pattern takes a fully year, as in department store sales. However, six months or even three months is a more appropriate time span in a life insurance agency. An advantage of the three or six months time period over the twelve months period is that it permits an earlier measurement of results and therefore makes possible necessary corrective and remedial action to bring achievement in line with target goals. Waiting twelve months before taking corrective action is too long a time period for a life insurance agent.

In completing step four, the agent does the "homework." He gathers the evidence in accordance with the procedures previously identified. He might be able to use reports and data presently available in the agency to indicate his results in achieving some targets. He might have to request that special reports be prepared to help him assess his progress toward some of his goals. Whenever possible, his targets should be expressed in quantitative terms to make the evaluation of results more precise. But some targets simply cannot be put in quantitative terms. For example, an agent might establish a goal of improving his professional relationship with a large corporate client. Even when there has been some progress with respect to this objective it may be very difficult to measure it in quantitative terms. In accordance with the prescribed procedures for management by objectives, the agent and his manager should have agreed upon a specific method of measuring progress when the target was set. In this example of the corporate client, a careful study of the target might have revealed that the opinions of two designated persons in the agency would provide the best index of accomplishment for that target. And in most instances an acceptable yardstick can be agreed upon if the matter is explored thoroughly at the time the specific target goal is established.

Not all results will be measured at the same point in time. For some targets it is merely enough to specify an arbitrarily selected date for the measurement of results, or to use existing reports. Targets other than sales goals can often be checked at some natural time point, such as a project completion, the date of a changeover to a new procedure, or after the C.L.U. examination.

5. Agent Discusses Results with Supervisor

Step five is the meeting at which the superior and subordinate talk over the results the subordinate has attained. Perhaps the best advice is this: hitting the bulls-eye is not the real test of success. Instead, the manager must look at the overall achievement of the agent. It is to be expected that he will surpass some targets and fall short of others. Indeed, should a person reach all of his targets we would be justly suspicious that he probably set only the safest possible targets.

There is a *total process* involved in every responsible job within a life insurance agency. That total process includes these interrelated steps: seeing agency needs, translating them into specific performance targets, devising actions to attain the targets, adjusting to unforeseen complications, and producing final results. The step five meeting focuses its attention on this total process. Its object is to explore and learn from all of the things that have happened between planned performance and actual results. Part of the discussion will focus on the suitability of the targets the agent selected. It will be helpful also to discuss the specific ways in which the agency as an entity facilitated the accomplishment of the agent's target goals and the specific ways the agency was deficient in providing assistance to the agent. The discussion does not stop there, however, but deals at length with the unplanned events that intervened as the agent attempted to reach his targets.

As in the step two meeting, the manager's role is to help the subordinate to learn from his own experiences. It is hardly necessary for the manager to worry about bestowing the proper praise or criticism during this meeting. The manager will probably be able to observe the subordinate's own gratification in his achievements. In addition, the meeting is focused on the results the agent attained, leaving little doubt about the presence of *earned recognition* for his efforts. Furthermore, the target-setting approach provides a framework for discussing the agent's work so that he can come to understand his failures in a manner far more meaningful than any criticism the manager could deliver.

SUMMARY AND CONCLUSIONS

Many companies have adopted target-setting management because of its power to motivate people. Many organizations have abandoned their customary performance appraisal systems as they have moved into results-oriented management that is achieved by the target-setting approach. The life insurance agency manager's appraisal of his agents and other subordinates should be much more useful if it is based on the *total process* that is the heartland of the step five meeting. The manager should have a clearer view of overall performance of his agents and other subordinates than that provided by the customary rating form.

The five basic steps are repeated again in the next time period. While it has been convenient to speak of the steps as if they were completely separated, in practice the lines between them tend to blur. The step five meeting focuses on the results just achieved, but it naturally gets into ideas useful for replanning and setting targets for the future. The information-providing function should be a continuous process, although there is still need for the concentrated attention of the target-setting discussion. So too, the assessment of the subordinate's progress will not be a once-a-year proposition but will tend to be an ongoing process. This is particularly true when the subordinate's checkpoints come at different times. However, it is still vital that there be an overall analysis of the subordinate's experience in trying to achieve the entire target program. Without this integrated size-up, the subordinate cannot chart his course for the next period.

What should the manager do when a subordinate does not show progress under the target-setting framework? Should the manager fall back on strict top-down authority and rebuild the maze of orders and instructions? It will be a very rare occurrence, yet some agents may fail to show significant progress when given the right to select their own performance goals. When this happens, three questions should be asked.

First, has the manager really given the agent the right to establish his own goals? Or has the manager somehow—perhaps unintentionally— given hints as to the targets that he as manager would like to see the subordinate establish?

Second, how well has the manager fulfilled his own responsibilities to be a helping resource to the agent in evaluating opportunities, resources, and limiting factors?

Third, if the manager has done his part well, should the agent be allowed to remain in the agency? If a person cannot succeed in an environment of self-direction, is he likely to have a prosperous career in life insurance sales? Is it worth the agency manager's time to deal with an agent who responds only to carrot-and-stick rewards? The possibility of termination takes on added significance when we recall the observation that the role of a life insurance agent is more like that of an independent businessman than that of an employee.

What are the drawbacks in supervising through agent target-setting? Managers considering its adoption often raise three criticisms. The first is that "it takes too much time." Yet managers who have actually used the target-setting framework report that they consider no other use of their time as productive as the time they spend helping their subordinates plan future achievement. They typically report the opinion that goals—and results—are higher than they would otherwise be. In addition, there are added bonuses of strengthened communication, greater understanding, and teamwork. Despite these advanatges, it cannot be denied that the target-setting and evaluation meetings take a considerable amount of time, especially in the first attempt. However, less time will be required for the five steps in succeeding cycles.

A second reaction to results-oriented supervision follows this line: "It might work in some places, but it won't work here. Some of our people will never do more than they absolutely have to." A close look reveals the fallacy in this argument. Recalling individuals who have thus far responded only to managerial force hardly disproves the theory because these individuals have been in situations wherein the dominant—if not the exclusive—method of motivation was authoritarian. Their failure to show commitment to agency goals in the past does not mean that they will not commit themselves toward self-set targets in the future, and it surely does not mean that they will not establish personal goals that will help the overall agency realize its potential.

A third reaction to target-setting supervision is this: "It's too theoretical. I want practical answers." For some, the only "practical" ideas are narrow, concrete answers to visible operating problems. They prefer a step-by-step recipe telling them what to do rather than a broader framework to help them find their own answers. Target-setting is just that—a broad framework for supervising the work of agents and other subordinates. Its practicality lies in its ability to serve the one continuing goal of supervision: the best possible performance from the persons being supervised.

We have discussed the target-setting procedure because many organizations have found it the most helpful structure or framework of supervision. It helps the agency achieve its collective objective because it assists the manager in helping each subordinate make good his own inner drive for competence and growth. Thus the target-setting approach has been suggested to show how the agency manager might apply the theoretical model presented earlier. By a skillful and continuous reading of the environment, the subordinate, and himself, the manager appropriately adapts his behavior in the five step management-by-objectives process to help each subordinate achieve success in his duties and growth in his skills.

29

Retaining Manpower
for Agency Growth

Bernard S. Rosen

The man has been found, selected, recruited and basic-trained. He has been associated with his agency selling life insurance on at least an acceptable level of performance for six months, or a year, or three years, or longer. Now the key job of his agency is to make certain this man will prefer to remain permanently in life insurance.

Preceding chapters have emphasized the interrelationship of recruiting, selection, training, supervision, public relations, and motivation to the sales success of agents and thus their interrelationship to retention of agency manpower. This interrelationship is exemplified in many ways. For example, meaningful selection of agents is possible only if a substantial number of new men are found each year who indicate an interest in life insurance selling. Effective training is possible only if the new agents selected have an aptitude for life insurance selling and have an inner drive to succeed. Supervision produces optimum results only if the supervisor has a group of carefully selected agents who are adequately trained and properly motivated to want to succeed in the life insurance business. All of these utopian circumstances are seldom realized in even the best agencies. Moreover, even in the best agencies an agent may terminate his contract for reasons that are only vaguely related to selection, training, and supervision.

The purpose of this chapter is to discuss some of the factors that an agency manager should consider in his attempt to improve retention of manpower in his agency. It is recognized that in many instances the manager may be unable to eliminate or ameliorate the factors that are unfavorably affecting manpower retention. Furthermore, in some instances terminations are not only wholesome for the agency but perhaps should be expedited so that a healthy organization can be preserved and developed into a productive entity.

Let's consider some of the reasons that an agent might terminate his contract with his agency. In doing so, it is essential to understand the problems, disquietudes, fears, and frustrations that beset a man during his early years in life insurance. And let us note that these problems and frustrations are not confined to men in just their early years. Some of the reasons an agent may not be fully committed to the life insurance business or to his agency are:

1. Worry about the adequacy and regularity of his income.
2. Desire for more status than "life insurance agent."
3. Frustration because he uses time ineffectively.
4. A nagging dissatisfaction with the agency management.
5. Loss of challenge, staleness, demoralization.
6. Various personal problems.

These are by no means a complete catalogue of reasons and they are not mutually exclusive. But they will serve two purposes. First, they do represent some of the major reasons why men leave agencies; therefore, a discussion of each will indicate some ways to help men want to stay. Second, they will provide a format for analyzing how an agency might go about the job of retention.

WORRIES ABOUT INCOME

In most cases the man who enters the life insurance business has worked as an employee on a salary basis. When he starts his life insurance career he is told that he has changed to a commission-type compensation, exchanging the regularity of salary for the opportunity to build his own business and to earn a larger income eventually. But he doesn't really comprehend what that means. In the very early months as a new agent, he doesn't readily see the difference in compensation method. He still has a relatively regular income made available through salary plans or advanced loan accounts.

Sooner or later, however, the agent finds that his income depends entirely on his commissions. At that point, if he is like most agents, concern about his income heightens. The very nature of commission income leads to variableness of paychecks and a difficult budgeting problem for the family.

In addition, in his early years in life insurance selling, even the ultimately successful agent will frequently have a very real income problem. But the new agent should recognize that almost every successful sole proprietor who is building a future equity in his business also has a problem of realizing adequate cash income during his early years. Building for the future means deferring present take-home monies so that future income will be greater. In a sense the life insurance agent is retaining earnings in his sole proprietorship. He is plowing back retained earnings in the form of deferred income. How important it is that both the agent and his family understand that he is building a new business, a new sole proprietorship! And that they comprehend the financial concept of this new sole proprietorship. Retained earnings mean larger and more dependable income in the later years.

The agency manager should make certain that both the new agent and the agent's wife understand this financial arrangement and realize that it is similar to most sole proprietorship financing but is not typical of most sales work. The manager might explain it in the following words:

"Mr. Prospective Agent, when you become a life insurance agent you create a new business entity, a sales sole proprietorship. If you were starting a business in most other product lines, you would need to invest some capital, either from monies you had accumulated previously or that you would now borrow. Another way you might invest in your business in its early years would be to take as little income out as possible for yourself and family; the difference between what you take as income and what you might have received working elsewhere as someone's employee is also your investment in your business. Therefore, low take-home pay in the inception years is not necessarily a sign of not doing well. It must be looked at in relationship to another measure of the financial results which you as a businessman have achieved during the same period of time. That is the growth in the value of your business. In life insurance this is represented by the dollar value of your renewal account.

"To understand this point, let's use the example of a young doctor who starts in private practice on January 1st of the current year. He too is starting a new sole proprietorship. Assume in his first calendar year the doctor provided professional services for patients and bills them in the amount of $15,000. Also, let's assume that by December 31st of that same first year, he has received remittances of $9,000 and that of the balance, he will collect $4,500 sometime during the following year and that $1,500 will prove uncollectable. The question to be asked and understood is: how much did the doctor proprietorship earn its first calendar year? $9,000? $15,000? Some other figure? Can you see that although $9,000 was his cash flow in his first year, the doctor's complete result for that year's work must include the $4,500 of collectibles he also created. So the financial result of the new doctor business entity in its first year was $13,500.

"Let's now relate this concept to you as an insurance agent. Assume that, like the doctor, you start your career January 1st of the current year, too. The policies you write by December 31st will provide some commission earnings in hand during that year, but the majority of the earnings from the year's work are going to come to you in subsequent years. It is what you receive that year plus what you can reasonably expect to receive in the future from the deferred commissions on the year's policies that represent your financial result for the year's work."

Reminding the agent of the above explanation at reasonable intervals during his early years can be most reassuring to him. Helping him judge the eventual profit accruing to himself from a particular year's production enables the agent to accept the slow build up of take home pay, which is a major worry, even despair, of most men in their first few years.

Income of Others Exaggerated

Compounding the agent's concern about slow growth of current income is his unrealistic view of what others around him earn, not only in the insurance business but in all other occupations, too. Many agency managers contribute to this disquietude. During recruiting interviews, and later in agency meetings, they place too much stress on the sales records of a few outstanding agents and their high income, making it sound as though that were the norm. When the new man cannot match such results, and in most cases he will never be able to even as a veteran, seeds of "am I in the wrong business or wrong agency" are planted. An agency manager can help avoid the needless resulting turnover by realistic discussions of average and medium incomes in the agency, the industry in general, and the cross section of incomes of all Americans. From the broad view the earnings of most agents may not always look glamorous, but will more than hold their own. And the average agent will be saved from much disillusionment as time goes on.

The agency manager can use many sources to find information about what Americans earn. Two good ones are Census Bureau figures and Chamber of Commerce studies. For example, Census Bureau figures of 1970 (the latest available at the time of the writing of this chapter) show that more than half of all families have before-tax money incomes of under $9,000. The statistics also indicate that only 2% of American families have before-tax incomes of $25,000. These figures are of family unit incomes and include the wife's income, too, if she works. The same kind of statistics for any locality can be found from local Chamber of Commerce studies. Except for a few unusual income areas, statistics indicate that incomes are suprisingly uniform throughout the United States.

An agent looking at his own results against a background of such information can and should regard his financial progress with more equanimity. It's the agency manager's responsibility to help him do so.

DESIRE FOR MORE STATUS THAN LIFE INSURANCE AGENT

From time to time, the agent is painfully aware that there remains a bit of a stigma attached to his occupation. Lists of job preferences by college graduates place "life insurance agent" low. The general public still doesn't attach much importance or status to life insurance sales work, though the old clichéd images are slowly disappearing. Families of new agents often gulp a little when they reply "life insurance man" to query about what a son or husband does. The agent himself in a social gathering frequently senses a freeze in the attitude of newly introduced persons or a supercilious comment when they learn he is an insurance agent. The numerous rejections the agent experiences each week in the sales process further humiliate and shake the confidence of even the hardiest agents.

Also in some cases the agent is bothered by the ambiguity of the role he feels is his within his agency and company. It takes the form of questioning what is his place and importance. Is there a hierarchy from the home office on down and is he low man on the totem pole?

It is no wonder that the status problem can become a nagging dissatisfaction. If this problem is not dealt with, the agent may leave the industry. Or he may leave his agency to seek a "titled" job of supervisor, or general agent, although the agent is neither desirous of nor does he possess the aptitudes for those duties.

Status of the Agent in the Marketing Process

What can the agency management do to bolster the agent in the difficult and nebulous area of status? Properly identifying to the agent his role in the life insurance industry is a good place to start. The earlier this is done, the better it will be for the new agent. As an example, the agency manager might use the following approach:

"The agent is the retailer of the life insurance product. The general agency (or branch office) can be compared to the wholesaler or distributor. The home office of the company is the factory which manufactures the product. It's not unlike the distribution system for practically all goods sold in this country. The fact that the agent handles only one factory's products doesn't alter the concept.

"In industries other than life insurance, the retailer has a different function from the wholesaler or the manufacturer, but is on an equal plane in importance in the business world. It would not be a promotion nor demotion as such for a retailer to give up retailing to become a wholesaler or to move to a job at the manufacturing plant. He merely has changed his place in the distribution system. Nor is it a promotion or demotion when the man in the sales department of the factory leaves to start or take over a business at the wholesale or retail level. The same reasoning applies to the agent, general agent or manager, or home office agency department. If a man changes from one to the other of the marketing functions, he is not moving up or down but merely to a new area of operation in the distribution of the life insurance products. Depending on the talents the man brings to the new area, the move can be profitable or costly to him."

The agency manager who describes the retailer-sole-proprietor concept, or in some other way defines the position of agent, helps the agent to understand the importance of the agent's role.

Prestige and Status Through Competence

What else can be done to help the agent with his status problem? Perhaps most important is making sure the agent develops superior competence in selling life insurance and serving his clients. The agent who does fine work and can communicate that fact to his customers is well on his way to status in their eyes and in his own. The agency, therefore, should provide a consistent continuing education and training program as part of its service to its associates. In particular, the agent should be encouraged to earn the C.L.U. designation at the earliest possible time because attainment of the C.L.U. designation provides, among other advantages, a status symbol for its holder. The man who is a C.L.U. or who is well on his way to achieving the C.L.U. designation rarely is a drop-out statistic for the life insurance business.

Prestige and Status Through Participation in Professional and Community Activities

There are many other ways the agency manager can provide leadership in assisting the agent to achieve personal security and personal status in life insurance work. For example, the agency manager can help the new agent to find opportunities to make talks, write articles, hold office in industry associations, and participate in meaningful community activities. Also, the agency manager can build the agent's morale and confidence by informing the agent's family, clients, and public about his significant and newsworthy achievements by means of news releases, advertisements, mailings and just plain personal comments when appropriate.

Prestige and Status Through Intraoffice Public Relations Management

From time to time the agency manager should examine long established routines in his office to determine whether they raise or lower agent prestige. For example:

1. Does agent stationery highlight the agent's name rather than the general agent's or manager's name? The agent would certainly feel more important in his many letter-writing contacts with his prospects and policy-owners if his name is the one stressed in the letterhead.
2. The terminology regarding relationships between general agent or manager and his agent associates should be reexamined. Patronizing comments about "my boys" should no doubt be eliminated once and for all from the manager's vocabulary.
3. What is the agency's policy regarding loans to agents? Lending money to an agent beyond the rookie stage lowers his self-image as a businessman, and should perhaps be replaced by assisting him to set up banking connections, as would any business owner.
4. How does the agency apportion its space? Is the agency office designed and square footage allotted in such a way as to play up the important status of agent?

Prestige in Marketing a Respected Product

Finally, a person feels important being associated with an industry or product of real economic and social significance. The agent must never be allowed to forget the remarkable value of his product to the financial security of the public. Through clippings from newspapers, articles in trade journals, case histories from the files of agency and company, and stories from any source, the agent should be reminded frequently how life insurance constantly is at work in the community safeguarding families and businesses. He should be made to understand the tremendous importance of the function performed by the life insurance agent in teaching people their financial responsibilities and persuading people to take the necessary action commensurate with those responsibilities.

The agency manager might well consider delegating to someone on his staff the responsibility for keeping up a steady flow of examples of life insurance-at-work. How much greater would be the agent's stamina then to withstand the occasional blows that strike at his feelings of status!

FRUSTRATION BECAUSE HE USES TIME INEFFECTIVELY

The lack of a set time schedule bedevils many people, but it is a particularly thorny problem for the life insurance man. Not only does the lack of an established time schedule lead to ineffectual use of time, it frequently becomes a rationale for not doing that which the agent fears or dislikes to do.

Most men have grown up with the "early to bed, early to rise" philosophy that is sparked by the regularity of their school years and the usual 9 to 5 job pattern of this country. The need for night work, much of it in the early years of the agent, causes a major fracture in the pattern of work hours to which he has been accustomed and which is being followed by his friends and neighbors. Feelings of discontent on the part of the man (and his wife too) can result when the new agent changes from the normal 9 to 5 routine to the pattern required of the life insurance agent in his first year. The agency should deal with this problem before it becomes a source of dissatisfaction.

Helping the agent understand what creates this dissatisfaction may help in dispelling it. He should be told in advance that at times he will feel resentment at working when others are not, accompanied by guilt feelings at not working when others are. Many agents tend to "work" many more hours than they need to, taking frequent coffee breaks with fellow agents, staying in the office more than necessary. This "hanging around" the office gives the agent the feeling that he is following a 9 to 5 routine and creates an alibi of working too many hours already so he needn't make any new appointments. Even though he knows the key to use of his time should be in seeing people, psychologically he may wish to avoid the rejection that seeing people creates and so makes busy work. The agency has to teach that it is not the number of hours worked, but the number of effective interviews that determines the success of the agent's work week.

The Fallacy of "No Night Work"

The fiction perpetuated by the industry itself, that a man can quickly outgrow all night work should be contradicted early in a man's career. Resentment at the industry will grow if the agent must discover for himself that it is not that easy, that a portion of his clientele will prefer to see him evenings, and that most successful life insurance men always work some evenings. The number of night appointments may become less as a man becomes a more mature salesman, but they seldom cease.

Importance of Time Control

As an accepted fact, a man can learn to cope with the pattern of work hours that is different from that followed by most people. It is up to the agency to help him arrive at a positive concept towards the required type of time scheduling. Part of early training should be the "how to" of organizing one's time, how to fill some of his daytime hours with effective appointments and how to use constructively some daytime hours away from work during the week with his family, if he is working most evenings.

A positive attitude toward irregular hours can be taught! The new agent can plan to attend his children's school programs, can play with a pre-school son at hours other than the evening when all members of the family are usually tired from the stresses of a full day. He can take the infant daughter to the park or the zoo in the sunlit hours. When he is a little more established in his career, he can go skiing on a weekday without guilt feelings or to the seashore or play golf when slopes and beaches and greens are uncrowded. And the insurance agent who plans family and pleasure time carefully will find he has more family life on a more exhilarating basis than 9 to 5 workers. Properly understood and properly implemented, time scheduling of both work and leisure becomes a bonus of job satisfaction for both the agent and his wife.

But time scheduling must be taught and re-taught. To enjoy his time off, the agent must feel his hours worked are utilized constructively. LIAMA studies indicate that the agent believes he has too little supervision, starting from the time he is just a few months along and that supervision progressively decreases as he is further along in his career. It is supervision of his effective use of time about which, among other things, he tacitly complains.

Hugh Bell in his *Book of Management Methods* wrote: "The most important and possibly the only really essential duty of the manager is to see to it that his men work! Do I startle you with a statement which you immediately believe to be an oversimplification? I confess that when I wrote that sentence, I, myself was startled. Could it be that all the complex procedures said to be involved in effective management can be reduced to a statement so primary, fundamental, and simple that even a child can understand it? Despite the risk of oversimplification, the more I reflected upon the statement, the more I became convinced that if we do not have in it the whole truth about the job of management, at least we have a good starting point."

If LIAMA and Hugh Bell are correct to any degree, then the agency manager can reduce the anxieties of the agent by frequently checking his use of time, his number of calls, and his ratios of effectiveness on those calls. But it must be done constructively, with imaginative suggestions as to how he might keep up his number of appointments, and how specifically he might increase his effectiveness. Discussions of training and supervisory techniques to accomplish these results are presented in the chapters devoted to those topics. Here the point to be made is that teaching the agent to understand, utilize intelligently, and live with a positive attitude toward the unusual hours of a life insurance man will help prevent his loss to the agency.

DISSATISFACTION WITH THE AGENCY MANAGEMENT

Stresses develop in every human relationship. There will be many times when the agent, for valid reason or not, will have grievances arising out of the agent's relationship with his manager. Even apparently minor grievances can, in fact, be like an iceberg with a large submerged section concealing potential danger. The agency manager needs to be constantly alert to these possible irritations because they can quickly destroy the morale of an associate group and lead to manpower loss.

Some of the irritations commonly voiced by the agent are, in brief form:

> 1. "The manager didn't tell me all the facts when he recruited me. He was extravagant in his claims about how much training I would receive, how quickly I could earn large commissions, and how relatively easy it would be to see prospective buyers if only I would follow his agency's instructions to the letter. He didn't tell me clearly enough the negatives and now I'm a bit disillusioned."
>
> 2. "There is no place in our agency to go for help on the advanced underwriting type case. The agency manager doesn't know any more about funding a stock retirement plan than I do. He hasn't kept up or increased his knowledge in years and has no one assisting him who can help in this area."
>
> 3. "Management is too busy with new manpower. A disproportionate amount of time, effort, and money is spent on new recruits, and most new men don't last anyway. The agency would be better off putting that work and money into helping me and the other agents already here, so that we can do better."
>
> 4. "There is too much attention and favoritism shown to just one or two large producers."
>
> 5. If the agency accepts brokerage business—"The broker seems to get faster and more attentive service than does the agent. The

agency manager or administrative staff drops everything to take care of the broker's questions. I have to wait my turn."

6. "I'm fed up with mandatory weekly agency meetings. They are uncreative. Frequently they are just harangues."

7. "The agency has too low standards. It allows the most marginal sort of producer to hang on forever. Management hasn't the guts to terminate anyone."

8. "The agency is unfair in how it dispenses its available money for services among the agents. For example, there is a different private deal with a favored few regarding secretarial help."

9. "The agency over-uses contests. We're no sooner through with one before we are involved in another. Most are childish, and really are just a substitute for more meaningful training and new sales ideas."

10. "When I was recruited I was told I would be building my own business. That implied some dignity and privacy. Yet the agency maintains a prominently displayed production board listing everyone's results day by day."

Many more could be added, of course. Frequently the comments are somewhat unfair. The agent, like everyone else, will tend to blame his dissatisfactions with himself and his progress on someone else, and the agency manager is a handy target. But fair or not fair, potential problems are there and must be kept from being magnified all out of proportion.

Communications Breakdown as a Cause of Agent's Dissatisfactions

It is of paramount importance that the agency head be acutely aware of any specific dissatisfaction and the extent to which it is bothering the agent involved. Frequently, strong negative feelings are expressed around the office and the agency manager is unaware of their magnitude or is deaf to their meaning. When that happens it is clear that communications between agent and his manager have broken down. Perhaps as a starting point, it would be best to understand why that happens and what might be done to prevent it.

Two major reasons for breakdown of communications seem to lead the list: first, the atmosphere in the agency does not make it conducive for an agent to express his grumblings directly to the agency manager; and second, the agency manager may not be skilled in listening.

When the agent uses roundabout methods for airing his gripes he is indicating that it is not accepted procedure in that agency to report grievances directly to the specific person involved. The agency manager himself must provide the leadership that inspires open and frank discussions between the people involved. He must be willing to hear complaints about himself and the management of the agency with an open mind and be willing to understand the complaints from the agent's point-of-view. An aggrieved air or the suggestion of resentment on his part will shut off a necessary safety valve. This direct confrontation should also exist when the agency manager must air a complaint he has with an agent. By stating it specifically to the man involved rather than griping about him to others in the office, management teaches the accepted way to handle such problems by example.

The Importance of Listening

Once it is understood that it is acceptable and correct procedure to express dissatisfactions directly and the agent does come to the manager with his complaints, the agency manager must listen, listen, listen! Listening is a most important element in inter-personal communication. It is a skill, like any other skill. It must be learned and constantly practiced with "correct form," like a golf swing.

Listening is a difficult skill for the typical life insurance agency manager to master. Criticism of what is going on in the agency is criticism of the agency manager himself. Therefore, so very often, after hearing just the first few sentences of an agent's complaint, the manager half-tunes out the speaker and begins thinking up rebuttals. Thus, he misses hearing clearly what is said subsequently. Furthermore, he may view his job as manager of the agency as one of telling people, not listening to them. He may subconsciously feel that the act of listening indicates weakness and endangers his role.

There are many excellent books and journal articles about listening. The following summarize the important ideas that are contained in the literature relative to listening:

> 1. *Be aware of the need* to listen more intently; that is the starting point in improved communication.
> 2. Listen longer before building up defenses against the complaint. Assume that what is being said is worth listening to, all the way through.
> 3. Focus on the person speaking; this is not merely courtesy but, more important, it tells him that you consider him worth listening to.
> 4. Give the speaker feedback. Repeat what he has said to make sure the meaning is being understood correctly; ask intelligent questions that are to the point.

These points may sound obvious and easy, but to master them requires hard work and considerable practice.

With better listening habits, the agency manager gives the agent a chance to ventilate fully. A person who has been able to have a full hearing on his complaint will tend to moderate his attitude. He is flattered when listened to intently. With his ego assuaged, he feels more warmth toward the agency manager. Most important of all, where the manager listens in depth, asking questions to the point, repeating what is said in a way to make sure total understanding is occurring, he begins to put himself in the other person's shoes, seeing the problem from the agent's point of view. In other words, the manager begins to empathize with the agent.

An agency manager might do well to save his rebuttals to use when he is alone and can think the problem through. This is a time when he must judge whether or not some of the typical agent's grumblings like those described above may be caused by errors or omissions on the part of the agency. If so, the manager should be willing to admit and correct mistakes.

Enlightened Management as Preventive Medicine

Part of this self-analysis should include means to prevent future problems. There is an old doctor's adage that "preventive medicine is a more noble art than curative medicine." Certainly the principle applies to management in an agency too. Such a preventive program would include the following ideas:

1. Management should formulate all general policies and procedures, especially regarding services and facilities that agents feel important to their status in the agency. This information should be stated clearly and restated at frequent intervals. The agency's policy with respect to allocation of secretarial help and amount and type of office space should be in writing for all to see and understand.

2. Management should go beyond a mere statement of the agency's policies by explaining why various decisions are made. For example, at times the agency's activities and goals in recruiting can be distasteful to some of the present members of the agency. Yet an early explanation can help the members of the agency understand and even sympathize when the agency manager occasionally becomes preoccupied with recruiting. One way of explaining the need for constant recruiting might be to show the similarity between the agent's need to prospect for new clients with the agency's need to add new manpower. The agent who does not consistently find new policyholders will someday wake up to the fact that his clientele, production, and financial results have shrunk because of move-aways, deaths and disabilities, and static client situations. Similarly the agency that does not add new men will find its new life sales declining.

3. Management should allow the agent to participate in many of the agency decisions that particularly affect him. On occasions the manager should invite the agents' counsel. There are some natural

spheres of agent participation. These would include plans and preparations for contests and incentives, agency social functions, agendas of most agency meetings and advanced underwriting programs. And there are many other areas for agent help and advice. Skilled management takes time to think through the possibilities for agent involvement in management decisions, knowing that agency programs in which the agent has a personal involvement in advance will be more acceptable and successful.

4. Management should be loud and clear in its expressions of appreciation to the agent. The words "thank you" are hard to overuse. Taking a person for granted, in work situations as in family situations will surely create future tensions. Everyone wants to be appreciated. An agent, performing adequately to justify retention, is worthy of a genuine expression of approval and thanks, and frequently.

These preventive measures will not totally eliminate agent dissatisfaction with management. However, they will help to minimize grievances. Then by maintaining a continuous awareness of complaints as they arise, the agency manager will keep to a minimum the level of general malaise and the danger of losing personnel.

LOSS OF CHALLENGE, STALENESS, DEMORALIZATION

The 7-year itch is not confined only to marriage. It frequently creates trouble in the relationship of the agent to his job. Any man with the capacity of feeling and thought necessary in a creative sales person is capable of being torn asunder in a search for meaning in his life. He sometimes feels that his daily work is a merry-go-round and senseless. He becomes confused as what he wants or who he is. He feels stale, anxious. An agent who is a year or two along in the life insurance business may have these feelings but they are more likely to strike at the man who has more tenure and who seems on the surface to be approaching success and permanency.

The symptoms are apparent to the perceptive agency manager. The agent begins making fewer calls. In particular, he sees few, if any, new prospects. His number of sales decreases even if his volume remains level for a while; a sameness of type of sale pervades his activity. He refuses to expend the energy and time necessary to study new areas and will not expose himself to a situation where he may lose face. When he misses a sale or suffers a lapse it becomes overly important and he finds something or somebody else to blame. He gripes about personalities, about his company, about people in general. He complains but he offers no solutions and will involve himself in very little that is constructive.

Since he is not forging ahead in sales and achieving what he defines as success the agent begins to believe he is a failure. He does not recognize the fact that success or failure is relative. In his anxiety, the grass looks greener everywhere else. He begins to ogle supervisor or home office jobs. He thinks very seriously about leaving the agency or the business itself in the hope that a different job will bring this elusive success he is searching for.

The agency can help this man, but not by a slap on the back or a resounding pep talk. A renewal of positive attitude and activity requires work and patience on the part of management. The agent's strong qualities must be pointed out to him clearly, but without magnification, and he should be reminded of where his successes have been and how he might measure his results.

Too often, the agent has worked himself into a frenzy, evaluating his results on a "black or white" basis. The agency manager must understand this very common ailment, the "black or white syndrome," if he is to help the agent combat it. It is best understood by reference to the customary Hollywood delineation of the good guy and the bad guy. The hero is all-good and wears a white hat. The villain is all-bad and wears a black hat. Everything is very simple. If something is not absolutely right, then it is absolutely wrong. There is no in-between.

In the distraught agent's mind, if he has not achieved absolute success he suspects he is an absolute failure. He sets idealistic goals for himself—goals that are quite vague and difficult to achieve, but nonetheless highly valued by him. He wants to earn a "great deal of money," but will not be pinned down to how much is enough. He wants "status," but cannot determine what will give him "status." He wants "happiness," but cannot define the word; he wants a "full life," but is not sure what this means. All he is sure about is that he has not succeeded in the feeling that he has attained any of his "goals" and therefore he must be failing. What he is anxiously pursuing is absolute success. And even though he does achieve a series of relative successes, all that anyone can expect, it is not enough. Thinking in absolutistic terms, he cannot view it as success and so in the midst of relative abundance he suffers the agonies of famine.

What can the agency head do to help?

> 1. A discussion of how the "black or white syndrome" makes people unrealistic may help the agent to understand the problem. If so, perhaps he can be made to realize that the difference between success and failure is closer to the difference between 51%–49% than 100%–0%, that most of life is lived by batting averages, not by perfect scores.

2. Management can urge the agent to choose goals that are reasonable, attainable, and definite.

3. Helping the agent measure his progress against these attainable goals on a frequent and regular basis will make it clear to the agent whether he is making progress or not. When he sees he is making progress he becomes less a target for demoralization.

4. To help the agent focus on his goal, management might find an incentive useful at this particular time. It will help definitize the specific goal so that success or failure can be clearly seen. The reward need not be costly, but should be immediate upon achievement. And it has the additional value of making the agent aware of the manager's personal attention to him, with its warming and salubrious effects.

To bring an agent out of feelings of staleness, a new sales idea, or a new way to present an old idea, is always good medicine. But just the presenting of the idea by the agency manager to the agent is not sufficient; he must be won over to a willingness to try it out. He will not try it unless he feels he can present it skillfully. Therefore good management technique requires more than merely teaching the agent the application of the idea; the agent must be drilled in exactly what to say to present the idea skillfully. The agency manager should remember how many repetitions are required before a new man gains confidence in his skill with a sales track or even a small part of a sales track. The established agent, to add to his repertoire, requires many drill repetitions, too. Only then will he feel comfortable and secure enough to utilize the new material.

Management should work with this agent to determine exactly where he will use the sales idea. A discussion of specific prospects, a schedule of when the agent will see the prospects, and a date for an evaluation of results are all required follow-through procedures by the agency leadership. Anything less brings poor results and the agent suffers another failure with its enervating consequences.

VARIOUS PERSONAL PROBLEMS

The agency manager finds many of his agent's personal problems landing on his desk. Marital problems, drinking, mental illness, complicated financial difficulties,—these and other similar problems can bring innumerable headaches for management. Loss of the agent to the agency could result and so the manager finds his interests involved, whether he likes it or not.

A chapter like this cannot give adequate advice on how to handle specific situations. All that can be attempted are a few words of caution:

1. Management's involvement should remain business oriented. The temptation to become adviser or go-between husband and wife, father and son, patient and doctor, must be resisted. It would be a rare case where the agency manager can really help. In the first place no one without specific training in the particular area of difficulty can really solve someone else's problems, and perhaps not even then. Second, only a person who is truly objective can give valid assistance in the efforts of the people attempting solution of personal problems. The agency head is poorly situated to maintain objectivity.

2. Management should recommend immediate professional help such as a minister, social worker, psychiatrist, child welfare clinic, marriage counselor, or someone, perhaps a banker, who can act as a financial adviser. The agent may resist the idea; like most people in trouble he may refuse to recognize the severity of the problem. If so, the agency manager, with patience and compassion, should nonetheless persist in recommending that help be obtained at once. When a man is forced to face a situation through a thorough discussion about it, his alternatives tend to become clearer to him.

3. The agency head must avoid becoming emotionally embroiled in the personal problem of any one agent. It serves no useful purpose and merely debilitates him. Management needs to conserve energies for all the other vital agency tasks. When one man receives a surfeit of agency time, other agents are short-changed. The agent in trouble, furthermore, is so much better off with objective professional care.

4. The manager must keep his composure when faced with an agent's problem of severe proportions; his job is to prevent the agent in trouble from demoralizing the other agents. In particular, care must be taken to keep the agent in trouble from crying on everyone's shoulder.

Despite all that good management may do, there are times when a man will leave the agency or the business. When an established man leaves, regardless of the reason, the agency's equilibrium will be shaken. This is another basic reason for the agency head having to remain objective when confronted with an agent's problem. Management's key job at such a time is to calm the rest of the agents and help them remain on the track to their desired goals. Otherwise there is a danger that an epidemic of uneasiness could result in the needless loss of another agent.

IMPROVING RETENTION THROUGH MANAGEMENT PLANNING SESSIONS

We have examined, in some depth, six of the reasons why men leave life insurance agencies. In looking at each reason carefully, it is apparent that management should have been able to anticipate and prevent some of the difficulties with its agents, but in other instances management could deal with the problems only as they arose. Is it possible that in most agencies more can be done on a preventive basis, thus eliminating some of the crises? What kind of planning might be done in an area of management as nebulous as "retention?" Certainly retention as a part of management's job overlaps recruiting, selection, training, motivation, and supervision. But are there some planning activities not normally considered by management that will improve retention?

One activity can be particularly valuable. It requires a form of planning that provides for each man's needs as an individual within the agency. This is implemented through a regular management planning session that is held not less than once a month and that is devoted to thinking about each person presently associated with the agency. The agency manager, together with his management assistants (including the "cashier" or office manager), should hold this meeting some place away from the office where there are no distractions and no disquieting time limitations. There must be a leisurely enough time schedule so that ideas may be brainstormed and the unusual considered.

An agenda for the monthly planning session is a must. The preparation of an agenda not only insures that all necessary matters will be covered and in logical sequence, but it forces the agency manager to give some preliminary consideration to various problems and this should make the session more productive. The agenda should be distributed in advance to all who will attend, so that everyone will have the opportunity to prepare.

The agenda should consider each agent or administrative employee as an individual item or main heading. Sub-headings for each agent should include: the agent's earnings; his rapport with management; quality and quantity of business; the trend of lives, premium, volume production; his continuing insurance education; development of markets; self-confidence; growth in new areas; progress in acquiring skills; standings toward conventions, company and industry awards and other important items. The final sub-heading on the agenda must include the scheduling of individual meetings between the agent and management for it is then that beneficial results are achieved.

To expedite planning and to assure thoroughness in planning, a technique of record keeping on each man must be developed. One possibility is the establishment of a file or dossier on each person in which all necessary data is kept. This might include a list of every educational course the agent has ever taken, including completion date; current and past production records; positions held in insurance industry organizations; plus the many other factors listed above as sub-headings to be discussed at the monthly "think session." One record often overlooked is that which indicates all the formal agency training sessions in which the agent has participated over the years. Even the established man should periodically be retrained and redrilled in such basic skills as asking for referred leads, use of power phrases, techniques of closing sales, and other similar skills. These records will help management to see which areas of training may have been neglected. They will also show trends and remind the agency manager of areas that need periodic shoring up.

It is important at this think-through session that the agent's point of view be continually kept in the foreground. The desires of each man and what he wants or needs from the agency, should be written down as management discovers them and this information placed in the dossier. Some agency managers will want to ask the agent to verify the list. Such a record could include the agent's desire for more income, his desire for a new challenge, his need to feel more secure, his need for reassurance of his progress, and his need to feel "in" and to feel important as an individual. It may be noted that this list is the counterpart to the negative list that agents often compile as a grievance pronouncement against an agency.

Other items suggested for the agenda of the management "think session" are plans for groups of agents, or groups of agency administrative people, or even all agency associates together. Agency contests, agency meetings of a general nature, social activities, and other similar activities, the need for which has been suggested in working with the dossiers of the individual agent, can be settled upon.

Finally, each management man leaving the staff session should leave with a schedule. Listed on each schedule will be individual conferences, group sessions and other duties that will be the specific person's responsibility. The schedules in the aggregate should require individual meetings with all the agents for the coming month.

Included with the scheduling of these individual conferences between management and agent should be a written memo or agenda setting forth the items to be covered. In other words, no meeting that is a business meeting should take place without a planned agenda. And when the meeting is concluded the written agenda with due notations on it should be placed in the agent's dossier. In the case of the management and individual agent meeting, the use of an agenda will not only prohibit meaningless chatter, but if different staff men take over they will have a record of material covered previously. The agenda helps to eliminate needless repetition that leads to stereotyped meetings.

By checking each dossier prior to each monthly meeting the agency manager can keep current on the developing pattern of all the agents. Even though he is in close contact with them day by day, this once-a-month survey of compiled results should clarify trends and make sure all bases are being touched. It is too easy for management to lull itself into believing there are no problems because the surface seems calm.

The important factor in retention of manpower is intelligent communication; inherent in communication is the art of listening. Therefore, agendas must make it possible for the agent to express himself fully. Flexibility in applying the agenda during the meeting should also be provided. However, a casual meeting or conversation will not suffice. Planned communication, covering all major items of importance to the agent, pays fine dividends in manpower retention.

Section IX

BUSINESS CONSERVATION
AS A RESPONSIBILITY
OF SALES MANAGEMENT

30

Business Conservation Policies and Practices

Robert E. Templin

THE MEANING OF CONSERVATION

One of the unique aspects of the life insurance product is the installment method of consumer payment. No other product can be purchased and then paid for over the life time of the purchaser. The level premium method of purchase solves the financial and budgetary problems of the purchaser. However, the level-premium-installment method of purchase creates so-called "conservation problems" for the life insurance business.

Conservation is the life insurance company's positive approach to negative consumer behavior. Conservation is the eclectic term that refers to all of the positive activities of a company designed to assure the continuation of a conditional sale. The sale remains in effect only if the customer meets the condition of paying the periodic premium. The customer's failure to meet this condition terminates the sale.

Conservation is variously referred to as: (1) keeping the business on the books; (2) maintaining the persistency of the business, (3) preserving the business, (4) conserving the business and (5) retaining the business. Regardless of the descriptive phrase used, the concept is the same: a company should make every practicable effort to persuade the purchaser of the value of his purchase so that he will make every effort to retain the benefits of his purchase by making the installment payments as they periodically come due.

All parties who have an interest in the continuation of a life insurance policy are affected adversely when a policy is terminated. Let's look at how these various parties are affected to their detriment. In looking at how conservation is beneficial to these various parties, we shall recognize the real meaning of conservation.

The Insured-Purchaser

First, the cost of the insurance protection for the terminating policyholder will be high, if the policyowner keeps the policy in force for only a short time. Most companies show very low cash surrender values for the first three years a policy is in force. It is only those policies that are kept in force for a period long enough for the company to amortize its acquisition costs, that develop substantial cash surrender values. In other words, low net cost is a function of the length of time the policy remains on the books.

Second, the cost for any new policy will almost inevitably be higher than the cost per $1,000 for the existing policy. This result would be expected since the new policy must bear a higher premium because of the insured's higher age. Also, acquisition costs will be incurred a second time for the new policy and the amortization of the new acquisition expenses will reduce cash values for the next few years.

Third, a new period of time must elapse to meet the requirements for the suicide clause and the incontestable clause.

Fourth, if the terminating policyowner does not replace his policy, he is leaving unsolved all of those financial problems that presumably he intended to solve by his purchase of the insurance in the first place.

The Insured's Family

First, the insured's family will be penalized by any increase in the cost of insurance which will be almost inevitable if a policy is cancelled and subsequently replaced by a policy in another company. Second, if the policy is not replaced, the family will be without the needed protection. Third, the family may be victimized by a new suicide clause or a new incontestable clause.

The Agent, the Agency and the Company

First, the agent, the agency and the company lose the renewal premium out of which each of the three parties receives some form of income. Second, an early termination means a shortened period for the company to amortize acquisition expenses. This means that this particular business did not pay its full costs of acquisition and handling. Third, a terminating policyholder no longer has any loyalty to the agent, to the agency or the company. Gone is a possible center of influence, a source of referrals and a contact point for information concerning newlyweds, births, new neighbors and prospective agents. Fourth, a short term policyholder frequently becomes embittered when he finds how small is his cash value at termination. Such a negative attitude can only have adverse consequences for the agent, the agency and the company. Certainly he will not be a good prospect for additional life insurance as his needs and income change. It takes a renaissance of dynamic proportions to convert subsequently a terminating policyholder into a loyal client.

The Life Insurance Industry

As suggested above, a terminating policyowner will frequently be a disgruntled and embittered individual. Moreover, such a policyowner frequently transfers to the life insurance industry in general any displeasures or grievances he associates wth his former insurer. Thus, a terminating policyowner may lose any affection or loyalty he previously had for life insurance and the life insurance industry. This negative attitude is likely to become particularly vindictive when the policyowner finds out the actual amount of his short term cash value. The position of the life insurance industry will not be enhanced by any event that develops unfavorable consumer attitudes.

BASIC FACTORS IN BUSINESS CONSERVATION

Every department in a life insurance company contributes at least to some extent in conserving business. These contributions may be evident at time of sale, since "the business that is well sold tends to hold, the business that is sold in haste tends to go to waste." Therefore, the underwriting department, by its careful selection of applicants, contributes to a company's persistency ratio because it determines what business will be exposed to possible termination. For example, among other things, the underwriting department must insist on a realistic relationship between the applicant's income and the premiums for his entire insurance program. An unrealistic premium burden relative to income means some or all of the applicant's life insurance is likely to lapse in a short period of time. Other departments also contribute to conservation or can worsen it by how they perform important functions involving policyowners. The claims department can antagonize a policyholder by the handling of a disability income claim. The policyholder service department can irritate the policyholder by poor record keeping. The agency department, however, has the greatest effect on conservation and it is in the operation of the agency department that significant improvements in conservation can usually be achieved.

The following paragraphs describe the basic operational factors in the agency department of a life insurance company that have an impact on the conservation of life insurance.

Market Planning

Market planning is the orderly structuring of the activities of the marketing department to achieve the company's marketing objectives. Market planning starts with the establishment of objectives. This necessarily requires sound, realistic thinking as to the relative importance of sales volume and persistency of sales. The maximizing of the former inevitably means compromising with optimum objectives relative to the latter. At one extreme the company may become so concerned about only writing quality business that sales volume suffers. At the other extreme, lack of concern for quality sales will impair persistency. The following opportunities for a company to broaden its market for life insurance are examined to determine their impact upon business persistency.

1. BROADENING THE PRODUCT PORTFOLIO

This will usually result in increased sales. Although the achievement of increased sales through broadening of the product portfolio does not necessarily result in a worsening of persistency, it usually does. So called "gimmick" policies or plans oftentimes give rise to customer dissatisfaction or misunderstanding. Some plans have great appeal at time of sale, but look less lustrous later.

2. BROADENING THE CHANNELS OF DISTRIBUTION

Management must decide whether to market its products through agents only, through agents and general insurance brokers, by mail, through somebody else's agents, over department store counters, by means of coin operated machines at railroad, bus and airline terminals, or through some combination of these channels of distribution.

The more sales outlets a company has for its products, the more sales it will make. This is another aspect of the law of large numbers. Some impairment to persistency, however, can be expected as a company increases the number of its sales outlets. Each company must decide whether the increased sales volume justifies the worsening of persistency that occurs. Oftentimes, the worsening of persistency is a function of the "span of control." The adequacy of management supervision and control is an inevitable problem associated with expansion in any business. Proper delegation of responsibility and authority, together with adequate controls will help to minimize the impairment to persistency from broadened operations.

3. BROADENING THE GEOGRAPHIC BOUNDARIES OF THE COMPANY'S MARKET

Growth in sales volume is usually more a function of the expansion of the marketing effort on a geographic basis than on a basis of either product expansion or expansion of distribution outlets. The larger companies write in all fifty states and several have entered the international market. Problems of "span of control," proper delegation of responsibility and authority, and maintenance of proper control devices are mandatory if persistency is not to be sacrificed to achieve sales growth.

4. BROADENING THE ECONOMIC AND SOCIAL STRATIFICATIONS OF THE COMPANY'S MARKET

Specific markets can be identified among families of different income and educational levels. Some companies have a basic marketing philosophy of prospecting only among families with incomes in excess of $15,000. Some companies sell only to the college market. Other companies, including some of the largest, have built their principal market in selling and servicing the blue collar and grey collar market. Contrary to the opinion of some, quality business is not the exclusive possession of companies writing in the upper economic strata. Quality business can be and is being sold at nearly every economic level. Frequently, families in the higher income levels overextend themselves in attempting to maintain a social life they believe necessary for their income, business or professional position. Too often, the reduction of their life insurance premiums is the first economy measure they employ in attempting to balance the family budget. Likewise, poor persistency is prevalent in the debit insurance market and companies operating in this market find that intensive efforts are required to keep industrial business on the books. If a company elects to broaden its market by moving either to higher or lower income families, it must be prepared to deal with the conservation problems that are unique in each of these markets, or actually experience lower persistency.

5. BROADENING THE MARKET THROUGH MONTHLY PREMIUM SALES

Families can sometimes be persuaded to purchase life insurance when the monthly premium is made to appear less burdensome than an annual premium. The only problem with this financial arrangement is that there are twelve times as many opportunities for the business to lapse than under an annual premium plan. However, some companies have achieved excellent persistency in making use of the pre-authorized check program on a monthly premium payment plan. With the increased propensity of families to think in terms of monthly payments for its various needs, there will probably develop an increasing use of some form of monthly budgeting of life insurance premiums. For the middle income family it might make more sense to arrange for annual premiums on six policies to be staggered approximately every two months rather than to use a monthly premium payment plan. The agent can oftentimes be helpful in counseling families on this particular matter.

6. BROADENING THE MARKET THROUGH SPECIAL FINANCING ARRANGEMENTS

Some companies have expanded their market by financing the first year or first two years of premium payments. For the college or graduate school student with a family, this arrangement is frequently attractive. Again, each company must decide whether the increased administrative costs of such financial arrangements and the problem of persistency of such sales are a small or large price to pay for the expanded sales volume. Minimum deposit and bank loan plans pose the same problem. These plans have produced disappointing persistency for some companies as a result of the 1969 tightness in the money market. With the prime interest rate at 8.5%, the carrying of life insurance with a bank loan became very expensive even with favorable tax treatment. Substantial policy loans are also a disadvantage to a company in a period of high interest rates because the company has no opportunity to take advantage of the high investment yield available for alternative investments.

Product Planning

Previous chapters have emphasized the close interrelationship between market planning and product planning. Probably no phase of life insurance sales management demonstrates this interrelationship more clearly than conservation of business. The right product for the right market will optimize persistency. The wrong product for the wrong market will maximize lapses. For the life insurance product to remain sold it must be a product that (1) meets the needs of the purchaser, (2) meets the premium paying capacity of the premium payer and (3) conforms to the purchaser's understanding of what he has purchased. A company needs a product portfolio that is broad enough to meet the needs of the various markets in which the company's sales force is selling. However, a company's sales representatives must be careful not to use one of the company's many products in making a sale for which that product is inappropriate. Therefore, in dealing with the conservation problem, a company should be more concerned with the appropriate use of its existing products rather than in the creation of additional products. Probably, the most important aspect of product planning, as far as conservation of business is concerned, is the company's abstention from developing and marketing products that will have poor persistency in the company's usual market. For example, a twenty-pay life policy for his full insurance program is usually not appropriate for a young man just out of college struggling to support a wife and two children. Frequently, such a sale will not persist because it should not have been made in the first place.

Manpower Planning

A company normally develops its agent recruiting policies and practices to conform to its marketing objectives and the products the company has developed to assist it in achieving its marketing objectives. A company which is concentrating on a market composed primarily of the self-employed, the professional, and the business executive, will recruit men who will be comfortable and effective in this type of market. Although this market does not necessarily require college men as salesmen, it is becoming increasingly evident that, since this market is composed primarily of college men, the salesman should also be a college man. Since it is the salesman who makes the sale rather than the company or the particular features of the policy, it will be primarily the salesman who will keep the policy in force. Therefore, if the client loses respect for the agent servicing his needs, he will likely transfer his loyalties and his business to the next prospecting agent in whom he has confidence and for whom he has respect. Old policies may be lapsed because the original agent does not have an opportunity to resell them.

The salesman is unquestionably the key factor in the persistency of business. Quality salesmen make quality sales and quality sales persist. A quality salesman is a product of (1) good recruiting, (2) careful selection, (3) excellent education and training, (4) competent supervision and (5) proper motivation. If we assume, in addition to the above ideals, that the quality salesman is employed by a quality agency, managed by a quality manager, and places his business with a quality company, (also possessing quality management) it would seem also inevitable that such a salesman would write quality business. Therefore, it is obvious that there are a large number of interrelated factors that have an impact on persistency.

Education and Training

Two basic factors affecting the persistency of business are the knowledge and skill of the salesman. They are extremely important both before the sale and in any conservation service work after the sale, sometimes referred to as the "resale." A company's education and training program depends to a large extent on the market being served, the products being sold and the previous educational background of the field force. A company that is concentrating its sales effort in business insurance and estate planning will need to devote considerable attention to continuing education. Dynamic changes in legislation and business operations can have considerable impact on whether certain aspects of previous sales need modification or changes by this purchaser to make them appropriate under changed conditions. Dynamic changes have significance for retention of existing business as well as for possible additional sales.

Some companies have a session in their home office career schools devoted exclusively to what constitutes quality business and its importance to the company, the policyowner, the agent and the agency. Some companies devote "career school" time to a discussion of "delivering the policy." A proper explanation to the insured and his wife at the time of delivery can do a great deal to prevent a future lapse.

Compensation

A company's compensation system can have a significant effect on the persistency of business. The system of paying renewal commissions is an incentive to an agent to preserve his business written. It can be argued that higher persistency would be achieved by reducing first year commissions and paying larger renewal commissions. There is some evidence that companies which spread out agent's compensation over a long period of time do experience higher persistency. However, a reduction in first year commissions to increase renewal commissions may provide such an incentive to preserve existing business that the agent will give his primary attention to the latter with a resulting reduction in the sale of new business. Another approach is to reward agents for persistency through annual quality awards and specific dollar bonuses for meeting certain persistency standards.

The agency manager is also a key person in conserving business. Regardless of the type of field management used, a company should provide compensation incentives to field management for persistent business. Companies using the general agency system typically provide renewal commissions to the general agent for eight or nine years. A collection fee is then paid to maintain the general agent's interest in keeping the business on the books. In later years, general agents realize their terminal renewal account is a major asset to produce continuing income and they make every effort to conserve this account.

Home Office Administration

Many companies have conservation departments whose efforts are devoted entirely to researching, reporting and recommending controls on the quality of the business produced and to administering company programs aimed at keeping the business on the books after it is written. Other companies are satisfied with periodic efforts at conservation made by different individuals in various departments such as actuarial, agency or secretarial, who assume this responsibility along with their regular duties. In any case, one person should be responsible to see that action is taken.

Service

Policyowner service is another vital link in the conservation chain. The Army motor pools refer to preventive maintenance as a means of forestalling equipment breakdowns. In a similar vein, there is much that both the home office and field people can do to provide the kind of policyowner satisfaction that will prevent lapse from occurring. Conservation of business after a lapse has occurred is difficult and resembles more than anything else, locking the barn door after the horse is gone.

Recognition

While the incentives for persistency inherent in a good compensation plan should be adequate encouragement for life insurance agents, the fact remains that home office recognition of a job well-done frequently inspires greater effort than dollars alone. A continuing program of recognition of good selling and servicing pays dividends. For example, as a minimum, the home office should applaud their National Quality Award winners. Some companies make a practice of mailing each winner a small engraved and personalized card of congratulations recognizing their number of years of qualifications. It is a little thing to do, but it does a lot of good. The men like to know that this accomplishment is recognized by the home office. It is also desirable to publish their names in the company's field magazine as well as arranging for recognition in each man's own agency.

SPECIFIC HOME OFFICE ACTIVITIES CONTRIBUTING TO THE CONSERVATION OF BUSINESS

The following home office activities may have considerable effect on the conservation of business. Although no one of these activities standing by itself would perhaps be significant, these various activities in the aggregate have a substantial effect in reducing policy lapsation.

A. Some home office underwriters take a realistic and almost paternalistic attitude toward the applicant. They try not to let him buy more than he can afford. If there is good reason to feel that the applicant will not be able to maintain his policy in force some home office underwriters look at the application very carefully and may decline it. Group underwriting standards also are important in achieving good persistency.

B. Some companies place limits on their acceptance of pension business and accept only the relatively small pension trust cases where employment is more stable and where other mass funding methods would not be a competitive factor for change of plan.

C. In developing new products some companies refrain from marketing so-called "gimmick" policies or life insurance plans where there is a future possibility of customer dissatisfaction or misunderstanding. A new policy, which appears to offer a company great potential in sales growth, may turn out to be a disappointment. A high lapsation in the first few years may reflect purchaser disenchantment with the "gimmick policy."

D. The inclusion of the automatic premium provision in a policy helps a company's lapse record and typically results in no undesirable side effects when properly used. Late payment offers for reinstatement after the grace period has expired can also be helpful.

E. Insisting upon the prepayment of premiums can be helpful, since the policyowner's ability to prepay is typically an indication that his policy will persist. In other words, if the applicant has a problem paying the first premium, he is a good candidate for future premium paying problems. An agency manager's periodic bulletins may be used to show production and prepayment of premiums. Agents with good prepayment records may be given special recognition. The importance of prepayment can be emphasized throughout a company's training course so its new agents will automatically assume that premiums are to be prepaid.

F. The presidents of some companies send a personalized letter of welcome to all first-time policyowners. This may be helpful in gaining a satisfied client and hopefully a consistent premium payer.

G. Some companies use their premium billing to provide the policy owner with a statement of his increase in cash value for the year. The statement will show the gross premium, the dividend for that year, the net premium payment and the increase in cash value, thereby giving the policyowner a clearer understanding of the value of his policy. This information will help the policyowner to recognize how little the continuation of his protection is costing him.

H. Some companies make an intensive effort to reduce the first year lapse rate on graded premium policies. A reminder can be helpful to the agent in seeing that his graded premium policyowners take the next premium step. Sometimes a graded premium policy is sold when it is inappropriate. An educational program to teach the agent the proper application of graded premium life insurance can be helpful.

I. Most companies find that their sales to previous policyowners represent a very persistent business. In order to encourage the writing of new policies on previous policyowners one company has prepared a policyowner's service program (ORE-Orphan Reclamation Effort). By the use of electronic data processing the company provides the agency manager with the names of all orphan policyowners in the agency's territory whether the premiums on the outstanding policies are collected through the agency or not. The ORE program then takes over under the direction of the agency manager. These orphan leads are distributed on an automatic basis followed up with calls from agents who use a structured interview technique. A reporting system concludes the cycle and assists in determining an agent's entitlements to additional leads. This simple system has proved effective in promoting good policyowner relations as well as resulting in substantial new business from old policyowners.

Some companies make an annual detailed first-year lapse study with a complete breakdown by agent's name, insured's name, sex, plan, policy number, amount, premium frequency and number of premiums paid. This usually points up the fact that one or two agents are primarily responsible for the lapses in an agency. The agency manager, with this record, can review the facts with each agent whose persistency is unsatisfactory and try to correct the situation. It may be poor prospecting, poor sales procedure or one of a number of other reasons. A listing of the lapsed business for each agency is sent to the agency manager along with a calculation of each agent's loss in income resulting from these lapses. The agency manager is advised also of the company's first year lapse rate, the agency's first year lapse rate and the agency's rank among the other agency managers of the company.

Some companies using the general agency system have so-called "district agents" which are actually branch offices within general agencies. Sometimes these branch office managers (district agents) are paid on a basis that requires more emphasis on persistency, particularly for the first three years, in order to receive the full compensation allowance. For example, a district agent might receive a first and second year margin on the work of his agents. He might receive also a development fee when a case is paid for, a second year fee if the policy renews, and another the third year if the policy is still in force.

Some companies pay their agents a persistency fee on premium paying business starting in the tenth year. Agents' retirement benefits sometimes are governed by their earnings with emphasis on their renewal accounts. The agents are made aware of these facts and are therefore motivated to create the largest possible retirement benefit for themselves by improved retention. Some companies frequently remind their agents of the value of persisting business by bulletin items such as the one below in Illustration I, (Dollar Cost of Poor Persistency).

Some companies prepare annually a complete breakdown of their agents' sales results by occupation, income, age of insured as well as the type of policy, premium and other vital factors. This permits a good review of the quality of agents' operations. Also provided is the value of this business with estimates as to the impact of varying degrees of lapse.

Some companies furnish their agents on the commission statement a complete recap of the factors of compensation. In this way, the agent will see the source of his first year and renewal commissions. He will also have listed for him the business that has lapsed and its value to him. The agent will have a valuation of his renewals before and after the current month's statement. Thus, he can see what he is building for the future. The impact of lapsation will clearly be brought to his attention in the form of dollars lost.

SUMMARY AND CONCLUSIONS

This chapter has described the nature of the conservation problem and has identified the specific adverse effects of poor persistency for (1) the insured, (2) the insured's family, (3) the agent, (4) the agency, (5) the

ILLUSTRATION I

Dollar Cost of Poor Persistency

If a 35 year old agent regularly produced business which had $10,000 of annual premiums, his total income actually received would depend upon the lapse rate of his business. Considering first-year and renewal commissions, persistency fees, and retirement benefits, the following chart shows the cost of higher lapse rates of gross earnings to age 65:

Lapse Rate	First Yr. Commis.	Renewal Commis.	Persistency Fees	Retirement Benefits	Total Earnings	Loss of Earnings Compared to 5% Rate
5%	$161,000	$110,000	$20,000	$26,000	$317,000	—
10%	158,000	95,000	15,000	22,000	290,000	$27,000
15%	154,000	83,000	11,000	19,000	267,000	50,000
20%	151,000	71,000	8,000	13,000	247,000	70,000
25%	147,000	62,000	6,000	14,000	229,000	88,000

GROSS EARNINGS to age 65—$10,000 Annual Premium per year

From Age 30		Lapse Rate	From Age 25	
Total Earnings	Loss of earnings Compared to 5% Rate		Total Earnings	Loss of earnings Compared to 5% Rate
$380,000	—	5%	$444,000	—
346,000	$ 34,000	10%	404,000	$ 40,000
317,000	63,000	15%	369,000	75,000
292,000	88,000	20%	339,000	105,000
271,000	109,000	25%	313,000	131,000

SOURCE: "The Importance of Persistency," by E. G. Newcomb, F.S.A. Supt. of Agcys, NML company and (6) the life insurance industry. Some of the basic positive actions that a company can take to improve business persistency include: (1) careful underwriting of new business, (2) establishing and maintaining effective policyholder service, (3) product planning that gives consideration to business persistency, (4) planning distribution channels that not only expand sales volume but also develop quality business, (5) recruiting and selecting quality agents, (6) providing education and training programs that develop quality agents, (7) providing supervision that inculcates good sales practices among agents, (8) establishing a compensation arrangement that provides incentives for maintaining business, and (9) maintaining a continuing program for recognizing agents for good persistency.

The establishment of company policy on the various aspects of conservation must be the starting point of any program and the decisions here will be the most important. Once the company has decided what it wants to do it will then find that there are numerous ways of doing it.

31

Business Conservation

Harry Krueger

Remember the perennial discussions about the sales process? Remember the controversy about whether the sales process can be broken down into segments— the pre-approach, the approach, the fact-finding interview, the closing interview, post-sales service and so forth, versus whether the close begins with the pre-approach and that the actual approach of the agent to the prospect has just as much to do with the eventual close as all the other elements leading to that close? Obviously, these discussions are more an exercise in semantics than inquiries into the significant elements of the sales process—but they continue nonetheless.

So it is with the question of conservation, the question of policy persistence, the question of quality business. When we think in terms of conservation and persistence, are we thinking in terms of what to do after the policy has been sold or after the policy has lapsed, or are we thinking about a prevention of such a circumstance in the first place? When we think of conservation, are we thinking about the final acts which keep the insurance in force, or are we thinking about all of the elements which create the sale of the policy in the first place?

In this electronic age in which we have almost more statistical and analytical information available to us than we know what to do with, it is possible to approach the subject as it is related to the entire sales process rather than as a unique problem to be dealt with separately. To conserve and to persist, we must first create; if conservation and persistence are desirable then that which is created must be good.

Poor Persistency Is Costly to the Insured

In 1964, the Life Insurance Agency Management Association revised a booklet entitled "Profitable Selling." In it, they said that, at the then current rate, over sixteen billion dollars of life insurance would lapse for non-payment of premiums during the first two policy years, and that over two million policies will lapse before the purchaser receives, in most cases, more than a small fraction of the benefits sought. If the insurance is re-placed, it means a second acquisition cost which is considerable. This is a dollar loss. But it is more than a dollar loss. It is the loss of a plan . . . a hope . . . a dream. It is more than that even. It is too frequently a loss of prestige for the life insurance business. It may mean a lowered opinion of those who sell life insurance and of the entire distributive procedure.

A lapsed life insurance policy is a pathetic document. No correspondence in an agency office is more poignant than that which comes from a widow who encloses a policy which she discovered in her decreased husband's be-longings and the inevitable question: "It's an old policy and I don't remem-ber anything about it. Is it worth anything?" The all-too-frequent reply is that the policy lapsed for "no value" years before.

Poor Persistency Is Costly to the Company

Early lapse means that the cost of acquisition is not covered. Poor per-sistency requires a constant, feverish effort to replace the lost policy with a new one with the consequent doubling of acquisition costs. It requires a more concentrated sales effort. A high lapse rate is not conducive to the creation of a desirable clientele. A client is generally described as a person who engages the professional services of another; a counseling relationship is essential to the creation of a client. A high lapse rate too frequently indi-cates that this relationship has not been established.

A Lapsed Policy Is Costly to the Agent

Up to now, in the great majority of life insurance companies, the com-pensation of an agent has been based in large part upon the persistence of the business and this will probably continue in the foreseeable future. A substantial first year commission is paid, followed by so-called renewals which, in turn, in many companies are followed by persistency fees or service fees.

A lapsed policy is indeed costly to an agent. Early lapse means that, from a dollar standpoint, at least half of the commission potential is lost to the agent. It is costly in other ways. It destroys the client-counselor rela-tionship so vital to professional growth. It necessitates the agent creating a new client, and a new sale, to replace the old one. It is, of course, axiomatic that the best business is repeat business—business sold to existing policyholders. In the degree to which lapses occur is the degree which militates against the possibility of repeat business.

Agent Termination

All the statistical evidence indicates that the persistency of life insurance business written by new agents is on the average less favorable than that of career agents. The highest percentage of lapsation occurs among policyowners of agents who have left the business. One large company found that for new business placed in force over a two-year period, the most significant factor affecting the persistency of that business was the status of the agent who sold that business. This study indicated that an astonishingly high percentage of lapsation occurred among those policyowners who were sold by an agent whose contract terminated before the lapse, as compared to agents still active. This same study showed that the longer the agent was under contract and active, the better the persistency of the business. For example, the study showed that the business produced by agents under contract less than a year had an 82% persistency rate as compared to a 90% persistency rate for agents under contract in their third year, a 93% persistency for business written by agents in their fifteenth to twenty-fourth years, and better than a 94% persistency for business produced by agents under contract for twenty-five years or more. As will be discussed in the next section, the same factors that affect the length of time an agent remains in the life insurance business affect the quality of the business the agent writes while he is in the life insurance business.

CHARACTERISTICS OF TERMINATING POLICYOWNERS

There is statistical evidence that policyowners can be grouped according to probability of lapse. The following are some of the statistical findings concerning probability of lapse for certain groups: (1) Persons having a partial high school education tend to have a higher lapse rate than persons with a partial college education. (2) Persons having a college degree have a higher persistency in the ownership of life insurance than persons with only a partial college education.[1] (3) Persons in the 20–24 age group have a higher lapse rate than persons over age 30. (4) Persons in the 35–50 age group have the highest persistency. (5) Farm proprietors and farm managers have a high persistency. (6) Professional people, semi-

---

[1] It should be noted that lapsation may be more a function of the stability of income and employment of college graduates rather than a function of scholarship.

professional and executives have a high persistency. (7) Unskilled laborers have a higher lapse rate than skilled laborers. (8) Persons in the higher income groups have a higher persistency than persons in the low income groups. (9) Persons who have been substantial purchasers of life insurance in a given company tend to be highly persistent with respect to any new insurance they purchase in that company.

It is important to emphasize, however, that any analysis of policyowner characteristics must be made with the realization that the characteristics are only barometers and are not the sole determining factors. There are quality people who are not educated. There are quality people who have menial jobs. There are quality people whose incomes are low. Quality business comes from quality people—and the opposite applies as well. External characteristics are not necessarily an index to basic character; it is good character which produces good quality.

Persistency Raters

Many agency managers find that the use of a Persistency Rater can be helpful in predicting persistency of new business. A Persistency Rater is a method of measuring the probability that a newly issued life insurance policy will remain in force. The method involves the assigning of debits and credits to specific factors that are known initially about the policyowner and the type of sale that is made. For example, debits and credits are assigned to such factors as: (1) age of applicant, (2) income level, (3) marriage status, (4) type of policy, (5) frequency of premium payment and (6) payment made with the application.

The LIAMA publishes a Persistency Rater (*The Persistency Raters, Research Report 1949–13, File No. 721*), which may be purchased from the Association. Several companies also have constructed their own raters based on their own experiences.. These various Persistency Raters are similar and for groups of policies are effective in predicting persistency. The ratings can be used by the agency manager in the following ways: (1) as a guide in supervising agents, (2) as a signal for the need for special emphasis in training and retraining, (3) as a factor in determining whether to continue financing of new agents and (4) as a factor in computing persistency bonuses.

AGENCY POLICIES AND PROCEDURES TO IMPROVE BUSINESS PERSISTENCY

Agency Objectives and Philosophy

There is no one factor that makes the difference between high persistency and low persistency of business written in a life insurance agency. However, if there is a starting point for implementing an agency program to improve business persistency, that starting point is the attitude, philosophy, and objectives of the agency as articulated and emphasized by the agency manager.

An agency should retain as its primary goal an increasing volume of sales. But a primary goal is not an exclusive goal. A family does not attempt to help a retarded child by devoting all of its attention exclusively to the one child. A quality agency keeps the goal of persistency constantly in mind and attempts to direct all of the significant agency activities in the direction of persistency. If it is true that "lapsation begins with the sale," then the agency manager must make an intensive effort to prevent unsound selling.

Agency Recruiting and Selection

Quality agents write quality business. Therefore, the agency that aspires to have high persistency must strive to recruit agents who will write quality business. Quality business has been defined as "the right policy for a specific need, purchased within the buyer's means, which is adequately understood by the purchaser and which continues to serve his best interests when regularly reviewed with him by his agent."[2] Implicit in this definition is the concept of a client-counselor relationship. "The right policy for a specific need" implies a selfless attitude on the part of the agent. "Which is adequately understood by the purchaser" implies education of the purchaser by the agent. "Which continues to serve his best interests when regularly reviewed by the agent" implies a continuing attitude of service.

The quality agency recruits and selects its sales force so as to continue to build a quality agency. This means recruiting and selecting people who will build a client-counselor relationship with their policyowners. Agents who sell by means of the gimmick or pressure techniques, typically, are more concerned with the one time sale rather than with building a client-counselor relationship.

Agency Education and Training

Early in the basic training of a new agent it is important to emphasize the significance of the client-counselor relationship. The new agent should be oriented to the concept of how the client-counselor relationship leads to repeat business. Some agencies insist on a monthly analysis of the quality factors of an agent's business, and in the "review of the month" interview, this can be an important part of the discussion.

---

[2] This is the definition accepted by the National Association of Life Underwriters.

It is desirable to inculcate in each new agent the idea that life insurance is a "prospecting" business as much as it is a "selling" business. A new agent should be trained in the careful keeping of records and in the following of procedures which, from the very beginning, make him conscious of the fact that new prospects can be generated extensively from satisfied, present policyowners.

Some agencies make effective use of a filing system which automatically reminds the agent to make calls on clients and prospects on a regimented basis at least twice a year: once on the birth date, and a second time six months thereafter prior to a change of age. (The latter is significant for those companies which base the issuing age upon the insured's age nearest his birth date.) The purpose of the call on the birth date is merely to maintain a continuing rapport, to solidify the "client-counselor" relationship. No attempt is made to sell life insurance at that time. If service is needed, the agent performs this, of course, as a part of his continuing program to preserve the client-counselor relationship. The client can be reminded that his is "policy review time" or "client-call day." Obviously, this latter approach can be scheduled for any time during the year and does not need to be tied in with a birthday.

At the time of the "age change" call, the existing program is reviewed and any service recommendations that are appropriate are made at that time. In addition, the agent reviews with the client the cash value increase of his policies. A part of this review is to compare the cash value increases with the amount of the premiums due. This procedure serves to remind the client again of the living values of his life insurance. This is a small step for the agent to take but a giant leap forward toward impressing the client with the specific values that are accumulating for him as he keeps his policy or policies in force.

The insured will be more inclined to continue his insurance if he recognizes that he actually is paying for his life insurance with the first or second premium payment and after this he is merely making savings deposits. At any time the insured surrenders this policy, the difference between the total premiums paid and the available cash value is no more than the first couple of premiums. This simple concept will have a tremendous impact on the insured and when properly presented, can make a significant contribution to persistence of in force business.

Many agencies use a various assortment of record keeping devices and techniques to improve agent planning of sales and conservation activities. For example, one company has each new agent make use of a so-called "Sales Builder." This is a continuing twelve month record not only of the agent's activities, but also a record of his follow-through on a continuing process of seeing his prospects and clients twice a year. Furthermore, this yearly record can be tied to a monthly booklet that facilitates better planning and, since the monthly booklet is with the agent at all times, provides a constant reminder of what needs to be done.

Many agencies include, as a part of each agent's bookkeeping system, special pages for determining the value of future income from business in force. A system used by one company is shown in the illustration on page 542. The agent is told to keep these records carefully and in so doing he is made conscious of the value of the business that persists.

Most agencies divide their "new agent" education and training program into phases. Some agencies conduct pre-induction training courses as a means of deciding whether the prospective candidate can measure up to the agency's rigid training and supervisory procedures and whether he has the imagination to recognize their desirability and necessity. This pre-induction training period can be invaluable for building wholesome attitudes toward conservation of business.

Most companies train their new agents to make use of a two-step process of selling, one interview being devoted exclusively to fact finding. Following this initial interview, the agent completes an analysis of the prospect's situation and prepares written recommendations. Following this, the agent arranges for a second interview in which he presents his recommendations and, if new life insurance is appropriate, an attempt is made to effect a sale. If the sale is made, a normal part of the whole procedure is to perform such post-sale service as is appropriate. This post-sale service includes an audit showing the client's total life insurance program as of that date. This audit is then kept up-to-date. Training new agents in this type of procedure can be a significant factor in conserving business that is sold. In addition, it makes an important contribution to the insured. The new agent's supervisor should check to make sure that the new agent follows through in performing the post-sale service. This service generates satisfaction among clients because they understand why they have bought what they have. Incidentally, this post-sale service also has the tremendous advantage of generating new referrals for the agent.

Many agents explain the "cost of insurance" concept to their clients at the time they deliver the policy. The time of delivery is a good time to make a sincere attempt to strengthen the client-counselor relationship and explaining the "cost of insurance" concept to the client will make him feel good about his purchase, the agent, and the company. A satisfied client is a more persistent purchaser than the buyer who is uncertain as to the merits of the product he has purchased. In all of its training the agency should attempt to create a realization on the part of the agent that life

GROSS VALUE OF DEFERRED FIRST YEAR AND RENEWAL COMMISSIONS EARNED

DATE PAID	INSURED	POLICY NUMBER	QUALITY FACTORS						ANNUAL PREMIUM OR EQUIVALENT	FULL FIRST YEAR COMS. INC. DEFERREDS	GROSS RENEWALS		
			WHEN TER-MINATED	INCOME OF INSURED	PRE-PAID	AMOUNT OF POLICY	PLAN	PAY-ABLE			RATE	YRS.	VALUE
	Gross commuted value of deferred 1st year and renewal com'd. as of Jan 1st									405 00			4680 00
Jan 2	Burke	3024689		2,000	mo	3000	O.L.	A.	89 72	4486	5	9	40 41
8	Carter	3025019		8,000	yes	15,000	L.65	S.	460 80	1843 32	5	9	207 32
12	Sims – Blank Ins Co rated			1,500	mo	2,000	O.L.	A.					
18	Johns	3052183		2,400	no	1,500	O.L.	S.	72 00	3600	5	9	32 40
26	Pane	3060167		3,600	yes	5,000	O.L.	A.	180 60	9000	5	9	81 00
	Total values created during January									760 18			504 1 17
	Less values received as income or lost through terminations									314 02			229 98
	Gross commuted value of deferred and rent'l com'd. as of Feb 1st									446 16			481 1 19

542

COMMISSIONS RECEIVED AS INCOME OR LOST THROUGH TERMINATIONS

DATE	INSURED	POLICY NUMBER	REMARKS: REASON FOR TERMINATION	ANNUAL PREMIUM OR EQUIVALENT	COMMISSIONS RECEIVED OR LOST THROUGH TERMINATIONS, ETC.*			
					FIRST YEAR	RATE	YEARS	RENEWALS
Jan 8	Clark	2918144	Poor quality—not employed	45 00	17 00	5	9	20 25
22	Dobbs	2508972	Moved from city—no contract	110 00		5	6½	35 75
31	Commissions rec'd during Jan—Totals from cash sheets				297 02			173 98
	Total comd. rec'd as income or lost through terminations				314 02			229 98

* INCLUDING CHANGES IN PLAN, SUBSTITUTION CASES AND CONVERSIONS

543

insurance is a solution to a problem, that it is an integral part of a family plan or a business plan, and that it cannot be discontinued without disrupting the entire plan.

Agency Use of Information Provided Electronically

Electronics have made it possible for life insurance company home offices to provide its agencies annually a complete sales inventory of each agent. This inventory can show each agent's sales results broken down as follows: (1) total sales volume, (2) total premiums, (3) number of lives, (4) types of policies, (5) amount per policy, (6) age of each insured, (7) ownership of policy (personal or business), (8) purpose of insurance (personal, business continuation, or key-man).

The sales information can be broken down further as follows: (1) according to income of purchasers, (2) according to age of purchasers, (3) according to the face amount of the policies, (4) according to sex of the purchasers, (5) according to whether the policies were issued standard or classified, (6) according to amount of insurance on previous policyowners and (7) according to the number of lives who were previous policyowners. This information can serve many purposes. Among the uses for this information is helping agents to evaluate the quality of their business and to assist them in identifying possible conservation problems before the problems arise.

Improving Persistency of Business of Terminating Agents

The persistency of the business of terminating agents is notoriously bad. Recognizing this, an agency should arrange immediately for a terminating agent's policyholder records to be turned over to another agent. The policyowner should then be informed of (1) the name, address and telephone number of the new agent, (2) the desire of the newly assigned agent to provide any service that he can, (3) the desire of the new agent to meet with the policyowners as soon as possible and that the new agent will try to arrange for such a meeting in the near future. The new agent should then follow through to set-up such a meeting and render such service as soon as he can. One of the forms that is frequently used in such a follow through appears on page 543.

Agency Recognition of High Persistency

Greater effort should be made at the agency level to encourage the sale of quality business. One form of encouragement is to recognize agents who achieve outstanding persistency for business written. This can be accomplished through: (1) the agency bulletin, (2) the agency system of honors, (3) the home office clubs and honor groups and (4) the attention and emphasis given to the National Quality Award of the National Association of Life Underwriters.

Reinstating Lapsed Policies

Reinstating lapsed policies is the action taken by the court of last resort. It is similar to attempting to rescue a drowning man after he has gone down for the second time. In other words, if conservation action isn't too late it is almost too late when a policy reaches the point that action taken during the thirty-one day waiting period was to no avail. Presumably, before this occurs, there have been the usual letters of persuasion and perhaps a telephone call. Most agencies are more active than this. Usually the home office will inform the agent of record that the particular policy is about to lapse. Sometimes the company's statistical division will provide information that will be helpful to the agent in his reinstatement attempt. Some companies provide that when a policy, that has been in a lapsed state for over six months, is reinstated by other than the agent who sold the insurance, the remaining renewals, if any there be, will be paid to the reinstating agent. This, needless to say, provides an excellent incentive to the agent to try to reinstate the policy.

SUMMARY

Business conservation is a sales management problem requiring the continued attention of management at both the home office and agency level. At the agency level the agency manager should deal with the conservation problem through implementation of the following policies and procedures:

(1) The writing of quality business should be an important objective of the agency.

(2) The importance of this objective should be communicated to all agency personnel.

(3) The agency should recruit and select quality manpower, because quality salesmen produce quality business.

(4) In the education, training, and supervision of its manpower, the agency should emphasize the importance of writing quality business.

(5) The agency should inculcate in each new agent the idea of the client-counselor relationship. Each agent should understand that

this is beneficial for maintaining business persistency as well as for writing new business and obtaining referrals.

(6) The sales force should make effective use of some type of filing system that automatically reminds the agent to make periodic calls on clients.

(7) The agency should encourage the writing of quality business by a formalized system for recognizing agents for excellence in writing persistent business.

(8) The agency should have a carefully organized procedure to follow as soon as a policyowner fails to pay his premium on its due date.

Section X

FINANCIAL MANAGEMENT

32

Agency Financial Policies and Practices

E. J. Moorhead

THE NEED FOR PROPER COMPANY POLICIES AND PRACTICES IN AGENCY FINANCIAL MANAGEMENT

Neither parsimony nor profligacy is a virtue in agency financial management. Spending as little as possible for agency operations can be as wrong as over-spending. The right approach is to make each dollar of expenditure work as hard and as effectively as possible in accordance with the company's objectives. Policies and practices in agency financial management should be designed to achieve not the company's sales objectives alone, but its total objectives when the latter have been appropriately defined.

In this industry in which achievement is measured so extensively in terms of growth, the danger is that the sales objectives will be a company's only clearly defined objectives. The result in such cases is that too little attention is paid to quality objectives, to profit objectives, to net cost objectives, and to the need for keeping the institution strong in an environment of competing devices for protection and savings.

The need, then, for proper agency financial management may be summed up in terms of the company's resulting ability (a) to compete with other companies, (b) to compete with other industries, (c) to operate within statutory expense limits, and (d) to remain solvent, i.e., capable of discharging its obligations to policyholders. Let us consider these four individually.

Competition with Other Companies usually comes to mind first. To meet competition in the cost of the life insurance product makes the difference in only a small proportion of total sales, but the ones affected are often the large and influential ones. But where a company stands in price of product can have a profound effect upon the morale and enthusiasm of its sales organization. Much field manpower loss can be attributed to unwillingness of agents to offer what they have recognized to be an inferior product.

Competition with Other Industries is a matter of immense importance to the future of our agency system. These "other industries" include all forms of life insurance marketing other than by agents, mass selling, life insurance organizations established by particular occupational groups, as well as competitors in the savings field in both the guaranteed and equity dollar categories.

The part of each premium dollar that is used for sales and service expense is substantial. Our practice is to justify this either by the comforting statement that life insurance is sold, not bought, or by showing that Ordinary Life cost compares favorably with term insurance supplemented by outside investment.[1] But it is the task of agency management to make sure that the services of our system are really worth what they cost—a task that demands, among other things, minimizing waste from agent turnover and seeing to it that service to policyholders through agents is rendered expertly and conscientiously.

Operating Within Statutory Expense Limits is a problem faced by companies that choose to operate in New York State. Agency officers of such companies should familiarize themselves with the impact upon their own company of the complex multiple limitation imposed by Section 213.[2] This multiple limitation includes (a) a limit on the discounted value of agents' and general agents' commission and benefit schedules, (b) a limit on the current expenditures of each year, including commissions, and (c) a limit on agent financing payments. These limits are interrelated among themselves. Situations in which imprudent agency financial management leads to problems with New York expense limitations can easily arise.

---

[1] As we view an exhibit showing that outside investments in conjunction with term insurance must provide unattainable yields to compete with Ordinary Life, we should ask ourselves whether the yield on Ordinary Life is really good, or whether the explanation is simply that the term rates that we have chosen to charge are relatively high.

[2] For a detailed discussion of the various financial problems associated with Section 213 of the New York State Insurance Code the reader is referred to Chapter 34, "Compensation and Incentive Arrangements."

Maintenance of Company Solvency is an obvious requirement but one which in the past has generally been less of a practical problem for established companies than it might have been. This is because, much more often than not, the premiums calculated by actuaries have turned out to have larger expense margins than could reasonably have been counted upon. These unexpected extra margins have come mainly from steadily declining mortality rates supplemented from time to time by upward swings in investment earnings.

Today, however, none of the four basic elements that determine whether premiums will prove to be redundant, adequate or insufficient—i.e., mortality experience, investment earnings, expense level, persistency rate— shows clear promise of future improvement. Mortality rates have remained static for a decade. The interest rate is at what history warns us is an abnormally high level. Expense rates face the prospect of a rising national price level and other upward pressures. Persistency rates are showing a tendency to become less satisfactory. Prudence therefore dictates an attitude of caution and points to the desirability of budgeting agency expenditures within expense margins that clearly can be counted upon. This applies with special force to a company that does not have on its books a large volume of business written at the higher premium rates that were characteristic of our industry in former days.

INGREDIENTS FOR SUCCESSFUL AGENCY FINANCIAL MANAGEMENT

For exercise of effective agency financial management the basic essentials are:

1. Understanding the characteristics, implications and philosophy of the system (general agency or branch office) which one's company uses.
2. Recognizing the situations in which heavy cost may arise.
3. Obtaining well-conceived, accurate and prompt expense data.
4. Disseminating operating rules *before* they must be put to the test.

To appreciate fully the significance of each of these four basic essentials one should consider the following:

1. The subject of *characteristics of the system* is so elusive and the variety so great that general categorical statements are useless. The following questions are illustrative of those that arise:

   (a) (General Agency.) Can we safely assume that expenses incurred by our general agents are their own concern, or had we better recognize that if they are excessive they may in due course become very directly the company's concern?

(Branch Office.) How can we encourage economical operation without inhibiting development, and without making too many decisions at the home office that could more intelligently be made locally?

(b) (General Agency.) Even though costs at the moment may be at a satisfactory level, have our renewal overriding contracts or guaranteed expense allowances committed the company to unduly heavy future expense?

(Branch Office.) Does heavy financial emphasis on production lead to unsatisfactory quality of the business being produced?

(c) (General Agency.) How can some management manpower that is being developed in agencies be made available for company expansion into new territories or for more intensive development of existing territories?

(Branch Office.) Should the manager be given a temporary special allowance when the company promotes one of his assistants?

(d) (General Agency.) How can adequate recruiting be achieved, particularly as a general agent approaches retirement age?

(Branch Office.) How can excessive expense of ineffective recruiting be avoided?

(e) (General Agency.) Is a system in which compensation is, other things being equal, in direct proportion to the quantity of business produced still economical when the company and its agencies grow very large?

(Branch Office.) How can the company attract a sufficient number of men capable of effectively operating large agencies, in competition with the rewards of the general agency system?

Questions such as these are difficult but are far from being insoluble when squarely faced and wisely explored.

2. *Situations in which heavy cost may arise* include development of new agencies, agent financing, second-line supervision, compensation plans and sales promotion activities. Careful attention to each of these areas can provide excellent opportunities for keeping costs under control. Costs will be heavy if ineffective agencies and agents are permitted to continue and if established general agents indulge in excessive delegation of their sales management responsibilities to subordinates.

3. The nature of needed *expense data* will be discussed in a separate part of this chapter. It should be emphasized here that data should be displayed in a manner and covering a sufficiently long period so that the agency vice president can observe what trends are occurring. Reliance on "this year versus last year" comparisons should be avoided.

4. *Advance dissemination of operating rules* is desirable because of many situations that arise, two of which serve as illustrations.

The first of these is inherent in the use of incentive pay systems which offer rewards for such independent activities as recruiting, office maintenance, collection of premiums. In the absence of clear home office statements of philosophy and intent, general agents and managers may interpret such systems too literally. Even though total expense allowances may be adequate to cover total expenses they may point to individual, sometimes minor, elements of their operations that are not covered by any specific compensation factor and say that they are "losing money" on those operations. The home office cannot effectively counter such arguments unless it has previously pointed out that the plan is not a cost accounting system intended to cover every phase of agency management activity but is designed to give at best rough justice while perhaps deliberately emphasizing certain activities considered of special current importance to company progress.

Another situation that requires advance understanding is what shall be done if agency territory is to be split or if an agent or supervisor is to be appointed to a management position elsewhere. This is unpalatable to discuss even in the abstract, but becomes exceptionally so if it remains unresolved until a specific case actually arises.

STATISTICS NEEDED FOR FINANCIAL MANAGEMENT

In agency management as in any other enterprise statistics are useless unless they answer questions that should be asked and that can be answered. So it is first necessary to decide what financial management questions can appropriately be asked, and then to discover what dollar and cent facts can be obtained to answer them.

A common question that actuaries are asked by agency officers is, "How much can we afford to spend for new business?" Even if the company is subject to the overall ceiling on field expenses imposed in New York, this question is extremely difficult to answer. It can be answered in a company whose financial condition is such that money for agency expansion just is not available. But in a company with ample resources the question itself is, at least in part, defective.

The fact is that a very large part of agency expense in a typical life insurance company is not spent "for new business," at least not for current new business. It is spent *for development of field manpower* which is likely to be reflected much more in the new business of several years hence than in the new business currently being written. Furthermore, the amount a company can "afford to spend" depends heavily upon the *quality* as well as the *quantity* of resulting new business. By quality is meant the persistency of the business and its handling cost.

Consider, for example, two companies that have identical scales of premiums, the same surplus conditions and similarity in other major operating factors. The question "How much can we afford?" would presumably be given the same answer in each of these companies. But in one the agency department might spend that money in such a way that the agency force would be expanded in a healthy manner. In the other the money might go to increasing the attractiveness of the franchise among existing agencies with relatively little resulting expansion and development. Clearly the first of these companies could "afford" that expenditure much more readily than the second company could. Agency expense must in large measure be visualized as an investment rather than as the mere payment of bills for current administrative operations.

On the other hand, if the agency officer and the actuary working together produce figures showing what agency plan of the future could be expected to result from a given expenditure, it should then be possible to produce what is called a model office indicating the effect upon the company of that expenditure. By this approach the question becomes not "How much can we afford?" but "How much money can we effectively use, and how can we most effectively use it, to strengthen and expand our agency operationt?"

Another common question is, "How does our expense compare with (a) our corresponding expense for any prior year, or (b) the results obtained by competing companies?" Although this question is subject to some of the same difficulties as the previous question it nevertheless can be the basis for development of enlightening statistics. This will be discussed further in this chapter under Agency Budgeting and Intercompany Expense Comparisons.

Another question sometimes asked is, "How can we determine the profitability of each of our agencies?" Facts can be developed to answer this question, but only after the purpose of the question has been clarified. This question may arise under either of two quite different circumstances. The first of these has to do with the desirability of opening an agency in a new territory, or of closing an agency that is observed to be working out poorly in terms of activity or quality of business, or expense. The other, more common, situation is when it is intended that the answer be used for the motivation, supervision or reward of field management.

In the first of these situations the company may obtain the answer by so-called "asset-share"[3] calculations incorporating the effect of mortality,

---

[3] An asset-share calculation is one that follows the profitability of a block of business through a period of years into the future using specified mortality, interest and expense assumptions.

persistency and expense elements to the extent that these can be isolated for the individual area. But in the other situation, in which the answer is to be used for supervisory purposes, it is important that each agency be viewed in terms only of fiscal elements over which the local field manager has some control. Recently opened agencies are usually much less profitable currently than long established agencies for obvious reasons having nothing to do with the competence of the incumbent agency manager. Likewise some areas in which a company may operate may be less salubrious than others from a persistency, mortality or operating expense viewpoint. The use of a single standard for agencies operating under different conditions can be extremely unfair. It does more harm than good to incorporate into profitability appraisals factors which the local manager is powerless to influence for better or worse.

On the other hand, every agency manager should be kept reliably informed of all the factors that determine the profitability of his agency, including the ones that are not directly or immediately controllable by him.

To sum up, the statistics needed for financial management are of two distinct types, namely

1. Projections showing what can be expected to happen in the future under differing future conditions.
2. Accounting statements showing what has happened in some recent period compared with a forecast previously made, or with the results of some prior periods, or with the results achieved in some other company.

In a company on the general agency system it is important to realize that two distinct sets of expense figures are needed for supervisory and planning purposes. The first set shows the cost *to the company,* reflecting the expense allowances that it pays to its general agents. The second is the cost, and resulting net income, *to the general agent,* reflecting the extent to which his actual incurred expense is more than, less than, or exactly equal to the expense allowances he received from the company.

Furthermore, as already mentioned, under the general agency system expense must be measured as the present value of the commitment that is created under the company's general agency contract by the production of a unit of new business. It is wrong and dangerous to look only at current outlay. The same situation may also occur under the branch office system under some forms of managerial contract.

It is extremely important to have for new agencies that are subsidized a realistic yardstick for measuring performance so that unsatisfactory developments will not be allowed to drag on unperceived for far too long.

AGENCY BUDGETING

In agency budgeting a company must take into account the principle already stated which is that the justification for a particular level of expense depends upon much more than just the quantity of current new business. It depends upon the quality as well as quantity of new business and it depends also upon the progress achieved in building effective agency manpower over the period under review.

Few companies have yet developed methods for agency budgeting that satisfactorily meet these difficult tests. As one surveys methods currently in use it is easier to see their shortcomings and superficialities than it is to point to a method that fully takes care of the basic requirements.

It is desirable, and some companies have taken the necessary steps, to analyze field manpower in a more illuminating and effective manner than simply counting the number of full time agents at any given time. A full-time agency force may be categorized into three segments, namely:

(1) Agents recently recruited, say within the past three contract years, whose performance and survival experience is just beginning to show itself. To these agents must go a large share of financing expense as well as training time. Much recruiting and selection expense is incurred also to fill the positions of the failures among these agents.

(2) Agents who have been under contract for more than three contract years who can be classified according to some criterion of their success. It should be noted that this criterion may change from time to time. The dollar-per-agent cost of maintenance and supervision in this established agent category is so heavy that company failure to establish a realistic criterion of success can prove very costly.

(3) Agents whose contracts are still in force but who are relatively inactive by reason of age, disability or non-life-insurance interests.

An agency budget can then be developed to provide rather substantial per capita amounts for agents in the first category, more modest sums for agents in the second category and small amounts for agents in the third category.

One difficulty that must somehow be overcome lies in the measurement of accomplishment (success) in each of these groups. Volume of new business is an unsatisfactory measure because it fails to distinguish between permanent and term insurance and fails to give recognition to persistency and handling cost. The most practical system seems to be to use a measure of prospective commission earnings that allows for earned cash commissions increased by a value of future earnings from business currently produced. The so-called "annualized first commission" method is a step in that direction, but it fails to make allowance on the one hand for the probability of lapse, and on the other hand for the value of renewal commissions.

For budgeting and control purposes agency expense needs to be classified into four categories which require differing treatment, namely:

(1) Commissions and security benefits for agents and general agents.
(2) Financing costs of new agents.
(3) Field office operating expense (salaries, rent and other such items) or expense allowances paid by the home office in lieu of such items.
(4) Agency expense emanating from the home office, particularly conventions, advertising, agency department salaries and expense.

(1) *Commissions and security benefits* are susceptible to effective control only at the times that new contracts and new coverages are introduced. When changes in these plans are under consideration the most careful analyses of prospective cost under realistic conditions, and comparisons with plans of competing companies should be made. Prospective cost should be examined on a present value (discounted) basis, and also by a projection that shows the incidence of cost year by year.

This expense category must, of course, also be examined in terms of value to the general agent, manager or agent who received the commission or security benefit. Special problems arise in measuring the compensation of general agents and agents.

Total compensation to a general agent for the activities of a calendar year is generally considered to be the net of the following five items (a), (b), (c), (d) and (e):

(a) the cash income received by him during the year in the form of overriding commissions, collection fees and expense allowances,

less (b) the operating expenses of the agency for the year (which the general agent should be asked to report to the home office),

plus (c) the amount by which the present value of general agent's future vested[4] first year and renewal overriding commissions on all the business of his agency at the end of the calendar year exceeds the corresponding present value at the end of the preceding calendar year.

(These present values should be calculated on a realistic basis for the particular general agent, recognizing the

---

[4] Some authorities prefer to measure total future commissions rather than the vested portion only.

anticipated persistency experience of his business as it may be deduced from his own past experience, and discounting for interest at an appropriate rate, at least 4% per annum under current conditions.)

plus (d) the cash income received by him on his personal production during the year.

plus (e) the amount by which the present value, realistically determined, of his future vested (or total) commissions on personal production at the end of the calendar year exceeds the corresponding present value at the end of the preceding calendar year.

The compensation of an agent is measured in the same way as described in (d) and (e) above.

(2) *Financing costs of new agents* require both a present value and a current cost approach. These also are controllable principally at the time that a new plan is being introduced. But in addition results should be regularly measured against the original assumption as to agents' survival and production. Also it may sometimes be found necessary to limit the number of new agents to keep financing costs from exceeding desired limits.

In addition to current review of each agent's financing outlay it is important to make regular studies of recruits contracted at different ages and financing levels so that recruiting effort will be exerted in the most desirable directions. Studies of this kind are quite likely to cause a company to change the advice it gives to its field managers about where recruits should be sought.

(3) If *field office operating expenses* are paid by the home office, analysis for control purposes should be accomplished by classifying these expenses into first year and renewal portions respectively. The procedure for making this separation is described elsewhere in this handbook (Chapter 33, Financial Planning for Profitable Agency Operation).

(4) *Agency expense emanating from the home office* likewise should be classified into its first year and renewal portions. Most of it is concerned with new business, but some administration work in the agency department may be involved in the renewal premium collection and service to policyholders functions of agencies.

When all these figures have been obtained and classified as indicated, it then becomes necessary to compare them with some index of quantity of business being done. (This is commonly done even though it may very properly be felt that some of the expense is for future rather than current new business.) Each of the available indices of quantity is subject to some objections and drawbacks,—volume of business because it fails to allow for differing proportions of term insurance; premiums because the effect of reducing gross premiums in a mutual company will be to raise the apparent expense rate and vice versa; commissions because they themselves are an element of expense; premium loadings because they do not genuinely represent the expense provision in a life insurance contract. The item among these that is subject to the smallest objection is either premiums or commissions, some preferring one, some the other. New business expense can be compared with first year premiums or commissions, renewal business expense with renewal premiums or commissions.

In addition, there may be developed a single index that represents total expense in terms of the premiums out of which that expense must be provided. To obtain this, the first step is to calculate the present value (discounted with allowance for interest and persistency) of all first year and renewal expenses over the lifetime of an Ordinary Life policy. The second step is to calculate the corresponding present value of all the premiums to be collected over the lifetime of an Ordinary Life policy. The expense rate is the value of the first of these items divided by the value of the second of these items expressed as a percentage. This is the manner in which the prospective quality as well as the quantity of the new business can be brought into the picture.

INTERCOMPANY EXPENSE COMPARISONS

Several possibilities exist for comparing agency expenses of one company with another. None so far devised is completely satisfactory, but, with care in compiling data and with caution in interpreting it, some useful and enlightening comparisons can be made.

One such method for comparison is the calculation of expenses in relation to the expense limits of New York Section 213 (Schedule Q). This can be done whether or not the company making the comparison happens to operate in New York State. It should be kept in mind, however, that the formula of Schedule Q tends to place substantial emphasis on renewal business. Hence a company that is growing rapidly, i.e., that has a relatively high proportion of first year as compared with renewal business, will tend to show a heavier expense ratio than a company that is growing more slowly even though the two companies may genuinely have identical first year and renewal expense rates.

Another method for comparison of expenses of one company with another is by developing an expense "formula" based on one's own company's actual results. The procedure is first to express one's own results as the sum of a percentage (f%) of first year premiums and another percentage (r%) of renewal premiums. Then, if the corresponding dollar expenses for another company that operates on a somewhat similar basis are available those expenses of that other company can be compared with what they would be if that company also incurred agency expenses equal to f% of its first year premiums plus r% of its renewal premiums.

The drawback to this method is that it gives no clue as to the location of whatever difference appears. The method also is beset by pitfalls attributable to the differences in operations, types of business and accounting practices of different companies. The shortcomings of annual statements from which such information must usually come have also to be recognized.

The best method for intercompany comparison is that upon which both the Life Insurance Agency Management Association and the Life Office Management Association have worked from time to time, i.e., to compare directly the first year expenses and the renewal expenses of various companies. This method which must be applied separately to different lines of business—individual and group, life and health—requires intercompany cooperation in the careful development of a set of rules so that the figures assembled are genuinely comparable. Even when comparability in the rules has been achieved, care is necessary in interpreting the figures because of difference in the patterns of company operations. For example, it is likely that one company performs functions in its agencies that another company performs in its home office.

THE STATE OF THE ART

Many of the procedures described in this chapter are widely used; others, it appears to this observer, are preached more often than practiced. Authorities on agency financial management agree that opportunity beckons us to broaden some of our concepts, to seek more and better facts to guide us, and particularly to develop a more clear-cut distinction between expenditures that merely maintain the status quo and expenditures that are genuine investments in agency development.

33

Financial Planning for Profitable Agency Operation

Armand C. Stalnaker

Profitable agency operation is a primary objective of both the individual agency head and the life insurance company. Whether the agency head is a general agent or an agency manager, the profitability of his agency operation will be an important factor in his survival, in his personal income and in his managerial success. For the company, profitability of agency operations will be an important factor in assuring survival, reducing net cost, increasing profits for the stock company and contributions to surplus for the mutual company, and preserving the approved Scheduled Q expense margins for companies authorized to do business in New York.

Financial planning for the agency must be accomplished within the constraints, resulting from (1) company policy, (2) company objectives, and (3) company plans, as well as the constraints resulting from the general environment in which the agency must operate. Within these constraints another level of objectives can be established at the agency level.

Many companies operating under a branch manager system evaluate the effectiveness of individual agencies by measuring their profitability, efficiency, or results in relation to costs. The degree of refinement employed, as well as the extent to which the component factors affect managerial compensation, will vary from company to company. Generally, the indices and compensation factors reflect measures of production, persistency, agency building, and controllable expenses. Some companies go further, incorporating measures of mortality and morbidity, in arriving at a measure of the long-term profitability of an agency.

Although this chapter will illustrate financial planning for a general agent, the basic techniques may be modified to provide a basis for financial planning for the manager of a branch office.

THE NEED FOR FINANCIAL PLANNING

Planning defines and prescribes the means of attaining an objective. Planning may be short-range or long-range in nature. Long-range planning provides a basis for short-range planning. Since a significant part of current agency expenses are for results in the future, long-range planning is particularly important in an agency.

A general agent may have many objectives, most of which affect the profitability of his operations. Some of these may be complementary and some may be conflicting. Let us consider a few examples:

(1) For the general agent's earnings to reach $30,000 in five years.
(2) To achieve company leadership in production in the current year.
(3) To meet minimum company standards for survival as a general agent this year.
(4) To build an agency of 35 successful agents in three years.
(5) To establish a successful pension sales operation.

Even when the objectives are complementary, some are of greater importance than others. Thus, as an aid to decision making, it is desirable to establish an hierarchy of objectives. The essential nature of the agency that will tend to evolve will reflect the philosophy and the objectives of the company, the philosophy, objectives and abilities of the agency head, and the opportunities that exist within the particular community involved.

The general agent is interested in maximizing his net income and profit, both currently and in the long run. Net income consists of his compensation, including expense allowance, less agency expenses (including any portion of his compensation required to pay commissions and salaries to supervisors and clerical employees). A portion of each year's income derives from agency activities in prior years (e.g., renewal overriding commissions on business written in prior years). Similarly the current year's operation of the agency will create income for the general agent in subsequent years, primarily in the form of vested renewal overridings. Renewal overriding commissions are termed vested if they are payable even after the general agent's termination. Profit consists of his net income for the year plus the increase for the year in the present value of his vested renewal overridings. The present value of his vested renewal overridings is obtained by discounting for interest and persistency renewal commissions payable in subsequent years. The increase for the year in the present value of his vested renewal overridings is the difference between (1) discounted renewal commissions stemming from that year's production, and (2) renewal commissions paid during the year.

The expenses incurred in selling life insurance can be justified only on the basis of certain assumptions about what will happen in the future to business that has been sold and is currently being sold. An understanding of the significance of a life insurance agency's financial operations becomes clear only if we bring down to the present the agency's expectations concerning the receipt of future premiums. The agency must take the long-term view of its life cycle. The installment payment of future premiums has a value to the agency only if the business stays on the books. But previous experience can be indicative of future expectation. Therefore, it is possible to predict realistically the ultimate consequences of agency actions currently taking place.

It is because of the relationship of every activity in the agency to the ultimate financial result that the need exists for careful planning of all agency activities to assure that each makes a favorable contribution to the financial success of the agency. The term "favorable contribution," of course, connotes a situation in which the income produced by or affected by a particular activity will be greater than the expense of conducting that activity. Regardless of the type of agency—general agency or managerial—an increasing volume of new business does not automatically produce satisfactory financial results, nor does cutting costs across the board always effectively correct a continuing problem of unsatisfactory financial results. Planning must be preceded by a careful examination of the causes of variations in rates of income and expenses. The subject of agency expense analysis will be treated in Chapter 35.

If required information for planning is not available in the agency, the agency head may be able to obtain assistance from the home office.

GENERAL AGENTS COMPENSATION

The compensation of general agents typically consists of most of the following elements:

(1) First-Year Overriding Commissions
(2) Vested Renewal Overriding Commissions
(3) Nonvested Collection Fees

(4) Expense Allowances

(5) Reversions (Some contracts provide that if an agent terminates, under certain conditions, all or part of the agent's renewal commissions revert to the general agent.)

(6) Personal Commissions

It is important that the general agent read his contract and understand the various sources of income in specific relation to his agency operation.

QUALITY BUSINESS

A life insurance agency should be interested in obtaining and retaining on its books business of high quality, both from the standpoint of service to the public and of course for its effect on profitable operation.

Some of the important numerical indices of quality business are average size policy, average premium per thousand, average collection frequency, and lapse ratio.

THE PLANNING OPERATION

The establishment of an objective, or a series of objectives, does not constitute a plan. Unless the general agent alters his operation the results that were obtained in the past will tend to continue in the future. Assume that an agency has been relatively static with respect to manpower for a number of years and the general agent is considering establishing an objective to increase the number of agents by 50 percent over a five-year period. Two questions must be answered: Is it feasible? Is it desirable?

To evaluate the feasibility of this possible objective, he must determine what its accomplishment entails. First, he might reduce it to an annual basis. Then he could consider how his recruiting and selection activities should be modified to obtain the additional manpower. He should determine whether the agency has the capacity to train the necessary number of men. Consideration must be given to space requirements. Will it be necessary for the agency to relocate and if so, when and where? At what point and to what extent will additional supervisors and clerks be necessary? Can the turnover rate of present personnel be reduced? What will be the probable short-range and long-range effect on the general agent's income and profit? Can this manpower growth be financed with capital which is available? The foregoing is illustrative of the analysis that should be undertaken to determine the feasibility of the objective.

The determination of the desirability of this possible objective should be based on comparison of the return in income and profit from the expenditure of effort and money with that which could be realized from other possible activities. Perhaps more desirable results might be obtained by providing the existing agents with additional staff support. Perhaps a less ambitious objective, within the limitations of the agency's present space and staff capacity, would be more desirable. Of all agency expenses involved in manpower expansion, additional supervisory and training staff is, by far, the most costly.

ESTIMATING RETURN TO THE GENERAL AGENT

In making plans for the future, the general agent will generally want to evaluate the financial effect of his plans. He may also want to set profit objectives and translate these objectives into meaningful production, conservation, and expense goals.

The example to be considered is not intended to be typical nor are the assumptions made applicable to any particular agency. The technique employed can be applied to a variety of planning situations. The general approach is to express income and expense as a percentage of applicable premiums. Calculations are based on a million dollars of new business. An average premium of $25 per $1000 of insurance for both new business as well as existing business is assumed.

The following table illustrates the persistency factors (Linton's A) and discount factors (7%) used:

Policy Year	Persistency Factor	Discount Factor	Product
1	1.000	1.0000	1.000
2	.896	.9346	.837
3	.838	.8734	.732
4	.791	.8163	.646
5	.751	.7629	.573
6	.716	.7130	.511
7	.684	.6663	.456
8	.656	.6227	.408
9	.631	.5820	.367
10	.608	.5439	.331
Sum: 2d to 10th years	6.571	—	4.861
11	.586	.5083	.298
12	.565	.4751	.268
13	.545	.4440	.242
14	.525	.4150	.218
15	.506	.3878	.196
Sum: 11th to 15th years	2.727	—	1.222
16	.488	.3624	.177

(*Continued*)

17	.470	.3387	.159
18	.452	.3166	.143
19	.433	.2595	.128
20	.415	.2765	.115
Sum: 16th to 20th years	2.258	—	.722
Sum: 2d to 20th years	11.556	—	6.805
Sum: 1st to 20th years	12.556	—	7.805

A first-year expense rate of $4 per $1,000 of insurance is assumed. This can be converted to a percentage of first-year premium by dividing the $4 by the average premium per $1,000 of $25 yielding a rate of 16%.

The following table summarizes the income and expense factors by policy years:

	First Year			Renewal		
	Income		Expense	Income		Expense
Policy Years	1st Year Overriding	Expense Allowance	16% 1st Yr. Expense	Vested Renewal Overriding	Collection Fee	1st Renewal Expense
1	5%	10%	16%	—	—	—
2–10				1½%	1%	1%
11–15				3%	2%	1%
16–20					2%	1%

First we shall calculate the estimated return to the general agent per million dollars of new business, without taking into consideration the element of interest.

Policy Year	Sum of Income Factors (from previous table)	Persistency Factors	Product (in % of new premium)
1	15.0%	1.000	15.000
2–10	2.5	6.571	16.427
11–15	5.0	2.727	13.635
16–20	2.0	2.258	4.516
		12.556	49.578%
Gross Income per Million		49.578% of $25,000	=$12,395
Renewal Expense per Million		1%×11.556×$25,000=	2,889
Available for First Year Expense and Income			$ 9,506
First Year Expense		4% of $25,000	= 4,000
Total Income per million			$ 5,506

It should be noted that this calculation of total income does not actually coincide with net income, since the income produced will be spread over a 20-year period, nor will it coincide with profit, since interest has not been taken into consideration. The result can be interpreted as representing the estimated income in the 20th year of operation from a level production of a million dollars of insurance per year.

If we take interest, as well as persistency, into consideration we have:

Policy Year	Sum of Income Factors	Combined Persistency and Discount Factors	Product
1	15.0%	1.000	15.000%
2–10	2.5	4.861	12.153
11–15	5.0	1.222	6.110
16–20	2.0	.722	1.444
		7.805	34.707

Gross Income per Million:	34.707% of $25,000=$8,677
Renewal Expense per Million:	1%×6.805×$25,000= 1,701
Available for First Year Expense and Income	$6,976
First Year Expense	4,000
Total Income per Million	$2,976

This calculation produces the present value, discounted for persistency and interest, of the income produced from $1,000,000 of new business.

There is another approach to the problem of estimating general agency income which, although somewhat longer, is more realistic due to its greater flexibility. Here, the method is to construct a model agency, reflecting expected future trends. Though in the interest of simplicity most factors are held constant, an increasing production assumption is frequently used —representing a gain in flexibility over the "short method."

CAPITAL BUDGETING

Planning and control of capital expenditures is an important factor in future profitable agency operations. The objective of capital expenditures is to make profits. Thus the need for growth should be measured by prospective profitability. Alternative possibilities should be evaluated on this basis.

An important constraint is the availability of funds. Long-range planning involves setting aside a portion of current profits for future capital requirements.

In the traditional "pure" general agency, capital required was supplied solely by the general agent. Today, in some instances, that is still true, while in other instances, changes in company practices have relieved the general agent of this burden in varying degrees. The fact remains, however, that it is still the general agent's responsibility to determine what capital is needed, and to plan and direct its use.

The types of capital needs in an agency are as follows:

1. For current agency operation when current income may be insufficient.
2. For acquiring furniture or equipment that may not be supplied by the company.
3. For headquarters space expansion, or for "district office" development.
4. For supervisor assistance.
5. For financing of agents (to the extent that it is not provided by the company).

With a need for capital once established in his mind, the general agent is confronted by the question of where to get it. One or more of several ways may be open:

1. From personal savings or other assets already accumulated, including the cash values of his personal life insurance.
2. From a reduction of the income he has been taking personally from the agency.
3. From his bank, on a simple demand note if possible, or by loan based on collateral other than agency assets.
4. From his bank on a loan based on his vested values in the agency.
5. From his company, if his plans for capital use are acceptable, and the security value seems adequate. Some companies will not make direct loans of this nature under any circumstances, but will by endorsement support the general agent's negotiations with his bank.

MEASURING THE LONG-RANGE IMPLICATIONS OF CURRENT DECISIONS

The general agent will want to estimate the future financial impact of alternate decisions presently being considered. These might relate to:

1. Changes in type and number of soliciting agents.
2. Changes in territorial activity.
3. Changes in kind of business sought.
4. Increase or decrease in office space allotment, including private offices.
5. Increase or decrease in special services to agents, such as policy audits, printed tax services, insurance journals, telephone use, and travel allowance.
6. Increased or decreased clerical and secretarial assistance to agents.

7. Increased use of mechanical devices.
8. Increase or decrease in supervisory assistance.
9. Increase or decrease in advertising and other stimulative activities.
10. Changes in training procedures.
11. Changes in the agency's policy on contests and awards.

If the contemplated decision will affect production, then a conservative estimate of the additional production that the change will produce should be obtained. Often it is desirable to have the estimate in the form of a range of values, i.e., a high estimate and a low estimate. Similarly, if the contemplated changes are likely to affect the persistency of business, an estimate of the effect should be made. The combined impact of these effects on the general agent's compensation should be calculated, not only for the current year but for a period of ten years. As an offset against increased compensation, it is necessary to determine the year by year impact of the change on expenses.

Admittedly, it is not easy to obtain reliable estimates of the factors of profit that will be affected by a change but even "guess-timates" are of some value. It is also important to use judgment and properly weigh the effect of the contemplated decision on factors that might not be directly associated with profit, e.g., morale and its ultimate effect on agency turnover.

34

Compensation and Incentive Arrangements

Charles F. B. Richardson

This chapter will discuss primarily compensation arrangements permitted by the New York Expense Limitation Law, commonly—but sometimes not too affectionately—known as Section 213. Restricting the discussion to compensation arrangements permitted by New York law seems appropriate because the latter's extra-territorial application to foreign companies operating in New York State makes Section 213 applicable to a large portion of the total life insurance business written in the United States.

It is true that Section 213 does not apply to companies that do not operate in New York State. However, the force of competition in the pricing of the life insurance product is such that non-New York companies must limit their expenditures in compensating the field force and in financing agency operations. If the non-New York companies were to be extravagant in such expenditures they would be forced to price themselves out of the market in order to recover the expenditures.

In many cases the non-New York companies pay out about the same amount in total, but they may pay it in forms not permitted by the New York law. While a new company may have to pay more to get business than a long established company, typically, total compensation costs tend to come down to somewhere near the New York standards as the new companies grow in size.

Because of space limitations this chapter will be confined to compensation arrangements for ordinary life insurance business, and will not attempt to discuss the many different considerations involved in compensation arrangements for the sale of industrial, health and group insurance or group pensions.

GENERAL CONSIDERATIONS

Philosophy and Objectives of Management

The philosophy of management of a company inevitably has a marked effect upon the types of compensation and expense structures that a company uses, especially for the upper levels of field management, e.g., general agents or branch managers, and to a lesser extent further down the line. For example, a company may desire to completely control or substantially dictate such things as (1) the types of market to be developed, (2) the methods used in such development, (3) the kinds of sales promotion to be used, (4) the systems of training and supervision of the agents, (5) the proportion of the manager's time permitted to be spent on personal production or upon the development of a sales force, (6) the emphasis to be placed on recruitment of full-time career agents versus various types of brokers, (7) the establishment of suboffices, and (8) the extent of centralization at the home office or decentralization at the agency office of policyholder service functions. On the other hand, the company may desire to give rather wide latitude to the local manager or general agent in some or all of these areas. The extent to which broad or narrow authority is given to the agency manager will, in turn, determine the extent and type of supervision furnished by the home office.

In practice there are wide differences in the objectives of different companies in most of these areas, and therefore in the methods of compensation and expense allowances used. It is not nearly as practical today, as it used to be, to give broad discretion to local management in its methods of operation. This results from a number of factors including (1) the effect of high income tax rates which make it difficult for the manager to repay out of after-tax income the large amount of borrowed capital needed initially, (2) the growing impact of mechanization (including centralization of services through the use of electronic data processing systems), (3) the development of costly financing and training programs for new agents, (4) the impact of national advertising programs, (5) the development of elaborate sales promotion systems in a business becoming more and more complicated which, in turn, necessitates some degree of standardization.

Finally, the cost of all these things, borne to an increasing extent by the company, usually results in more centralized and standardized systems. In essence, subsidy typically results in the imposition of greater central control.

Relative Importance of Income Stability versus Incentives

In designing a compensation plan for the various types of field personnel, one of the fundamental questions is the relative weight that should be given to (1) stability of income (renewal commissions, for example), (2) incentives to agents and managers to expand new sales, and (3) incentives to managers to develop new manpower. The degree to which these elements should enter a compensation plan will vary with the type of job involved, and there are wide differences of opinion as to the relative importance of the basic elements of stability of income and incentives.

It is generally held that for managers or general agents a greater degree of stability of income is desirable than in the case of agents,[1] and in any case the law dictates a considerable variation in the income of the agent in relation to his recent rate of production of new business. In the case of middle management, e.g., supervisors and assistant managers, whose main job is to develop new manpower, a substantial part of the compensation should depend on sales results and manpower development.

More difficult questions arise in the case of managers of group offices, group sales supervisors and group service representatives. Group offices generally serve several agencies and to some extent their results depend on the degree to which the agency managers choose to promote the group lines. Also, the group sales supervisors generally operate in the territory as a whole and more than one of them may work on a given case. Therefore, there is generally a sharing of the total sales results in the group office, sometimes related to the operating expenses and the growth of the business.

Compensation Competitive to Attract Manpower

The question as to the level of compensation that should be provided for a new manager or general agent will to a large extent be determined

---

[1] "The problem is that managers, like other people, are psychologically unable to accept the prospect of starvation or luxury as alternatives. If too large a portion of the compensation is related to variations in results, the minimum anticipated payment will come to be regarded as unrelated to results. A reasonably large, stabilized income, combined with a highly variable but relatively small performance incentive factor in the compensation, may actually provide much greater motivation." Stalnaker, Armand C., *Life Insurance Agency Financial Management*, Richard D. Irwin, Inc., Homewood, Illinois, 1956, p. 118.

by competition of other types of business for comparable manpower. This becomes a rather complicated matter because the manager of a life insurance agency has the opportunity to build a large income if he is successful, as compared to what he would receive in other types of industry, with comparable security and vesting of deferred income. It seems quite likely that the recruitment of competent managerial personnel in competition with other industries, and within the legal expense limitations that now prevail, may become one of the most difficult problems our business will have to face.

Compensation Controlled to Price Product Competitively

Finally, the total cost of distributing our product, including managerial and agent compensation, new agent financing and agency office expenses must be so controlled as to result in a competitive product in a mutual company, and a satisfactory profit to stockholders as well as a competitive product in a stock company. In this connection, it has been reliably estimated that these distribution costs in our industry comprise no less than two-thirds of our total operating expenses.

LEGAL RESTRICTIONS—SECTION 213 NEW YORK LAW

The New York expense limitation statute, which arose out of the Armstrong Investigation in 1905, but which has been greatly expanded and amended many times since then, has a pervasive and controlling effect on many phases of compensation, and must therefore be briefly described. The New York Insurance law requires all companies operating in the state to comply with the law with respect to their total operations, i.e., extra territorial supervision, and since most of the large companies operate in New York this statute effectively controls the level and type of compensation plans for a large proportion of the business in this country. It even applies to the foreign operations of the companies, which is an important reason why most United States companies do not engage in such operations.

The law is extremely complicated and there are several different limits applying to various types of expenses, and in more than one instance there are inside limits within an outside limit.

Limitations on Agents' Compensation

Agent compensation is affected by the following provisions of Section 213 of the New York law:

1. First year commissions may not exceed 55% of the premium.
2. There is a First Year Field Expense Limit covering first year commissions and advances to agents. While this is an aggregate limit, the formulas defining the limit result in a first year expense allowance for commissions lower than 55% for plans with premiums either higher or lower than ordinary life. While in theory it would be possible to pay a 55% first year commission on any plan, if the company did so and received too much business on that plan, the expenses, of which first year commissions comprise all but a fraction of the total, would inevitably exceed the limit. The result is that the grading of first year commission rates by plan is to a large extent dictated by the formulas contained in the law.
3. Renewal commissions, if vested in the agent, (i.e., payable if he leaves the company), are limited to a specified rate for the first ten years, a lower rate for the next five years and a still lower rate after the fifteenth year. They are lower on policies with premiums higher than 20 year endowments. These commissions may be rearranged on a basis actuarially equivalent to the scale in the law, and if they are wholly or partially non-vested, higher rates may be paid. For example, large renewals may be paid in the early policy years, but these must be spread over at least three years and not over 40% of the commuted value may be paid in any one year.
4. In addition to the renewal commissions allowed there is a small additional margin that may be used only to provide security benefits, (pension benefits, for example). If the value of these benefits exceeds this limit, the excess must come out of the value of the renewal commission scale.
5. In the case of new career agents, additional compensation, called training allowances, may be paid in the agent's first three years in the business and each such plan must be approved by the Insurance Department. Renewal commissions may never be vested on business written while the agent is receiving training allowances. There are restrictions with respect to eligibility to receive these allowances in the case of agents who have previously worked for another company. This is to prevent an agent from continually changing companies in order to get this extra compensation.

Limitations on Compensation of General Agents

The compensation of general agents, but not managers under a branch office operation, is also affected by the law.

1. Overriding commissions to the general agent cannot exceed 5% of the first premium if the agent gets 55% first year commissions. Renewal overridings are limited by a statutory scale which must cover commissions paid to general agents and agents combined. Here again the scale of renewal overridings may be rearranged on

an actuarially equivalent basis, more of the compensation being either paid in the earlier policy years or alternatively postponed to later years.

2. There are strict and detailed regulations governing agency expenses reimbursed to the general agent by the company designed to prevent evasion of the compensation limits through lax administration of expense allowances. The effect of this is that a general agent who runs an economical agency and spends less than the company's expense formula provides, cannot profit by his efficient operation because he can receive reimbursement only for expenses actually incurred. This aspect of the regulations has been frequently criticized.

3. If the general agent personally writes more than 50% of the agency's business, his overriding commissions are reduced.

4. New general agents may be subsidized for the first five years and on a restricted basis for another five years. Since it generally takes seven or eight years until the overriding commissions exceed the salary the company has to pay to keep the general agent, this portion of the law has been criticized because it hampers the development of new outlets under the general agency system. The result is that many companies are forced to start new general agents on the managerial system, changing them over to general agents when they have become established.

Besides the First Year Field Expense Limit mentioned above there is a Total Field Expense Limit. This covers all compensation to general agents, managers, supervisors and agents, including advances to agents, subsidies under financing plans and training allowances. The last item is further controlled by an inside limit. Other expenses included are the costs of operating the agencies, 60% of the cost of advertising and the current cost of pensions for agents. The formula for determining the limit is comprised of no less than 16 separate items.

Finally, there is a Total Expense Limit which covers all the expenses of the company except investment expenses (up to $\frac{1}{4}$% of assets) and taxes. This particular limit does not apply to stock companies selling only nonparticipating business.

The law applies only to ordinary and industrial business. It does not apply to health insurance or group insurance.

It is significant that the proportion of business in force in the United States in companies operating in New York State has declined from 80% in 1946 to 66% in 1965. The new business written in 1965 by companies admitted to New York was only 51% of the national total. The restrictive effects of this statute and the inflexibility which it imposes in so many areas must be among the most important reasons for this marked decline in the New York companies' share of the total market.

GENERAL AGENT COMPENSATION

The scale of compensation paid to the general agent in the form of overriding commissions cannot be considered alone without reference to the expense allowance formula which determines the amount of agency expenses to be paid by the company. Some companies pay generous overridings and modest expense allowances and in some cases the allowances are smaller than the cost of operating an agency under today's conditions. In these cases the general agent must use part of his compensation for expenses, especially if he wants to build his agency.

Forty years ago there were two typical scales of overriding commissions in general use by New York companies. The first provided 5% in the first year, 2½% for the second to tenth policy years, 5% for the eleventh to fifteenth years and 2½% thereafter. The second scale brought forward half of the commissions for the eleventh to the fifteenth years, resulting in 5% for the first year, 7½% in the second year and 2½% thereafter. These scales assume an agent contract providing 50% first year commission and nine 5's. Some general agents paid the agent 55% first year, thus eliminating their first year overriding. In recent years the New York law was amended to permit a total of 60% in the first year of which 55% could be paid to the agent.

TABLE 1
SCALES OF OVERRIDING COMMISSIONS TO GENERAL AGENT
Policy Year

Company	Total 1–15	1	2	3	4	5	6–10	11	12–15	16 On
A	34%	5%	5%	5%	2%	2%	2%	1%	1%	1%
B	26	0	4.5	4.5	1.5	1.5	1.5	6.5	0	0
C	47.5	5	5	5	2.5	2.5	2.5	2	2	2
D	46.3	5	7.5	2.5	2.5	2.5	2.5	1.75	1.75	1.75
E	36.5	0	6.5	2.5	2.5	2.5	2.5	2	2	2
F	32.5	5	5	5	2.5	2.5	2.5	0	0	0
G	52.5	5	2.5	2.5	2.5	2.5	2.5	5	5	2
H	40	0	2.5	2.5	2.5	2.5	2.5	3.5	3.5	0
I	45	10	2.5	2.5	2.5	2.5	2.5	2.5	2.5	0
J	42.5	5	2.5	2.5	2.5	2.5	2.5	3.0	3.0	0
K	29	5	4	2.5	2.5	2.5	2.5	0	0	0
L	45	0	2.5	2.5	2.5	2.5	2.5	4.5	4.5	1.5

NOTE: The above scales apply to policies with premiums no higher than 20 year endowment; a lower scale applies on higher priced plans.

TABLE 2
SCALES OF OVERRIDING COMMISSIONS WHICH VEST
ON TERMINATION

Company	Year	1	2	3	4	5	6–10	11	12–15	16 On
A		5	1.5	1.5	1.5	1.5	1.5	0	0	0
B		0	4.5	4.5	1.5	1.5	1.5	6.5	0	0
C		0	3.5	3.5	1	1	1	0	0	0
D		5	6	1	1	1	1	0	0	0
E		0	5.5	1.5	1.5	1.5	1.5	0	0	0
F		0	4	4	1.5	1.5	1.5	0	0	0
G		5	1.5	1.5	1.5	1.5	1.5	3	3	0
H		0	1.5	1.5	1.5	1.5	1.5	2.5	2.5	0
I		6	2.5	2.5	2.5	2.5	2.5	0	0	0
J		0	2	2	2	2	2	2.5	2.5	0
K		5	4	1.5	1.5	1.5	1.5	0	0	0
L		0	1.0	1.0	1.0	1.0	1.0	2.5	2.5	0

Today there is no really typical scale of overriding commissions for general agents, and there are many variations in the terms for vesting these commissions. The majority of companies pay 5% in the first year, but some pay nothing. Some companies pay rates larger than 2½% in the early renewal years and less in later years. Some companies terminate overriding commissions in the tenth or fifteenth policy years; few pay over 1½% or 2% after the fifteenth year; and some pay none. The actuarial commuted values of the various scales vary considerably and these values depend to some extent on the degree of liberality of the expense allowances.

Table 1 shows the scales used by twelve companies, all of which operate in New York.

Vesting Provisions in General Agents' Contracts

There is great variation in the vesting provisions in case of termination of a general agent's contract, as may be seen from Tables 2 and 3.

Some of the companies have no requirements for vesting while others grade the vesting by years of service. Some give more liberal vesting on death or retirement than upon termination of the contract. A majority of companies vest less than the full scale of overriding commissions, a number of them substantially less. No doubt the main reason is the fact that the company pays all, or a substantial part, of the operating expenses of the agency, including a subsidy to the new general agent.

TABLE 3

REQUIREMENTS FOR VESTING
(Same for death or retirement unless noted otherwise)

Company	
A	10 years service; between 5 and 10 years, vesting is for first 5 policy years; no vesting under 5 years of service.
B	None.
C	None.
D	Vesting reduced by 1/2% if less than 4 years service. Scale is 1/2% *more* on death or retirement.
E	None.
F	1% collection fee or part thereof may be deducted according to performance. Overriding is 1% more if terminated by death or retirement.
G	Vesting with 2–10 years service limited to policy years 1–20, less 2% collection fee.
H	3 years of service.
I	Vest one year for each year of service, maximum 9 years. On retirement an extra 7 1/2% of eleventh policy year premiums is paid.
J	1 year of service, 0; 2 yrs. 10%; 3 yrs. 25%; 4 yrs. 40%; 5 yrs. 60%; 6 yrs. 80%; 7 yrs. 100%. No service requirement for vesting on death or retirement.
K	1% *more* if terminated by death or retirement. On termination after age 55 and before 65, 50% of 1% extra vested after 10 years service increasing 5% a year to 100% after 20 years service.
L	None. On death overriding is 0.5% *more*.

Compensating General Agents for Expenses

Company arrangements for compensating general agents for expenses vary considerably with respect to (1) the types of formula used, (2) the liberality or conservatism of the total amounts involved and (3) the emphasis placed on the various factors.

A minority of the companies pay directly all or most of the operating expenses, these operations being rather like a branch office system as far as expenses are concerned. However, in these cases there is usually a factor rewarding the general agent for building new manpower, frequently a percentage of the new agent's commissions in his first two or three years.

The more common pattern is an expense formula which determines the maximum amount the company will pay towards expenses. The manner in which the money is spent is determined by the general agent. There is nearly always a first year factor expressed in terms of some measure of new business, i.e., a percentage of first year commissions or premiums, a renewal factor which is generally a small percentage of renewal premiums, and in many cases, but not all, a factor based upon the business written by new agents in their first two or three years. This last factor is coupled with a requirement that the general agent share in agent financing losses. Companies which collect premiums at the home office—a definite trend in these days of automation—pay no renewal expense factor or a small one to cover services in the agency.

Besides the expenses reimbursed by these formulas, it is common for the company to pay part of the expenses for such items as supervisors' salaries, district offices and agent financing losses. Most companies today provide all the funds for agent financing, a great change from the old days when the general agent had to do his own financing.

Another source of income to the general agent used to be the reversions arising from renewal commissions forfeited by terminated agents. However, this is becoming less common as many companies are financing the agents and therefore require these reversions to offset losses. Furthermore, many renewal commission scales anticipate reversions to the company to offset higher commissions provided for agents who survive.

No studies comparing the level of compensation and expense reimbursement offered by the various companies have ever been published. There are undoubtedly wide variations in the total compensation and expense allowances paid for a given performance. However, both of these items vary greatly according to such factors as the maturity of the agency, the expense rate, persistency, rate of growth, recruiting results, etc., and it becomes extremely difficult to make valid comparisons.

Perhaps the outstanding development in general agent compensation today as compared to 20 or 30 years ago is the fact that the general agent is no longer an independent contractor, free to develop his business in his own way.

One of the main reasons for this change is the fact that in these days of high income taxes it becomes impractical for the general agent to borrow money to finance his agency in the early years, as used to be widely practiced, because the profits that later emerge, from which the debt could be repaid, come from income which is taxed at high rates. This has made it necessary for the companies to take over the financing to a great extent and subsidy always brings with it a great degree of control over the operations by the companies. Another reason is that it is difficult to attract men who have the capital or borrowing power and also the qualities needed to become successful general agents.

COMPENSATION OF MANAGERS IN
BRANCH OFFICE COMPANIES

A manager, unlike a general agent, is an employee of the company and completely under the control of the company. Furthermore, he has no vested interest in the business of his agency upon termination of employment, even in case of death or retirement. However, pensions are quite generally provided based upon performance and in the majority of companies some vested interest in the accrued pension is provided in case of termination before retirement.

There is wide variation in the formulas used to determine the manager's salary, not only in the amount paid by various companies for a given performance, but in the emphasis placed upon the various factors which determine the compensation.

In 1958 an authoritative study was published by the Life Insurance Agency Management Association entitled Managerial Compensation (Research Report 1958—1), covering the plans then in use by 40 United States and Canadian companies. Among the factors that appear in the various formulas, not all in any one plan, are the following.

SALARY

In most cases there is a moderate fixed salary, but in a few cases this varies with the size of the agency. This means that the total cost of manager compensation, measured per unit of business, decreases with an increase in the size of the agency. This is one of the main differences between manager and general agent compensation since the latter varies directly in proportion to the size of the agency.

NEW BUSINESS

This factor is most commonly based on a percentage of first year commissions paid to agents. This automatically reflects early first year lapses. Sometimes the percentage is higher for full time agents than for brokers, and in some cases the rate is graded by the amount of production of each agent. Volume of business is still used by some companies, the rate being lower on term insurance than on permanent plans; such factors take no account of early lapses. A few companies use volume net of first year lapses and some have a factor based on gain in volume in force. Some companies employ more than one of these factors in their formulas.

RENEWALS

Some companies have no renewal factor. Others pay a percentage of agents' renewal commissions or a percentage of renewal premiums. If this factor is based on renewal commissions, part of which are non-vested to the agent, the result is to reward the manager who has low turnover and penalize one who has poor experience on agent survival.

AGENT DEVELOPMENT

Three types of factors are used here and they are found in most plans. The first is a factor based on the performance of each agent, not only new agents, and is generally graded according to the performance of the agent as measured by his first year commissions or premiums, more being paid for the substantial as compared to marginal producers. The second type is based upon the performance of new agents only, generally based on a percentage of first year commissions earned by all new agents in their first two or three years, and in some cases the factor varies by the agent's contract year. The third type of factor involves compensation paid only for new agents who meet certain standards of performance, and in some cases who are also validating the requirements of the financing plan. It usually takes the form of a percentage of first year commissions but some companies pay a graded dollar amount per qualifying man-month.

COSTS

The use of a cost factor is becoming more prevalent. Most of the plans give a reward or impose a penalty for expenses below or above a certain company standard. Some give a reward only. A few plans take account of the rate of growth of the agency; a cost factor ignoring this is of doubtful soundness.

PERSISTENCY

A special factor reflecting the first year lapse rate is being used by an increasing number of companies. It takes various forms, sometimes involving only a reward for good persistency, but in other cases also a penalty for high lapse rates. These factors are generally related to some standard, either a fixed one or a company average. Here, again, the rate of growth of the agency should be, but seldom is, taken into account, because the lapse rate of new agents is invariably much higher than that of mature agents.

SUPERVISORY COSTS

Most branch office companies pay the entire compensation of supervisors or assistant managers and these costs are taken into account in the manager's compensation only if there is a cost factor. In a few companies the manager has to pay supervisory compensation out of his salary.

FINANCING LOSSES

Agent financing losses are shared by the manager in some cases and in others the company bears the total losses. To some extent the treatment here depends on the degree of liberality of the factor for new agents.

PERSONAL PRODUCTION

Most companies permit the manager to write personal business but very few of the plans pay managerial compensation on such business. A small number of companies prohibits the manager from engaging in personal production.

The outstanding difference between the patterns of compensation under the managerial as compared with the general agency system is the small (in some cases zero) effect of renewal business upon managerial compensation and the overwhelming influence of new business. In contrast, the general agent must look to renewal business for all, or practically all, of his compensation. As a result, the persistency of the business has a far more important effect upon results in a general agency operation than in a managerial operation even in the case of managerial companies which use persistency factors, because such factors usually have a rather modest effect upon the total compensation.

In recent years there has been some evidence, though not yet widespread, of a tendency for some large companies to change from the general agency to the managerial system. Some of the reasons for this may be: (1) the desire of the company to reduce future commitments in vested commissions, (2) the need for greater incentive to build new manpower which is easier to provide under the managerial system, (3) the lack of flexibility under the New York law as it affects general agency operations, (4) the difficulty of opening new general agencies, (5) the opportunity to reduce compensation unit costs in the large agencies and (6) the greater degree of uniformity of operation and home office control offered by the managerial system. Hybrid systems, containing some of the features of both systems, are becoming more common.

COMPENSATION PLANS FOR CAREER AGENTS

In the early 1940's a Committee of the Life Insurance Sales Research Bureau, comprised of some of the leaders in the business, was appointed to study all aspects of agent compensation and they published five reports between 1940 and 1944. At that time there was growing criticism of a number of features of the plans then in use which, it was felt, had become outmoded. The scale in general use was 50% first year commissions followed by nine renewals of 5%. The renewals were frequently fully vested. At that time there were no service fees while pension plans and group life insurance for agents were rare. Some branch office companies paid 55% first year commissions but the prevailing scale for general agency companies was the traditional "50 and nine 5's," the reason being that the New York law did not then permit the present maximum of 60% in the first year, of which the agent could get 55% and the general agent 5%. The law did not then permit payment of service fees to agents.

The industry Committee laid down the following characteristics of a satisfactory compensation plan:

1. The agent should be able to earn an income selling life insurance, at least as large as that which a person of equal ability would be able to earn in other lines of business activity.
2. Business having a high degree of persistency should yield a larger return than at present as compared with business of poor persistency.
3. The commission schedule should as far as practicable be arranged to smooth out fluctuations in income.
4. It should also provide reasonable compensation to the agent for service rendered his policyholders during his active service in the business.
5. A margin should be available to provide a retirement income to agents who have made a reasonable contribution to the business over a minimum period of time.[1]

The Committee's first suggestions involved a scale of 40% first year, 15% and 10% in the second and third years vested, seven 5%'s followed by 2% service fees all non-vested. However, the large reduction in first year commissions proved unacceptable and while some companies went down to 45% for a short time, most did not and today a first year commission of 55% is used by the great majority of New York companies. Following the committee's reports certain amendments were made in the New York law in 1943, but it was not until 1954 that a major overhaul of the law was enacted. The years 1943–1954 were a period of evolution and reform and a number of important changes occurred in the pattern of compensation in most companies, among which were:

---

[1] *A Proposed Plan of Compensation,* First Report of Committee on Agents' Compensation presented at the joint annual meeting of Association of Life Agency Officers and Life Insurance Sales Research Bureau, October 29, 1940.

1. The introduction of service fees after the tenth year.
2. Pension plans and group insurance coverages were provided.
3. The former practice of vesting the renewal commissions in the first ten years was considerably modified in most companies to make it possible to pay large early renewals and also to pay more to the agent who stayed in the business and much less to the failures.
4. The problem under the New York law of providing adequate financing for new agents without encroaching on other margins affecting the compensation of mature agents or the general agent was eventually solved by the introduction, in 1954, of additional compensation in the agent's first three years. Today most companies provide the funds for financing new agents, although in most cases the general agent shares in the losses and this is also true, but to a lesser extent, for managers.

Today, one finds considerable variation in the basic commission scales used by New York companies. (See Table 4.) These rates are for an ordinary life policy; on plans with premiums higher or lower than ordinary life, lower first year rates are paid. A typical gradation is as follows:

Ordinary Life	55%
20 payment life	50
10 payment life	35
20 year endowment	35
10 year endowment	20
5 year term	35

Renewal commission rates are lower than the scales in Table 4 for plans of insurance with premiums higher than 20 years endowment and also on term plans.

Many companies pay a lower first year commission for policies under $5,000 and some have more than one gradation by size. The payment of additional compensation for good persistency, separately from the basic renewal scale, is quite rare among New York companies. In a few companies renewal commissions, and in some cases service fees, are forfeited on the business written in any year in which production falls below a certain minimum requirement, usually averaged over two or three years. The contracts of the majority of companies contain an automatic cancellation clause operative if new business falls below a certain level most commonly measured by first year commissions. However, these requirements are usually so low as to have little significance. The requirements are generally based on a two-year average and they are usually waived after the agent attains a certain age, becomes disabled or completes a prescribed number of years of service.

TABLE 4
Career Agents' Contracts
Basic Commission Scale for Ordinary Life

Policy Year	1	2	3	4	5	6	7	8–10	10 yrs. Total	11–15	16 on
Company											
1	55%	10%	10%	10%	5%	5%	5%	2%	106%	2%	2%
2	55	10	10	10	3	3	3	3	103	2	3
3	55	7	7	7	7	7	7	7–2–2	108	2	2
4	50	15	10	5	5	5	5	5–2–2	104	2	2
5	50	12	12	7	7	7	7	2	108	2	2
6	55	5	5	5	5	5	5	5	100	2	2
7	55	15	10	5	5	5	2	2	103	2	2
8	55	10	10	5	5	5	2	2	98	2	2
9	50	10	10	5	5	5	2	2	93	2	2
10	55	5	5	5	4	2	5	5	100	2	2
11	55	15	10	10	10	3	3	2	99	1½	1½
12	55	7½	7½	7½	7½	5	5	3	110	2	2
13	55	8	8	4(a)	4	4	4	3	110	2	2
14	55	8	5	5	5	5	5	4(a)	113	2(a)	2
15	55	5	7	7	7	5	5	5	100	2	2
16(b)	55	7	5	5	5	3	5	5	108	2	2
17	55	5	10	7½	7½	3	5	5	100	2	2
18	50	15	12	5	5	3	3	3	105	3	3
19	55	10	5	12	3	3	3	3	110	3	3
20	55	12	10	5	7	3	3	3	109	½	½
21	55	5	5	7	7	5	5	5	100	2	2
22	55	10	10	7	7	5	2	2	102	2	2

(a) Extra persistency factor payable in 4th, 9th, and 14th years based on persistency, new production and number of sales.

(b) Renewal scale is higher in 2nd to 5th, and lower in 6th to 10th years in first four contract years.

Table 5 gives a bird's eye view of the effect of the vesting provisions and reveals wide variations in practice. It shows the total, undiscounted, amount of renewal commissions payable after termination of contract or upon death. In case of early termination of contract, which generally means failure of the agent, vested rights are generally quite modest. In event of death, the provisions are usually generous. Service fees invariably cease upon death.

Companies which do not operate in New York are able to pay higher commissions, but not all do so; they can also employ certain types of factors illegal in New York, for example, a bonus for attaining a certain level of production. Most of these companies pay higher first year commis-

TABLE 5
COMPARISON of VESTING PROVISIONS
(Sum of renewal commissions vested)

Years of Service	Termination of Contract				Death		
	3	5	10	20	3	10	20
Company							
1	10%	30%	30%	30%	30%	30%	45%
2	0	30	30	48	48	48	48
3	7	21	49	49	49	49	49
4	15	25	25	25	30	30	30
5	22½	22½	22½	22½	22½	22½	22½
6	20	40	40	40	40	40	40
7	25	25	29	43	43	43	43
8	13	21	21	48	48	48	48
9	20	35	35	35	35	35	35
10	45	45	45	45	45	45	45
11	25	25	25	34	34	34	34
12	20	20	20	40	40	40	40
13	30	30	30	55	55	55	55
14	12	12	12	26	44	44	44
15	30	30	30	30	45	45	45
16	28	28	28	53*	53	53	53
17	20	20	20	45	45	45	45
18	25	25	25	25	40	55	55
19	25	25	30	45	45	45	45
20	0	0	0	0	54	54	54
21	20	20	20	45	45	45	45
22	20	20	20	39	20	20	39

*Agent must also meet certain production requirements.

sions. For example, in a group of 21 large companies the range in first year rates is from 55% to 70% with an average of over 60%. In a group of smaller companies the range is from 55% to 80% with an average of over 65%. Even though many of these smaller companies may pay more direct compensation to the agent, in many cases it will be found that they spend less money than the giant companies for such items as advertising, training, sales promotion of all kinds, availability of specialized products, home office assistance in the agencies, entertainment, travel, fringe benefits, and above all a highly competitive product, all of which contribute to the development of the agency and which, in the aggregate, involve heavy costs.

Recently, due largely to high tax rates, the more prosperous, well-established agents have expressed a desire for deferment of part of their compensation for payment either in a lump sum at retirement (subject to capital gains tax) or as an additional pension. There has been a gradual development of this type of deferred compensation or profit sharing plan, which usually permits election of several different types of investment including stocks, bonds or even shares in a stock company. Some of these plans are optional and some are mandatory.

FINANCING PLANS FOR CAREER AGENTS

The earliest forms of financing plans took the form of flat advances against the value of future commissions. There are several weaknesses in this type of financing. There is no incentive based on production. The recoveries on business written by agents who fail are almost always insufficient to liquidate the debt, largely because this business shows high lapse rates. Since these were generally advances with no recourse, substantial amounts of debt incurred by the failures were never collected, whereas the full amount of the debt had to be repaid from future commissions by those agents who succeeded and stayed in the business. In other words, the successes were paying for the failures. Frequently, it took several years for the agent to pay off these debts and this had a detrimental psychological effect on the new agent.

Today, there are many types of financing plans involving subsidies in various forms, although the old flat advance system is still used. Some of these are as follows, and each of them involves some form of validation which must be met if financing is to be continued.

1. A fixed salary for a period of two or three years. The performance is generally measured against cash commissions earned or annualized commissions net of unearned commissions on first

year lapses. Provision is generally made for payment of all or part of commissions in excess of the validation scale.

2. A fixed or variable salary measured against first year commissions, usually annualized net of lapses and weighted for the subsidy on a decreasing scale of percentages of such commissions. For example, the subsidy might be 60% of annualized first year commissions in the first contract year, 40% in the second and 20% in the third year. An account is maintained comparing the credits in the account, including subsidy, against the total salary paid and the debit balance is not permitted to exceed a certain amount, usually some multiple of the salary.

3. A decreasing salary with an increasing percentage of commissions earned, grading on to full commissions and no salary after a certain period such as three years.

4. A fixed income for a short period, e.g., two or three months, followed by advances determined as some percentage of net annualized first year commissions, varying by premium frequency to discount for expected lapses, plus a decreasing training allowance which generally varies each month according to net production.

These plans contain a built-in subsidy the amount of which may be fixed irrespective of starting salary, or it may be in proportion to the starting salary or in proportion to production measured in various ways. The subsidy is allowed for in setting the validation requirements and is designed to enable the agent to change over to straight commissions at the end of the financing period. However, since a change from salary or advances to cash commissions may be difficult, further advance financing usually based on annualized commissions is often continued for a limited period after the subsidized financing ceases.

The validation requirements are usually cumulative but there may also be production requirements based on recent performance designed to prevent the new recruit from coasting on the basis of excess production achieved some time ago. One of the most important attributes for success is steady, continuous production rather than spasmodic performance.

As already mentioned, most, but not all, companies require the manager or general agent to share in financing losses. This makes for better selection and more careful and regular supervision and training. Most compensation plans include a special factor rewarding the general agent or manager for building new agents, and the more successful of them make extra compensation in excess of the losses they must pay.[1]

---

[1] An excellent monograph discussing the philosophy underlying the design of agent financing plans was published by the Life Insurance Agency Management Association in 1961 and the reader is referred to this for more extended discussion of the complex subject.

COMPENSATION FOR BROKERS

There is a rather standard pattern in the commissions paid to brokers. Basically, commissions are the old 55% the first year and 5% for renewals over the next nine years, all vested. Occasionally, contracts are offered which involve "heaped" renewals confined to three years but these are rare. Generally, no service fees are paid to brokers.

However, there is a developing trend towards giving more generous treatment to large brokers, or general insurance houses which give first refusal on all their business to one company, or at least a minimum volume. In these situations, a number of companies will pay service fees, usually subject to a minimum production requirement.

A few companies offer group life coverage, while still fewer provide hospital and major medical benefits, including coverage for dependents. There are some instances of companies that offer modest pension plans for brokers, but this is rare. The fact that brokerage commissions are fully vested, whereas career agents' commissions have quite limited vesting, obviously justifies much more generous security benefits for career agents than for brokers.

Many of these brokers are not housed by the companies and maintain their own offices. It is not unusual, in such cases, if the volume of business justifies it, for the company to make certain expense allowances towards the part of the broker's office expenses attributable to the business he places with the life company. These allowances have to be supported by vouchers and are strictly controlled under the New York law. In most cases, these allowances have to come out of the expenses allowed to the general agent under his expense formula.

SECURITY BENEFITS

It is common practice today to provide security benefits for the sales forces, although there are considerable variations as between the benefits given to managers, general agents, agents and brokers.

MANAGERS OF BRANCH OFFICES

Managers, under the branch office system, frequently receive the same benefits as home office employees. Group life insurance for one or two years' salary with generous maximum amounts, decreasing after retirement, is usually offered on a contributory basis. Group health insurance covers hospital, surgical and major medical benefits. Temporary disability benefits usually vary in duration according to years of service and in some cases are followed by long-term disability benefits continuing to retirement age. Managers, being employees, may be, and usually are, covered under pension plans qualified with the Internal Revenue Service under which company contributions are not taxed to the employee before retirement, even if there is vesting as is usually the case. Such plans are commonly integrated with Social Security benefits.

GENERAL AGENTS

General agents are usually covered for group life and group health insurance on a contributory basis. However, since they are independent contractors, they cannot be covered by pension plans qualified with the Internal Revenue Service. Many companies provide no pensions for their general agents. Others supplement the decreasing income provided by vested overriding commissions with forfeitable, informal retirement benefits designed to place a floor under the ultimate income after retirement. Still other companies provide pension benefits separate from the overriding commissions after retirement, based on a formula reflecting earnings during their active service as general agents. If there are vested rights in the pension in event of termination before retirement, the company contributions would become taxable income to the general agent. Also, in order to avoid income tax problems, the pension benefits must be forfeitable.

CAREER AGENTS

For career agents it is common practice to provide generous group life insurance benefits, sometimes with very large limits. Such benefits are usually some multiple of earnings and most plans are contributory. Coverage usually grades down over a five year period after retirement to some modest ultimate amount. A small number of companies use plans which involve the accumulation of paid up insurance purchased by the agent's contributions. Group hospital, surgical and major medical benefits are generally provided on a contributory basis covering both the agent and his family. Long-term disability plans providing income to retirement age are a recent development.

Pension plans for agents take various forms, the most common being money-purchase accumulation plans, under which the agent contributes 3% to 5% of earnings, matched by the company. The accumulated funds are applied to purchase a pension at a guaranteed rate. A few plans provide pensions based on total earnings before retirement under unit credit formulas, sometimes integrated with Social Security, the agent making moderate contributions and the company paying the balance of the cost.

Nearly all these plans provide some degree of vesting of the company's contributions, if the agent terminates before retirement after a certain number of years of service, frequently 15 to 20 years.

BROKERS

No security benefits for brokers are offered by the majority of companies. However, an increasing number give group life coverages, and a few provide group health coverages, usually confined to substantial brokers who give the company first refusal on all their life business. Pension plans for brokers are quite rare.

In designing compensation plans and security benefits for all types of sales personnel, the companies are always influenced by the desire to offer an attractive career in our business, the effect of the New York law and the substantial impact of distribution costs upon the price of the product to the insuring public.

35

Agency Expense Analysis

Arthur I. Sternhell

The primary function of agency expense analysis is to provide a basis for planning and controlling agency expenses—a major element in profitable agency operations. In addition, analysis of agency expenses helps to provide a factual basis for decision making in all areas of an agency's operation.

AGENCY ACCOUNTS

In order to have adequate information to analyze agency expenses, appropriate records must be kept. An accounting system should produce the necessary data for properly measuring income and expenses in the form in which it will be most helpful to the general agent. It should also produce periodic statements of assets and liabilities.

At any time the assets of a business may be said to equal the total of the amount owned and the interests of the owners. This constant equality may be stated in the fundamental accounting equation, also called the balance sheet equation:

$$\text{Assets} = \text{Liabilities} + \text{Equity}$$

Assets	=	Liabilities	+	Equity
(Total Property Owned)		(Total Owed Creditors)		(Balance of Value Belonging to Owners)

As in any mathematical equation any change in one side requires a compensating change in the same side or the other side in order to perpetuate

591

the equality. Thus any change in an account included in one item of the equation (and every account is reflected in one of the three categories) must be compensated by corresponding changes in the same or different items so that the two sides of the equation are always in balance. It is for this reason that every transaction must be recorded so as to continue this balance.

The journal is the book of original entry in which is first recorded an analysis of a transaction in terms of increases and decreases of individual accounts. Normally a journal (1) chronologically sets forth the changes in the firm's accounts and (2) supplies a brief description of the transaction.

An agency will usually have a general journal for the transactions that do not occur with sufficient frequency to justify separate journals, and in addition, one or more specialized journals. Specialized journals permit division of work and facilitate use of mechanical bookkeeping devices for recording the transactions. Thus an agency would have specialized journals for cash receipts and cash disbursements.

Final entry is made in a ledger. This is a book in which are kept the individual accounts where all changes are recorded. Every account in the ledger will have appearing in its columns the changes that have been recorded in the journals, and at any given date the increases and decreases in the account may be totaled and a "balance" for the account determined. Most agencies have at least a general ledger and possibly one or more subsidiary ledgers.

A profit and loss statement is a summary of income and expenses for a period of time, the difference representing profit or loss for that period. It is prepared by summarizing the income and expense accounts of the ledger.

A balance sheet is a statement of financial position at a particular moment of time summarizing assets, liabilities, and the equity of the owners. It, too, is prepared by summarizing the corresponding accounts of the ledger.

The system of agency accounts will not produce all the information necessary for an effective analysis of agency expenses. As an example, it is desirable to keep records for each agent of business sold at least by amount, plan, premium, and mode of payment.

ANALYSIS OF AGENCY EXPENSES

A typical agency is conducting simultaneously two completely distinct functions—(1) obtaining new business and (2) collecting premiums and giving service to policyholders on existing business. For purposes of achieving an adequate analysis of agency expenses, it is first necessary to classify the various agency activities that involve an expense into one of these functions. The duties of each clerk must be recorded, the purpose of each area in the office must be noted, and so on, so that the general agent can allocate expenses to either (1) new business, or (2) renewal business.

Expenses for the following activities would be classified to "new business":

(1) Agent recruiting and selection
(2) Broker development
(3) Training
(4) Supervision of agents and brokers
(5) Sales assistance and service
(6) Sales development
(7) Administration of sales and supervisory staff
(8) Manager and supervisory training
(9) Agency promotion
(10) New-business processing
(11) Personal production

Expenses for the following activities are classified to "renewal business":

(1) Collection and premium accounting
(2) Policy service

Sometimes it is desirable to subdivide "new business" expense in two categories: that relating to the clerical expense of issuing the policy and the balance relating to agency development and acquisition of new business.

NEW BUSINESS EXPENSE

New business expense may be related to volume of new business for purposes of (1) comparing an agency's expenses as of different time periods, (2) comparing agencies in the same company, and (3) comparing specific agencies with agencies of other companies. Comparisons must be made with care since the bases for allocating expenses may differ or the product mix may differ.

Functional analysis of new business expense may also prove illuminating. The new business activities in an agency are devoted only indirectly to the task of obtaining new business. More directly they are concerned with (a) recruiting and establishing new agents in the business, and (b) housing, maintaining and providing services for established agents. This type of functional analysis may show that an agency whose expense per thousand of new business is low has achieved that result by failing to expend a sufficient amount of money for recruiting and training new agents.

RENEWAL EXPENSE

The expense of servicing business already in force may conveniently be expressed, for comparison purposes, either as (a) a percentage of renewal premiums collected, or as (b) cost per renewal collection. Collection of renewal premiums accounts for a large part of renewal expenses.

The most important factors affecting renewal expense are the quality characteristics of the business in force. The most significant of these are: (1) collection frequency, (2) average size policy in force, and (3) average premium per thousand of insurance in force.

The "renewal expense ratio" is an effective measure of the relative rate of renewal expense. It is determined by application of the following formula:

$$\text{Renewal Expense Ratio} = \frac{\text{Average renewal expense per policy}}{\text{Average premium per policy}}$$

This is arrived at by the use of the following formula:

$$= \frac{\text{Average cost per collection} \times \text{Average collection frequency}}{\text{Average size policy in \$'000's} \times \text{Average premium per \$1,000}}$$

Calculation of ratios and comparison with standards are but initial steps in expense analysis. Functional analyses carry the analysis a step further. However, these are but preliminaries to the major objective of increasing the profitability of the agency. An expenditure must be evaluated in terms of the results or benefits obtained. Thus, a reduction in cost at the expense of service may not be desirable.

INCOME AND PROFIT TO THE GENERAL AGENT

A general agent will want to follow his financial results from year to year. In the process, he can watch the over-all picture by determining two figures each year: net income and profit.

Net income consists of the general agent's compensation, including expense allowance, less agency expenses (including any portion of his compensation required to pay commissions and salaries to supervisors and clerical employees). A portion of each year's income derives from agency activities in prior years (e.g., renewal overriding commissions on business written in prior years). Similarly, the current year's operation of the agency

will create income for the general agent in subsequent years, primarily in
the form of vested renewal overridings. *Profit* consists of net income for
the year plus the increase for the year in the present value of his vested
renewal overridings. The present value of his vested renewal overridings
is obtained by discounting for interest and persistency renewal commissions
payable in subsequent years. The increase for the year in the present value
of his vested renewal overridings is the difference between (1) discounted
renewal commissions stemming from that year's production and (2) renewal commissions paid during the year.

By proper accounting, it is possible to determine the source of income
and, after allocation of expense between first year and renewal, to construct a useful income statement such as the following:

Renewal Income

	Vested	Nonvested	Total
Overriding commissions	$12,225	$5,138	$17,363
Collection fees	—	4,229	4,229
Personal renewals	1,445	—	1,445
Reversions	820	—	820
Total	$14,490	$9,367	$23,857
Less renewal expense			8,117
Net renewal income			$15,740

First Year Income

Overriding commissions	$17,921	
Personal first year commissions	2,037	
Expense allowance	10,000	
Total	$29,958	
Less first year expense	30,000	
Net first year income		— 42
Total net income		$15,698

This income statement is purely illustrative and no particular significance
should be attached to the specific figures. Other forms of income statements
are possible.

A manager's compensation plan is often composed of (1) a production
bonus for paid business in excess of allotment, (2) net gain of insurance
in force, i.e., new paid business less terminations of first and second year
business or less all terminations of existing insurance in force, (3) a bonus
based on the paid business of agents in their first or in their second or third
year of service with the company, (4) an "expense bonus" consisting of

some part of the amount which agency expense falls below the company's budget established for that agency. All four of the above elements of a manager's compensation are related to the profit margins which a general agent attempts to derive from a well-balanced agency operation.

GENERAL AGENCY ANALYSIS

If net income or profit is not up to expectations, the following are items to be investigated in determining what corrective action might prove helpful:

(1) *Average Premium per Thousand and Distribution by Plan of Insurance*—A low average premium, such as might result from excessive concentration of term business, might be the major factor behind a poor earnings picture. Much of the general agent's income is based on a percentage of premiums, and a reasonable distribution of business is normally a prerequisite to a healthy financial condition. A shift in emphasis on the type of selling may be necessary, implemented by a vigorous re-training program. The plans of insurance sold by each agent should be analyzed. If the sales of the agents appear to be concentrated in a very limited number of policies, this may be indicative of insufficient training.

(2) *Persistency*—Renewal compensation makes up the major portion of the general agent's income. Hence, poor persistency means a low level of return to the general agent. The early policy years' lapse rates usually will reveal the general level of persistency. Although improved conservation methods may help, the solution may require changes in sales, recruiting and training procedures.

(3) *Expenses*—An overly liberal attitude toward expenses may cut seriously into earnings. It is desirable to consider new business expense and renewal expense separately. Functional expense analysis is often helpful in locating areas that are out of line.

(4) *Profit Factors in the Renewal Expense Ratio*—Most general agents are charged with the responsibility of collecting renewal premiums and the company usually pays them a collection fee to cover this expense. These usually amount to not less than 1% nor more than 3% of the premium collected. The excess of collection fees received over the expense of collecting the corresponding premiums may have much to do with a satisfactory level of earnings. The cost of collecting renewal premiums customarily is expressed as a percentage of premiums and is called the "renewal expense ratio." Four factors enter into this ratio, three of which are "quality" factors—average collection frequency, average size policy and average premium per $1,000 of insurance:

$$\text{Renewal Expense Ratio} = \frac{\text{Average renewal expense per policy}}{\text{Average premium per policy}}$$

This is arrived at by the use of the following formula:

$$= \frac{\text{Average cost per collection} \times \text{Average collection frequency}}{\text{Average size policy in \$'000's} \times \text{Average premium per \$1,000}}$$

Thus if: Average cost per collection=\$0.75
Average collection frequency=2.2
Average size policy in \$'000's=\$5.5
Average premium per \$1,000=\$33.00

Then:

$$\text{Renewal Expense Ratio} = \frac{.75 \times 2.2}{5.5 \times 33} = \frac{1.65}{181.50} = .91\%$$

In this illustration, if collection fees average 1½% of renewal premiums, the earnings margin from this source would be .59% (1.50%–.91%). In an agency with unsatisfactory net earnings, the renewal expense ratio might approach or even exceed the collection fee. Noticeable improvement will take several years, for it takes time to offset low quality insurance in force with better quality new business. To effect an improvement, it is first necessary to obtain sufficiently detailed information. It is desirable to keep records for the agency and for each agent of collection frequency, average size policy and average premium per \$1,000 of insurance. Individual analysis may reveal that some agents are asking for the minimum premium. It may indicate that a particular agent has set his sights at too low a level.

(5) *Inadequate Production*—Too often poor agency earnings stem primarily from inadequate production, reflecting an unsatisfactory job of agency building. However, it is more meaningful to isolate the problem to individual agents. As a basis for analysis, it is desirable to evaluate the necessary level of production or first-year commissions for an agent to cover the expenses incurred to house, train, supervise and service him. If an agent is producing a low quality of business or an inadequate volume of business, all possible efforts should be used to train him to correct his inadequacies. If retraining and field supervision cannot bring about the necessary improvements, it would be well from a business standpoint, to assist him to find employment in some other line of work.

(6) *Agent Terminations*—The general agent should measure the effect of agent terminations on his income. A periodic appraisal of the selection, training, and supervision procedures may indicate unjustified expenses. Perhaps too much expense is being incurred in connection with inevitable failures. It might indicate an overemphasis on agent recruiting which often results in an oversupply of new agents thus preventing adequate absorption

of agents employed. Or the fault might lie in the selection process. More likely the training procedure is inadequate for the complicated task of selling life insurance in today's market. It is not always the money expended that causes financial disaster, more often it is the failure of some part of the operation to deliver adequate results.

(7) *Supervisory and Staff Personnel*—Each individual should be evaluated to determine his contribution to profit. All expenses attributable to a supervisor should be determined, less any related expense allowances received. This amount should be compared with the contribution to the general agent's profit as a result of the supervisor's activities. The general agent should be aware of the break-even points in his agency operation. Goals should be set and a realistic time-table established.

36

Budgeting and Expense Control

Joseph E. Boettner

THE NATURE AND PURPOSE OF BUDGETING

A budget is a financial tool whose purpose is to provide management with a blueprint of realistic expectations of income and expenses during a future period, and relate them to plans and objectives. In a sense, it is a combination of "educated estimates" and "projected probabilities." The former is based on experience and established fact, while the latter, in addition to those elements, contains a large degree of assumptive probability and a comprehensive knowledge and understanding of the factors that influence both expense and income.[1]

The mere attempt to prepare a budget represents disciplined conduct on the part of management, which is thereby forced to examine critically the various phases of operation and their relation to the financial status of the agency, and to make future plans in the light of what that examination discloses. Periodic re-examination is essential to give management the opportunity for re-evaluation of procedures and objectives. Management obtains the greatest benefit from budgeting only when it is guided by the results that periodic examination presents. It is at such check-points that coordination and control come alive.

---

[1] For a detailed and thorough treatment of agency budgeting and expense control, the reader is referred to *Life Insurance Agency Financial Management* by Armand C. Stalnaker, 1965, Revised Edition Richard D. Irwin, Inc., Homewood, Illinois. The author has developed this chapter from concepts originally discussed by Dr. Stalnaker in his text.

Agency planning, coordination and control rest to a high degree on the budget, especially in the "full" general agency whose head must depend upon total business results not only for expense money, but also for his personal income. In branch managerial types of agencies, budgeting of income has very limited significance, inasmuch as operational funds are provided in the main directly from the home office. This does not mean that an expense budget is less important in the managerial office. A vital part of agency budgeting is its function in controlling expenses, and this the agency manager must do in the same way as the general agent.[2] Many managerial companies require that the manager prepare a budget and submit a copy to the home office.

A Budget Formalizes Planning

A budget is a formalized statement of expectations. Notations on a memo pad setting forth future estimates of agency income and expenses may be helpful to the agency manager in formulating future plans, but such notations should not be accorded the dignity of being called a budget.

Each item in the budget should have specific dollar amounts assigned to it. It is this set of specific dollar amounts that articulates management's specific plans. In other words, since accounting is the language of business, businessmen become articulate in formulating future operational plans by specific allocation of dollar values to each item of expected future income and expense.

OBJECTIVES OF BUDGETING AND BUDGETARY CONTROL

Budgeting is the process of preparing a budget. This process requires management to focus on each specific phase of its operations that involves the receipt of income or the incurring of an expense. Thus, the primary purpose of preparing a budget (budgeting) is to assist the agency manager in performing his planning function.

Budgetary control focuses on the coordination and control of operations. Thus, after the budget is prepared it becomes an administrative tool for management to use in implementing, coordinating and controlling its operational plans. Deviations from these standards that have been specifically articulated by the budget, should be examined to determine if the causes for such deviations are wholesome and beneficial.

---

[2] It should be emphasized that an important aspect of controlling expenses is to make sure that expense dollars are being allocated so as to maximize the return from total expenditures. This aspect of expenditures might be referred to as "value management."

To some extent the preparation of the budget contributes to coordination of agency operations as well as being an integral part of agency planning. For example, the agency manager may establish as an objective for the next year a 25 per cent increase in the sale of new business. This decision will have budgetary implications as well as other administrative implications. In a small agency, the manager can use the budget estimates as a guide to coordinate the various activities that will be involved in the budgeted increase in new sales. In a large agency, the manager should communicate the new production objectives to the line and staff personnel, whose activities will be affected by the budgeted increase in producion. It is rather obvious that the budgeted increase in production will have an impact on recruiting, training secretarial and clerical personnel as well as expenditures for office space and furniture. The manager can use the budget as a guide to make sure he consults with all personnel affected or make sure he considers the impact on each phase of operations in the case of the small agency.

A considerable amount of motivation will usually result from effective use of an operational budget in the agency. For example, the communicating of the budget goal of a 25 per cent increase in new business for the agency in the illustration above can be expected to stimulate some excitement among all of the personnel in the agency. If the personnel in the agency have been involved in preparing budget estimates, they are likely to assume a responsibility for attaining the budgeted goals. Therefore, the manager should be sensitive to the importance of communicating and interacting with his key people during all phases of the preparation of the budget. Similarly, he must review the completed final version of the budget with all those who helped in its planning stages. The individual need for a feeling of accomplishment will be expressed in the acceptance of responsibility for the budget's execution. The process of budget preparation should be similar to the procedure outlined in Chapter 28, which discusses how management by objectives can be used in setting agent target goals for new production. "The targets established must be the agent's goals—not the manager's. They must be the agent's own objectives—not those suggested to him by his boss. He must be committed to the goals."[3]

OPERATIONAL AND CAPITAL BUDGETS

Operational budgets may be classified as: (1) fixed or static budgets and (2) variable or flexible budgets.

---

[3] See Chapter 28, "Supervision" by James Gatza.

Fixed Budgets

A fixed budget permits no changes in the dollar estimates for the various income items and expense items for the budget time period. Therefore, under a fixed budget an agency manager would make no change in his budgeted estimate for premium income even should he recruit an additional new agent whose new business had not been included in the budget estimates. Those agency managers who use a fixed budget emphasize the primary purpose of the operational budget as a planning tool. Some would see any favorable deviation from budgeted premium income as not financially significant for the remainder of the budget time period. However, in developing the agency's operational budget for the next time period the agency manager should modify the current budget accordingly. This entails several adjustments for both the estimated income and the estimated expenses.

The primary weakness of the fixed budget is that it provides a poor basis for controlling expenses when the level of incurred expenses varies with the actual level of business volume. For example, the agency manager may recruit two or three more agents than he originally planned when the budget was prepared. These additional agents will hopefully produce additional business and additional income. However, the new agents will also mean an increase in certain expenses which were not budgeted. Additional expenses will be necessary for such items as financing, training, housing and supplies. There certainly will be an increase in such expenses as telephone, secretarial services, proposal preparations, travel and direct mail items. It is necessary for the agency manager to calculate the increase in agency expenses that can be reasonably expected as a result of adding one, two or more new agents than contemplated when the budget was prepared. The agency manager must know what is the reasonable expected increase in costs associated with each increase in sales volume. In other words, controls over expenses should be available to the manager for various levels of production activity within a relevant range of expectations. A fixed budget, however, provides an estimate of expenses only for the specified level of production assumed in preparing the budget.

Flexible Budgets

A flexible budget permits periodic changes in the dollar estimates for each element of income and expense during the budget time period. Actually, a flexible budget is not one budget, but a whole series of *fixed* budgets providing estimates of dollar amounts for each item of income and expense at the various levels of agency production which may occur. For example, if it is expected that by the end of the third month the agency will have increased its premium volume by 10 per cent and the agency is expected to continue for the remainder of the year at this higher level, the agency manager must set his operational expense budget on the basis of the higher level of expected premiums. Some items may change very little, but other items of expense will increase by at least the 10 per cent increase in premium volume. These are the variable cost items. At the end of the budget period, the agency manager will be interested in determining how closely actual operational results matched the planned or budget results. If the manager compares actual expenses to the original amount estimated for the lower premium volume, he will have no meaningful basis of comparison. He will also be unable to determine efficiency of his agency's operations. The budget, brought out at the end of the third month based on the expectation of the 10 per cent increase in premium volume, is an excellent tool to use to compare actual performance with plans. Variations serve as signals to call attention to differences between expectations and achievements. The agency manager thus determines if efficiency of agency operations has been preserved as the agency has expanded operations.

Capital Budgets

A capital budget is an estimate of the various capital assets to be acquired by the agency during the budget time period and the proposed sources of funds or methods of payment for the capital assets. The acquisition of such capital assets as desks, filing cabinet, typewriters, dictating equipment and even a new agency building, frequently requires the expenditure or commitment of large sums of money. Therefore, capital budgets typically cover a longer period of time than an operational budget. In the case of a capital budget prepared in advance of the construction of a new agency office building, the time period covered by the capital budget might be one or two years. The point to emphasize is that the more substantial the capital expenditures, generally the longer will be the time period covered by the capital budget and the earlier such physical planning begins, the better. Even in the situation where the home office will provide total funding for the new agency office building, there will necessarily be a longer period covered by the capital budget than if only a few desks are to be acquired.

PREPARATION OF THE VARIOUS BUDGETS

The Agency Manager's Responsibility

Since the agency manager is responsible for overall planning in the agency, he should assume responsibility for the preparation of the agency's master budget. The master budget is actually a composite of several specific current budgets. It may also include a set of budgets for a number of future periods. Therefore, in a large agency, the agency manager will obtain recommendations and suggestions from his line and staff personnel. This will also have beneficial results for coordinating the various aspects of agency operations and for motivating and leading the people participating in the budgetary planning. In the small agency, the manager will probably receive less help from others. However, it is generally recommended that, wherever practical, budgeting should begin at the lowest level of management and move upward through the organization until it reaches the top level for final review and approval.

In a large agency the cashier, the comptroller, or perhaps the office supervisors, may actually perform the mechanical function of preparing specific dollar amounts for the various budget line items of anticipated costs and expected income. But the initiating of the preparation of the budget, the coordinating of the whole process and the final review and approval of the budget is the responsibility of the agency manager.

The Format for an Agency's Comprehensive Budget

The "Operating Expense" section of a comprehensive budget for a managerial agency is basically the same as that required for a general agency. The latter contains some specific expense items (for example, agents' commissions) which do not appear in a managerial agency's budget. However, most of the expense items of the general agency are included in the branch office version of a budget by the agency manager.

The "Income and Allowances" section of a budget for a general agency has little significance for a branch office. The latter is dependent upon the home office for its income and expense allowances, whereas the pure general agency must acquire the greater part of its income from new business and renewal commissions and allowances. An illustrative comprehensive budget for a general agency appears below. With some minor modifications its "Operating Expense" section could be used by a managerial agency.

ABC LIFE INSURANCE AGENCY

Comprehensive Budget
For the Year Ending December 31, 1971

AGENCY INCOME AND ALLOWANCES

Allowance for life insurance applications processed	$ 13,000
Allowance for health insurance applications processed	3,500
First year overriding life insurance commissions	8,000
First year overriding health insurance commissions	1,500
Life insurance expense allowance	38,500
Health insurance expense allowance	3,500
Life insurance renewal expense margins	18,500
Health insurance renewal expense margins	3,500
Life insurance collection fees	16,000
Total Gross Operating Income	**$106,000**

OPERATING EXPENSES

Salaries—regular office staff	$ 13,300
Salaries—general agent's staff	5,000
Salaries—assistant supervisor's staff	19,000
Overtime	
Total Salaries	**$ 37,300**
Legal fees and expenses	$ 250
Outside services	150
Recruiting fees	300
Total Outside Services	**$ 700**
Travel	$ 1,200
Entertainment	800
Dues	150
Local meetings and conferences	100
Total Travel and Entertainment	**$ 2,250**
Printing and stationery	$ 600
Books and stationery	450
Total Printing, Stationery and Books	**$ 1,050**
SUBTOTAL	**$ 41,300**

ABC LIFE INSURANCE AGENCY

Comprehensive Budget
For the Year Ending December 31, 1971

SUBTOTAL	$ 41,300
Equipment—maintenance	$ 90
Equipment—furniture and fixtures	700
Equipment—mechanical	300
Equipment—rental	160
Total Equipment	$ 1,250
Telephone Equipment	$ 5,400
Toll Calls	700
Telegraph and teletype	150
Total Telephone and Telegraph	$ 6,250
Advertising	$ 300
Direct Mail	—
Total Advertising and Direct Mail	$ 300
Rent	$ 21,000
Alterations	—
Total Rent	$ 21,000
Express	$ 25
Postage	850
Bank service charges	0
Total Postage and Express	$ 875
Employee relations and welfare	$ 85
Pre-employment examinations	25
Pre-employment reports	20
Social security taxes	1,600
Group insurance premiums	940
Total Employee Benefits	$ 2,670
Recruits—medical examinations	$ 50
Recruits—inspection reports	100
Total Agents' Benefits	$ 150
Allowance to Agents	$ 6,500
Donations	50
Miscellaneous	150
TOTAL—ALLOWANCES, DONATIONS AND MISCELLANEOUS	$ 6,700
GRAND TOTAL	$ 80,495

PREREQUISITES FOR AGENCY EXPENSE CONTROL

The prerequisites for effective agency expense control may be thought of as the ABC's of expense control.

A. *Attitude.* The key personnel must be favorably disposed toward the concept of controlling expenses and must cooperate with the agency manager in achieving this objective. With a favorable attitude toward the concept of expense control the agency personnel will provide a harmonious and receptive environment for the realization of the goal. Therefore, the starting point to successful expense control is selling the philosophy and the spirit of the planning idea to the agency personnel.

B. *Budget System.* Control requires setting standards to which to compare actual results. These standards are the budgeted amounts for each line item of expense for relevant ranges of expected productive activity levels. There must be periodic comparisons between actual expenses incurred and the budgeted expectation. Deviations from the expected must be summarily corrected. Expectations require continual re-appraisals and adjustments to meet changing conditions.

C. *Classifications of Expense Items.* A most important reason for classifying expense items is to distinguish between new business expenses and renewal expenses. Since the major objective is to control expenses, the manager must make sure that expenses associated with new business are not charged against the maintenance of existing business. A review will disclose more clearly that such new business expenses are in line with expectations. Another reason for classifying expenses is to provide meaningful records to facilitate preparation of future budget estimates. If expenses were unclassified, the manager would have no indications of cost experiences to use for reasonable bases to establish standards for a particular year.

D. *Definiteness of Relationship between Levels of Sales Activity and Expenses.* A useful control system assumes that some expenses will vary from the budgeted amounts for each activity level as production volume increases or decreases. However, not all expense items will vary directly with sales activity and those items that do vary directly, some may not vary proportionately with the rate of increase or decrease in sales. For example, a 25 per cent increase in new business sales can be expected to increase the expense item "Express and Postage," but it is unrealistic to expect a 25 per cent increase in this item as a necessary result of the 25 per cent increase in sales. Thus, the agency manager should determine precisely the relationship between the various budgeted expense amounts and various levels of production and service activities if his control is to be meaningful and effective.

E. *Estimates Carefully Prepared.* Is *any* budget estimate better than *no* estimate? An affirmative answer to this question has a small element of validity in the sense that some planning and some thinking is better than no planning and no thinking. However, with respect to the expense control function of the budget, the various expense estimates should be made carefully. If care is not taken, an expense estimate that is too high for the specific level of production can be an invitation to extravagance. The budget thereby ceases to serve as a control instrument.

Sequence of Steps in Budgetary Control of Agency Expenses

The following are the important steps in budgetary control of agency expenses.

1. Persuade key personnel of the vital importance of agency expense control.

2. Request the participation of all key functional personnel in the preparation of budget estimates of the expected expenses associated with their functions at the various levels of sales activity within the relevant range of anticipated performance or production.

3. Provide the key personnel preparing budget estimates with appropriate accounting records for previous accounting periods, with a cautionary memorandum to explain that these costs are not generally expected to be repeated and therefore serve only as a historical beginning point.

4. Determine overall objectives for the agency after consultation with key agency personnel and home office management in terms of sales, personnel levels and services to be performed.

5. Determine specific agency objectives after final approval of overall objectives.

6. Assign specific accountability and/or responsibility to the agency comptroller, cashier or other financially competent person who can work with the key personnel in making budget estimates for particular functions of agency operations.

7. Arrange for preparation of a capital budget and other supplementary budgets that will provide a more detailed breakdown of specific expenses to be incurred.

8. Establish an agenda for a monthly comparison between budget standards for each expense item and the actual amounts of expenses incurred.

9. Require the preparation of a periodic summary report of significant variations between such standards and actual costs with reasons for such variations and plans for corrective action. Such reports should be circulated among appropriate personnel with a request for written comments.

A CASE EXAMPLE

In any discussion of budgeting it is important to see how the parts fit into the whole. The illustrative budget appearing on pages 605 and 606 has indicated the source of the agency's income as well as its expenses. This chapter has also emphasized (1) the importance of the distinction between new business expenses and renewal business expenses and (2) the relationship between levels of Sales and Expenses. The primary purpose of any business is to make a profit and while this is true of the branch office system, it may not be as clearly defined as it is in the general agency system.

If the newly appointed and subsidized General Agent or a "Manager," who has the ultimate opportunity to go on to a pure general agent's contract, as some companies provide, can see beyond the budget and its goals to the ultimate and vital role budget control can and does play in the total profitability of an agency now and in the future, then budgets and expense control systems take on real meaning and purpose because they help the manager zero in on the bigger goal of attaining or improving profitability for both new and renewal business.

If the manager can develop, through budgeting, a cost awareness because of the agency's stake in total profitability, then he can exercise better judgment in the administration of expenses since he is tuned into the whole picture. The following case example illustrates the vital role that expense control can play in the attainment of the goals of overall agency profitability.

One major company is currently using the following data to determine the average value of new business income to a general agent:

First year O/R	$ .80
New business allowance	4.00
New manpower allowance & sup. allow.	1.75
Total average value per $1,000	$6.55

The same company is currently using the following data to determine the average value of renewal business to a general agent:

Renewal O/R	$3.15
Renewal collection allowance	1.00
Total average value per *$100.00* of prem. renewal	$4.15

The company has further determined that in moving a company subsidized agency to a full commission agency the general agent must move towards and ultimately attain the goal of acquiring his new business for no more than $7.50 per $1,000. The data indicate that with a reasonable amount of renewal business, and by getting his new business for $7.50 per $1,000, the general agent is making

95¢ per $1,000 investment in new business ($7.50−$6.55=95¢). The data indicate the general agent can operate profitably on a commission basis and thereby relieve the company of the necessity for further subsidy.

The practical achievements that are possible through expense control may be visualized from the following example of an agency that currently is producing $10 million of new business annually and has $1 million of annual renewal premium. The agency's total expenses including financing losses are $85,000 for the year. The agency determines that its renewal costs are $10,000 (this assumes that cost of collecting renewal premiums is $1 per $100 of premium). Deducting the $10,000 of renewal expense from $85,000 of total expenses leaves $75,000 to meet the cost of new business, which is $7.50 per $1,000 for the $10 million of new business.

Assuming that new business income is $6.55 per $1,000 as explained above, the agency will have $65,500 of new business income for the $10 million of new business written in the agency. This means that the agency must invest $9,500 in developing the new business ($75,000 new business expense minus $65,500 of new business income). Obviously the agency will recover this out of the renewal premium as the business remains inforce. In fact, according to the assumptions above, the agency will show $31,500 of renewal income in the current year for the $1 million of renewal premiums collected ($1 million x $3.15 net over-ride and collection allowance). Deducting the $9,500 invested in new business from $31,500 indicates a net income for the agency of $22,000, before group business income and personal production income are included.

The following is how the agency manager has allocated his total expense dollars ($7.50 per $1,000 of new business).

TOTAL AGENCY EXPENSES:

Office Salaries	$1.40
Supervisors' Salaries	.90
Supervisors' Incentive	1.35
Rent	1.45
Telephone	.60
Postage	.13
Office Supplies	.07
Group Insurance	.08
Bonds	.02
	$6.00
Sales & Promotional	.40
Recruiting	.30
Training	.30
	$7.00
Financing Losses	.50
	$7.50

Unit expense figures are included with agency's cost figures in respective areas.

The above allocations provide goals which the agency strives to achieve. The preciseness implied by the above allocations may not be realized. However, the agency can realize the $7.50 objective by offsetting small increases in expenses in some areas by decreases in expenses in other areas.

The remedy for high costs may be a matter of increased production instead of an actual reduction in costs. For example, increased production permits the spreading of such fixed expenses as salaries and rent to achieve a lower acquisition cost per $1,000 of new business. Such variable costs as sales promotion, training and financing of new agents can be reduced more readily than office salaries and rent, but even for these expense items, increased production may be the best way to reduce cost per $1,000 of new business.

BIBLIOGRAPHY

Section I
The Life Insurance Marketing Environment: Past and Present

Borch, Fred J., "The Marketing Philosophy As a Way of Business Life," in *The Marketing Concept: Its Meaning to Management* (Marketing Series, No. 99) New York: the American Management Association, 1957.

Bund, Henry and Carroll, James W., "The Changing Role of the Marketing Function," *Journal of Marketing,* 1957.

Cascino, Anthony E., "Organizational Implications of the Marketing Concept," in Eugene J. Kelley and William Lazar (eds.), *Managerial Marketing: Perspectives and Viewpoints* (3rd ed.); Homewood, Ill.: Richard D. Irwin, Inc., 1967.

Drucker, Peter F., "Insurance Opportunities in an Era of Change," *The Journal of Insurance Information,* July-August, 1969.

Felton, Arthur P., "Making the Marketing Concept Work," *Harvard Business Review,* July-August, 1959.

Holcombe, John Marshall, Jr., Library of Life Insurance Agency Management Association.

Johnson, Stanford L. and Tenge, John T., Jr., "The Men Behind the Marketing Concept," *Sales Marketing Today,* 1957.

Kephart, William M., "The Family, Society, and the Individual." New York: Houghton Mifflin Co., 1966.

Loman, Harry J., "Developing Trends in Environment Security and their Impact on Insurance," *Proceedings Fifth Annual International Insurance Seminar on Insurance Company Management and Economic Security.*

Morrison, Edward J., "Marketing Management Concepts Yesterday and Today, *Journal of Marketing,* 1967.

Nichols, Walter, "Annals of American Insurance, 1771-1876," *The Insurance Blue Book for 1876-1877,* New York: 1877.

Stalson, Owen J., "Marketing Life Insurance." Homewood, Ill., Richard D. Irwin, Inc., 1969.

Stone, Mildred F., "A Calling and Its College." Homewood, Ill., Richard D. Irwin, Inc., 1963.

Viebranz, Alfred C., "Marketing's Role in Company Growth," *MSU Business Topics,* Autumn, 1967.

Vizza, Robert F., Chambers, Thomas F., and Cook, Edward J., *Adoption of the Marketing Concept—Fact or Fiction?* New York: Sales Executives Club of New York, 1967.

Wattenberg, B. J., "This U.S.A." Garden City, New York: Doubleday & Co., Inc., 1965.

Life Insurance Agency Management Publications, Research Reports, Products and Services Bulletins and Annual Meeting Proceedings

Changes in the Marketplace, by Richard F. Neuschel. Proceedings, 1965, Speech

Early Results: Equity Products Sales. P & S Bulletin 72, 1970, Report

Equity Products and Life Insurance, by Kenneth C. Foster. Proceedings, 1967, Speech

Hats Off to the Past—Coats Off to the Future, by John M. Jackson, Jr. Proceedings, 1969, Speech

Life Insurance and Family Spending. RR 1956, Report

Life Insurance Attitudes and Expectations of American Youth; A Joint Study of High School Students by the Institute of Life Insurance and LIAMA. 1966, Report

Life Insurance in Focus; A Study by LIAMA and LUTC, Report

Markets and Marketing in the Age of Conglomerates and Congenerics, by John T. Fey. Proceedings, 1969, Speech

Mutual Funds; Soundings from the Marketplace. RR 1969, Report

People and Money—Challenge for the 70's, by Jan Meyer. Proceedings, 1969, Speech

Rendezvous With the Future, by Burkett W. Huey. Proceedings, 1968, Speech

The World of 1975-1985, by Frederik Pohl. Proceedings, 1966, Speech

Section II
Home Office Functions

Albers, Henry H., "Principles of Organization and Management." New York: John Wiley, 1965.

Beckman, Theodore N. and Davidson, William R., "Marketing." New York: The Ronald Press Co., 1967.

Copeland, Melvin T. and Towl, Andrew R., "The Board of Directors and Business Management." Boston: Division of Research, Graduate School of Business Administration, Harvard University, 1947.

Dale, Ernest, "Readings in Management." New York: McGraw-Hill, Inc., 1965.

Davis, Ralph Currier, "The Fundamentals of Top Management." New York: Harper & Brothers, 1951.

Drucker, Peter F., "The Practice of Management." New York: Harper & Brothers, 1954.

Emory, William and Niland, Powell, "Making Management Decisions." Boston: Houghton Mifflin Company, 1968.

Greenwood, William F., "Management and Organizational Behavior Theories." Cincinnati: South-Western Publishing Co., 1965.

Koontz, Harold and O'Donnell, Cyril, "Principles of Management" 3rd ed. New York: McGraw-Hill, Inc., 1964.

Koontz, Harold, "The Board of Directors and Effective Management." New York: McGraw-Hill, Inc., 1967.

LeBreton, Preston P., "General Administration: Planning and Implementation." New York: Holt, Rinehart, and Winston, 1965.

Miller, D. W. and Starr, M. K., Executive Decisions and Operations Research." Englewood Cliffs, New Jersey: Prentice-Hall, Inc., 1960.

Mooney, James D., "The Principles of Organization." New York: Harper & Row Publishers, Inc., 1947.

McGill, Dan M., Editor, *Life Insurance Sales Management.* Homewood, Ill.: Richard D. Irwin, Inc., 1957.

McGregor, Douglas, "The Professional Manager." New York: McGraw-Hill, Inc., 1967.

Newman, William H.; Summer, Charles E. and Warren, E. Kirby "The Process of Management." Englewood Cliffs, New Jersey: Prentice-Hall, Inc., 1967.

Scott, William G., "Organization Theory." Homewood, Ill.: Richard D. Irwin, Inc., 1967.

Tead, Ordway, "The Art of Administration." New York: McGraw-Hill, Inc., 1951.

Thayer, L. O., "Administrative Communications." Homewood, Ill.: Richard D. Irwin, 1961.

Tosdal, Harry R., "Introduction to Sales Management." 4th ed.; New York: McGraw-Hill, Inc., 1957.

Life Insurance Agency Management Publications, Research Reports, Products and Services Bulletins and Annual Meeting Proceedings

Marketing and Management by Objective, by Darrell Eichhoff. Proceedings, 1965, Speech

Responsibilities in a Computerized Management Information System, RR 1969, Report

The World of the Agency Vice-President, by James R. Martin. Proceedings, 1965, Speech

Section III
Fundamental Principles

Albers, Henry H., "Principles of Organization and Management." New York: John Wiley, 1965.

Bennis, Warren G., "The Personnel Management Process: Human Resources Administration." Boston: Houghton Mifflin Company, 1964.

Borch, Fred J., "The Marketing Philosophy As a Way of Business Life," in *The Marketing Concept: Its Meaning to Management* (Marketing Series, No. 99) New York: The American Management Association, 1957.

Bund, Henry and Carroll, James W., "The Changing Role of the Marketing Function," *Journal of Marketing,* 1957.

Cascino, Anthony E., "Organizational Implications of the Marketing Concept," in Eugene J. Kelley and William Lazer (eds.), *Managerial Marketing: Perspectives and Viewpoints* (3rd ed.) Homewood, Ill.: Richard D. Irwin, Inc., 1967.

Davis, Ralph Currier, "The Fundamentals of Top Management." New York: Harper & Brothers, 1951.

DeVoe, Merrill, "How to Tailor Your Sales Organization to Your Markets." Englewood Cliffs, New Jersey: Prentice-Hall, Inc., 1964.

Dill, W. R., Hilton, T. L., and Reitman, W. R., "The New Managers." Englewood Cliffs, New Jersey: Prentice-Hall, Inc., 1962.

Drucker, Peter F., "The Practice of Management." New York: Harper & Brothers, 1954.

Emory, William and Niland, Powell, "Making Management Decisions." Boston: Houghton Mifflin Company, 1968.

Felton, Arthur P., "Making the Marketing Concept Work." *Harvard Business Review,* July-August, 1959.

Jacobs, Lawrence, "The Meaning of Goals," *Business Horizons,* Winter, 1967.

Johnson, Stanford L., and Tenge, John T., Jr., "The Men Behind the Marketing Concept," *Sales Marketing Today,* June, 1967.

Kelley, Eugene J., and Lazer, William, 'Basic Duties of the Modern Sales Department," *Industrial Marketing,* April, 1960.

Koontz, Harold and O'Donnell, Cyril, "Principles of Management," 3rd ed. New York: McGraw-Hill, Inc., 1964.

Morrison, Edward J., "Marketing Management Concepts Yesterday and Today," *Journal of Marketing,* 1967.

McGregor, Douglas, "The Professional Manager." New York: McGraw-Hill, Inc., 1967.

Newman, William H. Summer, Charles E., and Warren, E. Kirby, "The Process of Management." Englewood Cliffs, New Jersey: Prentice-Hall, Inc., 1967.

Tosdal, Harry R., "Introduction to Sales Management." (4th ed.); New York: McGraw-Hill, Inc., 1957.

Viebranz, Alfred C., "Marketing's Role in Company Growth," *MSU Business Topics,* Autumn, 1967.

Vizza, Robert F., Chambers, Thomas F., and Cook, Edward J., "Adoption of the Marketing Concept—Fact or Fiction?" New York: Sales Executives Club of New York, 1967.

Section IV
Organizing for Life Insurance Sales

Albers, Henry H., "Principles of Organization and Management." New York: John Wiley, 1965.

Allen, Louis A., "Management and Organization." New York: McGraw-Hill, Inc., 1958.

Applewhite, P. B. and Porter, D. E., "Studies in Organizational Behavior." Scranton, Pa.: International Textbook Company, 1964.

Copeland, Melvin T. and Towl, Andrew R., "The Board of Directors and Business Management." Boston: Division of Research, Graduate School of Business Administration, Harvard University, 1947.

Dale, Ernest, "Organization." New York: American Management Association, 1967.

Davis, Ralph Currier, "The Fundamentals of Top Management." New York: Harper & Brothers, 1951.

DeVoe, Merrill, "How to Tailor Your Sales Organization to Your Markets." Englewood Cliffs, New Jersey: Prentice-Hall, Inc., 1964.

Drucker, Peter F., "The Practice of Management." New York: Harper & Brothers, 1954.

Greenwood, William F., "Management and Organizational Behavior Theories." Cincinnati: Southwestern Publishing Company, 1965.

Kelley, Eugene J. and Lazer, William, "Basic Duties of the Modern Sales Department," *Industrial Marketing,* April, 1960.

Koontz, Harold and O'Donnell, Cyril, "Principles of Management," 3rd ed. New York: McGraw-Hill, Inc., 1964.

Likert, R. A., "Human Organization: New Patterns of Management." New York: McGraw-Hill, Inc., 1967.

Litterer, Joseph A., "The Analysis of Organization." New York: John Wiley & Sons, 1965.

Lunger, J. B., *Yale Insurance Lectures,* Vol. I. Morehouse & Taylor Press, 1904.

Miller, D. W. and Starr, M. K., "Executive Decisions and Operations Research." Englewood Cliffs, New Jersey: Prentice-Hall, Inc., 1960.

Newman, William H., Summer, Charles E., and Warren, E. Kirby, "The Process of Management." Englewood Cliffs, New Jersey: Prentice-Hall, Inc., 1960.

Pfiffner, John M. and Sherwood, Frank P., "Administrative Organization." Englewood Cliffs, New Jersey: Prentice-Hall, Inc., 1965.

Rubenstein, Albert H. and Haberstroh, Chadwick J., "Some Theories of Organization." Homewood, Ill.: Richard D. Irwin, Inc., 1966.

Sayles, L. R., "Managerial Behavior." New York: McGraw-Hill, Inc., 1964.

Schlender, William E., Scott, William G., and Filley, Alan C., eds., "Management in Perspective." Boston: Houghton Mifflin, 1965.

Scott, William G., "Organization Theory." Homewood, Ill.: Richard D. Irwin, Inc., 1967.

Tosdal, Harry R., "Introduction to Sales Management." (4th ed.) New York: McGraw-Hill, Inc., 1957.

Woodward, Joan, "Industrial Organization: Theory and Practice." London: Oxford University Press, 1965.

Life Insurance Agency Management Publications, Research Reports, Products and Services Bulletins and Annual Meeting Proceedings

Managing an Agency, Field Publication

Organization for Marketing—A Boon or a Bogey? by W. J. D. Lewis. Proceedings, 1969, Speech

Responsibilities and Functional Activities of the Agency Department, 1963, Report

Responsibilities in a Computerized Management Information System. RR 1969, Report

The World of the Agency Vice-President, by James R. Martin. Proceedings, 1965, Speech

Section V
Market Planning for Life Insurance Sales

Ackoff, Russell L., "The Design of Social Research." Chicago: University of Chicago Press, 1953.

Albers, Henry H., "Principles of Organization and Management." New York: John Wiley, 1965.

American Marketing Association, "A Survey of Marketing Research." Chicago: 1959 and 1963.

Applebaum, William and Spears, Richard, "Controlled Experimentation in Marketing Research," *Journal of Marketing,* January, 1950.

Baxter, Brent and Kashnig, William, "Life Insurance Marketing Research." Bryn Mawr, Pa.: American College of Life Underwriters, 1962.

Bogart, Leo, "Inside Marketing Research," *Public Opinion Quarterly,* Winter, 1963.

Crisp, Richard D., "Company Practices in Marketing Research," Research Report No. 22. New York: American Management Association, 1953.

Crisp, Richard D., "What Can Be Tested?" *Marketing Research.* New York: McGraw-Hill, Inc., 1957.

Crisp, Richard D., "Marketing Research Organization & Operation." New York: American Management Association, 1958.

Dale, Ernest, "Readings in Management." New York: McGraw-Hill, Inc., 1965.

Davis, Ralph Currier, "The Fundamentals of Top Management." New York: Harper & Brothers, 1951.

DeVoe, Merrill, "How to Tailor Your Sales Organization to Your Markets." Englewood Cliffs, New Jersey: Prentice-Hall, Inc., 1964.

Drucker, Peter F., "The Practice of Management." New York: Harper & Brothers, 1954.

Eilers, Robert D. and Crowe, Robert M., "Group Insurance Handbook." Homewood, Ill.: Richard D. Irwin, Inc., 1965.

Emory, William and Niland, Powell, "Making Management Decisions." Boston: Houghton Mifflin Company, 1968.

Ferber, Robert; Blankertz, Donald F., and Hollander, Disney Jr., *Marketing Research.* New York: The Ronald Press Company, 1964.

Festinger, Leon and Katz, Daniel (eds), "Research Methods in the Behavioral Sciences." New York: The Dryden Press, 1953.

Kelley, Eugene J. and Lazer, William, "Basic Duties of the Modern Sales Department," *Industrial Marketing,* April, 1960.

Koontz, Harold and O'Donnell, Cyril, "Principles of Management." New York: McGraw-Hill, Inc., 1964.

LeBreton, Preston P., "General Administration: Planning and Implementation." New York: Holt, Rinehart, and Winston, 1965.

Miller, D. W. and Starr, M. K., "Executive Decisions and Operations Research." Englewood Cliffs, New Jersey: Prentice-Hall, Inc., 1960.

McGill, Dan M., editor, "Life Insurance Sales Management." Homewood, Ill.: Richard D. Irwin, Inc., 1967.

McGregor, Douglas, "The Professional Manager." New York: McGraw-Hill, Inc., 1967.

National Industrial Conference Board, *Organization for Market Research,* Studies in Business Policy No. 12 New York: 1945.

Newman, William H., "Administrative Action." Englewood Cliffs, New Jersey: Prentice-Hall, Inc., 1963.

Newman, William H., Summer, Charles E. and Warren, E. Kirby, "The Process of Management." Englewood Cliffs, New Jersey: Prentice-Hall, Inc., 1967.

Politz, Alfred N., "Science and Truth in Marketing Research." *Harvard Business Review,* January-February, 1957.

Roberts, Harry V., "The Role of Research in Marketing Management," *Journal of Marketing,* July, 1957.

Salisbury, Philip, "85¢ for Product Research; Only 15¢ for Market Research. Why?" *Sales Management,* March 15, 1950.

Scott, Brian W., "Long-range Planning in American Industry." New York: American Management Association, 1965.

"Survey of Buying Power," *Sales Management,* June 10, 1968.

Life Insurance Agency Management Publications, Research Reports, Products and Services Bulletins and Annual Meeting Proceedings

The Age of Planning, by Burkett W. Huey. Proceedings, 1966, Speech

A Case Study in Agency Planning; How to Use Our Agency Plans. 1968, Field Publication

LIAMA Research in Perspective, 1966, Report

Life Insurance and Family Spending, RR 1956, Report

Life Insurance Attitudes and Expectations of American Youth; A Joint Study of High School Students by the Institute of Life Insurance and LIAMA. RR 1966, Report

Life Insurance in Focus; A Study by LIAMA and LUTC, Report

Long-range Planning of Productive Resources, by Coy G. Eklund. Proceedings, 1964, Speech

Managing an Agency, Field Publication

Marketing and Management by Objective, by Darrell Eichhoff. Proceedings, 1965, Speech

A New Approach to Management Planning, 1968, Field Publication

The Opportunity to Buy; A Market Survey of United States Households. RR 1968, Report

Prospects and Agents; A Study of the Sales Process Sponsored by LUTC, LIAMA, and McCall's Magazine. RR 1967, Report

The World of the Agency Vice-President, by James R. Martin. Proceedings, 1965, Speech

Section VI
Public Relations and Sales Promotion

Applewhite, Philip B., "Organizational Behavior." Englewood Cliffs, New Jersey: Prentice-Hall, Inc., 1965.

Bass, Bernard, M., "Organizational Psychology." Boston: Allyn and Bacon, 1965.

Bradford, L. P., Gibbs, J. R., and Benne, K. D., "T-Group Theory and Laboratory Methods." New York: John Wiley, 1964.

Hayes, Samuel P., Jr., "Relating Behavior Research to the Problems of Organization." Ann Arbor, Mich.: University of Michigan, 1952.

Miner, John B., "The Management of Ineffective Performance." New York: McGraw-Hill, Inc., 1963.

McGill, Dan M., editor, *Life Insurance Sales Management.* Homewood, Ill.: Richard D. Irwin, Inc., 1967.

Sayles, Leonard R., "Managerial Behavior—Administration in Complex Organization." New York: McGraw-Hill, Inc., 1964.

Stalson, Owen J., "Marketing Life Insurance—its History in America." Cambridge: Harvard University Press, 1942.

Volk, Harry S., and Allsopp, Thomas, "Life Insurance Company Organization." Phila.: American College of Life Underwriters, 1955.

Life Insurance Agency Management Publications, Research Reports, Products and Services Bulletins and Annual Meeting Proceedings

Annual Reports Review, 1969, Report

Breaking the Ice; The Agent's Guide to Sales Promotion, 1956, Field Publication

LIAMA Research in Perspective, 1966, Report

Managing an Agency, Field Publication

Survey of Agency Opinion; A Survey Conducted by NALU and LIAMA. 1964, Report

Section VII
Manpower Development

Albright, Lewis and Glenn, J. R., Smith, Wallace S., "The Use of Psychological Tests in Industry." Cleveland: Howard Allen, Inc., 1963.

Anastasi, Anne, "Psychological Testing." New York: Macmillan Company, 1961.

Argyris, Chris, "Interpersonal Competence and Organizational Effectiveness." Homewood, Ill.: Richard D. Irwin, Inc., 1962.

Balinsky, Benjamin, "The Selection Interview: Essentials for Management." New York: Martin M. Bruce, 1962.

Bennis, Warren G., "The Personnel Management Process: Human Resources Administration." Boston: Houghton Mifflin Co., 1964.

Gekoski, Norman, "Psychological Testing." Springfield, Ill.: Charles C. Thomas Co., 1964.

Gross, Martin L., "The Brain Watchers." New York: Random House, 1962.

Guilford, S. P., "Personality." New York: McGraw-Hill, Inc., 1959.

Jewell, Keith, R., "Let's Take the Hocus Pocus Out of Hiring: Know What You're Looking For," *Sales Management,* February 7, 1964.

Jewell, Keith R., "Always Check with Others," *Sales Management,* March 20, 1964.

Josephson, Halsey D., "Josephson on Agency Management." New York: Probe, Inc., 1964.

Lapp, Charles L., "Training and Supervising Salesmen." Englewood Cliffs, New Jersey: Prentice-Hall, Inc., 1960.

Loen, Raymond O., "How to Spot Potential Salesmen," *Sales Management,* November 15, 1963.

Magee, Richard H., "The Employment Interview—Techniques of Questioning." *Personnel Journal,* May, 1962.

Mayer, David and Greenberg, Herbert M., "What Makes a Good Salesman." *Harvard Business Review,* July-August, 1964.

McMurry, Robert N., "Why You Must Plan Now to Meet Your Sales Manpower Needs for Tomorrow," *Sales Management,* November 10, 1957.

Koontz, Harold and O'Donnell, Cyril, "Principles of Management." 3rd ed. New York: McGraw-Hill, Inc., 1964.

LeBreton, Preston P., "Planning and Implementation." New York: Holt, Rinehart, and Winston, 1965.

Likert, R. A., "Human Organization: New Patterns of Management." New York: McGraw-Hill, Inc., 1967.

Miller, D. W. and Starr, M. K., "Executive Decisions and Operations Research." Englewood Cliffs, New Jersey: Prentice-Hall, Inc., 1960.

McClellen, David C., Atkinson, J. W., Clark, R. A. and Lowell, E. L., "The Achievement Motive." New York: Appleton-Century-Crofts, 1953.

McGregor, Douglas, "The Human Side of Enterprise." New York: McGraw-Hill, Inc., 1960.

McGregor, Douglas, "The Professional Manager." New York: McGraw-Hill, Inc., 1967.

Newman, William H., Summer, Charles E., and Warren, E. Kirby, "The Process of Management." Englewood Cliffs, New Jersey: Prentice-Hall, Inc., 1967.

Russell, G. Hugh and Black, Kenneth, Jr., "Human Behavior and Life Insurance." Englewood Cliffs, New Jersey: Prentice-Hall, Inc., 1963.

Sayles, L. R., "Managerial Behavior." New York: McGraw-Hill, Inc., 1964.

Schlender, William E., Scott, William G., and Filley, Alan C., eds., "Management in Perspective." Boston: Houghton Mifflin Company, 1965.

Stryker, Perrin, "The Incomparable Salesman." New York: McGraw-Hill, Inc., 1967.

Tannenbaum, A. S., "Social Psychology of the Work Organization." Belmont, California: Wadsworth Publishing Company, 1966.

Thayer, L. O., "Administrative Communications." Homewood, Ill.: Richard D. Irwin, Inc., 1961.

Vroom, V. H., "Work and Motivation." New York: John Wiley, 1964.

Whitmore, Eugene, "Helpful Prods Can Hinder Salesmen," *Sales Management,* July 15, 1960.

Whitmore, Eugene, "What Really Motivates Salesmen?" *Sales Management,* October 7, 1960.

"What's Wrong with Sales Contests?" *Sales Management,* September 10, 1967.

Research Institute of America, *Finding the Superior Salesman,* New York: 1967.

Robbins, Walter S., The National Underwriter—Life and Health Edition. March 30, 1968.

623

"Self-Made Men: Many Job Seekers Lie about Past in Resumes, but Concerns Are Wary," *Wall Street Journal,* January 22, 1968.

Thorndike, R. L., "Personnel Selection: Test and Measurement Techniques." New York: John Wiley, 1949.

Whisler, Thomas L. and Harper, Shirley F., "Performance Appraisal: Research and Practice." New York: Holt, Rinehart and Winston, 1962.

Life Insurance Agency Management Publications, Research Reports, Products and Services Bulletins and Annual Meeting Proceedings

Agency Manager Survey, RR 1966, Report

Career Orientation; Results of a Study in One Company, RR 1966, Report

Developing Management Manpower for You and Your Company, by George N. Quigley, Jr. Proceedings, 1969, Speech

Field Management Development, RR 1964, Report

50 of the Best Recruiting Ideas, 1966, Field Publication

A Guide for Assistant Manager Selection, Tool

Inventory of Job Attitudes Manual, Tool

LIAMA Research in Perspective, 1966, Report

The Life Insurance Career, 1969, Field Publication

Managers Handbook, Field Publication

Managing an Agency, Field Publication

Manpower and Its Development, by R. W. Donaldson. Proceedings, 1967, Speech

Manpower and Its Development, by Leland T. Waggoner, Proceedings, 1967, Speech

Manpower and Its Development, by Harold I. Weir. Proceedings, 1967, Speech

Manpower and Production Planning. RR 1963, Report

New Agent Characteristics Trends in Age and Education. Current Practices Bull. 327, 1968, Report

Precontract Orientation. RR 1970, Report

Predicting Supervisory Success. RR 1969, Report

Recruiting Career Men, 1965, Field Publication

Recruiting Trends, Survey

Research on Persistency, 1960, Report

Study Course in Agency Management, Course

Training Facilities; A Survey by Training and Communications Aids Committee, 1968, Report

Upgrading and Developing Management, by Marvin T. Benson, Proceedings, 1967, Speech

Upgrading and Developing Management, by C. A. Craig II. Proceedings, 1967, Speech

Upgrading and Developing Management, by Bernard S. Lyon. Proceedings, 1967, Speech

The World of Training, by Loran E. Powell. Proceedings, 1965, Speech

You've Taken the Test! Now What? 1968, Field Publication

Section VIII
Motivation, Supervision and Retention of Manpower

Albers, Henry H., "Principles of Organization and Management." New York: John Wiley, 1965.

Allen, Louis A., "Management and Organization." New York: McGraw-Hill, Inc., 1958.

Applewhite, P. B. and Porter, D. E., "Studies in Organizational Behavior." Scranton, Pa.: International Text-Book Co., 1964.

Argyris, Chris, "Interpersonal Competence and Organizational Effectiveness." Homewood, Ill.: Richard D. Irwin, Inc., 1962.

Bales, R. and Slater, P., "Family Socialization and Interaction Process." Glencoe, Ill.: Free Press, 1955.

Bennis, Warren G., "The Personnel Management Process: Human Resources Administration." Boston: Houghton Mifflin Company, 1964.

Burton, William M., "How to Use Motivation to Stimulate Your Salesmen," *Sales Management,* November 1, 1957.

Dale, Ernest, "Readings in Management." New York: McGraw-Hill, Inc., 1965.

Davis, Keith, "Human Relations at Work." New York: McGraw-Hill, Inc., 1962.

Dill, W. R., Hilton, T. L., and Reitman, W. R., "The New Managers." Englewood Cliffs, New Jersey: Prentice-Hall, Inc., 1962.

Drucker, Peter F., "The Practice of Management." New York: Harper & Brothers, 1954.

Flippo, E. B., "Management: A Behavioral Approach." Boston: Allyn and Bacon, 1966.

Gardner, John W., "Excellence." New York: Harper & Row, 1961.

Haring, Albert and Morris, Malcolm L., *Contests, Prizes, Awards for Sales Motivation.* New York: Sales and Marketing Executives-International, 1968.

Herzberg, F., "Work and the Nature of Man." Cleveland: World Publishing Company, 1966.

Homan, George, C., "The Human Group." New York: Harcourt, Brace and Company, 1950.

Jacobs, Lawrence, "The Meaning of Goals." *Business Horizons,* Winter, 1967.

Johnson, Marietta, "Youth in a World of Men." New York: John Day Co., 1929.

Life Insurance Agency Management Publications, Research Reports, Products and Services Bulletins and Annual Meeting Proceedings

Human Relations in Management, 1965, Field Publication
LIAMA Research in Perspective, 1966, Report
Managing an Agency, Field Publication
Managers Handbook, Field Publication
Motivation Through Campaigns, Contests, Conventions, Recognition, 1968, Field Publication

Section IX
Business Conservation as a Responsibility of Sales Management

Life Insurance Agency Management Publications, Research Reports, Products and Services Bulletins and Annual Meeting Proceedings

Conservation Programs, 1965, Report
LIAMA Research in Perspective, 1966, Report
Managing an Agency, Field Publication
Managers Quality Business Kit, 1966, Field Publication
Quality Business—Ideas on Persistency and Conservation, Report
Research on Persistency, 1960, Report
Training for Persistent Business, 1967, Field Publication
Use of Persistency Raters. P & S Bull. 61, 1967, Report

Section X
Financial Management

Anthony, Robert N., Dearden, John, and Vancil, Richard F., "Management Control Systems." Homewood, Ill.: Richard D. Irwin, Inc., 1965.
Catalog of Research and Statistical Projects of Life Insurance Organizations, 1950-1965, Institute of Life Insurance.
Johnson, Richard A., Kast, Fremont E., and Rosenzweig, James E., "The Theory and Management of Systems." New York: McGraw-Hill, Inc., 1967.
Lederer, R. Werner, *Home Office and Field Agency Organization—Life.* New York: Life Office Management Association, 1966.
Stalnaker, Armand C., *Life Insurance Agency Financial Management.* Homewood, Ill.: Richard D. Irwin, Inc., 1965.

Life Insurance Agency Management Publications, Research Reports, Products and Services Bulletins and Annual Meeting Proceedings

Compensation Handbooks: Agents' Ordinary Life and Health Contracts, Security Benefit Plans, Reports

Compensation Handbooks: General Agents' Compensation Plans, Managers' Compensation Plans, Security Benefit Plans, Reports

Compensation Handbook: New Agents' Financing Plans, Report

Developing New Agencies, RR 1964, Report

Financing Analysis Service, Tool

Financing. Current Practices Bull. 327, 1968, Report

Financing Details on Inexperienced Agents Employed in 1966, Current Practices Bull. 328, 1968, Report

Financing Validation and Postselection. RR 1959, Report

LIAMA Research in Perspective, 1966, Report

Managerial Compensation. Current Practices Bull. 303, 1965, Report

INDEX

629

H

I

Responsibility for sales promotion, 318-319

Responsiveness in supervisor, enhancing, 491-492

Retaining manpower for agency growth, 501-520
  frustration at ineffective use of time, 508-510
  income, worries about, 502-505
  loss of challenge; staleness, 514-516
  management of agency, dissatisfaction with, 510-514
  management planning sessions, 517-520
  personal problems, 516-517
  status, desire for more, 505-508

Retention of manpower, 457-520
  (see also "Motivation, supervision and retention of manpower")

Retention of personnel, assumptions about, 202

Return to general agent, estimating, 563-565

Reuther, Walter, 212

Reward vs. punishment as motivational theory, 459-460

Rewards, types of, 461

Rewards and recognition as motivation, 119-120

"Rifle" or "shotgun" approach to group insurance sales, 228

Richards, Max D., 57n

Robbins, Walter S., 373n

Robinson, Morris, 22

Rockefeller, Governor Nelson, 211-212

"Role of the Agency Department," 64n

"Role Differentiation in Small Decision-Making Groups," 462n

Rorschach test, 374

Roster publications as source of information for group insurance market analysis, 227

Russell, G. Hugh, 458n, 477

Russell, Winslow, 29, 31-33

S

Sales campaigns, motivational effects of, 472-477

Sales facilities of agencies, reviewing, 264-271

advertising, 267-268
contests, 265-266
established agents, continued training for, 264-265
morale-building activities, 266
new agent training program, 264
public relations program, 267
sales meetings, 265
seminars, 269-271
special activities, 266

Sales force, motivating, 457-477
communication and motivation, 471-472
hierarchy of needs of agent, significance of, 467-468
leadership and motivation, 470-471
motivation theory, fundamentals of, 459-464
achievement, need for, 461-462
and personal harmony, 464-466
prestige, 463-464
reward vs. punishment, 459-560
rewards, types of, 461
in selection and training, 463
shaping, concept of, 459-460
"motivational work environment," meaning of, 458-459
pleasure in selling, 466-467
process, motivation, 468-470
sales campaigns, motivational effects of, 472-477

Sales force, role of in implementing agency's public relations program, 310-311

Sales management, fundamentals of, 125-136
administration as direct skill, 126-127
administrator, fundamental responsibility of as staffing, 133
importance of, 135-136
marketing management and its evolution, 33-35
philosophy of management, 127-132
areas affected by, 128-132
(see also "Philosophy of management")
authority, 129-131
consistency, need for, 127-128
on control, 131-132
definition, 127